CONTENTS

WHY A SUMMER JOB WORLDWIDE?

The summer holidays are looming and weeks of gloriously un-timetabled free time are stretching ahead of you. You can do what-ever you want – you could go travelling, experience new places, meet some interesting people, try out exciting new things – the world is yours for the taking. Or it would be if it weren't for one problem: You're broke.

But why let a little thing like that ruin your summer? You could of course stay at home and slog it out at a local factory, or break your back stacking shelves at the local supermarket. But why would you when the alternative is working on a French campsite or behind a bar in Ibiza?

A wealth of CV-improving, mind-expanding and, most impor-tantly, interesting jobs is available throughout the UK, Europe and even further afield. Thousands of students and young people shake off the boredom and routine of living at home by packing their bags and heading off for a summer job worldwide. Why not join them?

The advantages of a summer job away from home

Experiencing new places and cultures

If it's a case of itchy feet you are hoping to cure, how better to see a new part of the world on a budget than to take a summer job? Working away from home is one of the ways that you can afford an extended period of travel. Many of the jobs you will find within these pages offer full bed and board as well as a wage. So all you have to fund is the travel. You will even find that many of the jobs on offer are set in some stunning locations, from remote retreats to five-star resorts.

By venturing away from your home town or city you will gain greater independence and expe-rience a destination from the inside rather than as an onlooker. If you don't fancy venturing too far from home, jobs abound all over the UK, from working on an activity camp on the shores of Lake Windermere in the heart of the Lake District, to working as a deckhand and tour guide on England's waterways.

But these days, with the number of cheap flights available, your job hunt should not be confined to Britain. With a bit of research you can find a budget return flight to many places in Europe for about £50. The added advantage of going abroad is that you can also use the trip to improve your knowledge of foreign languages and cultures. Working abroad offers an experience that is quite distinct from straightforward travel. If you are on holiday, you pass through rapidly, you see the sights and eat the food, but you very rarely leave feeling as though you have

Camp America workers taking some time off to explore

satisfied your curiosity about a place and its culture. By contrast, a summer job allows you to work at close quarters with local inhabitants, sometimes even lodge with local families, discuss local issues and build lasting friendships. And as for languages, whether you want to start from scratch or simply brush up your skills, there is no better way to do so than a few months of complete immersion.

Earning some cash

These days getting a decent education can cost a fortune. What with the astronomical financial burden of university tuition fees, added to the not inconsiderable social and accommodation costs, work-free summer holidays have become the sole preserve of the fortunate few. And the chances are, if you have bought this book, you are not one of them. Don't worry though. Working in the summer gives you the chance to boost your bank balance, with the average student earning over £1,600 during the long vacation.

Enhancing your CV

The summer is a great opportunity to get ahead of the game, and make yourself stand out as a candidate in an increasingly competitive job market. Employers notoriously favour candidates who have demonstrated initiative and spent their vacation time productively. Choosing a summer job that's relevant to a future career choice will stand you in good stead when it comes to entering the real world.

Improving your job prospects doesn't necessarily mean finding an internship with a New York investment bank. High-flying summer work is hard to come by, and anyway might not be that much fun. But increasingly employers are realising that transferable skills are what matter. And whatever you end up doing, it's the way that you sell it on your CV that matters. For instance, if you manage to find work on a holiday barge on the French waterways, you will have demonstrated language and communication skills, leadership abilities, client service and a hardy stomach. Even if you work behind a bar – you may well have demonstrated these same skills plus a degree of numeracy and a faculty for working long hours under pressure. Any summer job can be used to your advantage once you graduate.

The key is to go into it with the right attitude. Extract every last bit of experience that you can from a job that others would just turn up for. You need to go above and beyond – think about what else you can add to your role and show your employers you are capable of handling more. According to careers advisers, employers favour CVs that demonstrate how students have effected some change, regardless of the level or nature of work they have done.

Finding a job that is right for you

Given the opportunities available to enhance your CV, it is crazy to restrict yourself to the mediocre jobs in the local paper. If you want to gain experience in an unusual or competitive field, it is likely that you will have to travel to find the right job. Remember: there is a whole world of possibilities out there.

So, what's the down side?

Well there isn't one really. As long as you are realistic about what to expect. Quite often there is something of a gap between the expectations of the uninitiated summer worker who imagines his job to be some kind of paid holiday in the sun and his employer who regards him as someone who is, well, there to work. Of course it is inevitable that even the most interesting job will be complicated by the realities of day-to-day living and the expression 'working holiday' can be something of an oxymoron. Wherever you do it, a job is still a job, so it pays to try and think through the potential flaws a position might hold – thorns, heatstroke, isolation – all these practicalities are often overlooked during the grand conceptualisation. Nevertheless, as long as you do your research and ask the right questions of your future employer, there should be no nasty surprises.

Certain obstacles in the mind of the irresolute must be overcome: What jobs can I get? Do I need specific skills? What if I only speak English? This introductory section sets out to allay anxieties and to encourage readers to peruse details of the thousands of summer jobs available. Those who have shed their unrealistic expectations are normally exhilarated by the novelty and challenge of finding and doing a summer job worldwide.

You've already made a good start...

Finding a summer job abroad may strike you as a daunting task. However this book leads you through the process in a systematic way and provides sufficient listings to help you find a job suited to your needs. Some jobs listed pay very well and come with room and board; others are voluntary and therefore unpaid. Some last for the whole season (June to September or longer); others are just for a couple of weeks. Inside these pages you will find everything you need to know to make the most of your vacation time. Working abroad for a short period will enable the dream to become a reality, of being immersed in a different culture, meeting new friends and earning money at the same time.

The bulk of the individual opportunities in this book are in the UK and western Europe, though the rest of the world is also covered. Entries covering opportunities in a wide distribution of coun-

Club Med's Go Team summer group relax after work

tries or continents are included in the *Worldwide* chapter; while those with a distribution in three or more European countries are in the *Organisations With Vacancies Across Europe* chapter; others are listed in the relevant country chapter. At the start of each country chapter there are some general notes on employment prospects and regulations on work permits, visas etc. The information in the individual entries has been supplied by the organisations/employers themselves, and is included at their request.

We wish you the best of luck in landing a summer job that you have chosen from the selection within, please note however, that the publishers cannot undertake to contact individual employers or to offer any assistance in arranging specific jobs.

WHAT JOBS CAN YOU DO?

The listings in the 2008 edition of *Summer Jobs Worldwide* are as disparate geographically and occupationally as ever. They range from the practical (building, restoration work, organic farming) to the cerebral (writing reviews for a campsite guide), and from the artistic (theatrical animator, painting teacher) to the compassionate (working with the disabled) as well as an impressive array of workcamps, hotels, campsites, harvests, couriers etc. Here is a rundown of the types of job available to you worldwide.

Tourism

Working in Hotels

If you like the sound of working in some of the most beautiful corners of the world, from high in the Alps, to national parks in the USA, then hotel work might just be for you. The tourist industry is a mainstay of summer job seekers. The seasonal nature of hotel and restaurant work discourages a stable working population, so that hotel owners often rely on foreign and student workers during the busy summer season.

The earlier you decide to apply for seasonal hotel work, the better your chances. Hotels often recruit months before the summer season, so you should contact as many hotels as possible by March, preferably in their own language. Knowledge of more than one language is an immense asset for work in Europe. If you have an interest in working in a particular country and want to cast your net wider than the hotels listed in this directory, get a list of hotels from their tourist office in London or from a guide or the internet and contact the largest ones.

If you secure a hotel job without speaking the language of the country and lack relevant experience, you will probably be placed at the bottom of the pecking order, such as in the laundry or washing dishes. Reception and bar jobs are usually the most sought after and highly paid. However, the lowly jobs have their saving graces. The usual hours of chamber staff (7am-2pm) allow plenty of free time and of course you do not have to deal with guests.

Working in hotels, especially in the kitchens can involve hot working conditions, long hours and low wages but on good days hotel work is lively, varied and exciting. Before taking a job offer you should always ask for precise details about your duties. Many job

Hotel work in the USA with BUNAC's Work America Programme

titles do not provide a clear definition of the work and may vary in meaning between different establishments (and countries!) Small hotels tend to employ general assistants for a range of duties as diverse as cleaning rooms to working on reception.

There are loads of benefits to working in hotels. The vast majority provide their staff with accommodation and meals (a deduction may be made from wages for living expenses but in most cases this will not be unreasonable). You can also expect excellent camaraderie and team spirit, the opportunity to learn a foreign language, and enjoy beautiful surroundings. You will also be amazed at the ease with which wages can be saved when you are sleeping and eating on site.

Resorts and holiday centres

Camping holiday operators employ a huge number of students and young people for the summer season. The Holidaybreak group alone (see entry in *Europewide* section), which includes Eurocamp and Keycamp, recruits up to 2,000 campsite couriers and children's couriers.

The courier's job is to clean the tents and caravans between visitors, greet clients and deal with difficulties (particularly illness or car breakdowns), and introduce clients to the attractions of the area. The courier may even arrange and host social functions and amuse the children.

For this kind of work you will be rewarded with on average £100–£130 a week in addition to free tent accommodation. Many companies offer half-season contracts April to mid-July and mid-

The start of the show with the Haven Funstars

July to the end of September. Setting up and dismantling the campsites in March/April and September (known as *montage* and *démontage*) is often done by a separate team. The work is hard but the language requirements are nil. The majority of vacancies are in France, though the major companies employ people from Austria to Denmark.

Successful couriers make the job look easy, but it does demand a lot of hard work and patience. Occasionally it is very hard to keep up the happy, smiling, never-ruffled courier look, but most seem to end up enjoying the job since it provides accommodation, a guaranteed weekly wage and the chance to work with like-minded people.

The big companies interview hundreds of candidates and have filled most posts by Easter and sometimes by the end of January. But there is a high drop-out rate and vacancies are filled from a reserve list, so it is worth ringing around the companies later on for cancellations. Despite keen competition, anyone who has studied a European language and has an outgoing personality stands a good chance if he or she applies early and widely enough.

Sports

Sports holiday centres often specialise in sea, river or mountain activities and as such they are found in remote and beautiful places around the world. They almost always need to recruit live-in workers. While there are opportunities for some unskilled staff, most vacancies are for sports instructors and leaders. To apply for these positions you will need appropriate qualifications and a reasonable amount of experience.

Many specialist tour companies employ leaders for their clients (children and/or adults) who want a walking, cycling, watersports holiday, etc. Any competent sailor, canoeist, diver, climber, horse rider, etc. should have no difficulty marketing their skills abroad. A list of special interest and activity tour operators (to whom people with specialist skills can apply) is available from AITO, the Association of Independent Tour Operators (www.aito.co.uk). In the US, consult the *Specialty Travel Index* (www.specialtytravel.com).

Summer camp workers teaching horse-riding to children (BUNAC)

Agriculture

Fruit Picking

Farmers from England to Tasmania are unable to bring in their harvests without assistance from outside their local community and often reward their itinerant labour force well. Historically agricultural harvests have employed the greatest number of casual workers who have often travelled hundreds of miles to gather in the fruits of the land, from the tiny blueberry to the mighty watermelon. If you are looking for a satisfying job that is limited in duration, allows you to work outside, has free or cheap accommodation and will expand your cultural horizons by flinging you into a hard working environment with people from all over the world, then fruit harvesting may well be for you.

Part of the appeal of fruit picking is the ability to raise a fair amount of money in a short amount of time. Most fruit-picking work is paid at piece rates, so while you may start off barely scraping minimum wage, your pay will rapidly increase as you get more experienced. There is also little opportunity to spend your earnings on an isolated farm and most people are able to save several hundred pounds in say, a 10-day harvest.

Equally appealing is the opportunity to experience something completely different. There are few more authentic ways of experiencing an alien culture than working off the land in the most rural areas. The grape harvest, or *vendange*, in France for example, lures many for the pure romance of participating in an ancient ritual. While mechanisation may have completely replaced casual labour in some areas such as Cognac, the finest Grand Cru chateaux are unlikely to ever completely do away with hand-picking.

There is also a tremendous community spirit among fruit pickers, from the North African migrants and huge numbers of Eastern Europeans to international working holidaymakers. When thrust into such a hard-working environment, living together at close quarters with a large group of people, it is almost impossible not to make friends. Some of the larger farms offer communal

The grape harvest in France lures workers from all over Europe each year

excursions for workers on their days off, barbecue areas and shared sporting facilities. There is often a work hard, play hard atmosphere in fruit picking camps. During the *vendange* season for example, the free wine provided after a hard day's work often makes for sparkling evening company. Bear in mind though that an early start, and tiring work are not ideal companions for a hangover.

If your experience of farm work is limited to family excursions to the local PYO orchard, then the reality of a fruit-picking may be something of a rude awakening. Some physical fitness is a definite prerequisite and having a little experience is likely to make the work far more enjoyable. Without either, you are likely to find the first few days gruelling. Do not become disheartened. More experienced pickers will be happy to advise on technique and, after a week or so, your confidence and your earnings will have increased.

Fruit picking work is harder to find than it was a decade or so ago. But the jobs are still there for the taking and you will find several large Australian, British, Danish and Dutch farms listed in this book as well as interesting farm work schemes in Switzerland and Norway. There is no reason to restrict yourself to agricultural work listed here though. These are the kinds of jobs that are best found on the ground and via word of mouth.

Organic Farming

The organic farming movement is a very useful source of agricultural contacts. Organic growers everywhere take on volunteers to help them minimise or abolish the use of chemicals and heavy machinery. Various coordinating bodies go under the name of WWOOF – World Wide Opportunities on Organic Farms. National WWOOF coordinators compile a worklist of their member farmers willing to provide free room and board, and this list is sent to members. Organic producers are looking for volunteers who are genuinely interested in furthering the aims of the organic movement.

Each national group has its own aims, system, fees and rules. Some expect applicants to have gained some experience on an organic farm in their own country first. WWOOF is an exchange: in return for your help on organic farms, gardens and homesteads, you receive meals, a place to sleep and a practical insight into organic growing. (If the topic arises at immigration present yourself as a volunteer student of organic farming organising an educational farm visit or a cultural exchange but without mentioning the word 'work'.)

WWOOF has a global website *www.wwoofinternational.org* with links to the national offices in the countries that have a WWOOF coordinator. WWOOF organisations exist in many countries worldwide – developed and developing. Individual farm listings in other countries, ie those with no national organisation, are known as WWOOF Independents. It is necessary to join WWOOF before you can obtain addresses of these properties. If you are starting in Britain fill out the online membership application form (www.wwoof.org.uk). Membership costs £15 per year or £20 for joint membership and includes a subscription to their bi-monthly newsletter which contains small adverts for opportunities both in Britain and abroad.

English language teaching

One billion people speak, or are trying to speak, English around the world and those of us who speak it as a first language tend to take for granted how universally dominant it has become. There are areas of the world where the boom in English language learning seems to know no bounds, from Ecuador to Slovenia, Russia to Vietnam. The kind of people who want to learn English are just as numerous as the places in which they live, so there are jobs in this arena all over the world. A good source of information about the whole topic is *Teaching English Abroad* (576 pages) by Susan Griffith, available from www.crimsonpublishing.co.uk.

Teaching in Schools and at Summer Camps

Schools and English language institutes that run year round, sometimes run summer courses that require a huge influx of teachers and activity leaders.

To fix up a job in advance, make use of the internet and check adverts in the Education section of the *Guardian* every Tuesday. In a few cases, a carefully crafted CV and enthusiastic personality are as important as EFL training and experience. There is also increasing scope for untrained but eager volunteers willing to pay an agency to place them in a language teaching situation abroad (for example, see the entry for i-to-i in the *Worldwide* chapter).

In some private language institutes, being a native speaker and adopting a professional manner are sometimes sufficient qualifications to get a job. But these days it is more likely that you will require an ELT qualification (see box below). However, there are plenty of jobs in language schools that do not have this requirement. The majority of residential language schools often take on staff to work as social supervisors and organisers, both at the school outside of teaching time, and on day trips. The bigger ones may also require sports and activity instructors. These positions frequently require no qualifications other than interest and an ability to work with young people.

Short-term teachers are nearly always employed to stimulate conversation rather than to teach grammar. Yet a basic knowledge of English grammar is a great asset when more advanced pupils ask awkward questions. The wages paid to English teachers are usually reasonable, and in developing countries are quite often well in excess of the average local wage. In return you may be asked to teach some fairly unsociable hours since most private English classes take place after working hours, and so schedules split between early morning and evening are commonplace.

Working at English Summer Camps

Across the UK and Europe, a large number of short-term residential summer camps combine sports and outdoor activities with English tuition. Not only do they create short-term opportunities for teaching English, but they also provide a range of opportunities for camp counsellors, monitors, group leaders, activity instructors and sports coaches. English summer camps usually last from one to four weeks.

English Language Teaching Qualifications

Most language schools require their teachers to have a TEFL or TESOL qualification, though some will take on undergraduates. There are lots of TEFL/TESOL courses and qualifications on offer, varying widely in length, location and cost. Check the advertisements for those that seem most respected before committing to a course. It is important to choose a course which offers teaching practice as this will give you the skills and confidence you need to teach effectively. Courses cost between £800 and £1,100 including exam costs.

One of the most widely recognised certificates is the Cambridge CELTA (Certificate in English Language Teaching to Adults). CELTA courses can be taken at 250 approved centres in the UK and overseas. They can be taken full-time over four or five weeks, or part-time over a longer period. For more information and to find a centre, contact Cambridge Assessment (01223 553355; www.cambridgeesol.org/teaching).

The other major certificate, carrying equal recognition to the CELTA, the Cert TESOL, is awarded by Trinity College London (020 7820 6100; www.trinitycollege.co.uk), which stipulates a minimum of 130 hours of scheduled course input over a four- to five-week period (or part-time over a longer period – anything up to nine months).

Working with children

Summer Camps

Summer camps, once the preserve of the USA, now take place all over the world, becoming increasingly important as more and more parents go out to work and child-care costs rocket. Activities offered range from horse-riding and archery to learning how to perform circus tricks. And in order to maintain a broad appeal, new courses offered in the last few years include recording a CD, film-making and website design. These camps require a huge number of summer workers. Jobs available include sports instructors, monitors and group counsellors. Most camps last from two to four weeks.

Au Pairs, Nannies & Mothers' Helps

These days, young British women are much less likely to consider au pairing as a summer job than was formerly the case. Being an au pair is seen as an unadventurous option compared with helping to conserve an Amazon rainforest or teaching English to Nepalese children, which is the type of alternative offered by the many, rather expensive, gap year companies. Nevertheless, au pairing remains an excellent way to acquire fluency in a foreign language. Girls (and sometimes young men) can arrange to live with a family, helping to look after the children in exchange for pocket money.

The terms au pair, mother's help and nanny are often applied rather loosely, since all are primarily live-in jobs concerned with looking after children. Nannies may have some formal training and take full charge of the children. Mother's helps work full-time and undertake general housework and/or cooking as well as childcare. Au pairs are supposed to work fewer hours and are

A Club Med childcare instructor

expected to learn a foreign language (except in the USA) while living with a family. The Council of Europe guidelines stipulate that au pairs should be aged 17-30 (though these limits are flexible), should be expected to work about five hours a day, plus a couple of evenings of babysitting, with at least one full day off per week; they must be given a private room and full board, health insurance, opportunities to learn the language and weekly pocket money of €260–€280 per month in Europe (£55 per week in the UK), plus board and lodging.

A number of agencies both in the UK and in the destination countries are described in this book. Many leading au pair agencies and youth exchange organisations in Europe belong to IAPA, the International Au Pair Association, an international body trying to regulate the industry. The IAPA website (www.iapa.org) has clear links to its member agencies around the world. A list of agencies can also be found at *www.europa-pages.com/au_pair*. After satisfying an agency that you are a suitable candidate for a live-in childcare position, you will have to wait until an acceptable match can be made with a family abroad. Make enquiries as early as possible, since there is a shortage of summer-only positions. In the first instance contact several agencies to compare terms and conditions. If your requirements are very specific as regards location or family circumstances, ring around some agencies and ask them to be blunt about their chances of being able to fix you up with what you want. In the UK agencies are permitted to charge a fee of up to £40 plus VAT only after a placement has been verified.

The advantage of a summer placement is that the au pair will accompany the family to their holiday destination at the seaside or in the mountains; the disadvantage is that the children will be out of school and therefore potentially a full-time responsibility.

Voluntary Work

Charities and aid organisations offer a range of both structured and unstructured voluntary opportunities around the world. For example, enterprising summer workers have participated in interesting projects from helping a local native settlement to build a community centre in Arctic Canada, to working with hill tribes in the state of Haryana in northern India. Almost

Participants taking part on worthwhile projects on BUNAC's Volunteer Overseas Programme

without exception, volunteers must be self-funding, which serves to deter all but the most dedicated.

When starting your research for a longer stint abroad as a volunteer, it is important to maintain realistic expectations. Ideally, your research should begin well in advance of your intended departure so that applications can be lodged, sponsorship money raised, language courses and other preparatory courses attended, and so on. When you receive the literature or check the website of voluntary organisations, consider the tone as well as the content. For example, profit-making commercial companies that charge high fees for participating in their programmes are more likely to produce glossy brochures that read almost like a tour operator's, whereas underfunded charities or small grassroots organisations with no publicity budget will probably duplicate their information on an ancient photocopier. Most organisations, with big budgets or no budget have a website or at least an email address.

For anyone with a green conscience, numerous conservation organisations throughout the world welcome volunteers for short or long periods. Projects range from tree planting to gibbon counting. Unfortunately, the more glamorous projects such as helping to conserve a coral reef or accompanying scientific research expeditions into wild and woolly places charge volunteers a great deal of money for the privilege of helping.

For further information on volunteering, *The International Directory of Voluntary Work* (www.crimsonpublishing.co.uk) contains advice and listings of all types of voluntary work worldwide. The website World Wide Volunteering online database of 1,450 organisations offering a potential total of 1.1 million placements has recently been made free for all to use. See www.wwv.org.uk.

Workcamps

Every year the international workcamps movement mobilises thousands of volunteers from many countries to join a programme of conflict resolution and community development. As well as providing volunteers with the means to live cheaply for two to four weeks in a foreign country, work-

Concordia volunteers take a break from restoring an old stone
vineyard house in the South of France

camps enable unskilled volunteers to become involved in what can be useful work for the community (eg building footpaths, renovating schools and providing aid).

Workcamps are perfect for people who want to get some experience volunteering, as participants are not expected to have any skills or qualifications. They are also a great way to meet
people from many different backgrounds and to increase awareness of other lifestyles and social
problems.

There are workcamps each summer in more than 90 countries worldwide, although the
strongest movements are still in places like France, Germany and Italy. If you are based in the UK
you will find a huge number of workcamps that are available to you worldwide through the
Concordia website (www.concordia-iye.org.uk) as well as IVS (www.ivs-gb.org.uk), UNA
Exchange (www.unaexchange.org) and Youth Action for Peace (www.yap-uk.org).

Volunteering at the Summer Music Festivals

Music festivals are increasing in size and scope every year and behind the scenes huge numbers
of volunteers are involved in stewarding, first aid and clearing up the festival site. Each year thousands of enterprising individuals gain entry to sold out festivals, without paying a penny, by volunteering to fill these positions. Oxfam, for example, recruits several thousand volunteer
stewards for a range of festivals in the UK including Glastonbury (www.oxfam.org.uk).

As a volunteer, you are required to work quite hard, but in return receive ample time each day
to enjoy the festival atmosphere and see your favourite bands. In the majority of cases, volunteers are also provided with a separate camping area, warm showers and meal passes. You will
find the details of individual festivals and how to apply as a volunteer in the individual country
chapters of this book.

LANDING THE PERFECT SUMMER JOB

You have two choices: fixing up a definite job before leaving home, or taking a gamble on something on arrival. There is a lot to recommend prior planning, especially for people who have seldom travelled on their own and who feel some trepidation about being away from home.

If you have no predisposition to choose one country over another based on previous holidays, language studies at school or information from friends or relatives who live abroad, you are free to consider any job listed in this book. It will soon become apparent that there are far fewer listings in developing countries, simply because paid work in the developing world is rarely available to foreigners. Yet many students arrange to live for next to nothing doing something positive (see the section on Volunteering below).

Some organisations and employers listed in this directory accept a tiny handful of individuals who satisfy stringent requirements; others accept almost anyone who can pay the required fee, for example agencies that recruit paying volunteers for conservation work in exotic places or to teach English. Some work schemes and official exchanges require a lot of advance planning since it is not unusual for an application deadline to fall three to six months before departure.

The kind of job you find will determine the sector of society in which you will mix and therefore the content of the experience. The traveller who spends a few weeks picking olives for a Cretan farmer will get a very different insight into Greece from the traveller who looks after the children of an Athenian shipping magnate. And both will probably have more culturally worthwhile experiences than the traveller who settles for working at a beach café frequented only by his or her partying compatriots. The more unusual and interesting the job the more competition it will attract.

BUNAC workers teaching children how to sail on a summer camp

Ten tips for success

Summer work isn't difficult to find, but about half a million other students will be job hunting, so it pays to plan ahead.

1. Do your research

With over 50,000 vacancies, this book is a great starting point. But there is nothing to stop you using this directory as a jumping off point, and doing your own research. Once you have seen how many seasonal jobs there are around, and the kind of places to find them, you are sure to find more. Some people prefer just to turn up in a place and look for work. No matter how thorough this book is, there is no substitute for good old fashioned word of mouth.

The internet can also be useful. The only problem with it is that the plethora of resources in cyberspace can be bewildering and not infrequently disappointing – the number and range of jobs posted often fall short of the claims. Small-scale employers do not like to use the web as they are bound to be inundated with SPAM and applications from Merseyside to Mongolia. The internet as a job-finding tool works best for those with specific experience and skills, for example people looking for TEFL jobs abroad (see section below on last-minute job hunting for some recommended recruitment sites).

2. Timing

Apply early. Companies like to make their staff arrangements in good time. Some of the biggest employers may maintain reserve lists to cover late staff cancellations, so it might pay off to apply after the deadline, but don't be disappointed if you receive no reply.

Remember: most employers much prefer one person for the whole of the season rather than several people for shorter periods. If you are able to work for longer than the minimum period quoted, let the employer know at an early stage. This is often a deciding factor.

3. Cast your net wide

Apply for all of the jobs that appeal to you (plus a few that don't). The more you apply for the greater your chances of getting a great summer job. But do make sure that you are fully qualified for the job. Check any requirements and special qualifications needed, particularly if good knowledge of another language is called for. If there is any shortfall, emphasise other skills and qualifications that may be useful.

4. Get your approach right

Compose a short formal letter, explaining which position interests you, when you are available and why you think you are suitable. Always mention that the job has been seen in this book as many of the employers in it have a long-standing and trusting relationship with Vacation Work and its publications.

Try to address the potential employer in his or her language. It is not only polite to do so, but there is a possibility that he or she is unable to speak English.

5. Apply with a great CV

Enclose with your letter a well thought out *curriculum vitae* (CV or résumé). Always target your CV to the job in question, leaving out any irrelevant material and emphasising related achievements. Your CV should be on a single A4 sheet (2 sides if you must, but no more) covering the following points and any other details you consider relevant:

- Personal details (name, address, nationality, age, date of birth, marital status).
- Previous work experience, especially of similar type of work.
- Special qualifications, especially when they have some relevance to the job in question, e.g. canoe instructor's certificate, typing speeds or fluency in another language.
- Education (brief details of type of education, examinations passed).

Make sure you enclose a small recent passport-sized photo of yourself as this is often required. If you need some tips on improving your CV take a look at www.prospects.ac.uk.

6. Apply with care

Check and then double check the spelling and grammar in your application. If you are sending it via email, be sure to remember the attachment. Also if a CV is attached, make sure that it is written in a programme that is readable and receivable by the receiver (in Microsoft Word format or a pdf) and that it contains no viruses.

7. Chase it up

If there is no reply from the employer within a reasonable period of time (say two weeks), it may be advisable to follow up the application with a telephone call or another email. The employer may be impressed by your initiative and perseverance if it is matched by enthusiasm and politeness. If you are making a first approach to a potential employer by phone, smile while you are talking to them – it comes across in your voice.

In a few cases it is expected that applicants should make themselves available for an interview or visit the employer in person. Where this is the case, the applicant is likely to find more success if he can back up claims of suitability with a written CV and references.

8. Negotiate

When a job is offered to you, check details of wages, hours and other conditions of work with the employer. Do not be afraid to negotiate; you are always entitled to ask whether or not different terms are possible.

9. Check details carefully

The details given in this book have been supplied by the employer and will normally be correct, but it is wise to obtain written confirmation of them before taking up the position. You should insist that you receive a contract of employment before you set off for your job if the journey involves any great expense, or if the employer seems at all vague about the details of the work you will do.

10. Confirm

When you are offered a job, confirm acceptance or otherwise as quickly as possible. If plans change and you do not want to take up a job you have already accepted, it is only fair to let the employer know immediately. If you are offered more than one job, decide quickly which one you prefer and inform both employers of your decision as promptly as possible.

LEFT IT TO THE LAST MINUTE? DON'T PANIC!

If you're reading this, you are probably not the kind of well-organised jobseeker who plans ahead! Clearly it is far better to organise your summer job a long way in advance. The two main industries that survive on seasonal labour are tourism and agriculture, and managers from Canterbury to Cape Town need to have enough seasonal staff lined up before their busy season begins. So, the earlier that you can make contact with potential employers, as close as possible to the date indicating the start of the recruitment season provided in the entries that follow, the easier it will be to secure a summer job. Lecture over.

In the real world, it can be very difficult to focus on finding a temporary job until the summer is almost upon you. The good news is that not all is lost, especially for someone who already has a little relevant experience or a smattering of a foreign language. It is always worth contacting large seasonal employers at the last minute, since there is a high turnover in this field and a huge amount of demand. Eleventh-hour jobseekers from Britain will have to concentrate on the UK and Europe, since obtaining student work visas for Australia, New Zealand, the USA and Canada takes many months.

Patient searches of employment websites can also prove productive. A host of commercial websites promises to provide free online recruitment services for working travellers, and some of the job listings will show immediate start dates. These include the admirable Jobs Abroad Bulletin (jobsabroadbulletin.co.uk), a free monthly e-bulletin on working abroad and gap years, seasonworkers.com, natives.co.uk (originally for ski resort work but now also for summer jobs), anyworkanywhere.com, coolworks.com and jobsmonkey.com (though the latter two are mainly for North America). JobSlave.com is a network of recruitment sites aimed at the youth market covering everything from bar jobs in Sydney to banking jobs in London. Listings will be thinner than they would be before Easter but possibilities still exist.

As in any job hunt, networking is often the key to success. It is always worth telling family, friends and friends of friends about your plans in case they divulge the details of potentially useful contacts. And if you have no ready-made contacts in your chosen destination, you can seek them out in advance or after arrival through local clubs and organisations whose interests you share, e.g. cyclists, Hash House Harriers (social runners), jazz buffs, and so on. Irish pubs abroad often attract the ex-pat community who will offer free advice. To meet locals and get free accommodation, investigate membership in an international hospitality exchange organisation like Global Freeloaders, place2stay.net or couchsurfing.com, all of which are completely free to join.

Hot air balloon crew working in the Loire Valley, France

Finding a job on-the spot

If your patience gives out before you receive the promise of a job, there is one final recourse, which is simply to gamble on finding a job on-the-spot. Casual work by its very nature is changeable and unpredictable and can often best be searched out where it is happening. So whether you are going abroad, or just further afield than your home town, it may be that your best bet is to pack your bags and go for it.

Even if a prospective employer turns you down at first, ask again since it is human nature to want to reward keenness and he or she may decide that an extra staff member could be useful after all. Polite pestering pays off. Some go so far as to offer to work for an initial period without pay, hoping to make themselves first choice for any vacancy that occurs, though this may be a gamble too far. Boldness and initiative will usually be rewarded with some kind of remunerated job, though seldom will it be glamorous.

Your chances are better if you are willing to consider jobs that are unappealing and with awkward hours. For example while writing this, I received an email from someone who assures me that there are people in the state of Maine in the USA who dig for bloodworms to sell to fish bait dealers who pay 25 cents per worm and a good digger can collect 1000 worms in a day.

Less-structured possibilities abound. Enterprising travellers have managed to earn money by doing a bizarre range of odd-jobs, from selling home-made peanut butter to homesick Americans or busking on the bagpipes, to doing Tarot readings on a Mediterranean ferry or becoming film extras in Mumbai.

Top Tips for Finding a Job on-the-Spot

- Collect character/job references on headed paper, a short CV and any potentially relevant qualifications (driving, sailing, cooking, TEFL, computing, first aid). Scan and email copies to yourself so that you can access them anywhere.
- Pack a smart uncreasable outfit for interviews.
- Take a bilingual dictionary and teach-yourself language course on your iPod since you will be far more motivated to use these when you are actually living in the country.
- Broadcast your intentions to third cousins, visiting professors or in relevant chatrooms and be prepared to follow up every lead you are given. Contacts are often the key to success.
- On arrival, seek advice from expats and fellow travellers. If looking for casual work on farms or trying to fix up a passage on a transatlantic yacht, for example, a visit to a village pub frequented by farmers, yachties or the local expatriate community is usually worth dozens of speculative applications and emails from home.
- If going door to door, for example along a waterfront stretch of restaurants, ask at every single place, rather than just the ones that seem appealing. You may have to endure dozens of rejections, but the next door along might well be open to you.
- If there is something you are particularly keen to do but there are no vacancies, volunteer your labour so that you can showcase your ability and enthusiasm and then you will be on hand if an opportunity arises.
- Don't hang around waiting for something to turn up. Go out and sell yourself (not literally).

BEFORE YOU GO: ESSENTIAL PREPARATION

Travel

If you are a student, you can take advantage of a range of special discounts both at home and abroad which enable you to go almost anywhere in the world on the cheap. To qualify for these discounts on train, plane and bus fares, on selected accommodation, admission to museums and so on, you need an International Student Identity Card (ISIC) which is recognised all over the world. The card is obtainable for £9 from www.isiccard.com. The ISIC card is valid for 15 months from 1 September. If you are not a student, but still under 26, you can take advantage of the International Youth Travel Card (IYTC) available from www.isiccard.com for £9.

Both cards are available from STA Travel (0870 60 6070; www.statravel.co.uk), Student Flights (www.studentflights.co.uk) and some other student travel outlets. Applications should include proof of student status (if required), a passport photo, full name, date of birth, nationality, address and a cheque or postal order.

Flying

Valuable discounts are also available for air travel. Student and youth discount flights are operated by the major student travel organisations under the umbrella of the Student Air Travel Association – these include STA Travel and Student Flights, mentioned above. Most of the flights are open to ISIC card holders under 30 (some have different age restrictions) together with their spouses and dependent children travelling on the same flight or to young persons with a valid EURO<26 (www.euro26.org) or Go 25 card.

Specialist youth and student travel agencies are an excellent source of information for just about every kind of discount. Staff are often themselves seasoned travellers and can be a mine

Swimming lessons with Butlins lifeguards

of information on budget travel in foreign countries. But check out the no-frills airlines and cheap flights websites as well to compare prices before making a final decision. For complex routings, try Travel Nation (0845 344 4225; www.travel-nation.co.uk). A good starting place for independent flight research are websites that search and compare cheapest fares such as www.cheap-flights.co.uk and www.skyscanner.net.

The leading youth and budget travel specialist in the UK is STA Travel which can organise flexible deals, domestic flights, overland transport, accommodation and tours. STA is a major international travel agency with 450 branches worldwide including 65 in the UK. As well as worldwide airfares, they sell discounted rail and coach tickets, budget accommodation and insurance and many other packaged products, and have branches at many universities.

In America, in addition to the major student travel agencies such as STA Travel mentioned above in the context of student cards, discount tickets are available online on a standby basis from agencies like Air-Tech (+1 212-219-7000; www.airtech.com), Air Treks (1-800-350-0612; www.airtreks.com) and Air-Hitch (www.airhitch.org). The cheapest fares from the US are available to people who are flexible about departure dates and destinations; the passenger chooses a block of possible dates (up to a five-day 'window') and preferred destinations. The company then tries to match these requirements with empty airline seats being released at knock-down prices. The website www.studentuniverse.com is also worth a look for cheap flights.

From the UK to Europe it is usually cheaper to fly on one of the no-frills ticketless airlines than it is to go by rail or coach. Airlines like Ryanair and easyJet shuttle between regional airports and scores of European and Mediterranean destinations from Alta in northern Norway to Marrakesh in north Africa. The list of airlines below is only a selection. There are new companies and new destinations being added all the time so it pays to keep an eye on the press and use the internet. Note that quoted prices now have to include taxes (that add up to £35 on a return fare to Europe) and that you usually have to book well in advance to get the cheapest fares. These airlines do not take bookings via travel agents so it is necessary to contact them directly.

- *BMI Baby* – 0870 264 2229; www.bmibaby.com
- *EasyJet* – 0871 500 100; www.easyjet.com.
- *First Choice* – 0870 850 3999; www.firstchoiceairways.com
- *GB Airways* – 0870 8509850; www.gbairways.com
- *Ryanair* – 0871 246 0000; www.ryanair.com.
- *Thomsonfly* – 0870 1900 737; www.thomsonfly.com.
- *Flybe* – www.flybe.com
- *Jet2* – www.jet2.com

This style of flying has spread to the continent and discount airlines have proliferated including www.clickair.com (Spanish), www.airberlin.com and www.germanwings.com (German), www.transavia.com (Dutch), www.centralwings.com and www.wizzair.com (both Polish), www.smartwings.com (Czech), www.SkyEurope.com (Central Europe), www.blue1.com (Finnish), www.norwegian.no (Norwegian) and so on. Central sources of information include www.flycheapo.com and www.whichbudget.com. Scheduled airlines like BA have had to drop fares to compete and are always worth comparing. A company that offers an air pass for all of Europe is www.europebyair.com which mainly targets Americans. The Europe By Air Flight Pass is a flat-rate ticket ($99 or $129) per flight on participating airlines within Europe.

Rail and Coach Travel

If you want to reduce your carbon footprint, rail and coach travel are far better options and there are some cheap deals to be found if you know where to look.

InterRail is a great way to visit lots of countries cheaply. In the past, tickets were divided into zones, but this system was simplified in 2007. Now one Global pass covers the whole of Europe for one calendar month costing approximately £285 for those under 26 and £435 for those 26 and over. A shorter duration of 22 days is also available for £223/£338. If you plan to make a few long journeys in a certain number of days, investigate Flexipasses; they permit five days of travel within ten days, or ten days of travel within 22 days. A number of specialised agencies sell InterRail products and add slightly different mark-ups. Passes can be bought online (in which case you will probably have to pay an extra £5 or so for Special Delivery) or in person at branches of STA Travel and similar outlets. Websites to check include www.traineurope.co.uk,

'Which way now?' Taken by a Concordia volunteer in the Czech Republic

www.raileurope.co.uk, www.railpassshop.com or the marvellous site for train travellers everywhere www.seat61.com. Rail Europe can be contacted by telephone on 08705 848848.

The InterRail pass also entitles you to discounts on *Eurostar* and certain ferries in Europe.If you are travelling in Denmark, Finland, Norway or Sweden, you should investigate the ScanRail pass. Further details are available at www.scanrail.com.

Eurolines is the group name for 32 independent coach operators serving 500 destinations in all European countries from Ireland to Romania. Promotional prices start at £30 return for London–Amsterdam if booked 7 days in advance. Bookings can be made online at www.national express.com/eurolines or by phoning 08705 808080. So called 'funfares' mean that some off-season fares from the UK are even lower, e.g. £13 to Brussels, Paris or Dublin.

One of the most interesting revolutions in independent and youth travel has been the explosion of backpackers' bus services which are hop-on hop-off coach services following prescribed routes. These can be found in New Zealand (Stray Travel and the Magic Travellers Network), Australia (Oz Experience), Canada (Moose Travel) South Africa (Baz Bus) and Turkey/Greece (Fez Travel) as well as in Britain and Ireland. For example Busabout serves 30 destinations in 10 countries. You can buy a pass for a Western, Northern or Southern 'loop' (they are not so good on Eastern Europe) or a Flexitrip pass. All are valid for the entire operating season May to October. One loop currently costs £289. A Flexitrip Pass costs £239 and includes 6 stops (additional stops can be purchased on board). In North America trips run by *Green Tortoise* (1-800-867-8647; www.greentortoise.com) use vehicles converted to sleep 36 people and make interesting tours, detours and stopovers around the Americas and Mexico.

Visas and Red Tape

Visiting a foreign country as a tourist is quite distinct from going there in order to work. Tourist visas are not required in Europe nor to visit North America, Australia or New Zealand. Other countries may require a visa to enter. Up-to-date visa information is available from national consulates in London/Washington or on the internet. For example the visa agency *Thames Consular Services* in London (020 8995 2492; www.thamesconsular.com) allows you to search visa require-

A Club Med water sports instructor
wake boarding on the Mediterranean

ments and costs for individual countries and specialises in providing UK residents with visas for most countries (for an additional fee of £35–£45).

EU citizens have the right to work anywhere within the EU and in fact the bureaucratic procedures for nationals of the old EU states have become easier. In 2004 directives encouraged all member states to abolish the necessity for EU nationals to acquire a residence permit after three months. Usually some sort of registration process is necessary but the paperwork in most countries has been simplified. Slowly the impediments are being dismantled.

The accession of two new countries to the European Union in 2007 (Bulgaria and Romania) in addition to the ten new countries that joined in May 2004 means that the EU now consists of the original 15 member states (Austria, Belgium, Denmark, Finland, France, Germany, Greece, Ireland, Italy, Luxembourg, the Netherlands, Portugal, Spain, Sweden and the United Kingdom) plus Hungary, Poland, the Czech Republic, Slovakia, Slovenia, Estonia, Latvia, Lithuania, Malta, Cyprus, Romania and Bulgaria. However some transitional barriers to the full mobility of labour in the new EU countries will be in place for up to seven years. For up-to-date information on regulations regarding taking up work in all EU member states consult the EURES website at www.europa.eu.int/eures or the individual countries' embassies in your own country.

Work permits and residence visas are not readily available to Europeans looking to work elsewhere in the world or to North American and Antipodean jobseekers in Europe (see sections on

Red Tape in the country chapters). In most cases, a foreign job-seeker must first find an employer willing to apply to the immigration authorities on his or her behalf well in advance of the job's starting date and before the applicant enters the country. The alternative is to participate in an approved exchange programme where the red tape is taken care of by a sponsoring organisation. The same applies to non-European students looking for seasonal jobs in Europe. Established organisations with work abroad programmes are invaluable for shouldering the red tape problems and for providing a soft landing for first time travellers.

For example BUNAC (020-7251-3472; www.bunac.org.uk) is a student club that helps students and other young people to work abroad while BUNAC USA (www.bunac.org) assists a large number of Americans to work in Britain for up six months and in other countries around the world. BUNAC in the UK has a choice of programmes to the United States, Canada, Costa Rica, Australia, New Zealand, Peru, South Africa, Ghana and Cambodia, and in all cases assists with obtaining short-term working visas. In some programmes, jobs will be arranged for you, for instance as counsellors or domestic staff at American children's summer camps; in others, it is up to you to find a job once you arrive at your destination.

IST Plus, Ltd, in London oversees work abroad programmes for Britons in the USA, Canada, Australia, New Zealand, Thailand, Japan and China (020-8939 9057; www.istplus.com).

Many other youth exchange organisations and commercial agencies offer packages which help students to arrange work or volunteer positions abroad. For example *Camp America* and *Camp Counselors USA (CCUSA)* are major recruitment organisations which arrange for thousands of young people to work in the US mostly on summer camps (see chapter on the USA). Other agencies specialise in placing young people (both women and men) in families as au pairs, as voluntary English teachers or in a range of other capacities – see the entries for individual countries.

The Schengen Visa

The Schengen visa allows citizens of member states to cross borders freely without the need for a passport (although some form of government approved identification is needed for air travel). The 15 Schengen countries are: Austria, Belgium, Denmark, Finland, France, Germany, Iceland, Italy, Greece, Luxembourg, Netherlands, Norway, Portugal, Spain and Sweden. This is a visa for entry. It does not affect your ability to work in a certain country.

The Schengen Visa issued by an Embassy or Consulate of the above mentioned countries allows the holder to move freely in all these countries within the validity of the visa. To obtain this type of visa you will be required to hold a passport or travel document that is recognised by all of the Schengen member states and valid at least three months beyond the validity of the visa.

Estonia, Hungary, Latvia, Lithuania, Malta, Poland, Czech Republic, Slovakia and Slovenia are due to implement this agreement on 29 March 2008, providing that they fulfil all the prerequisites. Romania, Bulgaria and Switzerland will also be implementing it in the near future.

What to pack

Even if you are travelling directly to your place of work, don't load yourself down with excess baggage. Most people who go abroad for a summer job want to do at least some independent travelling when their job ends and will find themselves seriously hampered if they are carrying around a 30-kilo rucksack. When you're buying a backpack/rucksack in a shop try to place a significant weight in it so you can feel how comfortable it might be to carry on your back, otherwise you'll be misled by lifting something usually filled with foam.

While aiming to travel as lightly as possible you should consider the advantage of taking certain extra pieces of equipment. For example:

- A Swiss army knife (make sure it is not packed in your airline hand luggage) is often invaluable, if only for its corkscrew!
- A comfortable pair of shoes is essential since most summer jobs will involve long hours on your feet whether in a hotel dining room or in a farmer's field.
- A bin-liner to put inside your rucksack to keep your stuff dry.
- A basic sewing kit for mending backpacks or clothes.
- A couple of metres of light strong cord (such as dental floss) to make a washing line etc.

Ideally, talk to someone who has done the job before who might recommend an obscure piece of equipment you'd never think of, for example a pair of fingerless gloves for cold-weather fruit-picking. You might also allow yourself the odd lightweight luxury, such as an mp3 player or a digital camera. You can always post some belongings on ahead, with the employer's permission. Try to leave at home anything of either great monetary or sentimental value as their temporary absence is nothing compared to their permanent loss.

Good maps and guides are usually considered essential tools for a trip. If you are in London or Bristol, the famous map shop Stanfords (www.stanfords.co.uk) can supply most needs. The Map Shop (www.themapshop.co.uk) does an extensive mail order business and will send you the relevant catalogue. Another specialist is Maps Worldwide (www.mapsworldwide.com). There are dozens of travel specialists throughout North America; a good selection of maps and guides is available at www.netstoreusa.com/maps.

Accommodation

The vast majority of jobs listed in this book come with accommodation; usually shared with other workers. Even if there is no accommodation onsite, many of the employers listed regularly take on young people from all over the world and are used to helping their staff to find local lodgings.

You should always find out what the deal is way ahead of time. Ask the following questions of your potential employer:

- How much will be deducted from your wages to cover accommodation?
- What facilities (especially for self-catering) are provided?
- How close to your place of work are the lodgings?
- Will there be extra costs for food, utilities, etc.?
- Are staff allowed to move out if they find more congenial or cheaper accommodation?

Sometimes the accommodation provided is very basic indeed and you should be prepared for something rather more insalubrious than you are used to at home or at university. Certain jobs may provide more luxurious accommodation, for example: hotel/resort work or any live-in job. Live in jobs of course come with their own drawbacks, such as a lack of privacy and free time.

If accommodation is not provided with the job, try to arrange something in advance, and certainly for the first couple of nights. If necessary make the journey to your destination several days early to fix up a suitable room. In cities, if the backpackers' hostels are full, try universities, which might rent out student accommodation that has been vacated for the summer or whose notice boards may include details of housing. In holiday resorts, accommodation may be at a premium and you will have to use your ingenuity to find something you can afford.

Annual membership of the *Youth Hostels Association* costs £15.95 a year if you're over 26, £9.95 if you're not; you can join at any YHA hostel or shop over the phone on 0870 7708868 or online at www.yha.org.uk. Seasonal demand abroad can be high, so it is always preferable to book in advance if you know your itinerary. You can pre-book beds over the internet on www.hihostels.org or through individual hostels and national offices listed in the *Hostelling International Guide*, which contains details of 4,000 hostels worldwide. The Guide can be ordered from the YHA at the above number.

Hostels of Europe (www.hostelseurope.com) offer membership to a network of more than 500 Hostels on the best-travelled routes. Members get discounts of 5%–15% on accommodation, internet access, tours, etc. Information and on-line bookings can be made through www.hostels.net which is a searchable database of independent hostels in Europe, America and Down Under.

Money

Your average budget will vary hugely depending on where you are travelling. Obviously, India and Vietnam are going to be much cheaper than Switzerland or anywhere in Scandinavia. Whatever the size of your travelling fund, you should give some thought to how and in what form to carry your money. Travellers' cheques are much safer than cash, though they cost an extra 1% and banks able to cash them are not always near to hand. The most universally recognised brands are American Express, Thomas Cook and Visa. It is advisable also to keep a small amount of cash.

Euro notes and coins are the currency in Austria, Belgium, Finland, France, Germany, Greece, Ireland, Italy, Luxembourg, the Netherlands, Portugal, Slovenia and Spain (Cyprus and Malta will begin using it on 1 January 2008). Please note wages in this book are not always quoted in English pounds sterling. It depends on how the company in question prefers to pay their wages. Bear in mind then that exchange rates can fluctuate, so you are always advised to convert wages quoted at the current rate before accepting a job.

The easiest way to look up the exchange rate of any world currency is to check on the internet (e.g. www.xe.com/ucc or www.oanda.com).

Keeping your money safe

Theft takes many forms, from the highly trained gangs of children who artfully pick pockets in European railway stations to more violent attacks in South African or South American cities. You can reduce the risks by carrying your wealth in several places including a comfortable money belt worn inside your clothing, steering clear of seedy or crowded areas, and remaining particularly alert in railway stations. If you are robbed, you must obtain a police report (sometimes for a fee) to stand any chance of recouping part of your loss from your insurer (assuming the loss of cash is covered in your policy) or from your travellers' cheque company. Always keep a separate record of the cheque numbers you are carrying, so you can instantly identify the serial numbers of the ones lost or stolen.

In emergencies

If you do end up in dire financial straits and do not have a credit card, you should contact someone at home who is in a position to send money. You may contact your bank back home and ask them to wire money to you, often through the Swift service. This can only be done through a bank in the town you're in – something you have to arrange with your own bank, so you know where to pick the money up. Sample charges might be £15–£20 through high street banks.

Western Union (www.westernunion.co.uk) offers an international money transfer service whereby cash deposited at one branch can be withdrawn by you from any other branch or agency. Western Union agents – there are 90,000 of them in nearly 200 countries – come in all shapes and sizes (e.g. travel agencies, stationers, chemists). The person sending money to you simply turns up at a Western Union counter, hands over the desired sum plus the fee, which is £8 for up to £25 transferred, £21 for £100–£200, £37 for £500 and so on. It can also be done over the phone with a credit card, or online.

Thomas Cook, American Express and the Post Office offer a similar service called Moneygram (www.moneygram.com). Cash deposited at one of their foreign exchange counters is available within ten minutes at the named destination or can be collected up to 45 days later. The standard fee for sending £500 (for example) is £36. Ring 0800 897198 for details, or see the website.

Health and insurance

The National Health Service ceases to cover British nationals once they leave the United Kingdom. If you are travelling in Europe, you should get hold of a European Health Insurance Card (EHIC). The EHIC entitles you to free emergency medical treatment anywhere within the European Economic Area (the EU plus Liechtenstein, Norway and Iceland). You can apply for an EHIC in person (go into your nearest post office), over the phone (0845 6062030), or online (www.dh.gov.uk/travellers).

If you are planning to include developing countries on your itinerary, you will want to take the necessary health precautions, though this won't be cheap unless you are able to have your injections at your local NHS surgery where most injections are free or given for a minimal charge. Malaria poses an increasing danger and expert advice should be sought about which medications to take for the specific parts of the world you intend to visit.

Tap water is unsafe to drink in the more remote parts of the world so it will be necessary to give some thought as to the method of water purification you will use (filtering, boiling or chemical additives). Remember that water used to wash vegetables, brush teeth or make ice cubes is also potentially risky. Tap water throughout Western Europe is safe to drink.

MASTA (Medical Advisory Service for Travellers Abroad) runs Travel Health Centres throughout the UK (to locate your nearest health centre visit www.masta.org). It also maintains an up-to-date database on travellers' diseases and their prevention. You can also get a Travel Health Brief for £3.99 online, with health information on your destinations (up to ten countries).

Increasingly, people are seeking advice via the internet; check for example www.fitfortravel.scot.nhs.uk; www.tmb.ie and www.travelhealth.co.uk. The BBC's Health Travel Site www.bbc.co.uk/health/travel is a solid source of information about travel health ranging from tummy trouble to water quality and snake bites.

Foreign health services rarely offer as comprehensive a free service for emergency treatment as the NHS does; while some offer free treatment, others will only subsidise the cost and any part of the treatment not covered by the free health service is met by private health insurance top up schemes. In some countries the ambulance ride has to be paid for, but not the treatment. The cost of bringing a person back to the UK in the case of illness or death is never covered under the reciprocal arrangements so it is considered essential to purchase private insurance in addition to carrying an EHIC.

Travel insurance

Ordinary travel insurance policies cover only those risks that a holidaymaker can expect to face and will not cover work-related injuries such as treating backs damaged while grape-picking, or burns caused by an overboiling goulash in a restaurant kitchen.

The following companies should be able to arrange insurance cover for most people going to work abroad, as long as they are advised of the exact nature of the physical/manual job to be undertaken:

Club Direct: www.ClubDirect.com. Work abroad is covered as long as it does not involve heavy machinery

Columbus Direct: 0870 033 9988; www.columbusdirect.com. Provides a Globetrotter policy for those working abroad for short or long periods (up to 12 months).

The Travel Insurance Agency: 020-8446 5414; www.travelinsurers.com. Policies only for travellers, including those working abroad.

Worldwide Travel Insurance Services Ltd: 0870 112 8100; www.worldwideinsure.com. Comprehensive policies for most work abroad from 5 days to 24 months. Manual labour cover can be purchased from overseas for an additional premium.

Endsleigh Insurance: 0800 028 3571; www.endsleigh.co.uk. Offices in most university towns. Age limit 35.

FINDING A JOB IN THE UK

The summer has always been a period when employers in Britain look for large numbers of additional staff. Even when the recession of the early nineties was at its worst people still, for example, ate fruit and vegetables and went on holiday, so agriculture and tourism continued to provide a reliable source of short-term work. In this chapter we have collected details of job vacancies supplied to us by employers in England, Scotland, Wales and Northern Ireland. The jobs have been arranged under the following headings, complete with some UK specific information about each type of job: Business & Industry, Children, Holiday Centres & Amusements, Hotels & Catering, Language Schools, Medical, Outdoor and Sport, Voluntary Work and Vacation Traineeships & Internships, the latter providing on-the-job work experience for students in business and industry.

Further Sources of Information and Employment

Jobcentre Plus. The Department of Work and Pensions runs the Jobcentre Plus network where a full range of temporary vacancies can be found by searching on touch-screen terminals known as Jobpoints. Jobcentre Plus advertises all of its vacancies at www.directgov.gov.uk/employment and on its own website, www.jobcentreplus.gov.uk.

Jobseeker Direct (0845 606 0234) is a phone service designed to help you find a full or part-time job. Telephone advisors have access to jobs nationwide and can help match your particular skills and requirements to vacant positions.

Employment Agencies. While the number of agencies dealing with temporary work in London can be positively daunting, outside the capital the range is much narrower. It is worth registering with as many agencies as possible in order to enhance your chances of finding work. The jobs offered are frequently office based, though increasingly agencies specialise in different industry sectors. Under the Employment Agencies Act it is illegal for an agency to charge a fee for finding someone a job: agencies make their money by charging the employers.

National Institutes. One way of finding out more about vacation training opportunities within a specific field is to contact the relevant national professional body or institute. Institutes do not themselves offer traineeships, but may be able to offer general advice and/or give names and addresses of companies within their field. Here are a few – others can be found under *ASSOCIATIONS-TRADE* at www.yell.com.

> *Hotel & Catering International Management Association:* 020 8661 4900; www.hcima.org.uk
> *Institute of Chartered Accountants in England and Wales:* 01908 248040; www.icaew.co.uk/careers
> *Institute of Chartered Accountants of Scotland:* 0131 347 0100; www.icas.org.uk
> *Chartered Institute of Public Relations:* 020 7766 3333; www.ipr.org.uk
> *International Federation of the Periodical Press:* 020 7404 4169; www.fipp.com
> *Royal Institute of British Architects:* 020 7580 5533; www.riba.org

Tax and National Insurance

Income Tax. Single people are entitled to a personal tax allowance, which means that you do not pay income tax until your yearly earnings exceed £5,435 (2008/9 figure). Few people are likely to earn this much over the vacation. You may earn between £5,435 and £7,665 at a tax rate of 10%. If you earn any more than this you will have to pay tax at 22%.

To avoid paying tax you need to fill out the right form; if your employer uses the PAYE system, new employees will usually be taxed under an 'emergency code' until the Tax Office receives this form from your employer. Students working in their holidays should fill in form P38(S), and school/other students or individuals starting to work for the first time should fill in a P46. A P38 allows employers to pay students without the deduction of tax. However, if you are not planning to be a student after 5 April of the next year, or if your total income (excluding student loans, scholarships and educational grants) in the tax year exceeds £5,035, you should not fill in a P38. Students who work during term time as well as during holidays are also not eligible to fill out a P38. If you pay any tax before you are put on the correct tax code, then you can claim a rebate during the year if your estimated yearly earnings do not exceed the personal allowance. If you have not been put on the right tax code by the time you leave your job, send a repayment claims form (P50) to the Tax Office together with your P45, which you will get when you finish work. If you are being paid by cash or cheque, not PAYE, then worrying about codes and rebates should not be necessary, although strictly speaking any income should be reported to your local tax office. Further information can be found at www.hmrc.gov.uk/students.

National Insurance. National Insurance contributions are compulsory for employees over 16 years of age if they earn over a certain limit. The rate you pay is calculated according to your wages. Currently, anyone who earns less than £98 a week pays nothing and then 11% of earnings above that figure.

If you require information in addition to that given above, contact your local HM Revenue & Customs, the new department responsible for the former Inland Revenue and HM Customs and Excise offices, or visit www.hmrc.gov.uk or else your local Citizens Advice Bureau.

The National Minimum Wage

The UK has a national minimum wage, which on 1 October 2007 was raised to £5.52 per hour for those aged 22 and over and £4.60 per hour for those aged 18-21. Most workers in the UK, including home workers, agency workers, commission workers, part-time workers, casual workers and pieceworkers, are entitled to the national minimum wage. The minimum wage has been extended to cover 16 (who have ceased to be of compulsory school age) and 17 years olds, at a rate of £3.40 per hour.

This is a general overview. Those wanting more detailed information, leaflets or to register a complaint should call the National Minimum Wage (NMW) Helpline on 0845 600 0678 or visit www.dti.gov.uk/employment/pay.

Red Tape

Before writing letters to prospective employers, **overseas applicants** should clarify the terms under which they may visit and work in Britain. Anyone arriving at UK Immigration without the necessary visa, letter of invitation or other required documentation could be sent back home on the next available flight. An outline of the regulations is given below. For further information, contact the nearest British Consulate or High Commission.

The primary route for entry into the UK for the purpose of employment was previously the work permit system. Work permits were issued only where a genuine vacancy existed and where particular qualifications or skills were required that were in short supply from the resident and EEA labour force. In 2005, the government announced its intention to implement a Five Year Strategy for Immigration and Asylum. This represented a major overhaul of the work permit arrangements, as well as rules on immigration and asylum. Consequently, a new points-based system, designed to enable the UK to control immigration more effectively was introduced in March 2006 to replace the 80 different entry routes by which a non-EEA national could come to the UK to work.

Visa Requirements

All those who are **not** British or EEA nationals will need a visa or entry clearance for all stays in the UK over 6 months Since November 2003, nationals of 10 "phase one" countries require entry clearance for stays of over 6 months. These countries are Australia, Canada, Hong Kong SAR, Japan, Malaysia, New Zealand, Singapore, South Africa, South Korea, and the USA. From November 2006, nationals of a further 55 "phase two" countries also require the same entry clearance. These include much of South America, the Caribbean island states and some African nations. For the full list of "phase two" countries and for the latest information on visa requirements, it is advisable to check the UK visa website at www.ukvisas.gov.uk.

Entry under the Points-Based System for Migration

Wherever relevant, entries in this book specify if the company or organisation in question welcomes applications from overseas. Unfortunately, this does not mean that all foreigners can work for them legally in this country.

EEA Citizens. Nationals of the European Economic Area are free to enter the United Kingdom to seek employment without a work permit. At present this applies to citizens of EU countries, EEA member states of Norway, Iceland and Liechtenstein, and the European Free Trade Agreement (EFTA) member state of Switzerland. However EEA nationals still require a permit for the Channel Islands and the Isle of Man. However, nationals from most of the new EU states who find a job in the UK are required to register with the Home Office under the new Worker Registration Scheme as soon as they find work. This currently carries an initial charge of £90 (fees are reviewed regularly). This scheme was set up so that the government could monitor the impact of EU accession on the UK labour market and restrict access to benefits. Nationals from Malta and Cyprus have free movement rights and are not required to obtain a workers registration certificate. EEA nationals intending to stay longer than 6 months may apply for a residence permit, although there is no obligation on them to do so.

Non-EEA Citizens. Until the Points-Based Entry system (PBS) was introduced, the general position under the Immigration Rules was that overseas nationals (other than EEA nationals) coming to work in Britain should have work permits before setting out. Permits were normally issued only for specific jobs requiring a high level of skill and experience for which resident or EEA labour was not available. In other words, a UK employer could not receive a work permit for a non-EEA citizen unless it was a job for which there was no EEA national available.

The new points-based system of migration to the UK is still in the early stages of implementation. It is designed to control migration more effectively, tackle abuse and identify the most talented workers by consolidating entry clearance and work permit applications into one single-step application. The plan is to ensure that only those who benefit Britain can come here to work. These criteria are only for those workers from outside the EEA who wish to work or train in the UK. The system is based on 5 tiers:

- Tier 1: Highly skilled workers, e.g. scientists or entrepreneurs;
- Tier 2: Skilled workers with a job to offer, e.g. nurses, teachers or engineers;
- Tier 3: Low skilled workers filling specific temporary labour shortages, e.g. construction workers for a particular building project;
- Tier 4: Students;
- Tier 5: Youth mobility workers and temporary workers, e.g. working holiday makers.

For each tier, applicants will need sufficient points to gain entry clearance to the UK. Points can be scored for skills or attributes which predict a worker's success in the labour market. For Tiers 3-5, under which most summer employment falls, points will be awarded depending on whether the applicant has: a valid certificate of sponsorship from an approved sponsor; adequate funds to live in the UK; proven compliance with previous immigration conditions and in some cases English language ability. A web-based self-assessment programme, which allows applicants to understand whether they meet the UK's criteria for entry can be found on the Home Office website. The system is being introduced tier by tier, so whilst the new scheme automatically abolishes some of the previous work permit arrangements (see below), such as the Sectors Based Scheme, others will remain in place for the foreseeable future.

Further details about the PBS are available at www.workingintheuk.gov.uk and the Home Office Immigration and Nationality Directorate (www.ind.homeoffice.gov.uk). Queries should be directed to Work Permits (UK)'s Customer Contacts Centre on 0114-207 4074.

Citizens of Commonwealth Countries. Nationals of Commonwealth countries (including Australia, New Zealand, Canada and South Africa) between the ages of 17 and 30 are permitted to visit the UK under Tier 5 of the new system (previously known as the 'Working Holiday Maker' scheme). This allows them to take up casual employment which will be incidental to their holiday, but not to engage in business or to pursue a career. The period which can be spent in the UK is 2 years and of that time, 52 weeks may be spent working full-time or part-time at no more than 20 hours per week.

Canadian students, graduates and young people should contact the Student Work Abroad Programme (SWAP), which provides support to those wishing to work in Britain. It is administered by the Canadian Universities Travel Service, which has over 40 offices in Canada. For details see www.swap.ca.

Australians and New Zealanders should contact International Exchange Programmes (IEP), a non-profit organisation specialising in sending young Australians and New Zealanders on working holidays overseas. For more details visit www.iep.org.au or www.iep.co.nz.

Students from the USA. US students seeking temporary work in the UK will fall under Tier 5 of the new system (previously known as the 'Work in Britain Program'). This allows full-time US college students and recent graduates over the age of 18 to look for work in Britain, finding jobs through BUNAC listings or through personal contacts. Jobs may be pre-arranged, though most participants wait until arrival in Britain to job hunt. US students on study abroad programmes through an American university overseas are also eligible for the programme. When students apply to BUNAC they will receive a 'Blue Card'. The Blue Card must be presented to immigration on arrival in the UK. It is valid for 6 months and cannot be extended, although it is possible to obtain a second Blue Card in another calendar year if they again fulfil the eligibility requirements. The Blue Card costs $290 from BUNAC, (1-800 GO BUNAC; www.bunac.org).

Seasonal Agricultural Work Scheme (SAWS). This is one of the few schemes that remains in place after the PBS has come into effect. The government plans to maintain the scheme until 2010, from when it will fall under Tiers 3 and 4. Farm camps under this scheme are authorised by the Home Office and are the main hope for non-EEA and non-Commonwealth nationals wishing to work in this country. Special 'Work Cards' are issued to a certain number of non-EEA nationals each year. Places fill up very quickly and it is necessary to apply in November to have any chance of obtaining a card for the following year.

The recruitment for these farms is handled by nine agencies, known as SAWS operators, including Concordia. Between them they recruit pickers for over 160 farms throughout the year. Prospective participants should be aged 18 or over and full-time students in their own country. An invitation to work is only valid if the work card is issued by an official operator and *not* by individual farmers. The SAW scheme has undergone some large changes since 1 January 2004. Whereas in previous years the scheme only ran from May until November, it now runs all year long, taking in a much wider breadth of work for those involved, from daffodil picking to working with livestock. The numbers have been reduced, in the light of the addition of new EU states who can no longer participate in the scheme and would use the Workers' Registration Scheme route. The upper age limit of 25 has been removed. The only requirement is that the applicant is a full-time student, currently studying in higher education residing in a country outside of the EEA and not in their last year of studies. You can take part in the scheme for a minimum of 5 weeks and a maximum of 6 months at a time. Applicants should note that a reasonable charge may be made for the accommodation and other services provided. Applicants can participate in the scheme for longer than 6 months, as long as they return to their home country for a minimum of 3 months before applying again.

Voluntary Work. Overseas nationals seeking voluntary work in the UK will fall under Tier 5 of the new system. Overseas nationals may be admitted for up to 12 months for the purpose of voluntary work providing their sponsor is a charity or non-charitable philanthropic organisation and the applicant is receiving no remuneration other than pocket money, board and accommodation. The work which they do must be closely related to the aims of the charity, i.e. working with people, and they must not be engaged in purely clerical, administrative or maintenance work. Volunteers are expected to leave the United Kingdom at the end of their visit.

Vacation Traineeships & Internships. Again, these will fall under Tier 5 of the new system. Permission can be given for overseas nationals with pre-arranged work placements to obtain permits for professional training or managerial level work experience for a limited period of 12 months.

While many companies in this book are happy to employ overseas students as trainees since most of them run their schemes in order to try out potential employees, they may not be keen to take on anyone who cannot return to them after their studies.

Non EEA Students Studying in the UK. These students fall under Tier 4 of the new system. Overseas students studying in Britain who wish to take up vacation work no longer have to obtain permission to do so. This is on the basis that they do not pursue a career by filling a full-time vacancy or work for more than 20 hours per week during term time, except where the placement is a necessary part of their studies, with the agreement of the educational institution.

Au Pairs. Overseas Au Pairs now fall under Tier 5 of the new system (previously known as the Au Pair Placement scheme). For details of regulations affecting au pairs see the chapter *Au Pair, Home Help and Paying Guests* at the end of the chapter.

Japanese Students. Japanese nationals fall under Tier 5 of the new system (previously known as the *Youth Exchange Scheme*). This allows Japanese students aged between 18 and 25 to come to the UK for an extended holiday for up to 12 months with the intention of taking work as part of your holiday. There is a quota of 100 participants each year.

Further Information

Once in the UK, general information about immigration matters can be obtained from the Home Office Immigration and Nationality Directorate (0870 606 7766; www.ind.homeoffice.gov.uk): be prepared to wait in line for your call to be answered, it will be eventually. Guidance leaflets can be downloaded from www.ukvisas.gov.uk/forms. Further information and guidance can be found at www.ukvisas.gov.uk/guidance. Work Permits (UK): 0114 207 4074; www.workingintheuk.gov.uk can advise employers on the rules of the entry scheme.

THE UK

Business and Industry

This category includes working as drivers, temps, office workers, labourers and cashiers, among others.

Temping. Work as a 'temp' involves providing short-term cover for staff away on holiday, sick leave, and so on, and is usually arranged by an agency. Jobs are available in virtually all corners of business and industry, though the majority are clerical/office based and favour those with secretarial or computer skills, or experience of an office environment. Temping work is attractive as it is available at any time of the year, can offer flexible hours, and can be found at short notice. Temping can also be valuable to those looking for a more vocational experience as well as cash over the summer. You could secure a placement in a sector where internship schemes are rare, such as marketing or media, giving you vital insight as well as an edge over other candidates.

Shop Work. Recent developments in retail, such as the explosion of out-of-town retail parks with huge stores and 24-hour shopping, mean that there is sizeable demand for extra staff in the summer. Those willing to work antisocial hours are in demand, and working the night shift generally ensures a significantly bigger pay packet. If you are applying for a full-time job, then be aware that many shops will favour applicants with an interest in eventually working there permanently.

Cleaning. Office and industrial cleaning is another area that offers temporary vacancies. Most cleaning companies prefer to employ staff for long periods, but they will occasionally take people on temporarily for jobs such as cleaning newly-built or refurbished office blocks, or for the annual deep clean of those factories which still shut down for a couple of weeks each summer.

Factory Work. Spending the summer on a production line may not sound too thrilling, but the potential for work in this field is good. The factories most likely to require extra staff are those preparing for the Christmas rush—as they begin to increase production in August—or those that deal with the packaging and processing of seasonal food. Huge quantities of fruit and vegetables are harvested between late spring and early autumn and must be preserved by canning or freezing. The main vacancies in this business are for line workers, packers and delivery drivers. Be prepared for early mornings, shift work and high levels of boredom.

John Brownlee

Job(s) Available: Bottlers of spring water (2).
Duration: Work available all year round.
Pay: National minimum wage rates.
Accommodation: No accommodation available.
Application Procedure: By post to Mr John Brownlee at the above address. Overseas applicants welcome.

Head Office: Knockmakagan, Newtownbutler, County Fermanagh, Ireland
☎ +353 28 6773 8277
+353 28 6773 8275
+353 79 943 2131
✆ sales@fermanaghspringwater.com
🖥 www.fermanaghspringwater.com

Glen Lyn Gorge

Duration: Staff to work from April to September.
Working Hours: Hours are dependent upon the weather.
Pay: £200–£300 per week.
Company Description: A visitor attraction with self-catering holiday accommodation.
Job Description: Work to include being part of a boat crew, gardening and looking after the accommodation.
Requirements: No experience required, just enthusiasm.
Accommodation: Accommodation is available at a minimal price.
Application Procedure: By post to Matthew Oxenham at the above address from February for further information. Non-UK residents with suitable qualifications will be considered. An interview will be required.

Head Office: Glen Lyn Gorge, Lynmouth, Devon, EX35 6ER England
☎ 01598 753207
💻 www.theglenlyngorge.co.uk

Hay Festival

Job(s) Available: Box office staff (10).
Duration: Staff required for the build up to as well as during the Festival. The Festival runs from 22 May to 1 June.
Working Hours: Staff required for up to 39 hours per week.
Pay: Fair hourly rates of pay.
Company Description: An international festival production company celebrating great writing in every medium in Britain and around the world. Hay is a tiny market town in the Brecon Beacons National Park. It has 1,500 people and 41 bookshops. The Festival is a spectacular holiday party for people to enjoy their tastes for literature, food, drink, comedy, music, art and argument.
Requirements: Applicants need to be calm, good on the phone, familiar with computers and enjoy working with the public. Retail experience and a sense of humour are also useful.
Application Procedure: Applications should be made via the website from April. Overseas applicants are welcome to apply but must have a very high standard of spoken and written English.

Head Office: The Drill Hall, 25 Lion Street, Hay-on-Wye, Herefordshire, HR3 5AD England
☎ 0870 787 2848
💻 www.hayfestival.com

Lal Torbay (Summer Schools)

Job(s) Available: Office administrators, house parents, programme co-ordinators, welfare officers, activity leaders.
Duration: 4–6 weeks from July to August.
Working Hours: Flexible working hours, including day, evening and weekend work. An average working week would be 46.75 hours.
Pay: To be arranged.
Company Description: Summer school centres at Kelly College, Devon and Taunton School, Somerset.
Job Description: *Office administrators:* to run the office and administration aspects of a busy summer school. Experience with Microsoft Word and Excel a distinct advantage. *House*

Head Office: Conway Road, Paignton, Devon, TQ4 5LH England
☎ 01803 558555
✉ mark.cook@lalgroup.com
💻 www.lalgroup.com

parents: to assist in all welfare aspects of residential summer school, including the waking up and putting to bed of students in an accommodation house. Experience of working with children is extremely useful. *Programme co-ordinators:* to organise and supervise the leisure programme of a busy residential summer school. Good organisational and managerial skills essential. Microsoft Office and Excel skills a distinct advantage. *Welfare officers:* to run the welfare department of a busy residential summer school. Experience with working with children, languages and First Aid essential. *Activity leaders:* to assist, organise and lead activities for children aged 9–16, including leading sports, trips to theme parks, city tours, discos and transfers to and from the airport.

Requirements: Minimum age 18. Applicants must be good with children and enjoy the outdoor life.

Accommodation: Accommodation and food available.

Application Procedure: By post to Mark Cook, Summer School's general manager, at the above address.

Promotional Support Services

Job(s) Available: Temporary promotional contracts available.

Duration: Minimum period of work is one day at any time of year.

Working Hours: Staff to work 8–10 hours per day.

Pay: £50–£95 per day.

Head Office: 100 Sydney Place, Bath, BA2 6NE England
☎ 01225 443434
info@promotionalsupport.co.uk
www.promotionalsupport.co.uk

Company Description: Organises roadshows, exhibitions and events and supplies promotional staff for clients such as Walkers, Robinsons, Pepsi, L'Oréal, Bounty, Great British Chicken, Wellman, Benecol, Belvoir, Wykes Farm Cheeses and other blue-chip clients.

Requirements: Applicants should have bubbly, outgoing, attractive personalities.

Accommodation: No accommodation available.

Application Procedure: At any time to Promotional Support at the above address. Contact, by email, or post a CV and photograph with s.a.e. Overseas applicants considered. Interview preferred, but not necessary.

Pure Vacations Ltd

Job(s) Available: Multi-tasked administrators (2).

Working Hours: Hours will vary but very sociable and as required. All days of the week are optional and working conditions are good.

Head Office: Boughton Golf Club, Brickfield Lane, Boughton, Kent, ME13 9AJ England
☎ 01227 751999
steve@purevacations.com
www.purevacations.com

Pay: Salary will be based on experience and hours worked.

Company Description: Leading specialist tour operator based in Boughton, near Faversham. Programmes include showboarding, surfing, golfing and more.

Job Description: To follow booking enquiries, assist in ticketing and participate in, general basic administration duties. Job may lead to a good future career with a market leader.

Requirements: Minimum age 16. Must have a general interest in the travel industry and adventure travel, especially in outdoor activities including surfing, ranching, golf etc. Outgoing, fun, active but professional person. Any qualifications to do with activities including surfing will be advantageous but not necessary. Foreign language would be an advantage but again not necessary. Must be professional.

Accommodation: No accommodation available.

Application Procedure: By post to Wesley Baker, managing director, at the above address. **39**

Tony Fresko Ice Cream Ltd

Job(s) Available: Drivers (25).
Duration: Positions are available from March to October. Minimum period of work normally 6 weeks.
Working Hours: Approximately 11am–9pm. 7 days of the week available.
Pay: £6–£10 per hour.
Company Description: Mobile ice cream outlet, with a fleet of 15 vans.
Job Description: Drivers for mobile ice cream vans at various shows and fêtes and on rounds of industrial and housing estates.
Requirements: Full driving licence required.
Accommodation: No accommodation available.
Application Procedure: By post from February onwards to Mr J Sawyer at the above address. Foreign applicants with appropriate work permits and acceptable spoken English welcome. Interview necessary.

Head Office: Warren Farm, White Lane, Ash Green, Aldershot, Hampshire, GU12 6HW England
☎ 01252 315528
joesawyer@btconnect.com
www.fresko-icecream.co.uk

Wetherby Studios

Job(s) Available: Male photographic models.
Duration: Dozens needed throughout the year.
Pay: £100 cash for 2-hour sessions.
Requirements: Should be aged 18–40 years, but physique is more important than age. While more than half the models used are slim, it can be difficult to find men who have worked on their chest and arm definition, which is required if picture sessions promoting leisurewear are planned. Moustaches and beards permissible. No modelling experience necessary. Applicants must supply snapshots to show how they photograph facially and physically. Follow-ups are frequent, depending on the photographers' reactions to the first test shots.
Accommodation: No accommodation available.
Application Procedure: By post to Mr Mike Arlen, director of Wetherby Studios. Overseas applicants more than welcome, but must speak fluent English.

Head Office: 23 Wetherby Mansions, Earls Court Square, London, SW5 9BH England
☎ 020 7373 1107
mikearlen@btopenworld.com

Children

This category includes opportunities for individuals to work as leaders, playworkers, instructors and even managers.

In response to the desperation of parents trying to occupy their children in the long summer holidays, recent years have seen a boom in American-style holiday centres, camps and playschemes for the younger generation. These have become increasingly important as more parents go out to work and private child-care costs rocket. Centres vary in size and content; some are run by big operating chains, like PGL (www.pgl.co.uk), who attend to more than 140,000 children a year, and some others by local councils.

The main season is from around the start of April until mid-September, but longer-term work is available as PGL operate centres from February until October. The ages of many of those attending these centres range from 7-17, so anyone aiming to be a primary or secondary school teacher could gain valuable experience.

For these jobs, applicants will often not require formal qualifications. UK legislation, however, means that most employers will require successful applicants intending to work with children to undergo a Criminal Records Bureau (CRB) check - be aware that it may be expected even if not mentioned in the job advert. Preference is likely to be given to those with experience of working with children. Trainee primary school teachers are particularly well suited.

Acorn Adventure

Job(s) Available: Instructors, assistant instructors, support staff, village managers.
Duration: Seasonal work available from April until September.
Company Description: Acorn Adventure is one of the leading providers of outdoor adventure camps for schools, youth groups and families. They operate 9 activity centres in France, Italy, and the UK.

Head Office: Acorn House, Prospect Road, Halesowen, West Midlands B62 8DU
☎ 0121 504 2066
✉ jobs@acornadventure.co.uk
🖥 www.acorn-jobs.co.uk

Job Description: *Support staff:* maintenance and/or catering. *Village managers:* on-site representatives who welcome new groups, work closely with the children and organise evening events.
Requirements: *Support staff:* no experience necessary. Full training given pre-season. *Instructors:* should hold at least Instructor/Trainee Instructor status with a National Governing Body, eg BCU, RYA, SPA RLSS, GNAS, BOF or MLTB. Other nationally recognised coaching awards may be considered. *Village managers:* No experience necessary. Full training given pre-season. *Assistant instructors:* should be working towards the above qualifications/awards. Acorn runs an extensive pre-season training programme helping staff achieve these goals.
Application Procedure: For further information or applications go to www.acorn-jobs.co.uk or contact the recruitment department for a full information pack at the above address.

Acorn Educational/Halsbury Travel

Job(s) Available: Couriers (80).
Duration: University holiday periods and term time year round. Tours usually last around 1–2 weeks.
Working Hours: 35 hours per week.
Pay: £170 per week.
Company Description: Acorn Educational/ Halsbury Travel provide group and school tours to

Head Office: 35 Chruchill Park, Nottingham NG4 2HF
☎ 0115 940 4303
✉ acorn@halsbury.com
🖥 www.aee.eu.com or www.halsbury.com

western Europe and worldwide. They arrange sports tours, music tours, study tours, ski tours and tours for any academic theme including history, geography, media, travel and tourism, French, German, Spanish and Italian.
Job Description: Couriers, group leaders and tour guides are required for coach and air groups travelling to western European destinations.
Requirements: Minimum age 21. Must speak English and either French, German or Spanish.
Accommodation: Hotel accommodation half board, travel insurance and transportation all supplied.
Application Procedure: Applications taken in September, January and April. Apply to Rachel Weaver at ac1@halsbury.com.

Adventure & Computer Holidays Ltd

Job(s) Available: Camp leaders and teachers required for day camps.
Duration: Work available every half-term and school holiday throughout the year (mostly July to August). Minimum period one week.
Working Hours: 9am–4.45pm.
Pay: £180–£200 per week.

Head Office: PO Box 183, Dorking, Surrey RH5 6FA
☎ 01306 881299
✆ info@holiday-adventure.com
🖥 www.holiday-adventure.com

Company Description: A small, friendly company with 23 years experience in running activity holidays for children aged 4–13. Based at Belmont School, Holmbury St Mary, near Dorking.
Requirements: Qualifications or experience with children preferred. Minimum age 19.
Accommodation: Staff need to live in London or Surrey area.
Application Procedure: By post any time to Su Jones, director, at the above address. Interview required.

Allestree School's Out Holiday Club

Job(s) Available: Playworkers (4), sports coaches (2).
Duration: Staff are required during every school holiday.
Working Hours: Between 16 and 45 hours per week.

Head Office: 1 Kingscroft, Allestree, Derby DE22 2FP
☎ 01332 737947
✆ allestreeschoolsoutclub@hotmail.com
🖥 www.allestreeschoolsoutclub.com

Pay: Approximately £5.50 per hour.
Requirements: *Playworkers*: must have an NVQ 2 (or equivalent) in playwork/childcare. *Sports coaches:* must have previous sports experience and possibly be studying towards becoming a PE Teacher.
Accommodation: No accommodation available.
Application Procedure: By post to Amanda Hudson at the above address as soon as possible. Non-UK applicants with suitable qualifications and fluent English are considered.

Barracudas Summer Activity Camps

Job(s) Available: Camp managers (27), assistant camp managers (7), outstanding officers (15), group co-ordinators (150), group assistants (200), activity instructors (150), football coaches (50), arts and crafts instructors (50), dance and drama instructors (50), lifeguards (50).

Head Office: Bridge House, Bridge Street, St Ives, Cambridgeshire PE27 5EH
☎ 01480 497533
✆ jobs@barracudas.co.uk
🖥 www.barracudas.co.uk

Duration: Staff required from mid-July to the end of August. Minimum period of work 2 weeks.
Working Hours: All staff to work 40 hours per week.
Pay: *Group co-ordinators:* from £185 per week. *Group Assistants:* from £185 per week. *Activity instructors*: from £205 per week. *Football coaches:* from £175 per week. *Arts and crafts instructors*: from £185 per week. *Dance and drama instructors:* from £185 per week. *Lifeguards*: from £205 per week.
Company Description: Barracudas runs summer day camps for 5–14 year olds. Experience in teaching and management required.
Requirements: *Group co-ordinators:* experience with children/sports necessary. *Group assistants:* a wish to work with children and to ensure their safety is necessary. *Activity instructors:* confidence and the ability to give clear instruction. *Football coaches:* experi-

ence in football coaching and excellent knowledge of the game needed. *Arts and crafts instructors:* experience in arts and crafts needed. *Dance and drama instructors:* drama and dance experience necessary. *Lifeguards:* should be NPLQ/NARS or American Red Cross qualified. Minimum age 18.

Accommodation: Accommodation is available at some sites but is limited to qualified teachers, managers, lifeguards and instructors.

Additional Information: Training is available for all staff: Some courses lead to nationally recognised qualifications.

Application Procedure: By post from January onwards to Hayley Kendall at the above address or on the website. Foreign applicants with fluent English are welcome. Interview with references required. Police check and security checks made.

Calshot Activities Centre

Job(s) Available: Summer activity supervisors (4).
Duration: From mid-July to the end of August.
Working Hours: Required to work an average of 42 hours per week.
Company Description: Hampshire County Council-run outdoor activity centre providing dinghy sailing, windsurfing, canoeing, power boating, rock climbing, track cycling, skiing, snowboarding and archery.

Head Office: Calshot Spit, Fawley, Southampton SO45 1BR
☎ 023 8089 2077
carol.oneill@hants.gov.uk
www.calshot.com

Job Description: Duties include providing pastoral care for the children outside activity times; organising games and activities; supervising pre-bed drinks; organising roll calls; assisting with the supervision of some off-site activities; ensuring children are up and attending breakfast.

Requirements: Minimum age 18. Experience of working with children is an advantage, but a responsible and mature attitude and the ability to work as part of a close-knit team are just as important.

Accommodation: Board and lodging is available at a charge.

Application Procedure: By post to Carol O'Neill, at the above address, from April. Overseas applicants are welcome to apply as long as they have relevant work permits and are able to attend an on-site interview (usually mid-June).

CCUSA

Job(s) Available: Camp counsellors (500).
Duration: Applicants must be available for a 9 week period of commitment.
Pay: Wages dependent on position within the camp.
Company Description: With over 20 years experience and 150,000 participants from around the world, CCUSA offers renowned work and travel programmes.

Head Office: First Floor North, Devon House, 171–177 Great Portland Street, London W1W 5PQ
☎ 020 7637 0779
info@ccusa.com
www.ccusa.com

Job Description: Counsellors required to work at one of CCUSA's summer camps across the UK.

Requirements: Minimum age 18 or over by 1 July 2008. All staff must have previous camp experience or experience of working with children aged 11–17.

Accommodation: Board and lodging is available.

Application Procedure: Application forms and more information can be found online at the above website. Foreign applicants are welcome provided they speak English to the standard of a native speaker.

Cross Keys, Mini Minors And Experience UK

Job(s) Available: Group leaders and group assistants (20) to work in a daytime children's activity camp in north London.

Head Office: 48 Fitzalan Road, Finchley, London N3 3PE
☎ 020 8922 9686
🖥 www.campsforkids.co.uk

Duration: Camps take place in all school holidays; summer camps will take place July to August.

Working Hours: Working hours generally 8.30am–3.30pm but may vary slightly.

Pay: £175–£225 per week depending on position and experience.

Job Description: Staff required to work at a residential children's activity camp (XUK) based in Norfolk. Duties involve being responsible for junior or senior children aged 6–17 and include the care of children, the planning and running of activities and supervising trips. Will also work as part of a team of 3 adults per 24 children, running games and activities within a school environment.

Requirements: Full in-house training will be given. Should have an interest/background in childcare. Applicants for either camp must be enthusiastic team workers. Minimum age 18. Possession of lifeguard/first aid qualifications would be an advantage.

Accommodation: Includes accommodation, food and drink.

Application Procedure: Applications to Richard on 020 8371 9686 or go to 'staff zone' on the above website.

EAC Activity Camps Ltd

Job(s) Available: Camp directors (6), assistant camp directors (6), qualified instructors, group captains (40), group monitors (40), activity leaders (200).

Head Office: 45 Frederick Street, Edinburgh EH2 1EP
☎ 0131 477 7570
🖥 sdonnelly@eacworld.com
🖥 www.activitycamps.com

Duration: Required between June and August, with various contracts available.

Working Hours: All staff to work 42 hours per week.

Pay: Salaries dependent on position and experience but are very competitive.

Company Description: Multi-activity day and residential camps in Edinburgh, Glasgow, York, Ramsgate and Ashford for children aged 5–16. Plus International Summer Schools throughout the UK for young people aged 9–18.

Job Description: The work is hard but good fun and very rewarding.

Requirements: *Camp Directors:* must be qualified to NVQ Level 4 in childcare or equivalent. *Assistant Camp Directors:* must be qualified to NVQ Level 2 or equivalent. *Qualified Instructors:* required for archery, swimming, football and tennis. Relevant qualifications essential for lifeguard and archery positions: RLSS Life Saving/NPLQ/Bronze Medallion and GNAS for archery. Additional recognised coaching qualifications are a distinct advantage. Must have all-round sporting ability and enthusiasm. Sporting qualifications and coaching awards preferred.

Accommodation: Free accommodation and food available at most sites if required.

Application Procedure: Applications from February to Susan Donnelly, HR and recruitment manager, at the above email. All applicants must be available for interview. An enhanced CRB check is required for all successful applicants. Overseas applicants welcome but must have a police check from their own country before starting work.

Geos-Ltc International College

Job(s) Available: Activity leaders for junior summer school.
Duration: To work from the end of June to the end of August.
Pay: On application.
Requirements: Minimum age 18. Some experience with children required, though no formal qualifications necessary.
Application Procedure: By post to Jane Flynn, principal, at the above address.

Head Office:16–20 New Broadway, Ealing, London W5 2XA
☎ 020 8566 2188
✍ info@geos-london.co.uk
🖳 www.geos-london.co.uk

Ipswich Borough Council

Job(s) Available: Daycamp Leaders (2), activity camp leaders, activity camp assistants.
Duration: Monday to Friday.
Pay: *Activity camp leaders:* £5.94 per hour. *Activity camp assistants:* £5.08 per hour.
Requirements: Minimum age 18. Applicants must have experience of working with children. A standard disclosure is required for all positions.
Application Procedure: By post to HR at the above address from early March.

Head Office: Grafton House, 15–17 Russell Road, Ipswich IP1 2DE
☎ 01473 433514
✍ hr@ipswich.gov.uk

Junior Choice Adventure

Job(s) Available: Activity instructors (120), senior instructors (13), centre managers (13), watersports positions (10).
Duration: Required from March to July.
Working Hours: All positions average 40 hours work per week, 5 or occasionally 6 days a week.
Pay: *Activity instructors:* £240 per month. *Senior instructors:* pay to be arranged. *Centre managers:* pay to be arranged. *Watersports positions:* competitive wages.
Company Description: Provider of fun experiences for school children, with stunning locations throughout the south-west.
Requirements: *Activity instructors:* no experience required as full training and qualifications are provided, including a modern apprenticeship. *Senior instructors:* need industry experience, as will be leading a team of instructors, as well as giving necessary training. *Centre managers:* excellent communication, organisational and managerial skills necessary. Responsible for the day-to-day running of the activity centre. *Watersports positions:* level 2 and 3 watersports qualifications necessary; details on application.
Accommodation: *Activity instructors:* board and lodging available.
Application Procedure: By post at the above address.

Head Office: 14 Queensway, New Milton, Hampshire BH25 5NN
☎ 0870 513 3773
✍ jcajobs@travelclass.co.uk
🖳 www.juniorchoiceadventure.co.uk

Lakeside YMCA National Centre

Job(s) Available: Day camp leaders (40).
Duration: Minimum period of work 8 weeks between early July and the end of August.
Working Hours: To work 5 days a week.
Pay: £50 per week.

> **Head Office:** Ulverston, Cumbria LA12 8BD
> ☎ 0870 727 3927
> ✆ personnel@lakesideymca.co.uk
> 🖥 www.lakesideymca.co.uk

Company Description: The camp is set in 400 acres of woodland on the shores of Lake Windermere in the Lake District National Park and is one of the largest camps in Europe.
Job Description: The work involves leading groups of children aged 8–15 years in a wide range of activities, from environmental awareness to rock climbing.
Requirements: Minimum age 18. Some experience of outdoor activities is advantageous and experience of working with children necessary.
Accommodation: Free board and lodging.
Application Procedure: Application forms are available from January to May from personnel, YMCA National Centre, Lakeside, by email or via the website.

Leicester Children's Holiday Centre

Job(s) Available: Activity leaders (14), kitchen/dining room staff (5), cook/chef.
Duration: Staff needed from July to the end of August.
Working Hours: Activity leaders and kitchen/dining room staff work 48-hour weeks. Cook/chef to work a 6 day week.
Pay: National minimum wage rates.

> **Head Office:** Mablethorpe, Quebec Road, Mablethorpe, Lincolnshire LN12 1QX
> ☎ 01507 472444
> ✆ helen@lanzetta.freeserve.co.uk
> 🖥 www.childrensholidaycentre.co.uk

Company Description: A charity that provides free holidays for children from the inner city of Leicester, based on the east coast of England. For anyone interested in working with children this is a fairly unique opportunity offering practical experience and an excellent grounding for a future career.
Job Description: Activity leaders required to organise, instruct and supervise an outdoor activities programme for children aged 7–12. Energy, enthusiasm and a good sense of humour essential.
Requirements: Minimum age 18. No experience needed as full training is given.
Accommodation: Deduction made for board and lodging.
Application Procedure: Write or email for an application form (enclosing s.a.e.) from December to Helen Eagle-Lanzetta at the above address.

NST Travel Group Plc

Job(s) Available: Activity/ICT instructors (38), catering assistants (6), maintenance/cleaning assistants (2).

Duration: Staff required from January through to November. Minimum period of work 2 months.

Working Hours: Average working week 42 hours over 6 days.

Pay: National minimum wage rates.

Head Office: Discovery House, Whitehills Business Park, Brooklands Way, Off Preston New Road, Blackpool FY4 5LW
☎ 0845 671 1357
✒ info@nstjobs.co.uk
🖳 www.nstjobs.co.uk

Company Description: An outdoor activity and ICT residential centre for children aged 9–13. NST Travel Group is one of Europe's leading educational tour operators.

Job Description: *Activity/ICT instructors:* to instruct a range of outdoor and ICT activities and to assist with the evening entertainment programme. *Catering assistant:* to assist the catering manager and be involved in all aspects of kitchen work. *Maintenance/cleaning assistants:* to assist the maintenance manager.

Requirements: *Activity/ICT instructors:* while qualifications are valued they are not essential as full training will be given prior to working with guests. *Catering assistance:* no previous experience required. *Maintenance/cleaning assistants:* no previous experience required, but an interest in DIY useful.

Accommodation: All positions are residential.

Application Procedure: For more information and an application form please contact the above address.

PGL Travel Ltd

Job(s) Available: Activity instructors, group leaders, support staff.

Duration: Positions available from February to November, for the full season, as little as 8 weeks, or any period in between – although there are very few summer-only vacancies.

Pay: £70–£100 per week.

Head Office: Alton Court, Penyard Lane, Ross-on-Wye, Herefordshire HR9 5GL
☎ 0870 401 4411
✒ recruitment@pgl.co.uk
🖳 www.pgl.co.uk/recruitment

Company Description: PGL recruit around 2,500 staff each year to assist with the running of their children's activity centres throughout the UK, including locations in Devon, the Isle of Wight, Lincolnshire, the south coast, Surrey, Shropshire, Perthshire, and Wales. Europe's largest provider of adventure holidays for children has offered outstanding training and work opportunities to seasonal staff for more than 50 years. PGL jobs provide a break from the 9–5 routine. Staff need to be enthusiastic, energetic and looking for real experience and responsibility in a stimulating environment.

Job Description: *Activity instructors:* required for canoeing, sailing, windsurfing, fencing, archery, motorsports, pony trekking, and more. *Group leaders:* take responsibility for groups of children, helping then to get the most out of their holiday. *Support staff:* assist the catering, domestic and maintenance teams.

Requirements: *Activity instructors:* qualifications not essential for all positions as full training will be provided. *Group leaders:* previous experience of working with children is an advantage.

Accommodation: Free board and lodging.

Application Procedure: Applications can be made online, downloaded from the website. Alternatively call for an information pack.

Super Camps Ltd

Job(s) Available: Site managers (50), senior activity instructors (400), swimming pool lifeguards (40), trampoline coaches (15), activity instructors (500).

Duration: Staff needed for half terms, Christmas, Easter and summer (July and August).

Pay: *Site managers:* from £400 per week. *Senior activity instructors:* £300 per week. *Swimming pool lifeguards:* £245–£275 per week. *Trampoline coaches:* £275 per week. *Activity instructors:* from £225 per week.

Head Office: Park House, Milton Park, Abingdon, Oxfordshire OX14 4RS
☎ 01235 832222
✆ employment@supercamps.co.uk
🖥 www.supercamps.co.uk

Company Description: Runs multi-activity half term, Christmas, Easter and summer day camps for children aged 4–13 in schools in south and central England. Super Camps is committed to providing safe and fun-packed activities (including art/craft and sports) for all children attending its camps.

Job Description: *Activity instructors:* required to teach a range of activities to children aged 4–13 years. First aid and relevant childcare qualifications/camp experience an advantage. Training is provided, therefore enthusiastic individuals with an interest in sports or arts and crafts and a genuine interest in working with children are welcome to apply. Good experience for those wishing to go into a teaching, childcare or recreation/leisure profession.

Requirements: *Site managers:* qualified teachers with camp experience. *Senior activity instructors:* qualified/trainee teachers or individuals with substantial children's camp experience. *Swimming pool lifeguards:* must have experience and hold a recognised and up-to-date life saving/coaching qualification (NPLQ/NARS). *Trampoline coaches:* must have experience and hold a recognised and up-to-date qualification.

Application Procedure: By post all year round to personnel at the above address.

The Kingswood Group

Job(s) Available: Group leaders, activity instructors.

Duration: Camps run for 8 weeks from the start of July to the end of August. Activity instructors are employed on an initial 12-month training and development package.

Head Office: Kingswood House, Alkmaar Way, Norwich, Norfolk NR6 6BF
☎ 01603 309350
✆ jobs@kingswood.co.uk
🖥 www.kingswoodjobs.co.uk

Pay: National minimum wage rates.

Company Description: Kingswood operates year round educational activity centres for kids, including Camp Beaumont Summer Camps, which have been running for almost 3 decades at various locations across the UK.

Job Description: *Group leaders:* responsible for round-the-clock welfare of a group of children at Camp Beaumont Summer Camps, including overnight dormitory supervision. Also to instruct and initiate games and non-specialist activities, and to monitor the welfare needs of individual children in their group. Kingswood also recruits throughout the year for activity instructors to supervise various high and low adventure activities such as caving, go-karting, climbing and archery. Comprehensive training is provided.

Requirements: *Group leaders:* applicants must be aged between 18 and 25 and have some previous experience working with children. *Activity instructors:* No experience is necessary, though a friendly and outgoing personality and a love for working with children is a must. Telephone interviews and an assessment weekend required.

Accommodation: *Group leaders:* accommodation provided at a cost of £24.50 per week and food at a cost of £39.95 per week. Training and development package with food and accommodation.

Application Procedure: By post to the recruitment team at the above address. Foreign applicants with fluent English welcome.

THE UK

CHILDREN

World Challenge Expeditions

Job(s) Available: World Challenge's UK-based opportunities range from working as one of a team of leaders on a 1-day development programme to leading 5-day residential expeditions.

Duration: Ranges from 1 day to the whole summer.

Working Hours: Variable.

Pay: £10,000–£12,000 pro rata on a short-term contract.

Head Office: The Leadership Development Centre, Manchester Road, Buxton, Derbyshire SK17 6ST
☎ 01298 767900
✉ leaderinfo@world-challenge.co.uk
🖥 www.world-challenge.co.uk

Company Description: World Challenge run expeditions and adventure activities in the UK and overseas. All expeditions and activities are designed to enable education through exploration and to raise motivation in young people through developing skills in leadership, team building, decision-making and problem solving.

Requirements: All UK leaders working on residential expeditions should at least be trained in an NGB award eg ML, SPA, BCU, L2K, BELA. WGL also accepted. Leaders with good facilitation and youth development skills are also welcome. Minimum age 21.

Accommodation: May be provided.

Application Procedure: Email to the address above for more details.

Holiday Centres and Amusements

Tourism. The trend for short breaks and long weekends away within the UK is currently very strong, backed by industry pushes to promote such getaways. There has been a leap in visits to the UK's tourist attractions, including sites such as Alton Towers, in Staffordshire, and the London Eye, where over 20 million people have so far enjoyed its views across the capital. Attractions such as the Eden Project in Cornwall and the Imperial War Museum in Manchester are boosting regional tourism, while events like the Commonwealth Games have encouraged international interest in Britain, as will the Olympic Games due to be held in London in 2012. As a result, there has been an unprecedented growth in tourism and more than 2.1 million people are in employment related to UK tourism.

Holiday Centres. One of the greatest recent trends in UK tourism has been the growth of holiday camps, activity centres and theme parks. These centres are some of the largest seasonal employers in the country. Not only do they take on thousands of staff between them – the largest can take on hundreds each – but they also offer a diverse range of jobs, both unskilled and skilled. As a result of the number and type of posts offered, they are often popular and competitive as the opportunity to spend a summer working with many other young people in a holiday environment can prove quite attractive. It is essential to apply as soon as possible because many of the big employers start recruitment early in the year. Although extra people are hired later in the season, to cover bank holidays and busy weeks, these are frequently contacted from a reserve list compiled from the surplus of earlier applications.

If you fail to find employment with one of the centres listed in the book, try a speculative, personal approach. Visit Britain (020 8846 9000; www.visitbritain.com) can provide information on the major theme and leisure parks throughout England. Visit Scotland (0131 332 2433; www.visitscotland.com); Visit Wales (0870-830 0306; www.visitwales.com); and Visit Northern Ireland (078 6873 4813; www.visitnorthernireland.com) provide the same information for Scotland, Wales and Northern Ireland.

Allen (Parkfoot) Ltd

Job(s) Available: Bar and catering staff, cook/chef, adventure supervisor (1), secretary/receptionist (2).

Duration: Period of work Easter, May bank holidays and from June to mid-September.

Working Hours: *Bar and catering staff:* to work various shifts from 8am to midnight. *Cook/chef:* to work 8am–2pm and 6pm–11pm. *Adventure supervisor:* to work 10am–5pm Monday to Friday during school holidays. *Secretary/receptionist:* to work alternative early/evening shifts and shared weekends.

Pay: Negotiable according to experience.

Company Description: Family-run caravan and camping park by Lake Ullswater. Set in magnificent scenery only 6 miles from Penrith and perfect for outdoor activities.

Job Description: *Cook/chef:* to prepare cooked breakfasts, lunches and evening meals. *Adventure supervisor:* to run a children's action club from the park. Activities include archery, tennis, baseball, volleyball, football, arts and crafts and pool tournaments.

Requirements: Bar and catering staff minimum age 18. Secretary/receptionist must enjoy meeting people and have a pleasant telephone manner.

Accommodation: Accommodation can be arranged in shared staff caravans.

Application Procedure: Applications from Easter, enclosing colour photo, details of work experience and dates of availability. To be sent to Mrs B Allen or Mrs F Bell, Parkfoot Caravan Park.

> **Head Office:** Howtown Road, Pooley Bridge, Penrith, Cumbria CA10 2NA
> ☎ 01768 486309
> ✎ jobs@parkfootullswater.co.uk
> 🖵 www.parkfootullswater.co.uk

Althorp

Job(s) Available: Seasonal staff (approximately 40).

Duration: Staff are required from 1 July to 31 August.

Working Hours: Various shifts are available.

Pay: All staff are paid £5.50 per hour.

Company Description: The home of the Spencer family for over 500 years, Althorp House now welcomes visitors every summer to explore the house, gardens and their awarding-winning *Diana: A Celebration* exhibition.

Job Description: Staff required for both outdoor and indoor work including positions in the house, stable block, café, gift shop and grounds. Staff need to be friendly and enthusiastic.

Requirements: No qualifications are necessary.

Application Procedure: By post from February, to the visitor manager, at the above address. Overseas applicants are welcome to apply, as long as they have the relevant documents and can speak a high standard of English. An informal interview will be necessary.

> **Head Office:** Althorp House, Northampton, Northamptonshire NN7 4HQ
> ☎ 01604 770107
> ✎ jobs@althorp.com
> 🖵 www.althorp.com

Alton Towers

Job(s) Available: Up to 1,200 seasonal positions. *Rides and shows:* operators, ride assistants, hosts. *Retail:* food and beverage, shops, ride photos. *Front of house:* admissions and guest services. *Security, medical and traffic:* security officers, nurses, traffic management, car parking, monorail operators. *Finance:* strongroom team members. *Hotel:* housekeeping, restaurant and bar, conference and events, chefs and kitchen teams, reception, leisure. *Others:* lifeguards, Alton Towers PCV drivers.

> **Head Office:** Alton, Staffordshire ST10 4DB
> ☎ 0870 444 6998
> 🖵 www.altontowers.com

Duration: Positions are available from February to November in the park and year round in the hotels.

Working Hours: Full-time, 5 days a week, or part-time, including weekends and bank holidays.

Pay: *Lifeguards*: £6.25 per hour; *PCV drivers*: £7.54 per hour. Other wages are £5.65 per hour and above depending on position.

Company Description: Alton Towers is a large and nationally known theme park, part of the Merlin Entertainments Group, now the second largest visitor attraction business in the world. Two themed hotels, a Caribbean waterpark, spa and conference centre all offer excellent career opportunities for customer service-focused people who want to work as a team.

Requirements: No specific qualifications or experience are required as training is given. Minimum age 16.

Accommodation: Help with finding accommodation can be given.

Additional Information: Employees gain use of an active social club and a range of other benefits.

Application Procedure: Applications should be made from December onwards at www.altontowersjobs.com or the employment service at the above address. Interviews and assessment centres form the recruitment process. Overseas applicants with work permits welcome.

Archaeolink Prehistory Park

Job(s) Available: Guides to interpret reconstructions to the public.

Duration: Open from April to October.

Working Hours: To work between 20 and 37 hours per week all year.

Pay: To be arranged.

Head Office: Oyne, Insch, Aberdeenshire AB52 6QP
☎ 01464 851500
✆ info@archaeolink.co.uk
🖳 www.archaeolink.co.uk

Company Description: Archaeolink was started in 1997 to introduce the public to Aberdeenshire's rich archaeological heritage. It operates reconstructions including Stone Age camps, a Roman marching camp and an iron age farm based on archaeological evidence from north-east Scotland.

Requirements: Applicants should be good communicators and be able to demonstrate an interest in history. Some experience of archaeology would be useful.

Accommodation: Accommodation available in a local bed and breakfast.

Application Procedure: By post to the above address as soon as possible.

British Airways London Eye

Job(s) Available: Guest service assistants.

Duration: All positions are for the full season from the beginning of June to the end of September.

Working Hours: To work approximately 40 hours, 5 days a week, on a rota basis including weekends and bank holidays.

Head Office: County Hall, Westminster Bridge Road, London SE1 7PB
☎ 0870 443 9187
✆ recruitment@ba-londoneye.com
🖳 www.londoneyejobs.com

Pay: From £7.50 per hour. Holidays will be paid at the end of the contract.

Company Description: The Eye is one of the tallest structures in London, standing 135m high on the south bank of the Thames, opposite Big Ben and the Houses of Parliament. It provides stunning views over central London and beyond.

Job Description: Very busy working environment with some outdoor positions.

Requirements: Minimum age 18. Applicants must have a minimum of one year customer service experience. No qualifications are necessary, but the right attitude is.

Application Procedure: By post to Gurjit Sandhu, training and recruitment co-ordinator, from April onwards. Keep an eye on the website for more details. Foreign applicants must be available for an interview, have a relevant working visa and speak fluent English. Interview required.

Crealy Adventure Park

Job(s) Available: Retail assistants (10–15), catering assistants (20), play supervisors and ride operators (15).

Duration: Required for Easter and summer holidays. Play supervisors and ride operators for summer work.

Working Hours: Flexible hours to suit.

Pay: Dependent on age and experience.

> **Head Office:** Clyst St Mary, Exeter, Devon EX5 1DR
> ☎ 0870 116 3333
> ✆ fun@crealy.co.uk
> 🖥 www.crealy.co.uk

Job Description: *Retail assistants:* in the guest services department, *catering assistants:* for fast food outlets. Staff can expect full training and benefits.

Requirements: *Retail assistants:* experience in till operation an advantage. Minimum age 16. *Catering assistants:* experience not essential. Minimum age 16. *Play supervisors and ride operators:* must have outgoing personality and be able to adhere to strict working practices to comply with health and safety best practice. Minimum age 16.

Application Procedure: Apply online at the address above.

Drayton Manor Park Ltd

Job(s) Available: Seasonal caterers (150), seasonal ride operators (150), ticketing staff (30), retail staff (30).

Duration: Period of work from the end of March to the end of October.

Working Hours: Hours negotiable.

Pay: To be arranged; paid at an hourly rate.

> **Head Office:** nr Tamworth, Staffordshire B78 3TW
> ☎ 01827 287979
> ✆ info@draytonmanor.co.uk
> 🖥 www.draytonmanor.co.uk

Company Description: A family-owned and run theme park of 57 years standing, one of the top 5 theme parks in the UK. Owns a catering company.

Requirements: No experience necessary as full training is given. Minimum age 16. Foreign applicants with a work permit and able to arrange their own accommodation are welcome. Fluent English is not essential.

Accommodation: No accommodation available.

Application Procedure: By post from 1 January to HR department at the above address. Interview is generally necessary, but they do not expect applicants to travel long distances.

European Waterways Ltd

Job(s) Available: Deckhands, housekeepers, chefs, boat pilots, tour guides.

Duration: Applicants must be available for the whole season, which runs from early April until the end of October.

Pay: £160–£350 per week plus accommodation and meals.

> **Head Office:** 35 Wharf Road, Wraysbury, Middlesex TW19 5JQ
> ☎ 01784 482439
> ✆ sales@gobarging.com
> 🖥 www.gobarging.com

Company Description: Owners and operators of luxury hotel barges cruising rivers and canals in England, Scotland and France.

Requirements: All positions require applicants to hold a valid driving licence. Chefs must be fully qualified and hold a valid Food Hygiene Certificate and boat pilots need to have experience on rivers. Foreign applicants with a working visa, who are able to drive in the UK and have good English are welcome. Some knowledge of French is helpful.

Accommodation: Available.

Application Procedure: By post to Isabelle Price at the above address by February. Interview required.

Fantasy Island

Job(s) Available: Maintenance staff (25), ride operators (100+), cleaners (20+), arcade floorwalkers (20+), cashiers (12+).

Duration: Period of work from 1 March to 31 October. Ride operators, cleaners, arcade floorwalkers and cashiers required for seasonal work.

Working Hours: Staff required to work a 6-day week.

Head Office: Ingoldmells Ltd, Sea Lane, Ingoldmells, Skegness, Lincolnshire PE25 1RH
☎ 01754 874668
rides@fantasyisland.co.uk
www.fantasyisland.co.uk

Pay: *Maintenance staff:* to be arranged. *Ride operators, cleaners, arcade floorwalkers and cashiers:* national minimum wage rates.

Company Description: Fantasy Island is the largest indoor theme park in Britain, with a large funfair.

Requirements: Full training is provided and foreign applicants who speak English are welcome.

Accommodation: No accommodation available.

Application Procedure: By post, including 2 named photos, from January to the HR department at the above address.

GLL

Job(s) Available: Leisure assistants and lifeguards, kids activity instructors.

Duration: Positions are available from June to September. Minimum period of work 10 weeks.

Working Hours: 39 hours per week.

Pay: £5.80+ per hour.

Head Office: Middlegate House, The Royal Arsenal, Woolwich, London SE18 6SX
☎ 020 8317 5000 extension 4020
recruitment@gll.org
www.gll.org.uk

Company Description: The largest leisure centre operator in London, with more than 70 centres. As a worker-owned and controlled organization, GLL offers opportunities and benefits that exceed the rest.

Requirements: *Leisure assistants and lifeguards:* National Pool Lifeguard qualification an advantage but not essential; training is given. *Kids activity instructors:* coaching qualifications and experience of working with children required. Foreign applicants welcome with appropriate permits, must have a good command of the English language. Subsidised training courses are also offered to those who want to build a career in the leisure industry. All employees must undergo a CRB check.

Application Procedure: By post from early May onwards to the HR department, at the above address. Interview necessary.

Hoburne Naish

Job(s) Available: Bar and amusement arcade staff, waiting staff, kitchen staff, receptionists, lifeguards.
Duration: Required from 1 June to mid-September.
Working Hours: To work 40 hours per week. Bar and amusement arcade staff, waiting staff, kitchen staff and receptionists to work mainly evenings and weekends. Lifeguards for daytime and weekend work.
Pay: National minimum wage rates.
Company Description: Holiday park with 1,000 units of accommodation for holidaymakers, second-home owners and residents, situated midway between Bournemouth and Southampton. Overlooks the Isle of Wight and Christchurch Bay.
Requirements: *Lifeguards:* lifesaving qualification required.
Accommodation: No accommodation available.
Application Procedure: By post from 1 April to the general manager, at the above address. Interview required. Foreign applicants with fluent English welcome.

Head Office: Christchurch Road, New Milton, Hampshire BH25 7RE
☎ 01425 273586
✆ naish@hoburne.com
🖥 www.hoburne.com/park_naish

Legoland Windsor

Job(s) Available: Admission assistants, food and beverage assistants, retail assistants, rides and attractions assistants, environmental services assistants, security guards.
Duration: The operating season lasts from March to October. Staff must be available for a minimum period of 8 weeks.
Working Hours: Applicants will work an average of 40 hours over 5 days (variable, including weekends). Part-time positions are also available in the above areas.
Pay: Competitive rate of pay, with benefits offered.
Company Description: LEGOLAND Windsor is a theme park dedicated to the imagination and creativity of children of all ages.
Job Description: Applicants must have a passion for serving others, an exuberant personality and a natural affinity with children. To be part of the LEGOLAND team staff need to be willing to work hard and have fun whatever the weather (many positions involve working outside).
Requirements: No previous experience necessary; training will be given in all departments. Minimum age 16. Fluent English essential.
Accommodation: Help is available to find accommodation.
Application Procedure: Apply online at the above website from January.

Head Office: Winkfield Road, Windsor, Berkshire SL4 4AY (HR department)
☎ 01753 626143
✆ jobs@LEGOLAND.co.uk
🖥 www.LEGOLAND.co.uk

Madame Tussauds London

Job(s) Available: Customer service and retail positions.
Duration: Late June to mid-September.
Company Description: The Tussauds Group is one of Europe's largest operators and developers of visitor attractions with over 10 million guests a year.

Head Office: Marylebone Road, London NW1 5LR
☎ 0870 999 0046
🖥 www.madame-tussauds.com

Requirements: Experience in a customer-focused environment and a positive and energetic attitude is crucial for these fun roles.
Application Procedure: Apply online.

Motorsport Vision Ltd

Job(s) Available: Admission control/events stewards, litter pickers, catering team members, cleaning operatives, marshals.

Head Office: Brands Hatch, Fawkham, Longfield, Kent DA3 8NG
☎ 01474 872331
🖥 www.motorsportvision.co.uk

Duration: Staff are required from March to November, to work as and when required on a fixed term contract.
Working Hours: Hours worked for all positions will vary throughout the year, therefore, all candidates must have a high degree of flexibility. *Admission control/events stewards:* weekends only. *Litter pickers:* weekends only. *Cleaning operatives:* full-time hours on a fixed term contract could be available to the right applicant with mid-week and weekend positions available. *Marshals:* includes some weekend work.
Pay: Competitive salary.
Company Description: Motorsport Vision Ltd is the UK's largest motor racing circuit operator, owning Brands Hatch, Cadwell Park, Oulton Park, Snetterton and Bedford Autodrome. The group runs more than 150 racing events a year including major events such as A1, Grand Prix, WTCC, World Superbikes, DTM, British Superbikes and British Touring Cars.
Job Description: *Admission control/events stewards*: works at the entrance gates during race events. This role involves cash handling and as first point of contact for the venue, applicants must have excellent customer care skills. *Event Stewards:* carries out duties such as car parking and crowd control. *Litter pickers*: venue presentation is one of the most important aspects of events and reliable hardworking candidates are required to ensure high standards are maintained. *Catering team members:* required to work as part of the catering team within busy restaurants, bars and hospitality suites. *Cleaning operatives:* experienced cleaners to help maintain the high level of venue presentation. *Marshals:* required to marshal track activities. Must be flexible and able to work as part of a team.
Requirements: All positions require excellent customer care skills. Overseas applicants must have a valid work permit.
Application Procedure: By post to the HR administrator, from March, at the above address.

Pontins Ltd

Job(s) Available: Fast food assistants, restaurant staff, catering staff, bar staff, shop staff, reservations staff, security, lifeguards, leisure staff, accommodation staff, maintenance staff, cleaners/gardeners.

Head Office: Sagar House, Eccleston, Chorley PR7 5PH
☎ 0125 745 2452
📧 jointheteam@pontins.com

Duration: Staff are taken on for both seasonal and permanent contracts, but positions are available all year round. Minimum period of work 6 months.
Working Hours: To work 40 hours over 6 days a week.
Pay: National minimum wage rates and above.
Company Description: Pontins is one of the UK's leading holiday companies, entertaining over 600,000 guests every year at 8 coastal locations, and employing over 2,000 people throughout the UK. The centres are located in Blackpool, Lancashire; Burnham-on-Sea, Somerset; Rye, Sussex; Hemsby, Norfolk; Lowestoft, Suffolk; Clwyd, north Wales; Southport, Merseyside; and Brixham, south Devon.

www.pontins.com

Pontin's in one of the UK's leading holiday companies, entertaining 600,000 guests every year at 8 coastal locations. We employ over 2000 people throughout the UK. We are looking to recruit colleagues who have a passion for customer care and really want to make our guests feel welcome.

Positions available include
- Food and catering assistants
- Bar staff
- Cleaning and maintenance staff
- Accommodation staff
- Retail staff
- Lifeguards
- Reservations
- Leisure staff

Previous experience not essential as training will be given. Must be over 18 years and have an outgoing personality. Wages at national minimum and above, to work 40 hours over 6 days. Accommodation is available at most centres.

If interested why not visit one of our open days or visit your local job centre. Alternatively call the recruitment hot line on **01253 340128.**

Job Description: *Fast food assistants:* to serve food and drinks, operate the tills and perform general cleaning duties in a number of fast food outlets. *Restaurant staff:* to serve meals and clean dining areas in a variety of self and waiter service restaurants, which seat up to 2,000 people. *Catering staff:* including qualified and experienced chefs, cooks and kitchen assistants. Duties include catering for large numbers, preparing and cooking fast food, taking orders, collecting money and general cleaning of the catering areas. *Bar staff:* to serve drinks, operate the tills and clean in busy bars. *Shop staff:* to be responsible for sales, operating the tills and the merchandising of stock. *Reservations staff:* to book in guests and allocate apartments. *Security:* to patrol the centre and implement and report on health and safety measures. *Lifeguards:* to supervise the heated indoor pools and the safety of guests. *Leisure staff:* to supervise and operate all leisure amenities. *Accommodation staff:* to help prepare the accommodation for the arrival of guests, including the making up of beds and cleaning of kitchens and bathrooms. *Maintenance staff:* positions are available for qualified electricians, plumbers and joiners as well as those who have experience in general maintenance. *Cleaners/gardeners:* for internal and external cleaning and maintenance of gardens.
Requirements: Minimum age 18 for all positions. Qualifications and experience are not always necessary, except in specialist areas, as induction training is provided.
Accommodation: Limited accommodation is available. Food is subsidised.
Additional Information: Open days are held at all of the 8 coastal locations at various times throughout the year and are advertised in local newspapers and job centres. Road shows are also held across the country at Easter.
Application Procedure: To apply call the Recruitment Line (above) or email jointheteam@pontins.com from February onwards for summer positions.

Newlands Adventure Centre Ltd

Job(s) Available: Domestic assistants (4), kitchen assistant.

Duration: All positions run from March to October. Applicants must be able to start in April or May at the very latest and stay until September/October.

Working Hours: *Domestic assistants:* to work a 44-hour week. *Kitchen assistant:* to work a 44-hour week.

Head Office: Stair, Keswick, Cumbria CA12 5UF
☎ 01768 778463
✆ info@activity-centre.com
🖳 www.activity-centre.com

Pay: Further details of hours, salary and accommodation costs available on application.

Company Description: An outdoor centre located 3.5 miles outside Keswick offering multi-activity holidays in the heart of the Newlands Valley. Activities include climbing, abseiling, mountain biking, kayaking, archery and orienteering, among others.

Job Description: *Domestic assistants:* to maintain a clean and hygienic environment and to assist with the preparation of meals for guests and staff. *Kitchen assistant:* to help prepare meals and to maintain a clean environment in all food preparation areas. Staff have their own single room with shared bathrooms and TV lounge. There is also an opportunity to take part in the activities free of charge.

Requirements: Minimum age 18. No activity instructors required unless with 2 of the following UK qualifications: Summer ML, SPA, BCU Level 2 Coach Kayak, BCU Level 2 Coach Canoe.

Accommodation: All meals are provided.

Application Procedure: Applicants to send CV and letter of introduction by email to debbie@activity-centre.com. An application form will then be sent and 2 references required. Foreign applicants with a reasonable level of English and current visas and work permits welcome.

Pembrokeshire Coast National Park Authority

Job(s) Available: Visitor centre assistants, site guide assistants, coast path warden, car park attendants.

Duration: Staff are required from April/May to September.

Head Office: Llanion Park, Pembroke Dock, Pembrokeshire SA72 6DY
☎ 0845 345 7275
✆ pcnp@pembrokeshirecoast.org.uk
🖳 www.pembrokeshirecoast.org.uk

Working Hours: *Visitor centre assistants/site guide assistants:* to work 2–5 days a week including weekends. *Coast path warden:* to work Monday to Friday. *Car park attendants:* working hours will vary but will include weekends and holidays.

Pay: £5.68–£6.36 per hour for all positions.

Company Description: A national park authority that is responsible for planning control, conservation and education regarding the national park's environment.

Requirements: *Visitor centre assistants, site guide assistants:* applicants should have good communication skills and enjoy working with the public. It may be an advantage to have knowledge of the area. *Coast path warden:* applicants should have countryside skills. Main duty is maintenance of footpaths. *Car park attendants:* applicants should have good communication skills, experience of cash handling and practical skills for machine maintenance. Ability to speak Welsh is desirable, but not necessary for all jobs.

Accommodation: No accommodation available.

Application Procedure: Applications should be in response to vacancy advertised on website, no speculative applications. Send to June Skilton at the above address during February and March. Information, when recruiting, will be available on the website.

Pleasure And Leisure Corporation Plc

Job(s) Available: Ride Operators (50).
Duration: Positions are available from March to
September. Minimum period of work 8 weeks.
Working Hours: Working hours are variable
according to the time of the season.
Pay: At least national minimum wage rates, plus full
uniform and staff concessions on rides and food
outlets.

Head Office: Pleasure Beach, South
Beach Parade, Great Yarmouth,
Norfolk NR30 3EH
☎ 0493 844 585
✆ gypbeach@aol.com or
   nigelthurs@aol.com

Company Description: A family company operating a major leisure and amusement park
with over 25 rides, 2 amusement arcades and a bar over 9 acres. More than a million visitors
every year.
Requirements: Minimum age 18 with good spoken English. No previous experience necessary as training provided.
Accommodation: Accommodation not available.
Application Procedure: By post from March onwards to Nigel Thurston, personnel manager. Interview and drug screening necessary.

Potters Leisure Resort

Job(s) Available: Housekeeping staff, food and
beverage staff, kitchen and catering staff, lifeguard.
Duration: Positions available throughout
the year.
Working Hours: *Housekeeping staff:* to work part-
time, 18–20 hours over 6 days. *Food and beverage*

Head Office: Coast Road, Hopton-on-
Sea, Norfolk NR31 9BX
☎ 01502 734812
✆ recruitment@potters-leisure.co.uk
🖥 www.pottersholidays.com

staff: to work full-time and part-time positions up to 40 hours per week. *Lifeguards*: to work
full-time and part-time positions up to 40 hours per week.
Pay: Dependent on age.
Company Description: The UK's only privately owned 5-star holiday village. Operates all
year, good facilities.
Job Description: Food and beverage staff to work in bar, restaurant and catering positions.
Requirements: *Housekeeping staff:* minimum age 16. *Food and beverage staff:* bar staff
minimum age 18. *Kitchen and catering staff:* minimum age 16. *Lifeguard:* minimum age 16
and must hold a PLG lifeguard qualification.
Accommodation: Accommodation may be provided, depending on availability, at a cost of
£0.57 per hour worked, maximum of £22.75 per week.
Application Procedure: By post at any time to Beverley Read, HR officer, at the above
address. Interview required. Foreign applicants with good spoken English welcome.

The Abbey College

Job(s) Available: Activities staff/sports staff (15).
Welfare and administration staff (3).
Duration: Work available from the beginning of
June to the end of August.
Working Hours: To work 6 days a week.
Pay: *Activities staff/sports staff:* £150–£170 per

Head Office: Wells Road, Malvern Wells,
Worcestershire WR14 4JF
☎ 01684 892300
✆ jobs@abbeycollege.co.uk
🖥 www.abbeycollege.co.uk

week for 6 days work. *Welfare and administration staff:* £150–£200 per week for 6 days
work.

Company Description: A beautiful residential campus with students from more than 30 nations.

Requirements: Minimum age 18. Sports qualifications and experience of summer schools preferred.

Accommodation: Accommodation and meals provided for all staff, plus free use of all sports and leisure activities and excursions.

Additional Information: Overseas applicants welcome to work 3 weeks, they would not be paid, but will receive one week of free English classes (or work 6 weeks and get 2 weeks of free classes) and accommodation free of charge, worth £520 per week.

Application Procedure: By post from March to the personnel department at the above address.

The Sherlock Holmes Museum

Job(s) Available: Victorian maids (2), Sherlock Holmes lookalike.

Duration: Period of work from May to September.

Pay: By arrangement.

Job Description: *Victorian maids:* to receive visitors attending the museum. *Holmes lookalike:* to dress up as Sherlock Holmes and give out promotional literature to tourists.

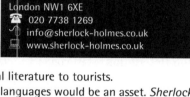
Head Office: 221b Baker Street, London NW1 6XE
☎ 020 7738 1269
info@sherlock-holmes.co.uk
www.sherlock-holmes.co.uk

Requirements: *Victorian maids:* knowledge of other languages would be an asset. *Sherlock Holmes lookalike:* must be slim, at least 6ft tall and well spoken.

Accommodation: No accommodation available.

Application Procedure: By post to Grace Riley, manager, at the above address.

Thorpe Park

Job(s) Available: Staff for food and beverages, cleaning, guest services, rides and attractions, sales, security admissions and car parking.

Working Hours: Flexible hours available.

Pay: £5.35–£7 per hour. Benefits include free uniform, free parking, staff canteen, social nights, discounted merchandise and complimentary tickets to any Tussauds group attraction.

Head Office: HR Department, Thorpe Park, Staines Road, Chertsey, Surrey KT16 8PN
☎ 01932 577302
www.thorpepark.com

Company Description: One of the top theme parks in the south, located off junction 11/13 of the M25 and accessible via trains from Waterloo to Staines; a short bus ride will take you to the park.

Job Description: Enthusiastic and friendly people of all ages are required to join the teams.

Application Procedure: Applications via the online form at the above website from January.

Vectis Ventures Ltd

Job(s) Available: General park assistants (up to 15).

Duration: Staff are required from April to September/October and must work from July to August for a minimum period of 6 weeks.

Working Hours: To work 5–6 days a week.

Pay: £5.35 per hour.

Head Office: Blackgang Chine, Ventnor, Isle of Wight PO38 2HN
☎ 01983 730330 or 01983 527352
info@blackgangchine.com,
info@robinhill.com

Company Description: Vectis Ventures Ltd are 2 visitor attractions on the Isle of Wight with a range of family amusements. Open daily throughout the summer, attractions include a small number of rides and also activity play areas.

Job Description: General park assistants to work on rides, in retail outlets and catering facilities, and for gardening and car parking.

Requirements: Minimum age 18. No experience is necessary but applicants should be friendly and outgoing.

Accommodation: No accommodation available.

Application Procedure: By post to Simon Dabell, managing director, at the above address between January and March. Interview necessary. Overseas applicants are welcome but must have reasonable English.

William Grant & Sons

Job(s) Available: Tour guides.

Duration: Minimum period of work: end of June to the end of August.

Working Hours: To work 5 days a week.

Pay: £200 for 32.5 hours.

Head Office: The Glenfiddich Distillery, Dufftown, Banffshire AB55 4DH
☎ 01340 820373
✆ brian.robinson@wgrant.com

Job Description: Staff conduct tours of Glenfiddich Distillery in an educational but informal way. The distillery is fully operational. The work may particularly suit people interested in Scottish history and culture. Tour guides to conduct members of the public on tours of the distillery.

Requirements: Minimum age 18. Must be fluent in at least one foreign European language. Experience with the general public very desirable but not essential. Job requires a bright, cheery and very outgoing personality. Only applicants with fluent English considered.

Accommodation: Limited accommodation may be available on site but local bed and breakfast costs approximately £60–£70 per week including evening meal. Self-catering accommodation can usually be found at £50–£60 per week.

Application Procedure: Between January and March to Mr B Robinson at the above address in writing or by email. All applicants must be able to attend an interview at the distillery. Interviews are held before or during the Easter vacation period.

Hotels and Catering

Hotels and catering establishments offer a range of jobs including work as waiting, bar and chamber staff, receptionists, chefs and kitchen assistants.

Many of the temporary hotel and restaurant jobs during the summer season are to be found in the country's main tourist resorts and beauty spots. Big hotel chains may provide the best opportunities for those based in or near cities, as they employ large numbers of staff and have a relatively fast turnover, meaning short-term vacancies can be available at any time of the year.

Working in a large and impersonal hotel in a city is likely to be more regimented and formal than spending the summer in an independent, family-run guest house on the coast, and so perhaps less friendly and enjoyable. If you choose a remote area with a lower cost of living and/or fewer opportunities to spend, such as the Scottish Highlands or the Black Mountains, you will find it easier to save the money you earn. Many hotels start advertising for summer staff before Easter, and generally applicants who can work for the entire season are preferred.

Standard pay in bars and restaurants tends to be at the national minimum rate, but higher for silver service and in London, and usually lower for fast food restaurants. Hotels usually offer a similar rate, but often offer added perks like use of their leisure facilities. Often, tips can be a substantial bonus to waiting and bar staff. However, centrally pooled and divided tips may be included in the national minimum wage, and a recent European Court of Human Rights ruling set a precedent for including cheque and credit card tips as part of waiters' minimum wage.

Youth Hostels. The Youth Hostels Association (www.yha.org.uk) employs Seasonal Assistant Wardens to help run its 227 Youth Hostels in England and Wales. Work is available for varying periods between February and October.

Appuldurcombe Heritage

Job(s) Available: Shop assistant, café assistant.
Duration: Minimum period of work is 2 months, from June until the end of September.
Working Hours: Hours to be agreed. Must be flexible about working days, including weekends.
Pay: From £5 per hour.

> **Head Office:** Appuldurcombe House, Wroxall, Isle of Wight PO38 3EW
> ☎ 01983 852484
> ⌨ enquiries@appuldurcombe.co.uk
> ▤ www.appuldurcombe.co.uk

Company Description: Comprises the Isle of Wight owl and falconry centre, and historic Appuldurcombe House.
Requirements: Minimum age 18. Fluent English is essential. Suitably qualified non-UK citizens will be considered. Experience in tourism preferred.
Accommodation: No accommodation available.
Application Procedure: By post to Jane or John Owen from Easter at the above address. An interview may be necessary.

Attingham Park (National Trust)

Job(s) Available: Part-time kitchen and tearoom assistants (2), full-time kitchen and tearoom assistant.

> **Head Office:** Attingham Park, Atcham, Shrewsbury, Shropshire SY4 4TP
> ☎ 01743 708196
> ⌨ elaine.deakinbothun@nationaltrust.org.uk

Duration: *Part-time kitchen and tearoom assistants:* from Easter until mid-September. *Full-time kitchen and tearoom assistant:* to work over the school summer holiday period.
Working Hours: *Part-time kitchen and tearoom assistants:* to work 6–8 hours per week, mainly at weekends.
Pay: Depends on age, but are above national minimum wage rates.
Requirements: Training will be given but knowledge of food hygiene would be helpful, and customer care experience is very useful.
Accommodation: Accommodation may be available free of charge for 5 weeks for full-time kitchen and tearoom assistant.
Application Procedure: By post from early March to Mrs Elaine de Akinbothun, catering manager, at the above address. Foreign applicants with fluent English are welcome to apply for the full-time position. Telephone interview required.

Aviemore Highland Resort

Company Description: The Macdonald Aviemore Highland Resort is located in the heart of the Cairngorms National Park. The resort consists of 4 hotels plus luxury self-contained woodland lodges, leisure and beauty arena and a large conference facility, which encompasses both a retail and food court thus offering boundless opportunities to enjoy the best of Highland hospitality.

Head Office: Aviemore, Inverness-shire PH22 1PN
☎ 01479 810771
✆ jobs@aviemorehighlandresort.com
🖥 www.aviemorehighlandresort.com

Requirements: Applicants need to be motivated and focused, have a desire to succeed, be committed to excellence, and wish to become part of a team.

Application Procedure: To apply visit the website, download and complete the application form and email or post to the addresses above. Alternatively, call the recruitment hotline on 01479 815256.

Balmer Lawn Hotel

Job(s) Available: Waiting staff (2–4).
Working Hours: To work 40 hours per week, including weekends, serving breakfast 6.30am–11am, lunch 11am–3pm, and dinner 6pm–11pm, on a shift basis.

Head Office: Lyndhurst Road, Brockenhurst, Hampshire SO42 7ZB
☎ 01590 623116
✆ info@balmerlawnhotel.com
🖥 www.balmerlawnhotel.com

Pay: To be arranged, minus £30 for accommodation.
Company Description: A friendly hotel situated in the heart of the New Forest with leisure facilities available. Approximately 20 minutes from Southampton and Bournemouth by train.
Requirements: Applicants should be over 20 and preferably have previous experience of the hotel industry, though training will be given.
Accommodation: Available. Costs £30.
Application Procedure: By post to Mark Albray, general manager at the above address.

Banham Zoo

Job(s) available: Catering assistants (12+).
Duration: Period of work from 1 July to 31 October; vacancies also at Christmas and Easter.
Working Hours: Flexible working hours, including bank holidays and weekend work.

Head Office: Kenninghall Road, Banham, Norfolk NR16 2HE
☎ 01953 715313
✆ lynn.mellish@banhamzoo.co.uk
🖥 www.banhamzoo.co.uk

Pay: National minimum wage rates.
Job Description: Catering assistants for general catering duties, serving at tills, clearing tables, serving hot and cold food and working in snack shacks within the zoo.
Requirements: Minimum age 18. Some positions will require a current health and hygiene certificate.
Application Procedure: By post to Lynn Mellish, HR manager, at the above address.

Bray Lake Watersports

Job(s) Available: Kitchen manager.
Pay: Negotiable, between £25 and £40 per day.
Company Description: Set next to a 50-acre lake, ideal for beginners and intermediate windsurfers, sailors and canoeists. Caters for both adults and juniors. Has a good range of equipment for teaching, hire and demo.

Head Office: Monkey Island Lane, Windsor Road, Maidenhead, Berkshire SL6 2EB
☎ 01628 638860
info@braylake.com
www.braylake.com

Job Description: Kitchen manager needed to run small coffee bar and be in charge of stock and health and safety. The ideal candidate would have an interest in water sports, and be looking to use the time to gain water sports experience and eventually become an instructor.
Requirements: Some catering experience preferable.
Application Procedure: By post to Lindsay Frost, centre manager at the above address.

Caledonian Thistle Hotel

Job(s) Available: Food service staff for the cafe/bar or dining room.
Duration: Minimum period of work 3 months from April to October.
Working Hours: To work split shifts for a 39-hour week.
Pay: National minimum wage rates.

Head Office: 10–14 Union Terrace, Aberdeen AB10 1WE
☎ 01224 640233
reservations.aberdeencaledonian@ thistle.co.uk
www.thistlehotels.com

Company Description: Part of the Thistle Hotel chain, the 77-bedroom Caledonian is situated in the heart of Aberdeen city centre.
Requirements: Staff should be at least 18, and experience is preferred.
Accommodation: Board and lodging available.
Application Procedure: By post to the above address from January onwards. Suitably qualified overseas applicants are welcome.

Camelot Castle Hotel

Job(s) Available: Chamber staff, waiting staff, kitchen staff, front of house staff, reception and, bar staff to work in busy hotel.
Duration: Required from May to the end of October.
Working Hours: To work 6 hours per day, 6 days a week.

Head Office: Atlantic Road, Tintagel, Cornwall PL34 0DQ
☎ 01840 770202
enquiries@camelotcastle.com
www.camelotcastle.com

Pay: £3.50 per hour with accommodation, breakfast and dinner provided.
Requirements: Applicants must be willing to do any aspect of hotel work.
Accommodation: Available.
Application Procedure: Applications to Irina Mappin at the above address or by email from March. Foreign applicants with appropriate visas and sufficient English welcome.

Clachaig Inn

Job(s) Available: General Assistants (12).

Duration: The minimum period of work is at least 3 months. Positions are available year round; those able to work over the New Year and Easter have priority when it comes to the summer months.

Head Office: Glencoe, Argyll PH49 4HX
☎ 01855 811252
📧 inn@clachaig.com
💻 www.clachaig.com

Company Description: A busy, vibrant country inn set in the heart of Glencoe. Popular year round with hillwalkers, climbers, mountain bikers, skiers and travellers. Specialists in real ale (award winning) with a significant food trade. A unique experience for customers and staff alike.

Job Description: General assistants required throughout the year to help in all aspects of the business; bar work (serving both food and drinks), waiting on tables and helping out in the kitchen, housekeeping and various odd jobs.

Requirements: Previous experience is helpful, but a friendly, outgoing personality and enthusiasm are more important. You must be clean and presentable, able to communicate well, and be able to work well as part of a team.

Accommodation: Excellent accommodation available in staff lodge or the fully refurbished staff bothy.

Application Procedure: Applications (with a covering letter and detailed CV) should be sent by email or post to Gordon Keppie, general manager, at the above address approximately one month before you are available for work.

Crieff Hydro Ltd

Job(s) Available: Food and beverage service assistants and commis chefs.

Duration: Positions are available year round. Minimum period of work is 6 months.

Working Hours: Approximately 39 hours per week with overtime available.

Head Office: Ferntower Road, Crieff, Perthshire PH7 3LQ
☎ 01764 651612
📧 janice.sneddon@crieffhydro.com
or sarah.glen@crieffhydro.com
💻 www.crieffhydro.com

Company Description: Crieff Hydro is a family-run hotel and leisure resort set in 900 acres of central Perthshire countryside, approximately 20 miles north of Stirling. The hotel has 215 bedrooms, 52 self-catering units and over 55 activities on site including quad biking, horseriding and golf.

Requirements: Applicants should have a good level of spoken English. Previous hospitality experience preferred.

Accommodation: Staff accommodation with meals available for approximately £30 per week; this does not include insurance or supplies (towels).

Application Procedure: By post to Janice Sneddon or Sarah Glen at the above address, or through the website. A phone interview is required. Overseas applicants welcome subject to valid work permits/visas and other travel documents.

Crown Hotel

Job(s) Available: General assistants.

Duration: Positions are available from April to September inclusive. Minimum period of work 2 months.

Head Office: Exford, Exmoor, Somerset TA24 7PP
☎ 01643 831554
📧 info@crownhotelexmoor.co.uk
💻 www.crownhotelexmoor.co.uk

Working Hours: To work 39 hours per week.

Pay: £200 per week minus board and lodging.

Company Description: Award-winning 17th-century coaching inn set in the heart of beautiful Exmoor National Park. Internationally renowned cuisine.

Job Description: General assistants needed for waiting in the restaurant, bar work, cleaning rooms and washing-up duties.

Requirements: Fluent English essential. Minimum age 19.

Accommodation: Board and lodging available, cost to be arranged.

Application Procedure: By post as soon as possible to Mr Chris Kirkbride at the above address. Suitably qualified foreign applicants welcome.

Dee Cooper

Job(s) Available: Live-in hotel staff.
Working Hours: Hours variable.
Pay: To be arranged.
Company Description: Agent working with more than 1,000 hotels in England, Scotland and Wales. Free service.
Accommodation: All positions live-in.

> **Head Office:** Culloch Schoolhouse, Comrie, Perthshire PH6 2JG
> ☎ 01764 670001 or 01764 679765
> 🖅 dee@livein-jobs.demon.co.uk
> 🖳 www.livein-jobs.co.uk or www.londonpubjobs.co.uk

Application Procedure: For a list of relevant available jobs, contact Dee Cooper using the above details. Foreign applicants with permission to work in the UK welcome.

Grange Moor Hotel

Job(s) Available: Waiting staff (10), dish washers (6).
Working Hours: To work hours to suit between 1 and 23 December for lunches and evening meals. Christmas Day work available between noon to 5pm.
Pay: From £5.50 per hour. Christmas Day work at £15 per hour.

> **Head Office:** St Michaels Road, Maidstone, Kent ME16 8BS
> ☎ 01622 677623
> 🖅 reservations@grangemoor.co.uk
> 🖳 www.grangemoor.co.uk

Company Description: A 50-bedroom family-run hotel with banquet room.

Job Description: Waiting staff required to provide plated service for Christmas dinners. Full training will be given.

Requirements: Applicants must be 17 or over, friendly, helpful and polite.

Accommodation: No accommodation available.

Application Procedure: By post to Mrs Christine Sedge at the above address.

Haven Passenger Cruises Ltd

Job(s) Available: Crew (5/6).
Duration: To work between May and September.
Pay: £5.35 per hour plus tips.
Company Description: The *Riverboat Georgina* is a fully appointed passenger craft on the river Cam, taking mainly private bookings for weddings, birthdays, corporate events and the group travel market.

> **Head Office:** PO Box 401, Cambridge CB4 3WE
> ☎ 01223 307694
> 🖅 info@georgina.co.uk
> 🖳 www.georgina.co.uk

Job Description: Crew for the *Riverboat Georgina*. Job involves bar work, serving food and general crewing tasks (tying/untying ropes, opening/closing locks on river).

Requirements: Full training given. Applicants must be at least 18 and proficient in English.

Application Procedure: By post to Amy Burns, operations manager.

Hilton PLC

Job(s) Available: Kitchen, restaurant, waiting, bar and housekeeping staff.
Duration: Staff required from June to October. Minimum period of work 12 weeks.
Working Hours: To work 39 hours over a 5 day week.
Pay: National minimum wage rates.

Head Office: Coylumbridge Hotel, Coylumbridge, Aviemore, Inverness-shire PH22 1QN
☎ 01479 813076
🖱 hr.coylumbridge@hilton.com
💻 www.hilton.co.uk

Company Description: Hilton Colyumbridge is a family-orientated hotel situated in the heart of the Scottish Highlands. Local attractions include golf, watersports and horse riding.
Requirements: Minimum age 18. Experience preferred.
Accommodation: Accommodation with basic facilities available.
Application Procedure: By post from April/May to the personnel department at the above address. Overseas applicants with basic English (communication level) welcome.

Hotel L'Horizon

Job(s) Available: Food and beverage service attendants, room attendants, kitchen porters, commis waiting staff/chef de rangs.
Working Hours: To work a 5 day week.
Company Description: A 4-star 106-bedroom hotel, located on one of the island's beautiful

Head Office: St Brelade's Bay, Jersey, Channel Islands JE3 8EF
☎ 01534 494404
🖱 sashford@handpicked.co.uk, lhorizon@handpicked.co.uk

beaches. Hotel L'Horizon offers a unique work experience for employees who prove themselves to be dedicated, responsible and efficient, with further employment prospects after the seasonal contracts terminate.
Requirements: All applicants must be presentable, have excellent customer care skills and have worked within a similar environment before. A good understanding and conversational fluency of English language is essential.
Accommodation: Uniform and meals on duty and accommodation provided.
Application Procedure: Applications should be made by application form available together with further information from the above address and website.

Kentwell Hall

Job(s) Available: Retail and catering staff (10).
Duration: The great annual Tudor re-creation takes place during June and July and is visited by up to 1,500 children on weekdays and the public on weekends.
Pay: To be arranged.

Head Office: Long Melford, Sudbury, Suffolk CO10 9BA
☎ 01787 310207
🖱 info@kentwell.co.uk
💻 www.kentwell.co.uk

Company Description: A privately owned moated Tudor Mansion, situated in its own park and farmland, approximately 1.5 miles from the historic town of Long Melford, famous for its great annual re-creations of Tudor life.
Job Description: Retail and catering staff needed. In order to keep the 16th and 21st centuries separate, the catering and shop are located outside of the main gates. Staff on the 21st century side ensure smooth running of the event for the public and school parties. Duties consist of serving in a temporary souvenir shop and restaurant in marquees and may also include marshalling school parties.
Requirements: Minimum age 16. Applicants need a pleasant manner and to be physically fit as they will be on their feet all day.

Accommodation: Employees must make their own accommodation arrangements.
Application Procedure: By post to estate office at the above address.

Knoll House Hotel

Job(s) Available: Waiting staff (6–10), housekeeping staff (6–10), general assistants (2–3), kitchen assistants (2–3), chefs (4).

Head Office Studland Bay, near Swanage, Dorset BH19 3AH
☎ 01929 452233
✆ staff@knollhouse.co.uk
🖳 www.knollhouse.co.uk

Duration: Positions available for a minimum of 6 weeks between March and October. Easter and summer vacation positions also available, as well as further positions for the entire season.

Working Hours: All staff to work 38 hours.

Pay: National minimum wage rates and above paid depending on position. *Chefs:* salary dependent on experience.

Company Description: A country house holiday hotel superbly located in a National Trust Reserve overlooking Studland Bay. Independent and family run, it has a reputation for service and care of its guests, many of whom return annually.

Job Description: *Waiting staff:* for dining room including wine service. *General assistants:* to work in children's own restaurant. *Kitchen assistants:* washing up and helping in kitchens.

Requirements: A happy disposition and a good attitude are more important than experience. Minimum age 17 years. *Housekeeping staff:* no experience required. *Chefs:* 706/1 or equivalent not always necessary.

Accommodation: Deduction made for board and lodging, available in single rooms.

Application Procedure: By post from the start of the year to the staff manager, Knoll House Hotel. EU applicants with good spoken English welcome. Interview is not always necessary.

Land's End and John O'Groats Company

Job(s) Available: Catering personnel and retail staff for various jobs at Land's End.

Head Office: Land's End, Sennen, Penzance, Cornwall TR19 7AA
☎ 0870 458 0099
✆ info@landsend-landmark.co.uk
🖳 www.landsend-landmark.co.uk

Duration: From spring to early autumn.

Working Hours: Hours depend on the level of business.

Pay: To be arranged.

Company Description: A leading tourist attraction in Cornwall located in a spectacular setting. It comprises various exhibitions and trading units operating throughout the year. In winter the operation is reduced.

Requirements: Minimum age 16. Those with previous experience preferred.

Application Procedure: By post to personnel at the above address.

Lion Hotel

Job(s) Available: General assistants (2), cook/kitchen assistant.

Head Office: Y Maes, Criccieth, Gwynned LL52 0AA
☎ 01766 522460
✆ info@lionhotelcriccieth.co.uk
🖳 www.lionhotelcriccieth.co.uk

Duration: *Cook/kitchen assistant:* minimum period of work 4 months.

Working Hours: *General assistant:* to work 39 hours per week over 6 days.

Pay: National minimum wage rates depending on age and experience.

Company Description: A busy 3-star hotel centrally situated in a seaside resort.

Accommodation: Single accommodation and food is available, at a price to be arranged.
Application Procedure: By post from 1 March to Mrs S Burnett, manager, at the above address.

Lochs & Glens Holidays

Job(s) Available: Kitchen, dining room, housekeeping and reception/bar team members.
Duration: Minimum period of work 12 weeks at any time of year. Dates of work negotiable.
Working Hours: Required to work 40 hours per week.

Head Office: School Road, Gartocharn, Dumbartonshire G83 8RW
☎ 01389 713713
✆ jobs@lochsandglens.com
🖥 www.lochsandglens.com

Pay: National minimum wage rates, plus live-in terms and conditions are available.
Company Description: A hotel and tour group with 6 hotels located in beautiful and remote areas of Scotland.
Additional Information: Both temporary and permanent positions available, as well as opportunity for career development.
Application Procedure: Apply at any time to jobs@lochsandglens.com or link through website.

London Hostels Association Ltd

Job(s) Available: General domestic staff, voluntary jobs.
Duration: *General domestic staff*: work available all year round, long stays welcome. Minimum period of work 3 months throughout the year. *Voluntary jobs:* minimum stay 8 weeks.

Head Office: 54 Eccleston Square, London SW1V 1PG
☎ 020 7834 1545
✆ ngrant@london-hostels.co.uk
🖥 www.london-hostels.co.uk

Working Hours: *General domestic staff:* to work an average of 30–39 hours per week (mornings and evenings). *Voluntary jobs:* working only 20 hours per week.
Pay: To be arranged, paid monthly.
Company Description: Established in 1940, London Hostels Association recruits residential staff for 11 London hostels run for young employed people and full-time bona fide students.
Job Description: *General domestic staff:* to do housework and help in kitchens.
Requirements: Common sense and willingness to tackle a variety of jobs required.
Accommodation: Board and lodging provided.
Additional Information: Opportunities to attend courses and improve English skills.
Application Procedure: By post 2 months before date of availability to the personnel manager, London Hostels Association, at the above address. Foreign applicants with permission to work in the UK are welcome.

Lundy Company

Job(s) Available: Travel staff (4).
Duration: Required from April to September.
Working Hours: To work a 5-day week.
Pay: Wages are variable.
Company Description: Lundy is an island off the north Devon coast owned by the National Trust with 23 letting properties, a pub and a shop.

Head Office: The Lundy Island Shore Office, The Quay, Bideford, Devon EX39 2LY
☎ 01237 423233
✆ admin@lundyisland.co.uk
🖥 www.lundyisland.co.uk

Job Description: Staff to assist with kitchen and bar duties.

Requirements: Applicants must have previous bar/kitchen experience.
Accommodation: Free board and lodging.
Application Procedure: By post from January to Derek Green at the above address. Interview necessary.

National Trust Enterprises

Job(s) Available: Catering assistants.
Working Hours: Hours vary but may include working over weekends and bank holidays.
Pay: Wages vary from property to property but will be at least in line with the recommended national minimum wage rates.
Job Description: Catering assistants to work in 17 National Trust properties catering to the general public in West Sussex, East Sussex, Kent and Surrey.

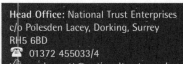

Head Office: National Trust Enterprises c/o Polesden Lacey, Dorking, Surrey RH5 6BD
☎ 01372 455033/4
✎ sue.knevett@nationaltrust.org.uk or louise.doe@nationaltrust.org.uk
🖳 www.nationaltrust.org.uk

Requirements: Experience of working in the catering industry and basic food hygiene are desirable but not essential; full training will be given.
Accommodation: Accommodation not available. Do not apply if accommodation is required.
Application Procedure: By post to Sue Knevett, catering operations manager, or Louise Doe at the above address. She will refer you to an appropriate property.

Now And Zen

Job(s) Available: Catering assistants.
Duration: Working around Britain at summer music festivals.
Pay: Pocket money paid.

✎ jobs@nowandzen.co.uk
🖳 www.nowandzen.co.uk

Company Description: Now and Zen has been one of the most popular festival caterers for music festivals for the past 20 years, specialising in vegetarian world foods (including Japanese noodles, French crêpes, and Italian pastas). This is a lively, friendly, happy, and efficient organisation.
Job Description: Catering assistants needed to help in busy vegetarian world food stalls. Duties include food preparation, light cooking, cleaning, serving, packing, and so on. You will become an important part of a mainly student team.
Requirements: Applicants must be able to work happily in a team and must have lots of energy and stamina, be lively and adaptable, conscientious, and good humoured. Will not suit a person who likes a 9–5 job.
Accommodation: Opportunity for home-stay with accommodation and food provided.
Application Procedure: Apply to Ron Zahl, proprietor.

Payne and Gunter

Job(s) Available: Waiting staff, catering assistants, bar staff, table clearers (200–1,200 per event).
Duration: Required from May to October.
Pay: £5.45 per hour.
Company Description: Payne and Gunter are the official caterers at Goodwood Racecourse and Festival of Speed and Goodwood Revival, supplying all catering staff.

Head Office: Goodwood Racecourse, Goodwood, Chichester, West Sussex PO18 0PS
☎ 01243 774839
✎ staffing.goodwood@compass-group. co.uk

Requirements: Minimum age 18.

Accommodation: Lunch provided.

Application Procedure: Send for an application pack at the above address or email staffing.goodwood@compass-group.co.uk.

Peppermint Events

Job(s) Available: Bar staff, trained bartenders, catering staff and cashiers (approximately 100).

Duration: Required from June to September, but recruitment is ongoing.

Working Hours: Staff usually needed to work 6–8 hour shifts.

Head Office: 19 Pensbury Street, Battersea, London SW8 4JL
☎ 0845 226 7845
✉ jobs@peppermintevents.co.uk
🖥 www.peppermintevents.co.uk

Pay: Both paid and unpaid positions. Wages depend on position and experience of applicant. Unpaid staff are reimbursed with free entry tickets to festivals, crew camping, plus a free meal and 2 free drinks per shift in exchange for 2 shifts per event.

Company Description: An event and bar management company that caters for events and festivals such as Glade Festival, Bestival, Skandia Cowes Week and other various music enents in London and the south-east.

Requirements: Minimum age 18. Experience of bar work is preferred, but not essential (except for trained bartender positions).

Accommodation: Camping accommodation provided at festivals only.

Application Procedure: By post to Adam Hempenstall at the above address, or via the website. Overseas applicants are welcome to apply provided they have the relevant documentation and speak English to the same level as a native speaker.

Porth Tocyn Hotel

Jobs Available: General Assistants

Duration: Minimum period of work 6 weeks between March and November.

Pay: Guaranteed above the national minimum wage.

Company Description: A country house hotel by the sea, filled with antiques. The house has been in

Head Office: Abersoch, Gwynedd LL53 7BU
☎ 01758-713303
✉ bookings@porthtocyn.fsnet.co.uk
🖥 www.porth-tocyn-hotel.co.uk

the family for 60 years, and has been in the *Good Food Guide* for more than 50 years.

Requirements: Intelligence, practical demeanour and sense of humour required. Cooking experience useful but not essential.

Accommodation: Free board and lodging and use of tennis court and swimming pool.

Additional Information: Travel expenses will be paid for those able to work for short stints over Easter and the spring bank holidays.

Application Procedure: Applications from those who are able to work over Easter and/or outside the summer university vacation period especially welcome. Applications with s.a.e. to Mrs Fletcher-Brewer, at the above address.

Queen's Hall

Job(s) Available: Bar staff/waiting staff (10).

Duration: Minimum period of work is 6 months.

Working Hours: To work 40 hours per week, all year around.

Pay: National minimum wage rates.

Head Office: The Queen's Hall, Warren Road, Minehead, Somerset TA24 5BG
☎ 01643 704186
✉ sue@kravis.co.uk
🖥 www.kravis.co.uk

Company Description: A food-led family pub.

Requirements: Minimum age 18. Applicants must have at least an intermediate level of English.

Accommodation: Available at a charge of £40 per week.

Additional Information: Staff also required for family entertainment centre, coffee shop and Subway in Minehead.

Application Procedure: By post at any time, to Marcus at the above address. An interview may not be required.

Rufflets Country House Hotel

Job(s) Available: Housekeeping assistant, restaurant assistant, lounge service assistant.

Duration: Minimum period of work is 6 months, between 1 April and 30 November.

Working Hours: All staff to work hours as required, 5 days a week.

Pay: National minimum wage rates.

Head Office: Strathkinness Low Road, St Andrews KY16 9TX
☎ 01334 472594
✆ reservations@rufflets.co.uk
🖥 www.rufflets.co.uk

Company Description: A privately owned 24-bedroom upmarket hotel which holds 2 AA rosettes for food quality. Young and friendly staff.

Requirements: Experience is not essential. Minimum age 18.

Accommodation: Available at approximately £4.50 per day.

Application Procedure: By post from January to the manager. Foreign applicants fluent in English considered. Interview not always necessary.

The Balmoral Hotel

Job(s) Available: Food, beverage and housekeeping staff.

Duration: Staff required for various casual and full-time positions.

Working Hours: Working 5 days out of 7.

Pay: National minimum wage rates.

Head Office: 1 Princes Street, Edinburgh EH2 2EQ
☎ 0131 622 8895
✆ hr.balmoral@roccofortecollection.com
🖥 www.roccofortecollection.com

Company Description: An elegant, 5-star hotel in the centre of Edinburgh. Part of the Rocco Forte Hotel group, with 188 bedrooms, Michelin star restaurant, brasserie, Palm Court Bar and NB's Bar, as well as extensive conference and banqueting facilities.

Requirements: Candidates must be flexible and motivated and enjoy delivering the best.

Application Procedure: Applications or CVs can be submitted from April to the HR department at the above address.

The Ceilidh Place

Job(s) Available: Cooks (3), housestaff (2), waiting staff (6), bar staff (2).

Duration: Work available between April and October, minimum period 3 months: no shorter period considered.

Pay: Wages paid monthly.

Head Office: West Argyle Street, Ullapool, Ross-shire IV26 2TY
☎ 01854 612103
✆ effie@theceilidhplace.com
🖥 www.theceilidhplace.com

Company Description: A complex of buildings including a small hotel with 13 rooms, a bunk house, bar, café/bistro, restaurant, bookshop, gallery and venue for music and drama.

Job Description: *Waiting staff*: serving food and drink and clearing tables. *Bar staff*: serving/stocking drinks and assisting with food service.

Requirements: *Cooks:* natural skill and enthusiasm. *Housestaff*: must be fit.

Accommodation: Board and lodging allowance included in wages.

Application Procedure: Email or write to the general manager at the above address for further information and an application form. Overseas applicants eligible to work in the UK and with necessary documentation welcome.

The Master Builders House Hotel

Job(s) Available: Commis waiting staff, bar staff and chamber staff.

Duration: Positions available from the end of April/May to the end of August/September.

Pay: £4.60–£5 per hour plus tips.

Head Office: Buckler's Hard, Beaulieu, Hampshire SO42 7XB
☎ 01590 616253
🖱 res@themasterbuilders.co.uk
🖥 www.themasterbuilders.co.uk

Job Description: *Commis waiting staff:* to work in the 2-rosette Riverview Restaurant. Serve at breakfast, lunch, afternoon tea, dinner and conference set-up. *Bar staff:* to serve drinks and pub food in the bar and galley. *Chamberstaff:* servicing guestrooms and evening turndown.

Requirements: Applicants need good English, a pleasant outgoing personality, to enjoy the countryside and be good team players in an international team.

Accommodation: Accommodation may be available; single room (£30 per week), shared (£25 per week), including 3 meals a day.

Application Procedure: By post to Sally Elcoate, general manager, at the above address.

The National Trust

Job(s) Available: Catering assistants, volunteer room stewards.

Duration: *Catering assistants:* required from July to the end of September.

Head Office: Belton House, Grantham, Lincolnshire NG32 2LS
☎ 01476 566116
🖱 angela.marshall@nationaltrust.org.uk

Working Hours: *Catering assistants:* to work any days from Wednesday to Sunday, including bank holiday Mondays. *Volunteer room stewards*: to work any days from Wednesday to Sunday, including bank holiday Mondays, from approximately 12.30pm to 4.45pm.

Company Description: The National Trust was founded in 1895 to preserve places of historic interest or natural beauty for the nation to enjoy.

Job Description: *Catering assistants*: to work with a friendly team in a busy assisted-service Stables Restaurant. *Volunteer room stewards:* receive a wonderful opportunity to help present one of the finest examples of a Restoration country house to the many visitors.

Requirements: Experience of working with the public desirable.

Accommodation: No accommodation available.

Application Procedure: By post from February/March to Sue Burkitt, catering manager, at the above address.

The Old Stocks Hotel

Job(s) Available: Housekeepers (2), waiting staff (2), kitchen assistants (2), bar staff (2).

Duration: Minimum period of work 3 months between April and November.

Head Office: The Square, Stow on the Wold, Gloucester GL54 1AF
☎ 01451 830666
🖱 info@oldstockshotel.co.uk

Working Hours: To work 40 hours, 5 days a week.

Pay: Approximately £180 per week.

Company Description: A small 18 bedroom family-run hotel with a friendly team of caring staff. Located in the highest point of the Cotswolds, a Grade II listed building.

Requirements: Previous experience not necessary as full training will be provided.

Accommodation: Accommodation available.

Application Procedure: By post to Helen E Allen, proprietor, at the above address.

The Radisson Sas Hotel Edinburgh

Job(s) Available: Waiting staff (10), chamber staff (15).

Duration: Minimum period of work is 4 months.

Pay: Wages for all positions at competitive rate, paid fortnightly.

Company Description: A busy 4-star deluxe city centre hotel situated halfway between a castle and a palace, aiming to provide first-class service for an international clientele.

> **Head Office:** 80 High Street, The Royal Mile, Edinburgh EH1 1TH
> ☎ 0131 473 6514
> Jenny.Mcglone@radissonsas.com
> www.edinburgh.radissonsas.com

Requirements: *Waiting staff:* minimum age 18. *Chamber staff:* minimum age 16. No experience necessary; full training is provided.

Accommodation: Assistance offered in finding accommodation.

Additional Information: Uniform and meals on duty as well as access to a range of discounts/benefits from day one.

Application Procedure: By post from March to HR department. Interview necessary (but could be conducted by telephone).

The Royal Castle Hotel

Job(s) Available: Waiting, bar, housekeeping and kitchen staff.

Duration: Work available all year round.

Working Hours: To work 40 hours over 5 days a week.

Pay: From £5.75 per hour.

> **Head Office:** 11 The Quay, Dartmouth, Devon TQ6 9PS
> ☎ 01803 833033
> enquiry@royalcastle.co.uk
> www.royalcastle.co.uk

Company Description: A busy 3-star hotel with 2 bars which employs around 50 staff.

Requirements: No experience necessary, just a bright personality, the right attitude, and the ability to work hard and play hard.

Accommodation: Available at a cost of approximately £25–£50 per week.

Application Procedure: By phone or email to the duty manager about 3 weeks prior to desired start. Interview sometimes required.

The Westin Turnberry Resort

Job(s) Available: A variety of positions are available depending on the time of year.

Duration: Required to work from the beginning of March until the end of October.

> **Head Office:** Turnberry Hotel, Maidens Road, Turnberry, Ayrshire KA26 9LT
> ☎ 01655 334164
> turnberry.hr@westin.com
> www.westin.com

Company Description: A 5-star luxury golf resort with 221 guest bedrooms set in 800 acres on the south-west coast of Scotland. The Resort is part of Starwood Hotels & Resorts Inc, the world's leading upscale hotel company spanning more than 80 countries.

Requirements: Applicants must be eligible to work in the EU.

Accommodation: Can be provided if required. This will be at a charge of approximately £150 per month and includes free transport from the resort to accommodation and all meals.
Additional Information: The resort offers excellent training and development facilities plus great career opportunities.
Application Procedure: By post to Jennifer Paton, HR co-ordinator at the above address or via email.

Topsail Charters Ltd

Job(s) Available: Bar worker, host/ess, catering assistants (3) for work on Thames sailing barges.
Duration: Positions are available from April to September.
Working Hours: Must be flexible about hours, up to 50 per week.
Pay: Approximately £7 per hour.

Head Office: Cooks Yard, The Hythe, Maldon, Essex CM9 5HN
☎ 01621 857567
✆ info@top-sail.co.uk
🖥 www.top-sail.co.uk

Company Description: Based in Maldon but also working in London and Ipswich. Private functions and public trips on historic sailing barges. A small company, very customer-orientated, with a great team of staff on board.
Requirements: Some bar/catering experience preferable; must be flexible and combine galley and bar work.
Accommodation: No accommodation available.
Application Procedure: By post to Stephanie Valentine from Easter onwards. Interview necessary.

Tors Hotel

Job(s) Available: Silver service waiting staff, chamber person, porters, kitchen porters.
Duration: Season lasts from March to January. Period of work must be for the whole period from April until September, applicants only available for summer vacation need not apply.

Head Office: Lynmouth, North Devon EX35 6NA
☎ 01598 753236
✆ Torshotel@torslynmouth.co.uk
🖥 www.torslynmouth.co.uk

Working Hours: All staff work 5 days a week. *Silver service waiting staff:* to work 39 hours, 5 days; split shifts. *Chamber person, porters, kitchen porters:* to work 39 hours per week.
Pay: £169 per week. Wages dependent on experience. Bonus paid on completion of season.
Company Description: A 3-star, 4-crown, 31-bedroom hotel situated on the north Devon coastline with stunning sea views across the Bristol Channel to Wales.
Requirements: *Silver service waiting staff:* experience or the ability to learn. *Chamber person, porters, kitchen porters:* no experience needed.
Accommodation: Free board and lodging provided.
Application Procedure: Send applications with details of previous experience and photograph to the manager.

Tresco Estate

Job(s) Available: Waiting staff (18), housekeeping staff (18), bar staff (4), chefs – all levels (18), kitchen assistants/porters (4), retail assistants (8), receptionists (5), cottage cleaners (6), maintenance person (1), tractor/transport driver (1), housekeeping supervisors (2), restaurant supervisors (3).

Head Office: Tresco, Isles of Scilly, Cornwall TR24 0QQ
☎ 01720 424110
✆ personnel@tresco.co.uk
🖥 www.trescojobs.co.uk

Duration: Period of work from February to November with further vacancies mid-season. Applicants will not be considered mid-season unless able to work a minimum of 10 weeks to include all of July and August.

Working Hours: To work 40 hours or more per week, generally split shifts over 5 – 5.5 days a week.

Pay: Starts at £5.52 per hour (2008). Tips for hotel staff are split at the end of the season for all who complete their contract.

Company Description: Private island holiday resort, 28 miles off the Cornish coast. Magnificent beaches and a mild climate.

Job Description: Staff needed to cover all duties in one of the Estate's 3 luxury hotels, the island stores, the holiday cottages department, or the Abbey Gardens shop and café.

Requirements: Applicants must be over 18 and have a valid work permit.

Accommodation: Live-in accommodation of approximately £30 per week, meals are included in the hotels; for other departments kitchen facilities are available.

Application Procedure: At any time, by post, fax or email (as above), stating the position you are interested in, and why you consider yourself suitable.

YHA (Youth Hostel Association)

Job(s) Available: General assistants needed to help run the YHA's youth hostels throughout England and Wales.

Duration: Work is available for varying periods (minimum 3 months), between January and October each year.

Company Description: The YHA, a registered charity, is the largest budget accommodation provider in Britain with 200 youth hostels in diverse locations throughout England and Wales.

> **Head Office:** HR Department (Recruitment Hostel Staff), Trevelyan House, Dimple Road, Matlock, Derbyshire DE4 3XA
> ☎ 01629 592570
> ✎ jobs@yha.org.uk
> 🖳 www.yha.org.uk

Job Description: Assistants undertake a variety of tasks including catering, cleaning, reception and general maintenance.

Requirements: Experience in one or more of the above areas is desirable, but customer service experience and enthusiasm are essential.

Application Procedure: For an application form call the YHA National Recruitment line on 01629 592570 between September and June. Alternatively, visit the YHA website at www.yha.org.uk. Non-EU nationals require a valid work permit. All posts are subject to an interview, usually at the hostel where the vacancy exists.

Language Schools

The staff needs of language schools are principally for EFL teachers and social organisers.

Teaching English as a foreign language (TEFL), also known as TESOL (Teaching English to Speakers of Other Languages), is perhaps no longer the major growth industry it was a decade ago, but it still offers a large number of summer jobs that often pay better than average. Starting from around June, people of all nationalities and ages, though usually teenagers and students, come to Britain to learn or improve their English and absorb some British culture. The schools that cater for them proliferate along the south coast and in major university/tourist cities like Oxford, Cambridge, Edinburgh and London.

The majority of residential language schools often take on staff to work as social supervisors and organisers, both at the school outside of teaching time and on day trips. The bigger ones may also require sports and activity instructors. These positions frequently require no qualifications other than interest and an ability to work with young people.

Briar School Of English

Job(s) Available: EFL teachers, sports instructors.

Duration: Busy seasons are over the Easter period and from the beginning of June to the end of August. Also entertain out of season school parties at different times of the year. Minimum period of work 3 weeks (June to August).

Head Office: 3 Dukes Head Street, Lowestoft, Suffolk NR32 1JY
☎ 01502 580203
✎ briar.school@set-uk.com

Working Hours: *Sports instructors*: required to work up to 6 hours per day.

Pay: *EFL teachers:* from £9 per hour. *Sports Instructors:* from £5.50 per hour. Successful applicants for both jobs can earn extra pay by leading half/full day excursions to Norwich, Cambridge, London and other local places of interest.

Company Description: Established since 1958. Offers English courses to international students aged 12–25.

Requirements: *EFL teachers:* TEFL qualifications or experience essential. Applicants must possess either a degree or a teacher's certificate. *Sports instructors:* ideal post for Physical Education students.

Accommodation: Accommodation not available.

Application Procedure: By post to Miss Lucy Oram, director of studies, at the above address.

Cambridge Academy Of English

Job(s) Available: EFL teachers to teach teenagers and young adults.

Duration: Required for 3 week courses between 23 June and 22 August.

Head Office: 65 High Street, Girton, Cambridge CB3 0QD
☎ 01223 277230
✎ cae@cambridgeacademy.co.uk
🖳 www.cambridgeacademy.co.uk

Working Hours: Job involves 21–24 hours teaching per week.

Pay: Approximately £1,000 per course.

Company Description: Situated in the leafy suburb of Girton, the Academy runs non-residential courses for teenagers and young adults, and residential courses for 9–13-year-olds and 14–16-year-olds.

Requirements: Must have RSA TEFL/Trinity CertTESOL or equivalent and experience.

Application Procedure: By post to S Levy at the above address.

Channel School Of English

Job(s) Available: EFL teachers (15), social organisers.

Duration: *EFL teachers:* to work June to August. *Social organisers*: to work July and August.

Head Office: Country Cousins Ltd, Bicclescombe, Ilfracombe, Devon EX34 8JN
☎ 01271 862834
✎ help@country-cousins.com
🖳 www.country-cousins.com

Working Hours: *EFL teachers:* to work 24-27 hours per week.

Pay: *EFL teachers:* £11.20 per hour. *Social organisers:* £5.51 per hour.

Company Description: Situated on the beautiful north Devon coast, the school offers a range of English courses with 12, 15 or 21 hours of lessons per week to those aged 7 to adult.

Job Description: *Social organisers:* supervising children and young adults on the school's sports and excursion programme.

Requirements: *EFL teachers:* must have TEFL qualification and should have experience with the age range 11–18. Ideally social organisers would be trainee teachers.

Application Procedure: By post to Maribel Cabrera at the above address.

Concord College

Job(s) Available: Residential summer course EFL teachers (10–15), summer course sports tutor (2–4), summer course outdoor education tutor (1–2).

Head Office: Acton Burnell Hall, Acton Burnell, Shrewsbury, Shropshire SY5 7PF
☎ 01694 731631
summercourses@concordcollegeuk.com
www.concordcollegeuk.com

Duration: Staff are required from the beginning of the month for July course (4 weeks) and/or August course (3 weeks).

Working Hours: Working hours are variable.

Pay: Salary is dependent on qualifications and experience.

Company Description: An independent international school.

Requirements: *Residential summer course EFL teachers:* applicants must hold as a minimum the RSA Certificate in TEFL. *Summer course sports tutor:* applicants must have the appropriate coaching qualifications.

Accommodation: Available at no charge. Fully residential with excellent facilities on campus.

Application Procedure: Applications and enquiries should be sent to John Leighton, director of summer courses, at the above address as soon as possible.

Concorde International Summer Schools Ltd

Job(s) Available: EFL teachers (150), course directors (approximately 5), assistant directors of study (approximately 5), centre managers (approximately 5), social assistants (25), social organisers (5).

Head Office: Arnett House, Hawks Lane, Canterbury, Kent CT1 2NU
☎ 01227 451035
info@concorde-int.com
www.concorde-int.com

Duration: The centres are open in June, July and August. Minimum period of work one week.

Working Hours: *EFL teachers:* required to teach in summer schools for full or part-time positions. An average working week consists of 15 hours tuition and 5 social activities, but weeks vary according to individual programmes. *Course directors:* to work 48 hours per week. *Assistant directors of study:* to work 35 hours per week. *Centre managers:* to work 48 hours per week. *Social organisers:* to work 48 hours per week.

Pay: To be arranged.

Company Description: Concorde International has been organising summer schools for more than 34 years in the south of England. They have a high return rate of international students and teachers.

Job Description: *EFL teachers:* both residential and non-residential positions are available. *Course directors:* to ensure the smooth running of the centre and liaise with head office, the local host family organiser and the group leaders. Other duties include holding staff meetings and weekly in-house training sessions, briefing teachers and standing in for them if required. Both residential and non-residential positions are available, depending on the centre. *Assistant directors of study:* required to ensure the smooth running of the social programme and take care of the students' health and welfare. Other duties include checking transfer arrangements, liasing with head office and regular staff at the centres.

Requirements: *EFL teachers:* applicants should have the RSA CELTA or Trinity CertTESOL or equivalent or PGCE in an appropriate subject, and some summer school experience. *Course directors:* applicants must hold a RSA Dip. TEFL or Trinity LTCL Diploma TESOL and have a minimum of 5 years of summer school experience. *Assistant directors of study:* applicants should hold DELTA/TEFL or Trinity LTCL Diploma TESOL preferred, but CELTA and experience will be considered. *Centre managers:* applicants should preferably hold a qualification in leisure management although other management qualifications/experience will be considered. *Social assistants:* experience preferred but not essential. *Social organisers:* qualifications and experience an advantage.

Accommodation: *Assistant directors of study:* positions are residential and non-residential. *Centre managers:* positions are residential.

Application Procedure: By post as soon as possible to the vacation course director at the above address or by email. Interview required. EU nationals preferred but non-EU applicants with necessary work permits/visas considered. Fluent English is essential.

Discovery Summer

Job(s) Available: Activity leaders (40).

Duration: Staff are required for a minimum of 2 weeks between July and mid-August.

Working Hours: One day off per week.

Pay: £235 per week.

Company Description: Organises summer courses for students learning English as a foreign language.

Head Office: 33 Kensington High Street, London W8 5EA
☎ 020 7937 1199
✆ mary@discoverysummer.co.uk
🖳 www.discoverysummer.co.uk

Job Description: Activity leaders required to supervise sports, arts and craft activities, parties and excursions for students aged 9–15.

Requirements: Experience of sports coaching or teaching/supervising children is desirable.

Accommodation: Available. Minimum age 18.

Application Procedure: From March to June to Mary Shipley, manager, via email to the above address.

EF International Language Schools

Job(s) Available: EFL teachers.

Duration: Required for July and August to work full-time.

Pay: Varies according to location and experience.

Requirements: Candidates should have at least a first degree and CELTA.

Application Procedure: By post with CVs to the director of studies at the above address.

Head Office: 74 Roupell Street, London SE1 8SS or 1–2 Sussex Square, Brighton, East Sussex BN2 1FJ or Palace Court, White Rock, Hastings, East Sussex TN34 1JP or 26 Wilbraham Road, Fallowfield, Manchester M14 6JX
☎ 020 7401 8399, 01273 571 780, 01424 428 458
✆ steve.allen@ef.com, sarah.williamson@ef.com, hastings@ef.com, david.bish@ef.com
🖳 www.ef.com

EF Language Travel

Job(s) Available: EFL teachers, leaders, activity co-ordinators.

Duration: Between June and the end of August.

Pay: *Teachers:* £26+ per half-day session (or £31 + if with a TEFL qualification). *Leaders:* £270+ per week.

Head Office: Plater College, Pullens Lane, Oxford OX3 0DT
☎ 01865 759670
✆ lt.oxford@ef.com
🖳 www.ef.com

Job Description: Staff needed to teach teenage overseas students and organise leisure activities.

Requirements: Minimum age 19. University students. Good knowledge of Oxford and London required.

Application Procedure: By post to the manager at the above address.

EF Language Travel

Job(s) Available: Group leaders and teachers (1,000 nationwide), activity co-ordinators (30 nationwide).
Duration: Minimum period of work 3 weeks between late May and late August.
Working Hours: All staff to work flexible hours, 6 days a week.

Head Office: 114a Cromwell Road, London SW7 4ES
☎ 020 7341 8500
lt.recruitment@ef.com
www.ef.com

Pay: Salary varies depending on region and experience.
Company Description: Language courses with free-time programmes for international students in locations throughout the UK.
Job Description: *Group leaders and teachers:* both residential and non-residential staff required. *Activity co-ordinators:* to plan an activity programme for all students in one particular town or residential centre.
Requirements: *Group leaders and teachers:* minimum age 19 years. Teaching or leadership experience preferred but not essential. Applicants must have a standard of English as high as that of a native speaker. *Activity co-ordinators:* minimum age 20 years. Previous organisational experience essential.
Accommodation: Full board and lodging available for residential appointments only.
Application Procedure: Apply online or by email at the above addresses. Alternatively contact Fraser Davis at fraser.davis@ef.com or at the above postal address for an application form or further information. All applicants must be available for interview.

EJO Ltd

Job(s) Available: Course directors, senior EFL teachers, EFL teachers, activity staff, qualified lifeguards and first aiders.
Duration: Staff are required for Easter, June, July and August.
Working Hours: Activity staff to work 5–6 days a week.

Head Office: Passfield Business Centre, Lynchborough Road, Passfield, Liphook Hampshire GU30 7SB
☎ 01428 751933
steve@ejo.co.uk
www.ejo.co.uk

Pay: Varies according to qualifications and experience.
Job Description: *Course directors, senior EFL teachers, EFL teachers:* required for residential and non-residential courses. *Qualified lifeguards and first aiders:* required for residential centres.
Requirements: *Course directors and senior teachers:* need to be TEFL qualified with a good degree (MA or TEFL/TESOL Diploma preferred) and 2 or more years of teaching experience. *Teachers:* need to have CELTA/Trinity CertTESOL qualification or QTS. *Activity staff:* should be studying towards or have graduated in a sports or arts qualification.
Accommodation: Available at residential centres.
Application Procedure: By post to the education department at the above address.

Embassy CES

Job(s) Available: Activity leaders (250), EFL teachers (350).
Duration: Positions are available from June to September.
Working Hours: To work 6 days a week.
Pay: Wages dependent on experience.

Head Office: Lorna House, 103 Lorna Road, Hove, East Sussex BN3 3EL
☎ 01273 322353
vacjobsuk@embassyces.com
www.embassyces.com/jobs

Company Description: Organises summer schools for international students, combining English lessons and an activity/excursion programme at schools and universities around the UK.

Job Description: Work includes running a full activity programme: discos, excursions, sports and local visits. *Activity leaders:* to organise a variety of daytime, evening and weekend activities. *EFL teachers:* to teach adults and children; to also assist with a programme of social activities/excursions.

Requirements: All applicants must speak fluent English, have enthusiasm and initiative and be hardworking. *Activity leaders:* experience of working with children or in the leisure or tourism industry is desirable but full training will be given. Graduates and undergraduates, minimum age 20. Qualifications in sports coaching, first aid, arts and crafts an advantage. *EFL teachers:* applicants must be 18+ and have RSA CELTA or Trinity CertTESOL. Previous experience is desirable.

Accommodation: Full board accommodation is available at residential centres.

Application Procedure: Applications from January. Go online (click on www.embassyces.com/jobs and follow the summer jobs links) or contact the recruitment department for an application pack. Interview necessary, usually by telephone.

Frances King School Of English

Job(s) Available: EFL teachers (30).
Duration: Period of work from the first week of July to the last week of August.
Working Hours: To teach up to 30 hours per week at various centres.
Pay: On an hourly basis.

Head Office: 77 Gloucester Road, London SW7 4SS
☎ 020 7870 6533
✆ info@francesking.co.uk
🖳 www.francesking.co.uk

Company Description: A large language school located on 2 sites in central London. Students come from all over the world, particularly Italy and Spain during the summer months.

Job Description: Optional leading of groups and taking part in activities with students.
Requirements: Must hold RSA/Cambridge TEFL certificates and have a minimum of one year's experience.
Application Procedure: By post to Drew Hyde, director of studies, at the above address.

Geos LTC London

Job(s) Available: EFL teachers (15).
Duration: To work from end of June to the end of August.
Working Hours: Teaching duties are for 3 hours per day Monday to Friday, helping with the social programme in the afternoons.

Head Office: 16/20 New Broadway, Ealing, London W5 2XA
☎ 020 8566 2188
✆ info@geos-ltc.com
🖳 www.geos-ltc.com

Pay: To be arranged.
Requirements: Applicants must have RSA, CTEFLA/CELTA, or Trinity CertTESOL.
Additional Information: Also has a school in Hove.
Application Procedure: By post to Jane Flynn, principal, at the above address.

Eastbourne Geos LTC

Job(s) Available: EFL teachers (5), residential welfare officers (4).

Duration: Staff required from end of June to mid-September.

Working Hours: *EFL teachers:* to teach 20 lessons per week; includes evening and some weekend social and residential duties. *Residential welfare officers:* to work 40 hours per week, including evenings and weekends.

Head Office: Compton Park, Compton Palace Road, Eastbourne, East Sussex BN21 1EH
☎ 01323 727755
info@geos-ltc.com
www.geos-ltc.com

Pay: *EFL teachers:* from £270 per week. *Residential welfare officers:* from £245 per week.

Company Description: A friendly private language school running courses for adult students and residential courses for young learners. Set in a mansion house in its own park, 20 minutes' walk from Eastbourne town centre.

Job Description: *Residential welfare officers:* would suit a student.

Requirements: *EFL teachers:* minimum of RSA/Cambridge CELTA or Trinity CertTESOL required. *Welfare officers:* first aid an advantage. Overseas applicants for teaching posts must have an advanced level of English (IELTS 9 or equivalent).

Accommodation: Free board and lodging.

Application Procedure: By post from February to Alisdair Goldsworthy, director of studies, at the above address.

Harrow House International College

Job(s) Available: English language teachers (15–20), residential sports/activities teachers (19–24), drama/art leaders (2), activities co-ordinator.

Duration: Staff required for a minimum of 7 or 8 weeks from approximately 16 June until the end of August.

Head Office: Harrow Drive, Swanage, Dorset BH19 1PE
☎ 01929 424421
info@harrowhouse.co.uk
www.harrowhouse.com

Working Hours: *English language teachers:* to work 6 days a week. *Residential sports/ activities teachers:* to work 6 days a week. *Drama/art leaders:* to work 6 days a week.

Pay: *English language teacher:* £340 per week. *Residential sports/activities teachers:* £208 per week. *Drama/art leaders:* £340 per week. *Activities co-ordinator:* £340 per week.

Company Description: A 38-year-old international language college set in the Purbecks in the heart of Dorset, which teaches English to students from more than 60 countries.

Job Description: *English language teachers:* required to teach children from age 8 upwards. *Activities co-ordinator:* required to provide students with a full leisure programme. Could be a residential position.

Requirements: *English language teachers:* applicants must possess a CELTA qualification or equivalent. *Residential sports/activities teachers:* must have relevant experience and qualifications. *Drama/art leaders:* relevant experience and qualifications required. *Activities co-ordinator:* relevant qualifications and experience required.

Accommodation: *Residential sports/activities teachers:* full board and lodging. Where accommodation is not included as a part of the wage, it is available at a cost of £80 per week.

Application Procedure: By post from February onwards to Sharon Patterson for the posts of English teachers and drama/art leaders, and to Paul Yerby for the posts of sports and activities teachers, at the above address. Foreign applicants are welcome to apply, but must have a level of English appropriate to the position.

International Student Club Ltd

Job(s) Available: Activity monitors (10).
Duration: Positions available between 6 July and 18 August 2008. Minimum period of work 2 weeks.
Working Hours: To work 6 days a week.
Pay: £220 per week.

Head Office: 21 Park Road, Hale, Cheshire WA1J 9NW
☎ 0161 929 9002
✆ info@student-club.co.uk
🖥 www.student-club.co.uk

Company Description: A small, family-run organisation offering English language and activity courses to foreign students aged 10–17.

Job Description: Activity monitors required to supervise young people during sports sessions, excursions, discos and competitions.

Requirements: Minimum age 19. Preference will be given to those with sports qualifications or experience in dance and drama.

Accommodation: Board and lodging available free of charge.

Application Procedure: By post to Jill Cutting at the above address from January onwards. Foreign applicants are welcome to apply but fluency in English is essential. Interview required.

King's School Of English

Job(s) Available: EFL teachers (40), social and sports supervisors (20), administrative assistants (10), course directors (4), residential course teachers and director of studies (15).

Head Office: 58 Braidley Road, Bournemouth BH2 6LD
☎ 01202 293535
✆ info@kingsschool.uk.com

Duration: Positions are available between mid-June and the end of August. Most posts available for 3–12 weeks.

Working Hours: *Course directors:* should be available all summer to work full-time. *EFL teachers:* to give 20–40 lessons per week. *Social and sports supervisors:* to work full-time 5–6 days a week. *Administrative assistants:* to work full-time 5–6 days a week.

Pay: *EFL teachers:* from £200–£450 per week. *Social and sports supervisors:* from £200–£275 per week. *Administrative assistants:* from £175–£250 per week. *Course directors:* from £350–£450 per week. *Residential course teachers and director of studies:* from £300–£450 per week.

Company Description: A private school of English for overseas students. Offers courses for all ages, but much of their work is with teenagers and children. The school is located 5 minutes from the centre of Bournemouth. It has a very busy summer period, offering a fun, vibrant but hard-working atmosphere. The school also runs residential summer camps in other places in the south of England.

Requirements: All applicants must be enthusiastic, versatile and enjoy working with young people. Fluent English absolutely essential for all posts. *EFL teachers:* must have TEFL certificate or diploma, and preferably a degree and relevant experience. *Social and sports supervisors:* must have relevant sports and social activities experience/qualifications. *Administrative assistants:* must have good computer, organisational and interpersonal skills. *Course directors:* must have a diploma in TEFL, university degree and considerable TEFL experience. *Residential course teachers and director of studies:* must be qualified TEFL teacher prepared to take part in sports, social activities and excursions and to act as houseparents. TEFL Diploma required for director of studies posts. Energy, enthusiasm and stamina required.

Accommodation: Not usually available, but included for teachers on residential courses.

Application Procedure: By post from March onwards to the school principal at the above address. Interview required. Foreign applicants may be considered for positions other than teaching posts.

King's School Of English (London)

Job(s) Available: EFL teachers (approxi-mately 10).
Duration: Teachers to work from mid–June to the end of August. Minimum 4 weeks.
Working Hours: Teachers to work 20–28 lessons per week.

Head Office: 25 Beckenham Road, Beckenham, Kent BR3 4PR
☎ 020 8650 5891
info@kingslon.co.uk
www.kingslon.co.uk

Company Description: The only year-round recognised school in Beckenham. Takes around 150–250 students from all over the world and specialises in teaching general English to international groups of adult learners. Established in 1966 and British Council accredited.
Job Description: Programmes for learners aged 14 and over.
Requirements: Only UCLES CELTA/DELTA qualified applicants need apply.
Application Procedure: By post from January to the director of studies at the above address.

Lal Torbay (Summer Schools)

Job(s) Available: EFL teachers/senior teachers.
Duration: Teaching staff required from July until August. 4 and 6-week contracts offered.
Working Hours: 15 hours per week.
Pay: To be arranged.

Head Office: Conway Road, Paignton, Devon TQ4 5LH
☎ 01803 558675
mark.cook@lalgroup.com
www.lalgroup.com

Company Description: Locations at Kelly College, Devon and Taunton School, Somerset; 2 residential summer schools with good resources.
Job Description: Young Learner workshops and observations provided as part of the support structure. Maximum class size of 15 students. *Teachers*: will also be involved in the leisure programme and take part in activities for the remaining sessions but are not involved in bedtime duties. *Senior and assistant senior teachers:* responsible for the execution of the academic programme, including arranging Trinity exams and extra lessons.
Requirements: Must be CELTA or equivalent or PGCE with TEFL experience.
Application Procedure: Application pack available at the above address.

Language Link

Job(s) Available: EFL teachers (20).
Duration: To work from the end of June to the end of August, Monday to Friday.
Pay: Dependent on qualifications and experience.

Head Office: 21 Harrington Road, London SW7 3EU
☎ 020 7225 1065
recruitment@languagelink.co.uk
www.languagelink.co.uk

Company Description: Language Link is accredited by the British Council and is a member of English UK. Located in the borough of Kensington and Chelsea, it is open all year, with a friendly, family atmosphere.
Requirements: Applicants must be Cambridge, Trinity or equivalent TEFL certified. This 4-week CELTA qualification can be taken at Language Link (email teachertraining@languagelink.co.uk).
Application Procedure: By post from May to the director of studies at the above address. An interview is required.

LTC International College

Job(s) Available: EFL teachers (5), residential welfare officers (4).

Duration: Staff required from the end of June to mid-September.

Working Hours: *EFL teachers:* to teach 20 lessons per week with evening and some weekend social and residential duties. *Residential welfare officers*: to work 40 hours per week, including evenings and weekends.

Head Office: Compton Park, Compton Palace Road, Eastbourne, East Sussex BN21 1EH
☎ 01323 727755
✆ info@geos-ltc.com
🖳 www.geos-ltc.com

Pay: *EFL teachers:* from £270 per week. *Residential welfare officers:* from £245 per week.

Company Description: A friendly private language school running courses for adult students and residential courses for young learners. Set in a mansion house in its own park, 20 minutes' walk from Eastbourne town centre.

Job Description: *Residential welfare officers:* would suit a student.

Requirements: *EFL teachers:* minimum of RSA/Cambridge CELTA or Trinity CertTESOL required. *Residential welfare officers:* first aid an advantage. Overseas applicants for teaching posts must have an advanced level of English (IELTS 9 or equivalent).

Accommodation: Free board and lodging.

Application Procedure: By post from February to Alisdair Goldsworthy, director of studies, at the above address.

Manchester Academy Of English

Job(s) Available: EFL teachers (6–7), EFL teachers for football programme, EFL teachers for young learners.

Duration: Positions are available between 1 July and 31 August. *EFL teachers for young learners:* positions available between 1 July and 15 August, for 2 weeks.

Head Office: St Margaret's Chambers, 5 Newton Street, Manchester M1 1HL
☎ 0161 237 5619
✆ info@manacad.co.uk
🖳 www.manacad.co.uk

Working Hours: *EFL teachers:* approximately 25 hours per week.

Pay: *EFL teachers:* approximately £12 per hour. *EFL teachers for football programme:* approximately £11.50 per hour. *EFL teachers for young learners:* approximately £500 for 2 weeks.

Company Description: City centre English language school for international students. A member of English UK, and British Council accredited.

Requirements: *EFL teachers:* applicants should have a degree and an RSA/Cambridge or Trinity CertTESOL or LTCL Diploma TESOL; 2 years of experience required. Minimum age 21. *EFL teachers for football programme:* candidates should be able to participate and support the activity programme. Applicants should have a degree and an RSA/Cambridge or Trinity CertTESOL or LTCL Diploma TESOL. One year experience preferred. Minimum age 20. CRB checked. *EFL teachers for young learners:* applicants should have a degree and an RSA/Cambridge or Trinity CertTESOL or LTCL Diploma TESOL. One year's experience preferred. Minimum age 20. CRB checked.

Accommodation: *EFL teachers:* no accommodation for any position. *EFL teachers for football programme:* residential accommodation included. *EFL teachers for young learners:* accommodation included.

Application Procedure: By post from February onwards to director of studies or Celine Cameron, director, at the above address. Interview required.

Oxford English Centre

Job(s) Available: EFL teachers (5–10), activities helpers (4), care staff (2).

Duration: Recruiting staff in July and August for summer courses. *EFL teachers*: required for July and August. *Activities helpers:* required between June and September. *Cafe staff:* required for July and August.

Head Office: 66 Banbury Road, Oxford OX2 6PR
☎ 01865 516162
info@oxfordenglish.co.uk
www.oxfordenglish.co.uk

Working Hours: *EFL teachers*: to work 15–30 hours per week. *Activities helpers:* to work full or part-time. *Cafe staff:* to work from 8am–3pm.

Pay: *EFL teachers:* salary by arrangement based on qualifications. *Café staff:* competitive wages.

Company Description: A year-round school of English.

Job Description: *Activities helpers:* job suits students on vacation. *Café staff*: required in international café.

Requirements: *EFL teachers:* applicants should have at least a first degree and RSA Preparatory certificate. *Activities helpers*: minimum age 19. *Café staff:* training given but applicants should be clean, quick and have good presentation skills.

Application Procedure: By post to Graham Simpson, principal.

Pilgrims English Language Courses

Job(s) Available: EFL teachers (25), programme staff (25).

Duration: Required to work from late June to August.

Pay: *EFL teachers:* £290 per month. *Programme staff:* £265 per month.

Head Office: 4–6 Orange Street, Canterbury, Kent CT1 2JA
☎ 01227 762111
gary.luke@pilgrims.co.uk
www.pilgrims.co.uk

Job Description: Programme staff required to lead sports, drama, art and music.

Requirements: EFL teachers must have recognised TEFL qualification.

Accommodation: Full board and lodging.

Additional Information: For details of working conditions see www.pilgrimsrecruitment.co.uk.

Application Procedure: By post to Gary Luke, director of training, at the above address.

Project International

Job(s) Available: Teaching/activity staff (50).

Duration: Staff needed for up to 6 weeks from early July.

Pay: £200–£450 per week.

Job Description: Teaching/activity staff to teach English and supervise activities at residential summer school centres.

Head Office: 20 Fitzroy Square, London W1T 6EJ
☎ 020 7916 2522
recruitment@projectinternational.uk.com
www.projectinternational.uk.com

Requirements: Possession of TEFL and PGCE qualifications an advantage but not essential.

Accommodation: Full board included.

Application Procedure: By post to summer staff at the above address.

Richard Language College

Job(s) Available: EFL teachers (20).
Duration: Minimum work period 2 weeks between 1 June and 30 September. Longer-term year-round placements for suitable applicants.
Working Hours: 8.30am–4.30pm, Monday to Friday. Teaching 6 or 7 lessons of 45 minutes per day.
Pay: £265–£285 per week depending on qualifications and experience.
Job Description: EFL teachers to teach adults of mixed levels and different nationalities, in classes of about 10 students.
Requirements: Must have first degree and RSA Preparatory certificate in TEFL.
Accommodation: Help cannot be given in finding accommodation.
Application Procedure: By post from 28 February to the academic manager at Richard Language College.

> **Head Office:** 43–45 Wimborne Road, Bournemouth, Dorset BH3 7AB
> ☎ 01202 555932
> acadman@rlc.co.uk
> www.rlc.co.uk

School Of English Studies Folkestone

Job(s) Available: EFL teachers (25), sports and activities co-ordinators (12).
Duration: Staff are required from 19 June to 29 August for a period of 2–8 weeks.
Working Hours: *EFL teachers*: to work 35 hours per week. *Sports and activities co-ordinators*: to work 35 hours per week.
Pay: *EFL teachers:* £300–£400 per week. *Sports and activities co-ordinators:* £225–£350 per week.
Company Description: Founded in 1957, the School of English Studies Folkestone is a serious, professional and successful language school.
Job Description: Both positions available involve working with students of English from overseas.
Requirements: *EFL teachers:* applicants must have a UK degree and a TEFL qualification. *Sports and activities co-ordinators:* applicants must have some appropriate qualifications. Minimum age 21.
Accommodation: Some accommodation is available in Folkestone.
Application Procedure: By post to Simon Himbury, principal, at the above address from January 2008 onwards.

> **Head Office:** 26 Grimston Gardens, Folkestone, Kent CT20 2PX
> ☎ 01303 850007
> info@ses-folkestone.co.uk
> www.ses-folkestone.co.uk

Severnvale Academy

Job(s) Available: EFL teachers (5–10).
Duration: Period of work late June to 15 August. To teach Monday to Friday daytime. Minimum period of work of 4 weeks.
Pay: From £290 per week.
Company Description: British Council Accredited English language school with separate adult and junior centres.
Requirements: *EFL teachers:* degree and TEFL qualification (eg CELTA/TESOL certificate) necessary. Spoken English to the standard of a native required.
Accommodation: Board and lodging available for £95 per week.
Application Procedure: By post from Easter onwards to Mr JWT Rogers, principal, at the above address.

> **Head Office:** 25 Claremont Hill, Shrewsbury, Shropshire SY1 1RD
> ☎ 01743 232505
> enquiry@severnvale.co.uk
> www.severnvale.co.uk

Southbourne School Of English

Job(s) Available: EFL teachers (20), residential teachers, sports organisers/assistants (8).

Duration: Staff required from mid-June to the end of August. *EFL teachers:* to work 15–30 hours per week. *Residential teachers:* required for 4 weeks to start work in July. *Organisers/ assistants:* to work 40–50 hours per week.

Head Office: 30 Beaufort Road, Bournemouth BH6 5AL
☎ 01202 422300
✆ jobs@southbourneschool.co.uk
🖳 www.southbourneschool.co.uk

Pay: *EFL teachers:* minimum £11.50 per hour. *Residential teachers:* £325 per week. *Sports organisers/assistants:* £180–£300 per week.

Company Description: A family-run school, working for more than 40 years teaching English as a foreign language. British Council accredited and a member of English UK.

Job Description: Residential teachers for junior courses.

Requirements: *EFL teachers:* must have one of the following qualifications; PGCE, BEd, Cert Ed, RSA Cert EFL, RSA Diploma EFL, TESOL, Trinity LTCL Diploma TESOL. *Sports organisers/assistants:* sports training useful.

Accommodation: Free accommodation on residential courses.

Application Procedure: By post from Easter to the director of studies at kathryn@southbourneschool.co.uk.

Stafford House School Of English

Job(s) Available: EFL teachers (40), activity organisers (20).

Duration: Minimum period of work 1 week between June and September.

Pay: Rates of pay on application.

Company Description: The summer school has mixed nationality classes with a maximum of 15 stu-

Head Office: 19 New Dover Road, Canterbury, Kent CT1 3AH
☎ 01227 452250
✆ info@staffordhouse.com
🖳 www.ceg-uk.com/staffordhouse_english/index.html

dents per class. Ages 12 to adult. Emphasis is on productive skills and fluency-based activities.

Requirements: *EFL teachers:* TEFL qualifications such as RSA/Trinity CertTESOL or RSA/Trinity LTCL Diploma TESOL required. *Activity organisers:* reliability, energy and enthusiasm essential.

Application Procedure: By post from February, to Naomi Cooper (teachers) or Betty Dagistan (activity organisers) at the above address. Interview required.

SUL Language Schools

Job(s) Available: EFL teachers.

Duration: Courses run for 2–4 weeks from April to September. Teachers required for a minimum period of 2 weeks. To work mornings and possibly afternoons, supervising activities.

Head Office: 31 Southpark Road, Tywardreath, Par, Cornwall PL24 2PU
☎ 01726 814227
✆ efl@sul-schools.com
🖳 www.sul-schools.com

Pay: Dependent on experience and qualifications but usually from £26 per morning of 2.5 hours.

Company Description: A well-established business that provides language holiday courses in Cornwall, Devon, Somerset, the Midlands, Scotland and Ireland for foreign teenagers.

Requirements: Applicants should be TEFL qualified or hold a languages degree or teaching qualification. Preferred CRB checked applicants.

Accommodation: Available at some centres.

Application Procedure: By post from January to director of studies at the above address. Interview usually required.

Thames Valley Summer Schools

Job(s) Available: Course directors, recreation directors, housemasters/mistresses, TEFL teachers, specialised recreation teachers, (arts and crafts, drama and aerobics/dance), sports instructors and administrative staff.

Head Office: 13 Park Street, Windsor, Berkshire SL4 1LU
☎ 01753 852001
✆ recruit@thamesvalleycultural.com
💻 www.thamesvalleycultural.com

Duration: During the months of July and August.

Company Description: TVSS has more than 30 years of experience in providing English language courses and activities for young learners from all over the world. Accredited by the British Council and a member of English UK, this summer school has 9 high-quality centres in prestigious locations in the south-east.

Requirements: *Course directors*: with relevant residential experience. *Recreation directors*: with residential and recreation administration experience. *Housemasters/mistresses:* with pastoral/residential experience. Staff should have appropriate skills, experience and qualifications relevant to the position.

Accommodation: Free full board and lodging for those undertaking residential positions.

Application Procedure: By post or email to Nin Kelay, director of education. Must include CV. Recruitment begins at the beginning of March for positions starting between the end of June and mid-July.

The Abbey College

Job(s) Available: EFL teachers (20).

Duration: Work available from the beginning of June to the end of August. Minimum period of employment 3 weeks. All year positions also available.

Head Office: Wells Road, Malvern Wells, Worcestershire WR14 4JF
☎ 01684 892300
✆ jobs@abbeycollege.co.uk
💻 www.abbeycollege.co.uk

Pay: £250–£310 per week.

Company Description: A beautiful 70-acre residential campus with students from more than 30 nations. The college has developed, over the last 30 years, an English course to meet every requirement alongside the main academic school. Wide range of on-site facilities.

Requirements: Must hold at least an RSA/Trinity CertTEYL. Previous summer school experience preferred.

Accommodation: Accommodation and meals provided.

Additional Information: Free use of all sports and leisure facilities and excursions open to all employees.

Application Procedure: By post from March to personnel department at the above address. Interview necessary.

University of Wales Aberystwyth

Job(s) Available: EFL teachers (6–10).

Duration: Work involves 20 hours of teaching per week, plus 16 hours of social duties per month and 12 hours of administration per month. Minimum period of work 1 month between mid-July and early September.

Head Office: Language and Learning Centre, Llandinam Building, Penglais Campus, Aberystwyth SY23 3DB
☎ 01970 622545
✆ tesol@aber.ac.uk
💻 www.aber.ac.uk/tesol

Pay: £400–450 per week.

Company Description: Attractive working environment in a secure seaside location between the coast of Cardigan Bay and the Cambrian Mountains. The centre offers courses to language learners and language teachers in a warm and welcoming academic environment.

Requirements: Applicants must have native-speaker competence in English. First degree, TEFL qualifications and 3 years of experience required.

Accommodation: Board and lodging available.

Application Procedure: By post from 1 January to Rex Berridge, director, at the above address. Interview necessary.

WELS Group of International House Schools

Job(s) Available: EFL teachers (40–50).

Duration: Staff required 16 June to 22 August. Minimum period of work 3 weeks.

Pay: £250–£350 per week.

Company Description: Offers English language programmes at 4 centres in Buckinghamshire, Oxford, Salisbury and Sussex. These are also 3 year-round schools running summer English programmes for juniors in Bath, Salisbury and Torquay. Part of a group with more than 120 affiliated schools in 40 countries.

Head Office: International House Summer in England, Ash Hill Road, Torquay TQ1 3HZ
☎ 01803 210943
richard@ih-westengland.co.uk
www.ihwelsgroup.com

Requirements: Must have a university degree and a minimum of a Cambridge CELTA or Trinity CertTESOL.

Accommodation: Provided free of charge at residential centres.

Application Procedure: By post to Richard Gubbin at the above address from February.

Medical

This category consists largely of opportunities for nurses and care and support workers.

Britain's care industry is currently suffering both from a shortage of health professionals and the pressure of an ageing population. Much of the work available is with the elderly, though some is available with the sick and disabled (applicants in these areas should be aware that UK legislation will require Criminal Records Bureau checks on those intending to work with vulnerable adults).

Overall there should be little difficulty in finding work in this field. Often agencies do not even require experienced applicants as on-the-job training is given. Generally, though, applicants must be over 18 and having your own transport can be an advantage. In addition to the vacancies in this book, specialist nursing agencies can be found in the *Yellow Pages* or at www.rec.uk.com.

Allied Healthcare Group

Job(s) Available: Health care assistants, support workers.

Duration: Positions are available all year. Minimum period of work 6 weeks.

Pay: *Health care assistants*: £5.35–£14.20 per hour, depending on the situation. *Support workers:* base wage of £7.67 per hour.

Head Office: The Old Chapel House, Bryants Bottom Road, Great Missenden, Buckinghamshire HP16 0JS
☎ 01494 488040/1
highwycombe@alliedhealthcare.com

Company Description: Nursing agency.

Job Description: *Health care assistants*: needed for work in the community, hospitals and nursing homes. *Support workers:* to work with children and adults with learning disabilities.

Application Procedure: By post to Mrs Vanessa Cracknell. Interview necessary. Overseas applicants with fluent English and valid work permits or student visas welcome.

Apex Nursing & Care Services

Job(s) Available: Trained/auxiliary nurses, support workers, care assistants.

Duration: Required for all vacations and during term-time.

Pay: Rates of pay will be discussed at interview.

Head Office: Emery House, 195 Fog Lane, Didsbury, Manchester M20 6FJ
☎ 0845 600 3041
✍ hr@apex-nursing.co.uk
🖥 www.apex-nursing.co.uk

Job Description: *Trained/auxiliary nurses, support workers, care assistants*: to work in hospitals, nursing homes and people's own homes. Social care roles may involve working with clients with learning disabilities and challenging behaviour.

Requirements: No experience is necessary as full free training is given. Minimum age 18.

Application Procedure: Enquiries for application forms can be made by emailing recruitment @apex-nursing.co.uk.

Consultus

Job(s) Available: Live-in carers.

Duration: Positions are available all year to work on 2-week live-in assignments.

Pay: From £57–£84.50 per day (£107+ for nurses).

Head Office: 17 London Road, Tonbridge, Kent TN10 3AB
☎ 01732 355231
✍ manager@consultuscare.com
🖥 www.consultuscare.com

Company Description: Founded in 1962 by the present managing director, Consultus is one of the major providers of live-in care in Britain. Their aim is to help the elderly remain happily and safely in their own homes for as long as possible.

Job Description: *Live-in carers:* needed nationwide to perform domestic duties and some personal care for elderly private clients. NMC-registered nurses also welcome. Duties may include cooking, cleaning, housekeeping, driving and shopping for the client. Work available across the UK.

Requirements: Minimum age 21. Some experience of care of the elderly/disabled preferred.

Accommodation: Own room and free meals in client's house while on assignment.

Application Procedure: By post at any time to the above address. Interview in either UK or South Africa. Overseas applicants with relevant permits and clear English welcome.

Home Comforts Community Care Ltd

Job(s) Available: Full/part-time care workers (15–20).

Duration: Positions available at all times of year.

Pay: £7 basic per hour plus travel expenses (average inclusive hourly earnings £9.25 per hour).

Head Office: Suite 6, Quarry House, Mill Lane, Uckfield, East Sussex TN22 5AA
☎ 01825 762233
✍ marie@hcccltd.fsnet.co.uk

Company Description: Care agency/employer with clients all over Sussex. Established 1995.

Job Description: *Full/part-time care workers:* to work various shifts in nursing homes, residential homes and homes for adults with learning disabilities in East Sussex, West Sussex and Kent. Some personal care: washing, dressing. A caring nature would be useful for this work.

Requirements: Own transport essential. Minimum age 18. Basic training will be given in first aid and manual handling.

Application Procedure: By post to Marie Ingram, HR director, at the above address. Foreign applicants with fluent English and eligibility to work in the UK are welcome.

Options Trust Staff Recruitment

Job(s) Available: Personal assistants (10–12).
Duration: Minimum period of work 6 months at any time of year.
Pay: £150–£250 per week.
Company Description: A non-profit-making organisation, set up and run by a number of disabled people who employ personal assistants to enable them to live in their own homes in the community.
Job Description: Personal assistants to carry out personal care, domestic duties and driving.
Requirements: Minimum age 18. Driving licence required but no previous experience is necessary.
Accommodation: Free board and lodging.
Application Procedure: By post to Mrs V Mason at the above address.

Head Office: 4 Plantation Way,
Whitehill, Bordon, Hampshire GU35 9HD
☎ 01420 474261
optionstrust@pvm.ndo.co.uk

Oxford Aunts Care

Duration: Temporary positions to live in the homes of the elderly and frail. Availability of 12 weeks required.
Company Description: Providing live-in services to older people who need general care and support and those with more complex health care requirements.
Requirements: Care experience and good standards of oral and written English essential, as well as an up-to-date police check from country of origin. Driving licence preferred.
Application Procedure: All applicants must be able to attend 4 full days (unpaid) induction training from Tuesday to Friday and an interview on the Monday beforehand.

Head Office: 3 Cornmarket Street,
Oxford OX1 3EX
☎ 01865 791017
enquiries@oxfordaunts.co.uk
www.oxfordaunts.co.uk

Westbourne Care Services

Job(s) Available: Care assistants (6), experienced care assistants (2), trained and experienced care assistants, NVQ trained care assistants (2).
Duration: Positions available all year round.
Working Hours: To work Monday to Sunday, various shifts available.
Pay: From £6 per hour according to experience, competence, qualification and past records on suitability, reliability, good health and trustworthiness.
Company Description: A care agency sending competent and trustworthy workers to care for elderly and disabled individuals.
Job Description: Work involves caring for elderly or disabled individuals either in their own home or in a registered home environment.
Requirements: Minimum age 21. Applicants should be in good health (a health screening is done as part of the recruitment process) and should preferably hold CRB vetted certificates and 2 references. A CRB check is imperative if applicants do not already hold certificates.
Application Procedure: Contact Westbourne Care Services at the above number at any time for an application form. Interview required. Foreign applicants who have been trained as auxiliary nurses and are fluent in English welcome.

Head Office: Claire Court, 128 Preston
Street, Yeovil, Somerset BA20 2EE
☎ 01935 410534
westbournecare@hotmail.com

Outdoor

The majority of vacancies in this category are for fruit pickers, farm staff and marquee erectors.

Agriculture. While increased mechanisation has reduced the number of pickers required at harvest time, agriculture remains the second largest source of seasonal work after tourism. The best areas for summer fruit and vegetable picking are from the Vale of Evesham over to the River Wye (in the Midlands), Kent, Lincolnshire, East Anglia (especially the Fens) and north of the Tay in Scotland (especially Perthshire). Harvest types and times vary between regions, so raspberries may ripen two weeks later in Scotland than in the south of England. Strawberries and gooseberries are among the first fruits to ripen in southern Britain, usually in June. Processing and packing work is generally available in the Vale of Evesham after the main harvest season. Work involving harvesting outdoor salad crops is also available in the Hampshire and West Sussex area. The apple harvest runs from August until mid-October and traditionally offers more lucrative work.

The fledgling English wine industry has been growing in reputation over recent years and there are some 350 vineyards throughout England and Wales, producing around two million bottles a year. These vineyards, located mainly throughout the southern half of England, may require workers, though the grape harvest is unpredictable as the sugar content depends on the often elusive sun. The grape harvesting season is fairly late, usually beginning in September and finishing mid-November, although it depends largely on a number of factors such as the region, the weather and the variety of grape. For more information contact English Wine Producers (01536-772264; info@englishwineproducers.com; www.englishwineproducers.com).

While fruit picking is generally short-term, it is possible to string several jobs together by following ripening crops around the country, or by choosing a farm with several crops that will ripen in sequence. On the spot applications are often productive, with no interview required, and it is sometimes possible to secure employment at very short notice (note that most farmers prefer the first approach to be via telephone).

Due to the temporary nature of much accommodation offered by farmers, a comfortable night's sleep may not always follow a tiring day's work. Some provide comfortable bunkhouses and meals, but others require you to bring your own tent and cater for yourself. Some provide communal cooking facilities, but these can sometimes be in a poor state of cleanliness as upkeep is no-one's direct responsibility. The Food and Farming Information Service also advises workers to take out insurance to cover personal belongings, and to visit farms in advance if possible.

Fruitfuljobs.com is a web-based agency which helps people find jobs with accommodation on UK farms; although the main season runs from March to October work is available throughout the year in the agricultural and horticultural industries - from organic farming to operating a fork-lift truck. You can also call 0870 0727 0050, or e-mail info@fruitfuljobs.com, for more information. Another useful website that details agricultural jobs in both the UK and overseas is www.pickingjobs.com.

Farmers can recruit students from any part of the EU. Some farms take part in the Seasonal Agricultural Workers scheme, enabling them to recruit student pickers from outside the EU. This is done through organisations such as Concordia (YSV) Ltd. (01273 422293; www.concordia-iye.org.uk).

Pay varies according to the fruit and the difficulty involved in the picking process. Many farmers pay piecework rates, which means that you are paid according to the quantity you pick. This method can be very satisfactory when a harvest is at its peak but when fruit is scarce earning more than the minimum can be much more difficult. However, even if you are paid on a piecework basis the amount you earn for each hour worked must average the rates set out in the

Agricultural Wages Order. The Agricultural Wages Board (020 7238 6523) sets minimum weekly and hourly rates for agricultural workers in England and Wales.

Removals and Marquee Work. While manual jobs with removal firms are available at any time of year, the summer is a real boom time for marquee erectors. During the sunny season there is a never-ending round of agricultural shows, festivals, wedding receptions and so on. And while a village fair may require just one marquee, a music festival will require a whole range of tents plus large amounts of furniture and equipment. All this has to be loaded and unloaded from lorries, as well as driven to and from a depot; for this and other driving work possession of an HGV driving licence would be a useful advantage. Overtime is often available, so marquee work can be lucrative. The disadvantage for women is that most employers specify a minimum height for loading work and only take on men.

Bamford Bros

Job(s) Available: Driver's mate (2), farm trail maintenance assistant.
Duration: Periods of work by arrangement around the year.
Working Hours: *Driver's mate:* to work 7am–5pm from Monday to Friday plus overtime at weekends.
Farm trail maintenance assistant: to work 4–6 hours daily, with hours to suit.
Pay: National minimum wage rates.
Job Description: *Driver's mate:* possibility of driver's job if applicants hold a driving licence.
Farm trail maintenance assistant: to see to the welfare and care of animals and maintain and build up a farm trail attached to the farm shop.
Application Procedure: By post to Margaret Bamford, manager, at the above address.

> **Head Office:** Law Farm, Law Lane, Southowram, Halifax, West Yorkshire HX3 9UG
> ☎ 01422 362788
> ✒ magsbamford@hotmail.com

Claremont Marquees

Job(s) Available: Marquee erectors/labourers (5).
Duration: Period of work 1 April to 1 October. Minimum period of work is 1 week.
Working Hours: Flexible working hours, normally 8–10 hours per day.
Pay: From £6–£7 per hour.
Requirements: Applicants must be fit and strong.
Accommodation: No accommodation available.
Application Procedure: By post to Robert Atkins, owner, at the above address from the start of April.

> **Head Office:** Fishers Hill House, Hook Heath Road, Woking, Surrey GU22 0QE
> ☎ 01483 720472
> ✒ robertatkins@tiscali.co.uk
> 🖥 www.claremontmarquees.com

D&B Grant

Job(s) Available: Fruit pickers (50).
Duration: Period of work from 10 July to 31 August.
Working Hours: To work 6 days a week. Shifts to be arranged.
Pay: To be arranged.
Job Description: Fruit pickers to pick strawberries and raspberries. Help also required to process fruit for freezing.
Accommodation: Caravan accommodation available.
Application Procedure: Apply to Colin M Grant via email or telephone only.

> **Head Office:** Wester Essendy, Blairgowrie, Perthshire PH10 6RA
> ☎ 01250 884389
> ✒ cmgrant99@yahoo.com

Danco International PLC

Job(s) Available: Marquee erectors (10–15), warehouse operatives.

Duration: Period of work from May to September.

Working Hours: *Marquee erectors:* to work 50–60 hours per week. Seven-day weeks are required, with days off once job is complete. *Warehouse operatives*: to work 50–60 hours per week, including weekend work.

Pay: *Marquee erectors:* £5.60 per hour plus a £10 night-out allowance when on site. *Warehouse operatives:* £5.60 per hour.

Job Description: *Marquee erectors:* to put up marquees around the UK. *Warehouse operatives*: to load and unload trailers and pack orders.

Requirements: Minimum age 20. Those with driving licences preferred.

Accommodation: *Marquee erectors:* basic accommodation provided but applicants need sleeping bag, pots, pans, cutlery and plates in addition to wet weather gear and steel toe-capped boots. *Warehouse operatives:* basic accommodation provided on site.

Application Procedure: By post to Elisa Lunt, personnel manager, at the above address.

Head Office: The Pavilion Centre, Frog Lane, Coalpit Heath, Bristol BS36 2NW
☎ 01454 250222
✒ elisa@danco.co.uk
🖥 www.danco.co.uk

E Oldroyd & Sons Ltd

Job(s) Available: Strawberry harvesters (20), rhubarb and vegetable harvesters (10).

Duration: Positions available from January to March and May to September. *Strawberry harvesters*: minimum period of work 1 month.

Working Hours: *Rhubarb and vegetable harvesters:* to work full/part-time, up to 8 hours per day for up to 3 months.

Pay: Piecework rates or hourly agricultural wage rates where applicable.

Company Description: Five generations of experience with fruit and vegetables. Britain's leading rhubarb producer – busy both in the winter and summer. Farms are close to Leeds city centre's excellent shopping and nightlife and only 5 minutes from the supermarket. Internet access available.

Requirements: Minimum age 17. Full training given.

Accommodation: Approved accommodation available.

Application Procedure: Early applications recommended to avoid disappointment. Write, enclosing a CV with references, to Mrs J Oldroyd-Hulme at the above address. Interview possibly required. Foreign applicants welcome.

Head Office: Hopefield Farm, Leadwell Lane, Rothwell, Leeds, Yorkshire LS26 0ST
☎ 0113 282 2245
✒ eoldroyd@btconnect.com

Field and Lawn (Marquees) Ltd

Job(s) Available: Marquee erectors.

Duration: Positions are available from May to November.

Working Hours: Required to work long hours.

Pay: Starts at £5.50 per hour.

Company Description: A young and enthusiastic company which takes pride in its product and employees. Work-hard, play-hard atmosphere.

Job Description: *Marquee erectors:* required to erect marquees throughout England and Wales. The work is very strenuous so fitness is essential.

Head Office: Southlands, Leeds Road, Thorpe Willoughby, North Yorkshire YO8 9PZ
☎ 01757 210444
✒ robbie.gibb-kirk@fieldandlawn.com
🖥 www.fieldandlawn.com

Application Procedure: By post from 1 April through to the end of September. Letters to the operations manager at the above address. Alternatively, telephone or email. Overseas applicants, particularly from New Zealand, South Africa and Australia, welcome.

Fridaybridge International Farm Camp Ltd

Job(s) Available: Picking and packing fruit, vegetables and flowers (approximately 450).

Head Office: 173 March Road, Fridaybridge, Cambridgeshire PE14 0LR
☎ 01945 860255
info@fridaybridge.com
www.fridaybridge.com

Duration: Required from February to December.

Working Hours: Usually 40 hours per week. Some extra work available at weekends.

Pay: Either the minimum hourly rate or piecework paid for actual work done.

Company Description: A unique company providing services to both workers and farmers. Offer accommodation and employment for people looking for work in the agricultural and food industries.

Job Description: Picking and packing.

Requirements: Minimum age 18. No qualifications or experience necessary. Fluent English not essential. Some qualifications such as tractor or forklift licenses are helpful.

Accommodation: Board and lodging available at £78.75 per week (inclusive of breakfast, dinner and use of all facilities). There is no charge for transport to and from work.

Additional Information: Participants will have the opportunity to earn money and gain experience in the working environment. They will also be able to meet and make friends with other young people of many different nationalities. Facilities include: bar/club, swimming pool, tennis, basketball, volleyball, football, table tennis, shop, internet, TV room, etc.

Application Procedure: Apply all year round to the bookings manager by email. No interview necessary. Applications from all nationalities eligible to work in the UK are welcome, but they must be physically fit.

Fruitgrowers Ltd

Job(s) Available: Apple and pear pickers (10).

Head Office: Turnover Farm, Decoy Road, Gorefield, Wisbech, Cambridgeshire PE13 4PD
☎ 01945 870749
p9ear@aol.com

Duration: Positions are available from 30 August to 30 September. Minimum period of work is 4 weeks.

Working Hours: 8 hours per day with some overtime.

Pay: Piecework rates, average £40–£50 per day depending on how hard you work.

Company Description: A family fruit farm with a small and friendly workforce.

Requirements: Minimum age 17. Applicants must be clean, healthy and able. No previous experience necessary.

Accommodation: Available in shared caravans at £28 per week. Showers and laundry facilities on site.

Application Procedure: By post from April onwards to Edward Newling at the above address. Foreign applicants with sufficient English to understand instructions welcome.

FW Mansfield & Son

Job(s) Available: Fruit pickers and packers (50–100).
Duration: Workers needed from May to November.
Working Hours: To work variable hours a week, plus overtime as desired.

Head Office: Nickle Farm, Chartham, Canterbury, Kent CT4 7PL
☎ 01227 731441
✆ rookc@mansfields.net

Pay: National minimum wage or piecework rates. Cash daily during harvest.
Job Description: Fruit pickers and packers to pick and pack apples, pears, strawberries, plums and cherries.
Requirements: Minimum age 18. Must be fit and hard working.
Accommodation: Available in caravans with communal kitchen and washing facilities at £30 per week.
Application Procedure: By post to the farms manager at the above address.

GE Elsworth & Son

Job(s) Available: Fruit pickers (6), crop thinners (6).
Duration: Fruit pickers to pick apples in September. Crop thinners required during June. Possibility of pruning work from January to March.
Working Hours: To work flexible hours between 9am and 5pm.

Head Office: Park Fruit Farm, Pork Lane, Great Holland, Frinton-on-Sea, Essex CO13 0ES
☎ 01255 674621
✆ s.elsworth@farmline.com

Pay: As set by the Agricultural Wage Board.
Accommodation: Available.
Application Procedure: By post to S Elsworth, partner, at the above address. Ensure job availability before arriving unannounced.

GL Events Snowdens

Job(s) Available: Marquee erectors.
Duration: From 1 April to 30 September.
Working Hours: To work an average of 10 hours per day 6 days a week (extra hours are available).
Pay: Average £300 per week, dependent on hours worked.

Head Office: Second Drove Eastern Industry, Fengate, Peterborough PE1 5XA
☎ 01733 294615
✆ adrian@snowdens.co.uk
🖥 www.snowdens.co.uk

Company Description: Snowdens is a subsidiary of GL Events, a leading marquee hirer in the show and hospitality market.
Requirements: Minimum age 18. Applicants must be physically fit and able.
Accommodation: Please note that accommodation is only provided when working away on site.
Additional Information: Successful applicants may visit some prestigious sporting locations, eg Ascot, Newmarket and Silverstone.
Application Procedure: By post from 1 March to Adrian West at the above address. Foreign applicants with all relevant work permits and an acceptable level of spoken English are welcome.

Harold Corrigall

Job(s) Available: Fruit pickers (10). Good English speaking personnel required for managerial posts for approximately 3 months (June to August).

Duration: Staff required for a minimum of 4 weeks between June and late August.

Working Hours: Required to work 6am–3pm per day, 6 days a week.

Pay: Approximately £35–£55 per day.

Company Description: A small farm growing 40 acres of strawberries under tunnels and 5 acres of raspberries.

Requirements: Minimum age 18.

Accommodation: Available at a charge of £4 per day.

Application Procedure: By post from February to Harold Corrigall at the above address. The farm takes many European students with appropriate permits or authorisation.

Head Office: Leadketty Farm, Dunning, Perthshire PH2 0QP
☎ 01764 684532
✎ haroldcorrigall@btconnect.com

HE Hall & Son Ltd

Job(s) Available: Fruit pickers (10).

Duration: Minimum period of work 1 day between mid-August and mid-October.

Working Hours: Required for work 8am–3pm, Monday to Friday, but flexible hours and days dependent on weather and crop.

Pay: Paid piecework based on national minimum wage rates.

Requirements: Minimum age 20. No previous experience necessary but it is useful.

Accommodation: Basic self-catering accommodation available at no cost.

Application Procedure: Apply from July onwards to Peter Hall by telephone. Overseas applicants considered if work authorisation is in order and English is spoken.

Head Office: Little Pattenden, Marden, Kent TN12 9QL
☎ 01622 831376
✎ peter.hall@targetfarm.co.uk

Hill Farm Orchards

Job(s) Available: Fruit pickers (10), fruit packers (5), pruners (5).

Duration: *Fruit pickers (10):* to work from September to October. *Fruit packers (5):* to work from October to March. *Pruners:* to work from January to April. Minimum period of work 1 month.

Working Hours: To work 8am–4.30pm, Monday to Friday, with occasional weekends.

Pay: As set by Agricultural Wages Board and piecework rates at the height of the season.

Company Description: Pleasantly situated between Portsmouth and Southampton, with shops and pubs nearby. Packing apples and pears for high class outlets.

Requirements: Minimum age 20. Applicants must be eligible to work in the UK and have a moderate level of English.

Accommodation: Minimum fee accommodation available.

Application Procedure: Apply by email (or post) to Mr Paul Roberts, farm manager, at the above address.

Head Office: Droxford Road, Swanmore, Hampshire SO32 2PY
☎ 01489 878616
✎ hifol@eur-isp.com.

HR Philpot & Son Ltd

Job(s) Available: Experienced machine operators, general farm workers.

Duration: Required to work the harvesting season from the end of June until October.

Company Description: Highly mechanised progressive large arable farming company based in Essex and Suffolk.

Head Office: Barleylands Farm, Barleylands Road, Billericay, Essex CM11 2UD
☎ 01268 290215
✆ robert@barleylands.co.uk
🖥 www.barleylands.co.uk

Job Description: Working on a farm with modern equipment, CAT 85, Fastrac, Vaderstat Cultivators, Drills/FC, Combine Harvesters, modern Potato Harvesting and grading equipment.

Requirements: Must be adaptable to take on any job when asked. Must have full UK driving licence, valid work permit and be able to understand and speak English.

Accommodation: Accommodation will be provided for single persons.

Application Procedure: By post to Robert Willy at the above address from December onwards.

International Farm Camp

Job(s) Available: Fruit pickers.

Duration: Minimum work period 4 weeks between early June and mid-July.

Working Hours: Hours 6am–3pm Monday to Friday; some weekend work.

Head Office: Hall Road, Tiptree, Essex CO5 0QS
☎ 01621 815496
✆ ifc@tiptree.com
🖥 www.tiptree.com

Pay: Piecework rates.

Accommodation: Accommodation available at £30 per week for overseas workers only. Caravan site available for British applicants.

Application Procedure: By post as early as possible to the above address. Overseas applicants welcome, but places for non-EEA nationals are open only to full-time students who have not completed their studies.

Jersey Cycletours

Job(s) Available: Cycle mechanic, bike issuer.

Duration: Needed from April to the end of September.

Head Office: 2 La Hougue Mauger, St Mary, Jersey JE3 3AF
✆ jerseycycletours@yahoo.co.uk

Working Hours: 20–40 hours per week.

Pay: Wages are according to age and experience.

Company Description: The company's bikes (Trek, Giant, Dawes) are the best maintained and equipped hire bikes in Jersey; they need people who are keen and able to maintain their standards.

Requirements: *Mechanic*: must have experience in bike building and repair. *Issuer*: should be clear-headed and enjoy cycling and helping people.

Application Procedure: Contact Daniel Wimberley at the above address.

John Brownlee

Job(s) Available: Fruit pickers (4–6).
Duration: Period of work September and October.
Pay: Piecework rates.
Company Description: Five apple orchards situated half an hour from Enniskillen, on the border with the Republic of Ireland. Many tourist attractions in the area.

Head Office: Knockmakagan, Newtownbutler, County Fermanagh BT92 6JP
☎ 028 677 382 77 07989 432131
✆ sales@fermanaghspringwater.com
💻 www.fermanaghspringwater.com

Job Description: Fruit pickers required for apple orchard work, either hand-picking or shaking.
Requirements: Applicants must be in good physical condition as work is heavy manual labour.
Accommodation: No accommodation, but workers can camp at farm.
Application Procedure: By post to Mr John Brownlee at the above address, in July. Overseas applicants, preferably from EU countries, welcome.

L Wheeler & Sons (East Peckham) Ltd

Job(s) Available: Apple pickers (20), hop pickers (20).
Duration: Minimum period of work 5 weeks between 21 August and 30 September. **Working Hours:** Required to work 8–9 hours per day for 5.5 days a week.

Head Office: Bullen Farm, East Peckham, Tonbridge, Kent TN12 5LX
☎ 01622 871225
✆ lwheelerandsons@yahoo.co.uk

Pay: Approximately £5.52 per hour with the possibility of bonuses.
Company Description: A hop farm within an hour's journey to London. Local facilities such as shops and pubs are available.
Accommodation: Available with just a charge for electricity.
Application Procedure: By post from June to the manager at the above address. Overseas applicants authorised to work in the UK welcome.

Leapfrog International Ltd

Job(s) Available: Events crew (up to 100).
Duration: Period of work between May and September.
Pay: Set figure per event. Hours of work vary from day to day.

Head Office: Riding Court Farm, Datchet, Berkshire SL3 9JU
☎ 01753 580880
✆ enq@leapfrog-int.co.uk
💻 www.leapfrog-int.co.uk

Job Description: Events crew needed to help set up and run outdoor activities such as team-building challenges, family fun days and 'It's a knockout' tournaments. Events take place all around the UK. Travel to events is organised by Leapfrog International from their headquarters in Datchet.
Requirements:. Applicants should be aged 18–40, enthusiastic and outgoing and should enjoy working with people. A clean driving licence is an advantage. Previous experience not essential as training will be given.
Application Procedure: Please call the event management team on 01753 589300 for an application form.

Leith UK Ltd

Job(s) Available: Marquee erectors (10).
Duration: Unlimited hours.
Pay: Good rates of pay.
Requirements: Minimum age 18, driving licence an advantage.
Application Procedure: By post to the above address.

Head Office: Sea View Business Park, Berwick upon Tweed, Northumberland TD15 1UP
☎ 01289 307264
✆ enquiries@leith-uk.co.uk
🖳 www.leith-uk.co.uk

Man of Ross Ltd

Job(s) Available: Fruit harvesters (60).
Duration: Minimum period of work 3 months between July and October.
Working Hours: Hours according to crop .needs, approximately 6–8 hours per day, 5–6 days a week.
Pay: Hourly and/or piecework rates.
Company Description: Situated in the Wye Valley, Man of Ross is a family-run, 250-hectare farm, supplying mainly to supermarkets.
Job Description: Fruit harvesters to work in cherry, plum, apple and pear orchards.
Requirements: Minimum age 18 years old.
Application Procedure: By post from January to William Jackson at the above address. Applicants from EU countries welcome.

Head Office: Glewstone, Ross-on-Wye, Herefordshire HR9 6AU
☎ 01989 562853
✆ fruitpick@yahoo.co.uk

Mobenn Hire Services

Job(s) Available: Marquee erectors for work all over the country.
Duration: Period of work by arrangement.
Pay: £50–£60 per day; same daily rate paid for long and short days. Students must complete P38; all others to produce CIS card and submit invoices for payment by Friday each week.
Copmany Description: This company is for those who like outdoor work. Hard days, good days and a great team spirit can all be found.
Requirements: Applicants need a clean driving licence. The work is quite strenuous so it is necessary to be fit and active.
Accommodation: No accommodation available.
Application Procedure: By post to Robin Bennett, administrator, at the above address.

Head Office: Mobenn House, Naunton Parade, Cheltenham, Gloucestershire GL51 7NP
☎ 01242 584515
✆ enquiries@mobenn.co.uk
🖳 www.mobennmarquees.co.uk

Peter Marshall & Co

Job(s) Available: Fruit pickers (250), farm assistants, raspberry field supervisors.
Duration: Minimum period of work one month between June and August.
Working Hours: To work 7 hours per day.
Pay: *Fruit pickers:* £40+ per day or piecework rates. New pickers often earn below average in their first week, while more experienced pickers earn far more. *Farm assistants, raspberry field supervisors:* to be arranged.

Head Office: Muirton, Alyth, Blairgowrie, Perthshire PH11 8JF
☎ 01828 632227
✆ meg@petermarshallfarms.com
✆ donna@petermarshallfarms.com

Company Description: Farm growing 100 acres of raspberries over extended season.
Job Description: Farm assistants and raspberry field supervisors to work on raspberry machines and tunnel building.
Requirements: Minimum age 18. Fluent English not essential. No experience necessary.
Accommodation: Available at a cost of £3.20 per night.
Application Procedure: By post from January to Meg Marshall, partner, at the above address. Foreign applicants welcome.

R & JM Place Ltd

Job(s) Available: Fruit picking.
Duration: Open all year round.
Company Description: Large soft fruit growers in the centre of the Broadland National Park.
Job Description: Fruit picking, weather permitting. Details on application.
Requirements: Must be in good health. No previous experience necessary.
Accommodation: Available for £57.75 per week, including breakfast, in purpose-built dormitory blocks. Tents and caravans are not permitted.
Additional Information: Social activities in camp include tennis, volleyball, badminton, basketball, football, pool and many more.
Application Procedure: By post with s.a.e. to the administrator, R & JM Place Ltd. Overseas applicants welcome.

Head Office: Church Farm, Tunstead, Norwich NR12 8RQ
☎ 01692 536337
info@ifctunstead.co.uk
www.ifctunstead.co.uk

Roustabout Ltd

Job(s) Available: Tent crew (5).
Duration: From May to September.
Job Description: Tent crew for setting up and dismantling tents at events all over the UK and expanding to mainland Europe. Long, unsocial hours, masses of travel.
Requirements: Driving licence useful, but not essential. Must be physically fit.
Accommodation: Stay in own tents at events.
Application Procedure: By post to Geoffrey Hill, managing director, at the above address.

Head Office: Frongouch Boatyard, Smugglers Cove, nr Aberdovey, Gwynedd LL35 0RG
☎ 01654 767177
info@roustabout.info

S&A Produce (UK) Ltd

Job(s) Available: Strawberry pickers (1,000).
Duration: Workers are required from 15 May.
Working Hours: Pickers are expected to work 39 hours per week.
Pay: National minimum wage rate. Overtime paid in accordance to the Agricultural Wages Order.
Company Description: S&A Produce is an independent strawberry grower supplying UK supermarkets. The company is managed and operated by a young dynamic team with a wealth of experience in growing and other related industries, who are able to cope with a fast moving and profitable business.
Requirements: Workers must be aged between 18 and 45. No experience is necessary, but applicants must be in good physical health. Fluent English is not essential as they have a number of interpreters on site.

Head Office: Brook Farm, Marden, Hereford, Herefordshire HR1 3ET
☎ 01432 880235
workers@sagroup.co.uk
www.sagroup.co.uk

Accommodation: Available.

Application Procedure: CV should be sent to Elena Tustin or Alex Fidoe via email to the above address. All applicants are registered on an internal system and receive a reply to their application within 1–3 working days. Overseas applicants are welcome.

Savoir Faire (Marquees) Ltd

Job(s) Available: Marquee erectors (up to 10).
Duration: Required from April to September.
Working Hours: To work Monday to Friday, 8am–5pm or 6pm plus occasional weekend work at time and a half.
Pay: From £5 per hour with occasional tips.
Requirements: Must be sociable, work well in a small team, preferably strong and at least 5ft 8 inches in height.
Accommodation: No accommodation available.
Application Procedure: By post to Richard Hall, managing director, at the above address.

Head Office: Lower Court Farm, Marlow Farm, Land End, High Wycombe, Buckinghamshire HP14 3JP
☎ 01494 883663
party@savoirfaire.co.uk
www.savoirfaire.co.uk

Sentance Marquees

Job(s) Available: Marquee erectors (2–6).
Duration: Required between April and the end of September. Minimum period of work is 2–3 months.
Working Hours: To work 5–6 days a week for 8–10 hours per day.
Pay: Starts at £5.50 per hour.
Company Description: A total event hire company.
Requirements: Minimum age 18. Must be strong and fit with a driver's licence or reliable transport to premises. Spoken English is an advantage.
Application Procedure: By post to Andrew Beamish at the above address or by phone or email at any time. Non-UK citizens will be considered.

Head Office: Hilltop Farm Caythorpe Heath, nr Grantham, Lincolnshire NG32 3EU
☎ 01400 275165
info@sentancemarquees.co.uk
www.eventsandtents.co.uk

Stanley & Pickford

Job(s) Available: Fruit pickers (30).
Duration: Period of work approximately 5 June to 5 August.
Working Hours: If the weather is suitable there is picking every day; hours of work are informal, but pickers can expect to work in the mornings and part of the afternoon.
Pay: Piecework rates.
Company Description: Runs a pick-your-own farm, and are suppliers of potatoes, strawberries, raspberries and other fruits.
Job Description: Fruit pickers to pick mainly strawberries and raspberries.
Requirements: Previous experience would be an advantage.
Accommodation: Available on the farm in mobile homes and caravans with cooking facilities, communal room, showers etc.
Application Procedure: Contact Mr RO Stanley, partner, at the above address for a full information pack giving information on the work available, rates of pay, accommodation, training etc.

Head Office: Rectory Farm, Stanton St John, Oxford OX33 1HF
☎ 01865 351214 or 07976 302404
s.and.p@farmline.com
www.rectoryfarmpyo.co.uk

Stuart Line Cruises

Job(s) Available: Boat crew (2).
Duration: Positions available for the summer.
Working Hours: Flexible hours.
Pay: £100–£150 per week.
Company Description: Passenger boat operator in Devon.

Head Office: 5 Camperdown Terrace, Exmouth, Devon EX8 1EJ
☎ 01395 279693
info@stuartlinecruises.co.uk
www.stuartlinecruises.co.uk

Requirements: Fluent English helpful. No experience necessary as full training is given. Minimum age 16.
Accommodation: No accommodation available.
Application Procedure: By post to Ian Stuart at the above address. Interview required.

The Dorset Blueberry Company

Job(s) Available: Pickers and packers.
Duration: Positions available from July to September.
Pay: Wages are calculated by kg performance and good workers can earn high wages.
Company Description: Britain's primary producers of fresh blueberries for major supermarkets.

Head Office: Littlemoors Farm, Ham Lane, Hampreston, Wimborne, Dorset BH21 7LT
☎ 01202 891426
info@dorset-blueberry.co.uk
www.dorset-blueberry.com

Application Procedure: Applications only accepted through the above website.

The Granta Boat and Punt Company

Job(s) Available: Punt chauffeurs (10), ice cream servers (2).
Duration: Staff required for a minimum period of 3 months from March to October.
Working Hours: Various hours are available for both positions. Applicants must be flexible as the hours will include weekend and evening work.

Head Office: Newnham Hill Pond, Newnham Road, Cambridge CB3 9EX
☎ 01223 301845
granta.boats@lineone.net
www.puntingincambridge.com

Pay: Competitive hourly rates.
Company Description: Boat and punt hire company situated on the River Cam.
Job Description: *Punt chauffeurs:* applicants must be able to provide informative verbal tours to guests, which will include memorising historical facts.
Requirements: *Punt chauffeurs:* Minimum age 18. Applicants must be outgoing, confident and physically fit. Previous experience of working in a customer service environment, as well as the ability to speak in a foreign language are preferable, but not essential. *Ice cream servers:* minimum age 16.
Accommodation: No accommodation available.
Application Procedure: By post from the end of February to Sarah Austen, director, at the above address. Overseas applicants are welcome to apply but must be able to speak English to the same standard as a native speaker.

Vibert Marquees

Job(s) Available: Marquee erectors (10).
Duration: Period of work runs from April to September; minimum period of work from June to August.
Working Hours: Required to work from 8am to finish, varied hours including overtime and weekends, approximately 50 hours per week.
Pay: From £7 per hour.

Head Office: Manor Farm, Rue du Manoir, St Ouen, Jersey JE3 2LF
☎ 01534 482970
✆ vibmarq@localdial.com
🖳 www.vibertmarquees.com

Company Description: Long-established, family-run business with 6 full-time and 20 seasonal workers.
Requirements: Minimum age 17. Applicants must be hard working.
Accommodation: No accommodation available, but there is a campsite within walking distance.
Additional Information: Working shirts are provided free; shorts are recommended.
Application Procedure: By post from January onwards to Gary Vibert at the above address. Foreign applicants who speak good English are welcome.

Wallings Nursery Ltd

Job(s) Available: Strawberry pickers (10).
Duration: Positions available from 20 March to 1 May.
Company Description: 3 hectares of glasshouses and 2 hectares of polytunnels, growing tabletop strawberries off the ground.

Head Office: 38 Harwich Road, Lawford, Manningtree, Essex CO11 2LS
☎ 01206 230163
✆ dtdunn@talk21.com

Accommodation: Board and lodging available in communal converted barns for £30 per week.
Requirements: Fluent English not essential.
Application Procedure: By post from February/March onwards to Christopher Batchelor at the above address. EU and Commonwealth citizens with permission to work in the UK welcome.

Wilkin & Sons Ltd

Job(s) Available: Fruit pickers (20–30).
Duration: Required from 10 June to 15 July (approximately). Minimum period of work 5 weeks.
Working Hours: 8–10 hours per day, 7 days a week.
Pay: £2 per kilo of fruit picked.

Head Office: International Farm Camp, Hall Road, Tiptree, Essex CO5 0QS
☎ 01621 815496
✆ ifc@tiptree.com
🖳 www.fruit-pickers.com

Company Description: Wilkin & Sons has been a world famous maker of the finest quality preserves at the Tiptree factory since 1885. The company own a freehold estate of about 1,000 acres and grow many choice varieties of fruit selected for their fine flavour.
Job Description: Strawberry picking.
Requirements: Minimum age 18. Fluent English not essential.
Accommodation: £30 per person per week to stay on site. Free pitch if they choose to camp.
Additional Information: Programmes offered in Bulgaria and Romania through SAWS programme.
Application Procedure: By post to Mrs Sonia Vanson from November to February. No interview necessary. Overseas students welcome to apply.

Special schemes for US Citizens
Bunac USA

Job(s) Available: Work in Britain is a government-approved programme allowing thousands of students every year to legally work and live in Britain.

Duration: Participants apply for the unique BUNAC Blue Card allowing them to work in the UK in any type of job for up to 6 months. Valid at any time of year.

Cost: $290.

Head Office: PO BOX 430, Southbury, CT 06488, USA
☎ +1 203 264 0901
info@bunacusa.org
www.bunac.org

Company Description: Work in Britain was established by BUNAC more than 40 years ago as part of a reciprocal student work exchange programme between the UK and the USA.

Job Description: Participants receive a programme handbook before they leave the USA, which is full of information including job listings, Income Tax, National Insurance, accommodation, travel and much more. BUNAC has well-established resource centres in London and Edinburgh to make finding work as easy and as stress-free as possible. Participants do a wide variety of jobs from working in a law firm to serving in a pub. Students can also take part in BUNAC's social programme ranging from Halloween Ghost walks to horse riding in Wales.

Requirements: To be eligible for the programme you must be a full-time degree level student at an American university, either in the USA or as part of a US university approved study abroad programme. So no matter where in the world you are currently studying, eligible US passport holders who are over 18 can apply to Work in Britain. Graduates can apply within a semester of graduating in the USA.

Application Procedure: For further information see www.bunac.org or contact BUNAC USA at the address or telephone above.

THE UK

SPECIAL SCHEMES FOR US CITIZENS

105

Sport

The range of jobs under this category includes, among others, instructors, coaches, boat crew, stable staff, and walk leaders.

Sports holiday centres often specialise in sea, river or mountain activities and as such are often found in remote and beautiful places such as Scotland and the Lake District. They almost always need to recruit live-in workers. While there are opportunities for unskilled staff, most vacancies are for sports instructors, teachers and camp managers. Applicants will normally require governing-body qualifications and a reasonable amount of experience. Growing concern about insufficient supervision and instruction at activity centres in the past has resulted in new tougher controls.

Teaching centres along the south and west coasts in particular are keen to recruit windsurfing, sailing and canoeing instructors in ever-increasing numbers. Several lake centres also advertise in this book. Anyone with life-saving qualifications could consider working as a lifeguard at a leisure centre. Several local authorities advertise such vacancies in this book.

Riding: Riding schools and trekking centres (which are particularly common in Wales) may take on experienced riders. Since a lot of the work is dealing with groups, the ability to get on well with people is also important. There might be a riding school or holiday centre in your area where you could ask about the possibility of a temporary job. The British Horse Society (0870-120 2244; www.bhs.org.uk) publishes a list of more than 900 approved establishments, available on the above website. The Association of British Riding Schools (01736-369440; www.abrs-info.org) provides a free directory of its members on their website. You should also contact them for information about trekking holidays and centres. Employment can also be found with racing stables, which sometimes require stable staff.

Albourne Equestrian Centre

Job(s) Available: Working pupils (2–3).
Duration: Staff are required at any time for a minimum of 6 months.
Working Hours: To work 5.5 days a week from 8am to 6pm.
Pay: Dependent on experience.
Company Description: An approved British riding school and livery yard, also council approved. Regularly holds affiliated and unaffiliated shows and clinics.

Head Office: Henfield Road, Albourne, West Sussex BN6 9DE
☎ 01273 832989
✆ enquiries@albourneequestriancentre.co.uk
🖳 www.albourneequestriancentre.co.uk

Job Description: Working pupils training for BHS exams needed. Work will consist of general yard work and riding tuition with the opportunity to compete at shows and events.
Requirements: Minimum age 16. Some experience with horses is preferred.
Accommodation: Available at a charge of £30 per week.
Application Procedure: By post to Megan Hughes at the above address. References required. Students of all nationalities are considered.

Alston Training & Adventure Centre

Job(s) Available: Assistant outdoor activity instructors, domestic staff.
Requirements: Should have current driving licence. MLC or canoe qualification useful.

Head Office: Alston, Cumbria CA9 3DD
☎ 01434 381886
✆ alstontraining@btconnect.com
🖳 www.alstontraining.co.uk

Accommodation: Free board, lodging and training provided.
Application Procedure: For further details and applications contact Dave Simpson, head of centre, at the above address.

Bradwell Outdoors

Job(s) Available: Sailing (3), canoeing (1), archery instructors.
Duration: Minimum work period 4 months between April and October inclusive.
Working Hours: To work approximately 8 hours per day.
Pay: To be arranged.

Head Office: Bradwell Waterside, nr Southminster, Essex CM0 7QY
☎ 01621 776256
🖂 info.bradwelloutdoors@essex.gov.uk
🖳 www.bradwelloutdoors.com

Company Description: A local authority-run high-quality multi-activity residential centre for young people and adults. Based on the edge of the River Blackwater in Essex, it is an excellent site for all water and land based activities.
Requirements: RYA Instructors Certificate essential or BCU/GNAS.
Accommodation: Includes board and lodging.
Application Procedure: By post in January/March to the manager.

Bray Lake Watersports

Job(s) Available: Seasonal watersports instructors (8).

Head Office: Monkey Island Lane, Windsor Road, Maidenhead, Berkshire SL6 2EB
☎ 01628 638860
🖂 info@braylake.com
🖳 www.braylake.com

Duration: Required from June/July to September to instruct adults and juniors in windsurfing, sailing and canoeing.
Working Hours: To work 5 days a week.
Pay: Dependant on qualifications.
Company Description: Set next to a 50-acre lake ideal for beginners and intermediate windsurfers, sailors and canoeists. Caters for both adults and juniors. Has a good range of equipment for teaching, hire and demonstration.
Job Description: Seasonal watersports instructors to teach windsurfing, sailing and canoeing.
Requirements: Instructors should hold RYA Windsurfing, RYA Sailing or BCU Canoeing Instructor's Certificates.
Accommodation: Some static caravan accommodation available on site.
Application Procedure: By post to Lindsay Frost, centre manager at the above address.

Cairnwell Mountain Sports

Job(s) Available: Ski instructors (2), activity instructors (2), lodge worker (1).

Head Office: Gulabin Lodge, Spittal of Glenshee, Blairgowrie, Perthshire PH10 7QE
☎ 01250 885255
🖂 admin@cairnwellmountainsports.co.uk
🖳 www.cairnwellmountainsports.co.uk

Duration: *Ski instructors:* required from 5 January to 10 March for 5–10 weeks. *Activity instructors:* required from 16 April to 16 June for a minimum of 4 weeks. *Lodge worker:* required from December to the end of May and July to the end of September.
Working Hours: *Ski instructors*: to work 6 days a week. *Activity instructors*: to work 5 days a week.

Pay: *Ski instructors*: £300 per week. *Activity instructors*: £250 per week. *Lodge worker:* £200 per week.

Company Description: A multi-activity centre and hostel for 35 people. Winter activities include ski school, snow board school and Nordic skiing; in summer climbing, walking, archery, zip wire, gorge ascents and more.

Requirements: *Ski instructors and activity instructors:* must have a national qualification. *Lodge worker:* no experience necessary.

Accommodation: Available at a cost of £50 per week.

Application Procedure: By post to Darren Morgan at the above address as soon as possible. Interview and references are necessary. Overseas applicants are welcome for the posts of lodge worker and ski instructor.

Caledonian Discovery Ltd

Job(s) Available: Mate/instructor, bosun, cook, assistant cook (part-time).

Head Office: The Slipway, Corpach, Fort William PH33 7NB
☎ 01397 772167
🖷 info@fingal-cruising.co.uk
🖥 www.fingal-cruising.co.uk

Duration: To work from mid-April to mid-October. Staff must be available for the whole season to qualify for a bonus with the exception of the assistant cook whose minimum period is one week.

Working Hours: All full-time staff to work 6.5 days a week and all crew live on board the barge.

Pay: *Mate/instructor:* £215–£290 per week net depending on experience. *Bosun:* £140–£160 per week. *Cook:* wages £215–£290 per week net. *Assistant cook:* to work their passage: no wage paid.

Company Description: Organises activity holidays based on a barge cruising the Caledonian Canal/Loch Ness. The 12 guests take part in various outdoor activities at numerous stops along the way. Activities include sailing, canoeing, windsurfing, walking, and biking, with other specialist weeks available. The work is hard, but varied and great fun.

Job Description: *Bosun:* main duties include maintenance of boat, driving of safety boat, helping on deck. Must be keen to learn, with practical nature. *Cook:* to prepare food for 18 people.

Requirements: *Mate/instructor:* experience and preferably qualifications in open canoeing and mountain walking required (windsurfing and sailing an advantage). *Bosun:* training provided. Personal experience of outdoor sports an advantage. *Cook:* must have experience in good cooking.

Application Procedure: By post from December to Martin Balcombe at the above address. A 2-day recruitment event will be held in February or March.

Clyne Farm Activity Centre

Job(s) Available: Activity instructor, riding instructor.

Head Office: Westport Avenue, Mayals, Swansea SA3 5AR
☎ 01792 403333
🖷 info@clynefarm.com
🖥 www.clynefarm.com

Duration: Minimum period of work 1 month between May and September.

Working Hours: To work 40 hours per week.

Pay: From £200 per week depending on qualifications and experience.

Company Description: Multi-activity centre in converted stone buildings with a wide range of client groups from school and youth groups to adults and families. Activities include everything from archery to windsurfing.

Accommodation: No accommodation available.

Application Procedure: By post to Geoff Haden at the above address from January. Interview required. Foreign applicants with recognised qualifications and good English welcome.

Contessa Riding Centre

Job(s) Available: Stable helpers.
Duration: Minimum period of work 2.5 months.
Working Hours: To work 8am–5pm (beginning at 8.30am on 2 days), 5.5 days a week, throughout the year, especially around the holiday periods.
Pay: Pocket money.

> **Head Office:** Willow Tree Farm, Colliers End, Ware, Hertfordshire SG11 1EN
> ☎ 01920 821792
> contessariding@aol.com
> www.contessa-riding.com

Company Description: Riding school and competition yard with a particular interest in dressage. Set rurally 30 miles north of London; easy access to Cambridge and Stansted Airport.

Job Description: Stable helpers to perform general yard duties including mucking out, grooming, tack cleaning and horse handling. Horses range from novice to grand prix standard.

Requirements: Minimum age 17. Qualifications and experience preferred.

Accommodation: Self-catering accommodation available.

Additional Information: Riding provided. Brochures available.

Application Procedure: Applicants should ideally be available for an interview and must apply with CV and references. Applications are welcome year round by post to Tina Layton BHSI at the above address.

FMC

Job(s) Available: Staff of all categories, including management and chefs.
Duration: The Championships at Wimbledon require 1,600 staff between Saturday 21 June and Sunday 6 July inclusive. Hours of work are by arrangement.
Pay: To be arranged.

> **Head Office:** All England Lawn Tennis and Croquet Club, Church Road, Wimbledon, London SW19 5AE
> ☎ 020 8971 2465
> resourcing@fmccatering.co.uk
> www.fmccatering.co.uk

Company Description: FMC is one of the largest outdoor event caterers in Europe. Its varied agenda covers some of the most prestigious events in the society calendar including The Championships at Wimbledon, Chelsea Football Club, the Harlequins Rugby Club at the Stoop Memorial Ground and The Brit Oval, Kennington, as well as numerous other outdoor and private catering events.

Job Description: Staff of all categories, including management and chefs are required to work at events.

Requirements: Applicants must be able to supply photocopied proof of their right to work in the UK with applications and provide the original on the date of their first assignment. Applicants for all events should be people who are outgoing and fun-loving with good communication skills.

Application Procedure: For more information on any of the above and to apply online visit www.fmccatering.co.uk.

Galloway Sailing Centre

Job(s) Available: *Instructors:* dinghy (15), windsurfers (5), canoes (5), climbers (3), archery leaders (2). Kitchen assistant (2), groundsman and maintenance, chalet girl.

Head Office: Shirmers Bridge, Loch Ken, Castle Douglas DG7 3NQ
☎ 01644 420626
✆ gsc@lochken.co.uk

Duration: Period of work from May to September, or peak season only.

Working Hours: Hours variable. Courses start at 10am and finish 5pm.

Pay: To be arranged.

Company Description: A family-owned centre in a picturesque setting, which aims to give its visitors an enjoyable yet educational time in a safe and friendly atmosphere.

Requirements: *Instructors:* must be NGB qualified. *Kitchen assistant:* no special qualifications needed but experience an advantage. *Groundsman and maintenance:* no special qualifications needed. *Chalet girl:* must enjoy working with children. Applicants should be versatile, good with people and prepared to accept responsibility. Knowledge of DIY an advantage.

Accommodation: Free board and lodging available.

Application Procedure: By post to Mr R Hermon, principal, at the above address. Overseas applicants with equivalent qualifications welcome.

HF Holidays Ltd

Job(s) Available: Walk leaders.

Duration: Applicants may choose where, how often and when they want to lead week-long walking holidays (from 2–30 weeks per year).

Head Office: Leader Recruitment Manager, Redhills, Penrith, Cumbria CA11 0DT
☎ 01768 214528 quoting SJA8
✆ walkleaders@hfholidays.co.uk
🖥 www.walkleaders.co.uk

Company Description: The UK's leading walking holiday company (founded 1913) is a non-profit-seeking organisation which owns 17 country house hotels based in some of the most scenic parts of Britain.

Job Description: Walk leaders required to lead walks catering for all levels of walker.

Requirements: Applicants should be experienced walkers with leadership potential, fully competent in the use of map and compass, considerate and tactful.

Accommodation: Full board and lodging, travel expenses and training opportunities will be provided.

Application Procedure: For applications or an information pack contact the above address or visit the website. Residential assessment courses are held during the winter and spring (difficult for applicants living abroad) so application by February is essential.

James Given Horse Racing Ltd

Job(s) Available: Stable staff.

Duration: To work from March until November or by arrangement.

Head Office: Mount House Stables, Long Lane, Willoughton, Gainsborough DN21 5SQ
☎ 01427 667618
✆ jamesgiven@bigfoot.com
🖥 www.jamesgivenracing.com

Pay: Dependent on experience.

Working Hours: To work 7.30am–1.30pm and 4.30pm–6pm, with overtime available.

Job Description: Duties including riding out, mucking out and all yard duties.

Requirements: Applicants must have previous experience of riding racehorses.

Additional Information: Staff will be able to take horses racing.

Accommodation: Available at approximately £70 per week.

Application Procedure: By post to Suzanne Maclennan, secretary, at the above address. An interview will be necessary.

Knowle Manor & Riding Centre

Job(s) Available: Riding instructor (1), ride leaders (2), in-house helpers (3).

Duration: Minimum period of work for all positions is July to the end of August or preferably September to October.

Head Office: Timberscombe, Minehead, Somerset TA24 6TZ
☎ 01643 841342
info@knowlemanor.co.uk
www.knowlemanor.co.uk

Working Hours: *Riding instructor:* to work 5 days a week. *Ride leaders:* to work approximately 42 hours per week. *In-house helpers:* to work approximately 35 hours per week.

Pay: *Riding instructor:* salary according to qualifications. *Ride leaders:* wages by the hour and according to the national minimum wage rates. *In-house helpers:* wages according to national minimum wage rates.

Company Description: Knowle Manor is a residential riding holiday centre based in Exmoor National Park and set in 80 acres of grounds with indoor heated swimming pool, trout lake, croquet and badminton areas.

Job Description: *In-house helpers:* to perform all household duties in the hotel, including cleaning and waiting.

Requirements: *Riding instructor:* applicants must have BHSAI. *Ride leaders:* tax and National Insurance deductions. Experience with horses essential. Recommended BHS Riding and Road Safety. First aid certificate and mature outlook needed. Minimum age 18. Staff training is undertaken. *In-house helpers:* no experience necessary but applicants must be cheerful.

Accommodation: Staff accommodation is £27.30 per week.

Application Procedure: By post from January onwards to Ruth and Kevin Lamacraft at the above address. Suitably qualified foreign applicants welcome.

Loch Insh Watersports & Skiing Centre

Job(s) Available: Watersports instructors, skiing instructors, restaurant staff.

Duration: Minimum period of work 4 months, with work available all year round.

Head Office: Insh Hall, Kincraig, Inverness-shire PH21 1NU
☎ 01540 651272
office@lochinsh.com
www.lochinsh.com

Working Hours: *Watersports instructors:* to work 5 days a week. *Skiing instructors:* to work 5 days a week. *Restaurant staff:* to work a 5–6 day week.

Pay: Dependent on qualifications.

Company Description: Loch Insh Watersports and Skiing Centre is nestled in the foothills of the Cairngorm Mountains in the scenic Spey Valley and has a lochside restaurant. Skiing from December to April.

Requirements: *Watersports instructors:* RYA and BCU qualified, or trainee instructor standard. *Skiing instructors:* BASI-qualified, or trainee instructor standard. *Restaurant staff:* experience preferred. Non-smokers preferred.

Accommodation: Bed and breakfast en suite accommodation and self-catering log chalets on site. Board and lodging provided at a charge of £60 per week.

Additional Information: Free watersports and skiing for staff.

Application Procedure: By post to Mr Clive Freshwater, at the above address. Overseas applicants with good spoken English welcome.

Medina Valley Centre

Job(s) Available: Seasonal temporary RYA sailing instructors.

Duration: Needed from the end of July to August.

Company Description: An outdoor education and activity centre providing fieldwork courses for schools in Biology and Geography, Key Stage 2 to A-level. Also provides RYA dinghy sail training and open (Canadian) canoeing courses for adults and children.

Requirements: Must have RYA dinghy sailing instructor qualifications.

Application Procedure: Applications to Peter Savory.

Head Office: Dodnor Lane, Newport, Isle of Wight PO30 5TE
☎ 01983 522195
✆ info@medinavalleycentre.org.uk
🖥 www.medinavalleycentre.org.uk

Northfield Farm

Job(s) Available: Trek leaders (2).

Duration: Work available from April to September; minimum work period June to August.

Working Hours: To work 8am–5pm, 5.5 days a week.

Pay: Dependent on age and qualifications.

Head Office: Flash, nr Buxton, Derbyshire SK17 0SW
☎ 01298 22543
✆ northfield@btinternet.com
🖥 www.northfieldfarm.co.uk

Company Description: BHS approved riding centre and working farm, situated in a small village. There is a post office and a pub less than 100m away. 30 horses are used, an Andalusian stallion at stud, a few breeding mares and young stock.

Requirements: Applicants must be competent riders, good with people and preferably drivers. Riding and road safety test plus first aid qualification also preferred. Applicants must speak the same standard of English as a native speaker.

Accommodation: Free accommodation.

Application Procedure: By post between March and May only (no applications before March) to Mrs E Andrews, Northfield Farm, at the above address. Interview required.

Peak District Hang Gliding Centre

Job(s) Available: Hang gliding instructor (1–2), telesales assistant/secretary.

Duration: *Hang gliding instructor*: to work from July to September. *Telesales assistant/secretary*: period of work by arrangement.

Head Office: York House, Ladderedge, Leek, North Staffordshire ST13 7AQ
☎ 07000 426445
✆ mike@peakhanggliding.co.uk
🖥 www.peakhanggliding.co.uk

Working Hours: *Hang gliding instructor*: hours by arrangement.

Pay: *Hang gliding instructor*: £80 per day. *Telesales assistant/secretary*: wages by arrangement.

Company Description: The longest established hang gliding school in the UK; based in the Peak District National Park.

Requirements: *Hang gliding instructor*: must be experienced. *Telesales assistant/secretary*: must have a good telephone manner.

Application Procedure: By post to Mike Orr at the above address.

Perth and Kinross Leisure

Job(s) Available: Relief leisure assistant (wet facilities), relief leisure assistant (dry facilities), sports coaches, relief catering assistants.

Duration: Positions are available at variable times throughout the year, especially holiday periods, weekends and evenings.

Head Office: Company Head Office, Caledonia House, Hay Street, Perth PH1 5HS
☎ 01738 450750
✒ dmgaffney@pkc.gov.uk

Working Hours: Hours are variable.

Pay: *Relief leisure assistant (wet facilities):* £7.59 per hour. *Relief leisure assistant (dry facilities):* £7.59 per hour. *Sports coaches:* £5.52–£10.25 per hour. Relief catering assistants: from £6.22 per hour.

Company Description: Provides leisure and community facilities throughout the Perth and Kinross area to promote development, health, fitness and wider leisure services.

Requirements: *Relief leisure assistant (wet facilities):* RLSS pool lifeguard qualification needed. *Relief leisure assistant (dry facilities):* first aid at work qualification needed. *Sports coaches:* appropriate coaching certificates needed.

Accommodation: *Relief catering assistants:* no accommodation available.

Application Procedure: By post to Diane Gaffney, HR and administration manager, by letter. Interview necessary. Foreign applicants welcome with appropriate work permit.

Rookin House Equestrian & Activity Centre

Job(s) Available: Trek leaders (2), activity instructor.

Duration: Staff are required from June to September and must work July and August.

Head Office: Troutbeck, Penrith, Cumbria CA11 0SS
☎ 01768 483561
✒ deborah@rookinhouse.co.uk
🖳 www.rookinhouse.co.uk

Working Hours: To work 40 hours per week.

Pay: From £220 per week.

Company Description: Situated on a hill farm, Rookin House is a multi-activity centre offering quad biking, go-karting and, archery. There is also an equestrian centre with 38 horses offering trekking, hacking and lessons.

Job Description: For both positions work will involve taking clients on activities and the maintenance of equipment and surroundings. There is also a self-catering unit which will require cleaning.

Requirements: *Trek leaders:* applicants must be 18 or over, hold riding and road safety qualifications and be able to ride well. *Activity instructor:* applicants must be 18 or over and preferably hold GNAS for Archery Leader Award, first aid certificate and ATV qualification. In-house training can be provided if applicant does not hold the above.

Accommodation: Available at a charge of £20 per week.

Application Procedure: By post to Deborah Hogg at the above address from March. Overseas applicants are welcome but must have a work permit and speak good English.

Snowdonia Riding Stables

Job(s) Available: Trek leaders (2).

Duration: Staff are required from mid-July to mid-September.

Head Office: Waunfawr, Caernarfon, Gwynedd LL55 4PQ
☎ 01286 650342
✒ riding@snowdonia2000.fsnet.co.uk
🖳 www.snowdonia2000.fsnet.co.uk

Working Hours: Required to work approximately 40 hours per week.

Pay: To be arranged.

Company Description: A trekking centre/riding school with 25 horses including dressage/event horses, young stock and liveries.

Job Description: Work includes care of horses, yard work, trek leading and light maintenance work.

Accommodation: Accommodation is available in self-catering caravans free of charge.

Requirements: Minimum age 18. Applicants must have good riding ability.

Application Procedure: By post to Mrs R Thomas at the above address from spring onwards. Overseas applications are welcome.

South Wales Carriage Driving Centre

Job(s) Available: Volunteer stable staff, carriage driving horse assistants (maximum 2 at any one time).

Working Hours: Hours to suit.

Company Description: Small company teaching people how to drive a horse and carriage for commercial work and just for fun.

Head Office: Llwyn Mawr Farm, Gowerton, Swansea SA4 3RB
☎ 01792 874299
✒ info@rowena-moyse.com
🖳 www.rowena-moyse.com

Requirements: Minimum age 16. Fluent English is essential.

Accommodation: Could be provided.

Application Procedure: By post to Rowena Moyse at the above address at anytime.

Travel Class Ltd

Job(s) Available: Activity instructors, group leaders, watersports instructors and support staff.

Duration: Positions available from March until September.

Pay: Excellent wages.

Company Description: A premier UK provider of

Head Office: 14 Queensway, New Milton, Hampshire BH25 5NN
☎ 0870 513 3773
✒ admin@travelclass.co.uk
🖳 www.travelclass.co.uk

adventure activity and environmental programmes for primary school children. Heroic and enthusiastic role models required.

Job Description: Activity instructors, group leaders, watersports instructors and support staff required for a summer job with a difference, to work with children in glorious coastal locations at Travel Class's 14 JCA Adventure and Environmental Activity Centres in Devon, Cornwall, the Isle of Wight, the Midlands, Wales, Norfolk and Somerset. Great lifestyle working as part of a multi-national, young and vibrant team.

Requirements: Training and qualifications provided but applicants must have enthusiasm, dedication and an affinity with children.

Accommodation: Superb food and quality accommodation.

Application Procedure: Call or email at any time for an application pack.

Vacation Traineeships and Internships

Listed below are placements and schemes that aim to provide young people with an opportunity to gain on-the-job training during their holidays. They are variously referred to by firms as 'work placements', 'internships', 'vacation schemes', 'training schemes' as well as a myriad of other names. They are generally short-term placements for students lasting from two weeks to the whole summer holiday.

Traineeships and internships may not appeal to those wanting a summer job just to have fun or to earn enough money for a holiday or to repay an overdraft. Some employers offer fantastic remuneration, with some City internships paying up to £650 a week. Others see the reward as the experience itself and just pay expenses. In the long run, a work placement can prove to have been the most valuable investment of your vacations.

The content and style of traineeships and internships varies from one firm to another. Some, especially large banks, accountants and consultancies, will put you into a position of real responsibility so you can learn the ropes of the business from its centre. Others operate more of a 'work-shadow' scheme where you are expected to follow and observe a member of staff, and perhaps help them with their work.

Advertised traineeships and internships tend to be most numerous in areas of Science, Technology and Engineering, since these industries have seen a serious decrease in numbers of students coming into them. In other areas, like finance and law, competition is likely to be strong. Traineeships and internships in oversubscribed areas tend to be the unpaid ones; media and marketing among others.

The Advantages of Vacation Training & Internships. Many schemes pay impressive salaries but the value of the experience gained far outweighs that of the salary. Traineeships/internships can give you a valuable insight into potential careers. It is an incredible advantage, when looking for permanent jobs, to have had a taste of various industries without having had to make a commitment to any, and perhaps more importantly to have it listed on your CV. Employers are more far likely to value a candidate who spent a summer gaining experience and skills, and probably cultivating a more mature approach to work, than one who worked sporadically at a local pub.

In addition, when it comes round to interview time for graduate jobs, you will have already been able to practice and will be better prepared as a result. Having done a traineeship/internship will also provide a good source of interview conversation. Employers frequently say that they are looking for work experience, practical business skills, personality and initiative, and if you are able to demonstrate these on your CV a minimum degree requirement for the job may be waived.

Many companies also treat their schemes as extended assessment periods: while you are getting an insight into them, they can assess your suitability for a permanent position. Some interns leave with a permanent job offer in the bag and even sponsorship for their final year. Even if the company does not make you a job offer, a good reference from them can help you find work elsewhere. Experience in sectors where placements are rare, like media or the arts, can enable you to build up a bank of contacts that would help enormously in future job hunts. Further guidance and advice on work placements and internships can be obtained from the National Council for Work Experience (www.work-experience.org).

Accountancy, Banking and Insurance

Coulsons

Job(s) Available: Trainees.
Duration: Mainly during the summer vacation.
Company Description: Coulsons, a firm of chartered accountants, occasionally takes on trainees to work in its Scarborough office.
Job Description: Candidates would normally be UK undergraduates intending to pursue chartered accountancy as a career.

Head Office: PO Box 17, 2 Belgrave Crescent, Scarborough, North Yorkshire YO11 1UD
☎ 01723 364141
postmaster@coulsons.co.uk
www.coulsons.co.uk

Requirements: Vacation work would be offered only to students giving an undertaking to take up a training contract with Coulsons on the completion of their academic studies.

Accommodation: Local candidates are at an advantage as accommodation is difficult to find.

Application Procedure: For further details contact Mr PB Hodgson, student training officer in April, at the above address. Please note that only those short-listed will be contacted.

Euromoney Institutional Investor PLC

Job(s) Available: Vacation and work experience placements.

Duration: Length of placements vary depending on the work available.

Pay: Varies depending on the work available.

Comapany Description: Euromoney Institutional

Head Office: Nestor House, Playhouse Yard, London EC4V 5EX
☎ 020 7779 8888
✉ people@euromoneyplc.com
🖥 www.euromoneyplc.com

Investor is an international publishing and events company based in central London. Vacation and work experience placements are available for university undergraduates or gap year students with excellent grades and an interest in finance.

Job Description: The work available includes research or project work for our editorial teams, or telesales and data entry work for our sales and marketing teams. Students of any discipline are considered, with economics, law and languages particularly useful.

Accommodation: Not provided.

Additional Information: For further information about these employment opportunities, visit the employment section of the company's website.

Application Procedure: Applications including CV and covering letter should be sent by email to the HR manager at people@euromoneyplc.com. Qualified overseas applicants who hold a relevant work permit are welcome to apply.

Financial Services Authority

Job(s) Available: The FSA Summer Internship.

Duration: The placements last for 10 weeks between July and September.

Pay: Approximately £400 per week.

Company Description: The FSA ensures integrity in the UK financial markets and protects consumer interests.

Head Office: 26 The North Colonnade, Canary Wharf, London E14 5HS
☎ 020 7066 3568 020 7066 1019
✉ fsa.graduates@fsa.gov.uk
🖥 www.fsa.gov.uk/careers

Job Description: The FSA summer internship is available to approximately 30 students in their penultimate year at university. Interns spend their time getting to know how the FSA upholds the highest standards and how that impacts on the world of business. Through project-based work in one department, interns will have the chance to gain a unique insight into the UK financial system.

Requirements: Candidates should have a minimum 300 UCAS points, be expecting a 2:1 degree and be able to show a keen commercial awareness. Candidates must have the unrestricted right to work in the UK.

Application Procedure: Applications should be made online via the FSA website. An interview and assessment centre test will be required.

JPMorgan

Job(s) Available: Summer internships (200).
Duration: 10 weeks.

Head Office: 10 Aldermansbury, London EC2V 7RJ
www.jpmorgan.com/careers

Company Description: Investment banking is a fast-moving world where talented people can achieve great things. If you want responsibility and the chance to make an impact at an early stage in your career, you'll find it at JPMorgan.

Job Description: Training programmes combine on-the-job learning with classroom instruction that is on a par with the world's finest business schools. Applicants will gain exposure to different lines of business, giving a multi-dimensional perspective of the company. As a result, those interested will emerge with a thorough grounding in a chosen business area as well as a broad understanding of the wider commercial picture. Interns will also gain a range of transferable business skills, from project management to team leadership. Applicants are given responsibility from day one.

Requirements: The work can be intense, so JPMorgan is looking for team players and future leaders with exceptional drive, creativity and interpersonal skills. Impeccable academic credentials are important, but so are achievements outside the classroom. Interns will need to express a preference for one business area when applying so it's important to understand the difference between them.

Application Procedure: The deadline for applications is 13 January 2008 and can be made online at www. jpmorgan.com/careers.

PricewaterhouseCoopers LLP

Job(s) Available: Summer Internship Programme; approximately 160 positions throughout the country.

Head Office: Cornwall Court, 19 Cornwall Street, Birmingham B3 2DT
☎ 0800 100 2200
recruitment@pwc.com
www.pwc.com/careers

Duration: Placements last for 8 weeks from the first week of July.

Pay: The internships are competitively paid.

Company Description: The member firms of the PricewaterhouseCoopers network provide industry-focused assurance, tax and advisory services to build public trust and enhance value for its clients and their stakeholders. More than 140,000 people in 149 countries share their thinking, experience and solutions to develop fresh perspectives and practical advice.

Job Description: The 8-week summer internship programme gives students an insight into what the company does, the way it works and its company culture. The programme runs in many of the national offices, in a range of business areas: assurance, tax, actuarial and advisory and strategy. Students are given a combination of business training and work experience similar to that of a graduate. Working with teams, students are able to make a direct contribution to the work of the firm while developing their own personal skills.

Requirements: PricewaterhouseCoopers are looking for outstanding penultimate year undergraduates of any degree discipline. As competition for places is fierce you will need a strong academic record, expecting at least a 2:1, with a minimum of a 280 UCAS tariff, and should be able to demonstrate excellent communication and interpersonal skills.

Application Procedure: Apply online at www.pwc.com/careers between October and 31 March 2008. Early applicants stand a better chance of gaining a position in their area of preference.

Business and Management

John Lewis

Job(s) Available: 2 placements.
Duration: Placements last 6 weeks.
Pay: Trainees receive a weekly salary.
Job Description: The John Lewis Partnership offers placements to penultimate year university students

Head Office: 171 Victoria Street, London SW1E 5NN
careers@johnlewis.co.uk
www.jlpjobs.com/graduates

of any discipline. Successful candidates gain an overall view of working in John Lewis. They gain experience of customer service standards, stock handling methods and everything else involved in working in a large retail business. This is backed up by insights into selling support functions and a project focusing on a commercial aspect of the business.
Accommodation: While no accommodation is provided, efforts are made to place trainees in branches close to where they live.
Requirements: You should have good written and verbal communication skills as you will be working with senior management, colleagues on the shop floor and customers and you will also make a presentation based on your project.
Application Procedure: Applications should be made online at www.jlpjobs.com/graduates.

Charity Work

British Red Cross

Job(s) Available: 15–20 internships at their central London office.
Duration: 8–10 weeks from July to September.
Working Hours: Interns should expect to work for 2–3 days a week.
Pay: The internships are unpaid but reasonable travel expenses are reimbursed and lunch is provided.

Head Office: 44 Moorfields, London EC2Y 9AL
020 7877 7077
mkemsley@redcross.org.uk
www.redcross.org.uk

Company Description: The British Red Cross helps people in crisis, whoever and wherever they are. They are part of a global network of volunteers, responding to natural disasters, conflicts and individual emergencies.
Job Description: Each internship has its own role description. All interns should be enthusiastic, committed and interested in pursuing a career in the voluntary sector. The internships are aimed at university students, school leavers or those in further education.
Application Procedure: Applications should be made from May via the above website. An interview will be necessary. They also accept applications from those changing career path. Overseas applicants are welcome to apply, provided they have the relevant documentation and funding.

Cancer Research UK

Job(s) Available: Internship prgogramme.
Duration: Applicants are required to work normal office hours for a period of 12 weeks from July to September.
Pay: Internships are unpaid, but travel and lunch expenses are provided.

Head Office: 61 Lincolns' Inn Fields, London WC2A 3PX
0845 009 4290
internships@cancer.org.uk
www.cancerresearchuk.org/internships

Company Description: One of the world's leading independent organisations dedicated to cancer research. They support research into all aspects of cancer through the work of more than 3,000 scientists, doctors and nurses.

Job Description: Cancer Research UK is seeking high-calibre individuals looking to gain work experience in the fields of fundraising, marketing, retail, communications and campaigning for their internship programme. Interns work on real projects that will make a difference to the charity. They are also provided with a thorough induction to the charity, as well as given mid-internship training on CV writing and interview techniques. Applicants are usually undergraduates, graduates or professionals looking for a career change.

Accommodation: No accommodation available.

Application Procedure: For more information and to download an application for completion visit the website from May. Selection process includes a written application form and an interview. Overseas applicants are welcome to apply provided they have the correct documentation to work in the UK and speak English to a very high standard.

Law

Allen & Overy

Job(s) Available: Placements.

Pay: Vacation students are paid £250 per week.

Company Description: Allen & Overy is an international legal practice with 5,100 staff in 24 major centers worldwide. Clients include many of the world's top businesses, financial institutions, governments and private individuals. Renowned for the high quality of its banking, corporate and international capital markets advice and strengths in dispute resolution, tax, employment and employee benefits, real estate and private clients.

> **Head Office:** One Bishops Square, London E1 6AO
> ☎ 020 3088 0000
> graduate.recruitment@allenovery.com
> www.allenovery.com/careeruk

Job Description: Placements will assist a partner or senior associate on real deals. Students will sit in 2 departments and asked in advance what area most interests them. They will also work with fellow vacation placement students on a case study project designed to sharpen research skills and expose students to a broad range of practice areas. Alongside legal work, placements will take part in workshops and attend presentations and talks aimed at helping to develop the skills needed to be a successful commercial lawyer, such as negotiation, presentation and interview skills. There is also time to socialise with other Allen & Overy staff. Students will work in a team, use their own initiative and manage their own time and workload. Evidence of teamwork, leadership and problem-solving skills will be looked for.

Requirements: Placements take place in the London office for students at the end of their penultimate year of study of their undergraduate degree, or at the end of the second year of a 4-year course (if the third year is spent abroad). Applicants are welcomed from both law and non-law students. A strong and consistent academic performance is expected at both school level and degree studies (typically AAB or equivalent) and a 2:1 (or equivalent) should have been achieved, or be predicted.

Application Procedure: Applications from 1 October 2007 to 18 January 2008. Details of all vacancies and a link to online application forms are available at www.allenovery.com/careeruk.

Ashurst

Job(s) Available: 55–60 placements in the summer and 25–30 at Easter.

Pay: £275 per week.

Company Description: International city law firm with 195 partners, around 550 solicitors and a total staff of 1,600. Main areas of practice are in: corporate, employment, incentives and pensions, energy, transport and infrastructure, EU and competition, international finance, litigation, real estate, tax and technology and commercial.

Job Description: During the schemes, students are placed in a different department each week and share an office with a solicitor or partner. The main aim is that students become involved in the solicitor's daily workload by completing 'real' tasks such as letter writing, drafting, legal research and attending client meetings. In addition, a series of lectures, workshops and social activities are arranged.

Requirements: Penultimate year law degree students and final year non-law degree students are eligible.

Accommodation: No accommodation is provided but help in finding some can be given.

Application Procedure: Applications should be made online to Stephen Trowbridge, by 31 January. Foreign applicants who speak fluent English are welcome.

> **Head Office:** Broadwalk House, 5 Appold Street, London EC2A 2HA
> ☎ 020 7638 1111
> ✉ gradrec@ashurst.com
> 🖥 www.ashurst.com

Burges Salmon Solicitors

Job(s) Available: 40 placements for 2008. 22 training contracts for September 2010.

Duration: 2 weeks.

Pay: Remuneration £250 per week. Full fees are paid for both the GDL and LPC.

Company Description: Based in Bristol, Burges Salmon is one of the UK's leading commercial law firms offering an exceptional quality of life combined with a concentration of legal talent unsurpassed by any other firm in the country. Burges Salmon provides national and international clients with a full commercial service through 6 main departments: Corporate and financial Institutions (CFI), commercial, property, tax and trusts, commercial disputes and construction (CDC), and agriculture, property litigation and environment (APLE). Specialist areas include: banking, competition, corporate finance, employment, IP and IT, and transport. The firm is ranked top tier by Chambers and Partners for 18 of its practice areas.

Accommodation: Maintenance grants of £6,000 to LPC students and £12,000 to students studying both the GDL and LPC (£6,000 per year).

Application Procedure: Applications can be made online via website. Queries to Miss Katy Edge, graduate recruitment manager, at the above address. Closing date for applications 31 January 2008.

> **Head Office:** Narrow Quay House, Narrow Quay, Bristol BS1 4AH
> ☎ 0117 902 2766
> ✉ katy.edge@burges-salmon.com
> 🖥 www.burges-salmon.com

Charles Russell LLP

Job(s) Available: 16 vacation scheme placements.

Duration: Placements lasting 2 weeks between June and July.

Working Hours: Interns will be expected to work for 35 hours per week.

Pay: £200 per week.

> **Head Office:** 8–10 New Fetter Lane, London EC4A 1RS
> ☎ 020 7203 5241
> ✉ graduate.recruitment@ charlesrussell.co.uk
> 🖥 www.charlesrussell.co.uk

Company Description: Charles Russell is a top 50 UK legal practice, providing a full range of services to UK and international companies, organisations and individuals with 75% of work carried out for corporate commercial clients whilst the other 25% is for private clients.

Job Description: Attendees will spend the placement in 2 different departments. In addition to gaining an insight into the practice, interns will participate in a number of structured activities including a 'mock trial'. Each candidate will be nominated a mentor (a recently qualified solicitor) as well as working closely with the current trainees.

Requirements: Charles Russell are looking for candidates who have or are expected to achieve a 2:1 degree, with good A-Level and GCSE results and who are eligible to start a training contract in 2010 or sooner.

Application Procedure: Applications should be completed using the online form which is available via the website. The application process lasts from 1 December to 31 January. Overseas applicants are welcome to apply, although a good command of English is required.

Clifford Chance

Job(s) Available: Vacation placements.
Duration: Take place during the spring and summer breaks.

Head Office: 10 Upper Bank Street, Canary Wharf, London E14 5JJ
☎ 020 7006 6006
✉ contacthr@cliffordchance.com
🖥 www.cliffordchance.com/gradsuk

Company Description: Clifford Chance is a truly global law firm operating as one organisation throughout the world, aiming to provide the highest quality professional advice by combining technical expertise with an appreciation of the commercial environment in which clients work.

Job Description: Trainees will gain breadth and depth in their experiences. Clifford Chance offers a global perspective and actively encourage lawyers to develop international experience. Most trainees interested in an international secondment spend 6 months abroad. The range of work performed by the firm worldwide can be divided into 6 main areas of business: banking and finance, capital markets, corporate, litigation and dispute resolution, real estate, tax, pensions and employment. The common theme in all areas is the provision of creative commercial solutions for the wide range of issues encountered by clients. The working style is characterised by a sense of energy, enthusiasm and determination to provide the best possible service to clients. Clifford Chance is committed to building the futures of all trainees and the recruitment strategy is based on a long-term view; that trainees will stay with the company on qualification and enjoy a rewarding career contributing to the success of the global business. It is a diverse multicultural firm and it expects and encourages trainees to develop in directions that reflect their individual talents and style. Vacation schemes provide students with real and interesting experience working on 'live projects' as part of a closely integrated and supportive team. In addition to the vacation schemes, Clifford Chance holds a series of workshops which run for one or 2 days. These offer a more compact way of gaining an insight into life at the firm, as well as the chance to start building networks.

Application Procedure: Apply online for both training contracts and vacation placements at www.cliffordchance.com/gradsuk.

CMS Cameron McKenna

Job(s) Available: Placements to students during Easter, summer and Christmas.
Duration: 2 weeks.

Head Office: Mitre House, 160 Aldersgate Street, London EC1A 4DD
☎ 0845 300 0491
✉ gradrec@cms-cmck.com
🖥 www.grad.law-now.com

Company Description: CMS Cameron McKenna, an international city law firm is distinctive, unstuffy and approachable; looking for creative, bright, commercially aware, committed people who have the potential to contribute to its future success.

Requirements: Positions are open to second year law students or final year non-law students who expect to achieve at least a 2:1 degree.

Application Procedure: To apply visit the firm's online application form or call 0845 300 0491 for an information pack. The closing date for the Easter and summer schemes is 28 February 2008. All training contract applications must be received by 31 July 2008.

DLA Piper

Job(s) Available: 200 vacation placements.
Duration: Placements are 2 weeks long.
Pay: Wages in London are £250 per week, £200 per week outside London.
Company Description: One of the world's largest law firms offering placements throughout their UK offices: Birmingham, Edinburgh, Glasgow, Leeds, Liverpool, London, Manchester and Sheffield.

Head Office: Victoria Square House, Victoria Square, Birmingham B2 4DL
☎ 0121 262 5675
✎ recruitment.graduate@dlapiper.com
🖥 www.dlapiper.com

Job Description: Involves shadowing a current trainee solicitor, attending talks, a visit to court, as well as social events.

Requirements: The scheme is open to undergraduates and graduates who are able to apply for training contracts; ie second year law students, final year non-law students. Applicants are expected to have at least 3 Bs at A-Level, with an expected or attained 2:1 degree.

Accommodation: Not provided, but advice given if necessary.

Application Procedure: Applications should be made on the company's online application form before 31 January.

Mills and Reeve

Job(s) Available: Formal placement scheme.
Duration: There are 25–30 placements throughout June or July for 2 weeks.
Pay: £200 per week.
Company Description: Mills and Reeve is a leading law firm based in Norwich, Cambridge and

Head Office: 112 Hills Road, Cambridge CB2 1PH
☎ 01223 222 336
✎ graduate.recruitment@mills-reeve.com
🖥 www.mills-reeve.com

Birmingham who offer a full range of corporate, commercial, property, litigation, and private client services to a mix of regional businesses and national household names.

Job Description: Mills and Reeve offer a formal placement scheme at each of their offices. Students gain experience in 4 main departments, attend seminars and take part in extra curricular events.

Requirements: Preference is given to penultimate year law students, final year non-law students and all those who have already graduated and are interested in a legal career.

Application Procedure: Applications should be made online via the firm's website and should be submitted before 31 January 2008. Overseas applicants are welcome but must have a valid work permit.

Nabarro

Job(s) Available: There are 60 places available in the Summer 2008 vacation scheme in London and 8 in Sheffield.

Duration: Each placement is for a period of 3 weeks.

Company Description: Nabarro is one of the country's leading commercial law firms offering a broad range of legal services to major national and international clients across a range of practice areas.

Requirements: Applicants must be in at least their penultimate year of a law degree or final year of a non-law degree (Mature Graduates, GDL, and LPC students are also welcome to apply).

Application Procedure: Apply online at www.nabarro.com or via www.cvmailuk.com. Students should submit an application form between 1 November 2007 and February 2008.

Head Office: Lacon House, 84 Theobalds Road, London WC1X 8RW
☎ 020 7524 6000
graduateinfo@nabarro.com
www.nabarro.com

Pannone LLP Solicitors

Job(s) Available: Pannone LLP offers 120 vacation placements in Manchester for students planning a legal career.

Duration: Placements last for one week, at Easter and over the summer vacation.

Company Description: A high-profile full service firm, the best law firm to work for in the UK, according to *The Sunday Times* 2007 survey.

Job Description: Students are given a real experience of the kind of work that trainee solicitors do, drafting correspondence or documents, researching, and spending time with trainees, fee-earners and partners. In 2008 placements are aimed at those seeking a training contract in 2010, mainly second year law and third-year non-law undergraduates. Non UK applicants will be considered as long as they are planning a career as a solicitor in Manchester.

Accommodation: No accommodation available.

Application Procedure: Applications online on above website. For enquiries email Julia Jessop at the above address. The closing date is 25 January 2008 for Easter placements and closing dates vary for summer placements. Full graduate recruitment information is available at the above website.

Head Office: 123 Deansgate, Manchester M3 2BU
☎ 01619 093 000
julia.jessop@pannone.co.uk
www.pannone.com

Pinsent Masons

Job(s) Available: Summer vacation scheme.

Duration: Placements run for 2 weeks between mid-June and the end of August.

Company Description: Pinsent Masons is one of the most highly regarded specialist law firms in Europe and the Asia Pacific region with 7 UK offices, as well as alliances in Europe, the US and Dubai. Pinsent Masons provide a complete legal structure to clients operating in banking and finance, corporate, dispute resolution and litigation, employment pensions and tax, insurance and reinsurance, international construction and energy, outsourcing technology and commercial, projects group, property and UK construction and engineering.

Head Office: City Point, 1 Ropemaker Street, London EC2Y 9AH
☎ 020 7418 7000
gradrecruiting@pinsentmasons.com
www.pinsentmasons.com/graduate

Job Description: The placements are designed to provide a real flavour of Pinsent Masons' culture while improving your skills and knowledge. Students have the opportunity to spend time in one area doing real work, as well as mixing with other students and staff through skills workshops, business presentations, group exercises and much more.

Requirements: Pinsent Masons is looking for bright, motivated second year Law students or final year non-Law students who are expected to achieve at least a 2:1 as their final degree classification and have a minimum of 300 UCAS points (excluding General Studies).

Application Procedure: Applications should be made online by 31 January at the above website.

Pritchard Englefield

Job(s) Available: Student placements (20).
Duration: Placements run for 2 weeks between the end of June and the end of August.
Job Description: Student placements to assist legal advisers in a variety of tasks at the office in London.
Requirements: Applicants should be undergraduates who have compleated at least one year of an English Law degree course, English Law graduates, or non-law graduates who have completed at least the Graduate Diploma in Law (or similar), as well as being fluent in German and/or French.
Additional Information: Travel expenses will be paid.
Application Procedure: Apply to Mr Ian Silverblatt between 1 January and 31 March.

> **Head Office:** 14 New Street, London EC2M 4HE
> ☎ 020 7972 9720
> ✆ isilverblatt@pe-legal.com
> 🖥 www.pe-legal.com

Reed Smith Richards Butler

Job(s) Available: 3 vacation schemes.
Duration: 2 weeks.
Pay: Trainees receive £250 per week.
Company Description: Reed Smith Richards Butler is a premier international law firm with its head office in the City of London and 20 other offices worldwide.
Job Description: Reed Smith Richards Butler offer 3 different 2 week vacation schemes during the summer to both law and non-law students in their second year or above. Students partake in skills training, presentations and work-shadowing.
Accommodation: Trainees will need to arrange their own accommodation.
Application Procedure: Applications between November and February should be submitted online via the website. Foreign applicants eligible to work in the UK are welcome.

> **Head Office:** Beaufort House, 15 St Botolph Street, London EC3A 7EE
> ☎ 020 7247 6555
> ✆ graduate.recruitment@reedsmith.com
> 🖥 www.reedsmith.com

Simmons & Simmons

Job(s) Available: Summer internship.
Company Description: Simmons & Simmons lawyers provide high quality advice and a positive working atmosphere in their 21 international offices. The firm offers their clients a full range of legal services across numerous industry sectors. They have a particular focus on the world's fastest growing sectors that include: Financial Institutions; Energy and

> **Head Office:** City Point, One Ropemaker Street, London EC2Y 9SS
> ☎ 020 7628 2020
> ✆ recruitment@simmons-simmons.com
> 🖥 www.simmons-simmons.com/traineelawyers.

Infrastructure; and Technology. They provide a wide choice of service areas in which their lawyers can specialise. These include Corporate and Commercial; Communications; Outsourcing and Technology; Dispute Resolution; Employment and Benefits; EU and Competition; Financial Markets; IP; Projects; Real Estate; Taxation and Pensions.

Job Description: Simmons & Simmons' summer internship is one of their primary means of selecting candidates for a career at the firm. It provides them with the chance to test suitability for a training contract. It is also a unique opportunity to get to know them and decide if they are the best firm for you. Undergraduates usually apply for internships in their penultimate year. However, Simmons & Simmons are also happy to offer internships to final year students, graduates, mature students, international students and those changing career.

Application Procedure: Applications should be marked for the attention of Anna King, graduate recruitment officer, from 1 November.

S.J. Berwin LLP

Job(s) Available: 60 placements on vacation training schemes.
Duration: 2 weeks.
Pay: Attendees receive £270 per week.
Job Description: Participants spend 2 weeks working in a department ideally suited to them, gaining hands-on experience in a wide range of legal tasks during the summer.

Head Office: 10 Queen Street Place, London EC4R 1BE
☎ 020 7111 2268 020 7111 2393
graduate.recruitment@sjberwin.com
www.sjberwin.com

Requirements: The placements are open to second year law students (and above) and third year non-law students (and above) who are expecting or have gained a 2:1 degree.
Accommodation: While accommodation is not provided suggestions on good hostels and university halls can be made.
Application Procedure: Applications should be completed online at www.sjberwin.com/gradrecruit. The deadline is 31 January 2008. Suitably qualified applicants from abroad who do not require a work permit are considered.

Stephenson Harwood

Job(s) Available: Work-shadowing (18 placements).
Duration: Placements last 2 weeks and take place in June and July in the firm's St Paul's Office.
Pay: £260 per week.
Company Description: Stephenson Harwood is an international City law firm with 7 overseas offices across Europe and Asia. A medium-sized law firm based in a spectacular location opposite St Paul's Cathedral, with a friendly culture and international practice. Their main areas of work are: Corporate, Employment and Pensions, Finance Group, Dry and Wet Shipping Litigation, Commercial Litigation, Real Estate, and Property and Insurance and Reinsurance.

Head Office: One, St Paul's Churchyard, London EC4M 8SH
☎ 020 7329 4422
info@shlegal.com
www.shlegal.com

Job Description: Stephenson Harwood offer students the opportunity to spend 2 weeks work-shadowing solicitors. Students spend one week each in 2 different departments.
Requirements: Applicants must be second year Law undergraduates or third year non-law undergraduates.
Accommodation: No accommodation available.
Application Procedure: Applications by online application form only to the Graduate Recruitment Department. Visit the above website for details of application dates. The application form can also be found at www.cvmailuk.com/shlegal.

Trowers and Hamlins

Job(s) Available: 30 vacation placements.
Duration: 2 weeks.
Pay: £225 per week.
Company Description: Trowers and Hamlins offers vacation placements for penultimate year law students and final year non-law students.

> **Head Office:** Sceptre Court, 40 Tower Hill, London EC3N 4DX
> ☎ 020 7423 8000
> ✆ hking@trowers.com
> 🖳 www.trowers.com

Job Description: Students assist solicitors and trainee solicitors for a period of 2 weeks during which time they spend a week in 2 different departments. Real work is given to successful applicants, for example, attending court and client meetings. Placements will take place in the firm's Head Office in London and Manchester offices.
Requirements: Successful applicants should have a minimum of 320 UCAS points and a 2:1 or above at degree level (predicted or obtained).
Accommodation: Accommodation cannot be provided.
Application Procedure: Applications to Hannah King, graduate recruitment officer, by 1 March 2008.

White & Case

Job(s) Available: Vacation placement programme for one week at Easter (30) and 2 weeks during the summer (50).
Company Description: White & Case is a leading global law firm with more than 2,000 lawyers in 35 offices across 23 countries. The firm works with

> **Head Office:** 5 Old Broad Street, London EC2N 1DW
> ☎ 020 7532 1000
> ✆ trainee@whitecase.com
> 🖳 www.whitecase.com/trainee

international businesses, financial institutions, and governments worldwide on corporate and financial transactions and dispute resolution proceedings. Clients range from some of the world's longest established and most respected names to many start-up visionaries.
Job Description: Our programmes provide a real opportunity to discover what working in a global law firm is really like. Students will work with lawyers on a daily basis and attend organised presentations, training events and social activities.
Application Procedure: To apply for a placement in 2008, complete the online application form available on the website and submit it by 31 January 2008.

Media

Birds Eye View Film Festival

Job(s) Available: A number of internships.
Duration: Staff required all year round.
Working Hours: Hours are flexible, but interns must commit to a minimum of 2 days a week over 2 months.

> **Head Office:** Unit 306 Aberdeen Centre, 22-24 Highbury Grove, London N5 2EA
> ☎ 020 7704 9435
> ✆ rosiestrang@birds-eye-view.co.uk
> 🖳 www.birds-eye-view.co.uk

Pay: All internships are voluntary.
Company Description: Birds Eye View presents the new generation of talented female filmmakers from across the globe. Through London-based festivals and UK touring programmes, they entertain audiences with innovative films, including shorts, features and documentaries.

Job Description: A number of internships are available across the office, including project assistant, office management, research assistant and marketing assistant positions.

Requirements: Minimum age 18. Office experience is preferred.

Accommodation: No accommodation available.

Additional Information: Travel expenses are paid.

Application Procedure: By post to Rosie Strang, Project Manager, at the above address. Overseas applicants are welcome, but must speak good English.

Globe Education

Job(s) Available: Administration work experience placements (30).

Duration: Minimum period of work 3 months. Positions available all year round.

Working Hours: Hours by arrangement.

Pay: Positions are unpaid, and expenses cannot be provided.

Head Office: Shakespeare's Globe, International Shakespeare Globe Centre, 21 New Globe Walk, Southwark, London SE1 9DT
☎ 020 7902 1400
✉ info@shakespearesglobe.com
🖥 www.shakespeares-globe.org

Company Description: Restored Shakespearean theatre on the banks of the Thames with exhibition, lecture programme and workshop. Caters for 70,000+ students each year.

Job Description: To work in the main areas of operation, including exhibitions, fundraising, communications, research, stage management, corporate events and front of house. Some stewarding and special events work will also be available in the summer.

Requirements: Minimum age 18.

Application Procedure: Applications should be made to Rob Norman, personnel manager, at the above address or by email to robert@shakespearesglobe.com. Internship descriptions and an application form for each placement is available within the education section of the website. Interview required. Foreign applicants with fluent English welcome to apply.

Meridian Records

Job(s) Available: 1 or 2 candidates.

Duration: The placements run for a varying number of weeks during any of the 3 main vacations.

Pay: The traineeships are unpaid.

Head Office: PO Box 317, Eltham, London SE9 4SF
☎ 020 8857 3213
✉ mail@meridian-records.co.uk

Company Description: Meridian Records is a small record company specialising in the recording and production of classical records.

Job Description: In 2008 the company will be seeking candidates who can demonstrate motivation and a keen interest in music. The successful candidate(s) will participate in a wide variety of tasks including the preparation of artwork, accounting, recording, editing and the maintenance of machines, buildings and grounds.

Requirements: No particular qualifications are required, although applicants should have a general interest in all aspects of running a record company. An ability to read music is useful but not essential. It is the policy of Meridian Records only to employ non-smokers.

Accommodation: The company may be able to offer accommodation on its premises.

Application Procedure: By post to Mr Richard Hughes, director, at the above address. Overseas applicants will be considered.

Royal Opera House Education

Job(s) Available: Work placements/internships for students with an interest in ballet or opera, though not necessarily in performance.

Duration: Both the period of work and the duration of the placement to be mutually agreed.

Job Description: Placements offered across the organisation but predominantly in technical and production areas.

Requirements: Minimum age 18.

Application Procedure: Contact Joanne Allen, work placement co-ordinator for further information.

> **Head Office:** Covent Garden, London WC2E 9DD
> ☎ 020 7212 9410
> 🖂 education@roh.org.uk
> 🖳 www.royaloperahouse.org

Public Sector

Government Economic Service

Job(s) Available: 50 economist summer vacation placements.

Duration: Placements last for 6 weeks between July and August.

Working Hours: 35-hour week.

Pay: £16,000–£17,000 pro rata.

> **Head Office:** HM Treasury, 1 Horse Guards Road, London SW1A 2HQ
> ☎ 020 7270 4577
> 🖂 ges.int@hm-treasury.gsi.gov.uk
> 🖳 www.ges.gov.uk

Company Description: The Government Economic Service is the UK's largest recruiter of economists with more than 1,000 professionals in more than 30 departments. The GES gives you access to a wide range of economist career options.

Job Description: Interns are expected to provide support to professional economists dealing with a range of issues affecting government policy.

Requirements: Applicants must be studying for a degree in economics, or, if it is a joint degree, economics must comprise at least 50% of the total course (including macro and micro economics). They should also be either UK nationals, Commonwealth citizens, Swiss nationals or members of the European Economic Area.

Application Procedure: Applications available from the GES website from mid-January 2008 and should be sent to ges.int@hm-treasury.gsi.gov.uk.

Science, Construction and Engineering

Black & Veatch

Job(s) Available: Placements.

Duration: The traineeships last for up to 10 weeks.

Company Description: Black & Veatch is a leading global engineering, consulting and construction company. Operating primarily in the water and envi-

> **Head Office:** Grosvenor House, 69 London Road, Redhill, Surrey RH1 1LQ
> ☎ 01737 774155
> 🖳 www.bv.com

ronmental sectors, Black & Veatch specialises in projects that make a difference to the quality of people's lives. It has more than 8,700 professionals worldwide, including 1,800 in the European business.

Job Description: The organisation offers 2 or 3 placements during the summer to civil engineering undergraduates. Traineeships take place in the company's Environmental or Water project centres.

Application Procedure: Applications should be sent to hrdept@bv.com by Easter.

Corus

Job(s) Available: Summer placements and 12-month placements.

Pay: £14,500 per year pro rata.

Company Description: Corus is a customer focused, innovative, solutions driven company. It manufactures, processes and distributes metal products as well as providing design, technology and consultancy services.

> **Head Office:** Ashorne Hill Management College, Leamington Spa CV33 9PY
> ☎ 01926 488025
> recruitment@corusgroup.com
> www.corusgroupcareers.com

Job Description: Every year Corus offers summer placements and 12-month placements around the UK in the following areas; engineering, manufacturing and operations management, metallurgical and technical services, research development and technology, commercial (sales and marketing), supplies, logistics, finance and HR. These positions are suitable for students in their first or second year at university.

Accommodation: Help can be given in finding accommodation.

Application Procedure: Register online at www.corusgroupcareers.com. Registration takes 5 minutes. A full application will then be invited by Corus should a vacancy arise matching your requirements.

ExxonMobil

Job(s) Available: Industrial placements and summer placements.

Duration: Summer placements run from beginning of July to the end of August each year.

Pay: For undergraduates, between £16,730 and £21,340 pro-rata depending on year of study. Salaries are generally reviewed each summer.

> **Head Office:** Recruitment Centre, MP02, ExxonMobil House, Ermyn Way, Leatherhead, Surrey KT22 8UX
> ☎ 0845 330 8878
> uk.recruitment@exxonmobil.com
> www.exxonmobil.com/ukrecruitment

Company Description: ExxonMobil is a worldwide leader in the petroleum and petrochemicals business, with both global and local customers. In the UK it serves around one million customers every day, 365 days of the year, through 900 service stations and owns the country's largest refinery.

Job Description: Graduate positions are offered across a range of functions, industrial placements and summer placements. A range of Summer Placements are split into 4 areas: Refining and Chemicals, Gas and Power Marketing, Business Services and Production and Development. All students will be given a project to complete and receive skills training and development and the opportunity to attend a 2-day outdoor team-building course. During the placement, students will have the opportunity to go through the graduate recruitment process, with the possibility of securing a graduate job before their final year of study.

Requirements: The placements are open to students who are in their penultimate year of study who are expecting to receive a 2:1 degree classification and have the current right to work in the UK.

Application Procedure: Apply via www.exxonmobil.com/ukrecruitment. Early applications are encouraged.

Faber Maunsell

Job(s) Available: Work placements/sponsorships/industrial placements.

Pay: Competitive package offered.

Company Description: An international multi-disciplinary buildings, transportation and environmental consultancy. Offices throughout the UK. One of *The Sunday Times* '100 Best Companies to work for' in 2007.

Head Office: Marlborough House, Upper Marlborough Road, St Albans AL1 3UT
☎ 020 8784 5736
✆ fran.smith@fabermaunsell.com
🖥 www.fabermaunsell.com

Job Description: Open to students looking to pursue a career within the industry.

Application Procedure: Applications online via careers at www.fabermaunsell.com. Interview required. Applicants considered who have the right to live and work within the UK.

Gardline Marine Sciences Ltd

Job(s) Available: Summer placements.

Company Description: The largest independent survey company which operates 10 fully equipped vessels covering Europe, the Far East and West Africa. Gardline Marine Sciences Ltd is involved in hydrographic and marine geophysical surveys.

Head Office: Endeavour House, Admiralty Road, Great Yarmouth, Norfolk NR30 3NG
☎ 01493 850723
✆ hr@gardline.com
🖥 www.gardlinemarinesciences.com

Job Description: The company offers a variable number of summer placements in several different fields, including seismic/hydrographic survey work for surveyors, geophysicists and electronic engineers; there will also be some office work opportunities. Trainees are based in Great Yarmouth from where they will be sent to work on survey.

Requirements: Vacancies are open to students on relevant degree courses, with a preference for those in their second or third year of study. Overseas applicants are welcome.

Accommodation: Shared accommodation is sometimes available.

Applicant Procedure: By post to Andrew Daniels, group HR manager, at the above address.

Gifford

Job(s) Available: Summer vacation traineeships for 15 to 20 students.

Duration: A summer placement will usually last between 10–12 weeks.

Company Description: Gifford is an award-winning consultancy, offering a comprehensive service in engineering and design. Prime disciplines cover

Head Office: Carlton House, Ringwood Road, Woodlands, Southampton SO40 7HT
☎ 023 8081 7500
✆ recruitment@gifford.uk.com
🖥 www.gifford.uk.com

civil, structural and building services engineering, together with complementary support from geotechnical, environmental, survey, transportation and archaeological departments. With more than 50 years in the industry, 700 staff worldwide and 9 UK offices, Gifford values creativity, clarity and the ability to appreciate the problem from the client's perspective, and pride themselves on their reputation for providing technically innovative engineering solutions.

Job Description: Summer vacation traineeships for students to work at offices located in Southampton, Chester, York, Leeds, London, Oxford, Manchester, and Birmingham. Student engineers work with a design team within a multi-disciplinary consultancy environment.

Requirements: Gifford welcomes applications from students studying any of the above disciplines.

Application Procedure: Apply by submitting a letter of application and CV online at www.gifford.uk.gtios.com or by post to the above address.

Niab

Job(s) Available: Vacation work (approximately 30).

Pay: £10,293 per year pro rata for experienced applicants and £8,562 per year pro rata for other applicants.

Head Office: Huntingdon Road, Cambridge CB3 0LE
☎ 01223 342203
jobs@niab.com
www.niab.com

Job Description: Vacation work involving working in fields and laboratories at regional trial centres and the head office.

Accommodation: Accommodation not provided although lists of accommodation are available.

Application Procedure: Applications from April 2008 for summer work to the people and professional development office at the above address.

Rolls-Royce PLC

Job(s) Available: Summer internships and full internships.

Duration: Summer internships are 10 week placements. Full internships are placements that last anywhere from 4 to 12 months, usually as part of a

Head Office: PO Box 31, Derby DE24 8BJ
☎ 01332 244344
peoplelink@rolls-royce.com
www.rolls-royce.com/university

degree course. Typically run from the end of June and last for one year, although it is possible to accommodate both shorter and longer placements.

Company Description: A global company operating in 4 dynamic markets: civil and defence aerospace, energy and marine.

Job Description: Although an engineering business, summer internships are offered in purchasing, supply chain management, finance, commercial and HR, operations management, as well as engineering. Placements have a structured programme and set objectives. They are designed for undergraduates in at least their second year of study. Full internships are designed for students in their second year of study so that they can apply knowledge gained from the course.

Application Procedure: To apply, visit the above website.

Shell Step Programme

Job(s) Available: Work experience placements.
Duration: 8 weeks over the summer.
Pay: Approximately £190 per week (tax and national insurance free).

Head Office: Step Enterprise House, 14-16 Bridgford Road, West Bridgford, Nottingham NG2 6AB
☎ 0870 036 5450
enquiries@shellstep.org.uk
www.shellstep.org.uk

Job Description: The Shell Step Programme offers work experience placements to undergraduates in small to medium sized businesses and community organisations throughout the UK.

Requirements: Applicants must be second/penultimate year undergraduates registered on a full-time UK university degree course.

Application Procedure: To apply visit www.shellstep.org.uk.

Sir Robert McAlpine Ltd

Job(s) Available: Summer placements. Maximum number of vacancies is 35.
Duration: Minimum 8 weeks.
Pay: Varies according to experience and qualifications.
Company Description: Sir Robert McAlpine Ltd is one of the UK's major building and civil engineering contractors, undertaking projects such as industrial plants, marine works, power stations, hospitals, offices, theatres, leisure and retail complexes.

Head Office: Eaton Court, Maylands Avenue, Hemel Hempstead, Hertfordshire HP2 7TR
☎ 01442 233444
✆ careers@sir-robert-mcalpine.com
💻 www.sir-robert-mcalpine.com

Job Description: University students reading degrees in construction-related subjects, or 'A' Level students considering such degrees, are offered summer placements. Students assist site engineers and quantity surveyors working on various major construction sites throughout the country.
Accommodation: Assistance in finding lodgings is provided.
Application Procedure: Applications should be made to the HR department, at the above address, or via the above website.

Textron Fluid & Power

Job(s) Available: Summer vacancies.
Pay: The salary is discussed at interview.
Company Description: As a worldwide resource for high quality technology solutions, Textron serves a comprehensive range of industries including utility, nuclear, oil, gas, water, petrochemical, mining, marine, defence, construction, paper, metals and

Head Office: Park Gear Works, Lockwood, Huddersfield, West Yorkshire HD4 5DD
☎ 01484 465500
✆ sbuczek@davidbrown.textron.com
💻 www.textronPT.com

food processing applications. Textron Fluid & Power specialises in the design and manufacture of industrial pumps, gears and gearboxes. It has built its business into what it is today by combining the collective strengths and expertise of some of the most highly respected gear and pump manufacturing specialists in the world. Familiar brand names include: Bell Helicopter, Cessna Aircraft, E-Z-Go and Greenlee, among others.
Job Description: Occasional summer vacancies for students, who will be employed in such areas as General Office Admin, Manufacturing Engineering, Production Control, Manufacturing and General Site Services. Applicants should be studying Business or Mechanical Engineering and have an interest in engineering manufacturing processes and/or gearing.
Accommodation: No assistance with accommodation is given.
Application Procedure: By post to Steve Buczek, HR manager UK, at the above address. Suitably qualified overseas applicants will be considered.

Travel and Tourism
Hotel Hougue du Pommier

Job(s) Available: Positions mainly in the restaurant.
Company Description: An attractive farmhouse style hotel on the west coast of Guernsey. Busy in summer with visitors from the UK, France, Germany and Switzerland.

Head Office: Castel, Guernsey, Channel Islands GU5 7FQ
☎ 01481 256531
✆ hotel@houguedupommier.guernsey.net
💻 www.hotelhouguedupommier.com

Job Description: Hotel Hougue du Pommier does not offer formal traineeships, but certain positions are open to catering students hoping to develop their skills and gain valuable work experience.

Accommodation: Board and lodging is provided at a cost of £50 per week.

Application Procedure: Further details about jobs available and applications from Julie Payne, director, at the above address. Applicants are not required to attend an interview.

Voluntary Work

The category of voluntary work encompasses a large range of activities including *Archaeology, Children, Conservation and the Environment, Heritage, Physically/Mentally Disabled, Social and Community Schemes* and *Workcamps.*

Many organisations throughout the UK need volunteers to help with a host of different types of work, from caring for people with disabilities or the elderly to taking part in conservation and archaeological projects. Festivals and events are also a good source of temporary voluntary work, though very short-term. Cheltenham Festival of Literature and the Hay Festival of Literature are among the larger advertisers here – you can apply personally to smaller local events, particularly in university or historical towns. You might be paid travel and other expenses and will usually get free entrance to all the events of the festival.

If you are interested in becoming involved in local issues in your area, contact Millennium Volunteers through the Department for Education and Skills (email millennium.volunteers @dfes.gsi.gov.uk; www.mvonline.gov.uk). Millennium Volunteers is a UK-wide, government-funded initiative providing 130 volunteering opportunities for young people aged between 16 and 24. Volunteers contribute to a range of voluntary organisations from their local Citizens Advice Bureau, to joining a conservation project organised by BTCV (see entry), to projects such as sports coaching and music and dance. A national online database of voluntary work is available at www.do-it.org.uk. Those completing 200 hours of voluntary activity in a year receive an award of excellence signed by the Secretary of State. Most UK universities also have thriving Community Action groups offering a range of volunteering opportunities in the local area.

Sources of Information. *The International Directory of Voluntary Work* (Vacation Work, £12.95) has been fully revised and includes information on both short- and long-term opportunities. The National Council for Voluntary Organisations (0800-279 8798; www.ncvo-vol.org.uk) publishes the *Voluntary Agencies Directory,* price £35 plus £5.50 postage and packing for non-members, which lists more than 2,000 organisations countrywide.

Volunteering England (0845-305 6979; www.volunteering.org.uk) produces information sheets on finding out about volunteering opportunities. The website details voluntary organisations, ideas about the types of volunteering available and where to find your nearest Volunteer Centre for local volunteering opportunities. Information on voluntary work in Wales can be obtained from Wales Council for Voluntary Action (0870-607 1666; www.wcva.org.uk).

Archaeology

Arbeia Roman Fort

Job(s) Available: Volunteers (5 per week).
Duration: Needed from June to 30 September.
Working Hours: 8.45am–4.45pm, Monday to Friday.
Company Description: Part of the Tyne & Wear Museums service and within easy reach of Newcastle by Metro. South Shields has good parks and beaches and is an ideal base from which to visit nearby cities or countryside.

Head Office: Tyne & Wear Museums Service, Baring Street, South Shields, Tyne & Wear NE33 2BB
☎ 01914 544093
✉ liz.elliott@twmuseums.org.uk

Job Description: Volunteers to excavate the site, record and process finds, draw the site and take photographs.
Requirements: Minimum age 16. Disabled people may find access to the site difficult.
Accommodation: Volunteers are responsible for their own travel, board and other costs.
Application Procedure: By post to Elizabeth Elliott, office manager, at the above address.

Archaeolink Prehistory Park

Job(s) Available: Volunteers are needed to work in reconstruction and living history.
Duration: From April to October.
Working Hours: Between 20 and 37 hours per week.
Company Description: Archaeolink was started in 1997 to introduce the public to Aberdeenshire's rich archaeological heritage. It operates reconstructions including stone-age camps, a Roman Marching camp, a bronze-age metalsmith workshop and an iron age farm based on archaeological evidence from northeast Scotland.

Head Office: Oyne, Insch, Aberdeenshire AB52 6QP
☎ 01464 851500
✉ info@archaeolink.co.uk
🖥 www.archaeolink.co.uk

Requirements: No experience is necessary and volunteers may be as young as 14 if they are accompanied by a guardian.
Accommodation: Available at a local bed and breakfast, and volunteers must pay for travel, food and accommodation. Lunch is provided by the company on days of volunteering.
Application Procedure: Contact the park, at the above address, for further information.

Bamburgh Research Project

Job(s) Available: Volunteers (35 per week).
Duration: Required from the end of June to the end of August.
Company Description: A project centred on Bamburgh Castle dedicated to using the most modern field techniques to provide training for both students and volunteers. The castle is located 50 miles north of Newcastle on the coast.

Head Office: Bamburgh Castle, Bamburgh, Northumberland
☎ 01904 769 836 (office hours)
✉ paulgething@bamburghre searchproject.co.uk
🖥 www.bamburghresearchproject.co.uk

Job Description: Volunteers needed for excavation, training, field walking, test pitting and media. There are many sites being excavated, including an early medieval gatehouse and a medieval metalworking site, within the castle. There is also a comprehensive survey programme and a media department dedicated to filming the archaeological process. The sites excavated range in period from medieval to modern.
Requirements: Volunteers of all ages and levels of experience are welcome.

Accommodation: Accommodation is provided at a fully equipped campsite but volunteers must bring their own camping equipment.

Additional Information: The nearest railway station is Berwick on Tweed and there is a regular bus service to Bamburgh, or pick up in Newcastle if arranged in advance. The cost of approximately £120 per week which includes tuition, travel to and from the site, food and space for camping.

Application Procedure: By post to the above address as soon as possible.

Council for British Archaeology

Job(s) Available: Excavations and fieldwork projects.

Company Description: Archaeology for all: The CBA is an educational charity working throughout the UK to involve people in archaeology and to promote the appreciation and care of the historic environment for the benefit of present and future generations. Details of excavations and other fieldwork projects are given on the Council's website and in the Council's publication *British Archaeology*. The magazine is published 6 times a year. An annual subscription costs £25 (£19 for the first year); however, it also forms part of an individual membership package which is available for £32 per year and brings extra benefits.

> **Head Office:** St Mary's House, 66 Bootham, York YO30 7BZ
> ☎ 01904 671417
> ✉ info@britarch.ac.uk
> 🖥 www.britarch.ac.uk

Application Procedure: Having studied the magazine you should make applications to the director of the projects which interest you.

Silchester Roman Town Life Project

Job(s) Available: Volunteers.

Duration: Required for July and August to work on the excavation.

Company Description: Situated midway between Reading and Basingstoke, a major long-term excavation of the industrial and commercial area of a Roman town.

> **Head Office:** Reading University, Department of Archaeology, Whiteknights, PO Box 227, Reading, Berkshire RG6 6AB
> ☎ 01183 788132
> ✉ archaeology@rdg.ac.uk
> 🖥 www.silchester.rdg.ac.uk

Job Description: The project is suitable for both beginners and those with more experience.

Requirements: Minimum age 16.

Accommodation: The cost is approximately £250 per 6 day week, which includes food and campsite facilities with hot showers, although volunteers must provide their own camping equipment.

Application Procedure: Visit the above website for further information, or contact Amanda Clarke at the above address.

Conservation and the Environment

Bardsey Island Bird and Field Observatory

Job(s) Available: Volunteer programme for assistant wardens.

Company Description: Situated on a bird island 2 miles off the tip of the Lleyn Peninsula.

> **Head Office:** Cristin, Bardsey off Aberdaron, via Pwllheli, Gwynedd LL53 8DE
> ✉ warden@bbfo.org.uk
> 🖥 www.bbfo.org.uk

Additional Information: On account of the location, postal mail can often be delayed due to bad weather, as can normal ferry service. Only Orange and Vodafone mobiles work.

Application Procedure: For further details contact the warden.

British Trust for Ornithology

Job(s) Available: Volunteers.

Duration: Surveys run by the BTO range from extremely long-term to short-term schemes.

Company Description: An organisation set up to promote the appreciation and conservation of birds.

Job Description: Volunteers needed to participate in surveys run by the BTO.

> **Head Office:** BTO, The Nunnery, Thetford, Norfolk IP24 2PU
> ☎ 01842 750050
> ✆ info@bto.org
> 🖥 www.bto.org

Application Procedure: By post to the above address at any time.

Conservation Volunteers Northern Ireland

Job(s) Available: Volunteers.

Duration: For those who wish to take on extra responsibility, a commitment of at least 6 months is requested.

Company Description: Conservation Volunteers Northern Ireland is part of BTCV, which involves more than 70,000 volunteers each year in environmental projects throughout Northern Ireland, England, Wales and Scotland, making it the largest practical conservation charity in the country.

> **Head Office:** 159 Ravenhill Road, Belfast BT6 0BP
> ☎ 028 906 451 69
> ✆ CVNI@btcv.org.uk
> 🖥 www.btcv.org.uk

Job Description: Volunteers to participate in projects to inspire people to improve the places they live in throughout Northern Ireland. These include community development work, biodiversity projects, health initiatives and use of practical skills etc. There are opportunities to suit all levels of commitment.

Requirements: All training, protective clothing and tools are provided according to the role the volunteer takes on. No experience is necessary. Minimum age is 18.

Accommodation: Limited amount of accommodation at tree nursery site for volunteer officers.

Application Procedure: By post to Kate Holohan, at the above address, at any time of the year.

Hessilhead Wildlife Rescue Trust

Job(s) Available: Volunteers (40 annually).

Duration: Minimum period of work 2 weeks, maximum 6 months in the period between April and October.

Company Description: A wildlife rescue and rehabilitation centre in Scotland.

> **Head Office:** Gateside, Beith, Ayrshire KA15 1HT
> ☎ 01505 502415
> ✆ info@hessilhead.org.uk
> 🖥 www.hessilhead.org.uk

Job Description: Volunteers help with a range of jobs involving rescue, daily care and cleaning of wild birds and animals, as well as treatment and hand-rearing, assessment for release and post-release monitoring.

Requirements: Experience with animals is advantageous, but not necessary, as full training is given.

Accommodation: Provided with heating and cooking facilities.

Additional Information: Costs £10 per week.
Application Procedure: For further details, contact Gay Christie at the above address.

John Muir Trust

Job(s) Available: Volunteers.
Duration: A programme of work parties is organised throughout the year.
Company Description: This Trust believes that the only way to protect wild land is to own and then manage it carefully. It currently owns more than 49,000 acres of land in the Highlands.

> **Head Office:** 41 Commercial Street, Edinburgh EH6 6JD
> ☎ 01315 540114
> ✆ admin@jmt.org
> 🖥 www.jmt.org

Job Description: Volunteers needed to participate in a number of ways, such as organising local meetings, raising funds and helping with general administration, as well as carrying out most of the practical conservation on the Trust's land.
Requirements: Volunteers need to bring their own tent, food and transport.
Application Procedure: For details, contact Conservation Activities, 69 Hyndland Street, Glasgow G11 5PS.

Marine Conservation Society (MCS)

Job(s) Available: Volunteers.
Duration: At certain periods of the year, large amounts of data need to be entered into databases; volunteers with computer skills are particularly welcome at these times.
Company Description: The MCS is the only charity in the UK devoted solely to protecting the marine environment.

> **Head Office:** Unit 3 Wolf Business Park, Alton Road, Ross-on-Wye, Hereford HR9 5NB
> ☎ 01989 566017
> ✆ info@mcsuk.org
> 🖥 www.mcsuk.org

Job Description: Volunteers are sometimes needed in the Society's offices and for participation in campaigns and surveys.
Additional Information: Unfortunately, the Society is unable to provide any financial payment, accommodation or transport. There are also several campaigns in which volunteers can participate. Check the website for further details.
Application Procedure: For further information, contact the Society at the above address.

Merryweather's Herbs

Job(s) Available: Vegetable gardeners (4).
Duration: Minimum period of work 4 weeks between March and October.
Working Hours: To work 10am–5pm, 1–2 days a week (Wednesday and Thursday).
Company Description: Garden development and wildlife project extending to nearly 6 acres and

> **Head Office:** Merryweather's Farm, Chilsham Lane, Herstmonceux, East Sussex BN27 4QH
> ☎ 01323 831726
> ✆ info@morethanjustagarden.co.uk
> 🖥 www.morethanjustagarden.co.uk

incorporating a small nursery, situated in the beautiful Sussex High Weald. Whole project managed organically.
Job Description: Volunteer gardeners to perform general garden maintenance and development, fruit and vegetable growing and wildlife habitat management, as well as some nursery propagation.
Requirements: Training will be given but some experience preferred. Non-smokers only.

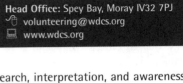

Accommodation: Accommodation not currently available.

Application Procedure: By post to Liz O'Halloran, Proprietor, at the above address from January. References required. Foreign applicants with good spoken English welcome.

Moray Firth Wildlife Centre

Job(s) Available: Volunteers.

Duration: Seasonal.

Company Description: The Whale and Dolphin Conservation Society takes on seasonal volunteers to work at the Moray Firth Wildlife Centre.

Head Office: Spey Bay, Moray IV32 7PJ
volunteering@wdcs.org
www.wdcs.org

Job Description: The work is varied and includes research, interpretation, and awareness-raising events around Scotland.

Accommodation: Accommodation is provided and a contribution is made towards expenses.

Application Procedure: For more information, email the above address.

RSPB Residential Volunteering Scheme

Job(s) Available: Volunteers.

Duration: Bookings start and finish on a Saturday and can be for a week or more.

Company Description: If you are interested in birds and conservation, here is an ideal opportunity to help conservation work at RSPB, gain practical work experience, meet new people, explore new

Head Office: The Lodge, Potton Road, Sandy, Bedfordshire SG19 2DL
☎ 01767 680551
volunteers@rspb.org.uk
www.rspb.org.uk/volunteering/residential

areas, enjoy a working holiday and simply make good use of spare time while keeping fit in the great outdoors. Nationally, the RSPB has more than 12,200 volunteers. There are 37 reserves within the scheme and the work varies from season to season and from reserve to reserve but physical management tasks are an important aspect of the RSPB's work on most sites. Visitor work is available at some sites.

Job Description: A willingness to help with mundane jobs and to work as part of a team is needed. At sites where work is (mainly) helping visitors to the reserve, you must feel comfortable talking to people.

Requirements: No special skills needed for most of the volunteering opportunities but a genuine interest in and enthusiasm for birds and wildlife conservation is essential. Minimum age 16 (18 on some reserves).

Accommodation: Volunteers need to organise and pay for their own travel to and from the reserve and to provide and cover the cost of their own food during their stay. The RSPB will provide accommodation free of charge.

Application Procedure: For a brochure on residential volunteering *Do Something Different* and an application form visit the website or write to The Volunteering Development Department (Residential), at the above address.

Suffolk Wildlife Trust

Job(s) Available: Volunteer education assistants (2), volunteer midweek team members.

Duration: *Volunteer education assistants:* hours vary but may include weekdays and weekends. *Volunteer midweek team members:* needed for 1 day a week (Tuesday, Wednesday or Thursday).

Head Office: Carlton Marshes, Burnt Hill Lane, Carlton Colville NR33 8HU
☎ 01502 564250
carlton@suffolkwildlifetrust.org
www.suffolkwildlifetrust.org

Company Description: Promotes and protects Suffolk Wildlife through education, including outdoor lessons and activities, games, crafts, events, family and adult talks and walks.

Job Description: *Volunteer education assistants:* environmental education for all ages, including assisting with preparation of resources and assisting with wildlife and conservation themed activities. Help with Clubs (Toddler, Arts and Watch Clubs).

Volunteer midweek team members: for practical conservation work on various nature reserves. Work includes building paths, cutting trees and maintaining reserve habitats.

Requirements: Minimum age 18.

Accommodation: None available.

Application Procedure: By post to the education officer at the above address. An informal trial day is required. Foreign applicants with some English welcome.

The Centre for Alternative Technology

Job(s) Available: Short-term and long-term volunteer programme.

Duration: Short-term programme from March to September inclusive, for stays of one or 2 weeks. Long-term programme for 6 months.

Head Office: Machynlleth, Powys SY20 9AZ
☎ 01654 705950
✆ info@cat.org.uk
🖥 www.cat.org.uk/volunteers

Company Description: Established in 1974, the Centre for Alternative Technology is an internationally renowned display and education centre promoting practical ideas and information on technologies, which sustain rather than damage the environment.

Job Description: *Long-term volunteer programme*: for individuals to help in specific work departments. Jobs include the following departments: biology, engineering, gardening, information, media and site maintenance. *Short-term volunteers*: could help with gardening, landscaping, site maintenance and preparation for courses.

Requirements: Applicants for either programme can be of any nationality. Applicants for the long-term programme should have relevant experience.

Accommodation: Cooked lunches and hot drinks are provided. Accommodation for short-term is basic, youth hostel style, shared with other volunteers. There are other arrangements for long-term volunteers; they would need to be self-supporting, for example by claiming state benefits payments if eligible.

Application Procedure: To apply for a long-term placement, send a full CV and covering letter (giving details about yourself and stating which department you would like to with) to Barbara Wallace. Contact Barbara or 01654 705955 or email barbara.wallace@cat.org.uk.

The Monkey Sanctuary Trust

Job(s) Available: Volunteers.

Duration: Summer volunteers required between April and September, winter volunteers between October and March.

Head Office: Looe, Cornwall PL13 1NZ
☎ 01503 262532
✆ info@monkeysanctuary.org
🖥 www.monkeysanctuary.org

Working Hours: 40 hours per week.

Company Description: Home to a colony of Woolly Monkeys and Rescue Centre for ex-pet Capuchins. The Sanctuary is a community dedicated to conservation, sustainable living and animal welfare. Education of the public in these areas is their main summer activity.

Job Description: Volunteers are required in the sanctuary, and are essential in allowing the team of keepers to care for the colony. Help is needed in the kiosk, and with cleaning while the sanctuary is open to the public. In the closed season volunteers assist with general maintenance work and cleaning.

Requirements: No qualifications are necessary but workers must have an interest in animal welfare and conservation. Minimum age 18.

Accommodation: Food and accommodation are provided, and volunteers are asked to make a voluntary donation to the Monkey Sanctuary Trust (suggested £45 per week waged, £35 per week students/unwaged).

Application Procedure: By post, 4 or 5 months in advance, to Volunteer Co-ordinator at the above address, enclosing stamped s.a.e. or International Reply Coupon. Overseas applicants with a good standard of English welcome.

The National Seal Sanctuary

Job(s) Available: Volunteers.

Duration: Taken all year round. Must be able to work for 2 weeks.

Company Description: The Sanctuary is a well-known marine animal rescue centre.

Head Office: Gweek Nr. Helston, Cornwall TR12 6UG
☎ 01326 221361
✆ seals@sealsanctuary.co.uk
💻 www.sealsanctuary.co.uk

Job Description: Volunteers are to help with the Sanctuary's work, including caring for seals and sea lions.

Requirements: Minimum age 18.

Application Procedure: By post to Marianne Fellows at the above address.

The National Trust

Job(s) Available: Volunteering opportunities.

Company Description: Leading conservation and environmental charity.

Head Office: Heelis, Kemble Drive, Swindon SN2 2NA
☎ 0870 609 5383
✆ volunteers@nationaltrust.org.uk
💻 www.nationaltrust.org.uk/volunteers

Job Description: The National Trust has a range of volunteering opportunities if you are looking to fill a gap year, change career or gain work experience. Roles range from assisting with house stewarding and interpretation to events and conservation. All located at beautiful Trust sites.

Requirements: Training is provided.

Accommodation: May be available; some placements are available through the New Deal scheme. Out-of-pocket expenses covered.

Application Procedure: For an information pack call 0870 609 5383, email, or visit the website.

The Wildlife Trust of South and West Wales

Job(s) Available: Voluntary assistant wardens.

Duration: Island volunteers will work for a full week (Saturday to Saturday) or a maximum of 2 weeks between Easter and October.

Head Office: The Welsh Wildlife Centre, Cilgerran, Pembrokeshire SA43 2TB
☎ 01239 621 212, 01239 621 600
✆ islands@welshwildlife.org
    wwc@welshwildlife.org
💻 www.welshwildlife.org

Company Description: The fourth largest wildlife trust in the UK, covering more than 100 nature reserves. Concerned with educating people about the Welsh environment, and its protection and potential.

Job Description: Voluntary assistant wardens required for Skomer Island, a national nature reserve off the Welsh coast. Work involves greeting visitors, census work, general reserve maintenance and wildlife recording, etc.

Requirements: Minimum age 16 with an interest in natural history.

Accommodation: Self-catering accommodation is available free of charge but food is not included.

Application Procedure: Application forms available from Island Bookings or website; apply via email if overseas. Overseas applicants welcome.

Trees for Life

Job(s) Available: Volunteers (10 a week, around 400 annually).

Duration: Volunteers needed for a week at a time. Weeks run from midday Saturday to midday Saturday, including 5 working days. Volunteers may participate in more than one week. Required mid-March to beginning of June and beginning of September to the end of October.

Head Office: The Park, Findhorn Bay, Forres IV36 3TZ
☎ 0845 458 3505
trees@findhorn.org
www.treesforlife.org.uk

Company Description: Scottish charity dedicated to the restoration of the Caledonian Forest to a large, significant area of the Highlands of Scotland.

Job Description: To carry out practical restoration work including tree planting, fence removal, tree-felling, wetland restoration, tree nursery work, stock-fencing and seed collecting.

Requirements: Minimum age 18. Applicants must understand English and be reasonably fit, as work is physical.

Accommodation: All food, accommodation and transport from Inverness provided. Cost is £90 per week/£55 concessions.

Application Procedure: By post to 'Trees For Life Work Week Booking' at the above address, or book online. Foreign applicants welcome.

Wildfowl & Wetlands Trust

Job(s) Available: Volunteers.

Duration: Full-time and part-time opportunities are available but some placements do require volunteers to commit to a minimum of 2 months at the centre to allow time for training.

Head Office: Volunteer Opportunities, Slimbridge, Gloucester GJ2 7BT
☎ 01453 891900
enquiries@wwt.org.uk
www.wwt.org.uk

Company Description: WWT is a charity aiming to promote the conservation of wildfowl and their wetland habitats as well as increasing the public's knowledge of these birds. The Centre has the world's largest collection of wildfowl.

Job Description: The WWT depends on help from volunteers to assist the teams at all 9 centres. At Slimbridge, volunteers assist throughout the grounds and centre including the Visitor Services, Education, Aviculture and Horticulture departments. Grounds and Reserve volunteers assist the wardens in their daily duties and gain practical conservation knowledge and experience. Duties for volunteers working in Visitor Services include manning the information desk, meeting and greeting groups, selling grain to visitors that want to feed the birds and generally being a friendly and helpful face for the public. Education volunteers assist with the development of educational material and help run teaching and informal learning sessions that includes pond dipping and story telling. Other areas where volunteers assist are Marketing, Administration and Maintenance. Volunteers in all areas will have the opportunity to help with a number of exciting new developments including Crane School (where cranes are being reared for release into the wild) and Toad Hall (a collection of amphibians from the UK and overseas) through helping project development, interpretation and giving talks and presentations to visitors.

Requirements: Minimum age 16. No previous experience or qualifications are required, only plenty of enthusiasm, a willingness to help and a capacity to learn.

Accommodation: Limited on-site accommodation is available.

Application Procedure: For further details contact the Sarah Aspden, volunteer co-ordinator, on 01453 891 137 or email sarah.aspden@wwt.org.uk. Other WWT centres also welcome the assistance of volunteers, contact the centre you are interested in for information, details on the website.

Festivals and Special Events

Broadstairs Folk Week

Job(s) Available: Volunteers (150+).

Duration: Minimum period of work 5 days between 8 and 15 August.

Working Hours: Volunteers work 4 hours per day.

Pay: Posts are unpaid, but staff receive a season ticket for access to all events.

> **Head Office:** Pierremont Hall, Broadstairs, Kent CT10 1JX
> ☎ 01843 604080
> 🖱 jo@broadstairsfolkweek.org.uk
> 💻 www.broadstairsfolkweek.org.uk

Company Description: The Broadstairs Folk Week Trust, a registered charity, organises events throughout the year and an annual festival. 2008 will be the festival's 43rd year. The whole town and its promenade, jetty, bandstand, taverns, halls, churches and streets become the venue for international music, song and dance.

Job Description: Volunteers are needed as door stewards, information and shop staff, PA and sound technicians, drivers, campsite stewards and collectors. Volunteers are also needed to handle publicity and liaise with international personnel.

Requirements: Free camping is available.

Application Procedure: By post from March to Jo Tuffs. Download the form from the website or phone. Interview is not necessary. Overseas applicants with good English are considered.

Hay Festival

Job(s) Available: Volunteer festival stewards (approximately 150).

Duration: Volunteers must commit to a minimum of 2 shifts during the festival which runs from 22 May to 1 June.

Working Hours: Shifts last for 3 to 4 hours per day.

> **Head Office:** The Drill Hall, 25 Lion Street, Hay-on-Wye, Herefordshire HR3 5AD
> ☎ 0870 787 2848
> 💻 www.hayfestival.com

Company Description: An international festival production company celebrating great writing in every medium in Britain and around the world. Hay is a tiny market town in the Brecon Beacons National Park. It has 1,500 people and 41 bookshops. The Festival is a spectacular holiday party for people to enjoy their tastes for literature, food, drink, comedy, music, art and argument.

Job Description: Volunteer festival stewards required to make sure both the authors and the audience are safe and happy, before, during and after each event. Stewards work in teams of 4 to 10 people. Stewards receive free entry to any talk, although the work must come first.

Accommodation: Accommodation is provided at a local campsite, for a small charge.

Application Procedure: Applications should be made via the website from April. Overseas applicants are welcome to apply but must have a very high standard of spoken English.

Oxfam Stewards

Job(s) Available: Festival stewards (up to 5,000).

Duration: The festivals run from June to September.

Working Hours: Stewards are required to work a minimum of 3 shifts per festival. Shifts last 8 hours.

Pay: Applicants are asked to pay a deposit (£155 in 2007) at the beginning of the summer, which is returned once all stewarding duties are completed. In return, stewards receive free entrance to the festival, a meal ticket for every shift worked, and a separate camping area with toilets and showers.

> **Head Office:** Brunswick Court, Brunswick Square, Bristol BS2 8PE
> ☎ 01179 166 483
> ✎ stewards@oxfam.org.uk
> ▢ www.oxfam.org.uk/stewards

Company Description: Oxfam has been providing volunteer stewards for music festivals since 1993 and now offer stewarding places at 10 festivals. This service forms part of the Oxfam Events team.

Job Description: Stewarding is about providing a safe environment for everyone at a festival. It usually involves talking to people and answering general enquiries. On occasions, you may be called upon to deal with serious incidents or emergencies. It is vital for the safety and security of a festival that the emergency services have competent stewards that can be relied upon to assist in the effective management of a major incident.

Application Procedure: Applications should be made from February/March. Please visit the website for an application form and further details.

The Times Cheltenham Festival of Literature

Job(s) Available: Festival volunteers (30).

Duration: The work is for 13 days from 8-20 October (the festival running 10-19 October).

Working Hours: The hours at the festival are fairly long, the festival day runs from 10am- midnight.

> **Head Office:** Cheltenham Festivals, 109-111 Bath Road, Cheltenham, Gloucestershire GL53 7LS
> ☎ 01242 775861
> ✎ clair.greenaway@cheltenham.com

Company Description: The Times Cheltenham Festival of Literature will be in its 59th year in 2008 and is the largest and most popular of its kind in Europe. There is a wide range of events including talks and lectures, poetry readings, novelists in conversation, creative writing workshops, exhibitions, discussions and a literary festival for children.

Job Description: Festival volunteers are required to look after both the authors and the audience as well as helping with the setting up of events, front of house duties, looking after the office and assisting the sound crew.

Requirements: Applicants should be graduates over 18, with an interest in literature, arts administration or events management.

Accommodation: Volunteers are given free accommodation, travel expenses and food and drink. Free entry to all events is also provided.

Application Procedure: By post to Clair Greenaway, festival manager, from May onwards to the above address. Overseas applicants are welcome but must be over 21 and must have a very high standard of spoken and written English.

Fundraising and Office Work

Oxfam

Job(s) Available: Volunteering programmes.

Pay: Oxfam reimburses reasonable local travel and lunch expenses.

Company Description: Oxfam runs a number of different volunteering programmes including volunteering in the shop network.

Job Description: For those interested in a career with Oxfam, volunteering is an excellent way to gain relevant experience and to get to know the organisation.

Additional Information: Call into your local shop for more details. Oxfam also advertises more specialised volunteer vacancies on its website at www.oxfam.org.uk/what_you_can_do/volunteer/latest.htm, all of which are UK based, and many of which are at its head office in Oxford. Follow the instructions from recruiting managers. Email the above address with any general questions or queries. See www.oxfam.org.uk/interns for more information.

Application Procedure: Further information is available from givetime@oxfam.org.uk, internship@oxfam.org.uk or call into your local Oxfam shop.

> **Head Office:** Oxfam House, John Smith Drive, Oxford OX4 2JY
> ☎ 01865 473 259
> givetime@oxfam.org.uk
> www.oxfam.org.uk/what_you_can_do/volunteer/index.htm

Heritage

Alexander Fleming Laboratory Museum

Job(s) Available: Volunteer guides.

Duration: In addition the museum offers a summer placement working as a volunteer in the archives of St Mary's Hospital and as a guide, offering experience in archives and museums.

Working Hours: *Volunteer guides:* hours from 10am to 1pm from Monday to Thursday. *Summer placement:* hours from 10 am to 5pm from Monday to Friday.

Company Description: The museum has been designated an International Historic Chemical Landmark and visitors come from all over the world.

Job Description: *Volunteer guides:* needed all year round to conduct visitors around the Alexander Fleming Laboratory Museum, which is based on a reconstruction of the laboratory in which Fleming discovered penicillin. The job includes making a short presentation and retail duties in a small museum shop.

Requirements: Full training will be supplied: knowledge of the subject matter is not required. Minimum age of 16.

Additional Information: The museum lacks disabled access. Situated close to Paddington Station, with good transport links.

Application Procedure: By post to Kevin Brown, trust archivist and museum curator.

> **Head Office:** St Mary's Hospital, Praed Street, London W2 1NY
> ☎ 020 7886 6528
> kevin.brown@st-marys.nhs.uk
> www.st-marys.org.uk/about/fleming_museum.htm

Ffestiniog Railway Company

Job(s) Available: Volunteers.
Duration: Throughout the year.
Job Description: Hundreds of volunteers are needed to help in the operation and maintenance of a 150-year old narrow gauge railway between Porthmadog and Blaenau Ffestiniog. The work done by individual volunteers depends on their skills,

Head Office: Harbour Station, Porthmadog, Gwynedd, North Wales LL49 9NF
☎ 01766 516035
tricia.doyle@festrail.co.uk
www.festrail.co.uk

many of which are built up over a period of regular commitment to the railway which provides on-the-job training. The railway is divided into various diverse departments, and so jobs range from selling tickets and souvenirs to the 'elite' task of driving the engines.
Requirements: Railway enthusiasts and non-enthusiasts of any nationality may apply provided they speak a good standard of English. Minimum age of 16 years.
Accommodation: Limited self-catering accommodation is provided for regular volunteers, for which a small charge is made. Food is extra. Camping space and a list of local accommodation is also available.
Application Procedure: Further information may be obtained from the Volunteers Resource Manager, Ffestiniog Railway Company.

House of Dun

Job(s) Available: Volunteers.
Duration: Period of work is from June to September.
Pay: Opportunity for both paid and voluntary work.
Company Description: Beautiful Georgian mansion dating from 1730 and designed by William Adam.

Head Office: House of Dun by Montrose, Angus DD10 9LQ
☎ 01674 810264
iturner@nts.org.uk
www.nts.org.uk

Job Description: Volunteers required to conduct guided tours and for gardening duties.
Accommodation: Free accommodation may be available.
Application Procedure: By post to Ingrid Turner, area manager, at the above address.

Kentwell Hall

Job(s) Available: Volunteer Tudors (700).
Duration: Annual re-creation of Tudor life takes place for 3 weeks during June and July. Most volunteers stay 1 or 2 weeks from May/June to August/September.

Head Office: Long Melford, Sudbury, Suffolk CO10 9BA
☎ 01787 310207
info@kentwell.co.uk
www.kentwell.co.uk

Working Hours: To work 6 days a week.
Company Description: A privately owned Tudor mansion, situated in park and farmland, approximately 1.5 miles from the historic town of Long Melford. Up to 1,500 schoolchildren visit on weekdays and the public at weekends.
Job Description: Volunteer Tudors needed for historical re-creations and for other smaller events throughout the year. Duties consist of demonstrating 16th century life and activities to visiting schoolchildren and the public.
Requirements: Take 16th century skills or learn them there. All ages and nationalities welcome. Applicants can be of any age; an interest in the 16th century would be helpful.

Accommodation: All meals, evening entertainment and space on campsite provided for volunteers only.

Applications Procedure: Applicants should email CV in January/February at the above address.

Lundy Company

Job(s) Available: Volunteer positions.

Duration: Volunteers are required from April to October and positions are available for 1 week.

Company Description: Lundy is an island off the North Devon coast managed by the Landmark Trust with 23 letting properties, a pub and a shop.

Head Office: Lundy Island, Bideford, North Devon EX39 2LY
☎ 01271 863636
📧 warden@lundyisland.co.uk
🖳 www.lundyisland.co.uk

Job Description: There are various positions available involving conservation or general island duties. The jobs are variable according to the time of year.

Requirements: Volunteers need no experience but must have lots of enthusiasm.

Accommodation: Basic, self-catering accommodation is provided free of charge and there is a reduced fare on boat trips.

Application Procedure: By post to the warden at the above address from January onwards.

Mid Hants Railway (Watercress Line)

Job(s) Available: Volunteers.

Duration: Both full-time and part-time positions. Staff are required from May to September for a minimum of 2 months.

Company Description: A preserved steam railway running trains between Alresford and Alton.

Head Office: Railway Station, Alresford, Hampshire SO24 9JG
☎ 01962 733810
📧 info@watercressline.co.uk
🖳 www.watercressline.co.uk

Job Description: Tourism students are particularly encouraged to apply, and there is the possibility of work for engineering students.

Application Procedure: By post to volunteer recruitment at the above address from the beginning of February.

River Stour Trust

Job(s) Available: Volunteer tea room helpers (6), volunteer event helpers (20), working party volunteers (20), Volunteer marketing/fund-raising advisors (2), boat crew volunteers (10), volunteer boat maintenance and engineers (2).

Head Office: The Granary, Quay Lane, Sudbury, Suffolk CO10 2AN
☎ 01787 313199
📧 administrator@rst1968.fsnet.co.uk
🖳 www.riverstourtrust.org

Duration: Voluntary positions available mainly in the summer season although there may be some in the winter and autumn. *Volunteer boat maintenance and engineers:* needed all year round.

Working Hours: *Volunteer tea room helpers*: to work Sundays and bank holidays. *Volunteer event helpers:* to work mainly Sundays and bank holidays. *Working party volunteers:* to work weekdays and weekends as required. *Volunteer marketing/fund-raising advisors:* to work when required. *Boat crew volunteers:* to work weekdays and weekends.

Company Description: The River Stour Trust is a charity dedicated to restoring and conserving the Essex/Suffolk River Stour navigation, by raising funds to rebuild locks, provide other navigation enhancements and encourage leisure boating.

Job Description: *Volunteer boat maintenance and engineers*: to help with electric launches.

Requirements: *Volunteer tea room helpers:* minimum age 18. *Volunteer event helpers:* full training given for each situation. *Working party volunteers:* skilled and unskilled applicants required. Full training given for each situation. *Volunteer marketing/fund-raising advisors*: must have successful track record in these areas. *Boat crew volunteers:* will be trained by charity and must meet appropriate standards.*Volunteer boat maintenance and engineers:* volunteers must have knowledge of electric boat engines and design. All volunteers welcome but fluent English is essential for dealing with the public.

Application Procedure: By post to the trust administrator at the above address. Interview required.

The Alice Trust

Job(s) Available: Volunteer gardeners. Other volunteer opportunities (including room wardens, gardeners, weekday and first Sunday of every month, garden guides, aviary assistants, raffle ticket sellers, buggy drivers, event assistants) may sometimes be available within the Collection.

> **Head Office:** Waddesdon Manor, Aylesbury, Buckinghamshire HP18 0JH
> ☎ 01296 653307
> liz.wilkinson@nationaltrust.org.uk
> www.waddesdon.org.uk

Duration: A limited number of full-time residential places are available, normally for a period of up to 6 months.

Company Description: Waddesdon Manor, a National Trust property, is a magnificent French Renaissance-style chateau, home to the Rothschild Collection of 18th century French furniture and decorative arts, with acclaimed Victorian gardens.

Job Description: Volunteer gardeners required for a diverse range of maintenance tasks, alongside the team of professional gardeners.

Requirements: Commitment and reasonable fitness are required and experience is preferred but not essential.

Accommodation: Rent-free accommodation and some assistance with food expenses may be available.

Application Procedure: By post with CV and references to Liz Wilkinson (ref SJ7) at the above address. Overseas applicants are considered, however, a good standard of English is required. Early application advised.

The Cleveland Ironstone Mining Museum

Job(s) Available: Museum guides (6+), visitor receptionists (2+), collection care (2+).

Working Hours: Museum is open Monday to Saturday. Minimum period of work is 4 hours per week.

> **Head Office:** Deepdale, Skinningrove, Saltburn, Cleveland TS13 4AP
> ☎ 01287 642877
> visits@ironstonemuseum.co.uk
> www.ironstonemuseum.co.uk

Pay: Expenses only are paid.

Company Description: The Cleveland Ironstone Mining Museum preserves and interprets the ironstone mining heritage of Cleveland and North Yorkshire. This is a unique, award-winning, small, independent museum run by volunteers on a day-to-day basis.

Requirements: Applicants should be interested in local history and heritage. Minimum age 16.

Accommodation: No accommodation available.

Application Procedure: By post all year round to the museum manager at the above address. Interview preferred.

Waterway Recovery Group

Job(s) Available: Volunteers.

Duration: Work is available year round; minimum period of work one day.

Working Hours: To work either on weekends or weeklong canal camps.

Company Description: The national coordinating body for voluntary labour on the inland waterways of Great Britain.

Head Office: PO Box 114, Rickmansworth, Hertfordshire WD3 1ZY
☎ 01923 711114
✆ enquiries@wrg.org.uk
🖥 www.wrg.org.uk

Job Description: Volunteers needed to restore Britain's derelict canals: work may involve restoring industrial archaeology, demolishing old brickwork, driving a dumper truck, clearing mud and vegetation and helping at a National Waterways festival.

Requirements: No experience or qualifications are necessary but volunteers should be between the ages of 18 and 70.

Accommodation: Accommodation and food provided for £42 per week/£6 per day.

Application Procedure: By post to the enquiries officer at the above address. Overseas applicants welcome, but must be over 21.

Wirksworth Heritage Centre

Job(s) Available: Voluntary general museum assistant.

Duration: Minimum period of work of 1 month. Positions are available all year.

Working Hours: To be arranged.

Company Description: The Centre is a small regis-

Head Office: Crown Yard, Wirksworth, Derbyshire DE4 4ET
☎ 01629 825225
✆ enquiries@storyofwirksworth.co.uk
🖥 www.storyofwirksworth.co.uk

tered museum telling the story of a small, formerly very important town in Derbyshire. The 'Wirksworth Story' in a former silk mill offers information about local customs and social history. A small gallery exhibits and sells the work of local artists, ceramicists, sculptors and photographers.

Job Description: Ideal post for a museum studies student.

Requirements: Must be able to communicate confidently with the public, be pro-active and enthusiastic and able to help with all aspects of running a small museum. Knowledge of museum documentation systems useful.

Accommodation: No accommodation available.

Application Procedure: By post to Mrs M Vaughan at the above address. Interview necessary.

Physically/Mentally Disabled

Beannachar

Job(s) Available: Volunteers.

Duration: Minimum work period 2 months between June and September, 1 year for long-term volunteers.

Working Hours: To work long hours, 6 days a week.

Company Description: Beannachar is one of the Camphill communities in which vulnerable children

Head Office: Banchory-Devenick, Aberdeen AB12 5YL
☎ 01224 869138
✆ elisabeth@beannachar.org
🖥 www.beannachar.co.uk

and adults can live, learn and work with others in healthy social relationships based on mutual care and respect. Beannachar is a training community for teenagers and young adults with learning disabilities.

Job Description: Volunteers are needed for household, workshop, garden and farm duties.

Requirements: Minimum age 19. Must have lots of enthusiasm and a positive attitude. Overseas applicants must speak fluent English.

Accommodation: Free board and lodging plus pocket money provided.

Application Procedure: By post at any time to Ms EA Phethean at the above address.

Independent Living Alternatives

Job(s) Available: Volunteers.

Duration: Vacancies arise all year round.

Pay: Volunteers receive £63.50 per week.

Job Description: Volunteers required to provide support for people with disabilities, to enable them to live independently in their own homes. The work involves helping them get dressed, go to the toilet, drive, do the housework, and so on. ILA offers a chance to learn about disability issues and see London at the same time.

> **Head Office:** Trafalgar House, Grenville Place, London NW7 3SA
> ☎ 020 8906 9265
> ✉ enquiry@ILAnet.co.uk
> 🖥 www.ILAnet.co.uk

Requirements: No qualifications required, except good English.

Accommodation: Free accommodation, usually in the London area or in Cumbria.

Application Procedure: By post to Tracey Jannaway at the above address.

Kith & Kids

Job(s) Available: Volunteers.

Duration: Minimum period of work 2 consecutive weeks in late July/early August or a week at Christmas/Easter. There is also a 3-day training course before each project.

> **Head Office:** The Irish Centre, Pretoria Road, London N17 8DX
> ☎ 020 8801 7432
> ✉ projects@kithandkids.org.uk
> 🖥 www.kithandkids.org.uk

Working Hours: 9.30am–5pm daily.

Company Description: A self-help organisation that provides support for families of children with a physical or learning disability.

Job Description: Volunteers needed to take part in social development schemes working with disabled children and young people, helping them with everyday skills and community integration.

Requirements: Minimum age 16. No experience necessary, but lots of enthusiasm essential.

Accommodation: No accommodation available. Lunch and travel expenses within Greater London provided.

Additional Information: The organisation does also run a one-week camping holiday in the second half of August with accommodation for volunteers.

Application Procedure: For further details contact the volunteer organiser at the above address.

Riding for the Disabled Association

Job(s) Available: Volunteer helpers.

Duration: Volunteers are needed for a minimum of 3 days between May and September.

Working Hours: Providing 24 hour care and supervision for between 3 and 7 days.

> **Head Office:** Lavinia Norfolk House, Avenue R, Stoneleigh Park, Warwickshire CV8 2LY
> ☎ 0845 658 1082
> ✉ info@rda.org.uk
> 🖥 www.rda.org.uk

Company Description: The RDA is a registered charity consisting of more than 500 member groups throughout the UK. Providing holidays for disabled people is one of the many services it offers to its members.

Job Description: Volunteer helpers are required to help on RDA holidays throughout the summer months.

Requirements: Knowledge of horse riding is preferable along with a first aid/medical qualification and work experience with disabled people. Minimum age 16.

Accommodation: Living expenses are provided along with free accommodation at some venues.

Application Procedure: To apply and for details of the holidays being run, contact the above address from January. Suitably qualified foreign applicants are welcome.

Speyside Trust

Job(s) Available: Volunteer care assistants (2 per week), seasonal care assistant/instructor.

Duration: April to October. *Volunteer care assistants:* for 2 or more weeks.

Working Hours: Volunteers are expected to work 10 hours per day with 2 days off a week. *Seasonal care assistant/instructor:* to work 40 hours over 5 days a week, with 2 evenings off a week.

Head Office: Badaguish Outdoor Centre, Aviemore, Inverness-shire PH22 1QU
☎ 01479 861285
✆ silvie.m@badaguish.org
🖳 www.badaguish.org

Pay: *Seasonal care assistant/instructor:* £15,000 to £17,000 pro rata. *Volunteer care assistants:* £30 pocket money per week.

Company Description: The Centre specialises in outdoor recreation holidays for children and adults with learning or multiple disabilities. Clients enjoy various adventure activities and 24-hour respite care in a spectacular setting. Badaguish is 7 miles out of Aviemore in the Greenmore Forest Park; nearest shops are 2 miles away in Glenmore. Volunteers must enjoy the outdoors and take part in all activities offered.

Job Description: *Volunteer care assistants:* to work with people with special needs.

Requirements: *Volunteer care assistants:* no qualifications necessary but applicants must want to work outdoors with people with special needs. Applicants must have experience of working with people and experience of special needs. They must also enjoy the outdoors. Minimum age 18.

Accommodation: Accommodation available at the centre in a chalet or caravan at no charge. Food is provided while on duty.

Application Procedure: For more information and applications write to Silvie Mackenzie at the above address from January onwards. Foreign applicants with related qualifications in care, nursing, social work or physiotherapy welcome.

The 3H Fund

Job(s) Available: Volunteers (approximately 90).

Duration: Holidays are usually for 1 week and take place between May and September.

Company Description: The fund organises subsidised group holidays for physically disabled children and adults with the support of volunteer carers, thus affording a period of respite for regular carers.

Head Office: 147a Camden Road, Tunbridge Wells, Kent TN1 2RA
☎ 01892 547474
✆ info@3hfund.org.uk
🖳 www.3hfund.org.uk

Job Description: Volunteers are asked to provide as much help as they feel comfortable with. This could range from assisting with cutting up a guest's food, to helping with lifting and pushing a wheelchair. Full training is provided. Each holiday has an experienced leader, co-leader and nurse as well as other supportive volunteers.

Requirements: A caring nature, the willingness to ensure that a disabled guest has an enjoyable holiday and the ability to cooperate as a team member are essential qualities. Minimum age 17. Applicants must have a reasonable level of physical fitness.

Accommodation: Board and lodging are provided in venues such as holiday centres but a financial contribution (50% for students) is requested. Advice can be given on raising this by sponsorship.

Application Procedure: By post to Lynne Loving at the above address as soon as possible for further information.

Vitalise (formerly Winged Fellowship Trust)

Job(s) Available: Volunteers.
Duration: Needed for 1 or 2 weeks at a time.
Company Description: Vitalise is a leading UK charity providing holidays for disabled people and breaks for carers.

Head Office: Shap Road, Kendal, Cumbria LA9 6NZ
☎ 0845 330 0148
volunteer@vitalise.org.uk
www.vitalise.org.uk

Job Description: Volunteers to help trained staff enhance the holiday atmosphere for the guests. Holidays are available at purpose-built centres in Essex, Nottingham, Cornwall, Southport and Southampton, where guests can enjoy a break with or without their regular carer.

Accommodation: Volunteers are provided with free accommodation and meals in exchange for their time.

Application Procedure: For an application form please contact the team at the above address. Overseas applicants with good English welcome.

Woodlarks Camp Site Trust

Job(s) Available: Volunteer carers/enablers.
Duration: Camps are held weekly from May to September. Volunteers are normally taken on for one camp lasting a week, though some help on more.
Company Description: Woodlarks Camp Site Trust provides a setting for people of all ages with disabil-

Head Office: Kathleen Marshall House, Tilford Road, Farnham, Surrey GU10 3RN
☎ 01252 716279
enquiries@woodlarks.org.uk
www.woodlarks.org.uk

ities to expand their capabilities and have fun. This small-scale camping site and woodland activity area has facilities including a heated outdoor swimming pool, an aerial runway, a trampoline, archery and more. A dining/recreation room, disabled-friendly toilet block and some indoor sleeping accommodation are alongside the camping area. Woodlarks is staffed and maintained entirely by volunteers.

Job Description: Six open camps accept individual disabled campers and require volunteer carers/enablers.

Accommodation: Tent accommodation provided. Helpers and disabled campers pay a modest fee to cover the cost of food, outings.

Application Procedure: Written applications to the honorary secretary, Kathleen Marshall House, at the above address, enclosing an s.a.e or international reply coupon.

Social and Community Schemes

Concordia

Job(s) Available: Volunteers working on community-based projects.

Duration: 2–4 weeks with a main season running from June to September, although there are some spring and autumn projects. Volunteers can also apply for long term volunteer projects through the EVS programme.

Cost: Volunteers pay a registration fee of approximately £150 for UK projects and must fund their own travel and insurance.

Company Description: Concordia is a small not-for-profit charity committed to international youth exchange. Its International Volunteer Programme offers young people the opportunity to join an international team of volunteers working on community-based projects ranging from nature conservation, restoration and construction to more socially based schemes.

Requirements: In general no special skills or experience are required but real motivation and commitment are essential.

Accommodation: Board and accommodation are available free of charge.

Additional Information: Concordia also recruits volunteers (20+) to act as Group Coordinators on UK based projects, for which training is provided and all expenses are paid. This training takes place in spring each year. Early application is advised.

Application Procedure: Applications should normally be made to the above address. Details of all projects can be found on the website from March/April. Please note that overseas applicants must apply through a voluntary organisation in their own country; if necessary Concordia can pass on details of partner organisations.

> **Head Office:** 19 North Street, Portslade, Brighton, East Sussex BN41 1DH
> ☎ 01273 422218
> info@concordia-iye.org.uk
> www.concordia-iye.org.uk

Hackney Independent Living Team

Job(s) Available: Independent living support volunteers (30).

Duration: Minimum period of work 4 months at any time of the year.

Working Hours: To provide 35 hours per week support on a shift basis.

Company Description: Helps adults with learning disabilities in Hackney to live in the community as independently as possible, and to continue to develop their independence and personal identity. Based in north east London.

> **Head Office:** Richmond House, 1a Westgate Street, London E8 3RL
> ☎ 020 898 555 11
> ☎ 020 851 054 52 (volunteer hotline)
> volunteers@hilt.org.uk
> shane@hilt.org.uk
> www.hilt.org.uk

Job Description: Volunteers may be involved in all projects and activities of HILT. Some of the ways in which volunteers have supported service users include sports, leisure and social activities, arranging and accompanying on holidays and in assessing education and training opportunities. Volunteers support service users in personal development and achieving goals.

Requirements: Applicants must be committed to enabling people with learning difficulties to have as much control over their lives as possible. They should also help provide a service which reflects the cultural, racial and religious needs of service users, and promote anti-discriminatory practice. They should have a willingness to understand service users' emotional needs, and attend regular meetings with supervisors and staff and communicate ideas and suggestions. Minimum age 18.

Accommodation: Living allowance of £60 per week, plus weekly zones 1-2 Travelcard and free accommodation. All volunteers have their own furnished room, including all bills apart from telephone. Food allowance is incorporated into weekly allowance.

Application Procedure: By post as far in advance of intended start date as possible to the volunteer co-ordinator. Overseas applicants must have a good level of conversational English, and the right to enter the UK. Interview necessary.

Great Georges Community Cultural Project/The Blackie

Job(s) Available: Volunteering opportunities.
Duration: Volunteers are expected to stay for at least 4 weeks. Volunteers are welcome throughout the year and particularly over the summer, winter and spring holiday periods.

Head Office: Great Georges Project/The Blackie, Great George Street, Liverpool L1 5EW
☎ 01517 095109
staff@theblackie.org.uk
www.theblackie.org

Working Hours: Wonderfully long hours.
Company Description: The Blackie is celebrating its 40th anniversary in May 2008.

Job Description: Volunteering opportunities for anyone to try alternative education and the arts together with some sport, recreation and welfare in an inner-city context. The programme of youth work, crafts and games; workshops with local youngsters; staging exhibitions and events; projects from cookery to contemporary and African dance, from photography to fashion on a local, regional, national and occasionally international level at home base and on tour will resume in 2008 following a major building programme. Endless opportunities to learn and unlearn, to teach and to create.

Requirements: Minimum age 18. Volunteers are expected to provide their own food costs.
Accommodation: Accommodation provided.
Application Procedure: For further information write to the duty office at 40 Canning Street, Liverpool L8 7NP until April 08, after that at the above address.

Iona Community

Job(s) Available: Volunteers.
Duration: Between 6 and 12 weeks between March and November.

Head Office: Iona Abbey, Isle of Iona, Argyll PA76 6SN
☎ 01681 700404
staffing.office@iona.org.uk
www.iona.org.uk

Working Hours: 5.5 days a week.
Pay: Pocket money of around £30 per week.
Company Description: An ecumenical Christian Community sharing work, worship, meals and programme with guests visiting the Macleod and Abbey centres on Iona, and Camas, the more basic outdoors centre on nearby Mull. Guests come and stay for a week to take part in the common life of work, worship and programme.

Job Description: Volunteers work in the kitchen, shop and office, help with driving, maintenance, housekeeping and with the children's craft work activities programme.

Requirements: Volunteers should be in sympathy with the Christian faith and the ideals of the Iona Community. Minimum age 18.

Accommodation: Full board and lodging and travelling expenses within the UK.

Application Procedure: For details and applications write to the administration team leader at the above address, enclosing a stamped addressed envelope if applying by post. Overseas applicants with a working knowledge of English are welcome. Recruitment begins in the autumn.

L'Arche

Job(s) Available: Volunteer assistants.
Duration: Assistants required all year, usually for 12 months, though shorter periods of time possible.
Pay: Volunteers receive £43 per week.
Company Description: Seeks to reveal the particular gifts of people with learning disabilities who

Head Office: 10 Briggate Silsden, Keighley, West Yorkshire BD20 9JT
☎ 01535 656186
info@larche.org.uk
www.larche.org.uk

belong at the very heart of their communities and who call others to share their lives. There are L'Arche communities in Kent, Inverness, Ipswich, Liverpool, Lambeth, Bognor, Brecon, Edinburgh and Preston where people with and without learning disabilities share life in ordinary houses.
Job Description: Volunteer assistants required to share life and work with people with learning disabilities in an ecumenical Christian-based community.
Requirements: Minimum age 18.
Accommodation: Free board and lodging.
Application Procedure: By post to the above address. After completing the application form candidates are invited to visit the community and interviews are held. Overseas applicants in possession of the necessary work visas are welcome.

Lee Abbey Community

Job(s) Available: Volunteers.
Duration: Minimum stay is 3 months.
Pay: Pocket money provided.
Company Description: A Christian conference, retreat and holiday centre on the north Devon coast, run by a 90-stong international community with a vision to renew and serve the church.

Head Office: Personnel, Lee Abbey, Lynton, Devon EX35 6JJ
☎ 01598 752621
personnel@leeabbey.org.uk
www.leeabbey.org.uk

Requirements: Volunteers must be committed Christians. No qualifications necessary. Minimum age 18.
Accommodation: Board and lodging provided.
Application Procedure: Applications should be made using the application form obtainable from the above address. Foreign applicants with fluent English welcome.

The Lilias Graham Trust

Job(s) Available: Volunteers.
Duration: Required throughout the year to work for a minimum of 6 months.
Working Hours: 40 hour week.
Pay: £40 pocket money.
Job Description: Volunteers required at a short stay

Head Office: Braendam Family House, Thornhill, Stirling FK8 3QH
☎ 01786 850259
cathmorrison@braendam.org.uk
www.braendam.org.uk

family house for disadvantaged families experiencing poverty. Tasks include direct support to families, participating in trips and outings, domestic chores, driving, organising children's activities and play and generally responding to the needs of families.
Requirements: Minimum age 18. Applicants must be willing to work long days and to carry out domestic chores and maintain enthusiasm and energy for supporting families in need. A clean driving licence would be an advantage.
Accommodation: Full board provided. Most accommodation is in a single room although it may be necessary to share.

Additional Information: Volunteers are entitled to holidays, use of house car and bicycles for a small charge, and access to internet/email, again for a small charge. Volunteers will also have the opportunity to explore Scotland on days off.

Application Procedure: Applications to Cath Morrison, chief executive, at the above postal or email address.

The Prince's Trust

Job(s) Available: Volunteers.
Duration: 12 week course.
Company Description: The Prince's Trust is the UK's leading youth charity. It helps young people overcome barriers and get their lives working.

> **Head Office:** 18 Park Square East, London NW1 4LH
> ☎ 020 7543 1234
> ✎ webinfops@princes-trust.org.uk
> 🖥 www.princes-trust.org.uk

Job Description: Volunteers for the Team programme, enabling young people to develop essential life skills of benefit to future employment. Some 10,000 people take part each year. The programme involves team building activities, an outdoor residential week away, work experience and projects in the community. They take place in over 300 different locations throughout the UK.

Application Procedure: For further information call the above number or visit the website.

Toc H

Job(s) Available: Project work.
Duration: Throughout the year in Britain, lasting usually from a weekend up to 2 weeks.
Company Description: Toc H offers short residential volunteering opportunities.

> **Head Office:** The Stable Block, The Firs, High Street, Whitchurch, Aylesbury, Buckinghamshire HP22 4JU
> ☎ 01296 642 020
> ✎ info@toch.org.uk
> 🖥 www.toch.org.uk

Job Description: Project work undertaken can include: work with people with different disabilities; work with children in need; playschemes and camps; conservation and manual work. These projects provide those who take part with opportunities to learn more about themselves and the world we live in.

Requirements: Minimum age 16. There is no upper age limit.

Additional Information: The Toc H events programme is published yearly and can be viewed on their website.

Application Procedure: There is no closing date for applications.

Workcamps

ATD Fourth World

Job(s) Available: Voluntary artists, craftsmen.
Duration: The camps, street workshops and family stays take place from July to September. Most last 2 weeks.

> **Head Office:** 48 Addington Square, London SE5 7LB
> ☎ 020 7703 3231
> ✎ atd@Atd-uk.org
> 🖥 www.atd-fourthworld.org

Company Description: ATD Fourth World is an international voluntary organisation which adopts a human rights approach to overcome extreme poverty. It supports the effort of very disadvantaged and excluded families in fighting poverty and taking an active role in the community. Founded in a shanty town on the outskirts of Paris in 1957, it now works in 27 countries on 5 continents.

Job Description: ATD Fourth World organises workcamps, street workshops and family stays in London and Surrey in the UK and other European countries. The workcamps are a combination of manual work in and around ATD's buildings and conversation and reflection on the lives and hopes of families living in extreme poverty and on the aims and objectives of the organisation. The street workshops bring a festival atmosphere to underprivileged areas. Voluntary artists, craftsmen share their skills with the children and their parents. These street workshops for painting, crafts, computing and books etc. take place in the streets of deprived areas and make it possible to break down barriers allowing freedom of expression and building confidence. The family stays allow families split up by poverty, perhaps with children in care, to come together for a break. The volunteers assist ATD Fourth World workers to give the families a holiday to grow together and learn new skills.

Accommodation: Participants pay their own travel costs plus a contribution to the cost of food and accommodation. ATD is willing to take on foreign applicants.

Application Procedure: For further information volunteers should see the ATD international website, or for UK opportunities, contact the above address.

International Voluntary Service (IVS)

Job(s) Available: Volunteers.

Duration: Work for 2–4 weeks. Most projects run between April and October. Some winter and long-term opportunities are available.

Company Description: IVS is the British branch of Service Civil International (SCI), a peace organisation working for international understanding and cooperation through voluntary work. IVS organises some 25 projects in Britain each year as well as sending volunteers to projects in 45 countries overseas.

> **Head Office:** IVS-GB England, Oxford Place Centre, Oxford Place, Leeds LS1 3AX
> ☎ 01132 469900
> ⌂ england@ivs-gb.org.uk
>
> **Head Office:** IVS-Scotland, 7 Upper Bow, Edinburgh EH1 2JN
> ☎ 01312 266722
> ⌂ Scotland@ivs-gb.org.uk
> 🖥 www.ivs-gb.org.uk

Job Description: Volunteers in an international team of 6 to 20 people, living and working together. The project types include work with children, disabilities, disadvantaged, peace, anti-racism, environment and arts and culture.

Requirements: Volunteers must be over 18 to go abroad, or 16 for projects in the UK.

Accommodation: Volunteers pay their own travel costs and a registration fee (abroad £185/£145, in UK £95/£50), which includes annual membership. Accommodation and food are provided by the project.

Application Procedure: For more information, contact one of the regional addresses above. The listing of summer projects is available from April on the website and in brochure form. Applicants from overseas should apply for IVS Projects through partner organisations in their own country, see www.sciint.org for a full list of offices.

Pilgrim Adventure

Job(s) Available: Volunteer team members.

Duration: Team members should be able to co-lead at least one Pilgrim Journey of about 7 days each year, and take an active part in the planning of Pilgrim Journeys throughout the year.

> **Head Office:** South Winds, Culver Park, Tenby, Pembrokeshire SA70 7ED
> ☎ 01834 844212
> ⌂ pilgrim.adventure@virgin.net
> 🖥 www.pilgrim-adventure.org.uk

Company Description: An ecumenical Christian organisation founded in 1987. Provides an annual programme of Christian journeys in small, informal groups to places on the edge – island, hill, shore. Most journeys take place in Britain and Ireland.

Job Description: Volunteer team members to help lead all age groups of 8 to 15 people taking part in Pilgrim Adventure's annual programme of Christian Journeys within Britain and Ireland.

Requirements: Training will be provided. Applicants must have a sense of adventure and Christian commitment.

Accommodation: Staying in hostels, monasteries, tents and small hotels.

Application Procedure: By post to Mr David Gleed at the above address.

Websites

www.fruitfuljobs.com

Job(s) Available: Seasonal work for backpackers and permanent positions for those looking to develop a career in the UK (anything from farm managers to logistics assistants). The seasonal work

077 400 865 55
info@fruitfuljobs.com
www.fruitfuljobs.com

Fruitful can offer on UK/European farms and within the produce industry includes working as field, packhouse and camp supervisors, quality controllers, drivers, pickers, packers, production operatives and tractor drivers.

Duration: Jobs can be from a few weeks to 12 months. Peak employment is from March until October, but work is available throughout the year.

Accommodation: The majority of seasonal jobs have cheap accommodation available; they are out of the city and in the countryside, giving the opportunity to earn some money.

Additional Information: The workforces are multi-national which is great for the social side of things and also means that the growers have plenty of experience employing overseas travellers.

Application Procedure: Please see www.fruitfuljobs.com or call 077 400 865 55.

www.seasonal-jobs.com

Job(s) Available: Summer jobs, cruise ships and yachts, ski resort and winter jobs, gap years, hospitality and leisure.

Head Office: 6 Vine Close, Welwyn Garden City, Hertfordshire AL8 7PS
020 3006 2608
info@seasonal-jobs.com
www.seasonal-jobs.com

Duration: *Summer jobs:* jobs from April to October. *Cruise Ships and Yachts:* jobs available around the year. Varied contracts.

Working Hours: *Summer jobs:* to usually work a 6 day week. *Ski Resort and Winter Jobs:* to work a 6 day week.

Pay: *Summer jobs:* start at £50 per week. *Cruise Ships and Yachts:* from £500 a month. *Ski Resort and Winter Jobs:* start at £50 per week.

Company Description: A seasonal recruitment website.

Job Description: Positions available in UK and Ireland, across Europe and around the globe. *Summer jobs:* Beach resort/camping/activity/lakes and mountains/barges/flotilla. Vacancies for instructors, nannies, couriers, chefs, bar and hotel staff. *Ski Resort and Winter Jobs:* Ski resort jobs including work in chalets, hotels, bars and ski and snowboard hire retail shops, ski technicians, ski instructors, as reps, ski guides, nannies, resort admin, accounts, sales, resort and area managers. *Gap year:* gap year job ideas for around the globe. Voluntary to TEFL, ski and snowboard instructor courses and useful information and links on gap year activities. *Hospitality and leisure:* other jobs on offer include hotel, restaurant and bar work, theme park jobs, TEFL and fruit picking.

Requirements: Minimum age 18.

Accommodation: *Summer jobs:* with accommodation and transport provided. *Ski Resort and Winter Jobs:* ski pass, transport to resort and accommodation/food provided.

Application Procedure: For further details see www.seasonal-jobs.com.

Au Pair, Home Help and Paying Guest Agencies

Among the types of job to be found in this category are positions for *au pairs, mother's helps, playscheme leaders and paying guests.*

Playschemes. Most local authorities organise playschemes for children during the summer holidays, as a cheaper alternative to private childcare. Throughout the country dozens of playleaders and assistants are needed to run activities for children of all ages. Cash limits mean that some councils ask specifically for volunteers. Councils will usually advertise in local newspapers a few months before the end of the school term, or you can contact their education or leisure departments to find out what they will be offering.

Domestic Work. Anyone preferring closer contact with children should consider working in a family as a mother's help or (for applicants from overseas) as an au pair. This work usually requires some experience and involves light housework and looking after children. Mother's helps and au pairs work to assist the mother, not replace her as a nanny might, and therefore qualifications are not usually necessary. There are many agencies in the UK which specialise in placing home helps. If you prefer to find work independently, job advertisements appear in *The Lady* magazine and occasionally in *Horse and Hound*, both available from newsagents.

A2Z Aupairs

Job(s) Available: Au pairs (20).
Duration: Required in May/June.
Working Hours: To work 25 hours per week
Pay: Pocket money of £60 per week.
Job Description: Looking after children and carrying out light housework.
Requirements: Applicants should be aged between 17 and 27.
Accommodation: Accommodation provided.
Additional Information: Summer jobs in the tourist industry also available.
Application Procedure: By post to Rebecca Haworth-Wood at the above address.

Head Office: Catwell House, Catwell, Williton, Taunton TA4 4PF
☎ 01984 632422
✎ enquiries@a2zaupairs.com
▣ wwwa2zaupairs.com

Abbey Au Pairs

Job(s) Available: Au pair placements.
Duration: Minimum period of work 2 months. Positions are available all year round.
Working Hours: 2/3 evenings per week babysitting. 25 hour week.
Pay: Wages £55 per week.
Company Description: Established in 1988, the agency places girls with families mainly around Bournemouth and Poole. Regular coffee mornings are held and advice is given on language classes and activities.

Head Office: 8 Boulnois Avenue, Parkstone, Poole, Dorset BH14 9NX
☎ 01202 732922
✎ ursula.foyle@ntlworld.com

Job Description: Normal housework and childcare duties.
Accommodation: Full board and lodging available.
Application Procedure: By post at any time to Mrs Ursula Foyle at the above address.

Angels International Au Pairs

Job(s) Available: Au pairs.
Duration: Placements can be anywhere in length from 3 months to 2 years.
Working Hours: To work 25 to 40 hours per week.
Pay: Pocket money between £55 and £150 per week.
Company Description: An au pair agency specialising in placements within the UK as well as abroad.

Head Office: Bristol & West House, Post Office Road, Bournemouth, Dorset BH1 1BL
☎ 01202 313653
✆ earnot@btinternet.com
🖳 www.aupair1.com

Angels International offers full support for both families and au pairs, offering information about language classes.
Requirements: Childcare experience necessary. Applicants applying from abroad pay no fees; applicants wishing to go abroad pay £100 in fees.
Application Procedure: To apply, email the above address.

Au Pair Connections

Job(s) Available: Au pairs and mothers helps (300).
Duration: Period of work mid–June to mid–September; minimum period of work 6 weeks.
Working Hours: To work 25 hours per week or more.
Pay: £60 per week.

Head Office: 39 Tamarisk Road, Hedge End, Hampshire SO30 4TN
☎ 01489 780438
✆ apconnect@ntlworld.com
🖳 www.aupairconnections.co.uk

Company Description: An au pair agency operating in Southern England; some of the loveliest locations in the UK.
Requirements: Must have a minimum of 2 years of childcare experience. Minimum age 18.
Accommodation: Available free of charge.
Application Procedure: By post from January to mid–June to Denise Blighe at the above address. Note that all applicants must enclose either an international reply coupon or s.a.e.

Bloomsbury Au Pairs

Job(s) Available: Au pairs placed in the UK and Ireland from EU countries.
Duration: Placements throughout the year.
Working Hours: 30 hours help with childcare and light housework.
Pay: Pocket money €90 per week.

Head Office: 14 Tottenham Court Road, PO Box 625, London W1T 1JY
☎ 020 3122 0025
✆ bloomsburo@aol.com
🖳 www.bloomsburyaupairs.co.uk

Company Description: This agency has been operating for over 30 years, and every placement is personally supervised by the principal, S Kerwick.
Requirements: EU nationals aged 18–25. EU nationals must have sufficient knowledge of English to communicate with their host families and children and a wish to attend an English language course.
Application Procedure: By post at the above address or online at www.bloomsburyaupairs.co.uk.

County Nannies

Job(s) Available: Au pairs.

Duration: Minimum stay 6 to 12 months, but summer stays of 2 to 3 months also available.

Pay: Pocket money is £60 per week for au pairs, £80 per week for au pair plus.

Job Description: Au pairs placed in the UK.

Head Office: Cherry Gardens, Nouds Lane, Lynsted, Kent ME9 0ES
☎ 01795 522544
info@countynannies.co.uk
www.countynannies.co.uk

Requirements: Applicants should be 17–27 years old, with some childcare experience and childcare references. All nationalities that are within the British au pair scheme can be accepted. Male applicants can also be placed.

Application Procedure: By post to Benedicte Speed, managing director. Country Nannies require 2 to 3 childcare references and 2 character references needed with application. Personal interview held wherever possible.

Euro Pair Agency

Job(s) Available: Au pairs (100+).

Duration: Minimum period of work of 6 months. It is possible to find summer positions but no guarantee is given. Positions are available all year.

Working Hours: 5 hours per day, 5 days a week.

Pay: £65 per week pocket money.

Head Office: 28 Derwent Avenue, Pinner, Middlesex HA5 4QJ
☎ 020 8421 2100
info@europair.net
www.euro-pair.co.uk

Company Description: The agency supplies French speaking au pairs to British families in Great Britain and British au pairs to families in France. Takes great care in the selection of posts available and has a back-up service if things do not work out.

Requirements: Minimum age 18. Childcare experience and driving licence helpful.

Accommodation: Live-in positions.

Application Procedure: By post at any time to Mrs C Burt at the above address. Telephone interview required.

Jolaine Au Pair & Domestic Agency

Job(s) Available: Au pair/plus and mother's help.

Duration: Minimum stay is 6 months. Positions in the UK throughout the year.

Pay: *Mother's help*: from £100 per week. *General helpers*: £160 per week. *Au pair*: £60 per week. *Au pair plus*: £80 per week. Also arranges paying guest

Head Office: 18 Escot Way, Barnet, Hertfordshire EN5 3AN
☎ 020 8449 1334
aupair@jolaine.prestel.co.uk
www.jolaineagency.com

family stays in the London suburbs throughout the year, from £100 per week.

Company Description: Jolaine Agency has been successfully placing applicants in the UK and abroad since 1975 and operates a follow-up system to ensure that all applicants are happy with their stay.

Accommodation: Accommodation available for individuals or groups of any size. Discounts given to groups and extended stays. Visits, excursions, activities and classes arranged on request.

Application Procedure: For further information and application forms write at any time enclosing s.a.e. or an international reply coupon to the above address or email your details.

Jolaine Au Pair & Domestic Agency

Job(s) Available: Paying Guests.

Job Description: Accommodation with British families for foreign students/visitors to the UK wishing to stay as a paying guest.

Application Procedure: For further information please contact Jolaine Agency via telephone/email.

Head Office: 18 Escot Way, Barnet, Hertfordshire EN5 3AN
☎ 020 8449 1334
✎ aupair@jolaine.prestel.co.uk
🖥 www.jolaineagency.com

Nanny & Au Pair Connection

Job(s) Available: Au pairs (70), au pair plus (40), mothers helps, foreign housekeepers, nannies (20).

Duration: From one month to 2 years.

Working Hours: *Au pairs:* for up to 5 hours per day with 2 days off per week. *Au pair plus:* for 35 hours per week plus babysitting 2–3 evenings a week. 2 days free each week. *Nannies:* for 8-9 hours per day.

Head Office: 435 Chorley Road, Horwich, Bolton BL6 6EJ
☎ 01204 694422
✎ info@aupairs-nannies.co.uk
🖥 www.aupairs-nannies.co.uk

Pay: *Au pair:* £60 per week. *Au pair plus:* £80 per week. *Mothers helps:* £150 per week. *Foreign housekeepers:* £200 per week. *Nannies:* £250 per week.

Company Description: Specialist au pairs agency, established since 1989, with opportunities to work with families in Britain and learn languages at a local college or university.

Requirements: All positions open for girls and boys aged 17–27 years old. Au pair plus for EC Nationals only and Nannies minimum age 18. *Nannies:* must have NNEB qualification or similar.

Accommodation: *Au pairs:* own room and meals provided. *Au pair plus:* room and meals provided free of charge.

Additional Information: *Au pairs:* opportunity to have English classes. *Au pair plus:* can sometimes attend English classes.

Application Procedure: Applications welcome from all EC Nationals and Andorra, Bosnia-Herzegovina, Croatia, Cyprus, Faroe Islands, Greenland, Liechtenstein, Macedonia, Malta, Monaco, San Marino, Slovenia, Switzerland and Turkey.

UK Nannies and Au Pairs

Job(s) Available: Au pairs and nannies.

Duration: From 1 month to 2 years.

Working Hours: Between 25 and 60 hours per week.

Pay: From £100–£400 per week; overtime is paid. Applicants are not charged any fees.

Company Description: Support for the au pair/nanny is offered by the company.

Requirements: Minimum age 18.

Application Procedure: Apply by emailing the above address.

Head Office: 19 The Severals, Newmarket CB8 7YW
☎ 01638 560812
✎ jobs@theuknannyagency.co.uk
🖥 www.theuknannyagency.co.uk or www.theukaupairagency.co.uk

Universal Aunts Ltd

Job(s) Available: House keepers, nannies, mothers helps.

Duration: Must be available to sign on with the agency for minimum of 6 months.

Company Description: Established in 1921.

Job Description: House keepers, nannies, mothers helps required, in both residential and non-residential positions.

Additional Information: Please note the agency does not place au pairs.

Application Procedure: By post at any time to Universal Aunts Ltd.

Head Office: PO Box 304, London SW4 0NN
☎ 020 7738 8937
✆ aunts@universalaunts.co.uk
🖥 www.universalaunts.co.uk

EUROPE

EUROPE-WIDE

WESTERN EUROPE

CENTRAL AND EASTERN EUROPE

ORGANISATIONS WITH VACANCIES ACROSS EUROPE

General

Jobcentre Plus

Company Description: Jobcentre Plus handles vacancies for work in the UK and overseas. Vacancies can be accessed through the job search facility on the Jobcentre Plus website or via touch-point screens called Jobpoints, available in all Jobcentre Plus offices and Jobcentres, or by calling Jobseeker Direct on 08456060234.

Head Office: International Jobsearch Advice, Jobcentre Plus Regional Office, Sixth Floor, Whitehall II, Whitehall Quay, Leeds LS1 4HR, UK
☎ 01133 078090
✉ international-jobsearch-advice@jobcentreplus.gsi.gov.uk
🖥 www.jobcentreplus.gov.uk

Additional Information: EURES website (www.eures-jobs.com): as part of the European Employment Services (EURES) network, Jobcentre Plus receives new jobs from Europe on a daily basis. To find out more about the EURES network and to get information about living and working in EEA countries visit the EURES job mobility portal www.europa.eu.int/eures. This site has a job bank of vacancies based in Europe and a facility to post CVs so that employers throughout Europe may view them.

Application Procedure: Check website, or call 0845 606 0234 or visit your nearest Jobcentre Plus office or Jobcentre.

InterExchange

Job(s) Available: Work exchange programmes including work and travel, volunteer, internship, au pair, language school and camp counselor programmes operate within the United States and around the world. In the USA they offer J-1 Visa programs and an H-2B Visa programme for au pairs and

Head Office: 161 Sixth Avenue, New York, NY 10013, USA
☎ +1 212 924 0446
✉ info@interexchange.org
🖥 www.interexchange.org

those undertaking seasonal work, internship, camp counselor and staff positions. Interexchange also offers Working Abroad placements for US residents in Australia, Costa Rica, France, Germany, England, India, Italy, Kenya, Namibia, the Netherlands, Peru, South Africa and Spain working as au pairs, interns, volunteers, seasonal workers and language students.

Company Description: InterExchange is a non-profit organisation dedicated to promoting cultural awareness.

Additional Information: Most interexchange programmes include placements.

Application Procedure: For further details contact InterExchange at the above address.

Boats

European Waterways

Job(s) Available: Cordon Bleu chefs, deckhand mechanics, tour guides, stewards/stewardesses.

Duration: Period of work is from April to October.

Head Office: 35 Wharf Road, Wraysbury, Staines, Middlesex TW19 5JQ, UK
✉ accounts@GoBarging.com
🖥 www.GoBarging.com

Pay: *Cordon bleu chefs:* £1,000-£1,200 per month. *Deckhand mechanics:* £750 per month. *Tour guides:* £750 per month. *Stewards/stewardesses:* £650 per month.

Company Description: Owners and operators of luxury hotel barges cruising rivers and canals in England, Scotland and France.

Job Description: *Stewards/stewardesses:* duties include cleaning, ironing, waiting on.

Requirements: *Cordon bleu chefs:* must have training to Cordon Bleu standard, hold a driving licence. Minimum age 25. *Deckhand mechanics:* must have a driving licence, some mechanical experience. Minimum age 25. *Tour guides:* full clean, driving licence required, an interest in culture and history and some experience in hospitality also necessary. *Stewards/stewardesses:* must be hard working and have some experience in hospitality. A knowledge of French is essential for all positions in France.

Accommodation: All positions include on-board accommodation, meals and uniform.

Application Procedure: Apply, sending a CV and photo, to the above address or email.

Hotel Work and Catering

Scott Dunn

Job(s) Available: Resort managers (12), chalet and villa chefs/cooks (33), chalet and villa hosts (35), nannies (20), beauty therapists (5), drivers/maintenance people (15).

> **Head Office:** Fovant Mews, 12 Noyna Rd, London SW17 7PH, UK
> ☎ 020 8682 5005
> ✆ recruitment@scottdunn.com

Duration: Work is available during the winter and summer season. *Resort managers:* summer only. *Drivers/maintenance people:* available in winter only.

Working Hours: Hours to be discussed at interview.

Pay: To be discussed at interview.

Company Description: A small, very professional company, that provides beautiful villas and chalets in stunning locations all over Europe. Scott Dunn expect on attitude of nothing is too much trouble from their team. They offer a competitive package to the right applicants.

Job Description: *Resort managers:* required to run all aspects of the resort operations in Moilets. *Chalet and villa chefs/cooks:* required to plan the menu and cook for the clients in their exclusive villas and chalets. *Chalet and villa hosts:* required to assist the chef, look after the guests and maintain a high level of service. *Nannies:* required to care for the younger guests. *Beauty therapists:* required to provide mobile beauty services to guests. *Drivers/maintenance people:* required to transport people and goods within the resort, to manage and maintain all Scott Dunn properties and equipment, and to carry out any repairs or maintenance as and when necessary.

Requirements: Knowledge of French, Spanish, Italian or Portuguese useful, but not mandatory. *Resort managers:* applicants must have previous management and hospitality experience, as well as fluency in the local language (French for summer positions). *Chalet and villa chefs/cooks:* applicants must have completed a 6 month cooking course, or have extensive experience and flair. Must be organised and outgoing. *Chalet and villa hosts:* no formal qualifications necessary, although hospitality experience is essential. Applicants must be outgoing, organised and have excellent customer service skills. *Nannies:* must have a recognised childcare qualification, at least one year's childcare experience and be organised, confident and outgoing. *Beauty therapists:* applicants must have a recognised qualification, at least one year's experience and be organised, flexible and pro-active. *Drivers/maintenance people:* applicants must be flexible and have a practical mind. Previous hospitality experience is desirable.

Accommodation: Board and accommodation are provided free of charge.

Application Procedure: For summer positions apply in January, or for winter positions apply from June.

Canvas Holidays

France
Spain
Italy
Austria
Germany
Switzerland
Luxembourg
Holland
Croatia

Come and join our team!

Do you have customer service experience? We are looking for hardworking, enthusiastic, flexible, level-headed individuals to join our team this summer..

- positions at over 100 campsites across Europe
- supervisory, childcare, courier jobs and jobs for couples available
- opportunities available from March – October (2 months minimum term contract)
- competitive salary + travel to site + accommodation provided

To apply, complete an on-line application form at

www.gvnrecruitment.com

Alternatively, call the Overseas Recruitment Department

 01383 629012

Industrial and Office Work

The American Scandinavian Foundation (ASF)

Job(s) Available: ASF offers short-term training placements in Scandinavia to American students and recent graduates. Recent fields for placement have been: hospital management, chemical engineering, forestry ecology, wildlife fieldwork, construction engineering, and marketing. There are also positions teaching English in Finland during the academic year.

Head Office: Scandinavia House, 58 Park Avenue, New York, NY 10016, USA
☎ +1 212 879 9779
✏ trainscan@amscan.org
🖥 www.amscan.org

Pay: An income is provided.

Cost: A non-returnable application fee of $50 is charged but this includes a one-year membership to the foundation. Trainees are expected to cover the cost of a round-trip airfare and have medical insurance.

Company Description: A non-profit organisation set up in 1910 to promote educational and cultural exchange between the USA and Denmark, Finland, Iceland, Norway and Sweden.

Requirements: Young Americans aged over 21 welcome. Knowledge of a Scandinavian language is not required.

Additional Information: If an American is able to arrange a job outside the ASF scheme, ASF offers help with arranging work permits. All that is required is written confirmation from the training firm specifying the dates of training, the income, type of work and the name of the training supervisor.

Application Procedure: Those interested should contact ASF at the above address.

Celtic Welcomes Ltd

Job(s) Available: Marketing trainees, administration trainees, sales trainees, reservations trainees.

Head Office: Eglinton Chambers,21 Wellington Square, Ayr KA7 1HD, UK
☎ 01292 885656
✏ diana@celticwelcomes.com
🖥 www.celticwelcomes.com

Duration: Minimum period is 3 months.

Working Hours: Working hours are flexible up to a maximum of 37.5 hours, 5 days a week.

Pay: To be arranged.

Company Description: Celtic Welcomes is a tour wholesaler and incoming tours agency specialising in tours throughout Great Britain and Ireland, also running outbound Tours to Europe. Clients are located all over the world.

Job Description: *Marketing trainees:* required for marketing tours to clients worldwide. *Administration trainees:* required for tour reservations and general administration. *Sales trainees:* required for the sales of tours to clients worldwide. *Reservations trainees:* required for administering to clients worldwide.

Requirements: Knowledge of English plus another EU language is essential. All positions require candidates to have good English, both spoken and written. Individuals must also have a university or college degree with language and/or tourism content.

Accommodation: Board and accommodation are provided as part of package.

Application Procedure: Apply at any time.

Sports, Couriers and Camping

Acorn Adventure

Job(s) Available: Instructors, village managers, catering supervisor, catering assistant, 300 seasonal staff.

Duration: Seasonal staff needed mid-April to September (some shorter contracts).

Pay: Excellent rates of pay, plus supplement/bonus subject to centre and position.

Head Office: Acorn House, Prospect Road, Halesowen. Birmingham B62 8DU, UK
☎ 01215 042066
✆ chris.lloyd@acornadventure.co.uk
🖥 www.jobs-acorn.co.uk

Company Description: Adventure Activity Holiday company offering groups multi-activity camping holidays in North Wales, the Lake District, Spain and Italy as well as France.

Job Description: Activities include sailing, canoeing, kayaking, climbing, abseiling and caving. All positions are available in the UK, France and Italy. Instructor and village representative positions also available in Spain.

Application Procedure: By post, marked for the attention of recruitment or apply online.

Acorn Educational Exchanges/Halsbury Travel

Job(s) Available: Couriers, group leaders, tour guides required for coach and air groups travelling to Western European destinations (80).

Duration: University holiday periods and term time year round. Tours usually last around 1–2 weeks. Minimum period of work one week.

Working Hours: 35 hours per week.

Pay: £170 per week.

Head Office: 35 Churchill Park, Nottingham NG4 2HF, UK
☎ 01159 404303
✆ enquiries@halsbury.com
🖥 www.aee.eu.com or www.halsbury.com

Company Description: Halsbury Travel/Acorn provide group and school tours to Western Europe and worldwide. The company arrange sports tours, music tours, study tours, ski tours, and tours for any academic theme; History, Geography, Media, Travel and Tourism, French, German, Spanish and Italian.

Requirements: Minimum age 21. Must speak English and either French, German or Spanish.

Accommodation: Half board hotel accommodation, and transportation all supplied.

Application Procedure: Applications to Rachel Weaver by email at ac1@halsbury.com. Applications taken in September, January and April. EU applicants with fluent English and a Western European language welcome to apply.

Alan Rogers Guides Ltd

Job(s) Available: Campsite inspectors.

Duration: May to September.

Pay: An inspection fee and expenses are paid.

Company Description: Alan Rogers Guides are one of Britain's leading camping and caravanning guides.

Requirements: Must have a thorough knowledge and experience of camping and or caravanning in Europe. Foreign language would be useful.

Head Office: Spelmonden Old Oast, Spelmonden Road, Goudhurst, Kent TN17 1HE, UK
☎ 01580 214037
✆ contact@alanrogers.com
🖥 www.alanrogers.com

Accommodation: Must have own caravan or motorhome.

Application Procedure: Applications should be made to the campsites director at the above address.

American Council for International Studies (ACIS)

Job(s) Available: Tour managers (100).

Duration: Busiest periods are March/April and June/July. Tour managers needed for both short and long periods are needed. Minimum period of work is 10 days.

Working Hours: Flexible.

Pay: Depending on experience. Generous tips.

Head Office: 38 Queen's Gate, London SW7 5HR, UK
☎ 020 7590 7474
✉ tm_dept@acis.com
🖥 www.acis.com

Company Description: ACIS has been offering quality educational travel for over 20 years. Tour managers are vital to the success of the company, and are given unequalled training and support.

Job Description: Tour managers to lead American high school teachers and students on educational trips through Europe. Tour Managers meet groups on arrival, travel with them, act as commentators and guides, keep accounts, direct bus drivers, troubleshoot etc.

Requirements: Fluency in French, Italian, German or Spanish is essential. Applicants must be over 21, and either have or be studying for a university degree.

Accommodation: Provided with the groups in 3 or 4 star hotels.

Application Procedure: Apply online via the website where there is an application form.

Bombard Balloon Adventures

Job(s) Available: Ground crew (15).

Duration: During the summer season (May to Oct), the team travels to France, Tuscany, Switzerland, Austria, and the Czech Republic; and to the Swiss Alps in winter (Jan and Feb). Period of work by arrangement.

Head Office: Château de Laborde, Laborde Au Château 21200 Beaune, France
✉ jobs2008@bombardsociety.org
🖥 www.bombardsociety.org/jobs

Company Description: Since 1977, Bombard Balloon Adventures has provided complete luxury travel programmes built around hot-air ballooning.

Job Description: Ground crew to assist in preparation and packing of ballooning equipment, driving, and general household chores. Complete job description is on www.bombardsociety.org/jobs.

Requirements: Requires a clean driving licence, excellent physical fitness, a cheerful personality, responsible driving skills, the ability to live with others, and a neat, clean-cut appearance. Language skills are a plus but not a requirement.

Application Procedure: Applicants should send a CV including height, weight, and nationality; a scanned ID photo and copy of driving licence; and dates of availability to Michael Lincicome by email (preferred) at the address above. Include the letters "SRO" in the subject line of inquiries.

Canvas Holidays

Job(s) Available: Campsite courier, children's courier.

Duration: Full season positions start in March, April or May and end in September/October. High season staff needed to work at least 2 months during the peak season.

Pay: Package includes competitive salary.

Head Office: GVN Camping Recruitment, East Port House, Dunfermline KY12 7JG, UK
☎ 01383 629012
✉ campingrecruitment@gvnrecruitment.com
🖥 www.gvnrecruitment.com

Company Description: Canvas Holidays provide luxury mobile home and tent holidays at over 100 campsites throughout Europe.

Job Description: *Campsite courier:* involves cleaning accommodation, welcoming families to the site and showing them to their accommodation. Visiting customers, providing local information and basic maintenance are very important parts of the job. Campsite courier Opportunities are also available for couples to work on site together. *Children's courier:* needed to work at Hoopi's Club.

Requirements: *Children's courier:* applicants must have formal experience of working with children. Children's couriers should be energetic, enthusiastic and have good communication skills. A tent is provided as a Club venue and for equipment storage; this has to be kept safe, clean and tidy. Visiting new arrivals on site is an important and fun part of the job. Children's couriers also help with other campsite duties as needed.

Accommodation: Package includes tent accommodation, medical insurance, uniform and return travel from a UK port of entry.

Additional Information: For details of management positions, see website. Visit recruitment website for information about working with teenagers (Buzz Courier) and wildlife and the environment (Wild and Active Courier).

Application Procedure: Please call the recruitment department for more information and an application form, or apply online.

Casterbridge Tours Ltd

Job(s) Available: Tour managers/guides.

Duration: Period of work by arrangement between March and June.

Working Hours: To work all hours necessary, 7 days a week.

Pay: From £280 per week.

> **Head Office:** Salcombe House, Long Street, Sherborne, Dorset DT9 3BU, UK
> ☎ 01935 810810
> ✎ sales@casterbridge-tours.co.uk
> 🖳 www.casterbridgetours.com

Company Description: Casterbridge operate customised Group Tours throughout Britain and Europe. They have 3 specialist divisions: Student Educational Study Tours; Concert Tours for Performing Choirs, Orchestras and Bands; Adult Special Interest Tours.

Job Description: Tour managers/guides to escort groups in Europe.

Requirements: Applicants are expected to attend a training course; knowledge of languages useful.

Accommodation: Board and lodging provided.

Application Procedure: Applications to the above address.

Club Cantabrica Holidays Ltd

Job(s) Available: Resort manager (12), campsite couriers (30), peak season couriers (15), children's courier (11), maintenance staff (11), hotel staff (8) and chef.

> **Head Office:** 146/148 London Road, St Albans, Herts AL1 1PQ, UK
> ☎ 01727 866177
> ✎ recruitment@cantabrica.co.uk
> 🖳 www.cantabrica.co.uk

Duration: From April to October, except peak season staff. Peak season staff to cover same tasks as couriers but for June to September only. Minimum period of work 3 months.

Working Hours: Approximately 40 hours per 6 day week.

Pay: *Resort manager:* Competitive including bonus and commission. *Campsite couriers:* £100 per week plus commission and bonus. *Peak season couriers:* Competitive plus commission and bonus. *Children's courier:* Competitive plus commission and bonus. *Maintenance staff:* Competitive and subject to experience plus commission and bonus.

Company Description: Club Cantabrica is an independent tour operator with 30 years of experience. It offers luxury coach, air and self-drive holidays on excellent sites in France (including the French Alps). Italy and Spain and Austria. Opportunities also available for their ski programme in the Austrian Tyrol and the French Alps.

Job Description: *Resort manager:* to manage sites varying in size from 25–100 units. *Campsite couriers:* to work on camp sites in France, Italy, and Spain. Work involves looking after clients, setting up and closing down site, tent and mobile home cleaning and maintenance, paperwork and excursion sales. *Children's courier:* to run Kids' Club on campsites. *Maintenance staff:* to carry out maintenance and upkeep work on tents and mobile homes. *Hotel staff:* to help run the Club Hotel in Chamonix Valley.

Requirements: Couriers should be enthusiastic and have plenty of stamina, with knowledge of languages an advantage. Applicants should be over 18 years old (over 21 for managers). Experience preferable. *Resort manager:* must have previous campsite rep experience and French, Italian or Spanish language skills. *Children's courier:* must have experience of working with children and relevant qualification. *Maintenance staff:* applicants should have excellent practical skills. *Hotel staff:* fluent French required.

Accommodation: Free accommodation provided.

Application Procedure: Applications with CV to the above address (please specify winter or summer); applicants can also email the above address or visit the website.

Club Europe Holidays Ltd

Job(s) Available: Concert tour manager.
Duration: Tour length varies from 3-8 days.
Pay: Increases with experience but starts at £55 per day.
Company Description: Club Europe Holidays employ concert tour managers on a freelance basis,

Head Office: Fairway House, 53 Dartmouth Road, London SE23 3HN, UK
☎ 020 8699 7788
✆ aferdita@club-europe.co.uk
🖥 www.club-europe.co.uk

to accompany school and youth ensembles on tour in Europe. The nature of their business means that most of the work is on offer during the spring and summer school holidays, making the positions ideal for students and teachers.

Job Description: Duties include reconfirming booked excursions and concerts; introducing the group at the venues; interpreting and communicating the client's needs with the accommodation and local agents; coordinating any minor alterations to the itinerary with the coach drivers and accompanying the group at all times including all concerts and excursions. Tours are to France, Germany, Italy, Austria, Spain, Holland and Belgium.

Requirements: Looking for friendly confident staff with excellent organisational and communication skills. Applicants should be fluent in English and at least one other European language.

Accommodation: Tour managers are provided with the same board and accommodation as the client.

Application Procedure: Applications invited from 1 January.

Crystal Finest

Job(s) Available: Resort representatives, chalet chefs, cooking chalet hosts, chalet assistants, nannies, drivers and massage therapists for the winter ski season.
Duration: November to April.
Company Description: Crystal Finest is part of TUI UK, one of the top specialist tour operators in the

Head Office: King's Place, 12-42 Wood Street, Kingston-Upon-Thames, Surrey KT1 1JY, UK
☎ 020 8541 2223
✆ SLArecruitment@s-h-g.co.uk
🖥 www.crystaljobs.co.uk

UK. They offer a selection of luxury catered chalet and hotel holidays on their winter ski programme in the World's Premier Ski Resorts.

Requirements: Crystal Finest representatives need to be independent and have a thorough understanding of customer requirements.

Application Procedure: Applications to Crystal Finest on the above email address.

Equity Travel

Job(s) Available: Representatives to work with school groups on cookery, language or sports tours in France, Germany, Italy and Spain.

Duration: Positions are available for periods varying from 2 days to 1 week between February and October.

Head Office: 1 Jubilee Street, Brighton, East Sussex BN1 1AL, UK
☎ 01273 886911
✆ recruitment@equity.co.uk
🖥 www.equityski.co.uk/

Pay: £30 per day.

Company Description: Equity Travel is a direct sell tour operator, organising educational tours, sports tours, ski holidays and weekend breaks with the emphasis on customer service, quality and value for money. Equity Travel require staff of all levels to work overseas including hotel managers, chefs, ski reps and tour reps.

Job Description: Reps have a briefing at the Brighton office before travelling and a day in resort to set up prior to the group's arrival. Duties include liaising between the group, hotelier and coach driver; organisation of pre-booked, course-related excursions and interviews; translating during demonstrations and helping pupils with course-related work.

Requirements: Applicants must be fluent in French, German, Italian or Spanish, well organised and able to work on their own initiative. They must be able to relate to children and will ideally have some experience of working with school groups or in a public service industry. A driving licence is required for most tours.

Accommodation: Full board, accommodation, travel expenses, insurance and uniform provided.

Additional Information: Equity Ski also require reps for peak season Ski weeks throughout the winter.

Application Procedure: By post with a CV and a covering letter to Sue Lloyd at the above address.

Esprit Holidays Ltd

Job(s) Available: Hotel/resort manager, nannies, alpies rangers.

Duration: All staff must be available from mid-June to mid-September.

Head Office: 185 Fleet Road, Fleet, Hants GU51 3BL, UK
☎ 01252 618318
✆ recruitment@esprit-holidays.co.uk
🖥 www.esprit-holidays.co.uk

Pay: Weekly wage.

Company Description: Esprit Family Adventures run alpine holidays (France, Italy and Austria) for families in catered chalets and hotels and provide childcare in nurseries and alpine adventure clubs for children aged 4 months to 15 years old.

Job Description: All staff assist with chalet cleaning, babysitting and hosting guests. Staff to run chalet hotels and chalets. *Nannies:* needed to run Esprit nurseries and alpies club. Required to take care of babies and toddlers. *Alpies rangers:* required to run adventure activity clubs.

Requirements: All staff must be EU passport holders. Ideal for anyone who has an interest in alpine activities, ie mountain walking and biking, white water rafting etc. Staff need friendly and out-going personalities and previous experience. *Hotel/ resort manager:* Minimum age 25. Good command of spoken French or German, hospitality and customer service experience. Management and supervisory skills. Full clean driving licence. *Nannies:*

Dedicated, fun-loving and enthusiastic. Minimum age 18. DCE NNEB, NVQ3, BTEC or NVQ level 3 trained. *Alpies rangers:* Minimum age 21. Experience as play scheme leaders, children's sports coaches or trained teachers. Should have a mature, fun loving personality.

Accommodation: Food and accommodation, uniform, swimming pool pass and transport provided.

Application Procedure: Further information can be obtained regarding vacancies on the website.

Eurocamp

Job(s) Available: Campsite Courier, Children's Courier, Courier Team Leaders, Children's Courier Team Leaders, Montage/Demontage.

Duration: *Campsite Courier:* Applicants should be available to work from April/May to mid-September or June/July to mid-September. *Children's Courier:* Applicants should be available from early May to September or June to September. *Courier Team Leaders:* Applicants should be available from April to mid-September. *Children's Courier Team Leaders:* Applicants should be available from early May until September. *Montage/Demontage:* Applicants should be available from Feb to May or August to October.

> **Head Office:** Overseas Recruitment Department (Ref SJ/08), Hartford Manor, Greenbank Lane, Northwich CW8 1HW, UK
> ☎ 01606 787525
> 🖳 www.holidaybreakjobs.com/camping

Pay: You will receive a competitive salary, comprehensive training, return travel to and from an agreed meeting point, accommodation, medical and luggage insurance and uniform.

Company Description: Eurocamp is a leading tour operator in self-drive camping and mobile home holidays in Europe. We offer our customers a wide range of holiday accommodation on over 200 premier campsites. Each year the company seeks to recruit up to 1,500 enthusiastic people to work the summer season in a variety of roles.

Job Description: *Campsite Courier:* A Courier's responsibility begins by ensuring that the customer's accommodation is both inviting and cleaned to the highest of standards. You will welcome new arrivals, be the customers main point of contact and will be expected to provide local and general information, give assistance and even act as interpreter if required. Part of the role will involve helping out with minor repairs to accommodation and equipment and will also involve basic administration and accounts. *Children's Courier:* You will be responsible for planning and delivering a fun, safe, daily activity programme to our customers' children. The age of the children attending the club will range from 5 to 12 years old although we also run a toddler service in low season for 12 months to 4 years. *Courier Team Leaders:* You must be able to deliver first class customer service and organize the daily workload of the courier team. Your role also includes all the duties of a Campsite Courier and you will be expected to lead by example. There are a variety of team leader roles available, dependant on team size; Courier in Charge, Senior Courier and Site Manager. *Children's Courier Team Leaders:* Your role will involve the management, motivation and development of the Children's Couriers to ensure they provide a varied range of quality activities. Your role includes all the duties of a Children's Courier. *Montage/Demontage:* Montage and Demontage assistants are employed to either help set up for the season or close down at the end of the season. This involves putting up or taking down tents, moving/distributing equipment and cleaning/preparing accommodation.

Requirements: Applicants must hold a UK/EU passport and the current minimum age is 18 years old on the day you start work in order to obtain the relevant insurance cover. *Campsite Couriers:* You should have lots of energy, basic common sense and a genuine desire to help people. *Children's Courier:* Previous childcare experience is essential. Successful candidates will be asked to apply for an Enhanced Disclosure. *Courier Team Leaders:* You must have previous experience of leading a team successful applicants may be asked to apply for a

Standard Disclosure. *Children's Courier Team Leaders*: Previous experience with Children and leading a team successful candidates will be asked to apply for an Enhanced Disclosure. *Montage/Demontage:* Previous experience of physical and repetitive work successful applicants will be asked to apply for a Standard Disclosure.

Accommodation: Provided.

Application Procedure: Applicants should apply on-line at the above website or telephone for an Application Pack.

Freewheel Holidays

Job(s) Available: Freewheel Hosts.

Duration: Work available early July to the end of August, minimum period of work is 4 weeks.

Working Hours: Hosts work approximately 30–35 hours per week, approximately 6 days a week (depending on guest numbers).

Pay: £200 per week.

Head Office: Minster Chambers, Church Street, Southwell, Nottinghamshire. NG22 0HD, UK
☎ 01636 815636
info@freewheelholidays.co.uk
www.freewheelholidays.co.uk

Company Description: Freewheel Holidays is a successful independent tour operator whose guests enjoy cycling through wonderful landscapes in Austria, Belgium, Denmark, France, Spain and Switzerland, experiencing sights, sounds and cultures of different regions while their hosts manage the luggage and logistics.

Job Description: Freewheel are looking for mature, outgoing, resourceful people with full driving licence and knowledge of bicycle maintenance to be Freewheel Hosts. Hosts provide information and support to guests, meet them at airports and stations, transfer luggage and liaise with hotels.

Requirements: All applicants must speak either native or fluent English as well as another appropriate language. Applicants should possess a full driver's licence and first aid qualification.

Accommodation: Accommodation and training provided.

Application Procedure: Apply online at www.freewheelholidays.co.uk/careers

Halsbury Travel

Job(s) Available: Group leaders (100), language tutors (20), couriers (50), ski reps (10).

Duration: Minimum period of 1 week.

Working Hours: 8 hours per day, 6 days a week. *Langauge tutors:* 3–4 hours work a day.

Pay: *Group leaders:* £165 per week. *Language tutors:* £25 per week. *Couriers:* £30 per day. *Ski reps:* £165 per week. Discount offered on your ski-pass.

Head Office: 35 Churchill Park, Colwick Business Estate, Nottingham NG4 2HF, UK
☎ 01159 404303
rachel@halsbury.com
www.halsbury.com

Company Description: Halsbury Travel is an ABTA/ATOL Bonded Tour Operator, specialising in School Group, European and Worldwide Tours. Established in 1986 they are one of the leading UK student group tour operators.

Job Description: *Group leaders:* required to work with touring groups in France, Germany or Spain. *Language tutors:* required to work with touring groups in France, Germany and Spain. *Couriers:* required to accompany History, Geography, Art and Business Studies, Sports and Travel, Leisure/Tourism Groups. *Ski reps:* required to accompany ski groups to French resorts, liaise with local partners, organise evening activities or assist the groups as required.

Requirements: All applicants should be fluent in the language/or a native of the country they wish to work in.

Accommodation: Accommodation and meals included in pay. *Ski reps:* ski equipment included.

Application Procedure: Applications are invited to the above address in May/June for the winter season, (skiing jobs), and in January/February for jobs in the summer season.

Inghams Travel

Job(s) Available: Representatives (approximately 160).

Duration: Minimum period of work 3–4 months from May to September.

Working Hours: All staff to work 6 days a week.

Pay: £900–£1,300 per month including commission.

> **Head Office:** 10-18 Putney Hill, London SW15 6AX, UK
> ☎ 020 8780 4400
> ✆ travel@inghams.com
> 🖳 www.inghams.co.uk

Company Description: Inghams Travel is the largest independent operator of lake and mountain holidays in the UK with an excellent reputation built up over the last 70 years; they offer quality lake and mountain holidays to Europe and aim to attract the best staff in the industry.

Job Description: Representatives needed for client service, administration, sales, guiding of excursions and general problem solving.

Requirements: Knowledge of French, German, Italian or Spanish is required. Minimum age 23. Applicants must be friendly, outgoing flexible team players with enthusiasm and a good sense of humour and must be customer care orientated and have a liking for the country and culture.

Accommodation: Free board and accommodation is provided.

Application Procedure: Applications all year round to the above address.

Siblu Holidays Across Europe

Job(s) Available: Park representatives, children's club representatives, assistant park representatives, lifeguards, reception team members, accommodation team members, bar team members, entertainers.

Duration: The season runs between March and October, with varying contract dates. Limited high season positions are available.

> **Head Office:** Recruitment Team, Bryanston Court, Selden Hill, Hemel Hempstead HP2 4TN, UK
> ☎ 01442 293231
> ✆ recruitment@siblu.com
> 🖳 www.siblu.com

Pay: Team members will receive a competitive salary.

Company Description: Siblu Holidays exclusively own holiday parks in France, and also operate on 12 fantastic parks in France, Spain and Italy.

Job Description: The following roles are offered in these countries for seasonal work: *Park representatives:* duties include cleaning and maintaining accommodation, welcoming new arrivals, reception duties, paperwork and administration. *Children's club representatives:* duties include creating and running a daytime entertainment programme for children between the ages of 5 and 12, associated paperwork and assisting park representatives. *Assistant park representatives:* duties include cleaning and preparation of accommodation, welcoming new arrivals and reception duties. *Lifeguards:* NPLQ qualified, duties include poolside supervision, cleaning of pool area and supervision of slides and flumes. *Reception team members:* duties include the welcome and check-in of guests, providing park and local information, cash handling (*bureau de change*) and problem solving. *Accommodation team members:* duties include cleaning and preparing guest accommodation, bed making and customer visits. *Bar team members:* applicants must be conversational in French. Duties include bar service, cash handling, cleaning and washing of glasses, terrace service and re-stocking of bar. *Entertainers:* dancers, vocalists and children's entertainers, working as part of a team to provide daytime and evening entertainment programme for guests of all ages.

Requirements: *Children's club representatives:* experience of working with children is desirable. *Lifeguards:* NPLQ qualified. *Reception team members:* applicants must be fluent in French.

Accommodation: Accommodation as well as uniform, medical cover and travel costs to park included in pay.

Application Procedure: Please telephone the above number for a recruitment pack or visit the website to apply online.

ACFEA Tour Consultants

Job(s) Available: Couriers/tour leaders (1–2 per tour).
Duration: Work is available for a minimum of 1 tour in spring and summer. Duration of each tour usually 10–20 days.

Head Office: 12-15 Hanger Green, London W5 3EL, UK
☎ 020 8799 8360
✉ info@acfea.eu
🖥 www.acfea.eu

Working Hours: Work will be full-time.
Pay: Wage level depends on the particular tour.
Company Description: Established in 1955, a tour operator specialising in concert tours of mainland Europe and the UK for both amateur and professional musical groups (choirs, bands and orchestras).
Job Description: Couriers/tour leaders to escort choirs, bands and orchestras from the USA on concert tours throughout the UK and Europe. To be responsible for all daily events, confirming accommodation, transportation, concert arrangements and leading sight-seeing excursions.
Requirements: Knowledge of touring and musical background is an advantage. Excellent organisational skills, leadership qualities and initiative required. Confidence in the native language of the country being toured is required.
Accommodation: Board and accommodation is included for the duration of each tour.
Application Procedure: Applications from EU nationals only are invited throughout the year to the above address.

Sport & Educational Travel Ltd

Job(s) Available: Couriers.
Duration: All durations of visits are organised from day trips to weeklong stays.
Pay: From £120 for a day trip; on longer trips it is £110 for first day and £65 for every subsequent day.

Head Office: 3 Dukes Head Street, Lowestoft, Suffolk NR32 1JY, UK
☎ 01502 567914
✉ info@set-uk.com

Company Description: Established in 1991, Sport & Educational Travel Ltd organises group travel for school parties, with students aged between 11–17 years old. Trips to France, Belgium, Germany and Spain range from an introduction to Northern France and visits to Paris (including Disneyland) to First and Second World War tours.
Job Description: For all of these visits couriers are needed to accompany the groups, provide factual information during the trip in both English and the local language, and manage checking-in procedures, visits and general timings throughout the visit.
Requirements: Must speak fluently one or more languages relevant to the destination. Knowledge of area would be an advantage but not essential as full training is given.
Accommodation: For overnight visits or longer, accommodation and meals are provided on the same basis as the groups accompanied.
Application Procedure: Applications for this post to Mrs M Savage, managing director at the above address.

TIME OUT Tourist Service

Job(s) Available: Animators from Italy, Netherlands, Germany, Swiss Austria, United Kingdom, Belgium and France. Tourist assistants, female dancers, choreographers, scene-painters, DJ's, sportsmen and cocktail bar pianists.

Duration: Minimum period of work 3 months.

Company Description: TIME OUT takes care of screening applicants, and training courses for positions within the tourist industry. From a 5-star village resort, incentive travel packages to guided tours.

Requirements: Applicants must speak English and German, other languages are also helpful.

Accommodation: Board and lodging provided free of charge.

Application Procedure: Fill in subscription form at www.timeouttourism.com/formAniE.htm or send CV and photo to info@timeouttourism.com

> **Head Office:** Prinzenalle 7, 40549 Dusseldorf, Germany
> ☎ +49 211 52391149
> ✆ deutschland@timeoutourism.com
> 🖥 www.timeoutourism.com

Tracks Travel Ltd

Job(s) Available: Drivers, tour managers, cooks.

Duration: Work is available throughout the year, but all applicants should be prepared to work for a minimum of 2 full seasons.

Working Hours: Hours of work vary, depending on the nature of the tour.

Pay: To be confirmed.

Company Description: Tracks Travel is a coach tour operator operating throughout the UK and Europe.

Requirements: Knowledge of languages other than English is not required. *Drivers:* with a valid UK PCV licence required. *Tour managers:* must be good with a microphone, and confident in dealing with large groups. *Cooks:* must be able to cook for large groups. Relevant experience preferred.

Accommodation: Board and accommodation are available.

Application Procedure: Applications should be made to the above address at any time of year.

> **Head Office:** The Flots, Brookland, Romney Marsh, Kent TN29 9TG, UK
> ☎ 01797 344164
> ✆ info@tracks-travel.com
> 🖥 www.tracks-travel.com

Venue Holidays

Job(s) Available: Supervisors, campsite representatives, montage/demontage assistants.

Duration: *Supervisors:* required March to October. *Campsite representatives:* minimum period of work is 2 months; the complete season runs from April to October. *Assistants:* required March to May and September/October.

Working Hours: Hours as required.

Pay: Competitive salary paid monthly.

Company Description: Venue Holidays is a family run independent tour operator offering self drive family holidays to first class camping resorts in France, Italy and Spain. Clients are offered a choice of fully equipped tent or mobile home accommodation with a range of travel, hotel and insurance services. Company has over 21 years of experience within the camping industry and employs around 40 staff for our overseas operation.

> **Head Office:** 1 Norwood St, Ashford, Kent TN23 1QU, UK
> ☎ 01233 629950
> ✆ info@venueholidays.co.uk
> 🖥 www.venueholidays.co.uk

Job Description: *Campsite representatives:* duties to include cleaning and maintaining holiday units, welcoming clients and looking after them during their stay, sorting out any problems, and liaising between the campsite's management and the UK office. *Assistants:* jobs include setting up tents, preparing the campsite units for occupation and cleaning accommodation prior to the season. In September/October the process must be done in reverse.

Requirements: *Supervisors:* must possess a clean driver's licence. Minimum age 20. *Campsite representatives and assistants:* minimum age 18. Must have a full clean driving license.

Application Procedure: Apply online at www.venueholidays.co.uk/UK/Jobs/application form.htm

Voluntary Work and Archaeology

Activity International

Job(s) Available: Dutch citizens (hundreds) for several work and volunteer placements outside the Netherlands.

Job Description: Includes work on farms, in national parks, in hotels, orphanages, as au pairs etc.

Application Procedure: Applicants should contact the above address for details.

> Head Office: PO Box 694, NL-7500 AR Enschede, The Netherlands
> ☎ +31 53 4800382
> ✆ info@activityinternational.nl
> 🖳 www.activityinternational.nl

Aktion Suhnezeichen Friedensdienste (ASF, Action Reconciliation Service for Peace)

Job(s) Available: Volunteers.

Duration: To work on the Summer camps (2 weeks long) between 1 July and 1 October.

Company Description: ASF works for reconciliation and peace through long-term and short-term volunteer service.

> Head Office: Auguststr. 80, 10117 Berlin, Germany
> ☎ +49 3028 395184
> ✆ asf@asf-ev.de
> 🖳 www.asf-ev-de

Job Description: Volunteers needed for the *Sommerlager* programme in Belarus, Belgium, Czech Republic, France, Germany, Great Britain, Israel, the Netherlands, Norway, Poland, Russia, Slovakia and the United States. To help with the maintenance of Jewish cemeteries and memorial centres, work in social facilities and involve themselves in projects that support intercultural experiences. In addition there is much discussion concerning historical and current issues.

Additional Information: For volunteers from West Europe, USA and Israel, the cost is €100 (approx £67.40). Volunteers must pay travel expenses.

Application Procedure: By post to the above address.

ATD Fourth World

Job(s) Available: Workcamps.

Duration: The camps, street workcamps and family stays take place from July to September, and most last 2 weeks.

Pay: Participants must pay for their own travel costs, plus a contribution towards food and accommodation.

> Head Office: 48 Addington Square, London SE5 7LB, UK
> ☎ 020 7703 3231
> ✆ atd@atd-uk.org
> 🖳 www.atd-uk.org

Company Description: ATD Fourth World is an international organisation which adopts a human rights approach to tackling extreme poverty, supporting the efforts of very disadvantaged and excluded families in fighting poverty and taking an active role in the community. As part of their work ATD organises workcamps, street workshops and family stays all over the European Union.

Job Description: The workcamps involve a combination of manual work in and around ATD's buildings, conversation and reflection on poverty. The street workshops take a festival atmosphere, involving artists, craftsmen, sportsmen and volunteers to underprivileged areas. The family stays allow families split by poverty with children in care and/or adults in homes to come together for a break.

Application Procedure: For further information write, enclosing a stamped addressed envelope or and International Reply Coupon.to the above address or ATD Quart Monde, Summer Activities Team, 107 avenue du General Leclerc, 95480 Pierrelaye, France or email engage.ete@atd-quartmonde.org.

Bridges for Education INC

Job(s) Available: Volunteer English Teachers. About 100 volunteers are placed each year.
Duration: Volunteers teach for 3 weeks together as a team in the summer.
Pay: The board and lodging and a modest stipend are provided by the host country.

Head Office: 94 Lamarck Drive, Buffalo, New York, NY 14226, USA
☎ +1 716 839 0180
📧 jbc@bridges4edu.org
🖥 www.bridges4edu.org

Company Description: The purpose of Bridges for Education (BFE) is to promote tolerance and understanding using English as a bridge. BFE sends Canadian and American volunteer teachers, educated adults and college students to teach conversational English in the summer in Eastern and Central Europe. Since 1994, BFE has organised 86 camps in 10 countries serving 12,000 students from 38 countries. High School students whose parents or teachers are participants may also join a BFE team. BFE is not a religious or ethnic organisation.

Requirements: Those skilled in teaching English as a second language are preferred but teachers who are certified in any area are welcome. The team is prepared in basic ESL prior to departure. Applicants must be in good health.

Accommodation: Voiunteers receive free room and board while they teach and an additional week of travel within the host country.

Application Procedure: Applications from US or Canadian citizens only should be sent to the above address or made online. Programmes are posted on website in December and January.

The Disaway Trust

Job(s) Available: Volunteers (about 60).
Duration: 8–14 day periods during the year. The organisation usually arranges 2–3 holidays a year which take place between May and October.
Cost: A 50% contribution is required toward cost of travel, accommodation, board and entertainment.

Head Office: 51 Sunningdale Road, Worthing, West Sussex BN13 2NQ, UK
☎ 01903 830796
🖥 www.disaway.co.uk

Company Description: The Disaway Trust relies on helpers to enable them to provide holidays for adults who would be otherwise unable to have a holiday.

Job Description: Volunteers are required to help disabled people on holiday. The holiday venues are in the British Isles and in the Mediterranean.

Requirements: No special qualifications or experience are required.

Application Procedure: Apply to Nicki Green for further details including information on dates and locations. The information pack for 2008 will be available mid–January 2008.

Emmaus International

Job(s) Available: Volunteers to take part in summer camps in several European countries.

Working Hours: 35–40 hours per week depending on camp and the number of participants.

Cost: Applicants must pay for round-trip travel, medical costs and other personal costs.

Company Description: An international movement to fight against extreme poverty and its causes.

Head Office: 183, bis rue Vaillant Couturier, Boite Postale 91, 94143 Alfortville, France
☎ +33 1 48 93 29 50
✉ contact@emmaus-international.org
▢ www.emmaus-international.org

Job Description: The work consists of rag-picking and recycling materials to raise money for the poor.

Requirements: Minimum age 18.

Accommodation: Applicants receive free food, accommodation and accident insurance.

Application Procedure: For further details see website.

European Voluntary Service

Job(s) Available: Volunteers.

Duration: 2 to 12 months.

Pay: Pocket money.

Company Description: EVS is an approved sending and hosting organisation for the European Commission's European Voluntary Service scheme.

Head Office: EVS Unit, EIL Cultural and Educational Travel, 287 Worcester Road, Malvern WR14 1AB, UK
☎ Freephone 0800 018 4015, 01684 562 577
✉ k.morris@eiluk.org

Job Description: EVS is for young people aged 18–30 who want to work in a community-based project in another country.

Accommodation: Travel, food, accommodation and medical insurance are provided free of charge.

Application Procedure: For more details contact the above address.

L'APARE GEC

Job(s) Available: Volunteers for Euro-Mediterranean campuses and international voluntary workcamps in Provence and the Mediterranean region.

Duration: *Euro-Mediterranean Campuses:* 3 to 5 weeks during the students' summer holidays. *International voluntary workcamps in Provence and the Mediterranean region:* projects last 2–3 weeks.

Head Office: 25 Boulevard Paul Pons, 84800 L'Isle sur la Sorgue, France
☎ +33 4 90 27 21 20
▢ www.apare-gec.org

Company Description: L'apare GEC is an NGO which promotes transnational cooperation by bringing together professionals, local participants and young volunteers from around Europe and the Mediterranean region. Its objective is to carry out projects that contribute to the protection and enhancement of the environment and local heritage. The GEC develops voluntary efforts in favour of the environment and heritage preservation across Europe and the Mediterranean regions.

Job Description: *Euro-Mediterranean Campuses:* The campuses are intended for students from Europe and Mediterranean countries. They take the form of workshops with about 15 participants working in multi-disciplinary international groups. They include field studies and surveys that use professional skills in the areas of heritage preservation and the environment (in the widest possible sense), architecture, history of art, regional development, sociology, law etc. *International voluntary workcamps in Provence and the Mediterranean region:* (carried out in the context of the European Voluntary Service) allow participants to invest their skills in voluntary projects abroad, to the benefit of local communities. They can be held in urban or rural settings. 10–15 participants in each group.

Requirements: *International voluntary workcamps in Provence and the Mediterranean region:* this programme is designed for young people who are 16 to 18 of whatever nationality or professional training, as long as they reside in a participating country of Europe. Preferably from different disciplines and cultural backgrounds.

Application Procedure: Applications to the above address.

Internationale Bouworde (International Building Companions)

Job(s) Available: Recruits volunteers for construction work camps on behalf of the socially, physically and mentally underprivileged.

Duration: Camps last for 2–3 weeks and take place between June and September. Bouworde in Belgium and Italy operates workcamps around the year.

> Head Office: Bouworde, Tiensesteenweg 157, 3010 Leuven, Belgium (Represents IBO as a whole)
> ☎ +32 16 25 91 44
> 🖅 bauorden@oebo.at

Working Hours: Volunteers work for 8 hours per day, 5 days a week.

Cost: Travel costs and insurance (approximately £60) are the responsibility of the volunteer.

Job Description: The camps take place in Austria, Belgium, the Czech Republic, France, Germany, Hungary, Italy, Lithuania, the Netherlands, Poland, Romania, Slovakia, Switzerland and the Ukraine.

Accommodation: Free board, accommodation and liability and accident insurance are provided

Application Procedure: Applications, mentioning the country preferred, should be sent to the relevant address.

TEJO (Tutmonda Esperantista Junulara Organizo)

Job(s) Available: Volunteers to join work camps in various European countries arranged by TEJO, the World Organisation of Young Esperantists.

Duration: Period of work normally from 1 to 2 weeks.

> Head Office: Nieuwe Binnenweg 176, 3015 BJ Rotterdam, The Netherlands
> ☎ +31 10 4361044
> 🖅 info@tejo.org or oficejo@tego.org
> 🖥 www.tejo.org/info/index.php?lingvo=en

Company Description: TEJO, the World Organisation of Young Esperantists. TEJO is an international non-governmental youth organisation founded in 1938, which works to foster peace and intercultural understanding among young people around the world through Esperanto.

Job Description: Work to be done may be on reconstruction projects.

Requirements: Applicants should be aged between 16 and 30. No previous experience necessary: all camps include Esperanto lessons for beginners, and a few are limited to Esperanto speakers.

Accommodation: Accommodation provided.

Application Procedure: For details contact the above address.

AU Pairs, Nannies, Family Helps and Exchanges

The Au Pair Agency

Job(s) Available: Au pairs.

Duration: Summer stays of 12 weeks possible – early applicants receive priority. At all other times, a minimum commitment of 9 to 12 months is required.

Working Hours: Approximately 25 hours per week.

Pay: Pocket money of approximately £65 per week.

Head Office: 231 Hale Lane, Edgware, Middlesex HA8 9QF, UK
☎ 020 8958 1750
✐ elaine@aupairagency.com
▢ www.aupairagency.com

Requirements: Applicants should be aged between 17 and 25. Non-smokers preferred; drivers always welcomed. A reasonable knowledge of the language of the chosen country is needed. All applicants must be EU citizens.

Accommodation: Full board and lodging.

Application Procedure: Apply online at www.aupairagency.com/applicants. For further details contact Mrs Newman on the above number at least 12 weeks before preferred starting date.

Au Pair Agency Bournemouth

Job(s) Available: Au pair 20 summer placements and 70 long-term placements.

Duration: Long-term placements lasting one academic year.

Working Hours: Au pairs are expected to work 25 hours per week, 5 days a week.

Pay: Minimum £55 per week (overtime is paid extra).

Head Office: 45 Strouden Road, Bournemouth BH9 1QL, UK
☎ 01202 532600
✐ andrea.rose@virgin.net

Company Description: The Au Pair Agency Bournemouth offers placements for British applicants throughout Western and Eastern Europe.

Requirements: Applicants must love children and have experience in childcare (eg babysitting) and a basic knowledge of cleaning. Applicants must speak English.

Additional Information: British applicants are charged £40 on departure. A 24-hour emergency mobile number is provided for au pairs during the placement.

Application Procedure: Apply to Andrea Rose. See above for contact details.

Au Pair Connections

Job(s) Available: Au pairs, mothers' helps.

Duration: Minimum stays normally 6 months, but some summer stays of 10 weeks.

Pay: Pocket money approximately £50 per week.

Head Office: 39 Tamarisk Road, Wildern Gate, Hedge End, Southhampshire SO30 4TN, UK
☎ 01489 780438
✐ info@aupair-connections.co.uk
▢ www.aupairconnections.co.uk

Company Description: Au pairs, mothers' helps placed mainly in France, Spain (including the Balearic Islands), and also in Italy, Austria and sometimes elsewhere in Europe. Applicants from overseas also placed in the UK.

Requirements: Applicants must have experience of childcare, babysitting etc; a good knowledge of English is also useful as some families want their children tutored in English.

Application Procedure: For further details apply to Denise Blighe at the above address or email.

County Nannies (incorporating Au-Pair International and The Nanny Agency)

Job(s) Available: Au pairs.

Duration: Throughout the year for the UK and Europe. Unlimited number of posts available for 6–24 months stay, also 8–12-week summer placements.

Working Hours: 25 hours work per week, 2 days off.

Pay: £55 per week minimum pocket money or equivalent.

Job Description: The families in the UK are mostly in London, London suburbs and the southern counties and south soast. Vacancies in Europe are mainly in cities and coastal towns.

Accommodation: Au pairs recruited live-in.

Additional Information: Au Pair International's sister company County Nannies provides fully qualified nannies, maternity nurses and mother's helps. County Nannies cover Kent, London, South East England and the Home Counties.

Application Procedure: Applications to the above address in writing, or by email.

> **Head Office:** Cherry Gardens, Nouds Lane, Lynsted, Sittingbourne, Kent ME9 0ES, UK
> ☎ 01795 522544 (au pair division)
> 🖅 kerry.godley@countrynannies.co.uk
> 💻 www.countynannies.com

EN Famille Overseas

Job(s) Available: Paying guest stays and homestays.

Job Description: Paying guest stays arranged in France, Germany, Italy and Spain. Homestays with attendance at small private schools also arranged. Families in England for non-English speakers too.

Application Procedure: Applications to the above address.

> **Head Office:** La Maison Jaune, Avenue du Stade, 34210 Siran, France
> ☎ +33 4 68 914990, 01206 546741
> 🖅 marylou.toms@wanadoo.fr
> 💻 www.enfamilleoverseas.co.uk

Jolaine Au Pair and Domestic Agency

Job(s) Available: Au pairs and mother's help.

Duration: Families in the UK prefer applicants who stay for 9 months or longer. Summer stays are limited in the UK.

Company Description: Jolaine Agency can arrange for applicants to be placed with families in Europe. Can book both individuals and groups.

Job Description: Placements for British nannies are mainly in Italy and Spain.

Accommodation: With British families as a paying guest, mainly in the London suburbs.

Application Procedure: For further information and application forms write at any time enclosing s.a.e. or an international reply coupon to the above address or email your details.

> **Head Office:** 18 Escot Way, Barnet, Hertfordshire EN5 3AN, UK
> ☎ 020 8449 1334
> 🖅 aupair@jolaine.prestel.co.uk
> 💻 www.jolaineagency.com

M Kelly Au Pair Agency

Job(s) Available: Summer placement (20), long-term placement (95–100).

Duration: Minimum stay is 6 weeks; maximum stay is 2 years.

Working Hours: 25 hours per week minimum.

> **Head Office:** 17 Ingram Way, Greenford, Middlesex UB6 8QJ, UK
> ☎ 020 8575 3336
> 🖅 info@mkellyaupair.co.uk
> 💻 www.mkellyaupair.co.uk

Pay: Pocket money £55 per week minimum.

Requirements: Applicants must be between 18 and 27 years old.

Additional Information: Placements are available in all countries offering the au pair programme. Depending on placement help with travel and languages can be arranged.

Application Procedure: Apply to Marian Kelly; see above for details.

UK Nannies and AU Pairs

Job(s) Available: Hundreds of placements available in Europe.

Duration: Placements can last between 1 month and 2 years.

Working Hours: Hours vary from 25 to 60 hours per week with overtime paid.

Pay: Vary from £50 per week to £400 per week.

Requirements: Minimum age 18.

Application Procedure: Apply via email at address above.

Head Office: 19 The Severals, Newmarket CB8 7YW, UK
☎ 01638 560812
✍ help@uknanniesandaupairs.com or jobs@theuknannyagency.com
🖥 www.theuknannyagency.co.uk or www.theukaupairagency.co.uk.

Other Work in Europe

Natives.co.uk

Job(s) Available: Season work.

Company Description: A season workers website where jobs in Turkey and across Europe are listed, as well as advice on how to get one. Search by job (campsite manager, bar staff, chefs, lifeguards and so on) and country.

Accommodation: Accommodation is usually available.

Requirements: Fluent English necessary.

Application Procedure: Apply year round to the email above or via the website.

Head Office: 263 Putney Bridge Road, Putney, London, SW15 2LJ, UK
☎ 020 8788 4271
✍ vicky@natives.co.uk
🖥 www.natives.co.uk or www.resortjobs.co.uk

WESTERN EUROPE

EMBASSY OF THE PRINCIPALITY OF ANDORRA
63 Westover Road, London SW 182 RF
☎ 020 8874 4806
🖳 www.andorra.ad

Only limited opportunities for finding temporary employment exist in Andorra, because of its small size. Opportunities are best in the tourist industry – particularly in the winter ski season: there is a chapter on Andorra in *Working in Ski Resorts – Europe & North America* (Victoria Pybus, Vacation Work, 2006).You might be able to get leads on hotel work in the summer through the Andorra Hoteliers Association (ADHA), Avenue de les Escoles, 9 2n 2a, Escaldes-Engordany –CP AD700, Andorra; email adha@andorra.ad. Once governed jointly by France and Spain, Andorra has been a sovereign country in its own right since 1993.

Red Tape

Visa information: While it straddles the borders of France and Spain, Andorra is not itself a member of the European Union. This means that all foreigners, including nationals of EU countries, need work permits before they can take up employment. Applicants from neighbouring countries and then EU countries are usually given precedence over other nationalities. Permits for temporary and seasonal work have to be obtained by the employer and are non-renewable. No visas are needed by EU nationals for tourist purposes.

Centre Andorrà de Llengües

Job(s) Available: Teachers (2–3) of English as a foreign language.

Duration: Minimum period of work 9 months between September/October and June.

Working Hours: 27 hours per 5 day week. Must be willing to work between 8am and 10pm.

Pay: €2000 per month.

Head Office: 15 Av del Fener, Andorra la Vella
☎ +376 804030
🖰 centrandorra.lang@andorra.ad
🖳 www.call.ad

Company Description: A small family-run language school established in 1976 in the very centre of Andorra La Vella. Students range from 6-year-old children to professional adult employees. All levels from beginners to British Council Exams preparations.

Requirements: A university degree, plus TEFL qualification, plus at least 3 years of experience is requested. Applicants should be between 23 and 65. Non-smokers preferred. A good knowledge of French or Spanish is an asset. The posts would be ideal for a teaching couple.

Accommodation: Board and lodging available for €500 per month.

Application Procedure: Applications in the first instance can be made by email.

AUSTRIA

AUSTRIAN EMBASSY
18 Belgrave Mews West, London SW1X 8HU
☎ 020 7344 3250
✒ london-ob@bmeia.gv.at
🖥 www.bmeia.gv.at/london

Austria Today (www.austriatoday is an English language internet magazine for Austria. It and the Austrian Embassy's website (www.bmeia.gv.at/london) are excellent sources of information on jobs, the social, cultural and economic conditions of Austria; in particular, the *Living and Working in Austria* section of the website contains details of immigration, work and residence permits and social security procedures as well as useful information for job seekers about Austrian Employment offices. Also see the Eures website (www. europa.eu.int/eures) and click on Living & Working, then click on Austria.

For many years Austria has offered seasonal work in its summer and winter tourist industries. Eastern Europeans, especially from the countries newly acceded to the EU take an estimated 25% of jobs in the tourist industry. Some knowledge of German will normally be necessary unless you are working for a foreign tour operator with English-speaking clients.

During the summer, fruit is grown along the banks of the Danube, and in the early Autumn chances of finding a job grape-picking are best in the Wachau area around Durnstein west of Vienna, or Burgenland on the Hungarian border around the Neusiedler Sea.

The public employment service of Austria, the *Arbeitsmarktservice (AMS)*, publishes its vacancies on its website, www.ams.or.at (or at Arbeitsmarktservice, Vienna, Weihburggasse 30, A-1011 Vienna; +43 151 5250) but you must be able to speak German. For hotel and catering vacancies in the South Tyrol Region try a season work bureau, BerufsInfoZentren (BIZ), such as the AMS Euro Biz/JobCenter International, Schöpfstrasse 5, 6020 Innsbruck (+43 512 586300; eurobiz.Innsbruck@702.ams.or.at). Private employment agencies operate in Austria, but most of these specialise in executive positions or seasonal positions in the tourist industry for German speakers. It may be possible to find employment by placing an advertisement in daily newspapers: try *Salzburger Nachrichten* (Salzburg; +43 662 83730; www.salzburg.com), *Kurier* (Vienna; +43 1 52100; www.kurier.at) and *Die Presse* (Vienna; +43 1 514140; www.diepresse.at). *Die Presse* also organises an annual initiative to get leading Austrian companies to take on students for summer traineeships. These papers advertise job vacancies as well on Fridays, Saturdays and Sundays. See also *Der Standard*, (www.derstandard.at) one of the biggest newspapers concerning job vacancies.

There are opportunities for voluntary work in Austria arranged by UNA Exchange.

Red Tape

Visa Requirements: Certain nationals do not require a visa providing their stay in Austria does not exceed 3 months. Citizens of original EU countries have the right to live and work in Austria without a work permit or residence permit, however citizens of newer member states may require working visas.

Residence Permits: *EWR Lichtbildausweis* is an ID card which EU nationals can apply for within 3 months of arrival, though it is not compulsory. For Non-EU nationals wishing to work or live in Austria must apply for a residence permit (*Aufenthaltsgesetz*). Once a work permit is granted, it must be presented together with an application for residence permit. The form can be obtained from the Embassy. As a rule, first application for a residence permit must be submitted from abroad either directly to the relevant authority or by means of the Austrian

Diplomatic Mission (not Honorary Consulates). A residence permit is also required if you intend to take up seasonal work in Austria. It will normally be valid for 6 months.

Work Permits: British and Irish citizens and nationals of other original EU countries do not need work permits. Owing to its proximity to many of the newer members of the EU (Estonia, Latvia, Lithuania, Poland, the Czech Republic, Slovakia, Hungary, Slovenia, Bulgaria and Romania), a seven-year transition phase has been set up between Austria and these countries to prevent a flooding of the national labour market and newer EU members are subject to the same regulations as non-EU countries. Non-EU nationals require work (*Sicherungs bescheinigung*) and residence permits for all types of employment. Work permits have to be applied for by the future employer in Austria and must be obtained prior to departure from the country of residence. Work permits are not granted while on a visit to Austria. A useful organisation with respect to au pair positions is Au Pair 4You (+43 1 9901574; office@au-pair4you.at; www.au-pair4you.at). Work permits are also required by non-EU nationals for work with recognised voluntary organisations. The website www.help.gv.at gives useful details of all aspects of working in Austria.

Agricultural Work

WWOOF Austria

Job(s) Available: Volunteers.
Cost: A year's membership for WWOOF Austria costs approximately €20 plus €2 for postage. Membership includes a list of Austrian organic farmers looking for work-for-keep volunteer helpers.

Head Office: Pichling 277/9, 8510 Stainz Austria
☎ +43 676 505639 (mobile)
🖥 wwoof.welcome@utanet.at
🖳 www.wwoof.welcome.at.tf

Company Description: WWOOF Austria received the Ford Conservation and Environmental Award 2001.

Job Description: Volunteers required to take part in a form of cultural exchange where you live with and help a farming family, learning about organic farming methods in the process. Work is available on more than 200 farms. Movement between farms is possible.

Accommodation: Board and accommodation will be provided, however a separate wage will not. Applicants from outside the EU must secure their own travel insurance and all wwoofers pay for their own travel. In Austria they are covered by an insurance against accidents.

Application Procedure: For more information contact Hildegard Gottlieb at the above address.

Hotel Work and Catering

Hotel Bristol

Job(s) Available: Please check website for availability.
Application Procedure: Please check website for availability.

Head Office: Markatplatz 4, A-5020 Salzburg Austria
☎ +43 6628 73557
🖳 http://bristol.algo.at

Sports, Couriers and Camping

Bents Bicycle & Walking Tours

Job(s) Available: Company representatives (4–5).
Duration: Minimum period of work 8 weeks between the end of May and the end of September.
Working Hours: To work varied hours as needs of work dictate, but generally around 40 hours per week up to 7 day week.

Head Office: The Blue Cross, Orleton, Ludlow, Shropshire SY8 4HN, UK
☎ 01568 780800
✆ info@bentstours.com
🖥 www.bentstours.com

Pay: Around £600 per month.
Job Description: Company representatives for a tour operator offering cycling and walking holidays in France, Germany and Austria. Duties to include meeting clients at the airport, maintaining bicycles, transporting luggage between hotels and generally taking care of the needs of clients.
Requirements: Applicants should have a reasonable grasp of either spoken German or French and, fluent English. They must also possess a full valid driving license.
Accommodation: Board and accommodation provided.
Application Procedure: By post with a photograph, to Stephen Bent at the above address from January.

Canvas Holidays

Job(s) Available: Campsite courier.
Duration: Full season positions start in March, April or May and end in September/October. High season staff needed to work at least 2 months during the peak season.
Pay: Package includes competitive salary, tent accommodation, medical insurance, uniform and return travel from a UK port of entry.

Head Office: GVN Camping Recruitment, East Port House, Dunfermline, KY12 7JG, UK
☎ 01383 629012
✆ campingrecruitment@gvnrecruitment.com
🖥 www.gvnrecruitment.com

Company Description: Canvas Holidays provide luxury mobile home and tent holidays at over 100 campsites throughout Europe.
Job Description: Involves cleaning accommodation, welcoming families to the site and showing them to their accommodation. Visiting customers, providing local information and basic maintenance are very important parts of the job. Campsite courier opportunities are also available for couples to work on site together.
Accommodation: Provided as part of package.
Additional Information: For details of management positions, see website.
Application Procedure: Please call the Recruitment Department for more information and an application form, or apply online at www.gvnrecruitment.com.

Eurocamp

Job(s) Available: Campsite Courier, Children's Courier, Courier Team Leaders, Children's Courier Team Leaders, Montage/Demontage.
Duration: *Campsite Courier:* Applicants should be available to work from April/May to mid-September or June/July to mid-September. *Children's Courier:* Applicants should be available from early May to September or June to September. *Courier Team Leaders:* Applicants should be available from

Head Office: Overseas Recruitment Department (Ref SJ/08) Hartford Manor, Greenbank Lane, Northwich CW8 1HW, UK
☎ 01606 787525
🖥 www.holidaybreakjobs.com/camping

April to mid-September. *Children's Courier Team Leaders:* Applicants should be available from early May until September. *Montage/Demontage:* Applicants should be available from Feb to May or August to October.

Pay: You will receive a competitive salary, comprehensive training, return travel to and from an agreed meeting point, accommodation, medical and luggage insurance and uniform.

Company Description: Eurocamp is a leading tour operator in self-drive camping and mobile home holidays in Europe. We offer our customers a wide range of holiday accommodation on over 200 premier campsites. Each year the company seeks to recruit up to 1,500 enthusiastic people to work the summer season in a variety of roles.

Job Description: *Campsite Courier:* A Courier's responsibility begins by ensuring that the customer's accommodation is both inviting and cleaned to the highest of standards. You will welcome new arrivals, be the customers main point of contact and will be expected to provide local and general information, give assistance and even act as interpreter if required. Part of the role will involve helping out with minor repairs to accommodation and equipment and will also involve basic administration and accounts. *Children's Courier:* You will be responsible for planning and delivering a fun, safe, daily activity programme to our customers' children. The age of the children attending the club will range from 5 to 12 years old although we also run a toddler service in low season for 12 months to 4 years. *Courier Team Leaders:* You must be able to deliver first class customer service and organize the daily workload of the courier team. Your role also includes all the duties of a Campsite Courier and you will be expected to lead by example. There are a variety of team leader roles available, dependant on team size; Courier in Charge, Senior Courier and Site Manager. *Children's Courier Team Leaders:* Your role will involve the management, motivation and development of the Children's Couriers to ensure they provide a varied range of quality activities. Your role includes all the duties of a Children's Courier. *Montage/ Demontage:* Montage and Demontage assistants are employed to either help set up for the season or close down at the end of the season. This involves putting up or taking down tents, moving/distributing equipment and cleaning/preparing acco modation.

Requirements: Applicants must hold a UK/EU passport and the current minimum age is 18 years old on the day you start work in order to obtain the relevant insurance cover. *Campsite Couriers:* You should have lots of energy, basic common sense and a genuine desire to help people. *Children's Courier:* Previous childcare experience is essential. Successful candidates will be asked to apply for an Enhanced Disclosure. *Courier Team Leaders:* You must have previous experience of leading a team successful applicants may be asked to apply for a Standard Disclosure. *Children's Courier Team Leaders:* Previous experience with Children and leading a team successful candidates will be asked to apply for an Enhanced Disclosure. *Montage/Demontage:* Previous experience of physical and repetitive work successful applicants will be asked to apply for a Standard Disclosure.

Accommodation: Provided.

Application Procedure: Applicants should apply on-line at www.holidaybreakjobs.com/camping or telephone 01606 787525 for an application pack.

Teaching and Language Schools

English for Children – Summer Camp

Job(s) Available: Camp counsellors.

Duration: It is a 4-week day camp Mondays to Fridays. Week 1 is orientation week for counsellors only, where we set up the camp, cement the team and go through the programmes. Weeks 2, 3 and 4 comprise of the ELDC itself where counsellors and campers are present. It is necessary that the counselors attend the entire 4 week camp.

Head Office: Weichselweg 4, A-1220 Vienna Austria
☎ +43 1 95819720
office@englishforchildren.com
www.englishforchildren.com

Job Description: Camp counsellors to instruct in sports, arts and crafts, music, drama/and or English. To work in a total immersion summer camp, motivating children to speak English through different activities: sports, English language classes, arts and crafts, music, and to acquaint children with the different cultures of the English speaking world through games and songs etc.

Requirements: Applicants must have experience of working with children aged 3-14, and of camps, be versatile, conscientious, oriented towards children and safety and have an outgoing personality. Experience in more than one subject area is preferable. All applicants must be native English speakers. All applicants must be able to work within the EU as we cannot apply for work permits. Minimum age 20.

Accommodation: Help with finding accommodation is available and lunch is included in the working day.

Application Procedure: Applications with photos from English speakers invited from March onwards to English Language Day Camp, at the above address or by email.

Young Austria

Job(s) Available: Camp counsellor.
Duration: 2 week blocks all summer.
Company Description: Young Austira has organised camps for children and youngsters between 9 and 17 for over 30 years and moves mountains to create an unforgettable stay in Austria.

Head Office: Alpenstrasse 108a, A-5020 Salzburg Austria
☎ +43 662 6257580
✉ office@youngaustria.at
🖥 www.youngaustria.at

Accommodation: All positions are residential.
Application Procedure: Application form available at www.camps.at.

English for Kids

Job(s) Available: TEFL teachers.
Duration: *Residential summer camps:* period of work 3 weeks in August. *Day camps:* period of work 4 weeks in July and August.
Pay: Varies depending on qualifications, ranging from €560.

Head Office: A. Postgasse 11/19, 1010 Vienna Austria
☎ +43 1 6674579
✉ magik@e4kids.co.at
🖥 www.e4kids.co.at

Company Description: The teaching venue is a beautifully renovated, 17th century, building around a large central yard and it is situated in 40 hectares of meadows and woods.

Job Description: Residential summer camps in upper Austria with pupils aged between 10 and 15. Day camps based in Vienna with pupils aged between 5 and 15. The teaching style is full immersion with in-house methods following carefully planned syllabus and teachers' manual, supplemented with CD-Roms etc.

Requirements: TEFL teachers (8-10) with CELTA or Trinity CertTESOL (minimum grade B) and some formal teaching experience.

Accommodation: 2 weeks plus full board and accommodation and travel expenses within Austria included in pay.

Application Procedure: By post to Irena Köstenbauer, principal, at the above address.

Au Pairs, Nannies, Family Helps and Exchanges

AU Pair Austria

Job(s) Available: Incoming au pairs (200), outgoing au pairs (30)

Duration: Minimum stay of 8 weeks for summer au pairs, and between 6 and 12 months for the academic year.

Company Description: In business since 2001 and a member of IAPA.

Application Procedure: Candidates submit a written application and must undergo an interview.

Application Procedure: Contact Jana Varga-Steininger, general manager or Margit Mauhart, programme manager. All nationalities placed.

> **Head Office:** Ignaz Kock Str: 8/3, A-1210 Wien Austria
> ☎ +43 1 4054050
>
> **Head Office:** Ahornstrasse 8, A-4481 Asten
> ☎ +43 7224 68359,
> +43 676 4140150 (24/7 hotline)
> ✆ office@aupairaustria.com
> 🖳 www.aupairaustria.com

BELGIUM

BELGIAN EMBASSY
17 Grosvenor Crescent, London SW1X 7EE
☎ 020 7470 3700
🖳 www.diplomatie.be/london
✆ london@diplobel.be

Unemployment in Belgium is fairly high compared with other Western European countries, but the economy is stable and there are work opportunities.

Although small in area, Belgium is densely populated and can seem complicated to the outsider, as three languages are spoken within the country's federal states. These languages are Flemish, French and German. In broad terms Flemish is spoken in the north (Flanders) and French in the south (Wallonia), with both being spoken in Brussels in the centre of the country; German is spoken mainly in the Eastern Cantons. With its coastal resorts Belgium has an active hotel and tourism industry in the north which makes seasonal work in Belgium a viable prospect. Adecco, a group of temporary jobs agencies has information for local employment agencies at http://www.adecco.be

EU nationals looking for work can get help from the Belgian employment services, which are organised on a regional basis. They cover three main areas: in the Flemish region the services are known as the *Vlaamse Dienst voor Arbeidsbemiddeling en Beroepsopleiding (VDAB)* (+32 2 5083811; info@vdab.be; www.vdab.be); in the French region they are *Office Wallon de la Formation Professionnelle et de l'Emploi (FOREM)* (+32 71 205040; communic@forem.be; www.leforem.be); and in the Brussels Region they are known as *Office Régional Bruxellois de l'Emploi (ORBEM)/Brusselse Gewestelijke Dienst voor Arbeidsbemiddeling (BGDA)* (+32 2 5051411; http://www.actiris.be). There are local employment offices in most towns.

There are also some employment offices specialising in temporary work, known as the T-Interim, which are operated as Dutch and French speaking offices under the aegis of VDAB and FOREM; as may be expected the VDAB T-Interim offices are in Flanders and the French T-Interim offices are found in Wallonia, with ORBEM/BGDA running the T-Interim offices for Brussels. These offices can only help people who visit them in person, and the staff are multi-lingual in most cases. They can assist in finding secretarial work, especially in Brussels where there are a large number of multinational companies needing bilingual staff. Other opportunities they may have available consist of manual work in supermarkets and warehouses or engineering and computing. They are most likely to be able to help you during the summer, when companies need to replace their permanent staff who are away on holiday. T-Interims can be found on the internet at www.t-interim.be

You could also try advertising yourself as being available for work. One of the main newspapers published in Belgium is *Le Soir* (French) (+32 2 2255500/5432; journal@lesoir.be; www.lesoir.be). The daily newspaper *De Standaard* (+32 2 4672211; www.standaard.be) is for Flemish speakers. There is a weekly English language magazine called *The Bulletin* (+32 2 3739909; www.thebulletin.be); it comes out on Thursdays and is available from newsstands. *The Bulletin* lists offers of work on their website www.xpats.com. Twice a year they publish a very useful magazine-type supplement called *Newcomer* aimed at new arrivals in Belgium.

Those looking for work on Belgian farms should be warned that most conventional Belgian farms are highly mechanised and thus offer little scope for casual work.

The *Fédération Infor Jeunes Wallonie-Bruxelles* (www.inforjeunes.be) is a non-profit organisation which coordinates 11 youth information offices plus 28 local points of contacts in French-speaking Belgium. These can give advice on work as well as leisure, youth rights, accommodation, etc. A leaflet listing the addresses is available from the *Fédération Infor Jeunes* can be found on their website. Among Infor Jeune's services, they operate holiday job placement offices (*Service Job Vacances*) between March and September.

Americans can apply through Interexchange in New York (see entry in *Worldwide* chapter) to be placed in a summer job, internship or teaching position in Belgium. CIEE in New York helps to place Americans in short term voluntary positions in this country, as does Service Civil International (see the International Voluntary Service entry).

Voluntary work in Belgium can be arranged for UK nationals by Concordia, International Voluntary Service, Youth Action For Peace or UNA Exchange (entries for these organisations can be found in the *Worldwide* chapter).

For more information see the Living & Working Belgium section of the EURES website (www.europa.eu.int/eures) or use the jobs section to and work.

Red Tape

Visa Requirements: Visas are not required by EU citizens, or those of many other countries (including the USA, Canada, Japan, Australia and New Zealand and listed at www.diplomatie.be/london) provided they have a valid passport and that the visit is for less than three months. Other nationalities will have to obtain an entry permit, which should be applied for at a Belgian Embassy or Consulate in advance of travel in the applicant's country of residence, see www.vfs-be-uk.com for more information.

Residence Permits: All non-Belgians must register at the local town hall within 8 days of arrival to obtain a residence permit. EU nationals should take documents proving that they have sufficient funds and a valid passport.

Work Permits: These are not required by EU nationals; others must first arrange a job, then the prospective employer should apply for a work permit at the regional ministry of employment. There are some exceptions to work permit requirements according to the employment to be taken up; consult embassies and consulates for details. It is not normally necessary to obtain permits for short-term voluntary work with recognised organisations.

Hotel Work and Catering

Hotel Lido

Job(s) Available: Waiting staff (2), kitchen assistants (1).

Duration: Minimum period of work 1 or 2 months between June and September.

Working Hours: *Kitchen assistants:* to work from 9am–12am, 1pm–3pm and 6pm–9.30pm.

Pay: *Kitchen assistants:* £650 net per month.

Requirements: *Waiting staff:* basic French required.

Accommodation: *Kitchen assistants:* board and lodging provided free

Application Procedure: Applications with a CV and recent photograph to A Simoens at the above address.

Head Office: Zwaluwenlaan, 18 Albert Plage, 8300 Knokke-Heist Belgium
☎ +32 50 601925
✆ info@lido-hotel.be,
 lido.hotel.knokke@vt4.net

Sports, Couriers and Camping

Ski Ten International

Job(s) Available: English teacher, tennis teacher and sports teacher.

Duration: Summer camp in July and August.

Working Hours: 6 hours per day.

Pay: Approximately £600.

Head Office: Château d'Émines, 5080 Émines Belgium
☎ +32 81 213051
✆ martine@ski-ten.be
🖳 www.ski-ten.be

Company Description: Ski Ten offers a marvellous experience of working a month in an international team at the Château d'Émines which has 14 hectares of grounds with lakes, swimming pool etc.

Job Description: Duties will include looking after, eating with and arranging games for the children in their care.

Requirements: Some knowledge of French and previous experience working with children would be useful.

Accommodation: Accommodation will be provided.

Application Procedure: Applications should be sent in writing, with a photograph, to the above address.

Venture Abroad

Job(s) Available: Resort representatives (2–3).

Duration: Five weeks minimum work from June to August.

Working Hours: 6 days a week, flexible hours.

Head Office: Rayburn House, Parcel Terrace, Derby, DE1 1LY, UK
☎ 01332 342050
✆ joannek@rayburntours.co.uk
🖳 www.ventureabroad.co.uk

Company Description: Venture Abroad organise package holidays for scout and guide groups to the continent. They arrange travel and accommodation and provide representatives in the resort.

Job Description: Resort representatives to work in Belgium and Switzerland; checking in groups, dealing with accommodation enquiries, organising and accompanying local excursions etc.

Requirements: Applicants should be practical, resourceful and calm under pressure. Speaking German an advantage.

Application Procedure: Applications to the above address.

DENMARK

ROYAL DANISH EMBASSY
55 Sloane Street, London SW1X 9SR
☎ 020 7333 0200
🖥 www.denmark.org.uk
🖱 lonamb@um.dk

Denmark's low level of unemployment (currently around 3.8%), and very high standard of living would appear to provide a big incentive for jobseekers to look for work there. However, until recent times foreigners have had a hard time, especially if they didn't have some notion of the Danish language. However, according to the Ministry of Science, Technology and Innovation 'English-speaking jobs in Denmark are becoming more and more common', as Denmark's large companies such as Carlsberg, Novo and Nordea, and increasingly smaller companies too, adopt English as their corporate language. Non-EU citizens will find it hard to obtain a job in Denmark, as work permits are only issued where an employer can prove that there is no EU citizen who can do that job. Citizens of the newer EU members from Eastern Europe also have restricted access to Danish jobs in the transitional phase of their membership.

Anyone serious about wanting to work in Denmark should consult the EURES website (www.europa.eu.int/eures) for further information about life there. The useful leaflet called *Working in Denmark* is available from *Use It* Tourist Information, part of the Youth Information (+45 33730620; www.useit.dk). Please note that *Use It* is not an employment agency but an information centre for low budget travellers. The Ministry of Science, Technology and Innovation website (www.workindenmark.dk), is also very informative.

Despite the increasing mechanisation of farming there is still a need for fruit pickers during the summer; up to 1,000 people are needed each year for the strawberry harvest. Be warned, however, that the hours can be very long when you are paid by the kilo with picking taking place between 6am and noon. The main harvests are strawberries in June/July, cherries in July/August, apples in September/October and tomatoes throughout the summer. Fruit producing areas are scattered around the country: some of the most important are to be found to the north of Copenhagen, around Arhus, and to the east and west of Odense.

You may be able to obtain a job on a farm or other work by contacting the pan-European agency EURES through your local job centre; vacancies for the fruit harvest and other seasonal work are announced in the spring on the Danish EURES website (www.eures.dk) where an online application can be made.

Another method is to advertise in the farming magazine *LandbrugsAvisen* (+45 33394700; www.landbrugsavisen.dk).

It is also possible to arrange unpaid work on an organic farm. Another possibility is to contact VHH (the Danish WWOOF) to obtain a list of their 25–30 member farmers, most of whom speak English. In return for three or four hours of work per day, you get free food and lodging. Always phone or write before arriving. The list can be obtained either online or on paper. To obtain a copy of the list send £5/€10 to Inga Nielsen, Asenvej 35, 9881 Bindslev for the paper version, or to Lasse Baaner, Horsevadvej 200, 9830 Taars for the online version (+45 98938607; info@wwoof.dk; www.wwoof.dk).

The Danish state employment service is obliged to help Britons and other EU nationals who call at their offices to find a job. The administrative headquarters of the employment service – the National Labour Market Authority (*Arbejdsmarkedsstyrelsen*) – is at Blegdamsvej 56, Postbox 2722, DK-2100 Copenhagen (+45 35288100; ams@ams.dk; www.ams.dk). When you are actually in Denmark, you can find the address of your nearest employment office under *Arbejdsformidlingen* in the local telephone directory.

WESTERN EUROPE

DENMARK

195

There are also opportunities for voluntary work in Denmark, arranged by International Voluntary Service, UNA Exchange, Youth Action for Peace and Concordia for British applicants and CIEE and Service Civil International for Americans (see the *Worldwide* chapter for details). It is also possible to work as a volunteer as the mid-June Roskilde Festival (+45 46371982; www.roskilde-festival.dk; www.gimle.dk;david@sonordica.org). Volunteers are expected to be self-funding. A camping ground is provided and shifts last 8 hours.

There are a number of private employment agencies in Denmark, but most are looking for trained secretarial staff who speak fluent Danish.

An advertisement in a Danish paper may bring an offer of employment. Crane Media Partners Ltd, 20-28 Dalling Road, Hammersmith, W6 0JB (020 237 8601) are advertising agents for *Berlingske Tidende*. *Morgenavisen-Jyllands-Posten* (+45 87383838; http://jp.dk) is one of the more important papers for job advertisements visit their website for details.

Red Tape

Visa Requirements: Visas are not required by citizens of EU countries.

Residence Permits: A residence permit (*Opholdsbevis*) should be applied for through Kobenhavns Overpraesidium at Hammerensgade 1, 1267 Copenhagen K, Denmark, (+45 33122380). EU nationals wishing to stay in Denmark for longer than 3 months and all visitors from non-EU countries must gain a residence permit.

Work Permits: The Royal Danish Embassy has indicated that nationals of countries not in the EU or Scandinavia will not be granted work permits except where the employer can prove that the applicant has a unique skill. The exceptions are Australian and New Zealand nationals aged 18–30, who are entitled to apply for a Working Holiday Visa, which entitles them to work in Denmark for up to six months. Further details can be obtained from the Danish Immigration Service website (www.nyidanmark.dk). EU, Australian and New Zealand nationals who wish to take up employment in Denmark may stay there for a period not exceeding 3 months from the date of arrival in order to seek employment provided they have sufficient funds to support themselves. All work, paid and unpaid, is subject to the above regulations.

Agricultural Work

Birkholm Frugt & Baer

Job(s) Available: Strawberry pickers.

Duration: Minimum period of work 3 weeks. The high season starts around 6 June and ends in the middle of July.

Working Hours: Picking normally starts at 5am. 5–8 hours per day, 6 days a week.

Pay: Payment at piecework rates of around £0.50 per kilo.

Head Office: V/Bjarne Knutsen, Hornelandevej 2 D, DK-5600 Faaborg Denmark
☎ +45 62602262
birkholm@strawberrypicking.dk
www.strawberrypicking.dk

Requirements: Applicants must be an EU national and have a European passport. Minimum age 18.

Accommodation: Workers must bring their own tent and camping equipment. The price for camping is 25Dkr. per day.

Application Procedure: Contact the above address or check the website for further information.

Voluntary Work and Archaeology

Mellemfolkeligt Samvirke (MS)

Job(s) Available: Volunteers to work in international work camps in Denmark and Greenland.
Duration: The camps last from 2 to 3 weeks between July and August.
Cost: Participants must provide their own travelling expenses.

Head Office: Borgergade 14, 1300 Copenhagen K Denmark
☎ +45 77310022
✒ globalcontact@ms.dk
🖳 www.globalcontact.dk

Job Description: The camps normally involve community projects such as conservation of playgrounds, renovation, conservation, archaeological work, nature protection, reconditioning of used tools to be later sent to Africa, etc.
Requirements: Minimum age 18.
Accommodation: Board and accommodation are provided.
Application Procedure: British applicants should apply through Concordia (Second Floor, 19 North Street, Portslade, BN41 1DH England www.concordia-iye.org.uk) and the UNA Exchange (Temple of Peace, Cathays Park, Cardiff CF10 3AP Wales www.unaexchange.org). Applications to the above address.

Roskilde Festival

Job(s) Available: Volunteers (60), Refuse collectors (700).
Duration: 4 days in July.
Working Hours: 100 hours over 12 days.
Pay: No wage but free entry to festival.
Company Description: Roskilde is the most exten-

Head Office: Havsteensvej 11, DK-4000, Roskilde Denmark
☎ +45 46366613
✒ info@roskilde-festival.dk
🖳 www.roskilde-festival.dk

sive music festival in northern Europe, running for almost 40 years. It is a non-profit organisation, with a humanitarian focus.
Job Description: Volunteers work in different areas of the festival. As a reward, volunteers not only receive a free ticket to the festival but also free camping and 3 meals a day. There are social events and a field trip is organised.
Accommodation: Camping and meals provided free of charge.
Additional Information: Applicants must be available for interview between 26 March and 16 April.
Application Procedure: See website for more details.

FRANCE

FRENCH EMBASSY
58 Knightsbridge, London SW1X 7JT
☎ 020 7073 1000
🖳 www.ambafrance-uk.org
✒ consulat.londres-fslt@diplomatie.fr

France has long been one of the most popular destinations for British and Irish people looking for summer work. This is due to its physical proximity: the fact that French is the first (and often only) foreign language learned; and, possibly most important of all, because during the summer France still needs many extra temporary workers for both its vibrant tourist trade and farm work, even

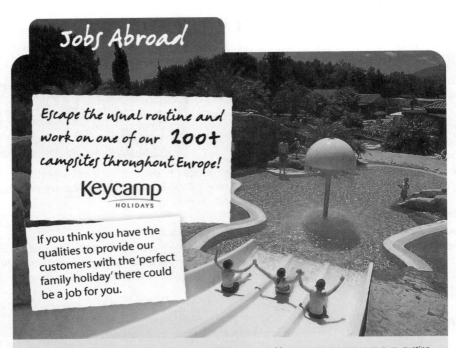
though there is currently fairly high unemployment of about 8.7% mainly amongst young people. Theme parks like Disneyland Paris or Parc Asterix need extra staff through peak times such as the summer holidays. Disneyland Paris alone employs many thousands of seasonal workers.

This chapter contains details of many jobs in the tourist industry: you can find others in the *Worldwide* chapter and in the weekly hotel trade magazine *L'Hotellerie* (+33 1 45486464; www.lhotellerie.fr) where you can check out the classified jobs section (arranged by region) at any time online.

British and Irish citizens, along with other EU nationals, are allowed to use the French national employment service (*Agence Nationale pour l'Emploi;* ANPE; +33 1 49317400; www.anpe.fr), although the offices in towns throughout France will know more about vacancies in their region. There is a comprehensive website detailing the services provided by ANPE in both French and English. British citizens can apply for work through the service by visiting any of almost 600 local ANPE offices around the country, see the website for details.

There are also a number of private employment agencies such as *Manpower, Kelly, Bis, Select France,* and *Ecco* in large cities which can help people who speak reasonable French to find temporary jobs in offices, private houses, warehouses, etc. They can be found in the Yellow Pages (*Les Pages Jaunes;* www.pagesjaunes.fr) under *Agences de Travail Temporaire*. These agencies can normally only find jobs for people who visit in person.

For further information relevant to working in France consult the EURES website (www.europa.eu.int/eures) and click on Living & Working.

Seasonal farm work can be difficult to obtain from outside France. If you cannot arrange a job in advance using the information in this chapter it is best to be on-the-spot and approach farmers in person, or ask at the local employment offices, town halls (*mairies*) or youth hostels. A word of warning: if you arrange to go grape picking with an organisation not mentioned in this chapter read the small print carefully: you may be buying just a journey out to France, with no guarantee of a job at the end.

For help in finding temporary work during the grape-picking season, you could contact ANPE. ANPE have offices in most large towns in France's main agricultural regions. Each office can offer around 1000 jobs to those who wish to work on farms up to 50km from the town. Apple-picking and grape-picking have the most prevalent jobs available.

Workers are needed to help harvest the following fruits (amoungst others), especially in the valleys of the Loire and the Rhône and the south east and south west of the country. The exact dates of harvests can vary considerably from year to year and from region to region: bear in mind that harvests tend to begin first in the south of the country.

- *Strawberries:* May to mid-June
- *Cherries:* mid-May to early July
- *Peaches:* June to September
- *Pears:* mid-July to mid-November
- *Apples:* mid-August (but chiefly from mid-September) to mid-October.

French farmers employ over 100,000 foreigners for seasonal work during the summer. Many of these are skilled 'professional' seasonal workers from Spain, Poland, Portugal and Morocco who return to the same regions every year: if there is a choice of applicants for a job, a farmer will prefer an experienced worker to a total beginner. In recent years there has also been an influx of people from Eastern Europe who are desperate for work and prepared to work for less than the minimum wage (*le SMIC,* approximately €8.44), for any farmer who will employ them illegally. Anyone going to France to look for farm work should be prepared to move from area to area in the search for a job: it would also be wise to take enough money to cover the cost of returning home in case of failure. Also be warned that payment is generally by piecework, so there are no wages if picking is suspended because of bad weather.

You could track down vineyards ahead of time using a detailed wine guide, and remove some of the uncertainty of the job hunt by visiting farmers to arrange a job before their harvests start: by doing so you should also be given an informed estimate of when the harvest will start. Note that although vineyard owners normally provide accommodation for grape pickers, workers on other harvests will normally need camping equipment. The increasing sophistication of the ANPE means that grape-picking and fruit picking jobs are advertised on their website (www.anpe.fr) in English.

France is rich in opportunities for voluntary work, as the entries in this chapter will testify. The CEI in Paris and Service Civil International (see the IVS entry) can assist Americans. International Voluntary Service (IVS), UNA Exchange, Youth Action for Peace and Concordia can help can UK residents to find short-term voluntary work; their entries can be found in the *Worldwide* chapter.

A great many archaeological digs and building restoration projects are carried out each year. The French Ministry of Culture has two departments dealing with antiquities, one focuses on archaeology and the other on the restoration of monuments (Ministère de la Culture, *Direction de l'Architecture et du Patrimoine, Sous-Direction de l'Archeologie*, 4 rue d'Aboukir, 75002 Paris (+33 1 40157781) and Ministère de la Culture, *Direction du Patrimoine, Sous-Direction des Monuments Historiques* at the same address (+33 1 40157681). Each year the ministry publishes a list of these archaeological fieldwork projects throughout France in a brochure and on the internet (www.culture.gouv.fr/fouilles) requiring up to 5,000 volunteers. Another brochure, *Chantiers de benevoles* published by Rempart (see entry under Voluntary Work), lists projects relating to building restoration.

Advertising for a job in France can be arranged in the Paris edition of the *International Herald Tribune*, contact the London office, 40, Marsh Wall, London E14 9TP (020 7836 4802; ukadv@iht.com), or New York Office, 850 Third Avenue, New York, NY 10022 (+1 212 7523890; usadv@iht.com), or at www.iht.com.

Red Tape

Visa Requirements: Visas are not required for visits to France by EU, American, Canadian, Australian or New Zealand nationals. Others should check with their nearest French Consulate.

Residence Permits: EU citizens are not obliged to have a *carte de séjour* (residence permit) for stays of any length. You can apply for one voluntarily as it can be a useful proof of ID for long-term foreign residents, but as the paperwork involved is so cumbersome, it is likely that most long-stayers will not bother. If you decide you want one, application for this permit should be made on a special form available from the *Prefecture de Police* in Paris, or the local *Prefecture* or *Mairie* (town hall) elsewhere. The following documents are required: passport, birth certificate, proof of accommodation, proof of payment of contributions to the French Social Security, 3 passport photos, a contract of employment, pension receipts or student status documents. Non-EU nationals need to possess a long stay visa before applying for a *carte de séjour*, and a work permit before obtaining either. Application for a long stay visa should be lodged with a French consulate in the applicant's country of residence.

Work Permits: Members of the EU do not need work permits to work in France. The standard procedure for non-EU nationals is that the prospective employer in France must apply to the agence nationale de l'accueil des etrangers et des migrations, 44 rue Bargue, 75732 Paris, Cedex 17. A work permit is required even for Voluntary Work.

Work Abroad Schemes for US Citizens: There is a special scheme allowing American students to work in France run by the Centre d'Echanges Internationaux (CIE; +33 1 40511186; wif@cei4vents.com; www.cei4vents.com)). To participate applicants must be in full-time higher education and have at least intermediate French skills (tests are available on request). Three types of scheme are available through the 'Work in France' department, the Job Placement, the Internship Placement and the Self-Service placement.

Self-Service Placement: Allows students a 3-month temporary work permit during their school holidays. Participants receive help finding jobs via a network of employers willing to employ foreign students and help finding housing.

Internship Placement: Offers an internship covered by a written work placement agreement, which must be signed by the student, the employer and the university. The work placement may not last longer than a year. The placement assigned to a student should have a direct link to the subject they are studying.

Job Placement: As an association recognised by the Ministry of Employment, the CEI is capable of validating a work permit for a placement found by the students themselves. For more information please visit or contact the CEI French Centre.

Agricultural Work

Appellation Controllee

Job(s) Available: Grape picking.
Duration: 1 to 4 weeks. Normal minimum stay on a farm is 3 weeks.
Working Hours: 8 hours per day, 7 days a week.
Pay: Either at piecework rate (average earnings £25–£40 per day) or at an hourly rate (approximately £30 per day).

Head Office: Neutronstraat 10, 9743 AM Groningen, The Netherlands
☎ +31 50 5492434
✆ info@apcon.nl
▤ www.apcon.nl

Company Description: An organisation that organises working holidays in France and England.
Job Description: Grape picking takes place in the Beaujolais, Maconais and Bourgogne regions in September. The job involves picking various fruits beginning with strawberries in May and followed by raspberries, bilberries and melons later on.
Requirements: Minimum age for all work is 18.
Accommodation: Board and lodging. Accommodation will be either camping or the farmer may provided clean, basic accommodation.
Application Procedure: By post to the above address.

Boats

Croisieres Touristiques Francaises

Job(s) Available: Chefs, drivers/guides, pilots, stewardesses, deckhands.
Duration: Must be available for work from April to early November.
Working Hours: For all positions the hours of work are long, over a 5 to 6 day week.

Head Office: 2 Route de Semur, F-21150 Venarey-les-Laumes France
☎ +33 3 80961710
✆ ctf.boat@club-internet.fr

Pay: *Chefs:* from £1,300 per month. *Drivers/guides:* from £1,100 per month. *Pilots:* from £1,300 per month. *Stewardesses:* from £900 per month. *Deckhands:* from £900 per month. Salaries quoted are for inexperienced crew members. Gratuities are divided equally amongst crew members.
Company Description: Croisieres Touristiques Francaises owns and operates 5 ultra-deluxe hotel barges, offering 6-night cruises in 5 regions of central France.
Job Description: *Chefs:* required to plan menus and prepare gourmet cuisine. *Stewardesses:* work involves cleaning cabins, general housekeeping, food/bar service and care of passengers. *Deckhands:* to assist the pilot during navigation and mooring and to carry out exterior maintenance of the barge.
Requirements: Crew members must be EU nationals, or possess appropriate visas permitting work in France. Minimum age 21. Applicants must be energetic, personable, and able to provide a consistently high standard of service. *Chefs:* Professional training and experience in haute cuisine establishments is essential, some knowledge of French useful. *Drivers/guides:* applicants must have a P.S.V. licence, should speak fluent French and have a concise knowledge of French heritage and culture. *Pilots:* must have French Inland Waterways Permit to drive 38m Hotel Barge and have mechanical experience. Some knowledge of French useful. *Stewardesses:* knowledge of French useful, but not essential. *Deckhands:* some knowledge of French useful.

Accommodation: Salaries include accommodation, full board and uniform.
Additional Information: Social Security coverage is taken care of by the company.
Application Procedure: Apply with CV, contact telephone number and recent photo to Mr. Thierry Bresson at the above address.

Holiday Centres

Disneyland Paris

Job(s) Available: Permanent or seasonal staff.
Duration: Temporary contracts lasting 2–8 months from March (minimum availability July and August) or permanent contracts starting at any time.

Head Office: Casting, BP110, F-77777 Marne La Vallée cedex 4 France
🖥 www.Disneylandparis.com/uk/employment

Working Hours: 35 hour working week.
Pay: £775 per month less social security contributions.
Job Description: Permanent or seasonal staff to work in the restaurants, on counter service or reception, in sales, for the attractions, sports and leisure attractions of the Disneyland Paris Resort situated 30 km east of Paris.
Requirements: Applicants should be at least 18, have a good working knowledge of French and be customer-service orientated. Experience not essential.
Accommodation: Assistance is given in finding accommodation and a contribution towards travel expenses is given to those who complete their contract.
Application Procedure: Applications in writing to the above address.

Hotel Work And Catering

Alpine Elements

Job(s) Available: Chalet hosts, resort managers, hotel chefs and reps.
Duration: 5 months.

Head Office: 1 Risborough Street, London SE1 0HF, UK
☎ 0870 011 1360
📧 info@alpineelements.co.uk
🖥 www.alpineelements.co.uk

Company Description: Alpine Elements arrange chalet and self-catering holidays in Chamonix, Morzine, Les Gets, Meriel, Alpe d'Huez, Val d'Isere, Les Arcs Courchevel and Tignes in France.
Requirements: Minimum age 18. Staff should be British passport-holders. Reps must hold a clean driving licence. Staff get 2 weeks of training in France and the UK.
Accommodation: Provided free of charge.
Application Procedure: Applicants should send their CV and a covering letter to the above address or email for the attention of Mr G Niedermann.

Alpine Tracks

Job(s) Available: Chef, cleaners (3), minibus driver, bar person, mountain bike and ski guides.
Duration: Between 1 June and 30 September; minimum period of work 2 months.

Head Office: 40 High Street, Menai Bridge, Anglesey LL59 5EF, UK
☎ 01248 717440
📧 info@alpinetracks.com, sales@alpinetracks.com
🖥 www.alpinetracks.com

Working Hours: Hours of work are 7am–10am and 5pm–9pm 7 days a week.
Pay: £350–£500.

Company Description: Alpine Tracks are a friendly and informal small professional holiday company operating chalets with a high level of personal service in the French Alps for skiers and mountain bikers.

Job Description: Dining and bar work, catering for up to 30 people.

Requirements: Applicants should be friendly, outgoing, preferably French speakers and hold relevant qualifications.

Accommodation: Board and lodging are provided at no cost.

Application Procedure: By post to the above address.

L'auberge Sur La Montagne

Job(s) Available: 1 or 2 chalet hosts.

Duration: Minimum period of work is 4 weeks.

Working Hours: Hours of work 2–4 hours per morning and 4–6 hours per evening (6–8 hours per day) 6 days a week.

Pay: €500 (£345) per month.

Head Office: La Thuile, F-73640 Sainte Foy Tarentaise France
☎ +33 4 79069583
✆ mail@auberge-montagne.com
🖳 www.auberge-montagne.com

Company Description: This private 8-bed hotel is situated in the French alps between Val D'Isère and Bourg Saint Maurice. There are great opportunities for, walking, cycling, water-sports and paragliding, as well as glacier skiing in summer.

Job Description: Required to clean rooms, public areas (bar, lounge and restaurant), wash up and serve breakfasts and dinner.

Requirements: Applicants should have some previous experience and speak English and French.

Accommodation: Free board and lodging.

Application Procedure: To apply contact Sue and Andy MacInnes from May onwards.

Hostellerie Le Beffroi

Job(s) Available: Reception assistant, bar, kitchen and restaurant staff.

Duration: Minimum period of work 3 months between April and the end of September.

Working Hours: 8 hours per day, 5 days a week.

Pay: Around €1100 per month.

Job Description: Duties by arrangement.

Head Office: BP 85, F-84110 Vaison la Romaine, Provence France
☎ +33 4 90360471
✆ ychristiansen@wanadoo.fr
🖳 www.le-beffroi.com

Requirements: Applicants should speak French (and German if possible) and must have experience of hotel or restaurant work.

Accommodation: Board and accommodation provided.

Application Procedure: Applications to Yann Christiansen at the above address.

Hotel Belle Isle Sur Risle

Job(s) Available: Waiter (1), receptionist (1).

Duration: Minimum period of work 1–2 months during the summer vacation: July and August.

Working Hours: 169 hours work a month.

Pay: SMIC

Head Office: 112 Route de Rouen, 27500 Pont-Audemer France
☎ +33 2 32569622
✆ hotelbelle-isle@wanadoo.fr
🖳 www.bellile.com

Requirements: Experience necessary. Good English and some French required.

Accommodation: Can be arranged.

Application Procedure: CV and photo by email.

Hotel Chateaurenard

Job(s) Available: General assistants (4).
Duration: To work minimum period of one week over Christmas/New Year, 4 weeks in February/March or 4–6 weeks during July to August/September.
Working Hours: 43 hours per week, 5 days a week.
Pay: SMIC

Head Office: F-05350 Saint Veran
☎ +33 4 92458543 France
✍ info@hotel-chateaurenard.com
💻 www.hotel-chateaurenard.com

Company Description: This 20-room chalet-style hotel, run by a French speaking Australian with her French chef husband is located at the foot of the ski slopes (2080m). It has spectacular views overlooking the 18th century village of Saint Veran, the Hautes Alpes, and the border with the Italian Piedmont.

Job Description: General assistants to clean rooms, work in the restaurant and the laundry.

Requirements: No special qualifications required except a happy nature and the ability to work with people and to work hard. Knowledge of French is essential.

Accommodation: Board and accommodation provided.

Application Procedure: Applications to the director at the above address.

Hotel-Restaurant Cheval-Blanc

Job(s) Available: Assistant waitress, kitchen assistant.
Duration: Period of work 3 months minimum from July to November.
Working Hours: 41 hours per week.
Pay: SMIC

Head Office: 11 rue principaleF-67510 Niedersteinbach France
☎ +33 3 88095531
✍ contact@hotel-cheval-blanc.fr
💻 www.hotel-cheval-blanc.fr

Company Description: A 25 room hotel combined with a 120 place restaurant located in a small village in a natural park. Facilities include a tennis court and a swimming pool.

Requirements: *Waitress:* Must have knowledge of German.

Accommodation: Accommodation provided free of charge. Meals not included.

Application Procedure: Email CV to contact@hotel-cheval-blanc.fr

Restaurant Cruaud

Job(s)Available: Summer staff to work in a hotel and restaurant.
Duration: From April to October.
Working Hours: 186 hours per month, 5 days a week.
Pay: By arrangement.

Head Office: 30, Avenue du Maréchal Joffre, 84300 Cavaillon France
☎ +33 6 80266998

Company Description: François Cruaud is also a Conseiller Culinaire and Officier du Mérite Agricole and offers cookery courses and formation for hotel and restaurant trainees. In 2005, he created the Association des Conseilles Alimentaires Français et Européens.

Requirements: Applicants must speak French and English.

Accommodation: Board and lodging provided.

Application Procedure: By post to Mr and Mrs Cruaud at the above address from January.

Domaine Saint Clair Le Donjon

Job(s) Available: Various dining room and kitchen positions, receptionist.

Duration: April to September.

Working Hours: 8 hours per day 5–6 days a week.

Pay: *Waiter:* from €850 per month. *Pastry chef:* from €1500 per month. *Receptionist:* from €1300 per month.

Head Office: 9 rue des Grands Champs, 75020 Paris France
☎ +33 1 43407779
direction@hoteletretat.com or contact@hotelspreference.com

Company Description: Hotel and restaurant with 21 rooms all with ensuite including jacuzzi. The restaurant is of gastronomic standard.

Job Description: Staff required for a 2-part organisation (hotel and restaurant) in reception and room cleaning and in the restaurant (service, bar and kitchen).

Requirements: *Dining room staff:* should speak French and English. *Kitchen positions:* require experience. *Receptionist:* must be fluent in French and English and have experience.

Accommodation: Board and lodging provided at no extra cost.

Application Procedure: By post to the director at the above address.

Hotel Edouard VII

Job(s) Available: Waiter/waitress, luggage porter, chamber maid.

Duration: Between June and September, minimum period of work is 2 months.

Working Hours: 39 hours per week, 5 days a week.

Pay: SMIC, average €1100 per month, depends on job and experience.

Head Office: 39 Avenue de l'Opéra, 75002 Paris France
☎ +33 1 42615690
reception@edouard7hotel.com
www.edouard7hotel.com

Company Description: The Edouard VII Hotel is a well-known, stylish, 4-star, family-run establishment that takes pride in the impeccable service offered to clients.

Job Description: *Waiter/waitress:* required to prepare, serve and tidy away after breakfast. Involves a lot of client interaction. *Luggage porter:* required to welcome clients and transport their baggage, to run occasional errands and supervise the lobby. This can be very physical work. Must be friendly, have a professional outlook and excellent people skills. Needs to be physically fit. *Chamber maid:* required for thorough cleaning of the rooms and bathrooms, bed making, stock taking and replacing. This can be a very physical job. Must have enthusiasm and professionalism.

Requirements: Minimum age 18. Good knowledge of English and French is essential. Other languages especially Spanish, Russian or Japanese an advantage.

Accommodation: Can be arranged.

Application Procedure: Email CV and cover letter to reception@edouard7hotel.com by April.

Hotel-Restaurant Le Fleuray

Job(s) Available: Hotel staff.

Duration: Minimum 4 months, between March and October.

Working Hours: 10 hours per day (split shift – mornings and evenings, with afternoons off) 6 days a week.

Head Office: F-37530 Cangey, Amboise
☎ +33 2 47560925 France
lefleurayhotel@wanadoo.fr
www.lefleurayhotel.com

Pay: Attractive weekly wage

Company Description: A small but expanding, friendly company, great opportunity for a language or hospitality student. Close to famous towns Amboise, Tours and Blois and surrounded by chateaux and vineyards. This highly acclaimed English-run, country house hotel is situated in the Loire valley, only 55 minutes from Paris by TGV. It is listed in many *Best Hotel* guidebooks worldwide and has appeared in *The Times*, the *Telegraph* and *San Francisco Chronicle* newspapers.

Job Description: Hotel staff required for all aspects of work in the hotel (including restaurant service, housekeeping, kitchen work and gardening). Male and female staff required.

Requirements: Candidates must be outgoing, friendly, keen to work closely with a sophisticated international clientele and not be afraid of hard work. Knowledge of French is useful but not essential. Applicants will ideally be students, although those taking time off or who have graduated will be considered.

Accommodation: Travel ticket and full board accommodation provided.

Application Procedure: Applications to the Newington Family at the above address.

Hotel Les Frenes

Job(s) Available: Waiter (2), room staff (2), chef de partie (2).

Duration: Minimum 3 months between 10 April and 15 November.

Pay: Negotiable salary.

Company Description: A small luxury hotel and restaurant.

Head Office: 645 Avenue Vertes Rives, 84140 Montfavet France
☎ +33 4 90311793
✆ contact@lesfrenes.com
🖥 www.lesfrenes.com

Job Description: *Waiter:* to work in the restaurant serving guests and other daily tasks. *Room staff:* to clean rooms and other daily tasks. *Chef de Partie:* daily kitchen duties.

Requirements: Must speak fluent French and English and a third language is an asset. *Waiter:* must have experience of working in high standard restaurants. *Chef de Partie:* must have experience in a high standard restaurant.

Accommodation: All staff get board and lodging included in salary.

Application Procedure: Apply from January to Jean-Philippe Fourier at the above address or email.

Garden Beach Hotel

Job(s) Available: Some housekeeping and front of house.

Duration: April to August. Minimum period of work 2 months.

Working Hours: 25 hours per week.

Pay: SMIC

Head Office: 15-17 Bd. Baudoin, F-06160 Juan les Pins France
☎ +33 4 92935757
✆ cilene.rollin@lemeridien.com
🖥 www.starwoodhotels.com

Requirements: English and basic French mandatory. *Front of house:* some Italian necessary.

Accommodation: Not available.

Application Procedure: Apply through Starwood Hotels website for specific jobs or apply speculatively to cilene.rollin@lemeridien.com

Hotel Imperial Garoupe

Job(s) Available: Chef de rang (3), commis chef (1), chamber maids (3).

Duration: At least 4 months between April and October.

Working Hours: 8 hours per day, 5 days a week.

Pay: Approximately £750.

Head Office: 770 Chemin de la Garoupe, 06600 Le Cap d'Antibes France
☎ +33 4 92933161
hotel-imp@webstore.fr
www.imperial-garoupe.com

Job Description: *Chef de rang, commis chef:* to prepare food in the restaurant. *Chamber maids:* required to clean and prepare bedrooms for guests.

Requirements: Applicants should be able to speak both French and English confidently.

Accommodation: Board and accommodation are provided free.

Application Procedure: Applications should be sent to Mr Gilbert Irondelle at the above address from January.

Jobs in the Alps (Employment Agency)

Job(s) Available: Waiting staff, porters, kitchen porters and housekeepers (150 in the winter, 50 in summer).

Duration: Periods of work: June to mid-September (minimum period 3 months including July and August), or December to April.

Working Hours: 5 days a week.

Pay: £500 per month

Head Office: Seasonal Recruitment Ltd, 3 Bracken Terrace, Newquay TR7 2LS, UK
info@jobs-in-the-alps.co.uk
www.jobs-in-the-alps.co.uk

Job Description: Staff for Swiss and French hotels, cafes and restaurants at mountain resorts.

Requirements: Good French and/or German required for most positions. Experience is not essential, but a good attitude to work and sense of fun are definite requirements.

Accommodation: Free board and accommodation.

Application Procedure: Applications should be sent by 30 April for summer and 30 September for winter to the above address.

Le Logis Du Fresne

Job(s)Available: Cleaners/waiting staff.

Duration: Minimum period of work 1 month between May and the end of September.

Pay: Approximately £600 per month plus bonus.

Head Office: F-16130 Juillac-le-Coq, France
☎ + 33 5 45322874
logisdufresne@wanadoo.fr

Company Description: A 3-star hotel run by Norwegian-French owners and situated 10km from Cognac in southwest France.

Job Description: Cleaners/waiting staff to provide general help in the hotel.

Requirements: Applicants should have a kindly attitude and speak English and conversational French; they must also either be EU nationals or have the correct permits to work in France.

Accommodation: Board and lodging available.

Application Procedure: By post to Tone Butler at the above address with a photo if possible.

Hostellerie De La Maronne

Job(s) Available: Waiting staff/receptionists, second chef.
Duration: Minimum of 2 months between 1 May and 15 September.
Working Hours: 8 hours per day, 5 days a week.
Pay: *Waiting staff/receptionists:* €1200 per month. *Second chef:* €1400 per month.

Head Office: Le Theil, F-15140 St Martin-Valmeroux France
☎ +33 4 71692033
maronne@maronne.com
www.maronne.com

Company Description: A hotel-restaurant in the countryside near Clermont-Ferrand with 21 rooms, heated pool, tennis courts and sauna, attracting customers from all over the world.
Job Description: *Waiting staff/receptionists:* to serve breakfast and supper along with reception duties. *Second chef:* serving preparing supper.
Requirements: Experience of working in 4 star hotels necessary; knowledge of French is preferred but not essential.
Accommodation: Board and lodging provided free.
Application Procedure: Apply from February to Alain Decock at the above address.

Hotel Du Pont Neuf

Job(s) Available: Waiter/waitress, kitchen staff.
Duration: May to October. Applicants must be able to work for a minimum of 3 months.
Working Hours: 5 days a week, approximately 39 hours per week.
Pay: SMIC

Head Office: Fauborg de Lorette 00320 Le Veurdre France
☎ +33 4 70664012
hotel.le.pontneuf@wanadoo.fr
www.hotel-lepontneuf.com

Company Description: This pleasant family-run hotel is situated in central France.
Job Description: The job includes breakfast, lunch and dinner service with a break in the afternoons. Placement would suit language students or those studying catering and hospitality.
Requirements: Previous experience helpful but not necessary. French language an advantage but not essential. Applicants should be confident, friendly and hardworking.
Accommodation: Full room and board provided.
Application Procedure: Applications from EU residents only, to the above address from January.

Chateau De Rochecotte

Job(s) Available: Maitre d'Hotel, chef de rang, receptionist, commis de salle.
Duration: Positions available from May to October.
Working Hours: 5 days and 39 hours per week.
Pay: *Maitre d'Hotel:* €1550 per month. *Chef de rang:* €1100 per month. *Receptionist:* €1100 per month. *Commis de salle:* €1020 per month.

Head Office: 37130 St Patrice
☎ +33 2 47961616 France
chateau.rochecotte@wanadoo.fr
www.chateau-de-rochecotte.fr

Company Description: A chateau hotel in the Val de Loire with 34 rooms and gastronomic cuisine.
Job Description: *Maitre d'Hotel:* in charge of the hotel. *Chef de rang:* to run the restaurant/dining room.

Requirements: *Maitre d'Hotel:* minimum of 10 years of experience. *Chef de rang:* minimum of 5 years of experience. *Receptionist:* good presentation. All positions require applicants to speak both English and French.

Accommodation: Can be arranged.

Application Procedure: Applications should be made to Mme Brosset by email with CV.

Simon Butler Skiing

Job(s) Available: Chalet people (4), handy men (2).

Duration: Minimum period of stay 3 months between June and September.

Working Hours: 6–7 hours per days, 6 days a week.

Pay: To be agreed on application.

Head Office: Portsmouth Rd, Ripley, Surrey GU23 6EY, UK
☎ 01483 212726
📧 info@simonbutlerskiing.co.uk
🖥 www.simonbutlerskiing.co.uk

Company Description: Simon Butler Skiing is a small independent company operating in Megève for the last 22 years and has many returning staff each year. The company also runs a summer activities programme with hotel accommodation.

Job Description: All jobs are in Megève, French Alps. *Chalet people:* required to clean, and make breakfast. *Handy men:* must be able to fix broken bed legs, toilets etc.

Requirements: Speaking French makes life easier but is not essential. Applicants should be confident and hard working.

Accommodation: Accommodation included.

Application Procedure: Applications invited from March 2008.

Simply Morzine

Job(s) Available: Chalet hosts (2), chalet chef (1), guide, driver, representative (3).

Duration: Early June until mid-September.

Working Hours: *Chalet hosts:* 7.30am–11am and 6pm–10pm, 6 days a week. *Chalet chef:* similar hours and days as chalet hosts (see above). *Guide, driver, representative:* 8.30am–6pm, 5–6 days a week.

Head Office: 118 Redwood Avenue, Melton Mowbray, Leicestershire LE13 1UT, UK
☎ 01664 568902
📧 info@simply-morzine.co.uk
🖥 www.simply-morzine.co.uk

Pay: *Chalet hosts:* £400 per month (approx) plus excellent package. *Chalet chef:* £550 per month (approx) plus excellent package. *Guide, driver, representative:* £500 per month (approx) plus excellent package.

Company Description: Simply Morzine is a professional, family-run company who have been offering specialist luxury Alpine holidays for over 10 years. Simply Morzine are the market leaders for summer family alpine activity holidays. Morzine is one of the world's premier ski, snowboard and summer alpine resorts. Simply Morzine's main clientele in June to September are artists, golfers and walkers while from July to August they operate well established family activity/adventure holidays. The company's summer programme has been featured in the national media, including *The Sunday Times*, *Irish Independent* and *Saga Radio*.

Job Description: Positions with Simply Morzine are an excellent summer opportunity, not only because of the splendour of the local area and the range of activities on offer, but also because the company are renowned for treating their staff very well! The work is demanding and tiring; yet alongside hard work it is fun, sociable and gives free time to enjoy the mountains. Positions require dedication, self-motivation, physical/mental toughness, decisiveness and a ceaseless attention to detail. Applicants are expected to be flexible and very much 'hands-on', working as part of a multi-functional team. The roles are an ideal opportunity to become involved with a progressive and forward thinking company, either for a short career break or post-university gap year, or for longer-term employment. Successful summer placements can lead to a placement for the winter season. *Chalet hosts:* required to clean chalets to a high standard, serve and clear meals, assist in the kitchen and generally have professional contact with guests to make sure they have the best possible holiday. *Chalet chef:* required to cater for approx 14–20 people to a very high dinner party standard. Responsible for breakfast, afternoon tea and 3 or 4 course evening meal 6 days a week. Needs to plan menus, budget, shop and maintain hygiene standards. *Guide, driver, representative:* A varied and challenging role. *Repping and coordinating:* welcoming clients, acting as a source of information and advice, booking activities, taking payments and solving problems to ensure the smooth running of their holiday. *Guiding:* to lead mountain biking, mountain walks and excursions. *Driving:* transporting guests in luxury resort minibuses including airport transfers, excursions, to/from activities and general chauffeuring around the resort. *General maintenance:* basic upkeep of Simply Morzine properties and vehicles.

Requirements: Minimum age 22. EU nationals only. *Chalet hosts:* must have experience of working in restaurants, and/or hotels, general customer service and cleaning. Must be hard-working with great attention to detail and have a friendly, outgoing personality. *Chalet chef:* must have minimum one year of experience with catering qualifications or 3 years of experience without a qualification. *Guide, driver, representative:* must be an experienced driver with working knowledge of French. Must have a keen interest and experience of outdoor pursuits and a high level of fitness.

Accommodation: We pride ourselves on treating our staff maturely, fairly and generously, with many becoming close family friends over the years. In return for your commitment to us, we provide a competitive rate of pay and many other benefits including full board and lodging in a beautiful private villa, return flights, comprehensive insurance, full area life pass, company clothing, free or discounted mountain equipment and an end of season bonus.

Application Procedure: For a job description and further information please send a CV and covering letter to the above email address, explaining why your skills, abilities and experiences meet the requirements of the position you are applying for. Applications are invited from Decmeber 2007. Unsuccessful applicants will not be contacted.

Hotel De La Tonnellerie

Job(s) Available: Room attendant (1–2), general help (1–2), breakfast attendant/bar worker.

Duration: Period of work May to September, with a minimum period of work of 2 months.

Working Hours: 35 hours per week, 5 days a week.

Pay: €950 (£665) per month.

Company Description: A 4-star, family-run hotel-restaurant with a young staff team, catering to discerning clients; located in a small village between Orleans and Blois.

Head Office: 12 rue des Eau Bleue, F-45190 Tavers France
☎ +33 2 38446815
✉ tonelri@club-internet.fr, reservation@tonelri.com
🖥 www.tonelni.com

Job Description: *Room attendant:* to clean rooms. *General help:* to carry luggage, warden duty and pool duty. No experience necessary. *Breakfast attendant/bar worker:* to serve breakfast and clean the dishes.

Requirements: Ideally candidates should speak French and English. *Breakfast attendant/bar worker:* some experience of waiting tables useful.

Accommodation: Some free board and lodging is available.

Application Procedure: Applications from 1 March to Marie-Christine Pouey at the above address.

TravelBound

Job(s) Available: Assistant managers, chefs, general assistants, kitchen porter/night porters, handypersons and lifeguards.

Duration: From February to October (shorter contracts available).

Company Description: TravelBound is a tour operator specializing with travel for predominantly schools groups as well as some adult groups. The chateau is situated in the beautiful Normandy countryside, and offers accommodation for up to 165 people in 40 rooms as well as a number of meeting rooms, a library, games room, lounge area and bar.

Requirements: Applicants must be 18, have a national insurance number and either an EU passport or relevant EU visa/permit.

Accommodation: We provide travel to and from France, emergency medical insurance, food and accommodation.

Application Procedure: Please visit the website.

> **Head Office:** Travelbound Recruitment Team, Sunsail, The Port House, Port Solent, Hants PO6 4TH, UK
> ☎ 02392 222329
> ✆ hr@sunsail.com
> 🖳 www.sunsail.co.uk/hr

Hotel-Restaurant Les Trois Colombes

Job(s) Available: Restaurant staff and chamber maids.

Duration: Period of work May to mid-August.

Company Description: A 3-star hotel restaurant in the heart of scenic Provence.

Job Description: *Restaurant staff:* for waiting service, place-setting, taking orders and washing up, preferably with 2–3 years of experience in restaurant work.

Requirements: Applicants must be smartly dressed, well-groomed non-smokers, and preferably good English speakers with some knowledge of French.

Accommodation: Free accommodation provided.

Application Procedure: See website for details.

> **Head Office:** 148 avenue des Garrigues, 84210 Saint-Didier-les-Bains, Provence France
> ☎ +33 4 90660701
> ✆ les3colombes@wanadoo.fr
> 🖳 www.hotel3colombes.com

UK Overseas Handling (UKOH) International Recruitment

Job(s) Available: UKOH recruit all kinds of resort/hotel staff for clients in France, but also offers a number of management trainee and student placement roles involved in all aspects of the resort and hotel management. Management trainee, restaurant, night audit, reception, housekeeping, pool cleaners, gardeners and maintenance/handy staff.

Duration: Staff required between May and October (winter season also available).

Job Description: To work in hotels and tourist residences in the south and south-west coasts of France, and also in the alps and cities of Paris and Montpellier.

Requirements: Successful candidates should be over 21 years of age and EU passport holders with a permanent British national insurance number. Must be flexible, keen and prepared for hard work. Experience and an excellent standard of French essential for reception and restaurant positions. Some knowledge of French is useful for other posts.

Accommodation: Package includes full board and shared accommodation.

Application Procedure: Applications to the above address.

> **Head Office:** Third Floor, Link Line House, 65 Church Road, Hove, East Sussex BN3 2BD, UK
> ☎ 0870 220 2148
> ✆ ukoh@ukoh.co.uk

211

Industrial and Office Work

The Automobile Association

Job(s) Available: Call handlers (up to 50).
Duration: Between March and September. Minimum period of work 8 weeks (July and August essential).
Working Hours: 35 hours per week on shifts.
Pay: Approximately €1,185 per month, overtime available.

Head Office: European Operations, 15th Floor, Fanum House, Basing View, Basingstoke RG21 4EA, UK
☎ 01256 492398
📧 elaine.badham@theaa.com

Job Description: Call handlers to work in the AA's multilingual European call centre in Limonest, north of Lyon: the centre provides 24-hour assistance to AA customers who have broken down or become involved in a road traffic accident in Europe.
Requirements: Applicants must be native English speakers, be fluent in French and preferably have one other European language. You will need to be efficient, responsible, compassionate and able to work under pressure.
Accommodation: Local accommodation can be arranged.
Application Procedure: Applications with CV and passport-style photo to Elaine Badham by email or to the above address.

Eurogroup

Job(s) Available: Internships.
Duration: Period of work by arrangement.
Company Description: A group managing 34 hotels and holiday residences in France.
Job Description: Internships involving work in the head office in Chambery in areas such as marketing,

Head Office: 472 rue du Leysse, BP 429, 73004 Chambery France
☎ +33 4 79650765
📧 alvalesni@eurogroup-vacances.com
🖥 www.eurogroup-vacances.com

reservations, purchasing, planning etc giving the opportunity to gain professional experience while improving language skills.
Requirements: Applicants must speak good French and be enrolled in an EU university or school.
Accommodation: Food and accommodation included in pay.
Application Procedure: By post to Mme Catherine Oldfield at the above address.

Sports, Couriers and Camping

Balloon Flights – France Montgolfieres

Job(s) Available: Balloon crew.
Duration: Required April to November.
Working Hours: No fixed days off. Hours can be very long.
Pay: £500-£600 per month.
Company Description: One of only 10 balloon

Head Office: 24 rue Nationale, 414 Montrichard
☎ +33 2 54322048
📧 jane@franceballoons.com
🖥 www.franceballoons.com

companies in France registered to carry passengers. The company has over 20 years of experience.

Job Description: Balloon crew to work for passenger-carrying operation with bases in the Burgundy and Loire Valley regions. Duties include maintaining and cleaning of vehicles and balloon equipment, driving and navigation of balloon chase vans, helping out in a balloon repair workshop, passenger liaison and secretarial work.

Requirements: Knowledge of French preferred. Minimum age 21, with clean driving licence (preferably class E).

Application Procedure: Please send CV, a photo, and a copy of your driving licence. Applicants should be EU nationals or possess correct working permits.

Belle France

Job(s) Available: Bike representatives (2).

Duration: Period of work from April to October. Minimum 2 months.

Working Hours: Approximately 35 hours per week.

Pay: Approximately £150 per week.

Company Description: Belle France is part of the Mark Hammerton Group Ltd., specialist in tour operating and publishing (*Alan Rogers Camping Guides*). A small, dynamic and friendly organisation.

> **Head Office:** Spelmonden Old Oast, Goudhurst, Kent TN17 1HE, England
> ☎ 01580 214010
> ✉ enquiries@bellefrance.co.uk
> 🖥 www.bellefrance.co.uk

Job Description: Bike representatives to work for a tour operator offering cycling and walking holidays in France. The job includes maintaining bikes, transporting luggage, collecting customers from station, etc.

Requirements: Applicants should be well organised and capable of working on their own. They should speak some French and hold a full clean driving license.

Application Procedure: Applications to the above address by the end of 2007.

Bents Bicycle & Walking Tours

Job(s) Available: Company representatives (4–5).

Duration: Minimum period of work 8 weeks between the end of May and the end of September.

Working Hours: To work varied hours as needs of work dictate, but generally around 40 hours per week.

> **Head Office:** The Blue Cross, Orleton, Ludlow, Shropshire SY8 4HN, England
> ☎ 01568 780800
> ✉ info@bentstours.com
> 🖥 www.bentstours.com

Pay: Approximatly £600 per month.

Job Description: Company representatives for a tour operator offering cycling and walking holidays in France, Germany and Austria. Duties to include meeting clients at the airport, maintaining bicycles, transporting luggage between hotels and generally taking care of the needs of clients.

Requirements: Applicants should have a reasonable grasp of either spoken German or French and fluent English. They must also possess a full valid driving licence.

Accommodation: Board and accommodation provided.

Application Procedure: By post with a photograph, to Stephen Bent at the above address from January.

Canvas Holidays

Job(s) Available: Campsite courier, children's courier.

Duration: Full season positions start in March, April or May and end in September/October. High season staff needed to work at least 2 months during the peak season.

Pay: Package includes competitive salary, tent accommodation, medical insurance, uniform and return travel from a UK port of entry.

Company Description: Canvas Holidays provide luxury mobile home and tent holidays at over 100 campsites throughout Europe.

Job Description: *Campsite courier:* involves cleaning accommodation, welcoming families to the site and showing them to their accommodation. Visiting customers, providing local information and basic maintenance are very important parts of the job. Campsite courier opportunities are also available for couples to work on site together. *Children's courier:* needed to work at Hoopi's Club. A tent is provided as a club venue and for equipment storage; this has to be kept safe, clean and tidy. Visiting new arrivals on site is an important and fun part of the job. Children's couriers also help with other campsite duties as needed.

Requirements: *Children's courier:* applicants must have formal experience of working with children. Should be energetic, enthusiastic and have good communication skills.

Accommodation: Provided as part of package.

Additional Information: For details of management positions, see website. Visit recruitment website for information about working with teenagers (Buzz Courier) and wildlife and the environment (Wild and Active Courier).

Application Procedure: Please call the Recruitment Department for more information and an application form, or apply online at www.gvnrecruitment.com.

Carisma Holidays

Job(s) Available: Site managers, couriers, and children's couriers to work on campsites on the west coast of France.

Duration: Late May to September.

Working Hours: Varied.

Pay: £125–£175 per week.

Head Office: Bethel House, Heronsgate Road, Chorleywood WD3 5BB, England
☎ 01923 287339
✍ personnel@carisma.co.uk
🖳 www.carismaholidays jobs.co.uk

Company Description: Specialises in self-drive, family holidays in mobile homes on private sandy beaches in the south-west of France. All Carisma's campsites are family-run and located on or very near to the beach.

Requirements: Full training is given on-site in France at the start of the season. Spoken French is preferable but not essential for all positions. *Children's couriers:* Minimum age 18.

Accommodation: Self-catering accommodation is provided. Travel costs to and from the resort are paid.

Application Procedure: See website for online application form.

Club Cantabrica Holidays Ltd

Job(s) Available: Resort manager (12), campsite couriers (30), peak season couriers (15), children's courier (11), maintenance staff (11), hotel staff including general duties rep, and chef (8).

Duration: From April to October, except peak season staff. Peak season staff to cover same tasks as

Head Office: 146/148 London Road, St Albans, Herts AL1 1PQ, England
☎ 01727 866177
✍ recruitment@cantabrica.co.uk
🖳 www.cantabrica.co.uk

couriers but from June to September only. Minimum period of work 3 months.

Working Hours: Approximately 40 hours per 6–day week.

Pay: *Resort manager:* competitive including bonus and commission. *Campsite couriers:* £100 per week plus commission and bonus. *Peak season couriers:* competitive plus commission and bonus. *Children's courier:* competitive plus commission and bonus. *Maintenance staff:* competitive and subject to experience plus commission and bonus.

Company Description: Club Cantabrica is an independent tour operator with 30 years of experience. Offering luxury coach, air and self-drive holidays on excellent sites in France (including the French Alps), Italy, Spain and Austria. Opportunities also available for ski programme in the Austrian Tyrol and the French Alps.

Job Description: *Resort manager:* to manage sites varying in size from 25–100 units. *Campsite couriers:* to work on camp sites in France, Italy, and Spain. Work involves looking after clients, setting up and closing down site, tent and mobile home cleaning and maintenance, paperwork and excursion sales. *Children's courier:* to run Kids' Club on campsites. *Maintenance staff:* to carry out maintenance and upkeep work on tents and mobile homes. *Hotel staff:* to help run the Club Hotel in Chamonix Valley.

Requirements: Couriers should be enthusiastic and have plenty of stamina, with knowledge of languages an advantage. Applicants should be over 18 years old (over 21 for managers). Experience preferable. *Resort manager:* must have previous campsite rep. experience and French, Italian or Spanish language skills. *Children's courier:* must have experience of working with children and relevant qualification. *Maintenance staff:* applicants should have excellent practical skills. *Hotel staff:* fluent French required.

Accommodation: Free accommodation provided.

Application Procedure: Applications with CVs to the above address (please specify winter or summer). Applicants can also send an email or visit the website.

Eurocamp

Job(s) Available: Campsite courier, children's courier, courier team leaders, children's courier team leaders, montage/demontage.

Duration: *Campsite courier:* Applicants should be available to work from April/May to mid-September or June/July to mid-September. *Children's courier:* Applicants should be available from early May to September or June to September. *Courier team leaders:* Applicants should be available from April to mid-September. *Children's courier team leaders:* Applicants should be available from early May until September. *Montage/demontage:* Applicants should be available from February to May or August to October.

> **Head Office:** Overseas Recruitment Department (Ref SJ/08) Hartford Manor, Greenbank Lane, Northwich CW8 1HW, England
> ☎ 01606 787525
> 🖥 www.holidaybreakjobs.com/camping

Pay: You will receive a competitive salary, comprehensive training, return travel to and from an agreed meeting point, accommodation, medical and luggage insurance and uniform.

Company Description: Eurocamp is a leading tour operator in self-drive camping and mobile home holidays in Europe. We offer our customers a wide range of holiday accommo-

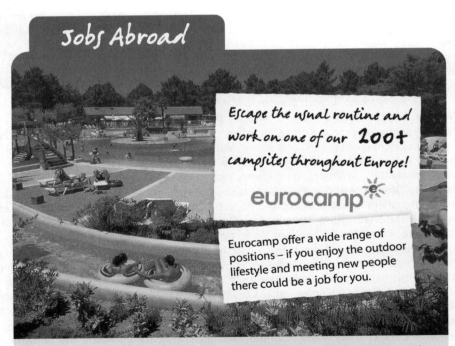

Jobs Abroad

Escape the usual routine and work on one of our **200+** campsites throughout Europe!

eurocamp

Eurocamp offer a wide range of positions – if you enjoy the outdoor lifestyle and meeting new people there could be a job for you.

For more information please call 01606 787525 quoting ref: SJ/08

or visit: **www.holidaybreakjobs.com**

dation on over 200 premier campsites. Each year the company seeks to recruit up to 1,500 enthusiastic people to work the summer season in a variety of roles.

Job Description: *Campsite Courier:* A Courier's responsibility begins by ensuring that the customer's accommodation is both inviting and cleaned to the highest of standards. You will welcome new arrivals, be the customers main point of contact and will be expected to provide local and general information, give assistance and even act as interpreter if required. Part of the role will involve helping out with minor repairs to accommodation and equipment and will also involve basic administration and accounts. *Children's Courier:* You will be responsible for planning and delivering a fun, safe, daily activity programme to our customers' children. The age of the children attending the club will range from 5 to 12 years old although we also run a toddler service in low season for 12 months to 4 years. *Courier Team Leaders:* You must be able to deliver first class customer service and organize the daily workload of the courier team. Your role also includes all the duties of a Campsite Courier and you will be expected to lead by example. There are a variety of team leader roles available, dependant on team size; Courier in Charge, Senior Courier and Site Manager. *Children's Courier Team Leaders:* Your role will involve the management, motivation and development of the Children's Couriers to ensure they provide a varied range of quality activities. Your role includes all the duties of a Children's Courier. *Montage/Demontage:* Montage and Demontage assistants are employed to either help set up for the season or close down at the end of the season. This involves putting up or taking down tents, moving/distributing equipment and cleaning/preparing accommodation.

Requirements: Applicants must hold a UK/EU passport and the current minimum age is 18 years old on the day you start work in order to obtain the relevant insurance cover. *Campsite Couriers:* You should have lots of energy, basic common sense and a genuine desire to help people. *Children's Courier:* Previous childcare experience is essential. Successful candidates will be asked to apply for an Enhanced Disclosure. *Courier Team Leaders:* You must have previous experience of leading a team successful applicants may be asked to apply for a Standard Disclosure. *Children's Courier Team Leaders:* Previous experience with Children and leading a team successful candidates will be asked to apply for an Enhanced Disclosure. *Montage/Demontage:* Pervious experience of physical and repetitive work successful applicants will be asked to apply for a Standard Disclosure.

Accommodation: Provided.

Application Procedure: Applicants should apply on-line at www.holidaybreakjobs.com/camping or telephone 01606 787 525 for an application pack.

Exodus Travels

Job(s) Available: Walking and trekking leaders, leaders for discovery and adventure and leisurely collection programmes, tour leaders.

Duration: Dates of work are from May to October plus Christmas and Easter. Periods of work of up to 7 months a year available. *Walking and trekking leaders:* work is available throughout the year. *Leaders for discovery and adventure and leisurely collection programmes:* trips of one or 2 weeks duration. The ideal candidate should be flexible and available to work between May and November at short notice.

Head Office: Grange Mills, Weir Road, London, SW12 0NE, UK
☎ 0870 240 5550
otownsend@exodus.co.uk
www.exodus.co.uk

Working Hours: *Tour leaders:* whilst away, tour leaders could be working 7 days a week.

Pay: *Tour leaders:* £24.50–£44.50 per day.

Company Description: Exodus is an adventure travel company that specialises in walking and trekking, discovery, cycling and multi-activity holidays. Applicants could be working in Europe, Africa, Asia, Central America and Cuba.

Job Description: *Leaders for discovery and adventure and leisurely collection programmes:* to lead trips based in Europe; either sightseeing, gentle walking or a mixture of both. *Tour leaders:* required to lead trips overseas.

Requirements: *Walking and trekking leaders:* with mountain walking experience and relevant qualifications such as SML and WML. Aged 25 and over. Must have a second language, interest in the outdoors, experience of independent travel and hill walking/group leading. *Leaders for discovery and adventure and leisurely collection programmes:* must also bring an aspect of cultural knowledge. A second language is also desirable. Suitable for older applicants. *Tour leaders:* must be 25 years and over. Knowledge of a second language eg Italian, Spanish, French is required.

Accommodation: *Tour leaders:* board and accommodation provided.

Application Procedure: Applications invited throughout the year. Please download an application form from the website: www.exodus.co.uk/vacancies.html

Fleur Holidays

Job(s) Available: Area controllers, representatives/ couriers, montage/ demontage.

Duration: *Area controllers:* period of employment may cover: start season Easter to July, and/or high season July to September. *Representatives/couriers:* period of employment may cover any or all of: start season Easter to July; mid-season Easter to July; mid-season May to July high season July to September. *Montage/demontage:* period of employment: 6 to 8 weeks from March to May and/or 6 to 8 weeks in September and October.

Head Office: 4 All Hallows Road, Bispham, Blackpool, Lancs FY2 0AS, England
☎ 01253 593333
reps@fleur-holidays.com
www.fleur-holidays.com

Pay: *Area controllers:* in the region of £650 per month, plus £14 per week bonus paid on completion of contract, dependent on service. *Representatives/couriers:* in the region of £470 per month plus £14 per week bonus paid on completion of contract.

Company Description: A company that offers mobile home and tent holidays on quality sites in France that are chosen for ambience.

Job Description: *Area controllers:* required to cover groups of campsites to ensure couriers are performing to the required standards. *Representatives/couriers:* required to meet clients at reception, prepare mobile homes and tents and organise social events and children's clubs. Each vacancy is an all round position with responsibility for the clients together with Fleur's representation at the campsite. *Montage/demontage:* required to assist in the preparation of mobile homes and the erecting of tents at the start of the season and /or the closing of mobile homes and taking down of tents at the end of the season.

Requirements: *Area controllers:* previous courier experience is essential. Vehicle provided or mileage allowance given. Experience of working within the service industry would be an advantage. Basic French required. *Representatives/couriers:* basic French an advantage. Experience of working within the service industry would be an advantage. *Montage/demontage:* applicants should physically fit and motivated. Minimum age 18 for area controllers and couriers.

Accommodation: Provided.

Application Procedure: For all positions, please send a full CV and covering letter with head and shoulders photograph, stating the exact dates that you are available to the above address. Alternatively, request an application form from the personnel manager.

Headwater Holidays

Job(s) Available: Overseas representatives, canoeing instructors.

Duration: Staff required for full season from April to October.

Working Hours: To work hours as required.

Pay: From £140 per week.

Company Description: Headwater looks to offer relaxed discovery and adventure holidays with personal service, warm friendly hotels and good regional cuisine. Headwater guides and information packs try to help clients make their own discoveries off the beaten track.

Head Office: The Old School House, Chester Road, Castle, Northwich, Cheshire, CW8 1LE, England
☎ 01606 720033
info@headwater.com
www.headwater.com

Job Description: *Overseas representatives:* to work in France, Italy, Spain and Austria. Duties include meeting clients at airports and stations, supervising local transport for them and their luggage, hotel and client liaison, bike maintenance and on the spot problem solving. *Canoeing instructors:* duties as for overseas representatives but also include giving canoe instruction.

Requirements: *Overseas representatives:* good, working knowledge of the language and full, clean driving licence required. Organisational skills, resourcefulness and cheerfulness essential.

Accommodation: Provided.

Application Procedure: Further information and an on-line application form can be found on the website, or an application form can be requested from the above address.

Keycamp Holidays

Job(s) Available: Campsite courier, children's courier, courier team leaders, children's courier team leaders, montage/demontage.

Duration: *Campsite courier:* Applicants should be available to work from April/May to mid-September or June/July to mid-September. *Children's courier:* Applicants should be available from early May to September or June to September. *Courier team leaders:* Applicants should be available from April to mid-September. *Children's courier team leaders:* Applicants should be available from early May until September. *Montage/demontage:* Applicants should be available from February to May or August to October.

Head Office: Overseas Recruitment Department (Ref SJ/08) Hartford Manor, Greenbank Lane, Northwich CW8 1HW, England
☎ 01606 787525
www.holidaybreakjobs.com/camping

Pay: You will receive a competitive salary, comprehensive training, return travel to and from an agreed meeting point, accommodation, medical and luggage insurance and uniform.

Company Description: Keycamp is a leading tour operator in self-drive camping and mobile home holidays in Europe. We offer our customers a wide range of holiday accommodation on over 200 premier campsites. Each year the company seeks to recruit up to 1,500 enthusiastic people to work the summer season in a variety of roles.

Job Description: *Campsite Courier:* A Courier's responsibility begins by ensuring that the customer's accommodation is both inviting and cleaned to the highest of standards. You will welcome new arrivals, be the customers main point of contact and will be expected to provide local and general information, give assistance and even act as interpreter if required. Part of the role will involve helping out with minor repairs to accommodation and equipment and will also involve basic administration and accounts. *Children's Courier:* You will be responsible for planning and delivering a fun, safe, daily activity programme to our customers' children. The age of the children attending the club will range from 5 to 12 years old although we also run a toddler service in low season for 12 months to 4 years. *Courier Team Leaders:* You must be able to deliver first class customer service and organize the daily workload of the courier team. Your role also includes all the duties of a Campsite Courier and you will be expected to lead by example. There are a variety of team leader roles available, dependant on team size; Courier in Charge, Senior Courier and Site Manager. *Children's Courier Team Leaders:* Your role will involve the management, motivation and development of the Children's Couriers to ensure they provide a varied range of quality activities. Your role includes all the duties of a Children's Courier. *Montage/Demontage:* Montage and Demontage assistants are employed to either help set up for the season or close down at the end of the season. This involves putting up or taking down tents, moving/distributing equipment and cleaning/preparing accommodation.

Requirements: Applicants must hold a UK/EU passport and the current minimum age is 18 years old on the day you start work in order to obtain the relevant insurance cover. *Campsite Couriers*: You should have lots of energy, basic common sense and a genuine desire to help people. *Children's Courier:* Previous childcare experience is essential. Successful candidates will be asked to apply for an Enhanced Disclosure. *Courier Team Leaders:* You must have previous experience of leading a team successful applicants may be asked to apply for a Standard Disclosure. *Children's Courier Team Leaders:* Previous experience with Children and leading a team successful candidates will be asked to apply for an Enhanced Disclosure. *Montage/Demontage:* Previous experience of physical and repetitive work successful applicants will be asked to apply for a Standard Disclosure.

Accommodation: Provided.

Application Procedure: Applicants should apply on-line at www.holidaybreakjobs.com/camping or telephone 01606 787 525 for an Application Pack.

Mark Warner

Job(s) Available: Accountants, receptionists, watersports instructors, tennis and aerobics instructors, chefs, kitchen porters, first aiders, nannies, handymen, nightwatchmen. Some reserve staff also needed throughout the season.

Duration: Corsica, Sardinia, Greece, Portugal and France: during the summer from April to October. Egypt, Sri Lanka and Mauritius: year round.

Pay: From £50 per week.

> **Head Office:** George House, 61-65 Kensington Church Street, London, W8 4BA, England
> ☎ 0844 844 3760, 0844 844 3770 (for childcare recruitment)
> ⌨ recruitment@markwarner.co.uk
> 🖥 www.markwarner.co.uk

Job Description: Staff required to work in hotels in Corsica, Sardinia, Greece, Portugal and France and in Egypt, Sri Lanka and Mauritius.

Requirements: Requirements for languages, experience, qualifications etc vary according to the job applied for.

Accommodation: Full board, medical insurance and travel expenses included in wages. Free use of watersport and activity facilities.

Application Procedure: For further details, please contact the Resorts Recruitment Department on the above number.

Matthews Holidays

Job(s) Available: Couriers/campsite representatives.

Duration: Should be available to commence work during April or May and work until mid/late September. A few vacancies available for the period July to September.

> **Head Office:** 8 Bishopsmead Parade, East Horsley, Surrey KT24 6RP, England
> ☎ 01483 284044
> ⌨ information@matthewsholidays.co.uk
> 🖥 www.matthewsfrance.co.uk

Working Hours: 35 hour, 6 day week.

Pay: £170 per week.

Job Description: To receive clients and maintain and clean mobile homes in western France, Brittany, the Vendée and the South of France.

Requirements: Knowledge of French essential. Minimum age 20.

Accommodation: Accommodation and board provided at the rate of £50 per week deducted from wages.

Application Procedure: Applications to the above email or postal address. If applying by post enclose an s.a.e.. Please give details of age, present occupation and other relevant experience, and date available to commence work.

Mastersun Holidays

Job(s) Available: Resort managers, assistant managers, resort representatives, hosts, housekeepers, chefs and assistant chefs, kitchen assistants, bar and restaurant staff, waterfront instructors, waterfront managers, children's and teen's workers.

Head Office: Thames House, 63-67 Kingston Road, New Malden, Surrey KT3 3PB, England
☎ 020 8942 9442
✉ rebecca@mastersun.co.uk
🖥 www.mastersun.co.uk

Duration: Numerous staff needed over the summer season. There are winter ski jobs as well.

Company Description: Mastersun is a Christian holiday company that organizes summer holidays in Greece, Turkey, Italy and Switzerland as well as winter ski holidays in the French Alps. Holidays are hotel or chalet based and the complete package includes watersports, skiing and other activities.

Application Procedure: Download an application form from the website or ask for a job pack from the above address or email. Applications welcome at any time.

NST Travel Group

Job(s) Available: Customer service assistants (French speakers 7), multi activity instructors (20), support staff (8).

Head Office: Recruitment Team, NST Travel Group plc, Discovery House, Brooklands Way, Whitehills Business Park, Blackpool FY4 5LW, England
☎ 0845 671 1357
✉ info@nstgroupjobs.co.uk
🖥 www.nstgroupjobs.co.uk

Duration: Minimum period of work 2 months.

Working Hours: 6 days a week.

Company Description: NST Travel has 2 residential centres in France. Le Chateau d'Ebblingham, offering educational and French language courses for secondary school groups and Lou Valagran which offers adventurous activity holidays for secondary school groups.

Job Description: *Customer service assistants:* for Le Chateau, to accompany guests on excursions around the French countryside. *Multi activity instructors:* for Lou Valagran, to instruct a range of outdoor activities including canoeing, kayaking and high ropes and to assist with the evening activities programme. *Support staff:* for Lou Valagran, including positions for drivers, boat loaders and bar, shop, support, cleaning and maintenance staff.

Requirements: Excellent working knowledge of French. *Multi activity instructors:* qualifications in canoeing, kayaking, caving or climbing would be advantageous. A full driving license is needed for driving positions.

Accommodation: All positions are residential.

Application Procedure: For more information and an application form please contact the recruitment team using the above details.

Orangerie De Lanniron

Job(s) Available: Bar person, shop attendant/cook, host/hostess, animateur, housekeeper.

Duration: 2–3 months. 6 months maxiumum.

Working Hours: 35 hours per week.

Pay: Based on SMIC and experience.

Company Description: A 10-acre campsite set in amongst 42 acres of woodland. Orangerie de Lanniron has holiday cottages, static caravans and space for touring caravans. It is 10 minutes drive away from Benodet and Quimper.

Head Office: Château de Lanniron, F-29336 Quimper France
☎ +33 2 98906202
🖰 camping@lanniron.com
💻 www.lanniron.com

Job Description: *Bar person:* required to run the bar, restock the bar and deal with money. Responsible for bar terrace and lounge. *Shop attendant/cook:* responsible for tending and restocking the grocery shop and preparation of takeaway food. *Host/hostess:* to care for the camping guests, register arrivals and departures, make telephone calls, handle money and show the guests their pitches. *Animateur:* responsible for entertaining both the young and older clients and organising garden parties and theme parties. Required to give information to guests about the entertainment programme. *Housekeeper:* to clean guest accommodation and to wash linen.

Requirements: Applicants for all the posts must speak English and French; and a third language such as Dutch or German would be useful. Applicants should be well educated, honest, punctual and be able to endure stress. Applicants must also have previous experience in hotel or restaurant work and good references. *Housekeeper:* must be female.

Accommodation: Accommodation will be in tents.

Application Procedure: Send CV with photo by email or view available jobs at the above website.

PGL Travel

Job(s) Available: Children's group leaders, children's activity instructors and general positions in catering, administration, driving (car or D1 towing), stores and site cleaning.

Duration: Vacancies available for the full season (February to October) or shorter periods between April and September.

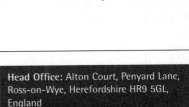

Head Office: Alton Court, Penyard Lane, Ross-on-Wye, Herefordshire HR9 5GL, England
☎ 0870 401 4411
🖰 recruitment@pgl.co.uk
💻 www.pgl.co.uk

Pay: £78–£224 per week.

Company Description: With 27 activity centres located in the UK, France and Spain, PGL Travel provides adventure holidays and courses for children. Each year 2,500 people are needed to help run these adventure centres.

Job Description: *Children's group leaders*: required to take responsibility for groups, helping them to get the most out of their holiday.

Requirements: *Children's group leaders*: previous experience of working with children is essential. *Children's activity instructors*: qualified or personally competent in canoeing, sailing, windsurfing, or multi-activities.

Accommodation: Full board and lodging.

Application Procedure: Applications can be made online or via a form obtained from the above address. Overseas applicants eligible to work in the UK welcome.

Rockley Watersports

Job(s) Available: Watersports instructors (over 100), couriers/ entertainment team (45).

Duration: From March to October. Minimum period of work 2 months.

Working Hours: Approximately 40 hours per week.

Pay: Competitive.

Head Office: Poole, Dorset BH15 4RW, England
☎ 0870 777 0541
✏ info@rockleywatersports.com
🖥 www.rockleywatersports.com, www.rockleyadventures.com

Company Description: Based in beautiful Poole harbour and South-West France, Rockley teach water sports to all abilities and ages. One of Europe's most highly regarded water sports centres. About 150 seasonal staff are employed at any one time.

Job Description: *Watersports instructors:* experienced RYA sailing, windsurfing, BCU kayaking instructors are required to work in south-west France at 3 of the largest RYA recognised water sports centres in Europe. *Couriers/ entertainments team:* for duties including evening entertainment, aiding water based sessions and general site duties. The jobs offer the opportunity to gain water sports experience and use all the facilities of the centres.

Requirements: *Watersports instructors:* RYA or BCU qualifications.

Accommodation: Full board and lodging in France. Optional at UK centres.

Application Procedure: Application forms available at www.rockleywatersports.com/wiw/how_to_apply

Sandpiper Holidays Ltd

Job(s) Available: Representatives (8).

Duration: Period of work from mid-May to mid-September. Applicants must be prepared to work for at least half the season.

Head Office: Walnut Cottage, Kenley, Shrewsbury SY5 6NS, England
☎ 01746 785123
✏ sandpiperhols@bigfoot.com

Pay: Wages by arrangement (approximately £400 per month plus an end of season bonus).

Company Description: Small friendly holiday tour operator specialising in self-drive camping holidays to France. Reps are chosen for their enthusiasm; they work hard, have a lot of fun and improve their French.

Job Description: Representatives to look after clients, clean and maintain tents and mobile homes and organise children's activities on camp sites in France.

Requirements: Applicants must be prepared to work hard, and have a sense of humour. Minimum age 19.

Accommodation: Provided in tents.

Application Procedure: Telephone the above number for an application form before the end of January.

Siblu Holidays

Job(s) Available: Park representatives, children's club representatives, assistant park representatives, lifeguards, reception team members, accommodation team members, bar team members, entertainers.

Duration: The season runs between March and October, with varying contract dates. Limited high season positions are available.

Head Office: Recruitment Team, Bryanston Court, Selden Hill, Hemel Hemptead, HP2 4TN, England
☎ 01442 293231
✏ recruitment@siblu.com
🖥 www.siblu.com

Pay: Team members will receive a competitive salary.

Company Description: Siblu Holidays exclusively own holiday parks in France, and also operate on 12 fantastic parks in France, Spain and Italy.

Job Description: The following roles are offered in France for seasonal work: *Park representatives:* duties include cleaning and maintaining accommodation, welcoming new arrivals, reception duties, paperwork and administration. *Children's club representatives:* duties include creating and running a daytime entertainment programme for children between the ages of 5 and 12 years old, associated paperwork and assisting park representatives. *Assistant park representatives:* duties include cleaning and preparation of accommodation, welcoming new arrivals and reception duties. *Lifeguards:* NPLQ qualified, duties include poolside supervision, cleaning of pool area and supervision of slides and flumes. *Reception team members:* duties include the welcome and check-in of guests, providing park and local information, cash handling (*bureau de change*) and problem solving. *Accommodation team members:* duties include cleaning and preparing guest accommodation, bed making and customer visits. *Bar team members:* applicants must be conversational in French. Duties include bar service, cash handling, cleaning and washing of glasses, terrace service and re-stocking of bar. *Entertainers:* dancers, vocalists and children's entertainers, working as part of a team to provide daytime and evening entertainment programme for guests of all ages.

Requirements: *Children's club representatives:* experience of working with children is desirable. *Lifeguards:* NPLQ qualified. *Reception team members:* applicants must be fluent in French.

Accommodation: Accommodation on uniform, medical cover and travel costs to park included in pay.

Application Procedure: Please telephone the above number for a recruitment pack or visit the website to apply online.

Snowcrazy Ltd

Job(s) Available: Chalet hosts (16 couples), team coordinators (16).

Duration: Summer 2008. Minimum period of work 6 weeks. Staff required from 19 July to 30 August.

Working Hours: *Chalet hosts:* 5 days per week, approximately 6 hours per day except transfer day, one day off. *Team coordinators:* 6 days, approximately 9am–6pm.

Pay: £100 per week.

Head Office: 55 Lancaster Drive, East Grinstead, West Sussex RH19 3XJ, England
☎ 01342 302910
✉ gosnowcrazy@aol.com
🖥 www.snowcrazy.co.uk

Company Description: A prestigious one week knock-out tournament for young people who are serious about playing football. The tournament concentrates on creating a competitive tournament between high quality teams from the same age groups and the same ability across Europe. The tournament is set in the heart of the French Alps. The area is better known for its famous ski areas. However, in the summertime, the snow covered pistes have transformed themselves into beautiful lush green mountains and valleys with meandering white-water rivers. Skis and snowboards have long been packed away and have been replaced by rafts, kayaks and mountain bikes.

Job Description: *Chalet hosts:* required to prepare and serve breakfast, pack lunch and 3 course evening meal for youth football teams ages 11 to 15 and the team coaches/parents. Very much in the style of a catered ski chalet with a simple child-friendly menu. *Team coordinators:* required to liaise between the team captains and the tournament organisers to ensure the smooth running of the tournament and the punctuality of the teams on the pitches.

Requirements: *Chalet hosts:* Preferably over 25. Experience running a catered chalet (minimum 12 bed) essential. No training provided. *Team coordinators:* Preferably over 25. Customer service and organisational skills a must.

Accommodation: Full board and lodging.

Application Procedure: Applications asap to Laura Clarke by email at the above address. Interviews May 2008.

Solaire Holidays

Job(s) Available: Site couriers (20).

Duration: Applicants can apply to work between April and October, May and September or July and August.

Working Hours: Hours of work vary according to demand, but applicants can expect to work for 6 days a week, on a rota system.

Head Office: 43 Milcote Road, Solihull B91 1JN, England
☎ 01217 054010
holidays@solaire.co.uk
www.solaire.co.uk

Pay: £280–£400 per month.

Company Description: Solaire Holidays provide self-drive self-catering holidays to France and Spain. They also have their own holiday park in Southern Brittany.

Job Description: Site couriers to look after clients and prepare accommodation.

Requirements: Knowledge of French/Spanish desirable.

Accommodation: Provided as part of contract. Food is not provided.

Application Procedure: Applications are invited from December 2007 for 2008. Please send a CV when applying to the above address or email.

Susi Madron's Cycling For Softies

Job(s) Available: Company assistants.

Duration: Minimum period of work 2 months between May and September.

Pay: Fixed wage plus bonus.

Job Description: Company assistants to work for a company offering cycling holidays in France. Full training in bicycle maintenance is given.

Head Office: 2-4 Birch Polygon, Rusholme, Manchester M14 5HX, England
☎ 01612 488282
info@cycling-for-softies.co.uk
www.cycling-for-softies.co.uk
website: www.alpirsbach.com

Requirements: Must be a keen cyclist, non-smoker, aged over 25 and speak French.

Application Procedure: Application forms can be obtained by telephoning the above number.

TJM Travel

Job(s) Available: Water sports instructors, beach lifeguards, mountain leaders and mountain bike instructors, holiday reps and various hotel staff.

Duration: Working periods are (summer) May to August and (winter) December to April.

Head Office: 40 Lemon Street, Truro, Cornwall TR1 2NS, England
☎ 01872 272767
jobs@tjm.co.uk
www.tjmtravel.com

Working Hours: 7 hours per day, 6 day per week.

Pay: Between £300 and £800 per month according to job and experience.

Company Description: TJM run hotels and activity centres in France, Spain and the UK in the summer months, and operate ski holidays from French Alpine hotels in the winter.

Requirements: Ideally 18 or over and available to work full or part season between May and September at the Adventure centres or December to April at the Ski centres. First aid qualification (except hotel staff and reps). *Water sports instructors:* need to be either fully qualified RYA dinghy instructors, fully qualified RYA windsurfing instructors, or fully qualified BCU instructors. *Sailors and windsurf instructors:* RYA power boat level 2 or above.

Accommodation: Board and lodging provided.

Application Procedure: Apply online at www.tjmtravel.com/tjm_jobs/index

Vendee Loisirs Vacances

Job(s) Available: Representative/children's entertainment (2).

Duration: Mid-May to beginning of September.

Working Hours: 1 day off per week, and most afternoons free.

Pay: €200 per week.

Head Office: 30 Parc des Demoiselles F-85160 St Jean de Monts, France
☎ +33 2 51580402
✆ v.l.v@wanadoo.f
🖥 www.vlv.fr

Company Description: Linda Aplin runs a small friendly business offering mobile home holidays on 2 campsites in St Jean de Monts. She lives locally and is on hand for help and advice.

Job Description: The job of the rep is to welcome, check out, and provide information for the client and to clean the mobiles. There is also a children's club to run 4 times per week in the morning and occasional evenings, plus afternoon activities such as boules, canoeing, horse riding etc.

Requirements: Ideal candidates would be French-speaking, experienced with children and would enjoy meeting people. Ideal for 2 friends.

Accommodation: Free on-site accommodation.

Application Procedure: Write to Linda Aplin at the above address enclosing a CV and photo.

Village Camps

Job(s) Available: Outdoor education and specialist instructors required for spring and autumn residential camps. Domestic and kitchen assistants required for the winter season. Nurses, receptionists, French/TEFL/German teachers, chefs, house counselors and domestic and kitchen assistants also required for Village Camps summer programmes.

Head Office: Recruitment Office, Department 808, Rue de la Morache, 1260 Nyon, Switzerland
☎ +41 22 9909405
✆ personnel@villagecamps.ch
🖥 www.villagecamps.com

Camps in Austria, England, Ireland, France and Switzerland.

Duration: Contract periods vary from 3 to 8 weeks between May and October.

Pay: A generous allowance is provided, paid in local currency.

Company Description: Village Camps has been organizing educational and activity camps for children from all over the globe for over 25 years with a serious commitment to client and staff alike.

Requirements: Applicants must be a minimum of 21 years old (18 for domestic/kitchen and facilities assistants) and have relevant experience and/or qualifications. A second language is desirable. A valid first aid and CPR certificate is required whilst at camp.

Accommodation: Room and board, accident and liability insurance and a weekly allowance provided.

Application Procedure: Recruitment starts in December 2007. There is no deadline to submit applications but positions are limited. Interviews are by telephone. Please specify department 808 on application. For information on dates, locations, positions available and to download an application form, visit www.villagecamps.com/personnel/Howto.html or contact the organisation at the above address.

Teaching And Language Schools

Centre International D'antibes/Institut Prevert

Company Description: The Centre is situated on the French Riviera, and teaches French to more than 5,000 foreign students a year.

Application Procedure: More details on the Work Experience Programme. Free French course and accommodation in exchange of work in the schools or residences.

Head Office: 38 Bd d'Aguillon 06600 Antibes, France
☎ +33 4 92907170 +33 4 92907171
⌨ wep@cia-france.com

Mrs Julie Legree

Job(s) Available: TEFL teachers (4) to teach English to 9-11 year old pupils, TEFL Teacher to teach 14-21 year olds.

Duration: Contracts run from October until May.

Working Hours: All posts require 20 hours per week teaching, per 4-day week, with no work on Wednesdays, weekends or school holidays.

Company Description: This is a local government scheme which has been running for fifteen years. They are looking for Francophiles who wish to develop their social and professional skills.

Head Office: Syndicat Mixte Montaigu-Rocheserviere, 23 avenue Villebois Mareuil, F-85607 Montaigu cedex, France
☎ +33 2 51464545
⌨ julie_legree@yahoo.co.uk
    eef@montaigu@wanadoo.fr
💻 www.explomr.com/english

Job Description: TEFL teachers to teach English to 9–11 year old pupils in 19 different primary schools in the Vendée. TEFL teacher to teach 14–21 year olds in a college and lycée as an *assistante*.

Requirements: Full training is given. Applicants should be outgoing, independent, organised and mature enough to act on their own initiative, as well as having a love of France and children. Candidates will need the maturity and self-confidence to deal with teenagers, and be able to relate to a large teaching staff.

Accommodation: Included in the remuneration package is free board and lodging with local families, and an allowance of approximately €177 per month, after national insurance contributions.

Application Procedure: Applications by post to Mrs Julie Legree at the above address.

Voluntary Work

Service Archeologique De La Communaute D'agglomeration Du Dousaisis

Job(s) Available: Volunteer-students (no more than 10 persons).

Duration: Minimum stay 2 weeks.

Cost: Application fee of €25.

Company Description: This is a local organisation

Head Office: 227 rue Jean Perrin, F-59500 Douai Dorignies, France
☎ +33 3 27088850
⌨ pdemolon@douaisis-agglo.com

for archaeology and the preservation of local cultural heritage. In 2008 an exploration of a merovingian cemetery will begin in collaboration with the university of Lille.

Job Description: Required to assist with the excavations, digging and drawing the finds. Classes on anthropology will be given.

Requirements: Applicants must have tetanus vaccination and valid passport. Volunteers should bring a sleeping bag and high boots.

Accommodation: Provided Monday to Friday.
Application Procedure: Applications to P Demolon at the above address from April.

Associations Des Paralyses De France

Job(s) Available: Assistants required for work in holiday centres for physically disabled adults.
Duration: Period of work 15–21 days during the summer vacation.
Pay: Expenses provided plus travel within France.
Requirements: Minimum age 18 years. Applicants should be able to speak French.
Accommodation: Board and accommodation provided.
Application Provided: Applications to APF Evasion at the above address.

> **Head Office:** 17 Boulevard Auguste-Blanqui, F-75013 Paris, France
> ☎ +33 1 40786900
> ✉ evasion.accompagnateurs@apf.asso.fr
> 🖥 www.apf.asso.fr

Les Amis De Chevreaux – Chatel

Job(s) Available: Volunteers.
Duration: Usually about 3 weeks.
Working Hours: About 30 hours per week.
Company Description: The château of Chevreaux is situated in a hilltop village above the Bresse Plains. Les Amis de Chevreaux is a place where young people of different nationalities can meet and spend time together.

> **Head Office:** 2 Rue du Château, 39190 Chevreaux, France
> ☎ +33 3 84859577
> ✉ accjura@free.fr
> 🖥 http://accjura.free.fr/chantiers/infos_ang (English)
> http://accjura.free.fr (French)

Job Description: The work site in the Jura requires willing volunteers to help with the restoration of the 12th century castle of Chevreaux. Duties involve cleaning, reconstruction of the ruins, stone working, carpentry, masonry, archaeology or topography.
Requirements: Volunteers aged 16 to 25.
Accommodation: Volunteers will be lodged on site (at the castle) in tents with camp beds; all sanitary and kitchen equipment provided.
Additional Information: A fee of €55 to cover insurance is required.
Application Procedure: Application forms online at the above website.

Bardou

Job(s) Available: Volunteer helpers.
Duration: During April, May and June. The minimum stay is 1 month.
Working Hours: 20 hours weekly is asked with tasks.

> **Head Office:** Klaus and Jeane Erhardt, Bardou, par Mons-La-Trivalle, F-34390 Olargues, France
> ☎ +33 4 67977243

Company Description: Bardou is a beautifully restored 16th century Hamlet owned by Klaus and Jean Erhardt. The Hamlet attracts many visitors during the year, especially musicians, orchestras and actors that are performing in the region. Volunteers are able to go to any of the cultural events locally.
Job Description: Volunteers to help with spring cleaning, gardening and maintenance such as painting and helping to keep the stone houses clean.
Accommodation: Provided. Shorter stays or those outside the project months cost from €8 per person/night in individual houses.

Additional Information: Mr Erhardt has published a book called *Bardou: A pioneer life in southern France.*

Application Procedure: Enquiries should be sent to Klaus and Jean Erhardt, enclosing an International Reply Coupon.

Club Du Vieux Manoir

Job(s) Available: Volunteers.

Duration: Long-term stays are a possibility for volunteers at the Château Fort de Guise. After a trial period of 15 days, board and lodging will be offered by the association. Minimum stay 2 months.

Working Hours: There are no set hours to work but everyone is expected to lend a hand when the group decides to work on a project.

Head Office: Abbaye du Moncel à Pontpoint, F-60700 Pont Ste Maxence, France
☎ +33 3 44723398
🖰 clubduvieuxmanoir@free.fr

Pay: Work is unpaid and volunteers are expected to contribute around £8 per day towards the cost of their keep.

Company Description: Founded in 1953, this is a volunteer association for young people who wish to spend some of their spare time doing rescue and restoration work on historic monuments and ancient sites.

Job Description: The volunteers share in the day-to-day organisation of the camp and site. The centres are at the Château Fort de Guise (Aisne), the Abbey Royale du Moncel à Pontpoint (Oise) and the Château d'Argy (Indre). Volunteers required for work on the restoration of ancient monuments and similar tasks.

Requirements: Minimum age 14. Training organised for participants of 16 years and over.

Accommodation: Accommodation is usually in tents.

Application Procedure: By post to the address shown above.

Rempart

Job(s) Available: Volunteer restorers and preservers.

Duration: Most stays are for 2 weeks.

Working Hours: 35 hours per week.

Job Description: Volunteer restorers and preservers needed for various castles, fortresses, churches,

Head Office: 1 rue des Guillemites, F-75004 Paris, France
☎ +33 1 42719655
🖰 contact@rempart.com
🖳 www.rempart.com

chapels, abbeys, monasteries, farms, ancient villages, Gallo-Roman sites on the 170 sites organised by REMPART during holidays every year. Work includes masonry, woodwork, carpentry, coating, restoration and clearance work.

Requirements: Most participants are 18–25 year olds. Some knowledge of French is needed. Previous experience is not necessary.

Accommodation: Board and accommodation are provided at a cost of €5–€8 per day.

Application Procedure: Application details available online.

Association Chantiers Histoire & Architecture Médiévales

Job(s) Available: Volunteers.

Duration: Placements are available from April, July and August and sometimes at other times of the year, with a minimum recommended stay of 2 weeks.

Working Hours: About 6 hours per day.

Head Office: 5 et 7 rue Guilleminot, 75014 Paris, France
☎ +33 1 43351551
🖰 cham@cham.asso.fr
🖳 www.cham.asso.fr

Pay/Cost: Volunteers pay their own travel and health insurance. Volunteer and teenage camps *(chantier):* €12 per day, plus €30 membership. Historic monument session *(stage):* €110 for the whole period. An extra €15 is required for registration payments from countries other than France to cover bank charges.

Job Description: Volunteers required for conservation workcamps at various locations in France. The work includes restoration and repair of historic monuments, châteaux and churches.

Requirements: Volunteers must be at least 16 years old and in good health. Volunteers receive on-the-job training under qualified supervisors.

Accommodation: Tent accommodation and cooking facilities are provided but volunteers need to bring their own bedding and work clothes.

Application Procedure: For full details of the workcamps write to CHAM at the above address.

Chantiers De Jeunes Provence Cote D'azur

Job(s) Available: Volunteers.

Duration: Camps run for 1 or 2 weeks during the summer, Christmas or Easter holidays.

Working Hours: Projects consist of 5 hours work in the morning and organised activities such as sailing, climbing and diving in the afternoons/evenings.

Head Office: 7 Avenue Pierre de Coubertin F-06150 Cannes, La Bocca, France
☎ +33 4 93478969
cjpca@club.internet.fr
stefvi@yahoo.com
www.club.internet.fr/perso/cjpca/

Job Description: Volunteers to take part in the restoration of historic monuments and in environmental protection projects. Camps take place in the country near Cannes or the island of Sainte Marguerite.

Requirements: Aged 13 to 17. Applicants must be sociable and speak French.
Accommodation: Provided.

Application Procedure: For further details send 2 International Reply Coupons to the above address with a letter written in French.

Concordia France

Job(s) Available: International volunteer projects.
Duration: Short-term.

Cost: Volunteers pay a registration fee of £150 and fund their own travel and insurance.

Company Description: Concordia offers volunteers the opportunity to take part in international volunteer projects in over 60 countries worldwide.

Head Office: 19 North Street, Portslade, Brighton BN41 1DH, England
☎ 01273 422218
info@concordia-iye.org.uk
www.concordia-iye.org.uk

Job Description: The work is community-based and ranges from nature conservation, renovation and construction to social work including children's play schemes and teaching.
Requirements: Minimum age 16.

Accommodation: Board and accommodation are free of charge.

Application Procedure: For further information on volunteering or coordinating please check the website or contact the International Volunteer Coordinator at the above address.

WESTERN EUROPE

FRANCE

231

Etudes Et Chantiers (Unarec)

Job(s) Available: Voluntary workcamps.

Duration: Work camps lasting for 2 or 3 weeks are held over the summer.

Cost: Application fees approximately £65 (including membership and insurance).

Company Description: Organises voluntary work-camps for the upkeep, development and preservation of the environment.

Head Office: Délégation Internationale, 3 rue des Petits-Gras, F-63000 Clermont-Ferrand, France
☎ +33 4 73319804
✆ unarec.di@wanadoo.fr eced. voluntariat@wanadoo.fr
💻 www.unarec.org/etudes.htm

Job Description: Tasks vary and include such activities as river cleaning, the preservation of old buildings and districts in small towns and organising local cultural festivals.

Requirements: Minimum age 18; camps are also held for younger teenagers aged 14 to 17.

Application Procedure: For further details by email contact unarec@wanadoo.fr. British volunteers must apply through Concordia or another UK organisation. An annual programme is produced in March.

Jeunesse Et Reconstruction

Job(s) Available: Volunteers needed for workcamps throughout France.

Duration: Most camps last for 3 weeks. There are also possibilities for voluntary work lasting for 3 months, where pocket money is provided. Longer term projects through ICYE (International Cultural Youth Exchange; www.icye.org).

Head Office: 10 rue de Trévise, Paris 75009, France
☎ +33 1 47701588
✆ com@voluntariat.org
💻 www.volontariat.org

Working Hours: About 7 hours work per day, 5 days a week.

Company Description: The national and international volunteer organisation Jeunesse et Reconstruction organises workcamps in France in the Auvergne, Basse Normandie, Pays de La Loire, Midi-Pyrénées, Rhône Alpes, Languedoc-Rouissillon and PACA.

Job Description: Type of work varies from camp to camp. Examples include sharing the daily lives and activities of disabled adults, laying out an orientation course and helping to organise a festival of music. Volunteers are likely to come from all over the world.

Requirements: Applicants should normally be at least 18 years old, though there are some vacancies for 17-year-olds.

Accommodation: Work is unpaid, but free board and accommodation are provided.

Application Procedure: Applications should be made online at the above address.

Neige Et Merveilles

Job(s) Available: Volunteers (4) to take part in international workcamps.

Duration: 2–3 weeks. Also has some longer term programmes.

Working Hours: 6 hours per day.

Cost: Volunteers must pay their own insurance costs of approximately £50.

Head Office: Association Neige at Merveilles, Miniere de Vallauria, 06430 Saint Dalmas de Tende, France
☎ +33 4 93046240
✆ doc@neige-merveilles.com
💻 www.neige-merveilles.com

Requirements: Minimum age 18.

Accommodation: Provided.

Application Procedure: Apply by email or post with CV and cover letter.

Madame De Montesquieu

Job(s) Available: Voluntary assistants (1 or 2).
Duration: Minimum 1 and a half months. Work available all year.

Head Office: La Bassie, Bloux, 03320 Lurcy-Levis, France
☎ + 33 4 70679613

Company Description: Madame de Montesquieu is the author of the cookery book, *Cuisinez La Nature*. The positions would be ideal for those who wish to perfect their French, French cooking and renovate old potteries. La Bassie is in a remote area with the next town 8km away so applicants must also love the country.

Job Description: Assistants to offer general help in and around a very pretty house with a garden and a swimming pool.

Requirements: Applicants must love cats and dogs (4 and 2 of them respectively), French cuisine and nature.

Accommodation: No wages are paid, but board and lodging is provided.

Application Procedure: For more details contact Mme Marie Laure de Montesquieu at the above address.

Au Pairs, Nannies, Family Helps And Exchanges

L'accueil Familial Des Jeunes Etrangers

Job(s) Available: Au pairs and paying guests.
Duration: *Au pairs:* summer placements from 1 to 3 months possible all over France; applications for these must be received by 15 May. Also placements for the school year, preferably from the beginning of

Head Office: 23 rue du Cherche-Midi, F-75006 Paris, France
☎ +33 1 42225034
⌁ accueil@afje-paris.org

September or January to the end of June. *Paying guest:* usual minimum of 2 weeks.

Working Hours: *Au pairs:* 30 hours per week.

Job Description: *Au pairs:* (boys and girls) to assist families with housework and look after children. *Paying guest:* stays in Paris and the suburbs (but in the provinces only during the holidays) also arranged for boys or girls.

Requirements: Minimum age 18.

Additional Information: Also now offer programmes for 1 year. Unpaid work experience in Europe, Canada, Columbia, Australia and China. Jobs in Australia and New Zealand.

Application Procedure: For further details contact the above address.

Angels International Au Pair Agency

Job(s) Available: Au pairs.
Working Hours: 25–40 hours.
Pay: Varies from £55 to £150. Pocket money for regular au pair and mother's helps.

Head Office: Bristol and West House, Post Office Road, Bournemouth, Dorset BH1 1BL, England
☎ 01202 571065
⌁ earnot@btinternet.com
🖥 www.aupair1.com

Company Description: Agency offering placements all over Europe and further afield. The agency offers full support for both families and au pairs, including language classes, trouble shooting.

Requirements: Must have childcare experience.

Application Procedure: Apply to above email address.

'Butterfly Et Papillon' School Of International Languages & Au Pair Agency

Job(s) Available: Au pairs.

Duration: Most positions last from 6 to 12 months. 3 month positions are available during the summer.

Working Hours: 30 hours per week plus 2 evenings babysitting.

Pay: Between €55–€90 per week.

Requirements: 18–26 years. Basic French required. Driving licence and experience with children preferred.

Accommodation: Board available.

Additional Information: Families in the au pair programme are obliged to pay €900 (approx £607.50) towards French lessons if the student stays over 9 months. Butterfly et Papillon also run a work exchange programme. Under the auspices of the EU's Leonardo scheme, this programme offers foreign students the unique opportunity to live and work in France for up to 13 weeks.

Application Procedure: Applications to Fleur Martin, main secretary, at the above address. Application forms available online.

> **Head Office:** 8, Av de Genève, F-74000 Annecy, France
> ☎ +33 4 50670133
> ✉ aupair.france@wanadoo.fr
> 🖥 www.butterfly-papillon.com

Institut Euro Provence

Job(s) Available: Au pairs.

Duration: Required for 6 months to a year. A few places for 2 months in the summer.

Working Hours: Required to work 30 hours per week plus 2 evenings baby-sitting.

Pay: €65 minimum per week.

Company Description: Institut Euro Provence is located in the centre of Marseille, a few minutes walk from the Vieux-Port, in the heart of the commercial district. Good bus and underground service. The Institut Euro 'Provence' offers an au pair option to learn French, to work and be paid in the South of France.

Requirements: Applicants must be between 18 and 30.

Accommodation: Board and lodging, own bedroom. Washing laundered.

Additional Information: Undertake a French course throughout your stay at the Institute Euro Provence.

Application Procedure: For more information contact the au pair placement representative from Monday to Friday, 9am to 1pm and 2pm to 4pm at the above number. Alternatively, email Myriam at the above address.

> **Head Office:** 69 rue de Rome, F-13001 Marseille, France
> ☎ +33 8 75825562, +33 4 91339060
> ✉ info@europrovence.org
> 🖥 http://perso.orange.fr/euro.provence/index

Soames International Services/Paris Nannies

Job(s) Available: Au pairs, nannies in France.

Duration: Minimum period of work 2 months.

Working Hours: 30 hours per week with 2 evenings babysitting.

Pay: *Au pairs:* €75–€80 per week. *Nannies:* minimum wage approximately €220 per week.

Requirements: Minimum age 18. Previous childcare experience desirable.

Accommodation: Provided.

Application Procedure: For further details contact the above address. Application form available online.

> **Head Office:** 64 rue Anatole France, 92300 Levallois Perrec, France
> ☎ +33 1 47304404
> ✉ soames.parisnannies@wanadoo.fr
> 🖥 www.soamesparisnannies.com

Other Employment In France

Centre D'echanges Internationaux

Job(s) Available: Jobs in hotels, restaurants, catering, sales etc.

Duration: Period of work covers university holidays, June to September and December to March.

Pay: Around €1200 per month or €8.48 per hour.

Description: Various jobs in France.

Head Office: 1 rue Gozlin, F-75006 Paris, France
☎ +33 (0) 14 40 51 11 86'
📧 wif@cei4vents.com
🌐 www.cei4vents.com

Requirements: Applicants must have an intermediate level of French and be university students.

Application Procedure: Application form available at www.cei4vents.com at least 3 months before arrival date. Foreign applicants welcome.

Centre D'information Et De Documentation Jeunesse

Job(s) Available: Temporary jobs.

Company Description: Advertises temporary jobs available to young people on a daily basis, mainly in Paris and the surrounding area. It also gives information on cheap places to stay, French university courses for foreigners and practical advice on regulations. CIDJ also publishes booklets on a range of subjects for young people.

Head Office: 101 quai Branly, F-75740 Paris Cedex 15
☎ +33 1 44491200
☎ +33 8 25090630 (information line)
🌐 www.cidj.com

Application Procedure: To get details of the jobs you must visit the centre personally as the CIDJ does not send out information on this subject. Opening hours are 10am–6pm, Monday, Tuesday, Wednesday and Friday, and from 1pm–6pm on Thursdays and 9.30 to1pm, Saturday. (Nearest metro: Bir-Hakeim).

Sejours Internationaux Linguistiques Et Culturels

Job(s) Available: Unpaid internship in a French company.

Duration: 4 weeks minimum.

Working Hours: 30 to 35 hours per week, 5 days a week.

Head Office: 32 Rempart de l'Est, F-16022 Angoulême Cedex
🌐 www.silc-france.com

Cost: €400 for 1–2 months.

Requirements: Minimum age 18. Upper-intermediate level of French (possibility to take French course prior to work placement to meet requirement).

Accommodation: Homestay. Full board, single room.

Additional Information: Also offers a variety of language study courses, international summer centers, individual homestays and private tuition.

Application Procedure: 12 weeks prior to the beginning of the work placement. Application forms are available from www.silc-france.com/students_WE.asp

GERMANY

EMBASSY OF THE FEDERAL REPUBLIC OF GERMANY
23 Belgrave Square, London SW1X 8PZ
☎ 020 7824 1300
🖱 www.london.diplo.de
📠 info@german-embassy.org.uk

The bad news is that Germany is no longer such a good prospect for seasonal work, as recent additions to the membership of the EU have flooded the market. Over the last couple of years German hotels have turned to Eastern Europe for their seasonal staff who now arrive by the bus-load delivered straight to the employers' doors. The other bad news is that unemployment is very high. However, though it requires great perseverance, it is not impossible for the truly determined with a grasp of German to get a job. The main opportunities are in the western and southern regions.

Many of the seasonal jobs available are in hotels, especially in tourist areas such as the Bavarian Alps, the Black Forest and resorts on the North Sea Coast. People going to work in a German hotel should note that managers may demand extra hours of work from their employees, and some will not always give extra time off or pay overtime as compensation. They may also ask workers to do jobs that are not specified in their contract by asking them to fill in for other members of staff. Anyone who feels that their contract is being breached and who cannot come to any agreement with their employer should appeal to the local *Arbeitsamt* (see below) for arbitration. Jobs in other sectors in the tourist industry can be found in this chapter and in the *Worldwide* chapter.

There are also fruit-picking jobs available, although not nearly as many as in France. During the summer the best region to try is the Altes Land which stretches between Stade and Hamburg in north Germany and includes the towns of Steinkirchen, Jork and Horneburg. The work there consists of picking cherries in July and August, and apples in September. Try also the Bergstrasse south of Frankfurt where apples and many other fruits are grown. Germany's vineyards also provide a source of work, particularly because in recent years German winemakers have found it increasingly difficult to find workers to help with the grape harvest. The harvest begins in October and continues into November: the vineyards are concentrated in the south west of the country, especially along the valleys of the Rhine to the south of Bonn and Moselle.

Au pair agencies in Germany no longer have to be licensed so there are now lots of private agencies. Agencies in Germany include IN VIA Germany (+49 761 200208; invia@caritas.de; www.aupair-invia.de) with 40 branches, and Verein für Internationale Jugendarbeit, (+49 228 698952; au-pair.vij@netcologne.de; www.au-pair-vij.org). The German YWCA (VIJ) has more than 20 offices in Germany and places both male and female au pairs for a preferred minimum stay of 1 year. Pocket money is paid and au pairs must be between 17 and 24 years of age. From January 2006, the monthly pocket money will be €260.

On arrival in Germany, EU nationals may go the *Arbeitsamt* (employment office) in the area in which they wish to work and obtain information on job opportunities. The address of the Arbeitsant will be in the local telephone directory. The system is computerised nationally and is highly efficient so it is not necessary to arrange a job in advance. However, if you prefer to have a job already arranged you can try to arrange a job through the EURES contact in your local employment office or through the Zentralstelle fur Arbeitsvermittlung (212.12 Internationale Nachwuchsförderung Studentenvermittlung, Postfach, 53107 Bonn; +49 228 7131330; www.arbeitsamt.de) which is the official government office dealing with job applications from abroad. The Zentralstelle may be able to help find work in hotels, on farms, or in factories: it has a special department to help students of any nationality find summer jobs, applications for which must be received before the end of February. For further information consult the EURES website (www. europa.eu.int/eures).

In addition to those listed in this chapter there are opportunities for voluntary work in Germany; British applicants can apply through International Voluntary Service, UNA Exchange, Youth Action for Peace and Concordia and CIEE. Service Civil International (see the IVS entry) can help US residents; their entries can be found in the *Worldwide* chapter.

An advertisement in a German newspaper may bring an offer of a job see *Rheinische Post* (+49 211 5052880; www.rp-online.de). The following weekly newspapers might also be of interest: The *Süddeutsche Zeitung*, (+49 89 21830; www.sueddeutsch.de); the *Bayernkurier* (+49 89 120040; redaktion@bayernkurier.de; www.bayernkurier.de), *Die Welt* (www.welt.de), or the *Frankfurter Allgemeine Zeitung*, (www.faz.net).

Red Tape

Visa Requirements: A visa is not required by citizens of EU nations, Iceland or Norway. Members of other countries who wish to go to Germany to do paid work need a Visa/Residence Permit before entering Germany.

Residence Permit: Within a week of finding permanent (ie not hotel) accommodation you should register your address (and any subsequent change of address) with the registration office (*Einwohnermeldeamt*), usually found in the town hall. A permit is required for any visit of more than 3 months or where employment is intended. Applications should be made to the Visa section of the nearest Embassy or Consulate General of the Federal Republic of Germany. In the case of EU Nationals already in Germany, applications should be made to the Foreign Nationals Authority *(Ausländerbehörde)* in the town or district *(Kreis)* of intended residence. Nationals of Switzerland, the USA, Australia, New Zealand, Japan, Canada and Israel can apply for a residence permit after arriving in Germany unless they have secured a job before arriving. A residence permit is usually provided within 2 weeks of application and is provided free of charge.

Work Permits: To find work in Germany it is essential to speak some German. The regulations for work permits are the same as for visas. EU Nationals intending to look for work for more than 3 months might have to show the local authority that they are self-supporting while conducting a job hunt. There are no restrictions on voluntary work.

Hotel Work And Catering

Hotel Alte Thorschenke

Job(s) Available: Positions for chambermaids, waiting staff, receptionists and kitchen staff.
Duration: Jobs available between April and October.
Company Description: A medieval hotel built in 1332.
Application Procedure: For more information contact Geschäftsfürer Herr Dudeck.

Head Office: Brueckenstrasse 3, 56812 Cochem (Mosel), Brückenstrasse Germany
☎ +49 2671 7059
✆ alte-thorschenke@t-online.de
🖥 www.castle-thorschenke.com

Hotel Bayerischer Hof/Hotel Reutemann/Hotel Seegarten

Job(s) Available: Waiting staff (9), kitchen assistants (8), chambermaids (8).
Duration: Minimum period of work 3 months.
Working Hours: 8 hours work per day, 5 days a week.
Pay: Approximately €880 net per month.

Head Office: Seepromenade, D-88131 Lindau Germany
☎ +49 838 29150
✆ hotel@bayerischerhof-lindau.de
🖥 www.bayerischerhof-lindau.de

Requirements: Applicants must be students. *Waiting staff:* must speak reasonable German. *Kitchen assistants* and *chambermaids:* knowledge of German not essential.
Accommodation: Board and accommodation available at a small charge.
Application Procedure: Applications to the above address.

Berghotel Johanneshoehe

Job(s) Available: Buffet assistants (2).
Duration: To work for at least 12 weeks; period of work by arrangement.
Working Hours: 40 hours per week.
Pay: Approximately £460 per month.

Head Office: Wallhausenstr. 1, D-57072 Siegen 1 Germany
☎ +49 271 3878790
✆ info@johanneshoehe.de
🖥 www.johanneshoehe.de/en

Requirements: Applicants must speak German.
Accommodation: Free board and lodging.
Application Procedure: Applications should be sent to the above address from 6 April.

Hotel Brudermuhle Bamberg

Job(s) Available: Hotel managers, waitresses (2), cook (1).
Duration: Minimum of 3 months.
Working Hours: 5 days a week, 8–10 hours per day at varying times during the day.

Head Office: Schranne 1, D-96049 Bamberg Germany
☎ +49 951 955220
✆ info@brudermuehle.de
🖥 www.brudermuehle.de

Pay: *Hotel managers and waitresses:* about £775 per month. *Cook:* about £840 per month.
Job Description: *Hotel managers and waitresses:* those working in the restaurant will serve food, drinks and wine. *Cook:* to help prepare food with the French cook.
Requirements: *Hotel managers and waitresses:* knowledge of German and relevant professional training required. *Cook:* cooking qualifications and knowledge of German is required.
Accommodation: Subsidised board and accommodation is available at around £100 per month.
Application Procedure: Applications are invited at any time to the above address.

Eurotoques

Job(s) Available: Kitchen assistants, waiting staff.
Duration: Minimum period of work 3 months at any time of year.
Working Hours: 9 hours per day, 5 days a week.
Pay: Unpaid.

Head Office: Winnender Str 12, D-73667 Ebnisee/Schwäbischer Wald Germany
☎ +49 7184 91055
+49 7184 2918107
✆ info@eurotoques.de
🖥 www.eurotoques.de

Job Description: Staff for placements in the restaurants of some of Germany's top cooks all over Germany.

Requirements: Applicants should speak German.

Accommodation: Free board and lodging is provided.

Application Procedure: Applications to the above address.

Familotel Allgauer Berghof

Job(s) Available: Chambermaids, kitchen assistants and restaurant assistants.

Working Hours: 40 hours work per week.

Pay: Approximately €900 net per month by arrangement.

Company Description: A 180 bed hotel with 50 staff situated in a hill-top ski resort, with access to world-cup races, hiking, tennis and mountain biking.

Head Office: D-87544 Blaichach, Southern Bavaria Germany
☎ +49 8321 8060
🖂 m.neusch@allgaeuer-berghof.de
🖥 www.allgaeuer.berghof.de

Requirements: Knowledge of German required. No previous hotel experience required. Minimum age 18.

Accommodation: Free board and lodging.

Application Procedure: Enquiries to Mrs Neusch at the above address.

Gashaus-Pension Erlenhof

Job(s) Available: Chambermaid, waiter/waitress, kitchen assistant, farmhand/groom.

Duration: Minimum period of work 2 months.

Working Hours: 8–10 hours per day, 5.5 days a week, in shifts. Time off by arrangement.

Head Office: Famille W. Scheerer, 72275 Alpirsbach-Ehlenbogen Germany
☎ +49 7444 6246
🖂 gasthof-erlenhof@alpirsbach.com

Pay: *Chambermaid:* around £400 per month. *Waiter/waitress:* around £400 per month including tips. *Kitchen assistant:* around £400 per month. *Farmhand/groom:* around £340 per month. Salaries quoted are net, deductions having been made for board and accommodation.

Company Description: Family run hotel restaurant and farm in the black forest between Stuttgart and France.

Job Description: *Chambermaid:* work includes helping with the laundry. *Kitchen assistant:* to prepare vegetables and wash up (using machine). *Farmhand/groom:* to work around the farm and/or help with the horses.

Requirements: *Waiter/waitress:* must have a knowledge of German and the ability to get on with people. Staff should be prepared to help in other departments.

Accommodation: Pay includes board and lodging.

Application Procedure: Applications throughout the year to Georg Dietel at the above address.

Holiday Inn Frankfurt Airport-North

Job(s) Available: Serving staff.

Duration: Minimum period of work 2 months.

Working Hours: Approximately 8 hour shifts per day, not including a 30 minute break, over a 5-day week. The hours worked will vary according to the shifts.

Head Office: Isenburger Schneise 40, 60528 Frankfurt Germany
☎ +49 696 7840
🖂 Sonja.thierer@queensgrouppe.de
🖥 www.frankfurt-airport-north-holiday-inn.com

Pay: Approximately €577 per month.

Company Description: Set in Germany's largest stretch of urban woodland near the old city, the Holiday Inn Frankfurt Airport-North is one of Frankfurt's premier hotels.

Job Description: Serving staff required for the hotel's restaurant, bar and beer-garden.

Requirements: Staff should speak English and German.

Accommodation: Board and lodging are available at a small charge.

Application Procedure: Apply by email to the above address.

Internationales Haus Sonnenberg

Job(s) Available: Internship or freelancer for seminars/training in pedagogical out-of-school youth work.

Duration: Between 2 and 8 weeks.

Working Hours: 30–35 hours per week, depending on task. Seminar times: 9am to 12pm and 7pm to 10pm.

Pay: Wages depending on responsibility. Information available on request.

Head Office: Sonnenberg-Kreis e.V./c.o. Internationales Haus Sonnenberg, Clausthaler Str. 11, 37444 St Andreasberg Germany
☎ +49 5882 9440
✆ info@sonnenberg-international.de
🖥 www.sonnenberg-internal.de

Company Description: The Internationales Haus Sonnenberg is the conference centre of the Sonnenberg-Kreis e.V., an independent provider of non school based education in Europe, which is registered as an educational charity under German law. The Internationales Haus Sonnenberg organise conferences throughout the year, normally with participants from several countries. Thanks to the international network, The Internationales Haus Sonnenberg is an experienced partner for international projects. Work takes place primarily in the following areas: the securing of human rights, peace, solidarity and social responsibility. The Internationales Haus Sonnenberg organises seminars and conferences with international, intercultural, socio-critical, political and ecological subjects for children, young people, school groups and adults. Additionally the Internationales Haus Sonnenberg offers in-service training for teachers and multipliers, interdisciplinary specialist conferences on educational subjects and programmes within the system of Educational Leave as well as training in competence for Europe, conferences for people with disabilities and leisure visits and seminars in other countries. The Internationales Haus Sonnenberg is also happy to offer rooms and services to conference organisers with their own programmes and leisure activities or can provide a tailor-made programme on request.

Requirements: Minimum age 18. Applicants should have a basic knowledge of German. To work as a freelancer applicants must have experience in pedagogical work. Any requisite work permits are required.

Accommodation: Provided free of charge.

Application Procedure: For further details email or telephone.

Hotel Jakob

Job(s) Available: General assistants.

Duration: Period of work from mid-May to mid-October.

Working Hours: 5 days a week.

Pay: Around €1500 per month.

Head Office: Schwarzeweg 6, D-87629 Fussen-Bad Faulenbach Germany
✆ info@kurhotel-jakob.de
🖥 www.kurhotel-jakob.de

Requirements: A basic knowledge of German is necessary.

Accommodation: Free board and lodging provided.

Application Procedure: Applications to Frau G Jakob at the above address.

Kloster Hornbach

Job(s) Available: Interns, waiters/waitresses.
Duration: Minimum period of work 3 months.
Working Hours: 40 hours per week.
Pay: Minimum €280 per month.
Company Description: Kloster Hornbach is a former monastery founded in 742, and rebuilt over the last 6 years into a 4-star hotel with 34 rooms, 2 restaurants, a large garden restaurant and several banqueting rooms.

Head Office: Loesch GmbH Im Klosterbezirk, D-66500 Hornbach
☎ +49 6338 910100
hotel@kloster-hornbach.de
www.kloster-hornbach.de

Requirements: Good level of German and hotel experience. Minimum age 18. Must be EU citizens.

Accommodation: Free accommodation and 2 meals a day.

Application Procedure: Applications by email with CV and cover letter to Christiane und Edelbert Loesch at the above address.

Posthotel

Job(s) Available: Chambermaids (2), kitchen assistants/washers up (2).
Duration: Minimum period of work 2 and a half months between July and October and between 20 December and 31 March.
Working Hours: 8-9 hours per day, 5 days a week. *Chambermaids:* from 6.30am–4pm, with an hour break. *Kitchen assistants/washers up:* from 7am–2pm and 5.30pm–9pm with a half hour break.

Head Office: Obermarkt 9, (Zufahrt Karwendelstr. 14), 82481 Mittenwald
☎ +49 8823 9382333
info@posthotel-mittenwald.de
www.posthotel-mittenwald.de

Pay: €850 per month.
Job Description: *Chambermaids:* to clean guest rooms, corridors, toilets, swimming pool etc. *Kitchen assistants/washers up:* to wash tableware and cooking utensils, peel potatoes, clean vegetables, etc.

Requirements: Some knowledge of German an advantage: other languages are not essential. Applicants only accepted from students holding EU passports or those studying in Germany who have the relevant work permit from the employment office.

Accommodation: Board and lodging available for around €160 per month.

Application Procedure: Applications, enclosing proof of student status from school, college or university stating that you are a full-time student there (International Student Identity Cards will not suffice) by email.

Hotel Schloss Hugenpoet GmbH

Job(s) Available: Gardeners, general assistants, chambermaids, laundry assistants needed.
Duration: Minimum period of work 2 months.
Working Hours: 8 hours per day over a 5 day week.
Pay: €600 approximately gross, monthly.
Company Description: The Hotel Schloss Hugenpoet is a beautiful building, not far from Düsseldorf. It belongs to the Relais and Chateaux Hotel Group.

Head Office: August-Thyssen-Strasse 51, D-45219, Essen-Kettwig
☎ +49 2954 120400
personal@hugenpoet.de
www.hugenpoet.de

Accommodation: Provided free of charge.

Application Procedure: Apply with CV and brief cover letter.

Schloss Reinhartshausen

Job(s) Available: Waiting staff (3), banqueting set-ups (3), kitchen helpers (2).

Duration: 6 months to 1 year.

Working Hours: 40 hours per week.

Pay: *Waiting staff:* approx £550 per month. *Banqueting set-ups:* approx £460 per month. *Kitchen helpers:* approx £550 per month.

Head Office: Hauptstrasse 41, Erbach m Rheingau, D-65346 Eltville, Germany
☎ +49 6123 676406
✆ isabel.oberdorf@kempinski.com
🖳 www.schloss-hotel.de

Company Description: Leading 5-star hotel with 54 rooms, 11 conference rooms, 3 restaurants, a beautiful terrace and a winery. Run by a young team.

Job Description: *Waiting staff:* required to prepare or serve food, clear tables, etc. Must be open minded, guest-orientated, friendly and enjoy serving. *Banqueting set-ups* required to prepare meeting rooms, serve food etc. *Kitchen helpers:* required to prepare food, especially for breakfasts and buffets. Cooking ability an advantage.

Requirements: Applicants must speak German and English.

Accommodation: May be available, depending on the number of requests, for approx £150 per month.

Application Procedure: Applications to the above address from December.

Hotel-Weinhaus-Oster

Job(s) Available: Waiting assistant, general assistant.

Duration: Minimum period of work 3 months between May and October.

Working Hours: 7 hours per day, 6 days a week.

Pay: Approximately £320 per month plus tips.

Head Office: Moselweinstrasse 61, D-56814 Ediger-Eller 2, bei Cochem/Mosel, Germany
☎ +49 2675 232
✆ hotel-oster@t-online.de

Company Description: A family hotel facing the magnificent river Mosel, with many attractions including the local wine festivals and wine-tastings arranged by the owner's brother.

Requirements: Applicants must speak German.

Accommodation: Free board and accommodation.

Application Procedure: Applications to Mrs ML Meyer-Schenk at the above address from January.

Hotel Wittelsbacher Hof

Job(s) Available: Chambermaids, dishwashers, kitchen assistants, restaurant assistants.

Duration: Minimum period of work 2 months from May to July, July to October or December to March. Positions also available from 20 December to 10 January, or for both the summer and winter seasons.

Head Office: Prinzenstrasse 24, D-87561 Oberstdorf, Germany
☎ +49 8322 6050
✆ info@wittelsbacherhof.de
🖳 www.wittelsbacherhof.de

Working Hours: 8 hours per day, 5 days a week.

Pay: Approximately €650 net per month plus help with travelling expenses.

Job Description: Chambermaids, dishwashers, kitchen assistants, restaurant assistants (male and female) to work in a 120 bed hotel.

Requirements: Knowledge of German preferable.

Accommodation: Board and lodging provided free of charge.

Application Procedure: Applications from EU citizens only to the above address enclosing a photograph, CV and proof of student status.

Sports, Couriers And Camping

Bents Bicycle & Walking Tours

Job(s) Available: Company representatives (4–5).
Duration: Minimum period of work 8 weeks between the end of May and end of September.
Working Hours: Varied hours as needs of work dictate, but generally around 40 hours per week, up to 7-day week.
Pay: Around £600 per month.

Head Office: The Blue Cross, Orleton, Ludlow, Shropshire SY8 4HN, England
☎ 01568 780800
✆ info@bentstours.com
🖳 www.bentstours.com

Job Description: Company representatives for a tour operator offering cycling and walking holidays in France, Germany and Austria. Duties to include meeting clients at the airport, maintaining bicycles, transporting luggage between hotels and generally taking care of the needs of clients.
Requirements: Applicants should have a reasonable grasp of either spoken German or French and fluent English. They must also possess a full valid driving licence.
Accommodation: Board and accommodation provided.
Application Procedure: By post with a photograph, to Stephen Bent at the above address from January.

Canvas Holidays

Job(s) Available: Campsite courier.
Company Description: Canvas Holidays provide luxury mobile home and tent holidays at over 100 campsites throughout Europe.
Job Description: Involves cleaning accommodation, welcoming families to the site and showing them to their accommodation. Visiting customers, providing local information and basic maintenance

Head Office: GVN Camping Recruitment, East Port House, Dunfermline KY12 7JG, England
☎ 01383 629012
✆ campingrecruitment@ gvnrecruitment.com
🖳 www.gvnrecruitment.com

are very important parts of the job. Campsite courier opportunities are also available for couples to work on site together.
Accommodation: Provided as part of package.
Additional Information: For details of management positions, see website.
Application Procedure: Please call the recruitment department for more information and an application form, or apply online at www.gvnrecruitment.com.

Eurocamp

Job(s) Available: Campsite courier, children's courier, courier team leaders, children's courier team leaders, montage/demontage.
Duration: *Campsite courier:* Applicants should be available to work from April/May to mid-September or June/July to mid-September. *Children's courier:* Applicants should be available from early May to

Head Office: Overseas Recruitment Department (Ref SJ/08) Hartford Manor, Greenbank Lane, Northwich CW8 1HW, England
☎ 01606 787525
🖳 www.holidaybreakjobs.com/camping

September or June to September. *Courier team leaders:* Applicants should be available from April to mid-September. *Children's courier team leaders:* Applicants should be available from early May until September. *Montage/Demontage:* Applicants should be available from Feb to May or August to October.

Pay: You will receive a competitive salary, comprehensive training, return travel to and from an agreed meeting point, accommodation, medical and luggage insurance and uniform.

Company Description: Eurocamp is a leading tour operator in self-drive camping and mobile home holidays in Europe. We offer our customers a wide range of holiday accommodation on over 200 premier campsites. Each year the company seeks to recruit up to 1,500 enthusiastic people to work the summer season in a variety of roles.

Job Description: *Campsite Courier:* A Courier's responsibility begins by ensuring that the customer's accommodation is both inviting and cleaned to the highest of standards. You will welcome new arrivals, be the customers main point of contact and will be expected to provide local and general information, give assistance and even act as interpreter if required. Part of the role will involve helping out with minor repairs to accommodation and equipment and will also involve basic administration and accounts. *Children's Courier:* You will be responsible for planning and delivering a fun, safe, daily activity programme to our customers' children. The age of the children attending the club will range from 5 to 12 years old although we also run a toddler service in low season for 12 months to 4 years. *Courier Team Leaders:* You must be able to deliver first class customer service and organize the daily workload of the courier team. Your role also includes all the duties of a Campsite Courier and you will be expected to lead by example. There are a variety of team leader roles available, dependant on team size; Courier in Charge, Senior Courier and Site Manager. *Children's Courier Team Leaders:* Your role will involve the management, motivation and development of the Children's Couriers to ensure they provide a varied range of quality activities. Your role includes all the duties of a Children's Courier. *Montage/Demontage:* Montage and Demontage assistants are employed to either help set up for the season or close down at the end of the season. This involves putting up or taking down tents, moving/distributing equipment and cleaning/preparing accommodation.

Requirements: Applicants must hold a UK/EU passport and the current minimum age is 18 years old on the day you start work in order to obtain the relevant insurance cover. *Campsite Couriers:* You should have lots of energy, basic common sense and a genuine desire to help people. *Children's Courier:* Previous childcare experience is essential. Successful candidates will be asked to apply for an Enhanced Disclosure. *Courier Team Leaders:* You must have previous experience of leading a team successful applicants may be asked to apply for a Standard Disclosure. *Children's Courier Team Leaders:* Previous experience with Children and leading a team successful candidates will be asked to apply for an Enhanced Disclosure. *Montage/Demontage:* Previous experience of physical and repetitive work successful applicants will be asked to apply for a Standard Disclosure.

Accommodation: Provided.

Application Procedure: Applicants should apply on-line at www.holidaybreakjobs.com/camping or telephone 01606 787 525 for an application pack.

Voluntary Work

Concordia Germany

Job(s) Available: International volunteer projects.
Duration: Short-term.

Company Description: Concordia offers volunteers the opportunity to take part in international short-term volunteer projects in over 60 countries worldwide.

Head Office: 19 North Street, Portslade, Brighton BN41 1DH, England
☎ 01273 422218
info@concordia-iye.org.uk
www.concordia-iye.org.uk

Job Description: The work is community based and ranges from nature conservation, renovation and construction to social work including children's play schemes and teaching.
Requirements: Minimum age 16.

Accommodation: Board and accommodation are free of charge.

Additional Information: Volunteers pay a registration fee of £150 and fund their own travel and insurance.

Application Procedure: For further information on volunteering or coordinating please check the website or contact the International Volunteer Coordinator at the above address.

IJGD Internationale Jugendgemeinschaftsdienste

Job(s) Available: Volunteers.

Duration: Periods of 3 weeks at Easter or between June and September.

Working Hours: 25 hours of work per week.

Company Description: An independent non-profit organization active in the field of international

> **Head Office:** Kaiserstrasse 43, D-53113 Bonn Germany
> ☎ +49 22822 80011
> 🖱 via website.
> 🖥 www.ijgd.de

youth work. One of the largest and oldest workcamp organizations in Germany which focuses on encouraging intercultural understanding. Aims to enable people to actively create community life while giving them the opportunity to broaden their horizons.

Job Description: Volunteers to work on summer projects such as environmental protection and the restoration of educational centres volunteers also needed to assist with city fringe recreational activities.

Requirements: Applicants should be aged between 16 and 26. Knowledge of German required on social projects.

Accommodation: Free board and accommodation provided.

Application Procedure: Applications should be made to the above address as early as possible. British volunteers should apply through Concordia or another UK organisation.

NIG EV

Job(s) Available: Volunteers.

Duration: 2–3 weeks.

Working Hours: 30 hours per week.

Job Description: Volunteers to work for a non-profit organisation, which organises 20 workcamps for people aged 18–30, in Germany and various

> **Head Office:** Carl-Hopp-Str. 27, 18069 Rostock Germany
> ☎ +49 381 4922914
> 🖱 nig@campline.de
> 🖥 www.campline.de/nig/fger

countries. The camps focus on environmental protection, nature conservation, archaeology and cultural projects. Some projects are aimed at conserving the remains of concentration camps and developing museum projects there to educate people about the Jewish holocaust.

Requirements: Aged 18–30.

Accommodation: Accommodation and food are provided free.

Additional Information: Volunteers will need to pay a registration fee of approximately £60. Further details can be obtained from the address above.

Application Procedure: British volunteers should apply through Concordia or another UK organisation.

Nothelfergemeinschaft Der Freunde

Job(s) Available: Volunteers for spring and summer work camps.

Duration: Camps normally last for 1 month.

Working Hours: Approximately 35 hours per week.

> **Head Office:** Post Fach 10 15 10, D-52349 Düren Germany
> ☎ +49 2421 76569
> 🖱 info@nothelfer.org
> 🖥 www.nothelfer.org

Pay: Work is unpaid but free board and accommodation and insurance against sickness, accident and liability are provided. Volunteers are responsible for their own travel costs.

Job Description: The work may involve building, gardening or social work.

Requirements: Applicants should be aged 16–20 years.

Accommodation: Provided.

Additional Information: Special workcamp with German language courses normally held mid-July–mid-August.

Application Procedure: Applications in April or May at the latest to the above address.

Open Houses Network

Job(s) Available: Restoration work.

Duration: 2 or 3 weeks (building weeks) or as long as you like for open houses. May to October for building weeks. Open houses run all year round.

☎ + 49 3643 502390
📧 info@openhouses.de
💻 www.openhouses.de

Cost: A contribution of €25–€40 per week depending on individual means.

Company Description: Formed in the mid-1980s when a group of young people voluntarily undertook to restore village churches in danger of decay, the network currently runs 6 historic buildings in the eastern part of Germany.

Job Description: Originally it was intended that anybody could help out with restoration work in return for board and lodging, and this policy continues today. Anybody can walk into an 'open house' and stay as long as they are prepared to work there. However, the project has grown to include building weeks, art workshops, workcamps and practical training for students. Building weeks allow participants to gain real restoration experience, working under the guidance of trained professionals.

Requirements: Open to all.

Accommodation: Basic lodgings provided in exchange for work. Meals are prepared by the group and are part of community life.

Application Procedure: See website for details.

Happy Hands

Job(s) Available: The programme arranges working holidays on farms or in family-run country hotels for British and European students.

Head Office: Anne von Gleichen, Roemerberg 10, 60311 Frankfurt Germany
☎ + 49 69 293733
📧 Anne.Gleichen@t-online.de
💻 www.workingholidays.de

Duration: 3–6 months, though a 6-week commitment is also allowed.

Working Hours: 36 hours per week with 1 day free.

Pay: Weekly pocket money of €51.

Requirements: Some knowledge of German.

Accommodation: Full board and lodging with families on farms or in country hotels.

Additional Information: The project is at present only for students coming from the old EU countries.

Application Procedure: Application form available online. Early requests are appreciated.

Au Pairs, Nannies, Family Helps And Exchanges

IN VIA

Job(s) Available: Au pair positions in Germany.

Duration: Minimum length of stay 6 months, but stays of 1 year preferred.

Company Description: With regional offices in 40 cities IN VIA can arrange to place au pairs with German families.

Requirements: Aged 18–24.

Application Procedure: For further information please contact the above address.

Head Office: Katholische Verband fur Madchen- und Frauensozialarbeit Deutschland eV, Karlstrasse 40, 79104 Freiburg Germany
☎ +49 761 200206
invia@caritas.de
www.aupair-invia.de

Verein Für Internationale Jugendarbeit

Job(s) Available: Au pairs.

Duration: Length of stay varies from 6 weeks (over the summer) to a year.

Pay: Pocket money of around €260 per month.

Job Description: Au pairs to be placed with families in Germany.

Head Office: Burgstr. 106, 60389 Frankfurt Germany
☎ +49 69469 39700
au-pair@vij.de
www.au-pair-vij.org

Requirements: Girls and boys between 18 and 30 years. Applicants should have a reasonable command of German.

Additional Information: Season ticket for local transport also provided.

Application Procedure: Those interested should contact the above address.

GREECE

EMBASSY OF GREECE
1A Holland Park, London W11 3TP
☎ 020 7229 3850
www.greekembassy.org.uk
consulategeneral@greekembassy.org.uk
Greek Consulate (regarding visas)
☎ 020 7313 5600

Every year Greece receives around 10 million foreign tourists, and it is the tourist trade, with employers such as those listed in this chapter, that offer foreigners the best chances of finding temporary work. Such work is best found by making enquiries when at the main tourist destinations. Even so, most Greek proprietors, in defiance of EU guidelines on male/female parity in the workplace, prefer to employ girls.

Other opportunities for foreigners involve domestic work with Greek families, helping with the housework and perhaps improving the family's English. Wages in Greece are generally low, but are enough to permit an extended stay. In recent years wage levels for unskilled work have been depressed in some areas because of the large number of immigrants – legal and otherwise –

from Albania and other countries in Eastern Europe who are willing to work for low rates. Unemployment remains constantly high at around 10%.

British, Irish and other EU nationals are permitted to use the Greek national employment service: local branches are called offices of the *Organisimos Apasholisseos Ergatikou Dynamikou*, or OAED (the Manpower Employment Organisation: +30 1 9989000; www.oaed.gr). For further information consult the free booklet *Working in Greece,* published by the UK Employment Service. Jobs are also advertised in the local major newspapers such as *Ta Nea* (www.tanea.gr), *Eleftheros Typos* (www.e-tipos.com), *Eleftherotypia* (www.enet.gr) and *Apogevmatini* (www.apogevmatini.gr).

Although people have succeeded in finding casual farm work; picking oranges and olives; it is almost impossible to arrange this from outside Greece. The large number of foreigners from Eastern Europe who are already present in Greece usually fill these jobs, so it is just as difficult to arrange this kind of work on arrival. Oranges are picked between Christmas and March, especially south of Corinth. Grapes are grown all over the mainland and islands, and growers often need casual help during the September harvest. Those who are prepared to take a chance on finding casual work in Greece will find further information on harvests in the book *Work Your Way Around the World* (see *Useful Publications*).

There are opportunities for voluntary work in Greece arranged by International Voluntary Service, Youth Action for Peace, Concordia and UNA Exchange for British applicants and Service Civil International for other nationalities: see the *Worldwide* chapter for details.

It may be possible to obtain a job by means of an advertisement in one of the English language newspapers in Athens. The *Athens News* is a weekly newspaper published every Friday whose classified department is at 9 Christou Lada str, 102 37 Athens, Greece (+30 10 3333404; email an-classified@dolnet.gr; www.athensnews.gr).

Red Tape

Visa Requirements: Citizens of the EU, Australia, Canada, New Zealand, Japan, Israel and the USA do not require a visa to travel to Greece providing that they stay no more than 90 days. If you intend to visit Greece for more than 90 days and are going to take up employment, you have to apply in person to the Consulate General of Greece for a national Visa.

Residence Permits: Non-EU citizens wishing to stay in Greece for longer than 3 months require permission to do so from the Aliens Department *(Grafeio Tmimatos Allodapon)* or Tourist Police in the area, along with your passport and a letter from your employer. The permit is normally granted on the spot.

According to EU regulations Greece should have scrapped its residence permit requirement for EU citizens by April 2006, however at the time of writing they had not done this and have had an official warning from the EU. Check the regulations regarding this before your 3 months expires. A summary of recent immigration regulations for Greece appears on the *Athens News* website at www.athensnews.gr.

Work Permits: A permit must be obtained by a prospective employer on behalf of a non-EU national prior to arrival in Greece. Failure to follow this procedure may result in refusal of entry to the country. EU nationals do not require a work permit to work in Greece. For more information see the Greek Embassy in London's website: www.greekembassy.org.uk. The residence permit also serves as a work permit.

Hotel Work and Catering

Doreta Beach Hotel

Job(s) Available: Barman, barmaid, waitresses.
Pay: Around £450 per month.
Requirements: Knowledge of German required.
Application Procedure: By post to Michalis A Yiasiranis, manager, at the above address.

Head Office: Theologos, 85100 Rhodes, PO Box 131, Greece
☎ +30 22410 8254363
🖃 alexia-doreta@otonet.gr
🖳 www.greekhotel.com/dodecane/rhodes/theologos/doreta/home.htm

Hotel ERI

Job(s) Available: Bar staff and couriers.
Job Description: Bar staff and couriers needed to work in this hotel in the Cyclades, on the Island of Paros.
Application Procedure: Applications to the above address.

Head Office: Parikia Paros Island Greece
☎ +30 22840 23360
🖃 rivolli1@otenet.gr
🖳 www.erihotel.gr

Mark Warner

Job(s) Available: Accountants, receptionists, watersports instructors, tennis and aerobics instructors, chefs, kitchen porters, first aiders, nannies, handymen and nightwatchmen. Some reserve staff also needed throughout the season.
Duration: During the summer from April to October.
Pay: From £50 per week.
Job Description: Staff required to work in hotels in Greece, along with various other locations.
Requirements: Requirements for languages, experience, qualifications vary according to the job applied for.
Accommodation: Full board, medical insurance and travel expenses included in wages. Free use of watersport and activity facilities.
Application Procedure: For further details, please contact the resorts recruitment department on the above number.

Head Office: George House, 61-65 Kensington Church Street, London W8 4BA, England
☎ 0844 844 3760 0844 844 3770 (for childcare recruitment)
🖃 recruitment@markwarner.co.uk
🖳 www.markwarner.co.uk/jobs

Rizos Resorts

Job(s) Available: Cooks (4).
Duration: Minimum period of work 4 months between 10 April and 1 October.
Working Hours: 8 hours per day, 6 days a week.
Pay: From £400 per month.
Company Description: Hotels in Aghios Gordios, St George South, Paleokastritsa, Pelekas Beach Regions, Corfu and Greece.
Job Description: Cooks to prepare food for around 400 people daily.
Requirements: Should have previous experience of professional cooking and international specialities, with an emphasis on Italian cooking.

Head Office: Rizos hotels, PO Box 70, Corfu 49100, Greece
🖃 rizosresorts@sympnia.com

Accommodation: No accommodation available.

Application Procedure: Applications to Dr Paul Rizos, manager, at above address or email (Mention ATTN HR – Dr Paul Rizos in the subject line.).

Sani Resort

Job(s) Available: Internships and training placements available for Hotel, Catering and Tourism trainees in this popular Greek resort.

Duration: Employees are expected to stay for 3–6 months. Staff required in winter for Oceania Club.

Working Hours: 8–9 hours per day, 5 days a week.

Pay: €400 per month.

Head Office: Kassandra 63077 Chalkidiki, Greece
hrd@saniresort.gr
www.saniresort.gr

Company Description: Sani Resort is one of the most unique resorts in Europe, comprising of 2 luxury 5-star hotels, 2 up-scaled 4 star hotels and the recently renovated biggest Marina in North Greece. This long established ecological resort, on the Haldiki peninsula, aims to guarantee its guests enjoyment by focusing on the training and motivation of its staff.

Job Description: Training programme includes financial, social and cultural elements, so that this is as much a cultural exchange as a working environment.

Requirements: Fluent English necessary. Minimum age 18.

Accommodation: Free accommodation provided.

Application Procedure: Email CV to hrd@saniresort.gr.

Village Inn

Job(s) Available: Entertainers/bar staff (2), mates/housekeeping (2).

Duration: Work is available between 1 May and 20 October.

Working Hours: 8 hours per day, 6 days a week.

Pay: *Entertainers/bar staff:* €850 per month. *Mates/housekeeping:* €800 per month.

Head Office: 400 Laganas St, Mouzaki, Zakynthos 29092, Greece
+30 269 551033
info@villageinn.gr
www.villageinn.gr

Company Description: Medium-size self-catering accomodation on the Greek island of Zakynthos.

Job Description: *Entertainers/bar staff:* to plan, organise and organise events such as music quizzes, karaoke nights etc, and to work as bar staff in the resort's pool bar. *Mates/housekeeping:* to work in the resort.

Requirements: Knowledge of Italian or Greek would be an advantage.

Accommodation: Not available.

Application Procedure: Applications to the above address are invited from 15 March.

Sports, Couriers and Camping

Mastersun Holidays

Job(s) Available: Resort managers, assistant managers, resort representatives, hosts, housekeepers, chefs and assistant chefs, kitchen assistants, bar and restaurant staff, waterfront instructors, waterfront managers, children's and teen's workers.

Head Office: Thames House, 63-67 Kingston Road, New Malden, Surrey KT3 3PB, England
020 8942 9442
rebecca@mastersun.co.uk
www.mastersun.co.uk

Duration: Numerous staff needed over the summer season. There are winter ski jobs as well.

Company Description: Mastersun is a Christian holiday company that organizes summer holidays in Greece, Turkey, Italy and Switzerland as well as winter ski holidays in the French Alps. Holidays are hotel or chalet based and the complete package includes watersports, skiing and other activities.

Application Procedure: Download an application form from the website or ask for a job pack from the above address or email. Applications welcome at any time.

Olympic Holidays

Job(s) Available: Overseas resort representatives (250), overseas transfer and guiding representatives (20), overseas administrators (30).

Duration: The season begins in March/April and runs until October, but high season positions (June to September) are also available.

Head Office: 1 Torrington Park, Finchley, London N12 9SU, England
☎ 0870 499 6742
julian@olympicholidays.com
www.olympicholidays.com

Working Hours: *Overseas resort representatives:* 6 days a week with variable hours and may be on call 24 hours a day, 7 days a week. *Overseas transfer and guiding representatives* and *overseas administrators:* 6 days a week. Hours are variable.

Pay: *Overseas resort representatives:* approximately £110 per week (tax free), plus generous commission (tax free), return flights, and insurance. *Overseas transfer and guiding representatives:* approximately £350 per month (tax free), return flights, and insurance. *Overseas administrators:* approximately £600 per month (tax free). Flights and insurance are provided.

Company Description: Olympic Holidays was one of the first tour operators in Greece over 40 years ago and they are now one of the leading independently owned tour operators to both Greece and Cyprus. They cover most resorts from young and lively to upmarket. In recent years they have added Bulgaria, Tunisia and Turkey to their portfolio. They also feature a range of more exotic destinations such as Egypt, The Gambia, Mexico and India.

Job Description: *Overseas resort representatives:* Acting as front line ambassadors of the company. Applicants must be professional, hardworking and possess unlimited stamina. Duties involve airport transfers, hotel visits, guiding excursions, administration duties, health and safety checks, complaint handling and attending welcome meetings. *Overseas transfer and guiding representatives:* applicants will be responsible for accompanying guests to and from the airport and their holiday accommodation. They will also guide day and evening resort excursions and assist the representatives whenever required. *Overseas administrators:* for office based administration work, arranging flights and transfers, accommodation allocation and guest related reports along with accompanying guests on transfers.

Requirements: Greek language skills are an advantage, but not essential. *Overseas resort representatives:* minimum age 18. Applicants should have at least 12 months customer service experience. Sales experience is preferable. Maturity, a calm manner and good organisation are all necessary skills. *Overseas transfer and guiding representatives:* minimum age 18. *Overseas administrators:* minimum age 18. Applicants should be able to use Word, Excel, and possess advanced PC skills along with good organisational skills.

Accommodation: Provided (meals not included).

Application Procedure: Applications can be made via the online application form on the Olympic website. Alternatively, applicants should call the above number to request an application form. Interviews start in November 2007.

Pavilion Tours

Job(s) Available: Watersports instructors.

Duration: Minimum period of work between May and October.

Working Hours: Variable, 7 days a week.

Pay: Approximately £100 per week.

Head Office: 1 Jubilee Street, Brighton, East Sussex BN1 1GE, England
☎ 0870 241 0425/7
✆ info@paviliontours.com

Company Description: An expanding, specialist activity tour operator for students with bases in Greece and Spain. Watersports include windsurfing, dinghy sailing, water skiing and canoeing.

Job Description: Watersports instructors required to instruct sailing/windsurfing etc and to assist with evening entertainments.

Requirements: The company are keen to recruit highly motivated staff.

Accommodation: Board and lodging included.

Application Procedure: Applications from November 2007 to the above address. Please include current instructor qualifications.

Skyros

Job(s) Available: Work scholars.

Duration: Period of work about 3 months; either April to July or July to October.

Working Hours: Variable working hours, but normally between 6 and 8 per day, 6 days a week.

Pay: Allowance of around £50 per week plus full board and accommodation.

Head Office: 92 Prince of Wales Road, London NW5 3NE, England
☎ 020 7284 3063
✆ john@skyros.com
office@skyros.com

Company Description: Skyros offer holistic holidays: they combine a holiday in a Greek island with the chance to participate in over 200 courses from yoga to sailing and cooking.

Job Description: Work scholars to assist in the smooth running of Atsitsa, a holistic holiday centre on Skyros island. Duties include cleaning, bar work, laundry, gardening and general maintenance. Work scholars live as part of the community; in exchange for their hard work they may participate in the courses (such as yoga, dance and windsurfing) where their duties allow.

Requirements: Applicants should be 21 or over. Qualified nurses, chefs and Greek speakers preferred.

Application Procedure: Applications should be sent to the above address between January and February.

Work at Sea

Setsail Holidays

Job(s) Available: Skippers, hostesses and engineers.

Duration: Starts April/May to end September/October 2008.

Pay: £120–£160 per week depending on job and experience.

Head Office: 40 Burkitts Lane, Sudbury, Suffolk CO10 2HB, England
☎ 01787 310445
✆ boats@setsail.co.uk
🖥 www.setsail.co.uk

Company Description: Setsail Holidays are a specialist tour operator providing flotilla sailing and bareboat charter holidays to Greece, Turkey and Croatia.

Job Description: Skippers, hostesses and engineers required to coordinate and run the flotilla sailing holidays which can consist of up to 12 yachts.

Requirements: Must have sailing experience and/or qualifications and the ability to work well with people.

Accommodation: Accommodation is provided on the 'lead yacht'.

Application Procedure: Applications to John Hortop at the above address or email. Applications must include a CV and recent picture.

Voluntary Work and Archaeology

Archelon Sea Turtle Protection Society of Greece

Job(s) Available: Volunteers.

Duration: The projects run from mid-May to mid-October. The minimum period of participation is 4 weeks, and there are greater needs for volunteers at each end of the project (May, June, September, October).

> **Head Office:** Solomou 57, GR-104 32, Athens, Greece
> ☎ +30 210 5231342
> ✒ stps@archelon.gr volunteers@archelon.gr

Pay: Volunteers will have to provide a participation fee of around £110 which goes towards supporting the project and includes a 1 year membership to the Archelon, with 3 issues of 'Turtle Tracks', their newsletter. Archelon cannot provide any financial assistance but estimates that volunteers will need to allow about £10 per day to cover food costs.

Company Description: Archelon is a non-profit-making NGO company that was founded in 1983 to study and protect sea turtles and their habitats and raise public awareness. Each year over 300 volunteers participate in STPS projects.

Job Description: Volunteers are required for summer fieldwork on the islands of Zakynthos, Crete and Peloponnesus, where the Mediterranean's most important loggerhead nesting beaches are to be found. Volunteers will participate in all aspects of the projects from tagging turtles to public relations. They will receive on-site training. The work can involve long nights in the cold or long days in the heat, so a resilient, positive and friendly attitude is essential, especially as the Society's work requires constructive co-existence with local communities. Volunteers are also required to work at the Sea Turtle Rescue Centre near Athens. This is a new centre set up on the coast 20km from Athens to help treat and rehabilitate turtles caught in fishing nets or injured by speedboats. Volunteers will help in the treatment of injured turtles, assist the ongoing construction of the site and carry out public relations work with visitors.

Requirements: A basic knowledge of animal care is helpful but not essential. Volunteers for either project need to be over 18 and willing to work in teams with people from other nationalities and backgrounds. Volunteers should be able to communicate in English and have their own health insurance.

Accommodation: *Islands of Zakynthos, Crete and Peloponnesus:* free accommodation provided at basic campsites. Volunteers will need to provide their own tents and sleeping bags; warm clothing will be required for night work as the temperature can get quite cold and smart clothes are needed when working in hotels and information stations. *Sea turtle rescue center:* free accommodation is provided in converted railway carriages.

Application Procedure: Application forms can be obtained by contacting the above address including an International Reply Coupon. Successful applicants will be informed within 1 month of application.

Conservation Volunteers Greece

Job(s) Available: Volunteers.
Duration: Minimum period of 2 weeks.
Working Hours: 5–6 hours per day over a 6 day week.

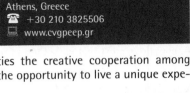

Head Office: Veranzerou 15, 106 77 Athens, Greece
☎ +30 210 3825506
🖥 www.cvgpeep.gr

Company Description: Since 1987 Conservation Volunteers Greece has promoted through its activities the creative cooperation among young people from all over the world. They are given the opportunity to live a unique experience.

Job Description: Volunteers will be working on projects that have a strong emphasis on Greek culture and the protection of Greek environment and take place in several areas of the country from remote villages to big cities.

Accommodation: CVG provides food, shared accommodation, and accident insurance.

Application Procedure: Applications can be sent to the above address from the beginning of April; prospective volunteers from the UK can also apply through UNA Exchanges and Concordia. Contact through website.

Greek Dances 'Dora Stratou' Theatre

Job(s) Available: Voluntary trainee assistants (2). Also trainees (2) to learn dance research.
Duration: Between May and October.

Head Office: 8 Scholiou Street, GR-10558 Athens Plaka, Greece
☎ +30 103 244395
📧 mail@grdance.org
🖥 www.grdance.org

Company Description: The official government-sponsored organisation for Greek folk dance, music and costume. The theatre provides daily performances, courses, workshops, field research programmes, books, CDs, CD-Roms, videos, costumes and more–all related to Greek dance and folk culture.

Job Description: Voluntary trainee assistants to learn theatre management, costume maintenance or computer production of cultural CD-Roms.

Requirements: No previous experience is necessary.

Accommodation: No accommodation available, but help may be given in finding it.

Additional Information: The cost will be around £20 per day.

Application Procedure: For further information contact Dr A Raftis, president, at the above address.

Medasset (Mediterranean Association to Save the Sea Turtles)

Job(s) Available: Conservation volunteers.
Duration: Minimum of 3 weeks.
Cost: Volunteers pay for their own transport costs etc.

Head Office: 1c Licavitou Str. 106 72 Athens, Greece
☎ +30 210 3613572
📧 mesasset@medasset.org
🖥 www.medasset.org

Job Description: Conservation volunteers needed to work in central Athens in office based roles with projects and campaigns.

Accommodation: Free accommodation is provided in central Athens.

Application Procedure: For further details contact through the above address or email.

Nine Muses Agency

Job(s) Available: Au pairs.

Duration: Summer placements from 1 to 3 months possible.

Working Hours: 30 hours per week.

Company Description: The owner Kalliope Raekou prides herself on her after-placement service, meeting regularly with au pairs at coffee afternoons.

Job Description: Au pairs to assist families with housework and look after children.

Requirements: It is requested that applicants are young European or American women.

Additional Information: Hotel positions sometimes also available. Can also place candidates after arrival in Athens.

Application Procedure: For further details contact the above address.

Head Office: Thrakis 39 and Vas. Sofias 2, 17121 Nea Smyrni, Athens, Greece
☎ +30 210 9316588
www.ninemuses.gr

ICELAND

EMBASSY OF ICELAND
2A Hans Street, London SW1X 0JE
☎ 020 7259 3999

The island of Iceland has a tiny population of about 300,000 inhabitants and has an unemployment rate that is low by European standards. Iceland is a member of the European Economic Area (EEA) and thus EEA citizens as well as European Union (EU) citizens have the right to live and work in Iceland without a work permit. Foreign nationals (not citizens of the EEA/EU) who wish to work and live in Iceland can only do so if they have arranged a contract of engagement with an Icelandic employer prior to entering Iceland; the employer will arrange for a limited Work and Residence Permit. Demand is greatest in the fish, farming, tourism and construction industries. The minimum period of work is usually 3 months.

There are 8 regional Employment Offices in Iceland and EURES advisors can be consulted at the main VMH (Jobcentre), Firdi, Fjardarjötu 13-15, 220 Hafnardjordur (+354 5547600; eures@svm.is). Efforts to recruit tend to be focused on the Scandinavian countries through the Nordjobb scheme (www.nordjobb.net), which arranges summer jobs for citizens of Scandinavia aged 18–25 able to work in Iceland for at least 4 weeks.

Red Tape

Visa Requirements: A visa is not required by citizens of most European countries if they are entering Iceland as a visitor.

Residence Permits: Those planning a stay of over 3 months must register with the Icelandic Directorate of Immigration (Utlendingastofnun), Skogarhlid 6, 105 Reykjavik, Iceland (+354 5105400; utl@utl.is; www.utl.is)

Work Permits: Work permits are not needed by nationals of the United Kingdom or any other EU country. If you are planning to take advantage of the freedom of all EU nationals to go to Iceland to look for work, take plenty of funds with you to cover the notoriously high Icelandic cost of living.

Ninukot

Job(s) Available: This agency originally found horticultural and agricultural jobs throughout Iceland but now also finds jobs babysitting, gardening and horse training as well as jobs in tourism and fisheries.

Head Office: Skeggjastadir 861, Hvolsvöllur, Iceland
☎ +354 4878576
✆ ninukot@ninukot.is
🖳 www.ninukot.is

Company Description: Private work and travel agency whose website is in English, offering the opportunity to pre-arrange a working holiday in Iceland.

Application Procedure: Applications to the website at the above address.

Worldwide Friends

Job(s) Available: Volunteers for work camps.
Duration: 2–4 weeks.
Working Hours: 6 hours per day, 5 days a week.
Job Description: Projects fall into 3 broad categories: physical work such as building, planting and restoration; social work, often with children or peo-

Head Office: Hafnarstraeti 15, 101 Reykjavik, Iceland
☎ +354 5518222
✆ wf@wf.is
🖳 www.wf.is

ple with handicaps and work/study, where work and learning opportunities are integrated.
Requirements: Minimum age 18.
Accommodation: Cost covers board and lodging, insurance, study visits and administration costs.
Aditional Information: Participation costs €50, €100 or €170 depending on the project and its duration.
Application Procedure: In order to join a work camp you need to contact the nearest partner organization in your country. Go to www.ivs-gb.org.uk for the UK, www.vsiireland.org for Ireland or surf the website.

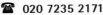

IRELAND

EMBASSY OF IRELAND
17 Grosvenor Place, London SW1X 7HR
☎ 020 7235 2171

The rapid growth of the Irish economy in recent years has produced an astonishing turnaround in the fortunes of a country which historically was one of the most poverty-stricken nations in Europe. It enjoys one of the lowest rates of unemployment in the European Union, and the rapid development of the economy has even resulted in shortages of skilled employees in some sectors such as IT, construction and nursing. Ireland offers a number of opportunities for seasonal work. The greatest demand for summer staff is in the tourist industry, which is concentrated around Dublin and in the west, south-west and around the coast. Dublin is a boomtown for the tourist industry and the rash of construction there shows no sign of abating. Unlike several other EU countries, Ireland has not imposed restrictions on the arrival of immigrants from the new (2004) member countries of Eastern Europe. Consequently, seasonal jobs are rapidly filled by workers from these countries. Ireland is, however, a notoriously expensive country to live in and has high taxes. Although it doesn't have the correspondingly high wages to compensate for such costs, wages are rising steadily.

There is a fair chance of finding paid work on farms and also scope for organising voluntary work. Two organisations can help those wishing to work voluntarily on Irish farms or who are interested in learning organic farming techniques; World Wide Opportunities On Organic Farms (WWOOF) and the Irish Organic Farmers and Growers Association. About 80 Irish hosts can be found on the WWOOF independents list; this can be found at www.wwoof.org. For information on the Irish Organic Farmers and Growers Association, contact them at Main Street, Newtownforbes, Co Longford, Ireland (+353 43 42495; www.irishorganic.ie).

FAS is Ireland's Training and Employment Agency. In addition to accessing details of Irish vacancies on their website www.fas.ie, job seekers can also register their CV and state what type of job they would like to do. Job seekers with a work permit in Ireland can call the local FAS EURES office for details of vacancies. The main one for foreigners is the Dublin office (27-33 Upper Baggot Street, Dublin 4, Ireland; +353 1 6070500; email info@fas.ie). Jobseekers from outside Ireland can also gain access to vacancies by using the European Commission's internet EURES placement system (http://europa.eu.int/jobs/eures). There are also listings of private employment agencies in the *Irish Golden Pages* (www.goldenpages.ie).

Those seeking temporary work in Ireland's hospitality and leisure industry who don't want to be based in Dublin can try the main tourist regions including most of the south-west and County Kerry. Some vacancies can be found on EURES, as prospective employees sometimes leave their details. Potential employers can then access the website's database and contact you to invite you to apply for jobs they are offering.

Foreign students are under certain employment restrictions in Ireland with the exception of students from the USA, Canada, Australia and New Zealand, which have reciprocal agreements with Ireland. Students from other nations studying in Ireland may work up to 20 hours per week in term and full-time in vacations only if they are attending a full-time course of at least a year leading to a recognised qualification. As their primary cause for being in Ireland is study, work permits are not required but working beyond the above limits will be construed as a breach of the student's study visa. This change in the availability of casual work for students does not remove the financial support requirements for student visas.

In addition to the opportunities listed in this chapter, voluntary work can be arranged by International Voluntary Service for British applicants and Service Civil International for Americans: see the *Worldwide* chapter for details.

Placing an advertisement in an Irish newspaper may lead to a job. Several newspaper websites carry information on job vacancies. You might also try the websites for job listings; these include the *Irish Examiner* (www.examiner.ie), the *Irish Independent* (www.independent.ie), the *Irish Times* (www.ireland.com), the *Sunday Business Post* (www.sbpost.ie) or the *Sunday Tribune* (www.tribune.ie).

Red Tape

Visa Requirements: If you are a citizen of an EU member state, you do not require a tourist visa to travel to Ireland. A number of other nationalities can enter Ireland without applying for a visa in advance including Australians, Canadians, New Zealanders and Americans. The full list of countries that do not require a visa in advance of entering Ireland is available on the Department of Justice, Equality and Law Reform website, www.justice.ie. Only nationals of EU countries, Iceland, Norway and Lichtenstein can become voluntary workers in Ireland without a visa.

Residence Permits: EU citizens do not require residence permits. However, nationals of the other EEA countries and Switzerland still need residence permits to stay in Ireland. On arrival in Ireland these citizens do not have to report their presence in the country immediately. However they must register within three months of their arrival and apply for a residence permit. If resident in Dublin, they should register with the Garda National Immigration Bureau. In other areas, they should register at the local Garda District Headquarters.

Work Permits: A work permit is granted by the Department of Enterprise, Trade and Employment to an employer in order to employ a non-EU national in a specific position in their company or organisation for a specific period of time. For further information contact Work Permits, Enterprise, Trade and Employment, Davitt house, 65a Adelaide Road, Dublin 2, Ireland, (+353 1 6313333; workpermits@entemp.ie; www.entemp.ie/labour/workpermits) .

'Work in Ireland Scheme' for Americans and Canadians: 'Work in Ireland' is a reciprocal programme which allows US students to work in Ireland for up to 4 months, and Canadian students for up to 12 months. For further information contact: BUNAC USA (+1 203 2640901; info@bunacusa.org; www.bunac.org/usa) or SWAP (www.swap.ca) for Canadians.

Working Holiday Permit for Australians and New Zealanders: Working Holiday Permits are available to Australians and New Zealanders for one year. For further information contact the relevant Irish Embassy.

Hotel Work and Catering

Ardagh Hotel

Job(s) Available: Chambermaids, waiting/bar staff, chefs, kitchen porters, reception/bar staff.
Duration: 3 months.
Working Hours: Flexible.
Pay: National minimum wage rates.

Head Office: Ballyconneely Road, Clifden, Connemara, Co Galway, Ireland
☎ +35 395 21384
ardaghhotel@eircom.net
www.ardaghhotel.com

Requirements: Applicants must speak English. Must have 1 year experience in the hotel trade, flexible and have an interest in catering.
Accommodation: Provided.
Application Procedure: Send CV, with telephone numbers for references, by email.

Best Western Eviston House Hotel

Job(s) Available: Bar staff, chefs, receptionists, waiter/waitress.

Duration: Minimum period of work 2 months between April and October.

Pay: €8.65 per hour.

Company Description: The Eviston House is a family-run hotel in the centre of beautiful Killarney. It comprises 75 rooms, the Colleen Bawn restaurant and the famous Danny Mann Pub.

Head Office: Best Western Eviston House Hotel, New Street, Killarney, Co Kerry, Ireland
☎ +353 643 1640
✍ christopherwalker@hotmail.com
🖳 www.evistonhouse.com

Requirements: Minimum age 18 years.

Accommodation: Not provided.

Application Procedure: Forward your CV to Mr Christopher Walker, general manager, at the above address.

Blue Haven Hotel

Job(s) Available: Bar/restaurant staff (5), kitchen junior chefs (3–4), receptionist (1), accommodation assistants (1–2).

Duration: Minimum period of work is 3 months between 1 May and 31 October.

Working Hours: 39 hours per week, 5 days a week.

Pay: *Bar/restaurant staff:* €8.65 per hour. *Kitchen junior chefs:* €8.65+ per hour (depending on experience). *Receptionist:* €9 per hour. *Accommodation assistants:* €8.65 per hour.

Head Office: 3 Pearse Street, Kinsale, Co Cork, Ireland
☎ +353 21 4772209
✍ info@bluehavenkinsale.com
🖳 www.bluehavenkinsale.com

Company Description: The Blue Haven is a small luxurious 17-bedroom hotel. They pride themselves on service, style and sophistication.

Job Description: *Bar/restaurant staff:* responsible for service and hygiene. Relevant experience and fluent English desirable. *Kitchen junior chefs:* working with preparation, presentation and service of food. Experience preferred. *Receptionist:* greeting, administration, hospitality tasks. Computer skills required. *Accommodation assistants:* cleaning of all bedrooms and public areas.

Accommodation: Not provided (about €80 per week locally).

Application Procedure: By post to the above address with CVs and a recent photograph.

Carrig House

Job(s) Available: Waitress, kitchen staff.
Duration: March to November.
Working Hours: Flexible.
Job Description: Staff to work in the restaurant and hotel of Carrig House, a family-run hotel, renowned for its hospitality.

Head Office: Carrig House, Caragh Lake, Killorglin, Co Kerry, Ireland
☎ +353 66 9769100
✍ info@carrighouse.com
🖳 www.carrighouse.com

Requiremets: Experience of 4-star dining.

Accommodation: Not available.

Application Procedure: Applications to Frank and Mary Slattery at the above email.

Castle Leslie

Job(s) Available: Waiting, bar and housekeeping staff.

Duration: Minimum period of work 3 months.

Working Hours: 7 days a week.

Pay: €8.65 per hour. €340 minimum per week.

Company Description: Irish country castle with specialist accommodation catering to local and international clientele.

Head Office: Glaslough, Co Monaghan, Ireland
☎ +353 478 8109
✏ carolineflanagan@castleleslie.com
🖳 www.castleleslie.com

Requirements: Restaurant and front of house staff should be fluent English speakers. Previous experience required but further training will be given.

Accommodation: Board and lodging is available at a negotiable cost.

Application Procedure: Go to www.castleleslie.com/careers for up to date vacancies or email CV to the above address.

Sinnott Hotels

Job(s) Available: Chefs/commis waiting staff, house assistants, bar staff, porters.

Duration: Minimum period of work 3 months between April and October.

Head Office: Furbo, Co Galway, Ireland
☎ +353 915 92108
✏ info@connemaracoast.ie
🖳 www.sinnotthotels.com

Working Hours: Shift work, 5 days a week.

Pay: By arrangement, depending on experience.

Company Description: A leading 4-star property in the west of Ireland with a strong emphasis on professional customer service.

Requirements: Applicants should be able to speak English. Previous experience is desirable but not essential.

Accommodation: Provided at a cost.

Application Procedure: Email CV to humanreosurces@sinnotthotels.com

Zetland Country House Hotel

Job(s) Available: Receptionist, commis chefs (2), waiting staff (4), housekeeper, chambermaids (4), kitchen porter (2).

Duration: 1 April to 31 October, with the minimum period of work 2 months.

Head Office: Cashel Bay, Connemara, Co Galway, Ireland
☎ +353 953 1111
✏ info@zetland.com
🖳 www.connemara.net/zetland

Working Hours: 10 hours per day, 5 days a week.

Pay: €1200 per month.

Company Description: A 4-star country house hotel on Ireland's west coast.

Job Description: *Receptionist:* for reception desk work, welcoming guests etc. *Commis chefs:* for breakfast and dinner catering. *Waiting staff:* to serve guests at breakfast and dinner. *Housekeeper:* to oversee upkeep of house and guest rooms. *Chambermaids:* to clean and tidy guest rooms. *Kitchen porter:* for general kitchen duties.

Requirements: Apart from the kitchen porter and chambermaid positions, some previous hotel/catering experience is necessary. All staff should speak English. Staff must be able to work in the EU.

Accommodation: Provided free of charge.

Application Procedure: Send CV by email.

Sports, Couriers and Camping

Errislannan Manor

Job(s) Available: Assistant gardener, junior trek leaders (2), instructors.

Duration: May to September. Minimum period of work 2 months.

Working Hours: 5 days a week. Half day Saturday.

Company Description: The manor is situated on Ireland's western seaboard, where the Gulf Stream allows palm trees and fuchsia to grow. The local habitat of sandy beaches and rock pools is home to seabirds, sea shells and wildflowers.

Head Office: Clifden, West Galway, Ireland
☎ +353 952 1134
✆ errislannanmanor@eircom.net
💻 www.connemara.net/errislannan-manor

Job Description: To work with 30 Connemara ponies at a trekking and riding centre mainly for children. The manor also breeds and schools ponies.

Accommodation: Accommodation provided. Meals not included.

Application Procedure: Applications to Mrs S Brooks at the above address during January and February.

Voluntary Work and Archaeology

Barretstown

Job(s) Available: Activity leader, summer cara, volunteer cara. (Cara is the Irish word for friend)

Duration: Length of contract is approximately the end of May to the end of August. *Volunteer cara:* 9 or 12 day volunteer positions are available throughout the summer and 3 or 4 day weekends during Spring and Autumn programmes.

Head Office: Barretstown Castle, Ballymore Eustace, Co Kildare, Ireland
☎ +353 4586 4115
✆ recruit@barretstown.org
💻 www.barretstown.org

Working Hours: Barretstown runs 7 10-day sessions each summer. There is no typical working day with contact hours varying, but staff can expect to work quite long days. Staff are given 3–4 days off between sessions with some time off every day during sessions including one 24-hour block.

Pay: Approximately €400 per week.

Cost: Travel costs are to be met by the applicant.

Company Description: Situated in the foothills of the Wicklow mountains in Ireland, children with cancer and other serious illnesses come to the castle for some serious fun. The children and their families, from Ireland and 22 European countries, take part in a unique programme which has become internationally recognised as having a profound and positive impact on the lives of children with serious illness and their families. The Barretstown staff and medical world call the programme 'therapeutic recreation', but the kids know it as 'serious fun'. The Spring and Autumn programmes focus mainly on the family, providing family camps and bereavement weekends. The 10 and 7-day summer programmes cater for children and teens aged between 7 and 17. Barretstown's programmes try to help children discover the courage they need to undertake the difficult journey of their illness and its treatment, and to encourage them to take part more actively in their own recovery process. Barretstown also recognises the impact of serious illness on the rest of the family and run sessions for the whole family as well as bereavement programmes.

Job Description: *Activity leader:* responsible for designing, planning and directing one or more activities. Will have overall responsibility for the safety and age appropriateness of the activities. *Summer cara:* to be responsible for supporting and encouraging each child to participate fully in all aspects of camp to ensure they have the best experience possible and to look after their day and night time needs. *Volunteer cara:* required throughout the day to accompany the children in their activity group to scheduled activities and to look after their night time needs.

Requirements: Applicants must possess experience in people guidance and group work. Applicants must be 18 years of age or over and must be fluent in English. Some experience with children or young people, particularly in terms of social, creative or sporting activities would be an advantage. Background checks will be performed.

Accommodation: All posts are residential. Full, shared accommodation and all food is provided.

Additional Information: *Summer cara and activity leader:* there is a training period of 1 week before sessions start. Volunteer interpreters, chaperones and onsite medical volunteers also needed.

Application Procedure: Application forms can be downloaded from the website or given by request from The Barretstown Gang Camp. Apply by the end of March.

Simon Communities of Ireland

Job(s) Available: Volunteers required for work alongside the homeless in Ireland.

Duration: A minimum commitment of 6 months is required.

Working Hours: Volunteers work shifts. Regular holidays.

Pay: £50 per week allowance.

Job Description: The main duties of the volunteer include befriending residents and general housekeeping.

Requirements: Minimum age 18.

Accommodation: Full board and lodging.

Application Procedure: For more information contact the above address.

Head Office: St Andrew's House, 28-30 Exchequer Street, Dublin 2, Ireland
☎ +353 1 6711606
✆ simon@simoncommunity.com

Voluntary Service International

Job(s) Available: Volunteers to work with VSI (the Irish branch of Service Civil International).

Duration: VSI organise 30 short-term voluntary workcamps in Ireland each summer.

Company Description: The aim of the organisation is to promote peace and understanding through voluntary service in Ireland and throughout the world. VSI welcome the participation of volunteers from other countries.

Head Office: 30 Mountjoy Square, Dublin 1, Ireland
☎ +353 855 1011
✆ info@vsi.ie
🖳 www.vsi.ie

Application Procedure: Enquiries and applications must go through your local Service Civil International Branch (see www.sciint.org) or workcamp organisation.

Other Employment in Ireland

Aillwee Cave Co. Ltd

Job(s) Available: Cave tour guides (5), catering staff (6), sales staff (2). Throughout the year a variety of positions become available.

Duration: Minimum period of work 2 months. Work commences March. Majority of staff needed by the end of April.

Head Office: Aillwee Cave,
Ballyvaughan, Co Clare, Ireland
☎ +353 6570 77036
✉ info@aillweecave.ie
🖥 www.aillweecave.ie

Working Hours: For all positions, 40 hours over 5 days a week. 2 days off each week. Working day from 9.30am to 6pm; 7pm during July and August.

Pay: *Cave tour guides:* approximately €1,100 per month gross, plus tips. *Catering staff:* from €1,100 gross per month. *Sales staff:* from €1,200 per month.

Company Description: Aillwee Cave is Ireland's premier show cave and has over 200,000 visitors each year. Its scenic location in the 'Burren' in Co Clare together with its reputation for a friendly welcome make it an attractive location for visitors and staff alike.

Job Description: *Cave tour guides:* to lead a maximum of 35 persons on a 45 minute tour through the caves. *Catering staff:* to work as counter hands for the salad bar, fast food outlet and potato bar. *Sales staff:* to work in the gift shop or to work in a farm shop in which cheese is made daily on the premises.

Requirements: Proficiency in English essential and a genuine wish to work in tourism. Leaving certificate or equivalent desirable. A desire to be friendly, helpful and flexible is essential. *Cave tour guides*: training will be given. Knowledge of geology a help but not essential. *Catering staff:* experience necessary. *Sales staff:* previous sales experience an advantage.

Accommodation: Hostel type accommodation is available. Rental charges are €50 per week.

Additional Information: Work is also now available from mid-November to the end of December for people with some drama/acting/singing experience to act as cave guides for the Santa Claus Project.

Application Procedure: By post with full CV, colour photograph and contact numbers for references. Apply to Mary Droney at the above address or by telephone.

ITALY

ITALIAN EMBASSY
14 Three Kings Yard, Davies Street, London W1K 4EH
☎ 020 7312 2200
🖥 www.amblondra.esteri.it
✉ ambasciata.londra@esteri.it

The rate of unemployment in Italy has fallen to under 8%. This can be a misleading figure, however, as there is a sharp divide between northern and southern Italy. In the industrial powerhouse of the north, unemployment is low (about 4%), while in the far south it can be as high as 20% in some regions. The best chances of obtaining paid employment in Italy are probably with the tour

WESTERN EUROPE

ITALY

operators featured in this and the *Worldwide* chapter. Other possibilities involve teaching English as a foreign language, though most who get jobs have a TEFL qualification and are prepared to stay longer than a few months of the summer. If you want to try and find this sort of job once you are in Italy look up *Scuole di Lingue* in the *Yellow Pages*. Those with special skills are most likely to find work. An experienced secretary, for example, with a good knowledge of English, Italian and German would be useful in a hotel catering for large numbers of German, British and American tourists. Otherwise it is surprisingly difficult to find work in hotels and catering as there are many Italians competing for the jobs as well as people from Eastern European countries that joined the EU in 2004 and 2007. People looking for hotel work while in Italy should try small hotels first as some large hotel chains in northern resorts take on staff from southern Italy, where unemployment is especially high.

Although Italy is the world's largest producer of wine, a similar problem exists with the grape harvest (*vendemmia*): vineyard owners traditionally employ migrant workers from North Africa and other Arab countries to help the local work force. Opportunities are best in the north west of the country; in the vineyards lying south-east of Turin in Piemonte, in the north-east in Alto Adige and to the east and west of Verona. The harvest generally takes place from September to October. For details of the locations of vineyards consult the *World Atlas of Wine* (Hugh Johnson and Jancis Robinson, Mitchell Beazley, 2007). The same publishers also produce the useful *Touring in Wine Country: Tuscany* (Maureen Ashley, Mitchell Beazley, 2000).

There are other possibilities for fruit picking earlier in the year, but again there will be stiff competition for work. Strawberries are picked in the region of Emilia Romagna in June, and apples are picked from late August in the region of Alto Adige and in the Valtellina, which lies between the north of Lake Como and Tirano. More information about finding casual farm work is given in *Work Your Way Around the World* (see *Useful Publications*) and when in Italy you should be able to get information on local harvest work from *Centri Informazione Giovani* (Youth Information Offices) which exist throughout the country for the benefit of local young people. Consult telephone directories for their addresses.

EU nationals are allowed to use the Italian state employment service when looking for a job in Italy. To find the addresses of local employment offices in Italy either look up *Centro per L'Impiego* in the telephone directory of the area where you are staying, or go to www.centroimpiego.it. Note that these offices will only deal with personal callers. For further information consult the jobs section of the EURES website (www.europa.eu.int/eures), or click on Living & Working for details.

International Voluntary Service (IVS), Youth Action for Peace, UNA Exchange and Concordia can assist British applicants in finding voluntary work in Italy, and Service Civil International can aid Americans; see the *Worldwide* chapter for details.

An advertisement in an Italian newspaper may produce an offer of employment. Smyth International, 1 Torrington Park, London N12 9GG (www.smyth-international.com) deal with *La Stampa* (Turin daily), and other provincial papers. The Milan paper *Il Giornale* is published at Via Gaetano Negri 4, I-20123 Milan (www.ilgiornale.it) and the Friday edition of *Corriere della Sera* (www.corriere.it) has a large section of employment adverts.

Red Tape

Visa Requirements: Full citizens of the United Kingdom, the United States, Australia, New Zealand and most western European countries do not require a visa for visits of up to 3 months.

Residence Permits: Visitors staying in a hotel will be registered with the police automatically. Those intending to stay for more than 3 months should apply to the local police at the *Questura* (local police headquarters) for a *permesso di sog-*

giorno which is valid for 90 days. If you arrive with the intention of working, EU nationals must first apply to the police *(questura)* for a *ricevuta di segnalazione di soggiorno* which allows them to stay for up to 3 months looking for work. Upon production of this document and a letter from an employer, you must go back to the police to obtain a residence permit – *permesso di soggiorno.* Then in some cases you will be asked to apply for a *libretto di lavoro* (work registration card) from the *ispettorato del lavoro* and/or *ufficio di collocamento* (although, in theory, this should not be necessary for EU nationals).

Special Schemes for Australians and New Zealanders: Australians and New Zealanders aged 18–30 are eligible for a working holiday visa for up to 12 months in Italy. Further details can be obtained from the Italian Embassy in Wellington (www.italian-embassy.org.ae).

Work Permits: a work permit is issued by the local authorities to the prospective employer, who will then forward it to the worker concerned. Non-EU citizens must obtain the permit before entering Italy.

Hotel Work and Catering

Darwin SRL

Company Description: Darwinstaff is a recruitment organisation dealing with hotels, resorts and tourist villages all over the world.
Application Procedure: Email CV from February.

Head Office: Piazza Del Pesce 1, 50122 – Firenze Italy
☎ +39 055 292114
✆ darwinstaff@yahoo.it
🖥 www.darwinstaff.com

Relai Ca'masieri

Job(s) Available: Waiters/waitresses, kitchen staff.
Duration: 3–6 months between the end of March and the end of October.
Working Hours: 8–12 hours per day, 5–6 days a week.

Head Office: I-36070 Trissino Italy
☎ +39 0445 490122
✆ info@camasieri.com
🖥 www.camasieri.com

Pay: Around £80 per week.
Requirements: Knowledge of German, Italian or French required.
Accommodation: Free board and accommodation provided.
Application Procedure: Applications as soon as possible to Mr Vassena Angelo.

Hotel Cannero

Job(s) Available: Receptionist assistant, waiter.
Duration: Period of work 6 months between April and September.
Working Hours: 10 hours per day, 6 days a week.
Job Description: *Waiter:* to help in the bar and the garden.

Head Office: I-28821 Cannero Riviera, Lake Maggiore Italy
☎ +39 0323 788046
✆ info@hotelcannero.com
🖥 www.hotelcannero.com

Requirements: *Receptionist assistant:* knowledge of English and basic German and Italian required.
Accommodation: Free board and accommodation.
Application Procedure: Applications to the above address.

Hotel Cavallino D'oro

Job(s) Available: Assistant manager, waiters (2), kitchen help (2), dish washers (2), chambermaids (2).
Duration: Minimum period of work 10 weeks.
Working Hours: 7 hours per day, 6 days a week.
Pay: Depends upon experience and qualifications.
Company Description: This carefully renovated hotel in the old village square of Kastelruth dates from 1326 and has a history of hospitality spanning 680 years.
Requirements: Knowledge of German and/or Italian would be an advantage, and is essential for the managerial position.
Accommodation: Free board and lodging provided.
Application Procedure: Applications to the above address from January.

Head Office: I-39040 Castelrotto, Sudtirol, Dolomiti, Italy
☎ +39 0471 706337
✆ cavallino@cavallino.it
💻 www.cavallino.it

Country Hotel Fattoria Di Vibio

Job(s) Available: Barman/waiter, chambermaid.
Duration: Minimum 2 month stay required between 15 June and 15 September.
Working Hours: 8 hours per day, 6 days a week.
Pay: Approximately £265 per month.
Company Description: A family-run country house.
Job Description: *Barman/waiter:* required to serve at tables in the restaurant/bar.
Chambermaid: required to clean rooms and carry out other general cleaning jobs.
Requirements: Applicants should have relevant experience, be 20 to 35 years of age and have a basic knowledge of spoken Italian and English.
Accommodation: Board and accommodation provided.
Application Procedure: By post to the above address from February.

Head Office: Doglio, I-06057 Montecastello di Vibio (PG), Italy
☎ +39 0758 749607
✆ info@fattoriadivibio.com
💻 www.fattoriadivibio.com

Hotel Des Geneys Splendid

Job(s) Available: Porters (2), one for day and one for night needed.
Duration: Minimum period of work July and August.
Working Hours: 6 day week of 48 hours.
Pay: €900 per month.
Company Description: A hotel with a youthful and family atmosphere. An ideal place to learn Italian, study and rest.
Accommodation: Free board and accommodation.
Application Procedure: Email CV to the above address.

Head Office: Via Luigi Einaudi 21, 10052 Bardonecchia, Casella Postale 45, Italy
☎ +39 0122 99001
✆ geneys@libero.it
💻 www.hoteldesgeneys.it

Hotel Morandi Alle Crocetta

Job(s) Available: Reception/breakfast clerk.
Duration: Minimum of 2 months.
Working Hours: 7.5 hours per day, 3 or 4 days a week.
Pay: €6 per hour.

Head Office: Via Laura 50, 50121 Firenze, Italy
☎ +39 0552 344747
✆ welcome@hotelmorandi.it
💻 www.hotelmorandi.it

Company Description: Small, 3 star hotel in the centre of Florence.

Job Description: *Reception/breakfast clerk:* to take care of the reception in the hotel cafeteria.

Requirements: Must be well-groomed, have fluent Italian and English and knowledge of French and/or German.

Accommodation: Not provided.

Application Procedure: Apply to Paolo Antuono at the above address.

IL Paretaio

Job(s) Available: Grooms (2), chambermaid, waiter/kitchen help.

Working Hours: 8 hours per day, 6 days a week (Monday to Saturday).

Pay: Salary negotiable.

Head Office: Strada delle Ginestra 12, Barberino Velsa-Firenze, Italy
☎ +39 0558 059218
info@il paretaio.it
www.ilparetaio.it

Company Description: Country house accommodation and horse riding school half an hour from Florence and Siena.

Job Description: *Grooms:* to look after horses. *Chambermaid:* to clean 10 rooms. *Waiter/kitchen help:* to be in charge of breakfast and serving dinner for 20 people. No cooking, just serving and cleaning.

Requirements: *Grooms:* must be experienced with horses.

Accommodation: *Grooms:* salary negotiable plus lodging, food and horse riding. *Waiter/kitchen help:* salary negotiable plus board and lodging.

Application Procedure: Applications at any time to Giovanni de Marchi at the above address or email.

Romantik Hotel Tenuta Di Ricavo

Job(s) Available: Waiter, reception assistant, night assistant.

Duration: From April to September/October. For waiters; from July to September/October with minimum period 2 months.

Working Hours: 40 hours per week, 6 days a week.

Head Office: Ricavo, 53011 Castellina in Chianti, Italy
☎ +39 0577 740221
ricavo@ricavo.com
www.ricavo.com

Restaurant and reception assistant: for morning, afternoon and evening shifts. *Night assistant:* on duty for night shifts from midnight to 7am.

Pay: *Waiter:* Approximately €1,000. *Restaurant and reception assistant:* €1,000.

Company Description: A 4 star hotel amidst typical Chianti landscape half an hour from both Siena and Florence.

Job Description: *Waiter:* to work at breakfast, lunch and dinner panding room and pool service, filling up stock, stocking minibar, cleaning restaurant. *Night assistant:* answer telephone/check-in late arrivals. Prepare buffet breakfast and prepare and serve early departures coffee.

Requirements: *Restaurant and reception assistant:* Besides English 2 languages requested, preferably French, German or Italian.

Accommodation: Room in staff house at hotel. Lunch and evening dinner at staff mensa.

Application Procedure: Apply January/February, May/June to the above address or email. Apply from October onwards for reception.

Hotel Zirmerhof

Job(s) Available: Waiting staff (2) and room maid.
Duration: Period of work is mid-May to 5 November.
Working Hours: 8am to 5pm, 6 days a week.
Requirements: Knowledge of German and Italian are required.
Accommodation: Board and accommodation are free.
Application Procedure: Apply in January to Sepp Perwanger at the above address.

Head Office: Oberradein 59, 39040 Radein, South Tyrol, Italy
☎ +39 0471 887215
✆ info@zirmerhof.com
🖥 www.zirmerhof.com

Sports, Couriers and Camping

Canvas Holidays

Job(s) Available: Campsite courier, children's courier.
Duration: Full season positions start in March, April or May and end in September/October. High season staff needed to work at least 2 months during the peak season.
Pay: Package includes competitive salary, tent accommodation, medical insurance, uniform and return travel from a UK port of entry.

Head Office: GVN Camping Recruitment, East Port House, Dunfermline KY12 7JG, Scotland
☎ 01383 629012
✆ campingrecruitment@ gvnrecruitment.com
🖥 www.gvnrecruitment.com

Company Description: Canvas Holidays provide luxury mobile home and tent holidays at over 100 campsites throughout Europe.
Job Description: *Campsite courier:* involves cleaning accommodation, welcoming families to the site and showing them to their accommodation. Visiting customers, providing local information and basic maintenance are very important parts of the job. Campsite courier opportunities are also available for couples to work on site together. *Children's courier:* needed to work at Hoopi's Club. Children's couriers should be energetic, enthusiastic and have good communication skills. A tent is provided as a Club venue and for equipment storage; this has to be kept safe, clean and tidy. Visiting new arrivals on site is an important and fun part of the job. Children's couriers also help with other campsite duties as needed.
Requirements: Applicants must have formal experience of working with children.
Accommodation: Provided as part of package.
Additional Information: For details of management positions, see website. Visit recruitment website for information about working with teenagers (Buzz courier) and wildlife and the environment (Wild and active courier).
Application Procedure: Please call the recruitment department for more information and an application form, or apply online at www.gvnrecruitment.com.

Collett's Mountain Holidays

Job(s) Available: Walk and Via Ferrata 'organisers' (20), resort managers (4), resort representatives (2), chalethosts/cooks (10), artists (2).
Duration: Dates of work are from mid-May to late September. Applicants are preferred who are willing to work a full season.

Head Office: Harvest Mead, Great Hormead, Buntingford, Herts SG9 0PB, England
☎ 01763 289660
✆ admin@colletts.co.uk
🖥 www.collets.co.uk/work

Working Hours: Between 7 and 10 hours per day, 6 days a week. *Chalet hosts/cooks:* required to provide breakfast and an excellent 3-course evening meal 3 days a week. *Artists:* to give casual 'on-location' watercolour tuition 4 days a week.

Pay: *Walk and Via Ferrata 'organisers':* €480 per month. *Resort managers:* €600 per month. *Resort representatives:* €120 per week. *Chalet hosts/cooks:* €150 per week.

Company Description: Collett's Mountain Holidays offers specialist holiday to the Italian Dolomites and South Tyrol for walkers, climbers, wildflower enthusiasts and painters. Each year they recruit people for the summer to join their small resort teams to do a variety of jobs based in 3 Alpine villages in the Central Dolomites. A rich and unforgettable 5 month experience spent in Europe's most spectacular mountains.

Job Description: *Walk and Via Ferrata 'organisers':* required to organise and accompany guests on high and low level walks or Via Ferratas in the area. Will advise guests on suitable walking and/or Via Ferrata routes and have a domestic commitment involving chalet cleaning and kitchen work. Also involved with airport transfer driving. *Resort managers:* couples welcome as well as individuals. Required to perform various management tasks in one of the 3 Alpine Resorts including hospitality tasks, staff support and general management. Overseeing the day-to-day running of the resort with food and laundry ordering, accounts, cleaning rotas and airport transfers. Would participate in the organised walk programme with guests. *Resort representatives:* required for office management, accounts, food and laundry ordering and management and supplier liaison. Role includes participation in organised walks and/or Via Ferrata, caring for well-being of guests, assistance, advice and suggestions. Also booking restaurants and activities and undertaking domestic tasks, cleaning and kitchen assistance. *Chalet hosts/cooks:* couples and individuals welcome to apply. Will work in an Alpine chalet hosting between 10 and 20 guests. Must have a warm, engaging, sociable and efficient manner. Responsible for domestic management of the chalet such as room cleaning, food ordering, chalet accounts, kitchen hygiene procedures etc. *Artists:* Keen walker with interest in the mountains and the outdoors. Optional participation in organised walks programme. Involvement with domestic tasks, cleaning, helping at dinner, kitchen assistance necessary. Responsibility for general care and well-being of guests.

Requirements: *Walk organisers:* must have excellent map reading and navigational skills. Outdoor and first aid qualifications are a bonus but not essential. *Via Ferrata organisers:* must have good ropework skills and climbing experience. *Resort managers:* must have a good level of spoken Italian or German. Must have experience of managing people, excellent interpersonal skills and the ability to think on their feet, as well as the experience and interest needed for the walk organiser role. *Resort representatives:* applicants must have an excellent level of spoken Italian and a good manner with people. Must have a patient and helpful personality. Experience of accounting and/or Microsoft Excel a bonus. *Chalet hosts/cooks:* applicants must have a good amount of cooking experience, but not necessarily professional. A passion for food and sharing it with other people is very important. Food hygiene certificate is a bonus. *Artists:* preferably qualifications up to degree level or experience of teaching art in some capacity. Untrained but talented individuals welcome to apply.

Accommodation: Board and lodging is provided free of charge.

Application Procedure: Applications invited at any time. Contact Phil Melia at phil@colletts.co.uk or telephone. The company are continually interviewing for summer and winter positions.

Esprit Family Adventures

Job(s) Available: Hotel/resort manager, nannies, alpies rangers.

Duration: All staff must be available from mid-June to mid-September.

Pay: Weekly wage.

Head Office: 185 Fleet Road, Fleet, Hants GU51 3BL, England
☎ 01252 618318
recruitment@esprit-holidays.co.uk
www.esprit-holidays.co.uk

Company Description: Esprit Family Adventures run Alpine holidays (France, Italy and Austria) for families in catered chalets and hotels and provide childcare in nurseries and Alpine adventure clubs for children aged 4 months to 15 years.

Job Description: All staff assist with chalet cleaning, babysitting and hosting guests. Staff to run Chalet Hotels and chalets. *Nannies:* needed to run Esprit Nurseries and Alpies Club. Required to take care of babies and toddlers in Esprit's nurseries. *Alpies rangers:* required to run adventure activity clubs.

Requirements: All staff must be EU passport holders. Ideal for anyone who has an interest in alpine activities, ie mountain walking and biking, white water rafting etc. Staff need friendly and out-going personalities and previous experience. *Hotel/ resort manager:* Minimum age 25. Good command of spoken French or German, hospitality and customer service experience and management and supervisory skills needed. Full clean driving licence. *Nannies:* must be dedicated, fun-loving and enthusiastic. Minimum age 18. DCE NNEB, NVQ3, BTEC or NVQ level 3. *Alpies rangers:* Minimum age 21. Experience as play scheme leaders, children's sports coaches or as a trained teacher required. Should have a mature, fun loving personality.

Accommodation: Food and accommodation, uniform, swimming pool pass and transport provided.

Application Procedure: Further information can be obtained regarding vacancies on the website.

Equipe Smile SRL

Job(s) Available: Animators/ entertainers (80).

Duration: Dates of work are from Easter (April/May) to 30 September. Minimum period of work is usually 2 months. Shorter 1 month jobs are available but board and lodging will be charged at a small fee.

Pay: The minimum for an animator is €400/€500 up to €1200 per month though there are no upper limits to earnings.

Head Office: Smile Animazione, Via Sbarre Sup. Dir. Lombardo 11, 89138, Calabria, Italy
☎ +39 03475 542564
✉ smileanimazione@gmail.com

Company Description: Smile Animazione is one of the leading tourist agencies in Italy. Established 20 years ago, they function all around the world but predominantly in Italy. Smile Animazione specializes in the training of animators, with most jobs taken by Europeans. A job with Equipe Smile requires reliability, seriousness and responsibility!

Job Description: Animators/entertainers required for entertaining in high quality Italian resorts such as Lake Garda and the Adriatic Coast in the North, Sardinia and Latium in central Italy, and Apulia in the South. Animators have the opportunity to work as sport-animators (tennis, swimming, organising archery tournaments), dance-animators, choreographers, fitness-animators (aerobic, step, trainer, water-gym, yoga), childcare-animators and scenographers. There are also opportunities in customer care/public relations as well as opportunities for musicians, DJs and clowns!

Requirements: Candidates must have artistic and/or sporting skills and a natural affinity for public relations. Must be open-minded and have a sunny disposition and enjoy interaction with guests. Knowledge of German, Dutch, French and/or English is essential.

Accommodation: Free board and accommodation are provided.

Application Procedure: Applications are invited from January. Candidates should fill in the application form on the website and send their CV with photos by post or email.

Eurocamp

Job(s) Available: Campsite courier, children's courier, courier team leaders, children's courier team leaders, montage/demontage.

Head Office: Overseas Recruitment Department (Ref SJ/08) Hartford Manor, Greenbank Lane, Northwich CW8 1HW, England
☎ 01606 787525
🖳 www.holidaybreakjobs.com/camping

Duration: *Campsite courier:* Applicants should be available to work from April/May to mid-September or June/July to mid-September. *Children's courier:* Applicants should be available from early May to September or June to September. *Courier team leaders:* Applicants should be available from April to mid-September. *Children's courier team leaders:* Applicants should be available from early May until September. *Montage/demontage:* Applicants should be available from Feb to May or August to October.

Pay: You will receive a competitive salary, comprehensive training, return travel to and from an agreed meeting point, accommodation, medical and luggage insurance and uniform.

Company Description: Eurocamp is a leading tour operator in self-drive camping and mobile home holidays in Europe. We offer our customers a wide range of holiday accommodation on over 200 premier campsites. Each year the company seeks to recruit up to 1,500 enthusiastic people to work the summer season in a variety of roles.

Job Description: *Campsite Courier:* A Courier's responsibility begins by ensuring that the customer's accommodation is both inviting and cleaned to the highest of standards. You will welcome new arrivals, be the customers main point of contact and will be expected to provide local and general information, give assistance and even act as interpreter if required. Part of the role will involve helping out with minor repairs to accommodation and equipment and will also involve basic administration and accounts. *Children's Courier:* You will be responsible for planning and delivering a fun, safe, daily activity programme to our customers' children. The age of the children attending the club will range from 5 to 12 years old although we also run a toddler service in low season for 12 months to 4 years. *Courier Team Leaders:* You must be able to deliver first class customer service and organize the daily workload of the courier team. Your role also includes all the duties of a Campsite Courier and you will be expected to lead by example. There are a variety of team leader roles available, dependant on team size; Courier in Charge, Senior Courier and Site Manager. *Children's Courier Team Leaders:* Your role will involve the management, motivation and development of the Children's Couriers to ensure they provide a varied range of quality activities. Your role includes all the duties of a Children's Courier. *Montage/Demontage:* Montage and Demontage assistants are employed to either help set up for the season or close down at the end of the season. This involves putting up or taking down tents, moving/distributing equipment and cleaning/preparing accommodation.

Requirements: Applicants must hold a UK/EU passport and the current minimum age is 18 years old on the day you start work in order to obtain the relevant insurance cover. *Campsite Couriers:* You should have lots of energy, basic common sense and a genuine desire to help people. *Children's Courier:* Previous childcare experience is essential. Successful candidates will be asked to apply for an Enhanced Disclosure. *Courier Team Leaders:* You must have previous experience of leading a team successful applicants may be asked to apply for a Standard Disclosure. *Children's Courier Team Leaders:* Previous experience with Children and leading a team successful candidates will be asked to apply for an Enhanced Disclosure. *Montage/Demontage:* Previous experience of physical and repetitive work successful applicants will be asked to apply for a Standard Disclosure.

Accommodation: Provided.

Application Procedure: Applicants should apply on-line at www.holidaybreakjobs.com/camping or telephone 01606 787 525 for an Application Pack.

WESTERN EUROPE

ITALY

271

Headwater Holidays

Job(s) Available: Overseas representatives, canoeing instructors.

Duration: Staff required for full season from April to October.

Working Hours: Hours as required.

Pay: From £140 per week.

Company Description: Headwater looks to offer

Head Office: The Old School House, Chester Road, Castle, Northwich, Cheshire CW8 1LE, England
☎ 01606 720033
✉ info@headwater.com
🖥 www.headwater.com

relaxed discovery and adventure holidays with personal service, warm friendly hotels and good regional cuisine. Headwater guides and information packs aim to help clients make their own discoveries off the beaten track.

Job Description: *Overseas representatives:* to work in France, Italy, Spain and Austria. Duties include meeting clients at airports and stations, supervising local transportation for them and their luggage, hotel and client liaison, bike maintenance and on the spot problem solving. *Canoeing instructors:* duties as for overseas representatives but also include giving canoe instruction.

Requirements: *Overseas representatives:* good, working knowledge of the language and full, clean driving licence required. Organisational skills, resourcefulness and cheerfulness essential.

Accommodation: Provided.

Application Procedure: Further information and an on-line application form can be found on the website, or an application form can be requested from the above address.

Keycamp Holidays

Job(s) Available: Campsite courier, children's courier, courier team leaders, children's courier team leaders, montage/demontage.

Duration: *Campsite courier:* Applicants should be available to work from April/May to mid-September or June/July to mid-September. *Children's courier:*

Head Office: Overseas Recruitment Department (Ref SJ/08) Hartford Manor, Greenbank Lane, Northwich CW8 1HW, UK
☎ 01606 787525
🖥 www.holidaybreakjobs.com/camping

Applicants should be available from early May to September or June to September. *Courier team leaders:* Applicants should be available from April to mid-September. *Children's courier team leaders:* Applicants should be available from early May until September. *Montage/demontage:* Applicants should be available from Feb to May or August to October.

Pay: You will receive a competitive salary, comprehensive training, return travel to and from an agreed meeting point, accommodation, medical and luggage insurance and uniform.

Company Description: Keycamp is a leading tour operator in self-drive camping and mobile home holidays in Europe. We offer our customers a wide range of holiday accommodation on over 200 premier campsites. Each year the company seeks to recruit up to 1,500 enthusiastic people to work the summer season in a variety of roles.

Job Description: *Campsite Courier:* A Courier's responsibility begins by ensuring that the customer's accommodation is both inviting and cleaned to the highest of standards. You will welcome new arrivals, be the customers main point of contact and will be expected to provide local and general information, give assistance and even act as interpreter if required. Part of the role will involve helping out with minor repairs to accommodation and equipment and will also involve basic administration and accounts. *Children's Courier:* You will be responsible for planning and delivering a fun, safe, daily activity programme to our customers' children. The age of the children attending the club will range from 5 to 12 years old although we also run a toddler service in low season for 12 months to 4 years. *Courier Team Leaders:* You must be able to deliver first class customer service and organize the daily workload of the courier team. Your role also includes all the duties of a Campsite Courier and you will be expected to lead by example. There are a variety of team leader roles available, dependant on team size; Courier in Charge, Senior Courier and Site Manager. *Children's Courier Team Leaders:* Your role will involve the management, motivation and development of the Children's Couriers to ensure they provide a varied range of quality activities. Your role includes all the duties of a Children's Courier. *Montage/Demontage:* Montage and Demontage assistants are employed to either help set up for the season or close down at the end of the season. This involves putting up or taking down tents, moving/distributing equipment and cleaning/preparing accommodation.

Requirements: Applicants must hold a UK/EU passport and the current minimum age is 18 years old on the day you start work in order to obtain the relevant insurance cover. *Campsite Couriers:* You should have lots of energy, basic common sense and a genuine desire to help people. *Children's Courier:* Previous childcare experience is essential. Successful candidates will be asked to apply for an Enhanced Disclosure. *Courier Team Leaders:* You must have previous experience of leading a team successful applicants may be asked to apply for a Standard Disclosure. *Children's Courier Team Leaders:* Previous experience with Children and leading a team successful candidates will be asked to apply for an Enhanced Disclosure. *Montage/Demontage:* Previous experience of physical and repetitive work successful applicants will be asked to apply for a Standard Disclosure.

Accommodation: Provided.

Application Procedure: Applicants should apply on-line at www.holidaybreakjobs.com/camping or telephone 01606 787 525 for an Application Pack.

Siblu Holidays

Job(s) Available: Park representatives, children's club representatives, assistant park representatives.

Duration: The season runs between March and October, with varying contract dates. Limited high season positions are available.

Pay: Team members will receive a competitive salary.

Head Office: Recruitment Team, Bryanston Court, Selden Hill, Hemel Hemptead HP2 4TN, England
☎ 01442 293231
recruitment@siblu.com
www.siblu.com

Company Description: Siblu Holidays exclusively own holiday parks in France, and also operate on 12 fantastic parks in France, Spain and Italy.

Job Description: The following roles are offered in Italy for seasonal work: *Park representatives:* duties include cleaning and maintaining accommodation, welcoming new arrivals, reception duties, paperwork and administration. *Children's club representatives:* duties include creating and running a daytime entertainment programme for children between the ages of 5 and 12 years old, associated paperwork and assisting park representatives. *Assistant park representatives:* duties include cleaning and preparation of accommodation, welcoming new arrivals and reception duties.

Requirements: *Children's club representatives:* experience of working with children is desirable.

Accommodation: Accommodation, uniform, medical cover and travel costs to park included in pay.

Application Procedure: Please telephone the above number for a recruitment pack or visit the website to apply online.

Teaching and Language Schools

ACLE

Job(s) Available: Summer camp English tutors
Duration: Vacancies are from the beginning of June to 6 September.
Working Hours: 40+ hours per week, 5-7 days a week depending on type of camp.
Pay: €200–€220 per week. Successful tutors also receive a bonus related to their performance.

Head Office: Via Roma 54, 18083 San remo (IM), Italy
☎ +39 0184 506070
✆ info@acle.org
🖥 www.acle.org

Company Description: The ACLE camp programme, now in its 25th year, is the only one of its kind recognised by the Italian Ministry of Education to use drama in education. ACLE are looking for enthusiastic and dependable people to work at English Camps throughout Italy for Summer 2008. Camps are held all over Italy including in the Alps and in small and big cities including Bologna, Milan, Naples, Rome, Siena, Venice, Verona Sardinia and Sicily.

Job Description: Italian language skills are not necessary and no teaching qualifications are needed as ACLE provides a specific introductory TEFL course. After this intensive and practical 4-5 day course tutors are sent to English camps to teach English in a fun and creative way. Each tutor is responsible for about 10 children. Games, songs, sports and drama are an essential part of the teaching-learning process. Tutors receive the Introductory TEFL certificate.

Requirements: Applicants must be native English speakers, between 20 and 30 years of age and love working with children. Experience in teaching and travelling abroad are an advantage.

Accommodation: On top of the wage ACLE provides transport within Italy to the camps, meals, accommodation and insurance while working at the camps.

Application Procedure: Applications should be made before 1 April 2008. Apply online at www.acle.org.

Keep Talking

Job(s) Available: English teachers for 2 language schools in Italy.
Duration: 9-month contracts.
Working Hours: 25 hours per week, with an occasional maximum of 30.
Pay: Dependant on qualifications, experience and special skills.

Head Office: Via Roma 60, 33100 Udine, Italy or Via Della Toree, 1,33028 Tolmezzo, Italy
☎ +39 0432 501525 (Uldine)
+39 0433 41601 (Tolmezzo)
✆ info@keeptalking.it
🖥 www.keeptalking.it

Company Description: Keep Talking was founded in 1989 and very quickly became the most highly-respected English language training organization in the area. Keep Talking have 2 schools in Friuli Venezia-Giulia; one in Uldine and the other in Tolmezzo in the mountains of Carnia (about 50km north of Uldine). Most of the students are adults (average age 20–40) learning English either for current or future jobs or personal interest/travel. Keep Talking also organize courses for children from 4–16. They have a large number of company clients. Keep Talking teach either at the school or at the client's office.

Requirements: All applicants must have a university degree and CELTA or equivalent plus minimum 1 year of experience. Native English speakers a passport from an EU member state or a current working visa only.

Accommodation: Can be provided.

Application Procedure: Please email your CV and a covering letter to the above address.

Lingue Senza Frontiere

Job(s) Available: Camp tutors (60).

Duration: Tutors work from early June for 2, 4 or 6 weeks.

Company Description: Italian non-profit association, officially recognized by the Ministry of Education.

Head Office: Corso Inglesi 172, 18038 Sanremo
☎ +39 0184 508650
christina@linguesenzafrontiere.org
www.linguasenzafrontiere.org

Job Description: Camp tutors needed for full-immersion summer camps. Camps are day-camps and are various locations north of Rome. In the morning children do worksheets and classroom games; in the afternoons arts, crafts and sports (all in English). At the end of the 2-week courses the children put on a show in English.

Requirements: All applicants must be fluent English speakers, over 21 and have experience teaching or working with children. Applicants should be able to lead sports, crafts or drama activities.

Accommodation: The association provides full board and accommodation, insurance, all materials, 3-day orientation and travel to and from the camps. Travel to Italy not included.

Application Procedure: Applications to Christina Nikenejad at the above address/email.

Theatrino

Job(s) Available: Native English Speaking TIE actors required. Also fluent French-speaking TIE actors.

Duration: January to June.

Working Hours: Flexible.

Pay: €250 per week.

Head Office: Via Roma 54, 18038 San Remo
☎ +39 0184 506070
camps@acle.it
www.acle.org

Company Description: Theatrino is part of ACLE, a non-profit organisation, which was the first to teach English to children and teenagers through Theatre in Education (TIE), and to organise drama courses recognised by the Italian Ministry of Education for Teachers. This small touring English language theatre company and the small routing French language theatre company both recruit from the UK. Should be young, enthusiastic actors with plenty of energy to work in Italy on a Theatre in Education tour.

Job Description: Actors tour Italian schools in groups of 3 and present graded interactive English language shows. These are followed by workshops consisting of sketches adapted for a particular age group focusing on a particular theme and grammatical point. The overall emphasis is on promoting spoken English in a fun way.

Requirements: Applicants must be flexible and able to work in a team. Must also be able to handle being 'on the road' and love working with children. Aged 20–30.

Accommodation: ACLE provides accommodation. Food not included.

Application Procedure: Applicants must visit the website for details and an application form. Auditions are held in London throughout the year.

Windsor School of English

Job(s) Available: English teachers (15-20).
Duration: To teach for 9–10 months in Italy.
Pay: According to experience.
Requirements: Teachers with minimum TEFL certificate. British or EU applicants only.
Accommodation: Provided.

Head Office: Via Molino delle Lime 4/F, 10064 Pinerolo (TO)
☎ +39 0121 795555
   +39 348 3914155 (mobile)
✆ info@windsorpinerolo.com

Application Procedure: Applications to Sandro Vazon Colla, director. Interviews can be carried out in UK.

Voluntary Work

Agape

Job(s) Available: Volunteers for manual work alongside the permanent staff.
Duration: 20 days to 5 weeks between the middle of June, and September.
Working Hours: 6 hours per day, 6 days a week.

Head Office: Centro Ecumenico, I-10060 Prali (Torino)
☎ +39 0121 807514
✆ ufficio@agapecentroecumenico.org
🖳 www.agapecentroecumenico.org

Company Description: AGAPE is an 'ecumenical centre', where believers of different faiths and denominational backgrounds can meet with non-believers in an open and relaxed atmosphere. AGAPE is situated in the village of Prali in the Germanasca valley, about 80 miles from Turin. The centre organises national and international 1-week seminars on theological, political, gender and homosexuality issues. Its isolated position provides the opportunity to experience life away from modern stresses, although this means that the volunteers should be good at entertaining themselves.
Job Description: Job includes helping with cooking, cleaning, laundering etc.
Requirements: Minimum age 18. Knowledge of Italian or English an advantage.
Accommodation: Board and lodging provided.
Application Procedure: Applications should be sent to the above address.

Concordia Italy

Job(s) Available: International volunteer projects.
Duration: Short-term.
Company Description: Concordia offers volunteers the opportunity to take part in international short-term volunteer projects in over 60 countries worldwide.

Head Office: 19 North Street, Portslade, Brighton BN41 1DH, UK
☎ 01273 422218
✆ info@concordia-iye.org.uk
🖳 www.concordia-iye.org.uk

Job Description: The work is community based and ranges from nature conservation and renovation to construction and social work including children's play schemes and teaching.
Requirements: Minimum age 16.
Accommodation: Board and accommodation are free of charge.
Additional Information: Volunteers pay a registration fee of £150 and fund their own travel and insurance.
Application Procedure: For further information on volunteering or coordinating please check the website or contact the International Volunteer Coordinator at the above address.

La Sabranenque

Job(s) Available: Volunteers (10).

Duration: Period of work 2–3 weeks between early July and August.

Working Hours: Work in the mornings, afternoons free.

Head Office: Centre International, rue de la Tour de l'Oume, F-30290 Saint Victor la Coste, France
☎ +33 4 66500505
🖂 info@sabranenque.com

Company Description: La Sabranenque is a non-profit organisation working with volunteers toward the preservation of traditional Mediterranean architecture. Participants learn skills and share experiences within a diverse group and live in these beautiful villages.

Job Description: Volunteers to help with the restoration of villages, sites and simple monuments using traditional building methods, in Altamura, Southern Italy and the hamlet of Gnallo, Northern Italy. Work includes restoration of walls, paths or the reconstruction of small houses. At least 1 day during each 2–3 week session is spent visiting the region.

Requirements: Applicants must be in good health. Minimum age 18.

Accommodation: Board and accommodation is included in the project cost, which is equivalent to £180 per 3 week project.

Additional Information: $710 for 2 weeks.

Application Procedure: Applications to the above address at any time.

Au Pairs, Nannies, Family Helps and Exchanges

Arce

Job(s) Available: Au pairs/mothers' helps for placements in Italy.

Duration: 6–12 months from September to June. 2–3 months in the summer.

Working Hours: 5–6 hours per day. 3 evenings babysitting.

Head Office: Attività Relazioni Culturali con l'Estero, Via XX Settembre, 20/124, 16121 Genova, Italy
☎ +39 0105 83020
🖂 info@arceaupair.it
🖳 www.arceaupair.it

Pay: €70 per week.

Job Description: To babysit and perform a little light housework.

Requirements: Aged 18–30. Single. Childcare experience essential. Knowledge of English and possibly Italian required.

Accommodation: Board and accommodation provided.

Application Procedure: Applications (male or female) from April to the above address.

LUXEMBOURG

EMBASSY OF LUXEMBOURG
27 Wilton Crescent, London SW1X 8SD
☎ 020 7235 6961
🖂 londres.amb@mae.etat.lu

The official language in Luxembourg is Luxembourgish but German and French are spoken and understood by almost everyone, and casual workers will normally need a reasonable knowledge of at least one of these. EU citizens can use the State Employment Service when they are looking for work and can get general information on the current work situation from them:

Administration de l'Emploi (ADEM; +352 4785300; www.adem.public.lu). ADEM also operates an employment service for students and young people (*Services Vacances;* freephone in Luxembourg 80024646; info.jeu@adem.public.lu) offering jobs in warehouses, catering etc. There is also useful information available from the jobs section of the EURES website (www.europa.eu.int/eures), or click on Living & Working for details.

Employment agencies specialising in temporary work include *Manpower-Aide Temporaire;* 42 rue Glesener, 1630 Luxembourg (+352 482323; manpower.lux@manpower.lu; www.manpower.lu). Employment agencies are listed in the *Yellow Pages* under *Agences de Travail.* In March or April of each year, a special forum for summer jobs is organised by the Youth Information Centre in Luxembourg City, where students can meet employees and firms offering summer jobs and be informed about their rights. The centre also runs a special service for summer jobs from April to August. The Youth Information Centre can be found at *Centre Information Jeunes;* 26 place de la Gare, L-1616 Luxembourg (+352 26293200; cij@info.jeunes.lu; www.cij.lu).

The internet can be used for obtaining contact details of hotels in Luxembourg; for instance check out the directory www.hotels.lu or the website of the Luxembourg Tourist Office www.luxembourg.co.uk.

People are sometimes needed to help with the grape harvest, which normally begins around 20 September and continues for 4 or 5 weeks.

To advertise in newspapers contact *Tageblatt* at 44 rue du Canal, L-4050 Esch-Alzette (+352 547131; www.tageblatt.lu) who also publish a French weekly called *Le Jeudi* aimed at foreigners living in Luxembourg.

Red Tape

Visa Requirements: no visa is necessary for entry into Luxembourg by members of an EU country or citizens of the USA, Canada, Australia or New Zealand.

Residence Permits: if you wish to stay in Luxembourg for longer than 3 months, you must obtain permission in advance from the Administration Communale of the Municipality of Residence unless you are an EU national. Non-EU nationals must produce a medical certificate and radiographic certificate issued by a doctor established in Luxembourg as well as the other documents required by all applicants: proof of identity and proof of sufficient means of support or a *Déclaration Patronale*.

Work Permits: are necessary for any non-EU national wanting to work in Luxembourg. Permits (*Déclaration Patronale*) are issued by the *Administration de l'Emploi* to the prospective employer. Non-EU nationals must obtain a job and a work permit before entering Luxembourg. Foreigners are free to carry out voluntary work for recognized international bodies.

Hotel Work and Catering

Hotel Le Royal

Job(s) Available: Stagiares (2).
Duration: 6 month placements.
Working Hours: 40 hours per week.
Pay: As a trainee, staff will earn: 1–2 months, €150; 2–4 months, €200; 4–6 months, €300; 6–12 months, €450.

Head Office: 12 Boulevard Le Royal, L-2449 Luxembourg
☎ +352 2416161
humanresources@hotelroyal.lu
www.hotelroyal.lu

Company Description: Located in the heart of Luxembourg City, this 5 star hotel has 210 rooms and suites, and prides itself on the attentive but discreet service of its staff.

Job Description: Stagiares required to take up placements in this leading hotel. Successful candidates may be employed as restaurant and banquet waiting staff or assistant receipt controllers and auditors.

Requirements: Applicants should ideally speak French.

Accommodation: Board and lodging available.

Application Procedure: Applications are invited immediately and should be sent to the HR manager at the above address.

Sports, Couriers and Camping

Canvas Holidays

Job(s) Available: Campsite courier.

Duration: Full season positions start in March, April or May and end in September/October. High season staff needed to work at least 2 months during the peak season.

Pay: Package includes competitive salary, tent accommodation, medical insurance, uniform and return travel from a UK port of entry.

Head Office: GVN Camping Recruitment, East Port House, Dunfermline KY12 7JG, Scotland
☎ 01383 629 012
✆ campingrecruitment@gvnrecruitment.com
💻 www.gvnrecruitment.com

Company Description: Canvas Holidays provide luxury mobile home and tent holidays at over 100 campsites throughout Europe.

Job Description: Involves cleaning accommodation, welcoming families to the site and showing them to their accommodation. Visiting customers, providing local information and basic maintenance are very important parts of the job. Campsite courier opportunities are also available for couples to work on site together.

Accommodation: Provided as part of package.

Additional Information: For details of management positions, see website.

Application Procedure: Please call the recruitment department for more information and an application form, or apply online at www.gvnrecruitment.com.

MALTA

MALTA HIGH COMMISSION
Malta House, 36–38 Piccadilly, London W1V 0PQ
☎ 020 7292 4800
💻 www.foreign.gov.mt/london
✆ maltahighcommission.london@gov.mt

It may be possible to arrange a holiday job in Malta with the Malta Youth Hostels Association mentioned below. Otherwise, jobs are likely to be mainly in the tourism sector. You can contact hotels in Malta via the Malta Tourism Authority (http://mta.com.mt) or contact hotel chains such as Hilton (www.hiltonmalta.com.mt) or Dolmen (www.dolmen.com.mt).

Red Tape

Visa Requirements: Citizens from to EU countries, USA, Australia, Japan and Canada do not need a visa to gain entry into Malta. Stays must not exceed 3 months. Visitors must not attempt to gain employment whilst they stay unless they are EU citizens who have applied for a work permit.

Work Permits: Malta joined the EU on 1 May 2004. However since it is a small island, it fears a disproportionate influx of labour from elsewhere in the EU. Therefore EU citizens still have to apply for a work permit until at least 2012 so that Malta can keep control of its labour market. An Employment Licence is obtained with a signed Employment Engagement Form from the employer which is then submitted to the Employment and Training Corporation, Head Office, Hal Far (etc@gov.mt). Information about opportunities to work in Malta for EU citizens can be obtained by emailing eures@gov.mt or on the website www.etc.gov.mt. Non-EU Citizens will find it is very difficult to get a permit to work in Malta; however in exceptional circumstances permits can be provided for a year.

Malta Youth Hostels Association (MYHA)

Job(s) Available: Volunteers to work on a short-term Work camps.

Duration: All year round. May stay for between 2 weeks and 3 months.

Working Hours: Minimum of 3 hours per day unpaid work as directed by the MYHA.

Head Office: 17 Triq Tal-Borg, Pawla PLA 1250, Malta
☎ +356 2169 3957
✆ myha@keyworld.net

Company Description: The MYHA offers temporary, free accommodation to persons needing social assistance. It also receives young travellers and workcamp volunteers to assist in the achievement of this aim. The MYHA operates workcamps all round the year. Volunteers are accommodated in return for work.

Requirements: Aged 18–25. Must be from EU countries.

Accommodation: Accommodation is in the youth hostels.

Application Procedure: Apply sending 3 International Reply Coupons (or $2 if International Reply Coupons are not available). Forms should be received 3 months before the camp is due to start.

THE NETHERLANDS

ROYAL NETHERLANDS EMBASSY
38 Hyde Park Gate, London SW7 5DP
☎ 020 7590 3200
🖥 www.netherlands-embassy.org.uk
✆ london@netherlands-embassy.org.uk

The Netherlands has one of the lowest unemployment rates in the EU at only 3.8%. Most Dutch people speak excellent English, and so knowledge of Dutch is not essential for those looking for unskilled seasonal jobs. The tourist industry employs large numbers of extra workers over the summer: it is worth noting that the bulb fields attract tourists from spring onwards so early application is therefore important. Information on living and working in The Netherlands can be found on the Dutch Embassy's website (www.netherlands-embassy.org.uk)

There are also a number of opportunities for voluntary work. International Voluntary Service, Youth Action for Peace, Concordia and UNA Exchange recruit Britons and Service Civil International (see the IVS entry) in the USA recruits Americans for camps there. See the *Worldwide* chapter for details.

The Netherlands has many private employment agencies (*uitzendbureaus*) which are accustomed to finding short term jobs for British and Irish workers. These jobs normally involve unskilled manual work, such as stocking shelves in supermarkets, working on factory production lines, or washing up in canteens. Most of the agencies will only help people who visit them in person. To discover nearby addresses look up *uitzendbureaus* in the *Gouden Gids* (Yellow Pages; www.goudengids.nl); Randstad, ASB, Unique and Manpower are among the best known names.

Some agencies handle vacancies for work in flower bulb factories, which need large numbers of casual workers from mid-April to October to pick asparagus, strawberries, gherkins, apples and pears: the peak period is between mid-June and the beginning of August. At the same time of year there are jobs in greenhouses and holiday parks. These jobs are popular with locals and usually can be filled with local jobseekers. From the end of September/beginning of October until January of the following year, jobs might be available in the bulb industry (bulb picking and in factories). Although bulbs are grown elsewhere in Holland, the industry is concentrated in the area between Haarlem and Lisse, especially around the town of Hillegom. There are also a limited number of jobs every year in the fruit and vegetable producing greenhouses of the 'Westland' in the province of Zuid-Holland.

EU nationals can make use of the service of the European Employment Services (EURES; www.europa.eu.int/eures) represented in their own Public Employment Service and in The Netherlands. EURES provides jobseekers with information and advice about living and working in another country of the EU. The Euroadvisers also have an overview of temporary and permanent vacancies available in The Netherlands. Contact the nearby local employment office for more information. In The Netherlands, addresses of local Dutch Euroadvisers can be obtained through the *Landelijk Bureau Arbeidsvoorziening*, look up *Arbeidsbureau* in a telephone directory. For further information consult the free booklet *Working in The Netherlands* published by the UK Employment Service (Jobcentre Plus).

Those wishing to place advertisements in Dutch newspapers may contact *De Telegraaf*, a major Dutch newspaper (+31 10 20 5852208; com.bin@telegraaf.nl; www.telegraaf.nl).

Red Tape

Visa Requirements: citizens of the United Kingdom, the USA, EU countries, Canada, Australia, New Zealand, Switzerland and Japan do not need a visa. Citizens of newer EU member countries (Bulgaria, the Czech Republic, Estonia, Hungary, Latvia, Lithuania, Poland, Romania, Slovakia, and Slovenia) will need to have a work permit to work in the Netherlands. Employers need to apply for the work permit. For more information see www.ind.nl. Members of countries needing a visa will have to apply for one at the Dutch embassy. The application will need to be accompanied by full details of means of support, accommodation and prospective employment. Entry may be refused to all travelers who are unable to show that they have the means to support themselves whilst in the Netherlands and to buy a return or onward ticket.

Residence Permits: Members of those countries not requiring a visa who intend to stay for more than 3 months must acquire a sticker in their passport from the local aliens police (*Vreemdelingenpolitie*) or Town Hall, normally over-the-counter, within 8 days of arrival. Non-EU members may be required to undergo a medical check for tuberculosis, take out comprehensive medical insurance, submit evidence of suitable accommodation and means of support, and sign a statement that they do not have a criminal record. Short-term residence permits can be authorised for paid employment and au pair placements.

Work Permits: Subjects of the older EU do not need work or employment permit. North Americans, Antipodeans and others who require no visa to travel to The Netherlands are allowed to work for less than 3 months, provided they report to the Aliens Police within three days of arrival and their employer has obtained a *tewerkstellingsvergunning* (employment permit) for them. In practice, the *tewerkstellingsvergunning* is unlikely to be issued for casual work. Non-EU nationals wishing to work for longer than 3 months must obtain a work permit before arrival in The Netherlands from the local labour exchange in the Netherlands. Permission to take voluntary work may be obtained on your behalf by the sponsoring agency in The Netherlands.

Working Holiday Scheme: The scheme is open to Australians, New Zealanders and Canadians who are aged between 18 and 30. They may obtain temporary work for up to a year to finance their holiday in the Netherlands. Applications must be made in person for a provisional residence permit (MVV) to the Dutch Embassy from which further details of personal requirements are available.

Hotel Work and Catering

Grand Hotel & Restaurant Opduin-Texel

Job(s) Available: Kitchen porters (2), assistant waiters (2), chambermaids (2).

Duration: Applicants for these positions must be available for at least 3–4 months during the period March to November.

Head Office: Ruyslaan 22, 1796 AD De Koog, Texel, The Netherlands
☎ +31 222317445
✆ info@opduin.nl
🖳 www.opduin.nl

Company Description: A luxurious 4 star hotel with 100 rooms, 50 employees, gourmet restaurant, and swimming pool. It is just 200m from the beach on a beautiful island in 'the top of Holland'.

Job Description: *Kitchen porters:* for general kitchen work including dishwashing and cleaning. *Assistant waiters:* for general work in their service department during breakfast, lunch and dinner. *Chambermaids:* for general cleaning work in the hotel.

Requirements: Knowledge of Dutch and English. Previous experience is recommended but not necessary. *Assistant waiters:* good appearance essential. *Chambermaids:* good health essential.

Accommodation: Available at a small charge.

Application Procedure: Applications with photograph from January to Luuk de Jong at the above address.

Sports, Couriers and Camping

Canvas Holidays

Job(s) Available: Campsite courier.

Duration: Full season positions start in March, April or May and end in September/October. High season staff needed to work at least 2 months during the peak season.

Pay: Package includes competitive salary, tent accommodation, medical insurance, uniform and return travel from a UK port of entry.

Head Office: GVN Camping Recruitment, East Port House, Dunfermline KY12 7JG, Scotland
☎ 01383 629012
✉ campingrecruitment@ gvnrecruitment.com
🖥 www.gvnrecruitment.com

Company Description: Canvas Holidays provide luxury mobile home and tent holidays at over 100 campsites throughout Europe.

Job Description: Involves cleaning accommodation, welcoming families to the site and showing them to their accommodation. Visiting customers, providing local information and basic maintenance are very important parts of the job. Campsite courier opportunities are also available for couples to work on site together.

Accommodation: Provided as part of package.

Additional Information: For details of management positions, see website.

Application Procedure: Please call the recruitment department for more information and an application form, or apply online at www.gvnrecruitment.com.

Eurocamp

Job(s) Available: Campsite courier, children's courier, courier team leaders, children's courier team leaders, montage/demontage.

Duration: *Campsite courier:* Applicants should be available to work from April/May to mid-September or June/July to mid-September. *Children's courier:* Applicants should be available from early May to September or June to September. *Courier team leaders:* Applicants should be available from April to mid-September. *Children's courier team leaders:* Applicants should be available from early May until September. *Montage/Demontage:* Applicants should be available from Feb to May or August to October.

Head Office: Overseas Recruitment Department (Ref SJ/08) Hartford Manor, Greenbank Lane, Northwich CW8 1HW, England
☎ 01606 787525
🖥 www.holidaybreakjobs.com/camping

Pay: You will receive a competitive salary, comprehensive training, return travel to and from an agreed meeting point, accommodation, medical and luggage insurance and uniform.

Company Description: Eurocamp is a leading tour operator in self-drive camping and mobile home holidays in Europe. We offer our customers a wide range of holiday accommodation on over 200 premier campsites. Each year the company seeks to recruit up to 1,500 enthusiastic people to work the summer season in a variety of roles.

Job Description: *Campsite courier:* A Courier's responsibility begins by ensuring that the customer's accommodation is both inviting and cleaned to the highest of standards. You will welcome new arrivals, be the customers main point of contact and will be expected to provide local and general information, give assistance and even act as interpreter if required. Part of the role will involve helping out with minor repairs to accommodation and equipment and will also involve basic administration and accounts. *Children's courier:* You will be responsible for planning and delivering a fun, safe, daily activity programme to our customers' children. The age of the children attending the club will range from 5 to 12 years old although we also run a toddler service in low season for 12 months to 4 years. *Courier team leaders:* You must be able to deliver first class customer service and organize the daily workload of the courier team. Your role also includes all the duties of a Campsite Courier and you will be expected to lead by example. There are a variety of team leader roles available, dependant on team size; Courier in Charge, Senior Courier and Site Manager. *Children's Courier Team Leaders:* Your role will involve the management, motivation and development of the Children's Couriers to ensure they provide a varied range of quality activities. Your role includes all the duties of a Children's Courier. *Montage/Demontage:* Montage and Demontage assistants are employed to either help set up for the season or close down at the end of the season. This involves putting up or taking down tents, moving/distributing equipment and cleaning/preparing accommodation.

Requirements: Applicants must hold a UK/EU passport and the current minimum age is 18 years old on the day you start work in order to obtain the relevant insurance cover. *Campsite Couriers*: You should have lots of energy, basic common sense and a genuine desire to help people. *Children's Courier:* Previous childcare experience is essential. Successful candidates will be asked to apply for an Enhanced Disclosure. *Courier Team Leaders:* You must have previous experience of leading a team successful applicants may be asked to apply for a Standard Disclosure. *Children's Courier Team Leaders*: Previous experience with Children and leading a team successful candidates will be asked to apply for an Enhanced Disclosure. *Montage/Demontage:* Previous experience of physical and repetitive work successful applicants will be asked to apply for a Standard Disclosure.

Accommodation: Provided.

Application Procedure: Applicants should apply on-line at www.holidaybreakjobs.com/camping or telephone 01606 787 525 for an Application Pack.

Volunteer Work

Pinkpop

Job(s) Available: Volunteers for barwork, backstage, catering, entrance and stewarding work (1000).

Duration: From 26 May to 28 May.

Working Hours: At least 8 hours per day.

Pay: Unpaid but volunteers receive a free ticket to the festival.

Head Office: Buro Pinkpop, Postbus 117 6160 AC Geleen, The Netherlands
info@pinkpop.nl
www.pinkpop.nl

Company Description: The Netherlands' most well-known open-air festival with over 30 bands on 3 stages across 3 days.

Accommodation: Free camping available.

Application Procedure: Information on volunteering appears on the website at least 6 months before festival. Apply by email to the above address.

Other Employment In The Netherlands

Job-Express

Job(s) Available: This agency seeks staff for a number of temporary and permanent jobs around the Netherlands.

Company Description: Dutch recruitment and international employment agency specialising in international positions in The Netherlands.

Requirements: EU citizen or valid work permit.

Application Procedure: Applications are invited all year round for these positions; contact Job-Express at the above address for more details.

> **Head Office:** Postbus 1459, 1300 BL Almere-Holland, The Netherlands
> ☎ +31 365 302000
> jobexpress@expatcompany.nl
> www.expatcompany.nl

NORWAY

ROYAL NORWEGIAN EMBASSY
25 Belgrave Square, London SW1X 8QD
☎ 020 7591 5500
www.norway.org.uk
emb.london@mfa.no

Norway voted not to join the European Union, but it is a member of the European Economic Area (EEA) which means that EU nationals can enter and look for work for up to 6 months. They can seek work through local offices of the Norwegian employment service (now part of NAV; www.nav.no), and work without needing work permits. Citizens of other Scandinavian countries are also free to enter Norway. The majority of other foreign nationals are required to get a visa once they have entered Norway. For full details check with the Norwegian Embassy (www.norway.org.uk).

There are a number of well-paid jobs available in Norwegian hotels over the summer. English is widely spoken but knowledge of Norwegian is advantageous. As elsewhere in Europe, the tourist industry appreciates people who can speak more than 1 language. People who are in Norway may also be able to find unpleasant but lucrative work in fish processing factories in such towns as Bergen, Vardø and Bodø, but over-fishing has reduced the possibilities of finding such work. When looking for work it is worth bearing in mind that Norwegian students are on vacation between 15 June and 15 August (approximately), and so there will be more opportunities before and after these dates. Those aged 18–30 can take advantage of a 'Working Guest' programme whereby visitors can stay with a Norwegian family in a working environment such as a farm, in tourism or as an au pair; details can be found under the Atlantis Youth Exchange Entry below, or at www.atlantis.no.

The Norwegian employment service is unable to help people looking for summer jobs. British citizens may be able to find voluntary work in Norway through Concordia or International Voluntary Service and Americans through Service Civil International (see the *Worldwide* chapter for details). For more information on living and working in Norway see the EURES website (www.europa.eu.int/eures), or the NAV website.

As in Copenhagen, Oslo has a Use It office (*Ungdomsinformasjonen*), one of whose aims is to find work and accommodation for young visitors while offering a range of services, which are all free of charge. The Oslo Youth Information Centre is located at Møllergata 3, 0179 Oslo (+47

22415132; post@unginfo.oslo.no; www.unginfo.oslo.no) and is open year round from 11am to 5pm with longer opening hours during the summer. Their website, in English, carries tips for living and working in Oslo.

Those wishing to advertise in Norwegian newspapers may contact Crane Media Partners Ltd, 20-28 Dalling Road, Hammersmith, London W6 OJB (020 8237 8601), who handle the national daily *Dagbladet* (www.dagbladet.no). *Aftenposten* (www.aftenposten.no/english) also has a job section.

Red Tape

Visa Requirements: A visa is not required by citizens of most EU countries for a visit of less than three months, provided that employment is not intended. If you are from a country that is not an EU member you must obtain a work visa or permit to work in Norway.

Residence Permits: This permit may be obtained before entering Norway through a Norwegian foreign service, or in Norway at the local police station for any stay of more than 3 months – your passport, two photographs and proof that you are financially self-supporting are required. Even if obtained before entering the country, you must report to the local police with a Confirmation of Employment within 3 months of arrival. EU nationals, with the firm intention of taking up employment, may enter and stay in Norway for up to 3 months (extendable to six months, if you are financially self-supporting) while seeking work. Should you obtain long-term work during this period you must apply for a residence permit and report to the local police. If you are from the EU and you take up short-term employment for a period not exceeding 3 months, you do not need a residence permit, nor do you need to report to the police.

Work Permits: British, Irish and nationals of other EU/EEA countries do not need work permits in Norway. Non-EU citizens must obtain a work and residence permit before entering Norway. Permits should be applied for at least 3 months before you intend to arrive in Norway. Having been offered a job and a place to live, you should obtain application forms for a work permit from the nearest Norwegian Embassy or Consulate General, which will send the completed applications to the Directorate of Immigration in Oslo for processing. Applicants may not enter Norway during the period in which the application for a work-and-residence permit is under consideration.

Permits for Skilled and Seasonal Workers: Skilled workers with higher level training whose position cannot be filled by Norwegian nationals or EU members may be provided with a work permit for at least 1 year. Non-EU nationals looking for seasonally-determined work may be granted a work permit for a period of usually no greater than 3 months. Applications for such permits should be made to the Norwegian Embassy.

Working Holiday Visas: A working holiday visa scheme exists between Norway and Australia; applicants must be Australian nationals, intend primarily to holiday in Norway for up to a year, be aged between 18 and 30 years at time of application and possess reasonable funds and travel insurance. Applications can be made through the consular offices of the Royal Norwegian Embassies in Australia or London.

Agricultural Work

Atlantis Youth Exchange

Job(s) Available: Working guest on a Norwegian farm.

Duration: Stays are for between 8 and 24 weeks all round the year. EU applicants can apply for up to 6 months.

Head Office: Rådhusgt 4, 0151 Oslo, Norway
☎ +47 22477170
✉ atlantis@atlantis.no
🖥 www.atlantis.no

Working Hours: Maximum of 35 hours per week. Usually 6 to 7 hours per day, 5 days a week.

Pay/Cost: Pocket money of approximately £56 per week. The registration fee is approximately £100 (£200 for a placement of 12–24 weeks); if not placed all but approximately £20 is returned.

Company Description: Atlantis, the Norwegian Foundation for Youth Exchange, arranges stays on Norwegian farms for people of any nationality to promote respect and understanding between cultures through youth exchange. They can also arrange an au pair programme in Norway.

Job Description: Participants share every aspect of a farmer's family life, both the work and the leisure. The work may include haymaking, weeding, milking, picking berries, fruit and vegetables, caring for animals etc.

Requirements: Applicants who are aged 18–30 and speak English.

Accommodation: Free board and lodging provided.

Application Procedure: Prospective applicants should contact the above organization direct for details of partner organizations in their own country.

Hotel Work and Catering

Fretheim Hotel

Job(s) Available: Waiting staff (15), bar staff (2), chefs (10), chamberstaff (12), café personnel (4).

Duration: 2 months.

Head Office: Post Box 63, 5742 Flåm, Norway
☎ +47 57636300
✉ mail@fretheim-hotel.no
🖥 www.fretheim-hotel.no

Working Hours: 35.5 hours per day, 5 days a week.

Pay: Approximately NOK18,880. *Chefs:* NOK20,000.

Job Description: *Waiting staff:* for silver service, buffet and à la carte. *Bar staff:* for hotel bar seating 80 persons. *Chefs:* all grades for buffet, à la carte, lunches and breakfast. *Chamberstaff:* for cleaning rooms and other parts of the hotel. *Café personnel:* to make salads/sandwiches/speciality coffee and to work in bar 2 nights per week.

Requirements: Experience necessary. Must speak fluent English; Norwegian would be a plus. *Chef:* Must have NVQ level 2.

Accommodation: Provided for NOK2350. per month.

Application Procedure: Applications between January and March to the above address or email.

Kvikne's Hotel

Job(s) Available: Chamber staff (10), waiting staff (15), bartender (5), chef (10), kitchen help (8), luggage porters (3), night porters (2).

Duration: Minimum period of work 1 June to 31 August.

Working Hours: 152 hours per month, 5–6 days a week.

Head Office: Box 24, 6898 Balestrand, Norway
☎ +47 57694200
✆ booking@kviknes.no
🖳 www.kviknes.no

Company Description: One of Norway's largest tourist hotels with 210 rooms, 400 guests, conference facilities.

Requirements: Previous experience is an advantage as are languages (German, French, Scandinavian).

Accommodation: Accommodation and board are provided for NOK1200 per month.

Application Procedure: Apply to the above address from 1 February.

Lindstroem Hotel

Job(s) Available: Hotel staff (20).

Duration: Minimum period of work 6 weeks between 1 May and 30 September.

Working Hours: 8 hours per day, 5 days a week.

Pay: NOK110 per hour.

Head Office: Laerdal, Norway
☎ + 47 57666900
✆ post@lindstroemhotel.no
🖳 www.lindstroemhotel.no

Job Description: Hotel staff to work in the kitchen, dining room and cafeteria and to clean rooms.

Requirements: No Norwegian necessary. Applicants should be aged at least 18 and speak English.

Accommodation: Board and lodging available at a charge.

Application Procedure: CV and cover letter to Knut Lindstrom at the above address from January.

Stalheim Hotel

Job(s) Available: Chefs (8), chambermaids (8), waiters/waitresses (10), pantry boys/girls (8), cooks (5), sales girls (5).

Duration: Minimum period of work 3 months between May and September.

Working Hours: 37.5 hours per week.

Pay: NOK19,000 per month gross.

Head Office: N-5715 Stalheim, Norway
☎ + 47 56520122
✆ info@stalheimhotel.com
🖳 www.stalheim.com

Company Description: This busy, first class family run hotel is situated in the Fjord country of western Norway, 140km from Bergen. It has an international clientele.

Requirements: Fluent English necessary. Must be an EU citizen. Minimum age 19.

Accommodation: Board and accommodation provided at approximately NOK2600 per month.

Application Procedure: Email or send CV and reference to above address.

PORTUGAL

PORTUGUESE EMBASSY
11 Belgrave Square, London SW1X 8PP
☎ 020 7235 5331
✎ london@portembassy.co.uk

Unemployment in Portugal is not one of the highest rates in Europe, although it stands at 7.4%. The best chances of finding paid employment are in the tourist industry. Though tour operators (see the *Worldwide* chapter), by teaching English as a foreign language, or in hotels and bars in tourist areas such as the Costa do Sol and the Algarve are normally good starting points. A drawback is that the minimum wage in Portugal is one of the lowest in the EU and approximately half that of Britain or France and that living costs, once correspondingly low, are rising faster than wages. Private employment agencies such as Manpower (www.manpower.com) may however be able to provide casual jobs, for which knowledge of Portuguese is necessary.

Short-term voluntary work can be arranged for British travellers by UNA Exchange and Youth Action for Peace. American and British citizens can also arrange some voluntary work places through International Voluntary Service/Service Civil International. See their entry in *Worldwide* for details.

British and Irish citizens and other EU nationals are permitted to use the Portuguese national employment service: look under *Centro do Emprego* in a telephone directory. The website of Portugal's national employment institute (*Instituto do Emprego e Formação Profissional*), has an English version of their website (www.iefp.pt). The EURES website (www.europa.eu.int/eures) has a comprehensive section on living and working in Portugal as well as a jobs section. There are also a number of private employment agencies, principally in Lisbon and Oporto: for agencies specialising in temporary work look under *Pessoal Temporàrio* in the *Yellow Pages* (*Pàginas Amarelas;* www.pai.pt).

An advertisement in the English language *Anglo Portuguese News (APN)* may lead to an offer of a job (+351 2 82341100; apn@mail.telepac.pt; www.the-news.net).

Red Tape

Visa Requirements: for holiday visits of up to 3 months a visa is not required by full citizens of EU countries. A visa is not required for either US or Australian citizens for holiday visits of up to 3 months. Portugal is a member of the Schengen agreement.

Residence Permits: for stays longer than 3 months a residence permit should be obtained from the nearest immigration office (*Serviço de Estrangeiros e Fronteiras*) in the area of residence. To obtain a residence permit, you must be able to provide a letter from your employer in Portugal confirming your employment. Non-EU nationals must provide a residence visa obtained from the Portuguese Consulate in their home country.

Work Permits: EU nationals do not require work permits to work in Portugal, only a residence permit as above. Non-EU nationals must provide an array of documents before they can be granted a work visa, including a residence visa obtained from the Portuguese Consulate in their home country, a document showing that the Ministry of Labour (*Ministerio do Trabalho*) has approved the job and a medical certificate in Portuguese. The final stage is to take a letter of good conduct provided by the applicant's own embassy to the police for the work and residence permit. There are no restrictions applied to volunteer work.

Hotel Work and Catering

Hotel Estalagem Vale Da Ursa

Job(s) Available: Waitresses/restaurant assistants (1-2), kitchen porters (1-2), reception staff.
Duration: Mid-June to the end of July.
Working Hours: 8 hour split shift. 6 days a week.
Pay: Minimum wages. Depends on experience.
Job Description: Staff to help in the dining room, bar and kitchen.
Requirements: Fluent English.
Accommodation: Provided, meals included.
Application Procedure: Applications should be sent to the manager at the above address in April and May.

Head Office: Estrada Nacional 238 KM 23, Cernache do Bonjardim, Portugal
☎ +351 2 74802981
✆ info@hotelvaledaursa.com
🖥 www.hotelvaledaursa.com

Mayer Apartments

Job(s) Available: Bar person.
Duration: From 1 May to 31 October.
Working Hours: 10am–7pm, 6 days a week.
Job Description: Outgoing, hardworking, independent individual to serve drinks and snacks at a busy poolside bar.
Requirements: No experience necessary since full training is given. Applicants must speak English.
Accommodation: Included.
Application Procedure: To apply send CV and photo to Mr Adrian Mayer at the above address from February onwards.

Head Office: Praia Da luz, 8600-157 Luz Lagos, Algarve, Portugal
☎ +351 2 82789313
✆ info@mayerapartments.com
🖥 www.mayerapartments.com

SPAIN

SPANISH EMBASSY
39 Chesham Place, London SW1X 8SB
☎ 020 7235 5555
🖥 www.conspalon.org
✆ conspalon@mail.mae.es

Unemployment has dogged the Spanish economy in recent years mainly due to regulations restricting fluidity in the job market. However, annual growth rates in GDP indicate a stable economy and unemployment hovers at around 8.5% having been in double figures for all the previous years since Spain joined the EU. Thus there are reasonable opportunities for finding temporary work. For foreigners these are best sought in the tourist industry or teaching English, both of which count knowledge of another language as an asset.

Some of the best opportunities for work in Spain are in the tourist industry, so that applications to hotels in tourist areas could result in the offer of a job. Since many of these hotels cater for tourists from northern Europe, a good knowledge of languages such as German, Dutch, French and English will be a great advantage to foreign workers. The website www.gapwork.com has information about working in Ibiza and provides the web addresses for clubs and other potential employers. It is estimated that about 6,000 Britons try to find work on Ibiza each year so it is important to offer a relevant skill.

It should be remembered that hotel workers in Spain work very long hours during the summer months and foreign workers will be required to do likewise. In many cases at the peak of the tourist season hotel and restaurant staff work a minimum of 10 hours per day and bar staff may work even longer hours. A 7-day week is regarded as perfectly normal during the summer. Despite these long hours, salaries are generally somewhat lower than elsewhere in Western Europe.

English and Spanish may help an experienced secretary to get bilingual office work with companies in large cities. There are also a number of jobs for teachers of English: the definitive guide to this type of work is *Teaching English Abroad* (see *Useful Publications*).

British and Irish citizens and other EU nationals who are in Spain and confident of their knowledge of Spanish may use the Spanish national employment service (www.oficinaempleo.com). For addresses consult the *Yellow Pages* (*Pàginas Amarillas;* www.paginas-amarillas.es),–look under *Oficina de Empleo*. Private employment agencies are known as *Empresas de Trabajo Temporal*. For further information consult the jobs section of the EURES website (www.europa.eu.int/eures), or click on Living & Working for details. Alternatively you can contact your nearest embassy: the Spanish Embassy in London has information on its website.

It is always worth checking the English language press for the sits vac columns which sometimes carry adverts for cleaners, live-in babysitters, chefs, bar staff, etc. Look for SUR in English (www.surinenglish.com) which has a large employment section and is used by foreign and local residents throughout southern Spain. It is published free on Fridays and distributed through supermarkets, bars, travel agencies, etc. If you want to place your own ad, contact the publisher through the website. Advertisements can be placed in Spanish newspapers including *El Mundo*, a national daily, which is handled by Smyth International (020 8446 6400; alastair@smyth-international.com; www.smyth-international.com). *El Pais* (www.elpais.com) is the leading national daily.

There are also opportunities for voluntary work in Spain arranged by Concordia, UNA Exchange, Youth Action for Peace and International Voluntary Service (for British citizens), and Service Civil International for US nationals. See the *Worldwide* chapter for details.

Red Tape

Visa Requirements: A visa is not required by citizens of the United Kingdom, the USA and EU countries for non-working visits to Spain. Non-EU nationals taking up a paid job must obtain a visa from the Spanish Consulate before travelling to Spain: this can take 3 months to process. To avoid delay, anyone requesting information or visa forms should write to the relevant consulate stating their nationality and the purpose of their intended stay, enclosing a s.a.e.

Residence Permits: Since March 2003, it has not been necessary for British and other EU citizens to apply for a residence card to reside in Spain. Residence cards can however be applied for on a voluntary basis (apply direct to the local *Comisaria de Policia* or *Oficina de Extranjeros*. Further details on the Ministry of the Interior's website; www.mir.es).

Non-EU citizens who intend to stay more than 3 months must apply for a residence card *(Tarjeta de Residencia)* within 30 days of arrival. Application should be made to the local police headquarters *(Comisaría de Policia)* or to a Foreigners Registration Office *(Oficina de Extranjería)*. This information can be confirmed with the Spanish Consulates General in your own country. You may also wish to register your stay in Spain with your country's consulate in Spain.

Further information on residing in Spain can also be obtained from the Spanish Consulates General in London, Manchester and Edinburgh and with the British Consulate General in Spain (c/ Marqués de la Ensenada 16-2, 28004 Madrid; +34 91 3085201; www.britishembassy.gov.uk).

NIE Number: all foreign nationals need to apply for a foreigner's identification number (*numero de identificación de extranjeros*) from the police as soon as they start work. The NIE is a tax identification number that allows you to undertake any kind of employment or business activity in Spain.

Work Permits: are not required by EU nationals. The immigration situation for non-EU citizens has become increasingly difficult forcing employers of non-Europeans to embark on an expensive, complex and lengthy process. Non-EU nationals must first obtain a *visado especial* from the Spanish Embassy in their country of residence (after submitting a copy of their contract), medical certificate in duplicate and authenticated copies of qualifications. In some cases a further document is needed, an *antecedente penale* (certificate proving that they have no criminal record). The employer must obtain a work permit on your behalf from the Spanish Ministry of Labour through the relevant *Delegacion Provincial de Trabajo y Seguridad Social*. There are no restrictions applied to voluntary work.

Hotel Work and Catering

Hotel Cap Roig

Job(s) Available: Waitresses (2), waiters (3), bar assistants, bar and pool assistants (2), chambermaids (3), assistant cook.

Head Office: 17250 Playa de AroCtr, Spain
☎ +34 972 652000
caproig@caproig.com
www.caproig.com

Duration: 3 months.

Working Hours: 6–8 hours per day, 6 days a week, either 8am–4pm or 2pm–10pm.

Pay: Approximately £500 per month. *Assistant cook:* approximately £575 per month.

Company Description: The hotel is situated directly over the sea. It is frequented by international clients and is open all year round.

Requirements: Good level of Spanish required. All applicants must have a valid EU passport.

Accommodation: Board and accommodation is included.

Application Procedure: Apply by email with CV.

Easy Way Association

Job(s) Available: Restaurant staff to work as fast-food staff, waiters and commis waiters.

Head Office: Calle Gran Via 80 Of. 1017, E-88013 Madrid, Spain
☎ +34 91 5428854
info@easywayspain.com
www.easywayspain.com

Duration: Minimum period of work is 4 weeks at any time of year.

Working Hours: Full and part-time positions available.

Pay: €180–€900 a month depending on hours worked and experience.

Company Description: A non-profit association for international cultural exchanges, specializing in work placements (long and short stays) and all types of programmes with accommodation in youth centers, apartments, residences and family accommodation in Madrid, Barcelona and the rest of Spain.

Requirements: Applicants aged 18–28.

Accommodation: Available in shared flats or homestays.

Additional Information: For some programmes no Spanish is required. Spanish lessons are available through the Easy Way School of Spanish.

Application Procedure: Applications to the above address or apply online at www. easywayspain.com/ingles/registration

Emilio's Bar & Apartment Rentals

Job(s) Available: Live-in bar staff and chambermaids required.

Duration: 2–3 months over the summer.

Working Hours: 6 hours per day, 6 days a week.

Pay: €100 per week pocket money plus tips.

Company Description: Busy beach bar and apartment rentals in the Puerto Sherry complex in El Puerto de Santa Maria on the Costa de la Luz.

Head Office: Paseo Maritimo 77, Puerto Sherry, El Puerro de Santa Maria, 11500 Cadiz, Spain
☎ +34 956 540112, +34 956 542394
✎ mail@emiliosbar.com
🖳 www.emiliosbar.com

Requirements: Spanish would be and advantage, but is not necessary.

Accommodation: Shared accommodation provided within walking distance of the beach.

Application Procedure: Email for more information or send CV to Apartado de Correos 880, Puerto Sherry, El Puerro de Santa Maria, 11500 Cadiz.

Hotel La Residencia

Job(s) Available: Waiters/assistant waiters (2 of each), chef de rangs, cooks, assistant cooks, chefs de partie (2 of each), chambermaids.

Duration: 3 months to 1 year.

Working Hours: 40 hours per week, 5 days a week.

Pay: Minimum €1020 per month.

Head Office: 07179 Deia, Mallorca, Spain
☎ +34 971 639011
✎ reserves@hotel-laresidencia.com
🖳 www.hotellaresidencia.com

Company Description: Part of Orient-Express Hotels. 160 staff to 110 guests maximum.

Accommodation: Accommodation and meals free.

Application Procedure: Apply all year round with CV by email or post.

Hotel-Restaurant Mont Sant

Job(s) Available: Chef (1), waiter (1).

Duration: From 3 to 6 months.

Working Hours: 8 hours per day, 5 days a week.

Pay: *Chef:* €800–€1200 per month. *Waiter:* €750–€1000 per month.

Head Office: Xativa, Valencia, Spain
☎ +34 96 2275031
✎ mont-sant@mont-sant.com
🖳 www.mont-sant.com

Company Description: Small (17 bedrooms) purpose-built hotel on the site of an ancient farmstead and situated in its own landscaped gardens with Michelin recognised restaurant, gymnasium and swimming pool.

Job Description: *Chef:* for cold starters, desserts, hot meals, sauces etc. *Waiter:* to serve food and undertake banquet work.

Requirements: Should speak Spanish plus another language (English, French or German etc.)

Accommodation: There is a charge of about approximately £30 per month for board and lodging.

Application Procedure: Apply to Javier Andrés Cifre, director, from February.

Nico-Hotel

Job(s) Available: Kitchen staff, waitresses (5), chambermaids (4), secretary.

Duration: The work period is April to October. *Kitchen staff:* needed all year round. *Waitresses:* minimum period of work 3 months. *Secretary:* minimum period of work 2 months.

Head Office: CN-II km 150, 42240 Medinaceli (Soria), Spain
☎ +34 975 326111
🖰 jaconto.3017@cajazuzal.com

Working Hours: *Kitchen staff:* 7 hours per day, 6 days a week. *Waitresses:* 8 hours per day, 6 days a week. *Chambermaids:* slightly shorter hours than waitresses. *Secretary:* 6 hours per day, 6–7 days a week.

Pay: Wages on application.

Company Description: This hotel is in a historic village 150km from Madrid, with a high class Spanish clientele. There is a staff of. 50 and customers are mainly Spanish, although other nationalities often visit in summer. The manager of this hotel wishes to stress that Medinaceli is not situated on the coast. There are also vacancies at the Hotel Duque de Medinaceli, CN-II 150, Medinaceli (Soria).

Requirements: All applicants must be at least 18 years of age. *Waitresses:* previous experience preferred. Some knowledge of Spanish required. *Secretary:* some knowledge of Spanish required.

Accommodation: Free board and accommodation provided.

Application Procedure: Applications from February to the manager at the above address, enclosing a full-length photograph.

Sports, Couriers and Camping

Camping Globo Rojo

Job(s) Available: Receptionist, waiter/waitress, qualified swimming pool guard.

Duration: Between 15 June and 30 August.

Working Hours: 8 hours per day, 6 days a week.

Pay: €565 per month.

Job Description: Staff required for campsite near Barcelona (40km).

Head Office: Barangé-Brun C.B.,
Carretera Nacional II, km 660,9 08360
Canet de Mar (Barcelona), Spain
☎ +34 93 7941143
🖰 camping@globo-rojo.com
🖳 www.globo-rojo.com

Requirements: Ideally applicants should speak English, German, and some Spanish.

Accommodation: Free board and lodging.

Application Procedure: Applications are invited from April onwards.

Canvas Holidays

Job(s) Available: Campsite courier, children's courier.

Duration: Full season positions start in March, April or May and end in September/October. High season staff needed to work at least 2 months during the peak season.

Pay: Package includes competitive salary, tent accommodation, medical insurance, uniform and return travel from a UK port of entry.

Head Office: GVN Camping Recruitment, East Port House, Dunfermline KY12 7JG, Scotland
☎ 01383 629012
✉ campingrecruitment@gvnrecruitment.com
🖥 www.gvnrecruitment.com

Company Description: Canvas Holidays provide luxury mobile home and tent holidays at over 100 campsites throughout Europe.

Job Description: *Campsite courier:* involves cleaning accommodation, welcoming families to the site and showing them to their accommodation. Visiting customers, providing local information and basic maintenance are very important parts of the job. Campsite Courier Opportunities are also available for couples to work on site together. *Children's courier:* needed to work at Hoopi's Club. Children's couriers should be energetic, enthusiastic and have good communication skills. A tent is provided as a Club venue and for equipment storage; this has to be kept safe, clean and tidy. Visiting new arrivals on site is an important and fun part of the job. Children's couriers also help with other campsite duties as needed.

Requirements: Applicants must have formal experience of working with children.

Accommodation: Provided as part of package.

Additional Information: For details of management positions, see website. Visit recruitment website for information about working with teenagers (Buzz Courier) and wildlife and the environment (Wild and Active Courier).

Application Procedure: Please call the recruitment department for more information and an application form, or apply online at www.gvnrecruitment.com.

Eurocamp

Job(s) Available: Campsite courier, children's courier, courier team leaders, children's courier team leaders, montage/demontage.

Duration: *Campsite courier:* Applicants should be available to work from April/May to mid-September or June/July to mid-September. *Children's courier:* Applicants should be available from early May to

Head Office: Overseas Recruitment Department (Ref SJ/08) Hartford Manor, Greenbank Lane, Northwich CW8 1HW, England
☎ 01606 787525
🖥 www.holidaybreakjobs.com/camping

September or June to September. *Courier team leaders:* Applicants should be available from April to mid-September. *Children's courier team leaders:* Applicants should be available from early May until September. *Montage/Demontage:* Applicants should be available from Feb to May or August to October.

Pay: You will receive a competitive salary, comprehensive training, return travel to and from an agreed meeting point, accommodation, medical and luggage insurance and uniform.

Company Description: Eurocamp is a leading tour operator in self-drive camping and mobile home holidays in Europe. We offer our customers a wide range of holiday accommodation on over 200 premier campsites. Each year the company seeks to recruit up to 1,500 enthusiastic people to work the summer season in a variety of roles.

Job Description: *Campsite courier:* A Courier's responsibility begins by ensuring that the customer's accommodation is both inviting and cleaned to the highest of standards. You will welcome new arrivals, be the customers main point of contact and will be expected to provide local and general information, give assistance and even act as interpreter if required. Part of the role will involve helping out with minor repairs to accommodation and equipment and will also involve basic administration and accounts. *Children's Courier:* You will be responsible for planning and delivering a fun, safe, daily activity programme to our customers' children. The age of the children attending the club will range from 5 to 12 years old although we also run a toddler service in low season for 12 months to 4 years. *Courier Team Leaders:* You must be able to deliver first class customer service and organize the daily workload of the courier team. Your role also includes all the duties of a Campsite Courier and you will be expected to lead by example. There are a variety of team leader roles available, dependant on team size; Courier in Charge, Senior Courier and Site Manager. *Children's courier team leaders:* Your role will involve the management, motivation and development of the Children's Couriers to ensure they provide a varied range of quality activities. Your role includes all the duties of a Children's Courier. *Montage/Demontage:* Montage and Demontage assistants are employed to either help set up for the season or close down at the end of the season. This involves putting up or taking down tents, moving/distributing equipment and cleaning/preparing accommodation.

Requirements: Applicants must hold a UK/EU passport and the current minimum age is 18 years old on the day you start work in order to obtain the relevant insurance cover. *Campsite Couriers*: You should have lots of energy, basic common sense and a genuine desire to help people. *Children's Courier:* Previous childcare experience is essential. Successful candidates will be asked to apply for an Enhanced Disclosure. *Courier Team Leaders:* You must have previous experience of leading a team successful applicants may be asked to apply for a Standard Disclosure. *Children's Courier Team Leaders:* Previous experience with Children and leading a team successful candidates will be asked to apply for an Enhanced Disclosure. *Montage/Demontage:* Previous experience of physical and repetitive work successful applicants will be asked to apply for a Standard Disclosure.

Accommodation: Provided.

Application Procedure: Applicants should apply on-line at www.holidaybreakjobs.com/camping or telephone 01606 787 525 for an Application Pack.

Keycamp Holidays

Job(s) Available: Campsite courier, children's courier, courier team leaders, children's courier team leaders, montage/demontage.

Duration: *Campsite courier:* Applicants should be available to work from April/May to mid-September or June/July to mid-September. *Children's courier:* Applicants should be available from early May to

> **Head Office:** Overseas Recruitment Department (Ref SJ/08) Hartford Manor, Greenbank Lane, Northwich CW8 1HW, UK
> ☎ 01606 787525
> 🖳 www.holidaybreakjobs.com/camping

September or June to September. *Courier team leaders:* Applicants should be available from April to mid-September. *Children's courier team leaders:* Applicants should be available from early May until September. *Montage/Demontage:* Applicants should be available from Feb to May or August to October.

Pay: You will receive a competitive salary, comprehensive training, return travel to and from an agreed meeting point, accommodation, medical and luggage insurance and uniform.

Company Description: Keycamp is a leading tour operator in self-drive camping and mobile home holidays in Europe. We offer our customers a wide range of holiday accommodation on over 200 premier campsites. Each year the company seeks to recruit up to 1,500 enthusiastic people to work the summer season in a variety of roles.

Job Description: *Campsite courier:* A Courier's responsibility begins by ensuring that the customer's accommodation is both inviting and cleaned to the highest of standards. You will welcome new arrivals, be the customers main point of contact and will be expected to provide local and general information, give assistance and even act as interpreter if required. Part of the role will involve helping out with minor repairs to accommodation and equipment and will also involve basic administration and accounts. *Children's courier:* You will be responsible for planning and delivering a fun, safe, daily activity programme to our customers' children. The age of the children attending the club will range from 5 to 12 years old although we also run a toddler service in low season for 12 months to 4 years. *Courier Team Leaders:* You must be able to deliver first class customer service and organize the daily workload of the courier team. Your role also includes all the duties of a Campsite Courier and you will be expected to lead by example. There are a variety of team leader roles available, dependant on team size; Courier in Charge, Senior Courier and Site Manager. *Children's Courier Team Leaders:* Your role will involve the management, motivation and development of the Children's Couriers to ensure they provide a varied range of quality activities. Your role includes all the duties of a Children's Courier. *Montage/Demontage:* Montage and Demontage assistants are employed to either help set up for the season or close down at the end of the season. This involves putting up or taking down tents, moving/distributing equipment and cleaning/preparing accommodation.

Requirements: Applicants must hold a UK/EU passport and the current minimum age is 18 years old on the day you start work in order to obtain the relevant insurance cover. *Campsite Couriers*: You should have lots of energy, basic common sense and a genuine desire to help people. *Children's Courier:* Previous childcare experience is essential. Successful candidates will be asked to apply for an Enhanced Disclosure. *Courier Team Leaders:* You must have previous experience of leading a team successful applicants may be asked to apply for a Standard Disclosure. *Children's Courier Team Leaders:* Previous experience with Children and leading a team successful candidates will be asked to apply for an Enhanced Disclosure. *Montage/Demontage:* Previous experience of physical and repetitive work successful applicants will be asked to apply for a Standard Disclosure.

Accommodation: Provided.

Application Procedure: Applicants should apply on-line at www.holidaybreakjobs.com/camping or telephone 01606 787 525 for an Application Pack.

Pavilion Tours

Job(s) Available: Watersports instructors.

Duration: Minimum period of work between May and October.

Working Hours: Hours of work variable, 7 days a week.

Head Office: 1 Jubilee Street, Brighton, East Sussex BN1 1GE, England
☎ 0870 241 0425
🖰 info@paviliontours.com

Pay: Approximately £100 per week.

Company Description: An expanding, specialist activity tour operator for students with bases in Greece and Spain. Watersports include: windsurfing, dinghy sailing, water skiing and canoeing.

Job Description: Watersports instructors required to instruct sailing/windsurfing and to assist with evening entertainment.

Requirements: The company are keen to recruit highly motivated staff.

Accommodation: Board and lodging included.

Application Procedure: Applications from November to the above address.

PGL Travel

Job(s) Available: Children's group leaders, children's activity instructors and general positions in catering, administration, driving (car or D1 towing), stores and site cleaning.

Duration: Vacancies available for the full season (February to October) or shorter periods between April and September.

Head Office: Alton Court, Penyard Lane, Ross-on-Wye, Herefordshire HR9 5GL, UK
☎ 0870 401 4411
🖰 recruitment@pgl.co.uk
🖳 www.pgl.co.uk/recruitment

Pay: From £78–£224 per week.

Company Description: The company has 27 activity centres located in the UK, France and Spain. PGL Travel provides adventure holidays and courses for children. Each year 2,500 people are needed to help run these adventure centres.

Job Description: *Children's group leaders*: required to take responsibility for groups, helping them to get the most out of their holiday.

Requirements: *Children's group leaders*: previous experience of working with children is essential. *Children's activity instructors*: qualified or personally competent in canoeing, sailing, windsurfing, or multi-activities.

Accommodation: Full board and lodging provided.

Application Procedure: Applications can be made online or a form obtained from the above address. Overseas applicants eligible to work in the UK welcome.

Siblu Holidays

Job(s) Available: Park representatives, children's club representatives, assistant park representatives.

Duration: The season runs between March and October, with varying contract dates. Limited high season positions are available.

Pay: Team members will receive a competitive salary.

Company Description: Siblu Holidays exclusively own holiday parks in France, and also operate on 12 fantastic parks in France, Spain and Italy.

Head Office: Recruitment Team, Bryanston Court, Selden Hill, Hemel Hempstead HP2 4TN, England
☎ 01442 293231
✆ recruitment@siblu.com
💻 www.siblu.com

Job Description: The following roles are offered in Spain for seasonal work: *Park representatives:* duties include cleaning and maintaining accommodation, welcoming new arrivals, reception duties, paperwork and administration. *Children's club representatives:* duties include creating and running a daytime entertainment programme for children between the ages of 5 and 12 years old, associated paperwork and assisting park representatives. *Assistant park representatives:* duties include cleaning and preparation of accommodation, welcoming new arrivals and reception duties.

Requirements: *Children's club representatives:* experience of working with children is desirable.

Accommodation: Accommodation, uniform, medical cover and travel costs to park included in pay.

Application Procedure: Please telephone the above number for a recruitment pack or visit the website to apply online.

Teaching and Language Schools

ABC English

Job(s) Available: Summer camp staff (20).

Duration: Required in July.

Company Description: ABC English organise summer English language camps in the Basque country. They are not a language academy.

Head Office: Calle Sol de Abajo 3, Antoñana, 01128 Alava, Spain
☎ +34 945 41045
✆ tulio@thefarmfun.com
💻 www.thefarmfun.com

Job Description: Summer camp staff to organise activities for Spanish children aged between 8–14.

Requirements: Applicants must be at least 18 years old and should have outdoor skills, a creative nature and complete proficiency in English.

Application Procedure: Applications, from EU citizens only, should be sent by post to Tulio Browning at the above address no later than 28 February.

English Educational Services

Job(s) Available: English teachers (80–110).
Duration: Standard length of contact is 9 months. Summer contracts available.
Working Hours: 5 hours per day. Teaching mainly in the evenings from 5pm onwards.
Pay: Salary depends on the client school the teacher is employed by.

> **Head Office:** c/ Alcalá 20-2, 28014 Madrid, Spain
> ☎ +34 91 5314783, +34 91 5329734
> ✉ movingparts@excit.com
>   richardinmadrid@gmail.com
> 🖥 www.eesmadrid.com

Company Description: Provides jobs in independent language schools in Spain.
Job Description: Positions available in various parts of the country including Madrid.
Requirements: English teachers with higher education and recognised EFL qualification such as CELTA or Trinity CertTESOL required by recruitment specialists for EFL in Spain. EU citizens are preferred.
Accommodation: Provision for accommodation depends on the client school the teacher is employed by. Most client schools will help their teachers find a place to live.
Additional Information: There is also an English-speaking theatre company operating from October to June, which has opportunities for candidates with a native speaker's standard of English.
Application Procedure: Applications with CV and 2 referees should be made to the above address. Interviews may be carried out in the UK and Ireland at peak times. Interviews also take place in Madrid throughout the academic year.

Voluntary Work

Festival Internacional De Benicassim

Job(s) Available: Volunteer stewards. Paid catering positions.
Duration: Minimum period of work 4 days in July.
Company Description: Europe's hottest summer music festival set by the beach, boasting some of the biggest names in indie and electronic music.

> **Head Office:** Benicassim, Valenica, Spain
> ✉ info@fiberfib.com
> 🖥 www.fiberfib.com

Job Description: Volunteers are required to fulfil a variety of roles. In return, volunteers receive entrance to the festival, insurance and meals during their shifts.
Application Procedure: Those interested in volunteering should fill in the online application form (available only in Spanish – click on *trabajo*) at any time after January. Catering positions are advertised 1 month before the festival begins.

VaughanTown

Job(s) Available: Native English-speaking volunteers.
Company Description: VaughanTown is the brainchild of an established English language school in Spain; Vaughan Systems. Founded by American Richard Vaughan in 1977, Vaughan Systems is the largest in-company language training firm in Spain,

> **Head Office:** Eduardo Dato, 3. Madrid 28010, Spain
> ☎ +34 91 5914880
> ✉ anglos@vaughantown.com
> 🖥 www.vaughantown.com

with over 300 teachers providing more than 350,000 hours of language training per year to over 5000 executives and technical personnel in more than 520 national and international companies.

Job Description: In VaughanTown, native English-speaking volunteers spend a free week at a 4-star hotel, near the Gredos mountain range, or in a restored 12th century monastery on the Camino de Santiago in the village of Carrion de los Condes. They spend time with a number of Spainards who have paid for the privilege of speaking English and interacting with them. During the week everyone will be involved in games and group dynamic exercises, amongst many other activities–all to help the Spanish participants practice their language skills.

Application Procedure: If you have the gift of the gab, check out the website where you will find all the necessary information and an application form.

Sunseed Desert Technology

Job(s) Available: Volunteers are required year round.

Duration: Short and longer-term contracts.

Cost: Volunteers make a weekly contribution of between £40 and £118 (depending on length of stay and hours worked).

Head Office: Apdo. 9, E-04270 Sorbas, Almeria, Spain
☎ +34 950 525770
✆ sunseedspain@arrakis.es
🖥 www.sunseed.org.uk

Company Description: Sunseed Desert Technology aims to develop, demonstrate and communicate accessible, low-tech methods of living sustainably in a semi-arid environment. It is a registered Spanish Association and a project of the registered UK charity The Sunseed Trust. Set in a beautiful rural location, there is an international community and delicious vegetarian food.

Job Description: Work includes helping with organic gardening, dryland management, appropriate technology, cooking (including solar cooking), construction, publicity and more. Longer-term volunteers can carry out their own projects in this field, which may be suitable for dissertation projects.

Application Procedure: See website or contact the project directly for further details.

Au Pairs, Nannies, Family Helps and Exchanges

ABB AU-Pair Family Service

Job(s) Available: Au pairs.

Duration: Placements are available all year, with a minimum stay of 2 months in the summer.

Working Hours: 25–30 hours per week, 5–6 days a week.

Head Office: Avendia Conde Sallent, 4, 1°C, E-07003 Palma de Mallorca, Spain
☎ +34 971 752027
✆ abbaupair@telefonica.net

Company Description: Friendly au pair agency with high quality services and carefully chosen host families.

Job Description: Au pairs required to help families look after children and carry out general housekeeping work.

Requirements: Applicants should have a mature outlook, be responsible and have a love of children. Applicants should speak either English or Spanish, English and French or English and German.

Application Procedure: Applications accepted all year, and should be sent to Clara Mangin at the above address. Remember to mention your telephone number.

Relaciones Culturales Internacionales

Job(s) Available: Au pairs, language assistants.
Duration: Usually 6–12 months. 1–3 month stays over the summer can be arranged.
Working Hours: *Au pairs:* 30 hours per week. *Language assistants:* 15 hours per week.
Pay: €65–€75 per week depending on location.

Head Office: Callez Ferraz no. 82, Madrid E-28008
☎ +34 91 5417103
spain@clubrci.es
www.clubrci.es

Company Description: Club de Relaciones Culturales Internacionales is a non-profit association with 26 years experience with Work and Study programmes in Spain.
Requirements: Non-smokers, 18–27 years old. *Language assistants:* must be native speakers of English, French or German and have studied at a higher education establishment.
Accommodation: Own room and full board provided.
Application Procedure: Application to the above address as soon as possible.

Other Work in Spain

Castrum Lenguas Culturas Y Turismo

Job(s) Available: Au pairs, hotel and restaurant staff, staff for theme parks and summer camps.
Duration: Minimum of 1 month.
Working Hours: Usually around 30 hours per week.
Pay: Depending on level of work.
Cost: From €300.

Head Office: Arda. Ramón Pradera no. 10-12 A, 47009, Valladolid
☎ +34 983 355343
info@castrum.es
www.castrum.org

Company Description: Castrum is a youth organisation operating language, business and cultural exchange programmes in France and Spain.
Requirements: Minimum age 18. Must be a citizen of an EU country. Intermediate level of Spanish.
Application Procedure: Further details of Spanish programmes can be obtained from Jesús G. Marciel, director of Castrum in Spain at the above address. Alternatively, email garcia.marciel@castrum.es or see the websites www.castrum.org; www.castrum.es.

Instituto Hemingway

Job(s) Available: Au pairs, internships, hospitality management staff.
Duration: Minimum period of work 3 months.
Working Hours: *Au pair:* 20 hours per week. *Internships and hospitality management staff:* full-time.

Head Office: Bailen 5, 2 Dcha, 48003 Bilbao
☎ +34 94 4167901
info@institutohemingway.com
www.institutohemingway.com

Pay: *Au pair:* pocket money. *Internships and hospitality management:* dependent on experience and job.
Company Description: Instituto Hemingway offers programmes that are designed for those who want to learn about other cultures whilst studying, travelling or working in Spain and other countries.
Requirements: Applicants should be aged 18–30.
Additional Information: Spanish lessons can be provided.
Application Procedure: Applications should be made via the above website.

EMBASSY OF SWEDEN
11 Montagu Place, London W1H 2AL
☎ 020 7917 6400
🖳 www.swedenabroad.com/london
🖐 ambassaden.london@foreign.ministry.se

Unlike its neighbour Norway, Sweden is a fully integrated EU member, and EU citizens are free to enter to look for and take up work through there are strict limits on the number of foreigners allowed to work in Sweden.

The Swedish Public Employment Service cannot help jobseekers from non-EU countries to find work in Sweden. General information and addresses of local employment offices may be obtained from *Arbetsmarknadsstyrelsen* at Vattugaten 17 45, S-113 99 Stockholm, Sweden (+46 8 58606000; arbetsmarknadsstyrelsen@ams.amv.se; www.amv.se; or in English at www. sweden. se). For further information consult the EURES website (www.europa.eu.int/eures). It is up to the individual to get in touch with employers.

The Scandinavian Institute in Malmö (Box 3085; +46 40 939440; info@scandinavianinst.com; www.scandinavianinst.com) makes au pair placements with Swedish families and throughout Scandinavia. There are also opportunities for voluntary work in Sweden arranged by International Voluntary Service for British people, and Service Civil International for Americans. See the *Worldwide* chapter for details.

Advertisements in Swedish newspapers may be placed through Crane Media Partners Ltd, 20-28 Dalling Road, Hammersmith, London W6 0JB (020 8237 860; www.cranemedia.co.uk), who handle *Dagens Nyheter*, *Goteborgs Posten* and *Sydsvenska Dagbladet*.

Red Tape

Visa Requirements: a visa is no longer required by many countries including all EU countries. Nationals of these countries are allowed to visit Sweden for up to 3 months. Visa information is available from the embassy website.

Residence Permits: Required if you are to live and work in Sweden for more than 3 months. EU citizens can apply for residence permits from within Sweden by contacting the Swedish Migration Board (Migrationsverket; 60170 Norrköping; +46 11 156000; migrationsverket@migrationsverket.se; www.migrationsverket.se) and completing the application forms. Applicants should note that the procedure of obtaining a Residence Permit can take between 2 and 5 months but that EU citizens are given preference over those from outside the EU.

Non-Europeans must submit to their local Swedish Embassy a written confirmation of work on form AMS PF 101704, at least 2 months before their proposed arrival. The procedure involves an interview at the Embassy. Immigration queries should be addressed to the Swedish Migration Board (see above for details). Full details are posted in English on their web pages or you can request printed leaflets.

Work Permits: Citizens of EU countries do not need work permits in order to work in Sweden. For others a work permit requires that an offer of employment has been obtained. Application forms for the necessary permit should then be obtained from your nearest Swedish Embassy. The application will be processed by the Swedish Migration Board and the procedure can take 1–3 months. Applications for work permits are not accepted from foreign visitors who are already in Sweden.

Teaching and Language Schools

The British Institute

Job(s) Available: English teachers.
Job Description: Teachers to work on a freelance basis at a school in Stockholm.
Requirements: Native English speakers. Applicants must have CELTA or DELTA qualifications.
Application Procedure: Email a CV to the above address.

> **Head Office:** Hagagatan 3, 11348 Stockholm Sweden
> ☎ +46 854 545 370
> ✆ corporate@britishinstitute.se
> 🖥 www.britishinstitute.se

Voluntary Work

Hultsfred Festival

Job(s) Available: Volunteers, stewards etc (5000).
Duration: 3 days in June. Minimum period of work 3 days.
Pay: No wages are paid but volunteers receive free entry to festival.

> **Head Office:** Hultsfred, Box 170 577 24, Hultsfred Sweden
> ☎ +46 495 69500
> ✆ info@rockparty.se
> 🖥 www.rockparty.se

Company Description: Hultsfred first started in 1986 and is one of the biggest and longest running youth-oriented music festivals within Scandinavia. It contains 7 stages and is located in a picturesque forest glade.
Job Description: Rockparty, a non-profit organisation, takes on 5000 volunteers a year, with around 4750 working only during the festival.
Accommodation: Volunteers receive a free ticket to the festival, as well as camping, uniform and free meals.
Application Procedure: Volunteers apply all year round but all volunteer places are allocated by February. Volunteers should send a CV and covering letter indicating their interest by January. Apply by email.

SWITZERLAND

EMBASSY OF SWITZERLAND
16/18 Montagu Place, London W1H 2BQ
☎ 020 7616 6000
🖥 www.swissembassy.org.uk
✆ lon.vertretung@eda.admin.ch

Switzerland has managed to maintain one of the lowest unemployment rates in the world at 3.8% in 2006 and to preserve that state it has traditionally imposed strict work permit requirements on all foreigners who want to work there. It is significant that unlike most of the other non-EU members of Western Europe, Switzerland did not join the EEA a few years ago, although there are long-term plans for it to do so. However, a bilateral treaty on free movement of persons was concluded with the EU and the main obstacles to free movement of labour were removed in 2004. In the same year the seasonal worker category of permit was abolished. As a result, EU job-seekers are able to enter Switzerland to look for work for up to three months. Permits are extendable for a potential period of up to five years, depending on the contract. Information on this can be found on-line at www.europa.admin.ch and www.auslaender.ch.

Switzerland has always needed extra seasonal workers at certain times of the year. The tourist industry in particular needs staff for both the summer and winter seasons (July to September and December to April). Jobs in the tourist industry are described both in this chapter and the *Worldwide* chapter. Students looking for hotel work should note the entry below for the Schweizer Hotelier-Suisse (Swiss Hotels' Association). Hotel work can be hard going: in the past some workers have found they have been expected to work longer hours than originally promised without any compensation in the form of overtime payments or extra time off, or be asked to do jobs other than those specified in their contracts. In return, however, wages should be higher than average for hotel work in the rest of Europe.

Farmers also need extra help at certain times of the year: see the entry below for the Landdienst-Zentralstelle, which can arrange working stays on Swiss farms. Opportunities in the short but lucrative grape harvest (particularly in the Lausanne area) are also worth seeking out although this takes place usually in October rather than summer. Some knowledge of German or French is normally needed, even for grape-picking. Italian is also spoken, particularly in the canton of Ticino.

Switzerland is also covered by the EURES programme (www.europa.eu.int/eures), and further information on job seeking and living and working in Switzerland can be found on their website. There are opportunities for voluntary work in Switzerland with the organisations named at the end of this chapter. British applicants can also apply through Concordia and International Voluntary Service, and Americans through Service Civil International; see the *Worldwide* chapter for details.

Placing an advertisement in a Swiss paper may lead to the offer of a job. *Tribune de Geneve* is published at 11 rue des Rois, CH-1211 Geneva (www.tdg.ch).

Red Tape

Visa Requirements: citizens of the UK, the US, Canada, Australia, New Zealand and most other European countries do not normally require visas for tourism. Nationals of most other countries need a visa.

Residence/Work Permits: For non-EU citizens the situation is now trickier as employers in Switzerland have to deal with sponsorship paperwork and must try harder to prove to the authorities that they need to employ a foreigner from outside Europe. An L permit has to be applied for by the employer in Switzerland and has to be issued in advance to the employee by the Swiss embassy in the employee's own country.

The L permits cover both the right of abode and employment. These are required for all persons entering to take up employment and entitle the holder to live in a specific canton and work for a specified employer. They also entitle the worker to join the state insurance scheme and enjoy the services of the legal tribunal for foreign workers, should they require an arbitrator in a dispute with their employer. Accident insurance is compulsory and is usually paid by the employer. This does not obviate the need of the temporary foreign employee to take out their own health insurance policy. Perks of having a Swiss L permit include discounts on public transport and discounted lift passes in mountain resorts. A work permit is required for volunteer work.

Agricultural Work

Landdienst-Zentralstelle

Job(s) Available: Farmers' assistants.
Duration: Minimum period of work 3 weeks between the spring and autumn; maximum period is 2 months.
Working Hours: 8 hours per day, 6 days a week.
Pay: £200 per month.

Head Office: Postfach 2050, CH-8401 Winterhur Switzerland
☎ +41 52 2640030
✆ admin@landdienst.ch
💻 www.landdienst.ch

Company Description: Landdienst is a non-profit making, publicly subsidised organisation which each year places around 3,000 Swiss and 500 foreign farmers' assistants.
Job Description: Farmers' assistants to work on family farms.
Requirements: Knowledge of German and/or French essential. Individual applicants should be aged 18–25. Individual applicants must be nationals of a country in western Europe and must pay a registration fee.
Accommodation: Free board and lodging.
Application Procedure: Applications are invited at least 4 weeks prior to desired starting date.

Hotel Work and Catering

Chalet-Hotel Adler

Job(s) Available: Barmaids, chambermaids, waitresses.
Duration: Minimum period of work 2.5 months from May/June to September/October.
Working Hours: 8.5 hours per day, 5 days a week.
Pay: Net salary approximately £790 per month.

Head Office: Fam. A & E Fetzer, CH-3718 Kandersteg Switzerland
☎ +41 33 6758010
✆ info@chalethotel.ch
💻 www.chalethotel.ch

Company Description: This hotel is set in the mountains of Switzerland, with rail access allowing excursions across the country.
Requirements: Knowledge of German required.
Accommodation: Provided.
Application Procedure: By post with a photo, from April to the above address.

Grand Hotel Bellevue

Job(s) Available: Waiting Assistants.
Duration: Period of work by arrangement between Christmas/New Year and July/August.
Working Hours: 42 hours per week.
Pay: Approximately £900 per month.

Head Office: 3789 Gstaad Switzerland
☎ + 41 33 7480000
✆ info@Bellevue-gstaad.ch
💻 www.bellevue-gstaad.ch

Requirements: Applicants should speak German, English and French.
Accommodation: Board and lodging available for around £285 per month.
Application Procedure: Applications to Mr Ferdinand D Salverda, general manager, at the above address.

WESTERN EUROPE

SWITZERLAND

Hotel Forni

Job(s) Available: Kitchen staff and waitresses.
Working Hours: 9 hours per day, 5 days a week.
Pay: Approximately £1,100 per month.
Job Description: To serve in the bar and restaurant.
Requirements: Must be presentable.
Accommodation: Board and accommodation available for £340 per month.
Application Procedure: Applications to the above address.

> **Head Office:** Marzio Forni, CH-6780 Airolo Switzerland
> ☎ +41 91 8691270
> ✆ info@forni.ch

Hotel Hirschen

Job(s) Available: Counter assistants/waiting staff (1–2).
Duration: Minimum period of work 3 months between June and October.
Working Hours: 9–9.5 hours per day, 5 days a week.
Pay: Approximately £1,100 per month.
Job Description: Required to serve hotel guests at mealtimes, present buffets, wash glasses, prepare coffee etc.
Requirements: Knowledge of German and previous experience of hotel work essential.
Accommodation: Board and lodging provided.
Application Procedure: Applications to S Walt at the above address from February.

> **Head Office:** Passhöhe, CH-9658 Wildhaus Switzerland
> ✆ info@hirschen-wildhaus.ch
> 💻 www.hirschen-wildhaus.ch

Jobs in the Alps (Employment Agency)

Job(s) Available: Waiting staff, porters, kitchen porters and housekeepers (150 in the winter, 50 in summer).
Duration: Periods of work: June to mid-September (minimum period 3 months including July and August), or December to April.
Working Hours: 5-day week.
Pay: £500 per month
Job Description: Staff for Swiss and French hotels, cafes and restaurants at mountain resorts.
Requirements: Good French and/or German required for most positions. Experience is not essential, but a good attitude to work and sense of fun are definite requirements.
Accommodation: Free board and accommodation.
Application Procedure: Applications should be sent to the above address by 30 April for Summer and 30 September for Winter.

> **Head Office:** Seasonal Recruitment Ltd, 3 Bracken Terrace, Newquay TR7 2LS, UK
> ✆ info@jobs-in-the-alps.co.uk
> 💻 www.jobs-in-the-alps.co.uk

Hotel Meisser

Job(s) Available: Service workers (1–2), general workers (1–2), kitchen staff.
Duration: Minimum period of work 3 months. June to October.
Working Hours: 9 hours per day, 5 days a week.

> **Head Office:** CH-7545 Guarda Switzerland
> ☎ +41 81 8622132
> ✆ banno@hotel-meisser.ch
> 💻 www.hotel-meisser.ch

Pay: CHF2075 per month.

Company Description: A medium-sized hotel, 2.5 hours from Zurich, led by a young dynamic team.

Requirements: Should have relevant experience. Ability to speak German and English is important; knowledge of French or Italian would also be useful.

Accommodation: Board and accommodation are available, the cost of which to be deducted from wages.

Application Procedure: Applications of CV and colour photo are invited to Benno Meisser by email from January onwards.

Hotel Postillon

Job(s) Available: Waiting staff.

Working Hours: 41 hours, 5 days a week.

Pay: Approximately £940 per month.

Job Description: Waiting staff to work in a busy restaurant on a motorway.

Head Office: CH-6374 Buochs Switzerland
☎ +41 41 6205454
✆ info@postillon.ch
🖳 www.postillon.ch

Requirements: Knowledge of German and English is necessary.

Accommodation: Board and accommodation available for approximately £125 per month.

Application Procedure: Applications to the above address.

Residence and Bernerhof Hotels

Job(s) Available: Waiters/waitresses, buffet assistants, laundry maids, general assistants.

Duration: Period of work from December to April, and from June to October.

Working Hours: 9 hours per day, 5 days a week.

Pay: Monthly salary.

Head Office: CH-3823 Wengen Switzerland
☎ +41 33 8552721
✆ bernerhof@wengen.com
🖳 www.bernerhof.wengen.net

Company Description: 2 hotel restaurants; à-la-carte, and pizzeria. Guests almost always are English, German, American, or Swiss. Located in the centre of Wengen.

Requirements: Knowledge of German required; knowledge of French an advantage.

Accommodation: Accommodation for 30 days. Meals: lunch/dinner (no breakfast) for 22 days.

Application Procedure: By post to Miss Lidice Schweizer at the above address.

Hotel Rigiblick Am See

Job(s) Available: Trainee assistant (waiter/waitress), trainee chef.

Duration: Period of work May/June-August/September.

Working Hours: 44 hours, 5 days a week.

Pay: Approximately €1800 per month.

Head Office: Seeplatz 3, CH-6374 Buochs Switzerland
☎ +41 41 6244850
✆ info@rigiblickamsee.ch
🖳 www.rigiblickamsee.ch

Company Description: A 4-star hotel and restaurant on the lakeside.

Requirements: Applicants must hold an EU passport and have a very good knowledge of German.

Accommodation: Board and accommodation provided for €600 per month.

Application Procedure: Applications as early as possible to the above address.

Romantik Hotel Säntis

Job(s) Available: Waiter/waitress.
Duration: Minimum period of work is 4 months between June and October.
Working Hours: 9 hours per day, 5 days a week.
Pay: Approximately €3300 per month.
Company Description: A traditional family-run 4-star hotel in one of the most beautiful areas of Switzerland; Appenzell is in the German-speaking region. The staff are mostly young people of various nationalities.
Requirements: Applicants must have experience and speak German. Temporary residence permits are only available for EU/EFTA nationals.
Accommodation: Board and accommodation available for €400 per month.
Application Procedure: Applications to Stefan A Heeb at the above address.

Head Office: CH-9050 Appenzell Switzerland
☎ +41 71 7881111
info@saentis-appenzell.ch
www.saentis-appenzell.ch

Romantik Hotel Schweizerhof

Job(s) Available: Chambermaids, maintenance assistants, assistant cooks, laundry assistants.
Duration: 3 months.
Working Hours: 42 hours, 5 days a week.
Pay: CHF2920 minimum practicum wage.
Company Description: The Schweizerhof, a truly traditional hotel in Grindelwald, is a world famous holiday and winter sports centre located at the foot of the Eiger in the Bernese Oberland.
Job Description: *Chambermaids:* to clean rooms and do laundry. *Maintenance assistants:* to carry out general maintenance tasks on the house and in the garden. *Assistant cooks:* to assist in the kitchen with preparation and washing-up.
Requirements: Knowledge of German is required.
Accommodation: Board and accommodation is available at a pre-arranged cost.
Application Procedure: Applications to the above address between January and March.

Head Office: CH-3818 Grindelwald Switzerland
☎ +41 33 8545858
info@hotel-schweizerhof.com
www.hotel-schweizerhof.com

Schweizer Hotelier-Suisse

Job(s) Available: General assistants.
Duration: Minimum period of work 3 months.
Pay: Minimum CHF3182 per month.
Company Description: The 'Swiss Hotel Association' has around 2500 hotels and restaurants as members.
Job Description: General assistants from EU countries to work in hotels in German-speaking Switzerland. Duties include helping with cooking, service and cleaning.
Requirements: EU citizens with good knowledge of German essential.
Accommodation: Board and accommodation available at a cost of approximately CHF900 per month.
Additional Information: Please note that jobs in the French and Italian speaking parts of Switzerland cannot be arranged.
Application Procedure: Applications to the above address.

Head Office: Monbijoustrasse 130, Postfach, CH-3001 Bern Switzerland
☎ +41 31 3704111
hoteljob.be@hotelleriesuisse.ch
www.hoteljob.ch

Hotel Sonne

Job(s) Available: Waiters/waitresses (3), buffet staff (2).

Duration: Minimum period of work 10 weeks. Winter season: December to March and Summer season: July to October.

Working Hours: 8.5 hours per day, 5 days a week.

Pay: *Waiters/waitresses:* £700 net, per month. *Buffet staff:* £600 net, per month.

Requirements: Good knowledge of German required.

Accommodation: Board and accommodation is available at £216 per month.

Application Procedure: Applications as soon as possible to the proprietor, Paul Beutler, at the above address.

Head Office: CH-9658 Wildhaus Switzerland
☎ +41 71 9992333
✆ beutler-hotels@bluewin.ch
🖳 www.beutler.hotels.ch

Hotel Waldhaus

Job(s) Available: General assistants (2).

Duration: Minimum period of work is 3–4 months in the summer or winter seasons.

Working Hours: 8–9 hours per day, 5 days a week.

Pay: £715–£858 per month.

Head Office: CH-7514 Sils-Maria, Engadin Switzerland
☎ +41 81 8385100
✆ staff@waldhaus-sils.ch
🖳 www.waldhaus-sils.ch

Company Description: A 5-star family hotel with guests from all over the world. 70% of guests are regulars.

Job Description: *General assistants:* to play an extensive role in service for the guest-rooms, lounge and terraces, and to see to the welfare of 220 guests as well as taking responsibility for their meals, under the direction of a superior.

Requirements: Must have knowledge of German, and the ability to take pleasure in working for guests.

Accommodation: Food and accommodation are available: a double-room costs about £70 per person per month.

Application Procedure: Applications are invited up until mid-March for the summer season, or mid-August for the winter. They should be sent to Irene Ryser, personnel manager, at the above address.

Sports, Couriers and Camping

Canvas Holidays

Job(s) Available: Campsite courier.

Duration: Full season positions start in March, April or May and end in September/October. High season staff needed to work at least 2 months during the peak season.

Pay: Package includes competitive salary, tent accommodation, medical insurance, uniform and return travel from a UK port of entry.

Head Office: GVN Camping Recruitment, East Port House, Dunfermline KY12 7JG, Scotland
☎ 01383 629012
✆ campingrecruitment@ gvnrecruitment.com
🖳 www.gvnrecruitment.com

Company Description: Canvas Holidays provide luxury mobile home and tent holidays at over 100 campsites throughout Europe.

Job Description: Involves cleaning accommodation, welcoming families to the site and showing them to their accommodation. Visiting customers, providing local information and basic maintenance are very important parts of the job. Campsite courier opportunities are also available for couples to work on site together.

Accommodation: Provided as part of package.

Additional Information: For details of management positions, see website.

Application Procedure: Please call the Recruitment Department for more information and an application form, or apply online at www.gvnrecruitment.com.

Eurocamp

Job(s) Available: Campsite courier, children's courier, courier team leaders, children's courier team leaders, montage/demontage.

Head Office: Overseas Recruitment Department (Ref SJ/08) Hartford Manor, Greenbank Lane, Northwich CW8 1HW, UK
☎ 01606 787525
💻 www.holidaybreakjobs.com/camping

Duration: *Campsite courier:* Applicants should be available to work from April/May to mid-September or June/July to mid-September. *Children's courier:* Applicants should be available from early May to September or June to September. *Courier team leaders:* Applicants should be available from April to mid-September. *Children's courier team leaders:* Applicants should be available from early May until September. *Montage/Demontage:* Applicants should be available from Feb to May or August to October.

Pay: You will receive a competitive salary, comprehensive training, return travel to and from an agreed meeting point, accommodation, medical and luggage insurance and uniform.

Company Description: Eurocamp is a leading tour operator in self-drive camping and mobile home holidays in Europe. We offer our customers a wide range of holiday accommodation on over 200 premier campsites. Each year the company seeks to recruit up to 1,500 enthusiastic people to work the summer season in a variety of roles.

Job Description: *Campsite courier:* A Courier's responsibility begins by ensuring that the customer's accommodation is both inviting and cleaned to the highest of standards. You will welcome new arrivals, be the customers main point of contact and will be expected to provide local and general information, give assistance and even act as interpreter if required. Part of the role will involve helping out with minor repairs to accommodation and equipment and will also involve basic administration and accounts. *Children's courier:* You will be responsible for planning and delivering a fun, safe, daily activity programme to our customers' children. The age of the children attending the club will range from 5 to 12 years old although we also run a toddler service in low season for 12 months to 4 years. *Courier team leaders:* You must be able to deliver first class customer service and organize the daily workload of the courier team. Your role also includes all the duties of a Campsite Courier and you will be expected to lead by example. There are a variety of team leader roles available, dependant on team size; Courier in Charge, Senior Courier and Site Manager. *Children's courier team leaders:* Your role will involve the management, motivation and development of the Children's couriers to ensure they provide a varied range of quality activities. Your role includes all the duties of a Children's courier. *Montage/Demontage:* Montage and Demontage assistants are employed to either help set up for the season or close down at the end of the season. This involves putting up or taking down tents, moving/distributing equipment and cleaning/preparing accommodation.

Requirements: Applicants must hold a UK/EU passport and the current minimum age is 18 years old on the day you start work in order to obtain the relevant insurance cover. *Campsite couriers:* You should have lots of energy, basic common sense and a genuine desire to help people. *Children's courier:* Previous childcare experience is essential. Successful candidates will be asked to apply for an Enhanced Disclosure. *Courier team leaders:* You must have previous experience of leading a team successful applicants may be asked to apply for a Standard Disclosure. *Children's courier team leaders:* Previous experience with Children and leading a team successful candidates will be asked to apply for an Enhanced Disclosure. *Montage/Demontage:* Previous experience of physical and repetitive work successful applicants will be asked to apply for a Standard Disclosure.

Accommodation: Provided.

Application Procedure: Applicants should apply on-line at www.holidaybreakjobs.com/ camping or telephone 01606 787 525 for an Application Pack.

Venture Abroad

Job(s) Available: Resort representatives (2–3).
Duration: 5 weeks minimum from June to August.
Working Hours: Flexible hours, 6 days a week.
Company Description: Venture Abroad organise package holidays for scout and guide groups to the continent. They arrange travel and accommodation and provide representatives in the resort.

Head Office: Rayburn House, Parcel Terrace, Derby DE1 1LY, UK
☎ 01332 342050
📧 joannek@rayburntours.co.uk
🖥 www.ventureabroad.co.uk

Job Description: Resort representatives to work in Belgium and Switzerland; checking in groups, dealing with accommodation enquiries, organising and accompanying local excursions etc.

Requirements: Applicants should be practical, resourceful and calm under pressure. Knowledge of German is an advantage.

Application Procedure: Applications to the above address.

Teaching and Language Schools

The Haut Lac International Centre

Job(s) Available: Language teachers: French (4), English (4), German (1), sports activity monitors (6), maintenance person, house staff.
Duration: Mid-June until the end of August, with a minimum requirement of 4 weeks work.
Working Hours: 45–54 hours, per 5–6 day week.

Head Office: CH-1669 Les Sciernes Switzerland
☎ +41 26 9284200
📧 stevie@haut-lac.ch
🖥 www.haut-lac.com

Language teachers: to take 4, 40-minute classes (Monday, Tuesday, Thursday, Friday) and one 40 min. study per day, supervise one test per week and have 1.5 days off per week. *Sports activity monitors:* 1 day off per week.

Pay: All positions are from £120 per week according to qualifications and experience.

Company Description: The Haut Lac Centre is a family-run business organising language and activity courses for an international clientele. The high client return rate is due to the Centre's work and play philosophy.

Job Description: *Sports activity monitors:* to organise and run a wide variety of sports and excursions. *Maintenance person:* to carry out garden upkeep, decorating tasks and repair work. *House staff:* for reception, cleaning, dishwashing or kitchen work.

Requirements: Applicants should speak English, French or German. *Language teachers:* candidates should have a degree and a TEFL qualification or equivalent, or be studying for a language or teaching degree. *Sports activity monitors:* a second language is preferable as are coaching qualifications or camping experience. *Maintenance person:* should have previous experience.

Accommodation: Board and accommodation are included, as is laundry.

Application Procedure: Applications are invited at any time to the above address.

Voluntary Work

Gruppo Voluntari Dalla Svizzera Italiana _____

Job(s) Available: Volunteers (15 per camp).
Duration: Minimum period of work 1 week between June and September.
Working Hours: 4 hours work per day.
Company Description: The Group of Volunteers of Italian Switzerland (GVSI) is an association of adults

Head Office: GVSI-CP. 12-6517 Arbedo Switzerland
☎ +41 91 8574520
📧 fmari@vtx.ch
🖥 www.gvsi.org

and youngsters, coming from Italian Switzerland. This organisation is open to all persons from other countries who believe it is useful to carry out community work such as volunteering in emergency situations.
Job Description: Volunteers take part in work camps in Maggia, Fusio and Borgogne carrying out tasks such as helping mountain communities, cutting wood, help the aged, in the orchards, etc.
Requirements: Applicants should speak Italian, German or French. The minimum age is 18. Volunteers must be able to present valid documents and a residence permit.
Accommodation: Board and accommodation available.
Application Procedure: Applications to the above address.

Internationale Begegnung in Gemeinschaftsdiensten Ev _____

Job(s) Available: Volunteers to attend international youth workcamps in Switzerland.
Cost: There is a registration fee of approximately £55.
Job Description: Typical projects might include restoring an old castle, environmental protection,

Head Office: Schlosserstrasse 28, D-70180 Stuttgart 1, Germany
☎ +49 711 6491128
📧 info@ibg-workcamps.org
🖥 www.ibg-workcamps.org

children's play schemes and media projects. Each workcamp consists of a group of about 15 people aged 18–30 from all over the world living and working together for the public benefit.
Accommodation: Food and accommodation are provided free on the camps.
Application Procedure: Applications to the above address. The annual programme is published in March. British volunteers should apply through Concordia or another UK organisation.

Mountain Forest Project: Stiftung Bergwaldprojekt _____

Job(s) Available: Volunteers (15–20 places per week)
Duration: Camps run from April to October. Volunteers may stay for 1 week per year.
Pay: Unpaid.
Company Description: An organisation of work-

Head Office: Hauptstrasse 24, CH-7014 Trin Switzerland
☎ +41 81 6304145
📧 info@bergwaldprojekt.ch
🖥 www.bergwaldprojekt.ch

camps for volunteers aged 18–80, working in the mountain forests of Switzerland, Austria and Germany.
Job Description: Places available in over 60 camps per year. Work involves reforestation and forest maintenance, building footpaths for access and fences.
Requirements: No experience is necessary. Volunteers should have a basic knowledge of German.

Accommodation: Free board and lodging is provided.

Application Procedure: Programme details will be available from January and applications will be accepted from then onwards. Apply online if possible.

Au Pairs, Nannies, Family Helps and Exchanges

Pro Filia

Job(s) Available: Au pairs.
Duration: 12–18 months.
Working Hours: 30 hours per week.
Pay: Weekly pocket money.
Job Description: Au pairs can be placed with families in the regions of Switzerland.

Head Office: 16 Beckenhofstr., Postfach, 8035 Zürich
☎ +41 44 361 5331
info@profilia.ch
www.profilia.ch

Requirements: Intermediate level of French or German (depending on region).
Accommodation: Full board provided.
Additional Information: Language lessons provided (French and German).
Application Procedure: Application forms available online from www.profilia.ch/aupairstellen.php

Perfect Way

Job(s) Available: Au pairs, nannies, domestic help.
Duration: Available for at least 6 months.
Pay: CHF800 per month approximately, plus other perks.

Head Office: Hafnerweg 10, 5200 Brugg
info@perfectway.ch
perfectway@bluewin.ch
www.perfectway.ch

Company Description: Au pair, domestic help and nanny agency that offers placements in Swiss, American and other international families in Switzerland.
Requirements: Applicants should be aged 18–29 *(au pair)* or 18+ *(nanny and domestic help)*. Good manners, common sense and references required.
Application Procedure: For further details contact the above address.

CENTRAL AND EASTERN EUROPE

CROATIA

EMBASSY OF THE REPUBLIC OF CROATIA
21 Conway Street, London W1T 6BN
☎ 020 7387 2022
🖱 consular-dept@croatianembassy.co.uk

The chances of finding paid summer work in Croatia are not very good although its tourist industry is burgeoning.

Sports, Couriers and Camping

Canvas Holidays

Job(s) Available: Campsite courier.
Duration: Full season positions start in March, April or May and end in September/October. High season staff needed to work at least 2 months during the peak season.
Pay: Package includes competitive salary, tent accommodation, medical insurance, uniform and return travel from a UK port of entry.
Company Description: Canvas Holidays provide luxury mobile home and tent holidays at over 100 campsites throughout Europe.
Job Description: Involves cleaning accommodation, welcoming families to the site and showing them to their accommodation. Visiting customers, providing local information and basic maintenance are very important parts of the job. Campsite courier opportunities are also available for couples to work on site together.
Accommodation: Provided as part of package.
Additional Information: For details of management positions, see website.
Application Procedure: Please call the Recruitment Department for more information and an application form, or apply online at www.gvnrecruitment.com.

> **Head Office:** GVN Camping Recruitment, East Port House, Dunfermline KY12 7JG, Scotland
> ☎ 01383 629012
> 🖱 campingrecruitment@gvnrecruitment.com
> 💻 www.gvnrecruitment.com

Work at Sea

Setsail Holidays

Job(s) Available: Skippers, hostesses and engineers.
Duration: Starts April/May to end September/October.
Pay: £120–£160 per week depending on job and experience.

> **Head Office:** 40 Burkitts Lane, Sudbury, Suffolk CO10 2HB, England
> ☎ 01787 310445
> 🖱 boats@setsail.co.uk
> 💻 www.setsail.co.uk

CENTRAL & EASTERN EUROPE
CROATIA

314

Company Description: Setsail Holidays are a specialist tour operator providing flotilla sailing and bareboat charter holidays to Greece, Turkey and Croatia.

Job Description: Skippers, hostesses and engineers required to coordinate and run the flotilla sailing holidays which can consist of up to 12 yachts.

Requirements: Must have sailing experience and/or qualifications and the ability to work well with people.

Accommodation: Accommodation is provided on the 'lead yacht'.

Application Procedure: Applications to John Hortop at the above address by fax or email. Applications must include a CV and recent picture.

Voluntary Work

Research-Educational Centre for the Protection of Nature

Job(s) Available: Conservation volunteers.

Duration: To work a minimum of 1 week between 15 January and 15 December.

Cost: Volunteers have to pay a volunteer fee, travel expenses to and from Croatia and food expenses.

Job Description: Conservation Volunteers to help with a variety of projects including the conservation of the Eurasian griffon vulture; cleaning and feeding griffons in the bird sanctuary, repairing dry stone walls, saving small ponds, interpretation centre, picking olives and helping local shepherds.

Head Office: Beli 4, 51559 Beli, Island of Cres Croatia
☎ +385 51 840525
✆ caput.insulae@ri.t-com.hr
🖳 www.caput-insulae.com
www.supovi.hr

Requirements: Applicants should be healthy, able to swim and speak English. Minimum age 18.

Accommodation: Provided.

Application Procedure: Apply to the address above.

THE CZECH REPUBLIC

EMBASSY OF THE CZECH REPUBLIC
26 Kensington Palace Gardens, London W8 4QY
☎ 020 7243 1115
🖳 www.mzv.cz/london
✆ london@embassy.mzv.cz

The Czech Republic is covered by the EURES programme (www.europa.eu.int/eures), and further information on job seeking and living and working in there can be found on their website.

The chances of finding paid summer work in the Czech Republic is low with the possible exception of TEFL. Voluntary work can be arranged for British people by International Voluntary Service, UNA Exchange, Youth Action For Peace and Concordia; Americans can be placed there by the CIEE and also Service Civil International (see the *Worldwide* chapter for details).

Red Tape

Visa Requirements: the Czech Republic became a member of the EU on 1 May 2004. EU Citizens are entitled to stay in the Czech republic on a temporary or permanent basis without any permit, irrespective of the purpose of the stay. For Non-EU Citizens a Visa must be obtained. Those unsure about whether they require a visa should check with their nearest Czech consulate. When applying for a visa, applicants must be able to present a passport valid for at least 15 months (or 9 months for a short-term stay) from the date of issue of the visa, 2 passport-sized photographs, a document proving the purpose of the stay (eg a work permit or a Long Term Residence visa), confirmation of available accommodation, proof of health insurance and proof that they have sufficient funds to cover their living expenses in the country.

Residence Permits: Permits are not required for EU citizens planning to stay for less than 3 months, however they are required to register with the Alien and Border Police within 30 days of arrival. If an EU citizen intends to stay longer than 3 months, they are entitled (but not obliged) to apply to the Alien and Border Police for a residence permit. Applicants will require: an application form completed and signed by the applicant, valid passport, 2 recent passport photographs and a document proving the applicant's compliance with the PRP. Full details are available from the Czech Embassy in your country. Any non-EU citizen who intends to work or for any other reason stay in the Czech Republic for longer than 3 months must obtain the permit in advance. Necessary documents include a work permit issued by the employer, proof of accommodation, etc all presented in the original or a notarised copy.

Work Permits: Must be obtained by your future employer from the local employment office *(Urad práce)*. They will need a signed form from you plus a photocopy of your passport and the originals or notarised copies of your education certificates. Work Permits will only be granted where the employer can prove that they cannot find a suitable Czech candidate to carry out the job. All of this takes at least 3 months.

Teaching and Language Schools

Caledonian School

Job(s) Available: Teachers (250).
Job Description: Teachers with TEFL background to teach English in a large Prague language institute.

Head Office: Vltavská 24, 15000, Prague 5 Czech Republic
☎ +420 257 313 650
✆ jobs@caledonianschool.com
🖳 www.caledonianschool.com

HUNGARY

EMBASSY OF THE REPUBLIC OF HUNGARY
35 Eaton Place, London SW1X 8BY
☎ 020 7201 3440
✆ office@huemblon.org.uk
🖳 www.mfa.gov.hu/emb/london

In addition to the opportunity listed below there are also opportunities for voluntary work arranged by Youth Action for Peace, International Voluntary Service and UNA Exchange for UK nationals, and for US nationals through the CIEE and Service Civil International: see the *Worldwide* chapter for details. Although the residence procedure for some foreigners has been much simplified, there is a considerable downside to working full-time in Hungary as EU nationals are subject to the same social security and pension deductions as Hungarians, namely 12.5% of wages. Employers' contributions total nearly 30%. This means employers are handing out fewer long-term contracts, which may increase the opportunities for summer teaching jobs and freelance work.

Hungary is also covered by the EURES programme (www.europa.eu.int/eures), and further information on job seeking, living and working there can be found on their website.

Red Tape

Visa Requirements: Hungary joined the EU on 1 May 2004. Citizens of the EU along with nationals of the USA, Australia, New Zealand, Norway and Canada do not require a visa to enter Hungary. Nationals of non-EU countries not listed above may need a visa.

Work Permits: Non-EU citizens must arrange work permits before leaving their own country. Nationals of some EU countries including Holland will still be required to have a work and residence permit until the end of the transitional period. UK citizens need only register their address and employment details. Further details are available from the Hungarian Ministry of Foreign Affairs (www.mfa.gov.hu).

Teaching and Language Schools

Central European Teaching Programme/CETP

Duration: Contracts are for 5 or 10 months.
Pay: Approximately $500 per month.
Company Description: CETP has a large presence in Hungary.
Requirements: Applicants must be university graduates, and have either a teaching certificate or a TEFL certificate (it may be earned online).

Head Office: NE 72nd Ave., Portland, OR 97213, USA
☎ +1 503 2874977
✆ mary@cetp.info
💻 www.cetp.info

POLAND

EMBASSY OF THE REPUBLIC OF POLAND
47 Portland Place, London W1B 1JH
☎ 087 0774 2700
💻 www.polishembassy.org.uk
✆ polishembassy@polishembassy.org.uk

Poland's unemployment rate has gone down slightly since it joined the EU, but that does not prevent it from having the highest unemployment in the EU (18%). While Polish professionals and the under-24s are leaving Poland to work in the richer EU countries, including Ireland and Britain, TEFL teachers can find relatively abundant employment and reasonable working conditions in

Poland. Teaching work in Poland can be found with the organisations listed below. Poland is also covered by the EURES programme (www.europa.eu.int/eures), and further information on job seeking, living and working there can be found on their website. In addition, voluntary work in Poland can by arranged through Youth Action for Peace, UNA Exchange and International Voluntary Service for British people, and the CIEE and Service Civil International for Americans (see the *Worldwide* chapter for details).

Red Tape

Visa Requirements: Poland joined the EU on 1 May 2004. EU nationals and those from the USA, Canada and New Zealand do not require visas to enter Poland but their stay is limited to anything from 14 to 90 days depending on country of origin. For stays of longer than three months EU citizens have to apply for a residence permit. The residence permit for EU citizens is renewable for periods of up to five years at a time. The website of the Polish Foreign Ministry is www.msz.gov.pl.

Work Permits: These are not required by EU citizens. Other nationalities should contact the Polish embassy in their home country for further details. For instance, American citizens should enquire at the Polish Embassy in Washington.

Teaching and Language Schools

Apass UK North, Anglo-Polish Universities Teaching Project

Duration: Placements are for either 4 or 8 weeks in July/August.

Head Office: 93 Victoria Road, Leeds LS6 1DR, UK
☎ 01132 758121

Working Hours: The course will be 2.5 hours English instruction in the morning (mainly conversational) followed by only 2 hours recreational activities either in the afternoon or evening. Weekends are free.

Pay: Generous pocket money given.

Job Description: The students are from grammar schools, roughly of the same age and ability.

Requirements: Applicants of all ages, from 17 upwards, are welcome (17-year-olds need written parental permission).

Accommodation: Accommodation, food and leisure/sporting facilities (swimming, walking, barbecue, horse riding, discos, visits to places of interest etc) are provided free of charge.

Additional Information: Some placements include a weekend trip to Prague. After 3 weeks out at the summer school, a week's 'grand tour of Poland' is organised, visiting Warsaw, Krakow, Auschwitz and the Tatra Mountains – all expenses are paid by the Polish host.

Application Procedure: For a comprehensive information pack, please send a 50p A5 stamped, self addressed envelope plus a £3 postal order to the above address.

ELS-Bell School of English

Job(s) Available: Teachers (8), activity leaders (8).
Duration: Begins in July. Minimum 2 weeks.

Head Office: ul. Niepodleglosci 792/2, Sopot, 81-805 Poland
☎ +48 58 5513298
recruitment@elsbell.pl
www.bellschools.pl

Working Hours: 14 days. *Teachers:* lead 3 hours of class per day, 5 days a week.

Pay: *Teachers:* PLN1,400 net. *Activity leaders:* PLN700 net.

Company Description: This is an international school of English based in Gdansk, Poland. Every summer residential camps are organised for mainly Polish students by the sea or in the Polish lake district.

Job Description: *Teachers:* lead classes and are also involved in drama, evening activities and excursions. *Activity leaders:* responsible for afternoon activities and other non-language sessions.

Requirements: *Teachers:* Degree/CELTA/native speaker of English. *Activity leaders:* must have finished first year of university and have Polish Kuritorium Camp Counsellors certificate C1 English.

Accommodation: Board and accommodation included.

Application Procedure: Contact Jo Raskin, head of schools. Phone interviews are conducted from March. Foreign applicants welcome.

The English School of Communication Skills (ESCS)

Job(s) Available: Teachers of English (60).

Duration: From October to June.

Working Hours: Part-time positions.

Pay: Salary according to experience and qualifications.

Company Description: ESCS school based in Tarnów, where the locals are reputedly the friendliest people in Poland.

> **Head Office:** Attn. Personnel Department, ul. Walowa 233-100 Tarnów Poland
> ☎ +48 14 6908749
> 🖂 personnel@escs.pl
> 🖥 www.escs.pl

Job Description: Job involves teaching English to Polish students of all ages.

Requirements: Applicants must hold an EFL methodology certificate and have a degree level of education. Minimum age 21.

Additional Information: ESCS holds EFL training courses in September.

Application Procedure: Applications to the above address or email.

PROGRAM-Bell

Job(s) Available: Teachers of English/sports monitors.

Duration: 6 weeks from the end of June.

Working Hours: 20 hours of teaching per week with a teaching hour of 50 minutes.

Pay: PLN1900 net per month.

> **Head Office:** AUL. Fredry 1, 61-701 Poznan Poland
> ☎ +48 61 8519250
> 🖂 office@program-bell.edu.pl
> 🖥 www.program-bell.edu.pl/ english/index.htm

Company Description: PROGRAM-Bell School of English is an ELT institution associated with the Bell Educational Trust. It operates a language school which is presently located at 2 centres in Poznan, one in Konin and one in Ostrow. PROGRAM-Bell offers tuition to approximately 1000 students, employing about 40 full-time qualified teachers from Poland as well as Britain and the US.

Requirements: Native English speakers with TEFL qualifications and a university degree.

Accommodation: Provided.

Application Procedure: Apply for a teaching post at PROGRAM-Bell by contacting the School by email. Selection is based on an interview.

ROMANIA

EMBASSY OF ROMANIA
Arundel House, 4 Palace Green, London W8 4QD
☎ 020 7937 9666
🖥 www.londra.mae.ro
🖐 roemb@roemb.co.uk

Romania is not currently covered by the EURES programme, but should soon be included. The following organisation offers voluntary work in Romania.

Red Tape

Visa Requirements: Romania joined the European Union on 1 January 2007 along with Bulgaria. Further to Romania's EU accession, the Romanian Government decided not to impose restrictions against the EU member states nationals looking for a job in Romania.

Work Permits: It is now not necessary for EU nationals to apply for a work permit as they have free access on the Romanian labour market. Concerning the other categories of foreigners (Americans, Australians and Canadians) they are still subject to the work permit obligation prior to their employment in Romania.

For further information, visit http://www.londra.mae.ro/index.php?lang= en&id=38313

Teaching and Language Schools

DAD International UK-Romania

Job(s) Available: Volunteer English teachers/activity leaders (50).

Working Hours: 4–6 hours per day.

Pay: Receive a benefits package while abroad, including full board, insurance, 24-hour support and assistance, transfers to place of work, training, internet access, a phrasebook and excursions to Transylvania, Moldavia etc.

Head Office: 1 Camil Petrescu, 705200 Pascani Iasi Romania
☎ +40 788 473523
🖐 dad@dad.ro
🖥 www.dad.ro

Company Description: DAD International UK Romania is a non-profit charity organisation and is an official partner of the Romanian Ministry for Education and Research. Its mission is to provide the highest possible quality summer and winter activity programmes in Romania, in order to meet the needs of both the Romanian and UK communities.

Job Description: To teach Romanian students through informal classes, games and fun.

Requirements: Minimum age 17. No previous teaching experience or special qualifications are required.

Accommodation: Full board.

Application Procedure: Apply online at www.dad.ro/main

RUSSIA

EMBASSY OF THE RUSSIAN FEDERATION
5 Kensington Palace Gardens, London W8 4QS
☎ 020 7495 7570
💻 www.visitrussia.org.uk
🖰 info@rusemblon.org

While there are occasional opportunities for finding paid temporary work in Russia it is still easier to find voluntary than paid work there. Even the English teachers in language schools are mostly home grown non-native speakers, although there are still sufficient high grade schools who are prepared to go to the expense of hiring foreign teachers with appropriate qualifications for TEFL. Don't forget that wages in Russia are shockingly low by Western standards, but those inspired by a genuine fascination with Russia will not be put off by this. In addition to the opportunities listed below British people should contact Youth Action for Peace, International Voluntary Service, UNA Exchange and Concordia while Americans should contact the CIEE and Service Civil International; for details see the *Worldwide* chapter.

Red Tape

Visa Requirements: Any person wising to travel to Russia must obtain a visa and register it within three working days of their arrival in the country (this does not apply to visits of three days or under). In order to obtain any sort of visa you must first obtain a special invitation from an inviting party in Russia (company, organisation, tourist agency, private person). The tourist visa is valid for three months but does not entitle the holder to undertake any work in Russia. Any person wishing to work in Russia (including volunteer work) must first receive an official invitation from the employer before they can apply for a working visa. As this takes time and effort very few national companies are willing to go through the process

Work Permits: In order to gain a work permit the foreign national must be able to produce a work contact from a company with an official invitation and the results of an HIV test. In certain cases a three-month stay can be lengthened to a year.

Teaching and Language Schools

British-American Langauge Centre

Job(s) Available: Teachers (3).
Duration: Minimum period of work 6 months.
Working Hours: 1,000 hours per month. Most classes are in the evening.
Pay: $700–$1,000 or $8–$10 per hour.
Company Description: A language school, with branches in Togliatti and Samara, Russia, which has been operating successfully for the past 8 years.
Job Description: To teach English to Russian students at all levels (elementary to advanced). Students are usually adults aged 15–40. Headway course books are used as the principal course of study but any supplementary materials are welcome.

Head Office: Office 526, 106 Novo-Sadovaya Street, Samara 443068 Russia
☎ +7 8462 703700
🖰 volgacentre@mail.ru
💻 www.the-world.ru

Requirements: BA, preferably in English, TEFL certificate or teaching experience required. Native English speakers only.

Accommodation: Accommodation is in a private flat, free for teachers.

Application Procedure: Applications to Olga Makarova, deputy director of studies at the above email or balins@mail.ru. Applications accepted all year round. Telephone interview necessary.

Language Link

Job(s) Available: Camp teachers (4).

Duration: Staff are required from 24 May to 15 August 2008. Preference given to teachers who are available for this period.

Working Hours: 40 hours per week, 5 days a week. This includes 30 academic hours (22.5 clock hours) of teaching. The remaining time can be taken up with lesson preparation and camp activities. Overtime will be renumerated.

Pay: $400–$500, depending on qualifications and experience.

Company Description: Language Link Russia, with its headquarters in London, has been teaching English as a foreign language since 1975. Each year it offers employment opportunities to more than 150 native speaking teachers. Language Link runs a number of English language summer camp programmes in the Moscow and St Petersburg regions.

Requirements: TEFL certificate is helpful but not necessary. All successful applicants will be put through a short training programme prior to undertaking their camp assignment. Minimum age 20. Experience of working with children is an advantage but not essential.

Application Procedure: Applications are accepted year round. Apply online at www.jobs.langauge.ru/jobs/application/apply_online_camp_programme.php. References are mandatory and telephone interviews are conducted. Applicants are accepted from the UK, Ireland, US, Canada, Australia and New Zealand.

> **Head Office:** Novoslobodskaya ultsa 5/2, 127055, Moscow
> ☎ +7 495 2506900
> ✉ jobs@languagelink.ru
> 🖥 www.jobs.languagelink.ru

Svezhy Veter

Job(s) Available: English teachers, au pair placement, work experience, Russia summer camp.

Duration: 2 weeks to 3 months (due to visa restrictions).

Pay: €50–€200 per month pocket money.

Requirements: Native speakers of English, French, Spanish or German. Good knowledge of Russian is an advantage. 18–55 years of age.

Accommodation: *Au pair and summer camp:* provided. *Work experience:* can be arranged.

Application Procedure: Application form available from website.

> **Head Office:** 426000 Izhevsk, PO Box 2040
> ☎ +7 3412 450037
> ✉ ask@svezhyveter.ru
> 🖥 www.sv-agency.udm.ru

SERBIA

EMBASSY OF THE REPUBLIC OF SERBIA
28 Belgrave Square, London SW1X 8QB
☎ 020 7235 9049
🖥 www.serbianembassy.org.uk

Serbia's status as an independent state is very recent. Serbia and Montenegro, two former provinces of former Yugoslavia, existed in a state union until Montenegro voted for separation from Serbia in June 2006. Short-term volunteer projects in Serbia can be arranged for British citizens by Youth Action for Peace and in Serbia by UNA Exchange. See their entries in the *Worldwide* chapter for more details.

Red Tape

Visa Requirements: the citizens of most EU countries as well as the United States of America, Canada, Singapore, the Republic of Korea, Australia and New Zealand do not need a visa to travel to Serbia.

Teaching and Language Schools

Galindo Skola Stranih Jezika (Sava Centar & Vozdovac)

Job(s) Available: English teachers.
Working Hours: 6–7 hours per day, 5 days a week.
Pay: Minimum wage rates, approximately £280 per month.

Head Office: Milentija Popovica 9, 11070 Novi Beograd Serbria
☎ +381 11 3114568
🖂 galindo@net.yu
🖥 www.galindo.co.yu

Company Description: The first private language school in the country, located in Novi Beograd's congress and shopping centre. Excellent working atmosphere, with students from pre-school to executives. Also has 2 other locations.
Job Description: English teachers to work with children, adolescents and adults.
Requirements: Applicants should have a BA in English and TEFL, TESL or TESOL qualifications. Knowledge of some Serbo-Croatian would be an advantage.
Application Procedure: Applications should be sent to Nada Gadjanski at the above address.

Voluntary Work

Exit Festival

Job(s) Available: Bartenders, promoters, security guards, stewards (approximately 150).
Duration: Required for 4 days in July.
Pay: No wage but free entry to festival.

☎ +381 21 4754222
🖂 info@exitservices.co.yu
🖥 www.exitfest.org

Company Description: This festival began life as an artistic antedote to the Milosevic regime and has grown into one of Europe's largest musical celebrations. It takes place in the grounds of a citadel and attracts mainstream rock, indie and hip hop artists.
Job Description: During the festival, Exit organisers engage around 1,500 workers and volunteers to work as bartenders, promoters, security, stewards and so on. Most of the volunteers are Serbian students, but a growing number of volunteers from all over Europe attend each year in return for a ticket.
Requirements: Fluent English is not necessary.
Application Procedure: Those interested in volunteering should keep an eye on the website from March each year when details about volunteering are made available.

SLOVENIA

EMBASSY OF THE REPUBLIC OF SLOVENIA
10 Little College Street, London SW1P 3SH
☎ 020 7222 5700
💻 www.gov.si/mzz-dkp/veleposlanistva/eng/london/index.shtml
🖱 vlo@gov.si

Slovenia is a great country to work in with a high standard of living. Most of the short-term possibilities for foreigners revolve around teaching English or voluntary work. The British Council in Ljubljana (www.britishcouncil.si) has a list of private language schools that may take teachers for summer schools. Slovenia is also covered by the EURES programme (www.europa.eu.int/eures), and further information on job seeking, living and working there can be found on their website.

The following organisation arranges voluntary work in Slovenia. British people can also find this type of work through International Voluntary Service or UNA Exchange, while US citizens can apply to Service Civil International; see the *Worldwide* chapter for details.

Red Tape

Visa Requirements: citizens of the majority of countries may travel to Slovenia without obtaining a visa, including those from the USA, New Zealand, Canada, Japan and Australia. Slovenia joined the EU on 1 May 2004. EU citizens are able to work in Slovenia under the same conditions as Slovenians. EU citizens also have the right to live in Slovenia, but a residence permit is obligatory for stays of longer than 3 months. For EU citizens working in Slovenia, the employer has to register their employment with the Slovenian Employment Service. Nationals of other countries may stay up to 90 days in any half a year depending on their country of origin. For more information go to the employment service of Slovenia website, www.ess.gov.si.

Voluntary Work

Zavod Voluntariat

Job(s) Available: International workcamp volunteers. Long and medium-term voluntary work.

Duration: Most workcamps are held from June to September and last 2 or 3 weeks.

Company Description: Voluntariat is a non-profit, non-governmental organisation which coordinates

Head Office: Zavod Voluntariat, Resljeva 20, 1000 Ljubljana
🖱 placement@zavod-voluntariat.si
irena@zavodvoluntariat.si
💻 www.zavod-voluntariat.si

voluntary work and international workcamps in Slovenia. Voluntariat aims to promote social justice, sustainable development and solidarity through voluntary service. Voluntariat sends volunteers abroad on long-term and mid-term projects.

Job Description: *International workcamps:* Voluntariat organises between 5 and 10 workcamps in Slovenia every year. The main topics of the workcamps are: ecology, children and handicapped people. *Long and medium-term voluntary work:* projects of LTV and MTV are based mostly in Ljubljana and they include: projects for youngsters from underprivileged backgrounds and projects for elderly people.

Requirements: Most workcamps do not require any special skills.

Accommodation: Accommodation and food is provided.

Application Procedure: Applications should be made through your local branch of Service Civil International, http://www.sciint.org

TURKEY

CONSULATE GENERAL FOR THE REPUBLIC OF TURKEY
44 Belgrave Square, London SW1X 8PA
☎ 020 7393 0202
🖥 www.turkishconsulate.org.uk
✆ turkishconsulate@btconnect.com

Opportunities for paid work in Turkey usually involve either teaching English or working for a tour operator. There are opportunities for volunteer work with the organisations listed below or through UNA Exchange, Youth Action for Peace, International Voluntary Service and Concordia for British citizens, or the CIEE and Service Civil International for Americans; see the *Worldwide* chapter for details.

Please note that those who enter Turkey as tourists with or without a tourist visa are not permitted to take up employment in the country.

Red Tape

See the website www.turkishconsulate.org.uk for up-to-date information.

Visa Requirements: All British, Australian, American, Canadian and Irish nationals can obtain a 3 months/multiple-entry visa at their point of entry to Turkey. New Zealand, Denmark, Finland, France, Germany, Greece, Holland, Iceland, Israel, Japan, Sweden and Switzerland citizens do not need visas for stays of up to 3 months as tourists. Any UK national entering Turkey is advised to have a minimum of 6 months validity on their passports from the date of their entry into Turkey. In the UK up-to-date details of visa and permit requirements can be obtained by telephoning 09068 347348. No paid work of any kind may be undertaken with only a tourist visa; in order to gain employment a working visa must be obtained.

Residence Permits: If you wish to reside in Turkey longer than the normal period allowed to tourists, you need to apply to the relevant Turkish consulate for a residence visa. After obtaining a residence visa, you must apply to the local police headquarters of the area where you are residing within a month following arrival in Turkey to be issued a residence permit. Nationals of European Union countries and nationals of Australia, Canada, Iceland, New Zealand, Norway, Switzerland and USA may be issued a 1-year resident visa in a week. If you are staying for a longer period of time or intend to work or study in Turkey you should check with the Embassy regarding visa requirements.

Work Permits: Work permit applications are always for a specific position and they are employer driven. Prospective employers must apply to the Turkish Ministry of Labour and Social Affairs in Ankara (www.csgb.gov.tr), for a work permit for their UK employees. Once this has been approved the person seeking employment must apply for a work visa through the Embassy of the Republic of Turkey (www.turkishconsulate.org.uk). Prospective English teachers must have a degree and TEFL certificate. Should the employer be related to the tourism business, a letter of approval should be obtained from the Turkish Ministry of Tourism before visa application. The application should be made from the country of origin, unless the applicant is the holder of a residence permit. Applications for an extension of a given work permit can be made if accompanied by a valid residence permit. The visa procedure in Turkey requires a double application - from the employee in their country of origin, and from the employer in Turkey, who must submit a file to the Ministry of Labour and Social Security, Department for Work Permits for Foreigners (www.yabancicalismaizni.gov.tr). There should not be more than 3 working days between the 2 applications. It usually takes 2 months for the applications to be processed. Foreigners who enter Turkey on the basis of a work visa are expected to get a residence permit within 30 days of arrival. Work permits are required for au pairs and voluntary work.

Agricultural Work

Omercan Ziraat Turizm As

Job(s) Available: Unlimited positions for field workers, technicians, farm workers.
Duration: From March to December.
Pay: Wages on application.
Company Description: Omercan is a new project operated by Canlar AS, set to become an integrated model organic farm for Turkey.

> **Head Office:** Omercan Ciftlik, Intepe, Canakkale 17060 Turkey
> ☎ +90 53 22336555
> ✆ organic@omercan.com.tr
> 🖳 www.omercan.com.tr

Job Description: This is a 150-hectare mixed organic farm. There is always a variety of jobs to be done. The farm is approximately divided equally into 3 types of landscape: forest, olives, fields.
Requirements: Enthusiastic and hard working.
Accommodation: Available. Price on application.
Application Procedure: Apply to Nurten Kam by email.

TaTuTa (The Bugday Association for Supporting Ecological Living)

Job(s) Available: Volunteer workers for organic farms.
Company Description: This is the new WWOOF exchange known as TaTuTa (an acronym of Agro Tourism and Voluntary Exchange, in Turkish)
Accommodation: Provided on organic farms.
Application Procedure: Via email, post, telephone or visit the Bugday office.

> **Head Office:** Istikal Street, No. 212, Aznavur Pasaji, Fifth Floor, 34430, Beyoglu/Galatasaray, Istanbul Turkey
> ☎ +90 212 2446230
> ✆ info@tatuta.org
> 🖳 www.bugday.org/tatuata

Work at Sea

Setsail Holidays

Job(s) Available: Skippers, hostesses and engineers.
Duration: Starts April/May to end September/October.
Pay: £120–£160 per week depending on job and experience.

> **Head Office:** 40 Burkitts Lane, Sudbury, Suffolk CO10 2HB, UK England
> ☎ 01787 310445
> ✆ boats@setsail.co.uk
> 🖳 www.setsail.co.uk

Company Description: Setsail Holidays are a specialist tour operator providing flotilla sailing and bareboat charter holidays to Greece, Turkey and Croatia.

Job Description: Skippers, hostesses and engineers required to coordinate and run the flotilla sailing holidays which can consist of up to 12 yachts.

Requirements: Must have sailing experience and/or qualifications and the ability to work well with people.

Accommodation: Provided on the 'lead yacht'.

Application Procedure: Applications to John Hortop at the above address by fax or email. Applications must include a CV and recent picture.

Voluntary Work and Archaeology

Concordia Turkey

Job(s) Available: International volunteer projects.

Duration: Short-term.

Cost: Volunteers pay a registration fee of £150 and fund their own travel and insurance.

Company Description: Concordia offers volunteers the opportunity to take part in international short-term volunteer projects in over 60 countries worldwide.

> **Head Office:** 19 North Street, Portslade, Brighton BN41 1DH, England
> ☎ 01273 422218
> info@concordia-iye.org.uk
> www.concordia-iye.org.uk

Job Description: The work is community based and ranges from nature conservation, renovation, construction and social work including children's play schemes and teaching.

Requirements: Minimum age 16.

Accommodation: Board and accommodation are free of charge.

Application Procedure: For further information on volunteering or coordinating please check the website or contact the International Volunteer Co-ordinator at the above address.

Genctur

Job(s) Available: International voluntary work-camps.

Duration: Camps last 2–3 weeks.

Company Description: Genctur is Turkey's leading youth and student travel organisation. Their main activities are international voluntary workcamps in Turkey.

> **Head Office:** Istiklal Cad. No 212, Aznavur Pasaji, K: 5 34430, Istanbul Turkey
> ☎ +90 212 2446230
> workcamps.in@genctur.com
> www.genctur.com

Job Description: Project volunteers are needed for mostly manual work including repairing and painting schools, digging water trenches, constructing schools or health care centres, gardening and environmental development works or social schemes such as helping handicapped people or practising English with children. Projects take place mostly in small villages and towns where the traditional way of life can be seen through contact with the local people. The language spoken at the camps is English.

Requirements: Minimum age 18.

Accommodation: Full board and accommodation is provided.

Application Procedure: Applications are only accepted through the following partner voluntary organisations: UNA Exchange, Concordia, IVS and Youth Action for Peace UK.

GSM Youth Services Centre

Job(s) Available: Workcamp volunteers.

Duration: The projects last for 2 weeks from July until the end of September.

Working Hours: 5 hours per day.

Cost: Volunteers pay their own travel costs.

Head Office: Bayindir Sokak, No.45/9 Kizilay, 06450 Kizilay-Ankara
☎ +90 312 4171124
📧 gsm@gsm-youth.org
💻 www.gsm-youth.org

Company Description: GSM Youth Services Centre is a non-governmental non-profit youth organisation that was founded by a group of young people in 1985, in Ankara, Turkey. Its main aim is to support common understanding, peace, friendship and intercultural learning among young people coming from different cultural backgrounds by organising international youth activities. It believes that these intercultural activities give space to young people to share their experiences and own cultural richness, which could help young people to break down barriers and prejudices. In order to achieve these aims the centre organises: international voluntary workcamps, international youth projects under European programmes, NGO capacity building seminars, youth information. GSM is a member of the Alliance of European Voluntary Service Organisations and YEN (youth express network).

Job Description: GSM organises around 20 workcamps throughout Turkey in cooperation with the local municipalities and universities. The projects, usually taking place in towns or on campus sites, can involve environmental protection, restoration, construction and/or festival organisations.

Requirements: Volunteers should be aged 18–28.

Accommodation: Board and lodging are provided in dormitories, small hotels/pensions, camp houses or with families.

Application Procedure: Applications through partner organisations including Concordia, Quaker International Social Projects and the United Nations Association (Wales).

Other Employment In Turkey

ICEP (International Cultural Exchange Programmes)

Job(s) Available: Au pair, interns with Turkish companies, English teacher.

Duration: Minimum of 3 months.

Pay: *Au pair:* minimum $200 per month. *Interns:* $150 per month. *English teacher:* $750 per month.

Head Office: Yuskel Cad. 9/10, Kizilay, Ankara
☎ +90 312 4184460
📧 info@icep.org.tr
💻 www.icep.org.tr

Company Description: The International Cultural Exchange Programme (ICEP) Scholarship Foundation is a not-for-profit organisation which was established in Turkey in 1995 under the auspices of the Turkish Prime Ministry Department of Charitable Foundations. The purpose of the Foundation is to provide cultural exchange opportunities for young people and students around the world, with the added aim of introducing Turkey, its history, heritage and culture to young foreigners.

Job Description: *Au pair:* babysitting, some light housework, caring. This work can include but is not limited to: preparing meals for the children, feeding them, playing with them, taking them to the park, taking them and picking them up from school, keeping their room tidy, washing and ironing their clothes. Vacancies are available for female applicants only. You may be asked to teach English to the children of your host family.

Accommodation: Available free of charge.

Application Procedure: Apply by email to icep@icep.org.tr.

ICEPworld

Job(s) Available: Student representative (2), marketing assistant (2).

Duration: The end of May or beginning of June to September. Can be longer. Minimum period of work 2 months.

Head Office: Barbaros Blv. 41B, D:2, Besiktas, Istanbul, 34353 Turkey
info@icep.org.tr
www.icep.org.tr

Working Hours: *Student representative:* 5 days a week, 7 hours per day. *Marketing assistant:* 5 days a week, 7 hours per day.

Pay: $150.

Company Description: ICEPworld is an international network for youths and students, work and travel, au pairs and language studies. ICEPworld partners are based all over the world including the UK, USA, Germany, Turkey, Ukraine and Romania.

Job Description: General office assistant position. Daily running of the office, completing projects as assigned.

Requirements: 18–30 years old. Basic IT skills.

Accommodation: Accommodation is provided and lunch meals are provided during office hours, both free of charge.

Application Procedure: Applications to Mr. Clement Yener by email at info@icep.org.tr. Applicants can be submitted from the beginning of April. There will be a phone interview only. Foreign applications welcome to apply.

WORLDWIDE

ORGANISATIONS WITH VACANCIES WORLDWIDE

Agricultural Work

IAEA/AgriVenture

Job(s) Available: Farming or horticultural working programmes.

Duration: Programmes depart all year round (applications required usually 2 months minimum before departure).

Costs: Programme costs start at around £2100 and include: return flights (and transfer to host family),

Head Office: Speedwell Farm Bungalow, Nettle Bank, Wisbech, Cambridgeshire PE14 0SA, UK
☎ 01945 450999, 0800 783 2186
📧 uk@agriventure.com
🖥 www.agriventure.com

full travel and work insurance, work permits, job placement, departure information meeting, seminar in host country and full emergency back-up through offices in hosting country.

Company Description: Farming or horticultural working programmes to Australia, New Zealand, Canada, USA and Japan are arranged by AgriVenture.

Requirements: Applicants must be aged 18–30, have no dependants, be British citizens, have a full driving licence and have experience or an interest in agriculture or horticulture.

Application Procedure: For a free brochure or more information telephone or email with your name, address and postcode, or visit the website to find details of your local office.

WWOOF (World Wide Opportunities on Organic Farms)

Job(s) Available: Volunteer farm labourers for work on organic properties.

Company Description: WWOOF exists to give people the opportunity of gaining first hand experience

📧 hello@wwoof.org.uk
🖥 www.wwoofinternational.org

of organic farming and gardening in return for spending a weekend or longer helping on a farm. Since WWOOF began in England in 1971, similar schemes have developed in other countries around the world. Each national group has its own aims, system, fees and rules, eg WWOOF Australia, WWOOF Italy. They are all similar in that they offer volunteers the chance to learn in a practical way the growing methods of their host. Each group will supply a booklet listing WWOOF hosts to members from which volunteers can choose a farm. Most national organisations expect applicants to have gained experience on an organic farm in their own country. Where countries do not have a national WWOOF organisation, individual hosts are listed with WWOOF Independents. Countries include Australia, Austria, Bulgaria, Canada, China, Costa Rica, the Czech Republic, Denmark, Estonia, France, Germany, Ghana, Hawaii, India, Israel, Italy, Japan, Korea, Mexico, Nepal, New Zealand, Spain, Sweden, Switzerland, Turkey, USA, UK.

Requirements: It is necessary to join the national WWOOF organisation before you can obtain addresses of their properties. This usually costs €15–€20 per year.

Application Procedure: For further information applicants should contact WWOOF (UK) (PO Box 2675, Lewes, Sussex BN7 1RB; hello@wwoof.org.uk; www.wwoof.org.uk), or WWOOF Independents in countries (addresses from www.wwoof.org), for information and application forms.

Hotel Work and Catering

Club Med Recruitment

Job(s) Available: Staff for children's clubs, sports instructors, hostesses/boutique, receptionists, public relations, bar staff and more.

Head Office: 132 rue Bossuet, 69 458 Lyon cedex 06, France

Duration: Applicants must be available for a period of 3 to 6 months. Shorter contracts for the childcare positions available.

Company Description: Club Med reps take part in all aspects of village life and help to create the international atmosphere which makes Club Med holidays unique.

Job Description: Staff are required for Club Med villages in Europe and North Africa.

Requirements: Applicants must possess excellent communication skills and a good level of spoken French. *Staff for children's clubs:* should have NNEB qualifications and/or experience in working with children. *Sports instructors:* should have relevant qualifications and experience to teach sailing, water-skiing, scuba diving (BSCA-advanced, CMAS), tennis, windsurfing, aerobic fitness and golf. *Hostesses/boutique receptionists:* should have relevant experience and speak 2 or 3 European languages.

Application Procedure: Applicants should apply online.

Crystal

Job(s) Available: Resort reps, qualified nannies and children's reps, chalet hosts, chefs, hotel staff, maintenance staff, qualified sailing and windsurfing instructors and various other qualified sports instructors.

Head Office: 12-42 Wood Street, Kingston-Upon-Thames, Surrey KT11JY, UK
☎ 020 8541 2223
💻 www.crystaljobs.co.uk

Duration: Crystal recruits for both winter and summer positions throughout the year.

Company Description: Crystal holidays has a number of different programmes.

Job Description: Crystal recruits for summer positions many exciting European and worldwide destinations. Work available in a variety of destinations throughout the year.

Requirements: Positions are available for qualified and unqualified staff with a flexible and friendly attitude. Must have a good understanding of customer requirements and the ability to work within a busy team.

Application Procedure: Please apply online at www.crystaljobs.co.uk

Industrial and Office Work

Global Choices

Job(s) Available: Internships, practical training abroad, working holiday, volunteering and work experience worldwide.

Head Office: Barkat House, 116-118 Finchley Road, London NW3 5HT, UK
☎ 020 7433 2501
📧 info@globalchoices.co.uk
💻 www.globalchoices.co.uk

Duration: From 2 weeks to 18 months.

Pay: Cost depends on programme.

Job Description: Destinations include Argentina, Australia, Brazil, Canada, China, Greece, India, Ireland, Italy, Spain, United Kingdom and United States. Placements are offered in many fields, industrial, business, science, conservation, agriculture, travel, tourism, and more.

Application Procedure: See website for details.

TUI
UK

A World Of Opportunities

TUI UK are part of the world's largest travel group, and as such we can offer virtually every holiday job under the sun – with fantastic opportunities for advancement to match.

Thomson Childcare and Holiday Reps

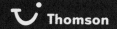 Thomson

From specialist Childcare Reps to our invaluable Holiday Reps, work with Thomson in any one of our overseas resorts and you'll come back a different person. You'll meet all sorts of people from all sorts of places, develop your already excellent customer skills and gain great experience of helping our customers make the most of their holiday by introducing them to our great range of days and nights out. We'll turn you into a slick sales person, problem solver and all-round crowd-pleaser. In short, you'll develop into someone who has the confidence to do anything! You could be based in any one of our many destinations worldwide, which means you'll get a real feel for working in different cultures and countries.

For more information and to apply, visit thomson.co.uk/jobs.

Crystal Reps

It's not just our customers who get to have the time of their lives with Crystal. So do our team. We're the no. 1 ski and snowboard specialists in the UK which means you'll enjoy the finest mountain scenery, and the most exhilarating slopes around – just like our satisfied customers. If you have what it takes to deliver outstanding service, you'll see your career take off in exciting directions, too. So for winters you won't forget, and sought-after career opportunities all year long, join us. Our summer programme includes Crystal Active and Crystal Lakes and Mountains.

For more information on available jobs and to apply, visit crystaljobs.co.uk.

Simply Travel Reps

As a Simply Travel Representative you'll ensure our guests' holidays run smoothly, so first-class customer service and troubleshooting skills will be second nature to you. And a keen eye for detail and expectation of high standards are also your forte. This is not your run-of-the-mill holiday. Travelling with Simply is all about living like a local. So like our guests, you'll need to be discerning, independent and a real culture connoisseur. Come and work with the finer things in life as a Simply Travel Representative. It's a million miles away from the usual tourist trails.

For more information and to apply, visit thomson.co.uk/jobs.

International Cooperative Education

Job(s) Available: Jobs include retail sales, banking, computer technology, hotels and restaurants, offices etc.

Duration: 2–3 months.

Working Hours: 30–40 hours per week.

Pay: Depending on the particular employment students earn a modest salary or stipend.

Head Office: 15 Spiros Way, Menlo Park, California 94025, USA
☎ +1 650 3234944
icemenlo@aol.com
www. icemenlo.com

Cost: Placement fee is $700 plus an application fee of $250.

Company Description: ICE provides American college and university students with the unique opportunity to become immersed in a culture other than their own, and gain practical cultural and work experience abroad.

Requirements: Aged 18–30. Full-time students. Most jobs require knowledge of the relevant language.

Accommodation: Either live with a homestay or with an employer sponsored housing programme.

Application Procedure: Apply online at www.icemenlo.com/apply

International Association for the Exchange of Students for Technical Experience (IAESTE)

Job(s) Available: Course-related traineeships.

Duration: Employed on short term contracts, usually for up to 3 months.

Pay: Students are responsible for their own travel and insurance costs, but are paid a salary by the host employer to cover their cost of living.

Head Office: IAESTE UK, 10 Spring Gardens, London SW1A 2BN, UK
☎ 020 7389 4114
www.iaeste.org.uk

Company Description: IAESTE operate an exchange scheme whereby students in undergraduate degree level scientific and technical studies are offered course-related traineeships in industrial, business, governmental and research organisations in over 80 countries.

Job Description: IAESTE selected trainees undertake specific scientific, or professional tasks.

Application Procedure: More information and applications available from the above address.

IS Recruitment

Job(s) Available: Private estate staff, corporate, health industry, childcare and hotel staff.

Duration: Minimum period of work 1 week.

Working Hours: 8–12 hours per day, 5–6 days a week.

Head Office: PO Box 12105, Abeckett Street, Melbourne, Victoria, 8006, Australia
admin@isrecruitment.com
www.isrecruitment.com

Pay: £125–£1,000 per week.

Company Description: An Australian agency that specialises in the introduction of 5-star quality service staff in domestic, corporate and private health sectors both temporarily and permanently throughout the world.

Requirements: Minimum age 21. Experience in a domestic world is needed. Tertiary education and/or foreign language a plus. Postgraduate degree and/or field experience required for specialist services (masseur, child psychologist, ski instructor). Clients are high profile, prestigious employers and all applicants must be trained or experienced in order to offer their services. CRB Check and first aid often required. Fluent English necessary.

Accommodation: Free accommodation and board available.

Application Procedure: Apply to Cassandra Haddad recruitment consultant at the above email address. Candidates may need to attend an interview but expenses are paid by the employer.

JPMorgan

Job(s) Available: Around 200 summer internships are available in locations such as America, India, Japan, South Africa, Europe and Asia Pacific.

Head Office: 10 Aldermansbury, London EC2V 7RJ
www.jpmorgan.com/careers

Duration: 10 weeks.

Company Description: Investment banking is a fast-moving world where talented people can achieve great things. Those 'great things' vary depending on where you go and what you do. If you want responsibility and the chance to make an impact at an early stage in your career, you'll find it at JPMorgan.

Job Description: JPMorgan's training programmes combine on-the-job learning with classroom instruction that is on par with the world's finest business schools. You'll gain exposure to different lines of business, giving you a multi-dimensional perspective of the company. As a result, you'll emerge with a thorough grounding in your chosen business area as well as a broad understanding of the wider commercial picture. You'll also gain a range of transferable business skills, from project management to team leadership. Interns are given responsibility from day one.

Requirements: The work can be intense so JPMorgan are looking for team-players and future leaders with exceptional drive, creativity and interpersonal skills. Impeccable academic credentials are important, but so are your achievements outside the classroom. You'll need to express a preference for one business area when you apply so it's important you understand the difference between them.

Application Procedure: The deadline for applications is 13 January 2008 and can be made online at jpmorgan.com/careers

Sports, Couriers and Camping

Broadreach and Academic Treks

Job(s) Available: Scuba instructors (35), skippers (17), Spanish, French, Chinese language instructors (8–16), wilderness leaders (8), marine biologists (8), surfing instructors (2).

Head Office: 806 McCulloch Street, Raleigh, North Carolina 27603, USA
☎ +1 888 8331907
staffinquiry@gobroadreach.com
www.gobroadreach.com
www.academictreks.com

Duration: Required from June to August. Minimum period of work 3 weeks.

Working Hours: 24 hours per day, 7 days a week for the duration of the trip. Each trip has several days of preparation and debriefing.

Pay: Wages for all positions depend on instructor's level of experience in the skill area as well as experience level as a trip leader.

Company Description: Broadreach and Academic Treks provide summer adventure and educational programmes for teens. These inspirational programmes focus on teamwork, exploration and skill-building. Academic Treks, is the academic and service adventure division of Broadreach. The division offers college-accredited summer programmes abroad for teenagers which combine experiential learning, traditional classroom learning and community service learning with wilderness adventure, international travel and cultural immersion to create unforgettable and enriching expeditions.

Job Description: All available positions are challenging. Instructors may have a 24-hour break and then the next session of summer begins. Instructors not only teach students about their area of expertise but also teach students all life skills required for life, in a confined space with a group of people. This includes but is not limited to cooking, cleaning, interpersonal counselling and group dynamic facilitation.

Requirements: Staff should be competent in their skill area. Staff should have experience travelling internationally, and working with teens on leading multi-day trips. Staff should enjoy working with teens, possess a positive, healthy attitude and be flexible. Fluent English is essential. *Skippers:* must be able to sail a 40ft–50ft sailboat. *Spanish, French, Chinese language instructors:* must have Masters or PhD. *Wilderness leaders:* must have backcountry experience. *Marine biologists:* must have Masters or PhD.

Accommodation: Board and lodging available. Meals, housing and some transportation are covered in addition to monetary wages.

Additional Information: Programmes are offered in more than one country but there is no sponsorship or visa reimbursement.

Application Procedure: Apply by email to Lauren Marchman. Overseas applicants welcome to apply.

Contiki Holidays

Job(s) Available: Tour managers and drivers.

Duration: Seasonal basis from March to October.

Company Description: A company that specialises in coach tours holidays for 18 to 35 year olds throughout Europe, Australia, the USA, New Zealand, and the UK.

> **Head Office:** Wells House, 15 Elmfield Road, Bromley BR1 1LS, UK
> ☎ 020 8290 6777
> ✉ travel@contiki.co.uk
> 🖥 www.contiki.com

Job Description: All successful trainees receive thorough training in the form of a 7 week road trip in Europe.

Requirements: Applicants must hold an EU passport or be able to obtain a valid visa which gives them the legal right to work in the UK. Must have a clean driving licence. *Drivers:* need a manual European coach licence.

Application Procedure: Applications to gary.willment@contiki.com or the above address. Recruitment starts in September for the following year's season.

Cosmos

Job(s) Available: Holiday consultants, children's/crèche representatives, operations assistants.

Duration: Summer season runs from March through to October.

Pay: *Holiday consultants:* from £400. *Children's/crèche representatives:* from £460. *Operations assistants:* from £650.

> **Head Office:** Wren Court, 17 London Road, Bromley, Kent BR1 1DE, UK
> ☎ 020 8695 4724
> ✉ overseasdept@cosmos.co.uk
> 🖥 www.cosmos.co.uk
> www.somewhere2stay.com

Company Description: Cosmos is an independent tour operator, providing holidays in the Mediterranean and further afield.

Job Description: *Holiday consultants:* customer service, sales, guiding excursions, airport duties. *Children's/crèche representatives:* to organise activities and provide activities for children aged 3–11. *Operations assistants:* to provide administrative support to a busy resort and management team.

Accommodation: Flights and accommodation are provided.

Application Procedure: Applications to the above address or email your CV.

Dragoman Overland

Job(s) Available: Crew to drive their expedition vehicles through developing countries.

Duration: Minimum of 15 months.

Pay: All crew on road (including trainees) receive daily living allowance. Once a qualified crew member you will start to earn a wage as well. When you are leading trips and/or are a trip mechanic you will also be eligible for bonuses based upon your performance.

Head Office: Camp Green, Kenton Road, Debenham, Suffolk IP14 6LA, UK
☎ 01728 862255
✆ recruitment@dragoman.com
🖥 www.dragoman.co.uk

Company Description: Overland adventure tours worldwide. Dragoman Overland employ overland crew to drive their expedition vehicles through developing countries. Showing travellers the wonders of the world.

Requirements: Minimum age 25. Valid driving license essential.

Application Procedure: Download an application form at www.dragoman.com/documents/crew_application_form.pdf

Exodus Travels

Job(s) Available: Walking and trekking leaders, leaders for discovery and adventure and leisurely collection programmes, tour leaders.

Duration: Dates of work are from May to October plus Christmas and Easter. Periods of work of up to 6 to 7 months a year available. *Walking and trekking leaders:* work is available throughout the year. *Leaders for discovery and adventure and leisurely collection programmes:* trips of 1–2 weeks. The ideal candidate should be flexible and available to work between May and November at short notice.

Head Office: Grange Mills, Weir Road, London SW12 0NE, UK
☎ 0870 240 5550
✆ otownsend@exodus.co.uk
🖥 www.exodus.co.uk

Working Hours: *Tour leaders:* whilst away, tour leaders could be working 7 days a week.

Pay: *Tour leaders:* £24.50–£44.50 per day.

Company Description: Exodus is an adventure travel company that specialises in walking and trekking, discovery, cycling and multi-activity holidays. Applicants could be working in Europe, Africa, Asia, Central America and Cuba.

Job Description: *Leaders for discovery and adventure and leisurely collection programmes:* to lead trips based in Europe, either sightseeing, gentle walking or a mixture of both. *Tour leaders:* required to lead trips overseas.

Requirements: *Walking and trekking leaders:* with mountain walking experience and relevant qualifications such as SML and WML. Minimum age 25. Must have a second language, interest in the outdoors, experience of independent travel and hill walking/group leading. *Leaders for discovery and adventure and leisurely collection programmes:* must also bring an aspect of cultural knowledge. A second language is also desirable. Suitable for older applicants. *Tour leaders:* must be 25 years and over. Knowledge of a second language, eg Italian, Spanish, French, is required.

Accommodation: *Tour leaders:* board and accommodation provided.

Application Procedure: Applications invited throughout the year. Please download an application form from the website link: www.exodus.co.uk/vacancies.html.

Explore!

Job(s) Available: Tour leaders.

Duration: 3–6 months. Work is available through-out the year, with the minimum period of work being 3 weeks, although the peak periods of Christmas, Summer holidays and Easter are the most popular times.

Working Hours: On duty 24/7 but the work is satisfying.

Pay: Fees start at £25 a day.

Company Description: Explore! is Europe's largest adventure travel tour operator.

Job Description: Tour leaders for leading tour groups of 16–24 clients per group, to 100+ countries around the world.

Requirements: Applicants with language skills and previous travel experience essential. Full training given. You must be available to leave the UK for certain set periods of time.

Application Procedure: Applications to the above address are accepted all year round and must be on an application form, which can be downloaded from the website.

> **Head Office:** Nelson House, 55 Victoria Road, Farnborough, Hampshire GU14 7PA, UK
> ☎ 01252 379553
> ✆ ops@explore.co.uk
> 🖥 www.explore.co.uk

First Choice Holidays

Job(s) Available: Resort representative, children's representative, transfer representative, finance and administration staff are just a few of the positions available on the summer sun programme.

Duration: For all positions, the period of work is flexible between March and October. 6 months contract.

> **Head Office:** Jetset House, Church Road, Lowfield Heath, Crawley, West Sussex RH11 0PQ, UK
> ☎ 0800 169 5692
> ✆ overseas.recruitment@firstchoice.co.uk
> 🖥 www.firstchoice4jobs.co.uk

enjoy a world of possibilities

Overseas Opportunities

The people. The place. The local cuisine and exotic drinks. There are a lot of things that make a good holiday a great one – not least our Overseas Resort and Support Teams.

Whether you're working as a **Resort** or **Children's Representative**, or as part of our **Finance** or **Administration** teams, you'll play an important role in ensuring that every one of our customers has the time of their life. It's a big challenge. A holiday experience that stands out from the rest calls for a real commitment to customer service and a personality that truly shines. Add to that a flair for sales and you'll be set.

Don't think of this as just a summer job though. Our training won't just prepare you for life overseas; it'll open the door to a range of opportunities – both in the UK and abroad.

If you're a strong team player, with a positive outlook and a full EU/EEA passport, we'd love to hear from you. Visit **www.firstchoice4jobs.co.uk** to apply online and for details of all our vacancies, including Cabin Crew and Retail.

Working Hours: 5.5 days a week. Hours vary.

Pay: Competitive plus benefits

Requirements: Applicants must have a national insurance number and either an EU/EEA passport or relevant EU/EEA work permit/visa.

Accommodation: Accommodation is provided free of charge.

Application Procedure: Full details of all the above positions and how to apply can be found on the website www.firstchoice4jobs.co.uk.

The Imaginative Traveller

Job(s) Available: Tour leaders (80–100).

Duration: At least 13 months overseas.

Company Description: A leading adventure tour operator that employs 80–100 tour leaders to work in adventurous locations around the world. Operates small group, active journeys worldwide.

> **Head Office:** TL Jobs, The Imaginative Traveller, 1 Betts Avenue, Martlesham Heath, Nr Ipswich, Suffolk IP5 3RH, UK
> 🖳 www.imaginative-traveller.com

Requirements: Comprehensive training is provided for those willing to work. Need to be a responsible, self-reliant traveller with great people skills and a positive attitude. Good spoken English is required.

Application Procedure: An application form and information pack is available from the above address. Applicants should include a letter explaining why they would be suitable for the role.

Kumuka Worldwide

Job(s) Available: Tour leaders, drivers.

Duration: 6 months minimum.

Working Hours: 24/7 with tour groups. Time off between tours.

Pay: Minimum £100 per week. Increases with experience.

> **Head Office:** 40 Earls Court Road, London W8 6EJ, UK
> ☎ 020 7937 8855
> 📧 humanresources@kumuka.com
> 🖳 www.kumuka.co.uk

Company Description: Leading specialists in worldwide Adventure Travel, Kumuka have been successfully operating exciting tours for the intrepid traveller for more than 23 years. Covering Africa, Latin America, Asia, Europe, the Middle East and Antarctica, Kumuka recruits outgoing people with a strong interest in travel.

Requirements: *Tour leaders:* Minimum age 23. Chosen according to experience and personality. *Drivers:* must hold PCV or HGV licence or be willing to obtain one.

Application Procedure: Applications via the above email address.

Mark Warner

Job(s) Available: Accountants, receptionists, watersports instructors, tennis and aerobics instructors, chefs, kitchen porters, first aid, nannies, handymen, night watchmen. Some reserve staff also needed throughout the season.

Duration: *Corsica, Sardinia, Greece, Portugal and France:* during the summer from April to October. *Egypt, Sri Lanka and Mauritius:* year round.

Pay: From £50 per week.

> **Head Office:** George House, 61-65 Kensington Church Street, London W8 4BA, UK
> ☎ 0844 844 3760, 0844 844 3770 (childcare recruitment)
> 📧 recruitment@markwarner.co.uk
> 🖳 www.markwarner.co.uk/jobs

Job Description: Staff required to work in hotels in Corsica, Sardinia, Greece, Portugal and France and Egypt, and Sri Lanka and Mauritius.

Requirements: Requirements for languages, experience, qualifications etc vary according to the job applied for.

Accommodation: Full board, medical insurance, travel expenses included in wages. Free use of watersports and activity facilities.

Application Procedure: For further details, please contact the resorts recruitment department on the above number.

Powder Byrne

Job(s) Available: Resort managers, children's club managers/assistants, crèche managers/assistants, resort drivers.

Head Office: 250 Upper Richmond Road, London SW15 6TG, UK
☎ 020 8246 5342
🖥 www.powderbyrne.com

Duration: Duration of contracts vary from 2 weeks to 6 months between April and October.

Working Hours: Like all resort work, be prepared for long hours. You will be expected to be up early and full of enthusiasm.

Pay: Wages according to job and experience.

Company Description: Powder Byrne is an exclusive tour operator offering tailor-made holidays, working alongside 4 and 5 star luxury hotels, to provide a top of the range holiday package. They are looking for highly motivated customer-focused team players to work in their summer resorts programme in exotic holiday destinations, such as France, Cyprus, Italy, Portugal, Tunisia, Mauritius, Dubai and Mallorca.

Job Description: *Resort managers:* required for managing a team of staff in resort, to provide a high calibre of services to Powder Byrne clients and to liaise with head office. *Children's club managers/assistants:* to organise and run the kids' clubs for 9 to 14 year olds. *Creche managers/assistants:* required for managing resort crèches for children aged 6 months to 3 years. *Resort drivers:* required for transporting guests in exclusive company minibuses and assist the Resort Manager in providing a high level of customer service to Powder Byrne clients.

Requirements: Knowledge of French, Italian and Spanish are desirable but not essential. No formal qualifications required unless you are managing one of the crèches, where a NNEB or equivalent is required. Training is provided.

Accommodation: Accommodation, food, transport, resort insurance and uniform provided.

Application Procedure: Applications are taken online.

Pure Vacations Ltd

Job(s) Available: Surf guide/instructor (10), resort manager (4), tour guide.

☎ 0845 299 0045
✍ info@purevacations.com
🖥 www.purevacations.com

Duration: Minimum period of work 12 weeks. Positions are available worldwide throughout the year.

Working Hours: Hours of work are variable.

Company Description: Pure Vacations Ltd is a world leading specialist tour operator. Programmes include snowboarding, surfing, golfing, rafting, ranching and more.

Job Description: *Surf guide/instructor:* surf tuition and surf guiding plus representative duties. *Tour guide:* to run guided tours to historical sites and activities such as rafting.

Requirements: Knowledge of languages is preferred, particularly Spanish, French or Portuguese. *Surf guide/instructor:* must have lifesaving qualification and surf training qualification from a recognised body such a BSA or ESF. Must have good organisational skills. *Tour guide:* must have qualification relevant to field.

Accommodation: Accommodation is provided.

Application Procedure: For more information contact the above email address.

Sunsail Ltd

Job(s) Available: Receptionists, beauty therapists, mountain bike leaders, tennis coaches, fitness instructors, childcare assistants (NNEB/BTEC/CACHE), activities assistants, watersports managers, RYA windsurf/dinghy/yacht instructors and BWSF water-ski instructors.

Head Office: The Port House, Port Solent, Portsmouth, Hampshire PO6 4TH, UK
☎ 02392 334600
recruitment@sunsail.com
www.sunsail.co.uk

Duration: To work from April to November, certain vacancies also available for summer holiday periods.

Working Hours: 6 days a week.

Company Description: Sunsail are the leaders in worldwide sailing holidays with 29 bases worldwide employing around 1000 staff. Most positions are seasonal, but as Sunsail is part of the First Choice Group there are opportunities for year round employment.

Job Description: *Receptionists, beauty therapists, mountain bike leaders, tennis coaches, fitness instructors, childcare assistants (NNEB/BTEC/CACHE), activities assistants:* In addition to the specific responsibilities of the role, staff also commit a great deal of time to socialising with guests and providing exceptional customer care. *Watersports managers, RYA windsurf/dinghy/yacht instructors and BWSF water-ski instructors:* are required to instruct RYA courses and provide rigging assistance and rescue cover for beach operations.

Requirements: Minimum age 18. Relevant qualifications essential.

Accommodation: Benefits include shared accommodation, all meals in the club, paid holiday, return flights on successful completion of the contracted period, full uniform, discounted holidays, bar discount in the club and free use of all the equipment.

Application Procedure: To apply or for more information visit the website www.sunsail.co.uk/hr and fill in an online application form.

Tucan Travel and Budget Expeditions Recruitment for South America

Job(s) Available: Tour leaders.

Duration: All year round.

Company Description: Tucan Travel is the world's leading adventure travel specialist for Latin America, operating tours throughout South and Central America, including Cuba, all year round. This is an exciting opportunity to relocate to a very interesting part of the world, to gain some fantastic travel

Head Office: 316 Uxbridge Road, Acton, London W3 9QP, UK
☎ 020 8896 6704
janine@tucantravel.com

experience and have a great adventure. Recruitment of drivers and tour leaders to run tours of international clients throughout Latin America, including Cuba and Mexico.

Job Description: Tour leaders are required to guide international groups on set itineraries within Latin America.

Requirements: Applicants must have some leadership experience, be a keen traveller, be self motivated and enthusiastic, speak at least a moderate level of Spanish, have travelled to Latin America previously, have an understanding or participated in group travel, be a minimum of 25 due to our liability insurance. Responsibility for the welfare and general enjoyment of clients, this entails being very friendly, helpful, outgoing and organized. Applicants need to display excellent communication skills and will be on call 24 hours a day.

Application Procedure: Please send your CV and job application (this can be found on the employment section of our website) to Janine at janine@tucantravel.com

TUI-UK Ltd (Thomson Holidays)

Job(s) Available: Holiday reps, Simply Specialist reps, qualified nannies and children's representatives and entertainment staff.

Duration: Recruitment of staff for both summer and winter throughout the year. *Simply Specialist Reps*: required during the summer season only.

Head Office: Wigmore House, Wigmore Place, Wigmore Lane, Luton LU2 9TN, UK
☎ 0845 055 0255
✆ TBRecruitment@thomson.co.uk
🖳 www.thomson.co.uk/jobs

Company Description: Thomson is part of The World of TUI, and incorporates Thomson Summer & Winter Collection, Simply Specialist Collection, Thomson Lakes and Mountains, Thomson Ski and Snowboarding and Thomson Faraway Shores. Staff are recruited for both summer and winter throughout the year in many exciting European and worldwide destinations.

Requirements: Positions are available for qualified and unqualified staff with a flexible and friendly attitude. Must have a good understanding of customer requirements and the ability to work within a busy team. Simply Specialist reps are required to speak the local language and must be able to work independently with excellent customer service skills.

Application Procedure: Please apply online at www.thomson.co.uk/jobs

VentureCo

Job(s) Available: Expedition leaders (8).
Duration: 4 months. Period of work is from January to May.
Working Hours: 24/7.
Pay: £600–£1,050 per month, plus expenses.

Head Office: The Ironyard, 64-66 The Market Place, Warwick CV34 4SD, UK
☎ 01926 411122
✆ mail@ventureco-worldwide.com
🖳 www.ventureco-worldwide.com

Company Description: VentureCo is a Gap Year and Career Gap provider operating in South America and the Galapagos, Central America, East Africa and Indochina.

Job Description: About 275 gap year students per year and those on a career break participate in projects which combine language schools, local aid projects and expeditions.

Requirements: Minimum age 25. Must be group-oriented and enjoy working with 18–25 year olds.

Accommodation: Board and accommodation provided.

Additional Information: Includes a travel safety course held in the UK, and expedition skills training in country.

Application Procedure: Apply immediately to the above address or email.

Weissman Teen Tours

Job(s) Available: Tour leaders (11).
Pay: All expenses paid while on tour.
Company Description: Family oriented teen tour company personally supervised by owners. The company offers programmes in USA, Canada, England, France, Holland, Belgium, Switzerland and Italy.

Head Office: 517 Almena Avenue, Ardsley, New York 10502, USA
☎ +1 914 6937575
✆ wtt@cloud9.net
🖳 www.weissmantours.com

Job Description: Trips include snorkelling, surfing or scuba diving in Hawaii, cruising to Mexico or horseback riding in Bryce Canyon.

Requirements: Minimum age 21. Relevant work visas and fluent English necessary. Must truly enjoy working with teens. No smoking or drinking alcohol permitted.

Accommodation: Accommodation and board provided.

Application Procedure: Apply by fax at +1 914 6934807. Own transportation to interview required. Must participate in interview in person.

World Challenge Expeditions

Job(s) Available: Expedition leaders (400).

Duration: Periods of work are 3–6 weeks between June and late August.

Pay: Fee negotiable and all expenses paid.

Company Description: World Challenge run expeditions and adventure activities in the UK and overseas. All expeditions and activities are designed to enable education through exploration and to raise motivation in young people through developing skills in leadership, team building, decision-making and problem solving.

> **Head Office:** Black Arrow House, 2 Chandos Road, London NW10 6NF, UK
> ☎ 0870 487 3173
> ⌕ leaderinfo@world-challenge.co.uk
> ▣ www.world-challenge.co.uk

Job Description: World Challenge Expeditions requires male and female leaders for expeditions to Central and South America, Africa and Asia.

Requirements: Should be trained in an NGB award eg ML, SPA, BCU, L2K, BELA and WGL also accepted. Leaders with good facilitation and youth development skills are also welcome. Minimum age 24.

Accommodation: May be provided.

Application Procedure: Apply to the leader recruitment team on the above details.

Work at Sea

Global Crew Network

Job(s) Available: Professional and amateur crewmembers wanted for permanent and temporary positions. Working holidays and working passages available, ideal for gap year students or people seeking low cost/free travel.

> **Head Office:** 23 Old Mill Gardens, Berkhamsted, Hertfordshire HP4 2NZ, UK
> ☎ 07773 361959
> ⌕ info@globalcrewnetwork.com
> ▣ www.globalcrewnetwork.com

Job Description: Luxury yacht jobs worldwide.

Application Procedure: For more info visit www.globalcrewnetwork or call the above number.

P&O Cruises Carnival UK

Job(s) Available: Port presenters, shore excursion staff.

Job Description: Staff required on board cruise ships to promote and manage operations of shore excursions in the Mediterranean, Caribbean and Americas.

> **Head Office:** Richmond House, Terminus Terrace, Southampton SO14 3PN, UK
> ☎ 02380 657030

Application Procedure: Applications should be made by CV and covering letter to Martin Young at the above address.

Voluntary Work

Africa and Asia Venture

Job(s) Available: Projects in teaching, community, sports coaching and environment in Africa, the Indian Himalayas, Nepal, China, Thailand and Mexico.

Duration: 5 weeks to 5 months. You can also take part in shorter vacation expeditions in Kenya, Uganda, Thailand and Mexico.

Head Office: 10 Market Place, Devizes, Wilts SN10 1HT, UK
☎ 01380 729009
✆ av@aventure.co.uk
💻 www.aventure.co.uk

Company Description: AV has 14 years of experience offering 18–24-year-old volunteers rewarding projects that combine community work with travel and adventure and opportunities for those keen to improve their Spanish, Mexico.

Job Description: Gap year with AV will start with an in-country orientation course covering customs, country and TEFL, then the experience of a rewarding project, followed by 3 weeks independent travel, and a 6–8 day safari, including travelling in game reserves, deserts, or white water rafting. All this supported by excellent back-up enabling you to experience first hand countries away from the tourist trail.

Application Procedure: Apply at the above number or online.

Global Vision International

Job(s) Available: Volunteers.

Duration: Length of projects varies from 2, 3, 4 or 5 weeks up to a year.

Pay: Costs also vary. £1,000 for 3 weeks in Madagascar, flights not included.

Head Office: 3 High Street, St Albans, Herts AL3 4ED, UK
☎ 0870 608 8898
✆ info@gvi.co.uk
💻 www.gvi.co.uk

Head Office: GVI North America, 252 Newbury Street, Number 4, Boston, MA, 02116, USA
☎ + 1 888 6536028
✆ info@gviusa.com
💻 www.gviusa.com

Head Office: GVI Australasia, PO Box 423, Chelsea, VIC, 3196, Australia
☎ +61 39 0185003
✆ info@gviaustralia.com

Job Description: Volunteers for projects in Belize, Brazil, Costa Rica, East Africa, Ecuador, Guatemala, Mexico, Madagascar, Nepal, Namibia, Panama, Rwanda, The Seychelles, South Africa, Sri Lanka, Sumatra, Thailand, USA, Kenya, Tanzania, New Mexico, Arizona, Guatemala, Nepal and the USA. Projects are very varied from volunteering with animal conservation projects to caring for orphans

Requirements: No special qualifications are required. Minimum age 18.

Application Procedure: For more information contact the programme director at the appropriate addresses.

Involvement Volunteers Association Inc (IVI)

Job(s) Available: Volunteers.

Duration: Volunteering placements in any number of countries over a period of 12 months. Placements of 2–12 weeks are currently available in Albania, Argentina, Australia, Austria, Bangladesh, Bolivia, Brazil, Cambodia, Cameroon, China, Columbia, East Timor, Ecuador, Egypt, Estonia, Fiji, Finland, France, Germany, Ghana, Greece, Guatemala, Guinea-Bissau, Iceland, India, Israel, Italy, Japan, Jordan, Kenya, Korea, Kosovo, Lebanon, Lithuania, Mexico, Mongolia, Namibia, Nepal, New Zealand, Palestine, Panama, Peru,

Head Office: PO Box 218, Port Melbourne, Victoria 3207, Australia
☎ +61 3 96469392
✆ ivworldwide@volunteering.org.au
💻 www.volunteering.org.au

Philippines, Poland, Sabah (Malaysia), Samoa, Serbia, South Africa, Spain, Tanzania, Thailand, Togo, Turkey, Uganda, UK, Ukraine, USA, Venezuela, Vietnam and Zambia.

Pay/Cost: IVI charges fees to cover administration costs in the organizing of a programme of one or more Volunteering Placements in any number of the countries.

Company Description: Involvement Volunteers Association Inc. was established in 1988 with the aim of making voluntary work available to people who wish to assist others and to learn from their volunteer experiences in any other country that would accept them as volunteers. IVI is a non-government, non-profit, organisation that is government registered in Australia. IVI associates and agents support the volunteers around the world.

Job Description: IVI volunteers participate as individuals or groups of individual volunteers in their own programme of placements, as unpaid participants – real volunteers. The aim of IVI is to enable volunteers to assist not-for-profit organisations in projects related to the natural environment (on farms, in national or zoological parks, animal reserves or historic places) or community based social service organisation (in homes for elderly people, camps or schools, orphanages etc in cities, towns or villages). Placement programs for one or more placements as required to provide valuable practical experience related to potential tertiary education, completed degree courses or completed careers for retirees).

Accommodation: Some placements have food and accommodation provided while some can cost up to about £50 per week for food and accommodation, depending on the economy of the country and the host organisation.

Additional Information: Where appropriate, IVI volunteers are met on arrival at the airport and provided with 24-hour back-up if need be during their visit. Advice is given where necessary.

Application Procedure: European applicants can contact Involvement Volunteers-Germany, Sudetenlandstrasse 23, DE-51688, Germany (+49 176 20088801; ivgermany@volunteering.org.au or ivworldwide@volunteering.org.au).

Projects Abroad

Job(s)Available: Sends around 3000 people abroad annually on a variety of projects in developing countries.

Job Description: Countries include: Argentina, Bolivia, Cambodia, Chile, China, Costa Rica, Ethiopia, Mexico, Moldova, Mongolia, Morocco, Nepal Peru, Romania, Senegal, Sri Lanka, South Africa, and Thailand.

Application Procedure: See website for further details.

> **Head Office:** Aldsworth Parade, Goring, Sussex BN12 4TX, UK
> ☎ 01903 708300
> ✎ info@projects-abroad.co.uk
> 🖳 www.projects-abroad.co.uk

Quest Overseas

Job(s) Available: They offer gap years, marine conservation (diving), career sabbaticals, 2–3 week ethical holidays and tailor-made group trips for companies, organizations and universities.

Duration: 2–3 week ethical holidays, 3-month combined expedition, some shorter volunteer projects and expeditions available from 2–6 weeks which can be done in summer breaks.

> **Head Office:** The North-West Stables, Borde Hill Estate, Balcombe Road, Haywards Heath, West Sussex RH16 1XP, UK
> ☎ 01444 474744
> ✎ info@questoverseas.com
> 🖳 www.questoverseas.com

Cost: Prices range between £1200 and £4900 depending on the duration and destination – prices include all accommodation, food, in-country transport and activities as well as a donation to support the project long-term. Flights and insurance are not included.

Company Description: Quest Overseas are project and expedition specialists in Latin America and Africa that have raised over £1 million in volunteer donations in 10 years.

Job Description: Gap year students can apply to join a 3-month combined expedition which consist of a 3 week language phase (South America only), 4–6 week conservation or community project phase followed by an explorer expedition. Expeditions vary but can include trekking, mountain-biking, white-water rafting, sand-surfing and bungee jumping whilst covering 3 or more countries. Quest Overseas also have shorter term projects. Choose to explore some of the most beautiful parts of South America or Africa, or carry out worthwhile volunteering work on a project to improve life for deprived communities, endangered rainforests or wildlife.

Additional Information: Quest regularly recruit project and expedition leaders to lead teams in Africa and South America. Check the careers section of the website for application criteria.

Application Procedure: Detailed information and pdf brochures can be found on the website or Quest Overseas are happy to advise over the phone.

Raleigh International

Job(s) Available: If you are aged 17–24 you will have the opportunity to work on sustainable community and environmental projects, plus an adventure challenge. For those aged over 25, volunteers to help lead and facilitate the expedition. Roles include project managers, medics, logistics, finance officers, administrators, communications officers, interpreters, photographers.

> **Head Office:** Third floor, 207 Waterloo Road, London SE1 8XD, UK
> ☎ 020 7183 1270
> ✆ info@raleigh.org.uk
> 🖥 www.raleighinternational.org

Duration: Adventure and challenge expeditions for 4–10 weeks. For those over 25 the commitment is either for 8 or 13 weeks.

Company Description: Raleigh International is a well established charity with over 22 years experience of providing adventure and challenge expeditions to destinations including Costa Rica and Nicaragua, Malaysia and India.

Job Description: Join a community of over 30,000 people who have enjoyed Raleigh. Be part of something amazing. You will be joining a group of venturers from all backgrounds and nationalities, including those from the host country. Over 25s will be taken out of their comfort zone into remote areas where applicants will learn about different cultures, make a valuable contribution and develop key life skills which will enhance your professional and educational prospects.

Requirements: We provide full training in-country for over 25 leaders.

Application Procedure: If you are interested, please attend an information event to find out more. More information on the website.

Scripture Union

Job(s) Available: Activity team (2000). Volunteers are expected to help organise Christian activity holidays for young people.

> **Head Office:** 207-209 Queensway, Bletchley, Milton Keynes, Bucks MK2 2EB, UK
> ☎ 01908 856177
> ✆ holidays@scriptureunion.org.uk
> 🖥 www.scriptureunion.org.uk

Duration: To work about 1 week throughout the summer.

Working Hours: Full-time.

Cost: Participation fee required.

Job Description: Programmes include Bible reading, missions and residential holidays for children and young people, work in schools, youth work and the publishing of Christian resources.

Requirements: Applicants must be in sympathy with the aims of Scripture Union, committed Christians and over 18 years old. There is always a need for those who have qualifications or interests in outdoor activities, sports, working with the disabled, first aid or life saving.

Application Procedure: Applications from December onwards to the holidays administrator, at the above address.

Travellers Worldwide

Job(s) Available: Structured voluntary placements.
Duration: Placements last from 2 weeks to a year, with flexible start dates all year round.
Cost: Costing from £745. Sample charges for 3 months in Sri Lanka are £1,495 and £1,095 in China.
Company Description: A Founder Member of the Year Out Group.

Head Office: 7 Mulberry Close, Ferring, West Sussex BN12 5HY, UK
☎ 01903 502595
✉ info@travellersworldwide.com
🖥 www.travellersworldwide.com

Job Description: Structured voluntary placements involving teaching conversational English (also music, sports, drama and other subjects), conservation (with urangutans, elephants, lions, dolphins, etc), language courses, structured work experience (journalism, law, medicine, etc) and cultural courses (photography, tango, etc) in Argentina, Australia, Bolivia, Brazil, Brunei, China, Cuba, Ghana, Guatemala, India, Kenya, Malaysia, Peru, Russia, South Africa, Sri Lanka, Zambia and Zimbabwe. Hundreds of projects are available worldwide and are described in detail on their website. If you have something not currently provided in mind, Travellers Worldwide will attempt to arrange it for you, so don't hesitate to ask.

Requirements: No formal qualifications required.

Accommodation: Prices include food and accommodation, collection from the nearest airport, plus support and back-up from local staff in destination countries, but exclude flights, visa costs and insurance. Travellers can arrange the latter but many volunteers prefer the flexibility of organising their own.

Application Procedure: Applications should be made to the above address.

Teaching and Language Schools

Cultural Embrace

Job(s) Available: English teacher in Chile (30–40). Many opportunities for: English teacher in Thailand, hospitality worker in the UK, hospitality worker in Spain, European childcare worker, English teacher in Latin America, English teacher in China.

Head Office: 7201 Bill Hughes Road, Austin, Texas 78745, USA
☎ +1 512 4699089
✉ info@culturalembrace.com
🖥 www.culturalembrace.com

Duration: Minimum period of work 4–6 months.

Working Hours: *English teacher in Chile:* 20 hours per week teaching, 10 hours per week extracurricular activities. *English teacher in Thailand:* approximately 20 hours per week. *Hospitality worker in the UK:* 35–50 hours per week. *Hospitality worker in Spain*: 35–50 hours per week. *European childcare worker:* 8–10 hours per day, 5 days a week. *English teacher in Latin America:* approximately 20 hours per week. *English teacher in China:* approximately 20–35 hours per week.

Cost: Programme fees.

Company Description: Cultural Embrace pre-arranges and guarantees placements for individuals and groups to work, intern, volunteer, teach, take cultural classes and live abroad. We offer programmes to Asia, Africa, Australia, Europe or Latin America, including major medical traveller's insurance, housing and visa assistance, pre-departure and local support. We specialise in programmes that integrate the authenticity of the local community, highlighting educational, cultural and/or humanitarian projects. We will customise an itinerary to fit your schedule, budget, interests, needs and academic curriculum.

Requirements: *English teacher in Chile:* Aged 21–50, fluent English, bachelor's degree, educated in English, beginning Spanish. *English teacher in Thailand:* under 65, fluent English, bachelor's degree. *Hospitality worker in the UK:* Minimum age 18. UK work visa, fluent English, US citizens must be recent grad or enrolled in university. *Hospitality worker in Spain:* Aged 18–35, intermediate or advanced level Spanish. *European childcare worker:* high school diploma, aged 18–25 for France and Switzerland, 18–27 for Spain, 18–30 for Italy, visa requirements vary per country. *English teacher in Latin America:* good command of English, Spanish helpful but not required, bachelor's degree. *English teacher in China:* good command of English, Chinese helpful but not required, bachelor's degree.

Accommodation: Almost all positions include accommodation. If not Cultural Embrace will help find a safe, clean, affordable room. Cost included in programme fees.

Application Procedure: Apply by email 3 months in advance. Phone interview required.

Mondo Challenge

Job(s) Available: Volunteers.

Duration: A normal stay lasts 2–4 months and start dates are flexible.

Cost: The cost for 3 months is £1200.

Company Description: Mondo Challenge is a non-profit organisation which sends volunteers (post university, career break, early retired, etc) to help with teaching and business development programmes in Africa, Asia, South America and Eastern Europe.

> **Head Office:** Malsor House, Gayton Road, Milton Malsor, Northampton NN7 3AB, UK
> ☎ 01604 858225
> ✆ info@mondochallenge.org
> 🖥 www.mondochallenge.org

Job Description: Programmes are community-based, providing volunteers with an insight into local cultures and a chance to experience a different way of life. Destinations include: Nepal, Sri Lanka, Tanzania, Kenya, The Gambia, Senegal, Chile, Ecuador and Romania. All nationalities and ages accepted (average age 34). About half of all volunteers are non-UK based with a large number of volunteers from North America, Europe and Australia.

Requirements: For teaching projects, the minimum qualification is A level or equivalent in the subject to be taught. For business development, a minimum of 4 years of business experience is required. Must be able to cope with remote posting and to relate to people of other cultures. Enthusiasm, flexibility and good communication skills are essential.

Accommodation: Board and lodging with a local family costs an extra £15 (approx) per week.

Application Procedure: Further information from the above address.

Conservation and Environment

African Conservation Experience (ACE)

Job(s) Available: Volunteers.

Duration: Voluntary conservation work placements last 4–12 weeks around the year.

Pay: Costs vary depending on reserve and time of year; support and advice are given on fundraising.

Company Description: ACE is a relatively small organisation that takes interest in each volunteer as an individual. It is the most experienced

> **Head Office:** PO Box 206, Faversham, Kent ME13 8RE, UK
> ☎ 0870 241 5816
> ✆ info@ConservationAfrica.net
> 🖥 www.conservationafrica.com

organisation for conservation projects in Southern Africa and has been arranging projects for over 5 years.

Job Description: Placements for people on game reserves in Southern Africa, including South Africa, Botswana and Zimbabwe. Tasks may include darting rhino for relocation or elephants for fitting tracking collars. Game capture, tagging, assisting with wildlife veterinary work, game counts and monitoring may be part of the work programme. Marine projects involve dolphin and whale research, seal and sea bird monitoring. Lion, Hyena and Leopard monitoring is often involved.

Requirements: Applicants must have reasonable physical fitness and be able to cope with mental challenges. Enthusiasm for conservation is essential. No previous experience or qualifications necessary.

Additional Information: The programme may be of special interest to students of environmental, zoological and biological sciences, veterinary science and animal care.

Application Procedure: Applicants are invited to attend open days at various venues across the UK. Applications to the above address.

Coral Cay Conservation Ltd

Job(s) Available: Expedition leaders, science officers, scuba instructors, medical officers.

Duration: Full-time expedition projects.

Pay: No wage is paid and expedition staff are required to cover the costs of their flights and insurance.

Head Office: 40-41 Osnaburgh Street, London NW1 3ND, UK
☎ 0870 750 0668
✆ recruitment@coralcay.org
🖳 www.coralcay.org

Company Description: Coral Cay Conservation recruits paying volunteers to help alleviate poverty through research, education, training and alternative livelihood programmes worldwide. Volunteers are needed to work for Coral Cay Conservation (CCC), a non-profit organisation established in 1986 to provide support for the conservation and sustainable use of tropical and marine resources. CCC maintains full-time expedition projects in the Philippines, Trinidad, Fiji and Tobago.

Job Description: *Expedition leaders:* to oversee running of marine or forest expeditions. *Science officers:* to oversee coral reef and/or tropical forest scientific training and survey programmes. *Scuba instructors:* to provide scuba training for expedition personnel and host country counterparts. *Medical officers:* to oversee all aspects of expedition medical health.

Requirements: Volunteers are provided with full training; no previous experience required. *Expedition leaders:* management experience is desirable. Plus, for marine expeditions scuba diving qualifications and for forest expeditions a mountain leader qualification is preferable. *Science officers:* minimum qualification: degree and proven field research experience. *Scuba instructors:* PADI OWSI and EFRI as minimum. *Medical officers:* minimum qualification: paramedic, registered nurse or doctor with A&E experience.

Accommodation: CCC covers accommodation, food and other subsistence costs.

Application Procedure: Either email, or send applications to the above address.

Earthwatch Institute (Europe)

Job(s) Available: Volunteers.

Duration: Over a period of 2 days or up to 3 weeks.

Cost: Project fees range from £150 to £2000.

Job Description: Volunteers to work with scientists as part of a team conducting research into a variety of environmental conservation and heritage projects in the UK, and all over the world.

Head Office: 267 Banbury Road, Oxford OX2 7HT, UK
☎ 0186 531 8831
✆ projects@earthwatch.org.uk (volunteer project enquiries)
info@earthwatch.org.uk (general enquiries)
🖳 www.earthwatch.org

Requirements: No formal qualifications or experience are required.

Application Procedure: For further details contact the above address.

Ecovolunteer Programme

Job(s) Available: Volunteers (500–600).

Duration: Projects lasting from 1 week to 6 months.

Company Description: The Ecovolunteer Programme organises wildlife conservation projects and wildlife research projects operated by local conservation organisations worldwide.

info@ecovolunteer.org
www.ecovolunteer.org
www.ecovolunteer.org.uk (British)

Job Description: Work varies from practical fieldwork to production and support jobs in wildlife rescue centres, to visitor education, maintenance work, and household duties, dependent on each individual project.

Requirements: Minimum age 18. Participants must be in good physical health.

Accommodation: Accommodation is provided.

Additional Information: A list of the national agencies can be found at www.ecovolunteer.org/contact.html or obtained from the above address as there are offices in Austria, Belgium, Brazil, Canada, France, Hungary, Italy, the Netherlands, Spain, Switzerland the UK. More than 30 projects; their latest projects include an animal sanctuary in Florida, a brown bear project in Russia, and a Toucan bird project in Brazil.

Application Procedure: Applications should be made to the national Ecovolunteer agency of the country in which the applicant is resident. If there is no agency in your home country, then apply through the agency in the UK.

Explorations in Travel

Job(s) Available: Volunteers.

Duration: Periods of work by arrangement; most placements are available throughout the year.

Company Description: Explorations in Travel arrange volunteer placements around the world, throughout the year, with placements arranged individually.

Head Office: 2458 River Road, Guilford, Vermont 05301, USA
+1 802 2570152
explore@volunteertravel.com
www.volunteertravel.com

Job Description: Volunteers to work with wildlife and domestic animal rescue organisations, rainforest reserves, organic farms, environmental and conservation projects, sustainable tourism and schools. Placements are in, Belize, Costa Rica, Ecuador, Guatemala and Puerto Rico.

Requirements: Minimum age 18.

Accommodation: Volunteers most often pay a local family for room and board.

Application Procedure: For further details contact the programme director, at the above address.

Frontier

Job(s) Available: Work in coral reefs, African savannahs, forests and mangrove areas as part of conservation programmes in far-off destinations. 250 placements per year.

Head Office: 50-52 Rivington Street, London EC2A 3QP, UK
020 7613 2422
info@frontier.ac.uk
www.frontier.ac.uk

Duration: Placements are for 4 weeks or longer and take place throughout the year.

Cost: Depending on location and duration, costs are between £1,100 and £3,950. This covers all individual costs, including a UK training weekend, scientific and dive training, all internal travel and airport pick-ups, visas, food and accommodation, but excludes international flights and insurance.

Company Description: Frontier is a non-profit international conservation and development NGO operating since 1989.

Job Description: Programmes are established in response to problems; surveys of damaged areas are carried out so that possible solutions can be identified. For example, dynamite fishing in Tanzania was destroying the delicate web of marine life so Frontier volunteers carried out more than 6000 dives in order to establish a marine park where marine life will be protected. As Frontier is a professional agency, volunteers get the chance to work on real wildlife and habitat conservation programmes. Volunteers also work on capacity-building initiatives aimed at developing sustainable livelihoods for the world's most impoverished and marginalized communities.

Requirements: The minimum age is 17 and no specific qualifications are needed as training is given.

Accommodation: Provided.

Application Procedure: Contact the above website for more details, a free information pack and application form.

Inkanatura Travel

Job(s) Available: Resident naturalists. Volunteers are also needed for projects in Peru, Bolivia and Brazil.

Duration: Duration is 90 days, with an option to extend.

Cost: A deposit of £166/$300 will be required to cover the first month, which will be forfeited if the volunteer leaves before the end of the 90 day period without good cause. If a volunteer should abandon the project without good cause he/she will also have to pay for his/her own transport home.

Head Office: Manuel Bañón 461, San Isidro, Lima, Peru
☎ +51 14 402022 +51 14 228114
✉ reservascus@inkanatura.com.pe
🖥 www.inkanatura.com

Company Description: Two conservation organisations, Selva Sur and Peru Verde have formed a non-profit travel agency to promote ecotourism and assist conservation work in order to save Peru's unique biodiversity.

Job Description: Resident naturalists required for 4 lodges in south-eastern Peru to guide tourists and take on small research projects. Possible wildlife studies include tapirs, spider monkeys (and 5 other small monkey species), peccaries, macaws, bats, deer, large macaws and the endangered giant river otter. After training and depending on experience, the applicant may be able to get a contract for guiding tourists.

Accommodation: Free food and lodging will be provided as well as transport from Cusco.

Application Procedure: Full details of these projects, costs and how to apply can be obtained from the above address or on the website.

International Conservation Holidays

Job(s) Available: Volunteers.

Duration: Projects take place throughout the year and last from 1–3 weeks.

Pay/Cost: Volunteers must pay their own travel expenses.

Company Description: BTCV is the UK's leading practical conservation charity. Founded in 1959, they help over 130,000 volunteers per year to take hands on action to improve urban and rural environments.

Head Office: Sedum House, Mallard Way, Potteric Carr, Doncaster DN4 8DB, UK
☎ 01302 388883
✉ information@btcv.org.uk
🖥 www.btcv.org

Job Description: Volunteers to take part in international conservation projects in Bulgaria, Canada, France, Germany, Iceland, Japan, Albania, Lesotho, Italy, Estonia, Romania, Kenya, South Africa, Portugal and the USA.

Requirements: Minimum age 18, knowledge of languages not essential.

Accommodation: Board, accommodation and insurance provided from £350 per week.

Application Procedure: For full details of BTCV's Conservation Holiday programme, contact BTCV for an up-to-date brochure. Full project details are also available on the BTCV website.

Operation Wallacea

Job(s) Available: Volunteer PADI divemasters (approximately 20), habitat/forest structure surveyors (approximately 12), logistics/admin, various scientific/field work positions.

Duration: Approximately 2 months from late June to early September.

Working Hours: Variable, approximately 8–15 hours per day.

> **Head Office:** Operation Wallacea Ltd., Hope House, Old Bolingbroke, Near Spilsby, Lincolnshire PE23 4EX, UK
> ☎ 01790 763194
> ✏ jobs@opwall.com
> 🖥 www.opwall.com

Company Description: Operation Wallacea is a series of biological and social science expedition projects that operate in remote locations across the world. These expeditions are designed with specific wildlife conservation aims in mind– from identifying areas needing protection, through to implementing and assessing conservation management programmes. What is different about Operation Wallacea is that the large teams of university academics, who are specialists in various aspects of biodiversity or social and economic studies, are concentrated at the target study sites. Therefore, research assistants and general surveyors joining the surveys have the option of customising their own itinerary from a range of training and science options at each of the sites. It also provides an excellent environment for students to complete their dissertations or senior theses and over 60% achieve a first for their field studies with Operation Wallacea.

Requirements: *PADI divemasters:* PADI divemaster qualification and appropriate insurance. *Habitat/forest structure surveyors:* tropical forest mensuration, summer or winter mountain leadership, advanced life-guarding, advanced first aid, biology or geography degree/background, work with 16–19 year olds. *Logistics/admin:* office work experience, basic Spanish and/or competency to learn, clean driving license, 4x4 experience. *Scientific/field work positions:* varies depending on area of research (small mammals, herpetology, etc), field research experience.

Accommodation: Varies depending on location. See website for further details.

Application Procedure: Please send any expressions of interest or letters of application together with a comprehensive CV to jobs@opwall.com

Overseas Development Institute

Job(s) Available: 40 Fellowships are awarded annually.

Company Description: ODI runs the Overseas Development Institute Fellowship Scheme which enables recent young economics graduates to gain

> **Head Office:** 111, Westminster Bridge Road, London SE1 7JD, UK
> ☎ 020 7922 0300
> 🖥 www.odi.org.uk

practical experience in the public sectors of developing countries in Africa, the Caribbean and the Pacific.

Requirements: Candidates may be of any nationality but must have (or be studying for) a postgraduate qualification in economics or a related field.

Application Procedure: Online applications are accepted from November each year via the website at www.odi.org.uk/fellows.

Trekforce Worldwide

Job(s) Available: Volunteers for remote conservation projects, teaching placements and challenging expeditions in the rainforest.

Duration: Choose from 4 weeks to 5 month expeditions. *Teaching placements:* 2–5 months.

Company Description: Trekforce worldwide is one

Head Office: Way to Wooler, Wooler, Northumberland NE71 6AQ, UK
☎ 0845 241 3085
info@trekforceworldwide.com
www.trekforceworldwide.com

of the experts in delivering remote conservation projects, teaching placements and challenging expeditions in the rainforest which actively protect sustainable and vulnerable environments and assist rural communities throughout the world.

Job Description: Concentrating on conservation and community development in the rainforest, the project could be anything from building ranger stations to discourage illegal logging, to building tourist huts and clearing trails to increase visitors to the area, or painting and restoring school classrooms. If teaching is what you're interested in then speak to Trekforce Worldwide about taking part in a teaching assistant role. You can choose from traditional subjects including English and maths or use your creative side and help run a drama group or art club. The only limit is your imagination.

Requirements: Trekforce Worldwide will talk to you about your skills and interests so that the school benefits from your skills and you enjoy the experience to the full!

Accommodation: *Conservation placements:* applicants will call a hammock home for the duration of the expedition and the alarm clock will be the local primates as they call across the canopy as the sun rises. *Teaching placements:* applicants will live with host families in pairs for the duration of the placement, a real cultural experience.

Application Procedure: Trekforce can put applicants in touch with past volunteers so they can speak to them about their experiences or attend event to hear more about the projects and jungle life. Call 0845 241 3085 for details.

Gap Year Organisations

Gap Activity Projects Ltd

Job(s) Available: Voluntary work opportunities.

Duration: Successful volunteers undertake full-time work for between 3 and 12 months.

Pay: Usually a living allowance is provided.

Company Description: Gap is a registered charity based in Reading which organises voluntary work

Head Office: GAP House, 44 Queen's Road, Reading, Berkshire RG1 4BB
☎ 01189 594914
volunteer@gap.org.uk
www.gap.org.uk

opportunities for 17–25-year-olds who wish to take a 'year out' between school and higher education, employment or training. Gap places over 2000 volunteers abroad each year and has been sending volunteers on placements that make a difference for over 35 years.

Job Description: Currently opportunities exist in Argentina, Australia, Brazil, Canada, China, Ecuador, Fiji and the South Pacific, Germany, Ghana, India, Japan, Malawi, Malaysia, Mexico, New Zealand, Russia, South Africa, Tanzania, Thailand and Vietnam. There is a variety of projects on offer including teaching English as a foreign language, general duties in schools, assisting on community projects or caring for the sick and people with disabilities, outdoor activities and sports coaching, conservation work and scientific surveys.

Requirements: Gap welcomes applications at any time from year 12 onwards.

Accommodation: Receive food and accommodation.

Application Procedure: Gap has no closing date for applications, although you stand a better chance of being placed on your first choice project, if you apply early. Every applicant is invited to interview with interviews taking place from the middle of October onwards in Reading, Leeds, Dublin, Belfast, Glasgow and other regional locations. If you are up for the challenge apply online at www.gap.org.uk

Outreach International

Job(s) Available: Volunteers.

Duration: Between 1 and 4 months. Departures are throughout the year but in the summer they are carefully coordinated with the vacations.

Cost: The cost of £2,700 (for 3 months) includes full health, baggage and public liability insurance, a generous food allowance and comfortable accom-

Head Office: Bartletts Farm, Hayes Road, Compton Dundon, Somerset TA11 6PF, UK
☎ 01458 274957
✆ info@outreachinternational.co.uk
🖳 www.outreachinternational.co.uk

modation, a comprehensive language course on arrival and a CD language course in the UK, full in-country support, visa, all project-related travel, a weekend trip, and training in the UK including a fund-raising awareness day.

Company Description: A small, specialist gap organisation with carefully selected projects in specific parts of Cambodia, Sri Lanka, Costa Rica, Ecuador, Galapagos Islands and on the Pacific Coast of Mexico. The projects have enough variety to ensure that the interests and skills of individual volunteers can be put to good use.

Job Description: The placements include helping at orphanages, supporting a busy centre for street children, horse riding with disabled children, teaching English in coastal schools, helping at a medical centre and offering support at a busy children's hospital, humanitarian work, physiotherapy, carrying out conservation work in the Amazon rainforest, working at a centre for rescued wild animals and arts and crafts projects. These are humble, grass root initiatives where you can make a significant difference to the lives of local people. The projects are well organised and have a clear and genuine need for volunteer support. Each one is regularly visited and assessed by the Outreach International director. In addition to providing a challenging experience a number of volunteers have used this as a stepping-stone towards a career in overseas work.

Requirements: No specific skills or qualifications are normally required and most placements are ideal for people taking a gap year. However trained physiotherapists and people with office skills are needed for some projects.

Application Procedure: Applications would be welcome from confident, energetic people with a desire to travel, learn a language and offer their help to a worthwhile cause. All potential volunteers are interviewed informally to help them make an informed decision about whether the placement is right for them. Further details from www.outreach international.co.uk or from the UK Head Office on 01458 274957.

Project Trust

Job(s) Available: There are a wide variety of projects on offer, from teaching to development work, outward bound activities, and child and health care.

Head Office: 12 East Passage, Long Lane, London EC1A 7LP, UK
☎ 020 7796 1170
✆ info@projecttrust.org.uk
🖥 www.projecttrust.org.uk

Duration: Placements are for 12 months.
Working Hours: Varies by project.
Cost: The cost is £4,480 for the year which includes insurance and travel, full support overseas, food and accommodation. Fundraising workshops are held throughout the country to help volunteers raise the necessary finance.
Company Description: Project Trust arranges for volunteers to spend a whole year in an exciting country, becoming part of a community and learning another language.

Project Trust is an educational charity, which sends 200 school leavers overseas every year to over 20 countries around the world. At present these are: Bolivia, Botswana, Brazil, Chile, China, Dominican Republic, Guyana, Hong Kong, Honduras, Japan, Malawi, Malaysia, Morocco, Namibia, Niger, Peru, South Africa, Sri Lanka, Swaziland, Thailand, Uganda and Vietnam.
Requirements: Minimum age 17–19 at time of project. Scottish Highers students can apply at 16.
Accommodation: Food and accommodation included.
Additional Information: All volunteers attend a selection course on the Isle of Coll in the autumn before they go overseas. Week-long training courses take place on the Isle of Coll after final exams in the summer, and following a year overseas the volunteers assemble again on the Isle of Coll to debrief on their experiences before dispersing to university or their future careers.
Application Procedure: Apply online at www.projecttrust.org.uk. Apply as early as possible to avoid disappointment.

Social and Community Schemes

AFS Intercultural Programmes UK

Job(s) Available: Volunteer programme and school programme.

Head Office: Leeming House, Vicar Lane, Leeds LS2 7JF, UK
☎ 01132 426136
✆ info-unitedkingdom@afs.org
🖥 www.afsuk.org

Duration: 6 month placements. Departures from the UK are between July and September.
Cost: £3,300.
Company Description: AFS is an international non-profit association of 54 national organisations and is one of the world's largest voluntary organisations providing over 11,000 participants with an intercultural learning experience each year.
Job Description: *Volunteer programme*: with AFS International Volunteer Programmes in Latin America or Africa on voluntary projects dedicated to healthcare, education, social welfare, environmental protection and other pressing human issues such as homelessness

among urban poor, (with a special emphasis on meeting the needs of children). Participants live with a local volunteer host family and are provided with an excellent support structure. *School programme:* A unique opportunity for young people to spend an academic year studying in one of over 20 countries. Participants live with a local host family and enrol in the local school/college system.

Requirements: *Volunteer programme:* applicants must be aged 18–29 and no language skills or qualifications are required. *School programme:* aged 16–18. Must be able to fundraise for both programmes.

Application Procedure: By post to the above address.

Concordia Worldwide

Job(s) Available: Offers volunteers aged over 16 the opportunity to join international teams of volunteers working on community-based projects in over 60 countries worldwide.

> **Head Office:** 19 North Street, Portslade, Brighton BN41 1DH, UK
> ☎ 01273 422218
> ✆ info@concordia-iye.org.uk
> 🖳 www.concordia-iye.org.uk

Duration: Projects last for 2–4 weeks with the main season from June to September and smaller winter/spring programmes.

Cost: Volunteers pay a registration fee of £150 and fund their own travel and insurance.

Company Description: Concordia is a small not-for-profit charity committed to international youth exchange.

Job Description: Projects are diverse ranging from nature conservation, restoration, archaeology, construction, art and culture to projects that are socially based including work with adults or children with special needs, children's play-schemes and teaching.

Requirements: Generally the work doesn't require specific skills or experience, though real motivation and commitment to the project are a must.

Accommodation: Board and accommodation is free of charge.

Additional Information: Concordia also recruits volunteers (20+) to act as group co-ordinators on UK based projects, for which training is provided and all expenses are paid. This training takes place in spring each year. Early application is advised.

Application Procedure: For further information on volunteering or coordinating please check the website or contact the international volunteer co-ordinator at the above address. Concordia can only place volunteers who are resident in the UK. Volunteers applying from abroad should contact a volunteer organisation in their country of origin or country in which they are based.

VOLUNTARY WORK

WORLDWIDE

358

Cross-Cultural Solutions

Job(s) Available: Volunteers.

Duration: Volunteer programmes operate year-round in Africa, Asia, Latin America and Russia and range from 1 to 12 weeks.

Cost: Prices start at £1422 for a 2-week programme.

Head Office: Tower Point 44 North Road, Brighton BN1 1YR, UK
☎ 0845 458 2781/2782
✆ infouk@crossculturalsolutions.org
🖳 www.crossculturalsolutions.org

Company Description: Established in 1995, Cross-Cultural Solutions is a registered charity and a recognised leader in the field of international volunteering, sending thousands of volunteers overseas every year.

Job Description: Volunteers work side-by-side with local people on locally designed and driven projects, enabling them to participate in meaningful community development and see a country from a whole new perspective. The CCS experience also includes cultural and learning activities so that volunteers learn about the local culture. These include an in-depth orientation, language training, guest speakers and more. There is also plenty of free time to relax, reflect, or explore the community.

Accommodation: CCS provide a home-base for all volunteers. Here, all daily needs are taken care of, including lodging, meals and transportation. Through each of these elements volunteers are able to immerse themselves into the culture of the country and fully realise their experience. Programme fees cover the costs of accommodation in the CCS home base, meals and ground transportation, plus individual attention and guidance from an experienced and knowledgeable programme manager, coordination of the Volunteer Placement, perspectives programming activities, a 24-hour emergency hotline in the USA, and medical insurance.

Application Procedure: For more information please contact Cross-Cultural Solutions using the above contact information. Please contact us for latest pricing. See website for details of offices in other countries.

Global Citizens Network

Job(s) Available: Volunteers.

Duration: Volunteer trips last 1 to 3 weeks and are ongoing throughout the year.

Pay: Volunteers pay a programme fee of $800–$2200 (£400–£1100). The airfare is extra.

**Head Office:** 130 N. Howell Street, St Paul, Minnesota 55104, USA
☎ +1 651 6440960
✆ info@globalcitizens.org
🖳 www.globalcitizens.org

Company Description: Connect with indigenous peoples and contribute to peace throughout the world with Global Citizens Network, an organisation offering short-term volunteer trips that last a lifetime.

Job Description: Volunteers for projects in Kenya, Tanzania, Guatemala, Nepal, Thailand, Ecuador, Peru, Brazil, Canada, USA and Mexico. Build, plant, grow, learn. Programmes involve volunteers building a health centre, teaching in a school, harvesting shade grown coffee and working with a women's co-op.

Requirements: No special qualifications are required but the minimum age is 18. Volunteers under 18 years must be accompanied by parent or guardian.

Accommodation: Cost includes most in-country costs (food, lodging, transportation etc).

Application Procedure: For more information contact the programme director at the above address.

VOLUNTARY WORK

WORLDWIDE

Habitat for Humanity Great Britain

Job(s) Available: Teams of 10–15 volunteers.
Duration: Each trip lasts about 2 weeks.
Pay/Cost: Each applicant pays for their direct costs and raises money to build more houses.
Company Description: Habitat for Humanity is an international house-building charity. Each year teams of 10–15 volunteers travel overseas to help build simple, decent houses alongside local people, who are in desperate need of shelter.

Head Office: 46 West Bar Street, Banbury, Oxon OX16 9RZ, UK
☎ 01295 220188
✆ globalvillage@habitatforhumanity.org.uk
💻 www.habitatforhumanity.org.uk

Job Description: Trips are ideal for those interested in travel and a volunteer experience. Trips are designed to promote cross-cultural understanding and raise awareness of the urgent issue of substandard housing.
Requirements: Minimum age 18. No experience or building skill is necessary.
Accommodation: Costs include food, insurance and sight-seeing activities during rest days.
Application Procedure: For further information on trips for individuals or groups, please visit the website or contact the global village department (see above).

Learning Enterprises

Job(s) Available: Volunteer English teacher (130).
Duration: From mid-June to mid-August. Minimum period of work 6 weeks.
Working Hours: Approximately 3–6 hours. Depends on the village.

Head Office: P.O. Box 20053, Stanford, CA 94309, USA
✆ info@learningenterprises.org
💻 www.learningenterprises.org

Company Description: Learning Enterprises sends college aged students overseas to teach English in underdeveloped areas. Its mission is to expand the horizons of disadvantaged youth through global volunteerism.
Job Description: Most volunteers are college students. Each volunteer will teach in a rural or underdeveloped area. Volunteers are placed with host families. Student ages range from 6 through to adults. Volunteers are required to develop their own lesson plans. Positions available in Mexico, Panama, Honduras, China, Indonesia, Mauritius, Egypt, Ethiopia, Hungary, Slovakia, Romania, Croatia, Poland and Lithuania.
Requirements: No teaching experience necessary. Minimum age 18. Latin American countries require basic Spanish.
Accommodation: Board and accommodation available.
Application Procedure: Apply online to the programme director for specific programmes. Interviews between 1 January and 1 February. There are 2 rounds of interviews.

Skillshare International

Job(s) Available: Projects cover a wide-range of activities and general management, agricultural, technical, educational and medical skills are all required.
Duration: Placements are usually for 2 years.
Cost: Skillshare offers a modest living allowance,

Head Office: 126 New Walk Street, Leicester LE1 7JA, UK
☎ 01162 541862
✆ recruitment@skillshare.org
💻 www.skillshare.org

flights/travel to the placement and return, medical cover, and pre and post placement grants to assist with relocation. The living allowance is adequate to cover your living costs whilst in the country of placement but not adequate for savings or meeting other costs you may have in your country of residence.

Company Description: Skillshare recruits professionals to share their skills and experience with local communities for further economic and social development in Botswana, Kenya, Lesotho, Mozambique, Namibia, South Africa, Swaziland, Tanzania, Uganda, India and Nepal. Its vision is a world without poverty, injustice and inequality where people, regardless of cultural, social, and political divides come together for mutual benefit living in peaceful co-existence.

Requirements: Applicants should be aged 21, have relevant qualifications and experience, particularly in training others.

Application Procedure: An information pack is available from the above address.

Tearfund Transform International Programme

Job(s) Available: Volunteers.

Duration: Volunteers to work for 4–6 weeks from early July to the end of August.

Cost: A contribution of approx £1,800 which includes orientation, travel, food and accommodation is required.

> **Head Office:** 100 Church Road, Teddington, Middlesex TW11 8QE, UK
> ☎ 020 8943 7777
> ✍ transform@tearfund.org
> 🖳 www.youth.tearfund.org/transform

Company Description: Tearfund is an evangelical Christian development charity working with local partners to bring help and hope to communities in need. In 2007 Tearfund supported hundreds of projects in over 90 countries.

Job Description: Volunteers to join teams of 8–12 people. Assignments are in a number of countries and include practical work, renovation and work with children.

Requirements: Applicants should be over 18 and committed Christians.

Application Procedure: Details are available from the enquiry unit at the above address and applications should be received by mid-February.

Workcamps

International Voluntary Service (British Branch of Service Civil International)

Job(s) Available: Volunteers.

Duration: Volunteers work for 2 to 4 weeks. Most workcamps are between April and September and last 1 to 4 weeks. There are some short-term projects.

Cost: Volunteers must pay for membership of IVS, this is included in a registration fee to IVS of £185 for projects abroad and £95 for projects in Britain. Volunteers pay for their own travel costs.

Company Description: IVS-GB aims to promote peace and intercultural understanding through vol-

> **Head Office:** IVS Registered Office, Oxford Place Centre, Oxford Place, Leeds LS1 3AX, UK (England)
> ☎ 01132 469900
> ✍ england@ivs-gb.org.uk
>
> **Head Office:** 7 Upper Bow, Edinburgh EH1 2JN, UK (Scotland)
> ☎ 0131 226 6722
> ✍ scotland@ivs-gb.org.uk
> 🖳 www.ivs-gb.org.uk

unteering and international voluntary projects. IVS-GB organises international short-term projects in Britain and across a choice of 45 countries around the world.

Job Description: Volunteers work for 2 to 4 weeks in an international team of 6–20 people, sharing domestic and social life as well as the work. The projects include work with children, with socially disadvantaged people, north-south solidarity, arts and culture, and the environment and conservation. For example helping an intercultural centre in Guatemala, helping at a centre for disabled children in Latvia or building a solar water heater on a Scottish island.

Requirements: English is the language of most projects, (languages are required for the north/south programme). For our north/south programme (Africa, Asia and Latin America for over 21s) previous experience of voluntary work is preferred.

Accommodation: Projects provide food and accommodation.

Additional Information: If you want to receive more information, please contact an IVS-GB office. To find an IVS/SCI branch in your country please see www.sciint.org or contact IVS-GB at the above addresses.

Application Procedure: IVS can only accept applications from people with an address in Britain. Applications should be posted to IVS at the relevant address. Application forms are available online or from an office. Project listings for each summer are compiled each year and available from March on the website, which has all the up to date project information IVS is working towards equal opportunities.

UNA Exchange

Job(s) Available: Volunteer projects.

Duration: Most projects last 2–4 weeks between the months of April and September but there are also ones at other times of year and longer-term opportunities. There are longer-term (6–12 month) projects available, mainly in Europe, through the European Voluntary Service (EVS) and Medium Term Volunteer (MTV) programmes.

Head Office: Temple of Peace, Cathays Park, Cardiff CF10 3AP, UK
☎ 02920 223088
✆ info@unaexchange.org
🖳 www.unaexchange.org

Cost: There is an administration fee of £110–£140 for projects abroad, which covers all food and accommodation by the host organisation during the project.

Company Description: Organises projects in Wales for international volunteers and sends volunteers to projects abroad.

Job Description: Projects include a huge variety of social, environmental and renovation work from helping to set up a festival in France to working with children in the Ukraine. UNA Exchange also operates a 'north-south' programme of projects in Africa, Latin America and South-East Asia.

Requirements: To participate in this programme, volunteers need to attend a training weekend in Cardiff.

Accommodation: Included in cost.

Application Procedure: Further details available on the constantly updated website

Volunteers for Peace, International Voluntary Service (VFP)

Job(s) Available: Voluntary service projects.

Duration: *Short-term voluntary service projects:* (2–3 weeks) and a smaller number of *medium-term projects* (1–3 months) and *long-term projects* (3–6 months).

Head Office: 1034, Tiffany Road, Belmont, Vermont 05730, USA
☎ +1 802 2592759
✆ vfp@vfp.org
🖳 www.vfp.org

Company Description: Coordinates international voluntary service projects in over 100 countries worldwide.

Job Description: There are many types of work available because projects arise from grass-lands local community needs (construction, environmental, agricultural, and social work).

Accommodation: Accommodations vary widely but usually volunteers share the same living space, doing all their own cleaning and food preparation on a rotating basis.

Application Procedure: A full listing of VFP's programmes can be found in VFP's International Workcamp Directory ($30 post-paid in the USA or online at www.vfp.org). For further details phone, write or email for a free newsletter.

Youth Action for Peace (YAP)

Job(s) Available: Volunteers needed to take part in voluntary work projects (workcamps).

Duration: Projects generally last for 2 to 3 weeks each, and take place all year round, but mainly in the summer. There are possibilities of longer-term projects (3–12 months).

Head Office: Yap UK, POB 43670, London SE22 OXX, UK
☎ 0870 165 7927
action@yap-uk.org
www.yap-uk.org

Working Hours: Participants will usually be working for around 30–35 hours per week.

Cost: There is an extra fee (on average $200) payable on arrival for projects taking place in Africa, Asia and Latin America. Volunteers must organise their own travel.

Company Description: Voluntary work projects organised by YAP in the UK and its sister organisations in 80 countries in Europe, the Americas, Africa and Asia.

Job Description: The work undertaken may consist of tasks such as restoration, entertaining children in need or environmental, social or artistic work. Applicants will work with volunteers from different countries and local people.

Requirements: No particular qualifications are necessary, but applicants must normally be aged at least 18.

Accommodation: Food, accommodation and leisure activities are provided.

Application Procedure: For further details check the above address.

Au Pairs, Nannies, Family Helps and Exchanges

A-One Au-Pairs and Nannies

Job(s) Available: Au pairs and au pairs plus.
Working Hours: 5 days a week.
Pay: Vary according to hours worked.
Job Description: Au pairs/au pairs plus required for light housework and childcare.
Requirements: Applicants should be 18–27 years old.

Head Office: 35 The Grove, Edgeware, Middlesex HAB 9QA, UK
☎ 0800 298 8807, 020 8905 3355
info@aupairsetc.co.uk
www.aupairsetc.co.uk

Accommodation: Board and lodging vary according to hours worked.

Additional Information: Places available throughout Europe and America.

Application Procedure: Contact Hillary Perry, proprietor, for details.

Au Pair Select

Job(s) Available: Au pairs, mother's helps, nannies.
Duration: Period of work varies from country to country but is usually 6 months and 2–3 months during the summer.
Working Hours: *Au pairs:* 30 hours per week.
Pay: *Au pairs:* £55 per week. *Mother's helps:* £120+ per week. *Nannies:* £200+ per week.

Head Office: 42 Milsted Road, Rainham, Kent ME8 6SU, UK
☎ 01634 310808
enquiries@aupair-select.com
www.aupair-select.com

Job Description: Applicants are placed in the following countries: England, France, Germany, Spain, Italy, The Netherlands, Belgium, Austria, Switzerland, Canada and Australia and occasionally other countries.

Requirements: Applicants must have childcare experience and be aged between 18 and 28.

Application Procedure: To register as an au pair in the UK visit www.aupair-select.com.

Childcare International

Job(s) Available: Au pair and nanny stays in the USA.

Duration: Visa-supported 1 year stay.

Pay: Up to $157.94 per week for qualified nannies and a minimum of $139.05 per week for au pairs. Families provide full round trip airfare, medical insurance and part-time college course plus 2 weeks paid holiday.

Head Office: Childcare International Ltd, Trafalgar House, Grenville Place, London NW7 3SA, UK
☎ 020 8906 3116
✆ sandra@childint.co.uk
🖥 www.childint.co.uk

Company Description: Childcare America allocate positions to applicants aged 18–26 with good childcare experience. Full local counsellor support is provided to introduce friends and give guidance with every aspect of the stay.

Job Description: Choose from a wide range of approved families from across the USA. Four days' orientation is provided in the USA.

Requirements: Applicants must drive.

Application Procedure: By post to the above address.

Cosmopolitan Nannies

Job(s) Available: Various childcare positions.

Duration: Minimum period of work 1 month.

Working Hours: 5–6 day week, 8–12 hours per day.

Pay: £200–£700 per week.

Head Office: PO Box 12105, Abeckett Street, Melbourne, Victoria, 8006, Australia
☎ +61 390 163581
✆ admin@cosmopolitannannies.com
🖥 www.cosmopolitannannies.com

Company Description: An Australian agency that specialises in the introduction of English, French, German and Spanish native speaking childcare professionals both temporarily and permanently throughout the world.

Requirements: Minimum age 21. Experience with children required. A child friendly nature mandatory. Tertiary education and/or a foreign language a plus. Fluent English necessary. CRB check and first aid certificate often required.

Accommodation: Free board and accommodation available.

Application Procedure: Apply to Patricia Leader, recruitment consultant at the above email. Candidates may have to attend an interview. Introductions are made worldwide and interviews are often held in major capital cities.

Inter-Sejours

Job(s) Available: Au pairs placed in Australia, Austria, Canada, Denmark, France, Germany, Ireland, Italy, the Netherlands, New Zealand, Spain, Sweden, the USA and the UK.

Duration: We accept stays for 2–3 months during the summer holidays and from 3–12 months during the rest of the year. An immediate start is possible.

Head Office: 179 Rue de Courcelles, F-75017 Paris, France
☎ +33 1 47630681
✆ aideinfo.intersejours@wanadoo.fr
🖥 http://asso.intersejours.free.fr

Working Hours: 25–30 hours per week.

Pay: Pocket money minimum €300 per month.

Company Description: Inter-Sejours is a non-profit making organisation with 37 years of experience.

Requirements: Applicants should be aged 18–30; previous childcare experience an advantage.

Accommodation: Full board and lodging provided.

Application Procedure: Application forms available from the website.

Neilson

Job(s) Available: Child minders (30).

Duration: Summer and winter (ski) work is available.

Working Hours: 6 days a week.

Pay: From £95 per week.

Company Description: Neilson is a holiday company committed to providing excellent quality

Head Office: Locksview, Brighton Marina, Brighton, East Sussex BN2 5HA, UK
☎ 0870 241 2901
✎ recruitment@neilson.com
💻 www.neilson.com/recruitment

activity holidays. They pride themselves on having a high staff/client ratio and the exceptional calibre of their overseas staff.

Job Description: To care for 0–5 year olds in the resorts.

Requirements: NNEB, BTEC or equivalent preferred. Applicants should be at least 18 years old with experience of working with children, a sense of fun, and be creative team players.

Accommodation: Flights paid to and from resort, accommodation, insurance and uniform provided.

Application Procedure: Contact the overseas recruitment team, at the above address.

Roma Au Pair Associazione Culturale

Job(s) Available: Au pair, au pair plus, mother's help.

Duration: From May to July, and August to September. Minimum period of work 8 weeks.

Working Hours: 6–8 hours per day.

Pay: €80–€100 per week.

Head Office: Via Pietro Mascagni, 138 00199 Roma, Italy
☎ +39 06 86321519
✎ info@romaaupair.com
💻 www.romaaupair.com

Company Description: Roma au pair has been working with the youth cultural programme since 1998. We personally take care of good placements for both the au pairs and families.

Job Description: The au pair programme is a cultural exchange for young people willing to live abroad and who wish to learn the culture and life style of their host country. A perfect way to experience life abroad without expensive costs and learning new languages.

Requirements: Minimum age 18. Childcare experience essential. Fluent English and driving license would be an advantage.

Accommodation: Full board and lodging paid for by host family.

Application Procedure: Apply to Giuseppina Pamphili at info@romaaupair.com between March and May. Phone interview required.

Solihull Au Pair & Nanny Agency

Job(s) Available: Au pairs, au pair care.

Duration: *Au pair care:* 5 day training session in the Sheraton Meadowlands Hotel, New Jersey. Two weeks paid vacation, and the possibility of staying for a further 12 months as an au pair if you wish to stay in the USA.

Head Office: 5 Parklands, Blossomfield Road, Solihull B91 1NG, UK
☎ 07973 886979
🖂 aupairs1@btconnect.com
🖥 www.au-pairs4u.com

Pay: *Au pairs:* pocket money £180–£240 per month. Pocket money is paid in Euros. *Au pair care:* weekly stipend of $158–$200 per week is paid. The higher amount is for those who have a recognised childcare qualification.

Company Description: Based in Birmingham, Lorraine regularly travels to London and can arrange interviews all over the UK and in Ireland. Established some 40 years, Lorraine uses her vast experience to place au pairs.

Job Description: *Au pairs:* placed in major European countries, France, Italy, Spain are the most popular countries and Lorraine works with overseas contacts to locate bonafide host families. *Au pair care:* round-trip airfare from your home country to the USA. Medical insurance provided plus private room and full board with carefully screened host family. A local area director lives nearby and regular social and cultural activities are arranged with other au pairs. You will receive $500 towards your education as you are required to study in the USA. There is a 24-hour telephone helpline. Opportunity to travel in the 13th month. Comprehensive training and support.

Requirements: For the American programme, you must be aged 18–26 and be able to drive, have a good knowledge of English and be able to commit to a 12-month stay.

Additional Information: The agency will deal with all visa requirements, tickets and arrange the interview and paperwork.

Application Procedure: Contact www.aupairs2usa.com or the above website and fill in the online pre-application form.

The Childcare Company

Job(s) Available: Ski/summer resort nannies, au pair and nanny programme to the USA, au pair programme in Europe.

Duration: Qualified nannies required for just a few weeks. Applicants must be available for the whole summer season (or whole winter season if applying for a ski resort job).

Head Office: 7 Garth Road, Sevenoaks, Kent TN13 1RT, UK
☎ 01234 352688
🖂 mary_elder@thechildcare company.co.uk
🖥 www.thechildcarecompany.co.uk

Working Hours: 25 hours per week.

Pay: *Au pairs:* £65 per week.

Company Description: The Childcare Company is a leading childcare recruitment agency, which was established in 1980.

Requirements: Minimum age 18. All applicants should have childcare training and qualifications in childcare. *In the USA:* Placements for qualified NNEB, BTEC National Diploma and NVQ level III in childcare to work with young babies. Also placements for unqualified applicants to work with school-age children.

Accommodation: Full board and lodging provided.

Additional Information: *Winter season:* perks include free skiing lessons, lift pass, and tuition.

Application Procedure: Applications to the above address.

Travel Active

Job(s) Available: Work exchange, au pair and high school programmes on a global scale.

Company Description: Travel Active is Holland's largest youth exchange organisation. Travel Active is a member of the Federation of International Youth Travel Organisations (FIYTO), Association of Language Travel Organisations (ALTO), International Association for Educational Work Exchange Programmes (IAEWEP) and a founding member of the International Au Pair Association (IAPA).

Head Office: PO Box 107, N5800 AC Venray, The Netherlands
☎ +31 478551900
✉ info@travelactive.nl
🖥 www.travelactive.nl

Job Description: Travel Active receives students from all over the world on its incoming high school, au pair and work exchange programmes. For these programmes Travel Active also offers its own tailor-made insurance. Youngsters may choose from a variety of work programmes, with or without job placement. Internships are also available. Several programmes combine a language course with a job placement.

Application Procedure: For further details contact the above address.

UK and Overseas Domestic Agency

Job(s) Available: Live-in, live-out nannies, au pairs, housekeepers and maternity nurses.

Duration: The minimum period for summer work is 3 months. The usual period of stay is 1 year. Recruitment is ongoing. It will normally take between 2 and 3 weeks to find a suitable overseas placement.

Head Office: 27 Old Gloucester Street, London WC1N 3BR, UK
☎ 020 7808 7898
✉ london@nannys.co.uk
🖥 www.nannys.co.uk

Working Hours: Conditions vary, as do hours of work.

Company Description: Established over 35 years ago, the UK and Overseas Agency places live-in, live-out nannies, au pairs, housekeepers and maternity nurses in locations worldwide.

Job Description: Nannies, au pairs, mothers' helps, house keepers: offers jobs throughout the UK, Europe and in the Middle East, Australia, Japan, Singapore, as well as many other countries.

Requirements: All applicants must speak English. The agency employs both experienced and inexperienced staff. The only stipulated requirements are good references and police clearance.

Accommodation: All positions provide board and lodging free of charge.

Application Procedure: Apply through the website. Completed applications with photos and references must be sent by post.

Other Employment Abroad

Alliance Abroad Group

Job(s) Available: Customised internship, work, teach and volunteer programmes.

Duration: 2 weeks to 12 months.

Company Description: Founded in 1992, Alliance Abroad Group, LP offers programmes for students and graduates in and outside of the USA. Opportunities include working in Australia and New Zealand, teaching in China, Argentina and Spain, interning in the USA and volunteering in South America and South Africa.

Head Office: 1221 South Mopac Expressway, Suite 250, Austin, TX 78746, USA
☎ +1 512 457 8062
✉ vnoel@allianceabroad.com
🖥 www.allianceabroad.com

Accommodation: For most programmes airport pickup, salary/stipend, meals and accommodation are provided.

Additional Information: All programmes include guaranteed placement, visa assistance, orientation materials, health and travel insurance, 24/7 emergency support, personal in-country co-ordinators.

Application Procedure: Contact the above address or email for details. Applications usually 3 months in advance.

Anywork Anywhere

Job(s) Available: Tour guides, overland drivers, ski/board instructors and guides, chalet chefs and hosts, all levels of hotel and pub staff, nannies, barge  and yacht crew, care workers, teachers, nurses, holiday and theme park, campsite and summer resort staff are amongst the jobs listed as well as a wide and changing variety of many others.

Company Description: This organisation provides a free source of information to people looking for work throughout the UK and worldwide via their web site.

Additional Information: The site also provides a broad range of other resources for work and travel worldwide.

Application Procedure: Interested candidates can simply contact their chosen advertiser and apply direct, with no registration necessary. For further information consult www.anyworkanywhere.com.

Bunac

Job(s) Available: There are a great variety of programmes on offer including summer camp counselling in the USA and work and travel programmes to the USA, Canada, Australia, New Zealand, South Africa, Ghana, Costa Rica, Peru, Cambodia and China.

Head Office: 16 Bowling Green Lane, London EC1R OQH, UK
☎ 020 7251 3472
✉ enquiries@bunac.org.uk
🖥 www.bunac.org

Company Description: BUNAC, a non-profit organisation, has enabled over 250,000 gap year, full-time students and other young people to work overseas since 1962. BUNAC is a national club and helps members to obtain jobs, work permits and affordable flight packages. BUNAC provides help and advice on jobs, accommodation and travel as well as providing back-up services while working and travelling.

Application Procedure: For further information contact the above address.

Global Choices

Job(s) Available: Internships, practical training abroad, working holiday, volunteering and work experience worldwide.

Head Office: Barkat House, 116-118 Finchley Road, London NW3 5HT, UK
☎ 020 7433 2501
✉ info@globalchoices.co.uk
🖥 www.globalchoices.co.uk

Duration: From 2 weeks to 18 months.

Pay: Cost depends on programme.

Job Description: Destinations include Argentina, Australia, Brazil, Canada, China, Greece, India, Ireland, Italy, Spain, United Kingdom and United States. Placements are offered in many fields, industrial, business, science, conservation, agriculture, travel, tourism, and more.

Application Procedure: See website for details.

Greenforce

Job(s) Available: Guaranteed work in the Australian outback in 1 of 3 areas; agriculture, hospitality or teaching. Greenforce also run volunteer projects working on animal rescue, marine conservation, humanitarian or community projects.

Head Office: 11-15 Betterton street, Covent Garden, London WC2H 9BP, UK
☎ 020 7470 8888
✉ info@greenforce.org
🖥 www.greenforce.org

Duration: *Volunteer projects:* range from 2 to 10 weeks. Required from 24 September.

Pay: *Work in Australia:* union agreed pay levels of £650 minimum per month.

Company Description: Greenforce are a non-profit organisation who have worked along side the WWF, UNESCO, UN, Red Cross, African Wildlife Fund, and various governments around the world. Last year they invested over £300,000 into the communities they work with and all expeditions, volunteers and staff are carbon neutral.

Job Description: *Agriculture:* cattle ranch, polo farms, rural outback station etc. *Hospitality:* road house, outback pub, etc. *Teaching:* as part of the Australian Government's distant learning project. *Volunteer projects:* in Ecuador, Tanzania, South Africa, Fiji, Bahamas, Nepal, and China to name a few. Again fully training is provided in research techniques, scuba diving, data collection, animal handling etc. These trips are a real adventure and should be checked out. Other opportunities include teaching English in South America or working as a game ranger in Africa.

Requirements: Minimum age 18. Full training is provided.

Accommodation: Food and accommodation is provided.

Requirements: For further details, and to choose your expedition, check out the website or contact Laura at Greenforce directly on the above details.

InterExchange

Job(s) Available: Work exchange programmes including work and travel, volunteer, internship, au pair, language school and camp counsellor programmes within the USA and around the world.

Head Office: 161 Sixth Avenue, New York, NY 10013, USA
☎ +1 212 9240446
✉ info@interexchange.org
🖥 www.interexchange.org

Company Description: InterExchange is a non-profit organisation dedicated to promoting cultural awareness.

Job Description: In the USA they offer J-1 Visa programs and H-2B Visa programs for au pair, seasonal work, internship, camp counsellor and staff positions. InterExchange also offers working abroad placements for US residents to travel to Australia, Costa Rica, France, Germany, England, India, Italy, Kenya, Namibia, the Netherlands, Peru, South Africa and Spain as au pairs, interns, volunteers, seasonal workers and language students. Most InterExchange programmes include placements.

Application Procedure: For further details contact InterExchange at the above address.

i-to-i

Job(s) Available: Volunteer projects, paid work overseas, TEFL training. More than 5,000 volunteers are placed each year.

Head Office: 261 Low Lane, Leeds LS18 5NY, UK
☎ 0870 333 2332, quoting SJ1006
✉ info@i-to-i.com
🖥 www.i-to-i.com

Duration: *Volunteer projects:* from 1–24 weeks in duration. Projects are available all year round from 1 week to a complete year out. *TEFL training:* range of TEFL courses including intensive weekend TEFL courses.

Pay: *Paid work overseas:* i-to-i also provides paid teaching placements across the globe and working holiday programmes in Australia.

Cost: All prices include pre-departure training (TEFL for teaching placements), comprehensive insurance and 24-hour support from the UK. *TEFL training:* Fees start from £195.

Company Description: i-to-i is an award-winning organisation providing worthwhile work and travel opportunities throughout the world. i-to-i offers around 500 volunteer projects across 23 countries worldwide along with self-development programmes and paid work programmes. It also provides onsite and online TEFL (Teaching English as a Foreign Language) training for those who want to combine teaching as part of their travel experience or find work overseas. All projects are thoroughly researched and volunteers are met and supported whilst away by in-country co-ordinators.

Job Description: *Volunteer projects:* project types include voluntary teaching, conservation, community development, building, sports and media as well as humanitarian tours. Current projects include a panda conservation project in China, surfing programmes in South Africa, reporting for an English newspaper in Sri Lanka, and teaching English to orphans in India. *TEFL training:* in the UK, the US, Ireland and Australia. An online TEFL course is also available at www.onlineTEFL.com allowing study from any location worldwide. Further courses add practical training with teaching practice sessions overseas. All courses are designed for travellers and include a module on finding work abroad. i-to-i also offers a database of more than 8,000 job contacts for TEFL tutees.

Requirements: i-to-i projects are suitable for all ages with special projects available for school students and corporate groups.

Accommodation: Food and accommodation are included on most projects and some also offer local language courses on arrival. *Volunteer projects:* accommodation varies from homestays with local families to guesthouses, and apartments.

Application Procedure: For further details contact the above address quoting SJ1006.

SeasonWorkers.Com

Job(s) Available: SeasonWorkers is a website that lists hundreds of rep, ski, outdoor, education, TEFL and childcare jobs and gap year opportunities.

Company Description: Season Workers has won various awards including Best Recruitment website at the 2004 Travel and Tourism Web Awards in London.

Head Office: Houdini Media Ltd, PO BOX 29132, Dunfermline KY11 4YU, UK
☎ 01383 851166
🖷 info@seasonworkers.com
🖳 www.seasonworkers.com

Job Description: You can use SeasonWorkers to thoroughly research every avenue and apply online for information packs on hundreds of different summer jobs.

Requirements: Whatever your age, experience or aspirations there will be a summer job on SeasonWorkers for you.

Additional Information: The site also includes a vibrant messageboard for help and chat about summer jobs, and when you return, and have lost contact with all the people you met, the 'Season Workers Reunion' service helps get you reunited.

Application Procedure: Go to www.seasonworkers.com and get started.

Travel Active

Job(s) Available: Work exchange, au pair and high school programmes on a global scale.

Company Description: Travel Active is Holland's largest youth exchange organisation. Travel Active is a member of the Federation of International Youth

Head Office: PO Box 107, N5800 AC Venray, The Netherlands
☎ +31 478551900
🖷 info@travelactive.nl

371

Travel Organisations (FIYTO), Association of Language Travel Organisations (ALTO), International Association for Educational Work Exchange Programmes (IAEWEP) and a founding member of the International Au Pair Association (IAPA).

Job Description: Travel Active receives students from all over the world on its incoming high school, au pair and work exchange programmes. For these programmes Travel Active also offers its own tailor-made insurance. Youngsters may choose from a variety of work programmes, with or without job placement. Internships are also available. Several programmes combine a language course with a job placement.

Application Procedure: For further details contact the above address.

Twin Work and Volunteer Abroad

Job(s) Available: *Work programmes*: include paid jobs and working guest, internships, work and travel. Positions available in hospitality, travel and tourism, manual trades, retail, business, administration, agriculture and many more. *Volunteer programmes*: include conservation, community and teaching.

Head Office: Twin Group, Second Floor, 67-71 Lewisham High St, Lewisham London SE13 SJX, UK
☎ 0800 804 8380
✉ workabroad@twinuk.com
🖥 www.workandvolunteer.com

Duration: Ranging from 2 weeks to 1 year.

Pay: Fully funded Leonardo da Vinci programmes through the EU available.

Company Description: Whether you are taking time out from study, a gap year or a break from a busy career Twin Work and Volunteer Abroad can help turn your dreams into an experience of a lifetime!

Job Description: *Work programmes: paid jobs and working guest:* improve your language skills abroad with year-round flexible paid opportunities. *Internships:* develop your career prospects and polish your language skills on professional career training programmes. *Work and travel:* travel the world outside Europe and fund your adventures with temporary seasonal work. *Volunteer programmes: conservation:* dedicate some time to wildlife and habitat protection from Ghana to the Galapagos. *community:* contribute to developing people's lives by volunteering on a wide range of social and community projects. *Teaching:* teach English and other subjects to eager children and adults of all ages.

Application Procedure: See website for further details.

AFRICA AND
THE MIDDLE EAST

EGYPT

CONSULATE GENERAL OF THE ARAB REPUBLIC OF EGYPT
2 Lowndes St, London SW1X 9ET
☎ 020 7499 3304
🖥 www.egyptianconsulate.co.uk
✍ info@egyptianconsulate.co.uk

Chances of finding a paid summer job in Egypt are slight but there may be possibilities in the tourist industry for example in the diving resort of Dahab. Otherwise opportunities for temporary work are normally restricted to voluntary work. There is also a need for English teachers to teach summer schools to Egyptian children and adults. Prospective teachers can advertise in the Egyptian expat press *Egypt Today* (www.egypttoday.com).

Teaching and Language Schools

International House

Job(s) Available: Teachers of English (6).
Duration: Between June and September, minimum period of work 6 weeks.
Working Hours: 20–25 hours of work per week.
Pay: Approximately £300 per month.
Job Description: Teachers required to teach intensive English courses to adults and young learners aged 5–15.

Head Office: International Language Institute Heliopolis, 2 Mohamed Bayoumi Street, Off Merghany Street, Heliopolis, Cairo Egypt
☎ +20 2 291295/4189212
✍ affiliates@ihworld.co.uk
🖥 www.ihworld.com

Requirements: Applicants should be Cambridge/RSA or CELTA qualified and preferably have experience of working with young learners.
Accommodation: Free accommodation.
Application Procedure: Applications to IH World Organisation Ltd, Unity Wharf, 13 Mill St, London SE1 2BH, UK. Please go online for more details.

Voluntary Work and Archaeology

Wind Sand & Stars

Job(s) Available: Participants for work on an annual environmental, scientific, historical expedition.
Duration: Operated during August.
Cost: There is a fee attached for travel to the area.
Company Description: Wind Sand & Stars is a small specialist company that organises a wide range of journeys and projects within the desert and mountain areas of South Sinai, Egypt.

Head Office: PO Box 58214, London N1 2GJ, UK
☎ 020 735 97551
✍ office@windsandstars.co.uk
🖥 www.windsandstars.co.uk

Job Description: Expeditions in the desert and mountains of Sinai.
Requirements: Minimum age 16.
Application Procedure: Applicants should contact the above address any time.

GHANA

OFFICE OF THE HIGH COMMISSIONER FOR GHANA
13 Belgrave Square, London SW1X 8PN
☎ 020 7201 5900

Voluntary work for Britons in Ghana can be organised by Concordia, UNA Exchange and Youth Action for Peace (See entries in the *Worldwide* chapter). The Student and Youth Travel Organisation in Accra (www.sytoghana.com) works with many partner organisations to bring volunteers to Ghana, but individuals can also apply to them direct via the website though this has to be done 10 weeks in advance. The organisations below also offer opportunities to work in Ghana.

Red Tape

Visa Requirements: the citizens of most countries are required to apply for a visa before travelling to Ghana. Please check with your local Embassy or Consulate.

Voluntary Work and Archaeology

Africatrust Networks

Job(s) Available: Tropical work experience.
Duration: 3–6 months.
Company Description: Africatrust Networks offers tropical work experience in North and West Africa with disadvantaged young people in Cameroon (French/English speaking), Ghana (English speaking)

Head Office: Africatrust Chambers, P.O Box 551, Portsmouth, Hampshire PO5 1ZN, UK
☎ 01873 812453
🖳 www.africatrust.gi

and in the southern parts of Morocco (French and Arabic speaking). Africatrust Networks is looking for volunteers who can work as part of a team, wish to learn as well as to give, can cope with limited resources and adapt their skills to a very different and often difficult work situation overseas.

Job Description: The UK office carries out the selection, interviewing, pre-departure briefings and helps with the fundraising for self-funded volunteer programmes. Each in-country director then leads the post-arrival and in-country 2-week induction course; acclimatisation, language, health, security, culture, music, history, geography, experimental living etc. Volunteers then choose from selected programmes and meet their host family. The in-country director then presides over the regular volunteer/host review meetings throughout the programme. Donations raised by volunteers are grouped and then distributed by the same team of volunteers. One vote per person not per pound raised. There are no deductions. Teams consist of 6 or 8 volunteers who are usually graduates, university gap year students, or students on placements – seeking supervised work experience in tropical development environments with the possibility of using French or Arabic. Such field experience might lead to careers with the British Council, UN, Save the Children, Oxfam, CNN/BBC or World Bank.
Application Procedure: For more information visit www.africatrust.gi or contact Africatrust Network at the above address.

Rural Upgrade Support Organisation (RUSO)

Job(s) Available: Volunteers for community projects in Ghana.

Duration: Placements vary in length. Usually short term is 3–4 weeks and long term is 4–8 weeks.

Cost: There is an initial registration fee of $200 (which includes the first month's stay). 1–3 months costs $25 per week.

Head Office: P O Box CE 11066, Tema
☎ +233 21 513147/8
✉ ruralupgrade@yahoo.com
🖥 www.ruso.interconnection.org

Company Description: RUSO is a non-political, non-sectarian and non-governmental organisation that aims to assist community upgrading using sustainable and environmentally friendly means. It employs volunteers to help implement community-based solutions after a thorough environmental impact assessment and total commitment to the 'green' approach.

Job Description: Projects include providing healthcare, education and small scale business management, cultural exchange and social development.

Requirements: Minimum age 18. Volunteers must be in good health, willing to work hard and live within the rural community.

Accommodation: Provided. Food and transport around the Keta district is not included.

Application Procedure: Apply direct, or via email, but not through the website.

Voluntary Workcamps Association of Ghana (VOLU)

Job(s) Available: Around 1,500 volunteers are needed for workcamps.

Duration: Needed at Easter, Christmas and from June to October. Volunteers can stay throughout each period.

Head Office: PO Box GP 1540, Accra
☎ +233 21 663486
✉ voluntaryworkcamp@yahoo.com
🖥 www.volu.org

Cost: Volunteers pay their own travelling costs and an inscription fee of approximately £120.

Company Description: VOLU organises workcamps in the rural areas of Ghana for international volunteers.

Job Description: Tasks involve mainly manual work; construction projects, working on farms and agro-forestry projects, tree planting, harvesting cocoa and foodstuffs, working with mentally disabled people, teaching, etc.

Requirements: No special skills or experience are required but volunteers should be over 16 years old and fit to undertake manual labour.

Accommodation: Accommodation and food are provided at the camps.

Application Procedure: Applications to the above address. VOLU supplies official invitations to enable volunteers to acquire visas before leaving for Ghana.

Volunteer In Africa

Job(s) Available: Volunteers.

Duration: Participants of programmes can stay for a period of up to 12 weeks. Students can do internships during the summer.

Head Office: 10 Tackie Tawiah Avenue, Adabraka, Accra
✉ ghana@volunteeringinafrica.org
🖥 www.volunteeringinafrica.org

Working Hours: 5 days a week, 5 to 8 hours per day, depending on the number of hours volunteers want to work daily.

Cost: Participation fees: £397 (1–4 weeks), £597 (6 weeks), £797 (8 weeks).

Job Description: Volunteer programmes social welfare teaching health care education (HIV/AIDS education), conservation, media and journalism law.

Requirements: Volunteers aged 16–60, of any religion, race or nationality.

Accommodation: Host families provide accommodation.

Application Procedure: Contact ebensten73@yahoo.com or the above address for application forms.

BUNAC: Volunteer Ghana

Job(s) Available: Volunteer.

Duration: Departures are all year round. Spend between 3 and 6 months working and travelling in West Africa.

Cost: Placements on these programmes are unpaid and participants will be expected to make a small weekly contribution towards living costs.

> **Head Office:** BUNAC, 16 Bowling Green Lane, London EC1R 0QH, UK
> ☎ 020 7251 3472
> ✆ volunteer@bunac.org.uk
> 🖥 www.bunac.org

Job Description: Placements range from teaching positions or development projects to administrative roles.

Requirements: Recent graduates aged 18.

Application Procedure: For further details about this programme contact BUNAC at the above address or visit www.bunac.org.

ISRAEL

EMBASSY OF ISRAEL
2 Palace Green, London W8 4QB
☎ 020 7957 9500
🖥 http://london.mfa.gov.il
✆ info-assist@london.mfa.gov.il

The number of foreigners wishing to work in Israel has dwindled considerably since the escalation of the conflict between the Israelis and Palestinians. The election of Hamas to the parliament in 2006 by the Palistinians continues to cause unrest in the country. Since the death of Yasser Arafat, the Palistinians have been deeply divided. His political party, Fatah, has lost much of its support and now focuses much of its energy on a territorial struggle with Hamas. Suicide bombers and rocket attacks are frequent, with no real end in sight. The Foreign and Commonwealth Office advises against all travel to Israel and Occupied Territories (www.fco.gov.uk). However, even so, tourists flock to Israel each year, and almost all visits are trouble-free. If you do decide to visit Israel, maintaining a high level of vigilance and taking security precautions for your personal safety is essential.

A special visa exists for volunteers to Israel to work on kibbutzim and moshavim, and there are organisations sending volunteers to Palestine, though it is becoming increasingly difficult for such organisations to operate there because of the instability of the Palestinian territories.

There are some opportunities for paid employment in the tourist industry, especially around the resort of Eilat on the Red Sea and the Old City in Jerusalem. However, most people who wish to work in Israel for a few months choose to work on kibbutzim or moshavim. These are almost wholly self-sufficient settlements which take on volunteers for a normal minimum of 8 weeks. The main difference between the two is that the property is shared on a kibbutz, while most houses and farms are privately owned on a moshav. So on one volunteers work and share the farm tasks with permanent staff, while on the latter they are paid and there is less community spirit. However, the whole kibbutz system has undergone so many dramatic changes from its origins in socialist, pioneering communities to the transfer of kibbutzim from state to private ownership. In the moshavim movement private ownership of land has always been the norm.

On a kibbutz the work may consist of picking olives, grapes or cotton in the fields, domestic duties, or factory work; on a moshav the work is usually agricultural. In return for a six-day week volunteers receive free accommodation, meals, laundry and cigarettes. Volunteers are normally given pocket money on kibbutzim, while on a moshav a small wage is paid but the working hours are liable to be longer. Other programmes available on kibbutzim include Kibbutz Ulpan (which is intensive Hebrew study) and Project Oren Kibbutz Programmes (which is intensive Hebrew study, as well as travel and study of Israel).

Kibbutz Representatives, Golders Green, London which, for decades, arranged for Britons to work on kibbutzim has shut up shop due to lack of demand and commercialisation within the kibbutz movement. Anyone interested in working on a kibbutz is advised to contact the Kibbutz Programmes Centre in Israel (kpc@volunteer.co.il). Americans can contact Kibbutz Program Center (+1 800247 7852; +1 212 3186130; kpc@jazo.org.il; ulpankad@aol.com); volunteers need to bear in mind that with this organisation they must be prepared to make a commitment of at least six weeks. Registration costs $150 + $80 for insurance. There are many other placement offices around the world: Israel's diplomatic missions should be able to advise on the nearest one to you.

The following organisation may be able to place people who are actually in Israel. In recent years the authorities have been discouraging volunteers from travelling to Israel on one way tickets without having a written assurance of a place on a kibbutz, and with insufficient money for their fare home: the official line is that volunteers must have a return ticket and a reasonable sum of money (around £150/$225) in their possession when they enter the country. Contact the Kibbutz Program Centre, Volunteers Department, 18 Frishman Street, Third Floor, Cr. Ben Yehuda Tel Aviv 61030 (+972 3 5246156; +972 3 5278874; kpcvol@inter.net.il; www.kibbutz.org.il); it is open 9am–2pm, Sunday to Thursday. The centre advises people who do not pre-arrange a place before entering Israel that there might be a wait of days or even weeks before one is found, especially in the summer. However in the current political circumstances, there is a general shortage of foreign volunteers. All volunteers must be available for a minimum of 2 months, be between the ages of 18 and 35, speak a reasonable level of English and be in good mental and physical health.

The other major form of voluntary work in Israel consists of helping with archaeological excavations, often of Old Testament sites. The minimum stay for volunteers is normally two weeks. In the majority of cases volunteers must pay at least £15/$25 a day for their expenses on a dig. British citizens wishing to find voluntary work in Israel can obtain placements through Concordia.

Placing an advertisement in the English language paper *The Jerusalem Post* may also lead to an offer of a job. They can be contacted at the *Jerusalem Post* Building, (PO Box 81, Romena, Jerusalem 91000; www.jpost.com).

Red Tape

Visa Requirements: to work in Israel you must have a foreign worker's visa for Israel which has to be arranged before arriving in Israel. This is the only visa that allows a visitor to work (other than for voluntary work, eg kibbutz) in Israel. For volunteer work a work visa is not normally required prior to arrival by citizens of the UK, USA and some Western European countries.

Residence Permits: on entering the country, a visitor is likely to be given permission to stay for up to 3 months. Permission for a longer stay should then be obtained from the Ministry of the Interior.

Work Permits: your prospective employer should obtain the necessary permit from the Ministry of the Interior in Israel. You should have the permit with you when you enter the country.

Voluntary Work: a B4 volunteer visa is required of participants doing voluntary work (which includes kibbutzim and moshavim). The fee is NIS75 ($17) which covers 3 months. If you have pre-arranged your stay before arrival and have a letter of invitation you can obtain the B4 at the point of entry: otherwise, you can obtain it within 15 days of beginning voluntary work, provided you obtained the position through official channels. The B4 can be renewed only once.

Kibbutzim and Moshavim

Kibbutz Programme Centre

Job(s) Available: Kibbutz volunteers.
Duration: Required all year round. Period of work 2 months (minimum) to 6 months.
Working Hours: 7–8 hours per day, 6 days a week.
Pay/Cost: Volunteers need to pay a registration fee of $70 and receive £60 pocket money per month.

> **Head Office:** 6 Frishman St (corner of Hayarkon St), Tel Aviv 61030
> ☎ +972 35246156/4
> kpc@volunteer.co.il
> www.kibbutz.org.il

Company Description: The Kibbutz Programme Centre is the only office officially representing all the 250 kibbutzim. The centre is responsible for their volunteers and provides for them from arrival until they leave the kibbutz.
Requirements: Volunteers must be able to converse in English.
Accommodation: Volunteers receive full board and accommodation, plus free laundry.
Application Procedure: To apply contact the centre with details of your name and date of birth, date of arrival, passport number and a covering letter describing yourself. Applications are accepted all year round, but apply at least 3 weeks in advance of your arrival in Israel.

Teaching and Language Schools

Unipal

Job(s) Available: English teachers.
Duration: The programmes take place each summer from mid-July and usually last 4–5 weeks.
Cost: Summer volunteers are expected to pay around £500 to cover air fare and insurance. Extra spending money should be budgeted for.

> **Head Office:** BCM Unipal, London WC1N 3XX, UK
> info@unipal.org.uk
> www.unipal.org.uk

Company Description: Unipal (Universities' Trust for Educational Exchange with Palestinians) seeks to facilitate a two-way process of education, providing English language teaching in Palestinian refugee camps in the West Bank, Gaza and Lebanon and introducing British students to a knowledge and understanding of the situation and daily lives of refugees.
Job Description: English teachers to teach school children aged 12–15. Sometimes additional teaching with older students or with women's groups can be arranged.
Requirements: Previous experience with children is essential and previous teaching experience would be a real advantage. TEFL/TESL qualifications are also an advantage but are not

necessary. Personal qualities needed include sensitivity, tolerance, adaptability, readiness to learn, political awareness, reliance and tenacity. It is also vital that each volunteer is able to work successfully as part of a team. Minimum age 20.

Accommodation: Food and accommodation are provided.

Application Procedure: Written enquiries preferred. Closing date for applications at the end of February.

Voluntary Work and Archaeology

Department of Classical Studies

Job(s) Available: Volunteers (up to 40).

Duration: Volunteers are recruited for 2-week periods in July and August; it is possible to stay for more than 1 period.

Job Description: Volunteers are needed to take part in archaeological excavations.

Accommodation: Volunteers must pay for their own food and accommodation (cost around £470 per 2 week period).

Application Procedure: For further details contact Professor Moshe Fischer or Mr Ilan Shancar at the above address or visit; http://itp.lccc.wy.edu/bibint2/articles/yavnehyam.htm.

Youth Travel Bureau

Job(s) Available: Archaeological excavations or educational tour members.

Duration: *Archaeological excavations:* minimum period of 2 weeks. *Educational tours:* minimum of 2 months.

Head Office: 1 Shazar Street, PO Box 6001, Jerusalem 91060
☎ + 972 2 6558400
iyha@iyha.org.il
www.iyha.org.il

Company Description: Can help groups of Youth Hostel Association members to participate either in archaeological excavations or other educational tours.

Application Procedure: Apply to the above address for details.

Other Employment In Israel

Weizmann Institute of Science

Job(s) Available: Undergraduate research students to join a research project.

Duration: Projects last for between 10 weeks and 4 months in the summer.

Head Office: PO Box 26, Rehovot 76100
greta1.rosenberg@weizmann.ac.il
www.weizmann.ac.il/acadaff/students

Pay: A small stipend is provided.

Job Description: A research project involving the life sciences, chemistry, physics and mathematics and computer science.

Requirements: Applicants must have finished at least 2 years at university and have some research experience.

Application Procedure: Application forms should be downloaded and completed online at www.weizmann.ac.il/acadaff/kkiss. Please note that this application is for foreign students. The programme for Israeli students is advertised only in Israel.

KENYA

KENYA HIGH COMMISSION
45 Portland Place, London W1N 4AS
☎ 020 7636 2371
🖥 www.kenyahighcommission.net
🖐 consular@kenyahighcommission.net

Chances of finding a paid summer job in Kenya are minimal, but there are opportunities to part-icipate in voluntary work with the following organisations. In addition, Concordia and UNA Exchange can place British, and Service Civil International, American nationals in voluntary work in Kenya (see the *Worldwide* chapter for details). For short-term teaching assignments in rural areas of Kenya, Americans can apply to Global Citizens Network (www.globalcitizens.org).

Red Tape

Visa Requirements: according to the Kenyan High Commission in London, all non-Kenyan citizens have to be in possession of an entry/work permit issued by the principal immigration officer, Department of Immigration, PO Box 30191, Nairobi, before they can take up paid or unpaid work.

Voluntary Work

Kenya Voluntary Development Association (KVDA)

Job(s) Available: Volunteers.

Duration: Short-term voluntary service programme takes 21 days and the schedule runs from January to December every year. Medium and long-term proj-ects take between 3 months and 1 year.

Working Hours: *Short-term:* 6 hours per day, 6 days a week.

Pay: There is a registration fee to be paid on arrival, of approximately $260 for 21 day workcamp while medium and long-term volunteers pay $250 every month.

Head Office: PO Box 48902 - 00100, GPO Nairobi, First Floor, Unit 5, Kampus Towers Kenya
☎ +254 20 225379
  +254 721 650357 (mobile)
🖐 kvdakenya@yahoo.com
  info@kvdakenya.org
🖥 www.kvdakenya.org

Company Description: KVDA is an indigenous, non-political, membership organisation which is non-sectarian and non-profit-making which started in 1962 as a workcamp organ-isation. In 1993, KVDA was registered as a non-governmental organisation by the establish-ment of the NGO coordinating act.

Job Description: *Short-term programmes:* volunteers will work on projects in remote villages aimed at improving amenities in Kenya's rural and needy areas, working alongside members of the local community. The work may involve digging foundations, building, making building blocks, roofing, awareness campaigns, environmental programmes. Every project is based on specific themes relevant to the socio-economic challenges of the local communities. This brings together 20–25 volunteers per project. The projects are thematic in nature with focus on socio-economic situations of the local people and motivated to provide impetus for empowerment of the marginalised segments of the local population especially the youth and women. *Long-term programmes:* entailing placement of both pro-fessional and non-professional volunteers drawn from various countries in the world. The projects are based on themes such as awareness on HIV/AIDS, drug abuse, agriculture, income-generating activities, renovation of learning institutions and infrastructure in general, conservation of the environment, volunteering in hospitals, among others.

Requirements: Minimum age 18.

Accommodation: Accommodation is normally provided in school classrooms or similar buildings by the local community; foreign participants are expected to adapt to local foodstuffs and cultures without imposing values on other people. Participation fee is inclusive of meals, accommodation and general administration.

Additional Information: Volunteers participating in KVDA projects are invited to participate in KVDA Educational tours designed to take them to spectacular places of interest that include historical and archaeological sites, wildlife and game parks, among others. The participation fee is $90 per day and there are different packages for 3–10 days. For details about this programme, kindly email KVDA.

Application Procedure: For further information visit the website. For more information about the work of KVDA and volunteers, in the United Kingdom, can apply through KVDA partner organisations like Concordia-UK, Youth Action for Peace (YAP-UK), and UNA-Exchange. You can also get links to KVDA partner organisations through the global voluntary service network, the coordinating committee for International Voluntary Service (CCIVS) based in Paris, France: ccivs@unesco.org

Skillshare International Kenya

Job(s) Available: Projects cover a wide-range of activities and general management, agricultural, technical, educational and medical skills are all required.

Head Office: 126 New Walk Street, Leicester LE1 7JA, UK
☎ 01162 541862
✎ recruitment@skillshare.org
🖥 www.skillshare.org

Duration: Placements are usually for 2 years.

Cost: Skillshare offers a modest living allowance, flights/travel to the placement and return, medical cover, and pre and post placement grants to assist with relocation. The living allowance is adequate to cover your living costs whilst in the country of placement but not adequate for savings or meeting other costs you may have in your country of residence.

Company Description: Skillshare recruits professionals to share their skills and experience with local communities for further economic and social development in Botswana, Kenya, Lesotho, Mozambique, Namibia, South Africa, Swaziland, Tanzania, Uganda, India and Nepal. Its vision is a world without poverty, injustice and inequality where people, regardless of cultural, social, and political divides come together for mutual benefit living in peaceful co-existence.

Requirements: Applicants should be aged 21, have relevant qualifications and experience, particularly in training others.

Application Procedure: An information pack is available from the above address.

MADAGASCAR

EMBASSY OF THE REPUBLIC OF MADAGASCAR

8-10 Hallam Street, London W1W 6JE
☎ 020 3008 4550
🖥 www.embassy-madagascar-uk.com
✎ embamadlon@yahoo.co.uk

Opportunities for paid temporary work in Madagascar are rare. The following organisations can arrange voluntary placements there.

Voluntary Work

Blue Ventures Expeditions

Job(s) Available: SCUBA diving research volunteers (120 per year).

Duration: Minimum period of work 3 weeks.

Working Hours: 6 days a week.

Cost: Prices from £1,147 for 3 weeks.

Head Office: 52 Avenue Road, London N6 5DR, UK
☎ 020 8341 9819
Richard@blueventures.org
www.blueventres.org

Company Description: An award-winning, non-profit organisation dedicated to coral reef conservation and sustainable development in Madagascar. Through marine expeditions, volunteers work with the field research team, in partnership with local communities.

Requirements: Minimum age 18. No previous experience necessary. Working understanding of English is required.

Accommodation: Included in cost.

Application Procedure: Email Madagascar@blueventures.org. Applications ongoing. Telephone interview required. Foreign applicants welcome.

Reefdoctor

Job(s) Available: Volunteers (4).

Duration: Minimum of 6 weeks and a maximum of 3 months.

Cost: £1,400 for 6 weeks, £2,500 3 months, excluding travel to Madagascar and in-country personal expenses.

Head Office: 14 Charlwood Terrace, Putney, London SW15 1NZ, UK
☎ 020 8788 6908
volunteer@reefdoctor.org
www.reefdoctor.org

Company Description: Reefdoctor is a young organisation which started a volunteer programme in reef conservation in Madagascar in 2005. Research is conducted in conjunction with Madagascar's only marine research institute, IHSM.

Requirements: Volunteer researchers need to be qualified up to PADI Advance Diver. Courses for this can be arranged in Madagascar. Volunteers can also hire diving equipment from Reefdoctor for free. Volunteers should also have an interest and enthusiasm for marine conservation though training in research techniques is given. Applicants to be aged 18-60.

Accommodation: Accommodation is in reed huts on the beach is heat, humidity and insects are the norm.

Application Procedure: Applications to the above address.

EMBASSY OF THE KINGDOM OF MOROCCO
49 Queen's Gate Gardens, London SW7 5NE
☎ 020 7581 5001
✆ ambalondres@maec.gov.ma

Work permits are necessary for employment in Morocco: they are generally only given to people who speak French and/or Arabic, and have some particular skill or qualification that is in demand (eg teaching or IT).

There are, however, possibilities of seasonal work in the expanding tourist industry, especially around the resorts of Agadir, Marrakesh and Tangier. Several European holiday companies operate in Morocco and employ summer staff. Knowledge of French will normally be expected: this is also the language most likely to be used in voluntary workcamps, although English should be understood.

Concordia, International Voluntary Service, Youth Action for Peace and UNA Exchange can help UK nationals, and the CIEE and Service Civil International Americans, find voluntary work in Morocco: see the *Worldwide* chapter for details.

Red Tape

Visa Requirements: a visa is not required by citizens of most European countries, Australia, Canada, New Zealand, the USA if they are entering Morocco as tourists for up to 3 months.

Residence Permits: those planning a stay of over 3 months must register with the police and be able to provide evidence of how they are supporting themselves.

Work Permit: any foreigner taking up paid employment in Morocco must have a valid work permit: this will be obtained by the prospective employer from the Ministry of Labour (or by applying directly to the Ministry of Labour if self-employed). Work permits (*Contrats de Travail*) can be obtained while in Morocco if a job is found. A foreigner does not need a work permit or special visa in order to take part in an organised voluntary work project in Morocco providing the scheme lasts for less than 3 months and the work is unpaid.

Teaching and Language Schools

American Language Centre

Job(s) Available: Teachers (50).
Duration: Typically semesters start in September and January but shorter contracts may be available.
Working Hours: 18–24 contract hours per week during the main terms, but teaching takes place on weekday evenings and Saturdays.

Head Office: 4 Zankat Tanja, Rabat 10000 Morocco
☎ +212 37 767103
✆ amalz@alcrabat.org
▣ http://www.alcrabat.org

Pay: Full-time salaries offered by ALC Rabat usually allow teachers to live comfortably in Rabat. Salaries are in Moroccan dirhams.
Company Description: Commercial language school, largest of a chain of 10 schools in Morocco.

Requirements: Bachelor's or Master's degree. A certificate in TEFL or TESL and attendance at an orientation programme before teaching begins.
Application Procedure: Application forms available from www.alcrabat.org/jobs.htm

SOUTH AFRICA

HIGH COMMISSION FOR THE REPUBLIC OF SOUTH AFRICA
South Africa House, Trafalgar Square, London WC2N 5DP
☎ 020 7451 7299
🖥 www.southafricahouse.com
✆ civicservices@rsaconsulate.co.uk _____

The government is, understandably, not keen to hand out work permits to Europeans and other nationalities when so many of their own nationals (40% at times) are unemployed. Work permits are granted only in instances where South African citizens or permanent residents are not available for appointment or cannot be trained for the position. The weakness of the land has lead to a 'brain drain' out of the country and positions exist for professionals.

Most people who do casual work have only a 3-month tourist visa, which must be renewed before it expires. A 90-day extension can be obtained from the Department of Home Affairs in Johannesburg or Cape Town for a fee. After you have done this a few times, the authorities will become suspicious.

A solution to the problem is to consider BUNAC's work and travel programme in South Africa. Full-time students or those within 12 months of graduation aged 18 or over may be eligible for a 12-month working holiday permit (see entry) which allows them to look for work on the spot. Unfortunately for summer job seekers, the time when jobs are likely to be found is the high season of October to March.

Voluntary work is organised for British citizens in South Africa by UNA Exchange and Youth Action for Peace (see their entries in the *Worldwide* chapter for details). Work can be found in South Africa through the organisations below.

Voluntary Work

Skillshare International South Africa _____

Job(s) Available: Projects cover a wide-range of activities and general management, agricultural, technical, educational and medical skills are all required.
Duration: Placements are usually for 2 years.
Cost: Skillshare offers a modest living allowance,

Head Office: 126 New Walk Street, Leicester LE1 7JA, UK
☎ 01162 541862
✆ recruitment@skillshare.org
🖥 www.skillshare.org

flights/travel to the placement and return, medical cover, and pre and post placement grants to assist with relocation. The living allowance is adequate to cover your living costs whilst in the country of placement but not adequate for savings or meeting other costs you may have in your country of residence.
Company Description: Skillshare recruits professionals to share their skills and experience with local communities for further economic and social development in Botswana, Kenya, Lesotho, Mozambique, Namibia, South Africa, Swaziland, Tanzania, Uganda, India and Nepal. Its vision is a world without poverty, injustice and inequality where people, regardless of

cultural, social, and political divides come together for mutual benefit living in peaceful co-existence.

Requirements: Applicants should be aged 21, have relevant qualifications and experience, particularly in training others.

Application Procedure: An information pack is available from the above address.

BUNAC: Work South Africa/Volunteer South Africa

Job(s) Available: *Work South Africa*: many participants work in hotels and restaurants or in jobs within the tourist industry. Many also take up shop-based or office work or community developmental work. *Volunteer South Africa:* enables applicants with suitable skills to become involved with volunteer projects in one of 4 main areas: the environment; tourism; education; and social welfare.

Head Office: BUNAC, 16, Bowling Green Lane, London EC1R 0QH, UK
☎ 020 7251 3472
✆ volunteer@bunac.org.uk
🖳 www.bunac.org

Duration: *Work South Africa*: the work visa is valid for up to 12 months and departures from the UK are year round. *Volunteer South Africa:* placements last from 5 to 17 weeks. Participants may then stay on in South Africa to travel. Departures are available on a year-round basis.

Requirements: *Work South Africa*: students who are to graduate in 2008 and who are aged at least 18 to take up legally any job anywhere in South Africa. BUNAC can provide help in arranging work on arrival.

Accommodation: *Work South Africa*: BUNAC arranges flights, visas, insurance and the first 6 nights' accommodation. *Volunteer South Africa:* accommodation and meals are included in the programme fee.

Application Procedure: For further details contact BUNAC at the above address or visit their website www.bunac.org.

SANCCOB – The Southern African National Foundation for the Conservation of Coastal Birds

Job(s) Available: Volunteers.

Duration: The period May to October is the busiest but help is needed year round, the minimum stay is 6 weeks.

Head Office: PO Box 11116, Bloubergrant 7443, Cape Town
☎ +27 21 5576155
✆ carole@sanccob.co.za
🖳 www.sanccob.co.za

Cost: Volunteers must meet their own living costs.

Company Description: The coastal waters of South Africa are a major shipping route and oil pollution is a recurrent problem, the main bird types dealt with are African penguins, gulls, gannets, terns and cormorants.

Job Description: Volunteers required to help with the cleaning and rehabilitation of injured, oiled, ill and abandoned coastal birds, in particular the African penguin. The main tasks involve keeping the rehabilitation centre clean (scrubbing pools and pens), feeding and caring for the birds.

Requirements: Volunteers must be willing to work in hard conditions with wild and difficult birds. Minimum age 18.

Accommodation: Help is given with finding bed and breakfast accommodation.

Application Procedure: To apply contact SANCCOB at the above address.

TANZANIA

HIGH COMMISSION FOR THE UNITED REPUBLIC OF TANZANIA

3 Stratford Place, London WIC 1AS

☎ 020 7569 1470

💻 www.tanzania-online.gov.uk

🖱 balozi@tanzania-online.gov.uk _____

In addition to the following entries, Concordia and UNA Exchange can offer short-term volunteer projects to Britons wishing to work in Tanzania for a few months, while Americans may be able to apply through Service Civil International (their entries in the *Worldwide* chapter give more details). There are other organisations which operate in a similar way to Volunteer Africa (below), ie you pay the organisation for your voluntary work placement of four weeks or longer: try also the UK-based Frontier (www.frontier.ac.uk) and Madventurer (www.madventurer.com).

Red Tape

Visa Requirements: All visitors wishing to enter the United Republic of Tanzania need to obtain a visa, which must be obtained before entering Tanzania. A tourist or visitor visa is valid for up to 3 months (90 days).

Work Permits: One of 3 types of work permit must be applied for, an 'A Class' permit is for self employed foreigners, a 'B class' is for other foreign employees and a 'C Class' permit is for students, volunteers and missionaries etc.

Voluntary Work

Skillshare International Tanzania _____

Job(s) Available: Projects cover a wide-range of activities and general management, agricultural, technical, educational and medical skills are all required.

Head Office: 126 New Walk Street, Leicester LE1 7JA, UK
☎ 01162 541862
🖱 recruitment@skillshare.org
💻 www.skillshare.org

Duration: Placements are usually for 2 years.

Cost: Skillshare offers a modest living allowance, flights/travel to the placement and return, medical cover, and pre and post placement grants to assist with relocation. The living allowance is adequate to cover your living costs whilst in the country of placement but not adequate for savings or meeting other costs you may have in your country of residence.

Company Description: Skillshare recruits professionals to share their skills and experience with local communities for further economic and social development in Botswana, Kenya, Lesotho, Mozambique, Namibia, South Africa, Swaziland, Tanzania, Uganda, India and Nepal. Its vision is a world without poverty, injustice and inequality where people, regardless of cultural, social, and political divides come together for mutual benefit living in peaceful co-existence.

Requirements: Applicants should be aged 21, have relevant qualifications and experience, particularly in training others.

Application Procedure: An information pack is available from the above address.

Volunteer Africa

Job(s) Available: Volunteers.

Duration: Volunteers can participate for 4–12 weeks depending on which programme they choose.

Head Office: PO Box 24 Bakewell Derbyshire DE45 1YP, UK
support@volunteerafrica.org
www.volunteerafrica.org

Cost: The cost of participating during 2008 is £1050 for 4 weeks, £1,710 for 7 weeks, £1,950 for 10 weeks. Of these fees, approximately 60% goes to the host organisations to support development work in Tanzania. Participants also need to budget around £600 for flights and medical insurance.

Company Description: Providing volunteers and fundraising to community-based organisations working in Tanzania, Volunteer Africa is run largely by volunteers to keep down running costs.

Job Description: There are 2 programmes: Singida rural development and Tabora resource centre. Fundraising advice is given and the first week is spent in language and cultural training.

Requirements: Applicants must be aged 18 or over when they are due to travel overseas.

Application Procedure: Applications can only be made through the organisation's website.

UGANDA

UGANDA HIGH COMMISSION

Uganda House, 58/59 Trafalgar Square, London WC2N 5DX
☎ 020 7839 5783
🖥 www.ugandahighcommission.co.uk
🖱 info@ugandahighcommission.co.uk

The following organisations can arrange voluntary placements in Uganda

Voluntary Work

Skillshare International Uganda

Job(s) Available: Projects cover a wide-range of activities and general management, agricultural, technical, educational and medical skills are all required.

Head Office: 126 New Walk Street, Leicester LE1 7JA, UK
☎ 01162 541862
🖱 recruitment@skillshare.org
🖥 www.skillshare.org

Duration: Placements are usually for 2 years.

Cost: Skillshare offers a modest living allowance, flights/travel to the placement and return, medical cover, and pre and post placement grants to assist with relocation. The living allowance is adequate to cover your living costs whilst in the country of placement but not adequate for savings or meeting other costs you may have in your country of residence.

Company Description: Skillshare recruits professionals to share their skills and experience with local communities for further economic and social development in Botswana, Kenya, Lesotho, Mozambique, Namibia, South Africa, Swaziland, Tanzania, Uganda, India and Nepal. Its vision is a world without poverty, injustice and inequality where people, regardless of cultural, social, and political divides come together for mutual benefit living in peaceful co-existence.

Requirements: Applicants should be aged 21, have relevant qualifications and experience, particularly in training others.

Application Procedure: An information pack is available from the above address.

United Children's Fund Inc

Job(s) Available: Volunteers.

Duration: Placements last 1 or 2 months at any time of year.

Cost: $1,850 (1 month), $2950 (2 months). This covers all food, transportation and local fees when in Uganda.

Company Description: United Children's Fund pro-
vides volunteer opportunities in East Africa for those wanting to use their talents and skills to make a difference in someone's life.

Head Office: PO Box 20341, Boulder, Colorado, 80308-3341, USA
☎ +1 303 469 4339, 1800 615 5229 (toll-free in the US)
📠 united@unchildren.org
🖥 www.unchildren.org

Job Description: United Children's Fund, places volunteers on projects in Uganda including health care, working in village clinics, teaching in local village schools, assisting teachers, school construction, working with women's groups on income-generating projects and more. Volunteers are needed to work on projects where they think they can make the biggest difference.

Requirements: Special skills are not prerequisite. Minimum age 18.

Application Procedure: For further details check the website above.

Uganda Volunteers for Peace (UVP)

Job(s) Available: International workcamps and medium/long term volunteering projects.

Duration: 1–2 weeks or over 3 months.

Working Hours: 30–40 hours per week.

Company Description: UVP reach out to needy communities.

Head Office: PO Box 3312, Ki Wooya House, 256 Kampala
☎ +256 77 402201
📠 uvpeace@yahoo.co.uk
🖥 www.uvp.org.uk

Job Description: Members do the following: renovations (buildings), painting schools, moulding bricks, construction using local materials, talking to communities about HIV/AIDS awareness and counselling.

Requirements: Aged 18–25 years.

Accommodation: Usually provided.

Application Procedure: Apply through website.

THE AMERICAS

CANADA

CANADIAN HIGH COMMISSION
38 Grosvenor Street, London, W1K 4AA
🖳 www.canada.org.uk

The employment of foreigners in either short or long-term work in Canada is strictly regulated. Even with Canada's relatively strong economy, it is illegal to work in Canada without a work permit; with some exceptions, a job must be obtained from outside the country, and even then the employer will face difficulty in obtaining permission to employ you unless they can show that they are not depriving a Canadian citizen or permanent resident of the job.

Anyone seeking employment in Canada should write directly to Canadian employers before arrival to enquire about employment prospects. Information on jobs in Canada can also be obtained from Canadian newspapers or trade journals, which are available at larger newsagents. Addresses of potential employers can also be found in the *Canadian Trade Index* or the *Canadian Almanac and Directory*, both of which can be found at large libraries.

Teachers from British Commonwealth nations may be able to arrange exchange placements by contacting The League for the Exchange of Commonwealth Teachers (0870 770 2636; info@lect.org.uk; www.lect.org.uk).

To work legally in Canada, you must obtain a work permit from a Canadian High Commission or Embassy before you leave your home country. The exceptions are the special schemes for different categories. The other and more flexible option is to obtain an Open Work Authorisation through BUNAC's Work Canada programme which offers about 3000 students and non-students the chance to go to Canada for up to a year and take whatever jobs they can find. Participants on this programme can depart at any time between February and December. The great majority of participants go to Canada without a pre-arranged job and spend their first week or two job-hunting. The Canadian High Commission in London administers the scheme for British and Irish passport holders. There are similar schemes for Australians and New Zealanders.

Interested students should check the website www.canada.org.uk or www.cic.gc.ca or you can telephone 020 7258 6350. Note that if you applying to work in Québec, there are separate and additional immigration procedures.

Concordia arrange voluntary placements in Canada, and UNA Exchange can organise voluntary work in French-speaking Québec; the CIEE can arrange voluntary work in Canada for Americans. For details of all these see the *Worldwide* chapter.

Red Tape

Visa Requirements: citizens of the United Kingdom and most other countries in Western Europe, of UK dependent territories, Australia, New Zealand, the United States and Mexico do not normally require a visa for a visit to Canada. Citizens of other countries may need to obtain one. No matter what the length or purpose of the proposed stay, permission to enter and remain in Canada must be obtained from the immigration officer at the port of entry. If the purpose is any other than purely for a tourist visit to Canada, you should consult the Canadian High Commission or Embassy abroad before departure. The length of stay in Canada is decided at the port of entry. Normally entry is granted for 6 months.

Work Permit: in almost all cases it is necessary to have a valid work permit which authorises an individual to work 'at a specific job for a specific period of time for a specific employer'. It must be applied for before arrival. Non-students aged 18–35 may be eligible for a 12-month general working holiday permit.

Student General Working Holiday Programmes: are open to full-time students aged 18–35 from the UK (see www.canada.org.uk), Ireland, Sweden and Finland. Citizens of the latter four countries can apply directly to the immigration section of their local embassy, providing a letter of university acceptance and a letter confirming return to studies or proof that they have completed their studies within the previous 12 months and sufficient funds must be proven for voluntary work). There is also the Student Work Abroad Programme (SWAP) available for Australian and New Zealand citizens. This programme is coordinated through STA (travel) offices in Australia and New Zealand. Prospective SWAP applicants must contact the STA office for information on the programme for that year.

Voluntary Work: a special category of work permit covers voluntary work which takes about two to four months to process if you have found a placement through a recognised charitable or religious organisation.

Agricultural Work

Agricultural Labour Pool

Job Description: Seasonal and permanent agricultural jobs in the USA and Canada.
Application Procedure: See website for details

☎ +1 604 8557281
✆ info@agri-labourpool.com
🖥 www.agri-labourpool.com.

World Wide Opportunites on Organic Farms (WWOOF CANADA)

Job(s) Available: Volunteers to work on organic farms.
Duration: Opportunities may be available all year round.
Company Description: Hundreds of young people, from 30 different countries, every year go

Head Office: 4429 Carlson Road, Nelson, British Columbia, Canada VIL 6X3
☎ +1 250 3544417
✆ wwoofcan@shaw.ca
🖥 www.wwoof.ca

'WWOOFing' in Canada. There are 650 hosts available from the east to the west coast of Canada.
Job Description: Volunteers to work on 650 organic farms in Canada ranging from small homesteads to large farms. Duties include general farm work and may include going to market, working with horses, garden work, milking goats, etc.
Requirements: Minimum age 16. Only EU nationals with valid tourist visas need apply.
Accommodation: Board and lodging provided free of charge.
Application Procedure: Applications enclosing C$50 (cash) includes postage, for a farm list and description booklet, should be sent to the above address.

Summer Camps

Camp Artaban

Job(s) Available: Kitchen helpers (3), head guard (1), lifeguards (2), maintenance workers (2).

Duration: 22 June to 1 September.

Company Description: Camp Artaban has been providing Christian Camping on its Gambier Island site since 1923, making it one of the oldest camps in British Columbia. The site was chosen by a group of ministers and businessmen under the leadership of Bishop Heathcote and the first camp was held in 1923.

Head Office: Camp Artaban Society, 1058 Ridgewood Drive, North Vancouver, BC V7R 1H8 Canada
☎ +1 604 9800391
✉ inquire@campartaban.com
🖥 www.campartaban.com

Job Description: The camp have the following objectives for employees to fulfil and encourage: experience living in a Christian community, a fuller understanding of the Christian faith, not only through relationships, but also through appropriately structured periods of instruction, join regularly in appropriate acts of corporate worship, develop recreational skills, sense of adventure and fun, learn to use freedom responsibly.

Requirements: Fluent English is necessary. *Kitchen helpers:* must have food safe level 1. *Head guard:* NLS and pleasure craft operators card required. OFA Boat level III an asset. Boating experience an advantage. *Lifeguards:* pleasure craft operator card required. Boating experience an asset. *Maintenance workers:* previous construction or other related experiences an asset. Must have a valid driver's license.

Accommodation: Board and accommodation available.

Application Procedure: email staffhire@campartaban.com. Application deadline 19 March.

Voluntary Work and Archaeology

Frontiers Foundation/Operation Beaver

Job(s) Available: Volunteers.

Duration: Minimum period of 12 weeks. The greatest need for volunteers is in June, July and August. Long term placements of up to 18 months are possible provided that the volunteer's work is deemed satisfactory after the initial 12 week period.

Head Office: 419 Coxwell Avenue, Toronto, Ontario M4L 3B9 Canada
☎ +1 416 6903930
✉ volunteers@frontiersfoundation.ca
🖥 www.frontiersfoundation.ca

Pay: Living allowance of C$50 per week.

Company Description: Frontiers Foundation is a non-profit voluntary service organisation supporting the advancement of economically and socially disadvantaged communities in Canada and overseas. The organisation works in partnership with requesting communities in low-income rural areas. Projects help to provide and improve housing, to provide training and economic incentives and to offer recreational/educational activities in developing regions.

Job Description: Volunteers are recruited from across the world to serve in native and non-native communities across Canada for a variety of community construction and educational projects.

Requirements: Minimum age 18. Skills in carpentry, electrical work and plumbing are preferred for construction projects. Previous social service and experience with children are sought for recreational/educational projects.

Accommodation: All accommodation, food and travel, within Canada is provided. Travel to and from Canada is the responsibility of the volunteer. Accommodation is normally provided by the community; volunteers must be prepared to live without electricity, running water or roads in some communities.

Additional Information: Medical insurance, food and travel within Canada is provided.

Application Procedure: Application forms available at www.frontiersfoundation.ca/node/19. Once an applicant has sent in application forms there can be a delay of 3–12 weeks as references come in and possible placements are considered. Acceptance cannot be guaranteed.

Au Pairs, Nannies, Family Helps and Exchanges

European Inhome Services INC

Job(s) Available: Summer nanny/au pair (2–3).
Duration: From 1 July to September 1. Minimum period of work 8 weeks.
Working Hours: 20 hours plus C$8/hour overtime.
Pay: C$100–C$150 per week.
Company Description: European Inhome Services places Western European au pairs, babysitters, caregivers, nannies and tutors in Canadian families. The families seek native speaking German/French/Spanish speakers who also understand and speak fairly good English.

> **Head Office:** 2585 W. Second Avenue, Vancouver BC, V6K 1K7 Canada
> ☎ +1 604 647 0951
> +1 604 828 8788 (mobile)
> ✆ welcome@europeaninhomeservices.com
> 🖳 www.europeaninhomeservices.com

Job Description: Families expect nannies to do minimum childcare at set hours, along with light housekeeping. Other families enjoy having a nanny that can drive or cook or do housekeeping and even run errands such as grocery shopping. Other families wish the nanny to do laundry or vacuum cleaning etc. The main thing is that the nanny can be independent and self-sufficient, especially in the hours that she has off. Some families will supply the nanny with a bus pass and a city map, while other expect the nanny to look after themselves. There are 3 different situations you may be in: mum and dad both work, or mum stays home but needs help, or a single parent situation.

Requirements: Minimum age 19. Infant or toddler or preschool experience. Our agency caters to families seeking au pairs and nannies from Western Europe, especially those with a second language such as English, French and Spanish. We do not accept applications from anyone else.

Accommodation: Available as part of wages.

Application Procedure: Apply to Elke Porter at info@europeaninhomeservices.com. Applicants will need to attend an interview at least 6 months prior to coming. May have a family call for a phone interview. 2 references needed.

Other Employment in Canada

Internship Canada Programme

Job(s) Available: Work experience programme.
Duration: Period of work experience of up to 1 year in Canada.
Pay/Cost: Programme costs start at £225 for a 2 month stay which includes IST Plus insurance cover for the length of their stay.

> **Head Office:** IST Plus Rosedale House, Rosedale Road, Surrey TW9 2SZ, UK
> ☎ 020 8939 9057
> ✆ info@istplus.com
> 🖳 www.istplus.com

Company Description: Assisting over 1500 students undertake practical training in North America each year, IST Plus is a worldwide organisation helping people develop skills and acquire knowledge for working in a multicultural, interdependent world.

Requirements: Students must hold British or Irish passports. Minimum age 18. Applicants must be enrolled in full-time further or higher education (HND level or above) or a recent graduate within 12 months of finishing, or a gap year student with an unconditional offer of a university place. Before applying applicants must have secured a full-time work placement in Canada directly related to their studies.

Additional Information: Official documentation and assistance with visa application are provided, as are orientation materials covering taxes, housing, Canadian culture and transportation; plus 24-hour emergency assistance with any problems whilst in Canada.

Application Procedure: Applications can be made at any time of year, but should be made at least 2 months before the desired date of departure.

BUNAC Work Canada

Job(s) Available: There are approximately 3,000 places on the Work Canada programme.

Duration: The Work Authorisation is valid for 1 year.

Head Office: BUNAC, 16 Bowling Green Lane, London EC1R 0QH, UK
☎ 020 7251 3472
✎ canada@bunac.org.uk

Job Description: Enables participants to work and travel anywhere in Canada. Approximately 90% of participants go to Canada without a pre-arranged job and take an average of 6 days to find one.

Additional Information: BUNAC also offers advice on job-hunting, various travel deals and on-going support services whilst in Canada.

Application Procedure: For further details contact the above address or visit the website www.bunac.org.

COSTA RICA

COSTA RICAN EMBASSY
Flat 1, 14 Lancaster Gate, London W2 3LH
☎ 020 7706 8844

Under Costa Rica law it is illegal for foreigners to be offered paid work, but the organisations listed in this chapter offer voluntary work. US nationals may be able to obtain voluntary work through the CIEE allowing for yearly changes in their project planning. Britons may find opportunities arranged by UNA Exchange (see their entries in the *Worldwide* chapter for details).

Red Tape

Work Permits: For paid employment of 1 year or less, foreigners may apply for a temporary working visa. The application should be made to the Department of Temporary Permits and Extensions at the General Directorate of Migration (GDM) while you are staying in Costa Rica. For longer stays in Costa Rica, you need to apply for Residency in Costa Rica.

Voluntary work: EU nationals may volunteer for up to 3 months without a visa

Sports, Couriers and Camping

Costa Rica Rainforest Outward Bound School

Job(s) Available: Summer marketing intern (1), surf interns (2), whitewater raft captain intern (2), land hiking intern (3).

Duration: All staff required to work from 1 June to 25 August. Minimum period of work 2 months.

Working Hours: *Summer marketing intern:* Monday to Friday, 9am–5pm. *Surf interns:* 15-day courses. *Whitewater raft captain intern:* 3–5 days a week. *Land hiking intern:* 15-day courses.

Pay: *Summer marketing intern:* $200 a month. *Surf interns:* $200 a month. *Whitewater raft captain intern:* $200 a month. *Land hiking intern:* $200 a month.

Company Description: An experimental education facility providing 15–60 day adventure trips in Costa Rica, Nicaragua and Panama for students and adults from around the world.

Requirements: *Surf interns:* past surf instructional experience necessary. *Whitewater raft captain intern:* past whitewater experience needed. *Land hiking intern:* past trip leading experience necessary.

Accommodation: Room and board included in wages.

Application Procedure: Applications to the communications director at the above email address from 15 January. No interview required.

> **Head Office:** CRROBS, SJO 829, PO Box 025216, Miami FL 33102, USA
> ☎ +1 506 2786062
> info@crrobs.org
> www.crrobs.org

Voluntary Work and Archaeology

Iyok Ami

Job(s) Available: Volunteers.

Working Hours: Volunteers are expected to work 4 hours per day, Monday to Friday. Weekends are free for visiting other places (the beach etc).

Pay/Cost: Iyok Ami is a private organisation that receives no funding and so volunteers pay $650 per month.

> **Head Office:** PO Box 335-2100, San José
> ☎ +506 3422123
> iyokbosque@yahoo.es
> www.ecotourism.co.cr/iyokami

Company Description: An extensive private reserve that includes both tropical cloud and tropical rain forests, and an Indian reserve. These wild areas have been set aside to protect flora, fauna and water resources, and also to serve as areas of scientific and research study.

Job Description: Volunteers' help is needed to build and maintain trails and for reforestation, help with labelling and transplantation of flowering plants around the trails, making topographical and pictorial maps of the area, constructing signposts, teaching English in schools, protecting and stimulating the Quetzal bird reproduction. Volunteers also help with the classification of plants, birds and fungi, and other work depending on the volunteer's interest and specialist knowledge.

Requirements: Anyone is welcome to apply.

Accommodation: Cost covers board, laundry and accommodation (overlooking the forest, the Irazu, and Turrialba volcanoes).

Additional Information: Volunteers will receive a free daily hour of basic Spanish teaching.

Application Procedure: Applications to the above address.

Rainforest Concern

Job(s) Available: Volunteers (18).

Duration: Minimum period of work 7 days. Required at any time.

Cost: For costs and availability please see the website for individual project contact details.

Head Office: 8 Clanricarde Gardens, London W2 4NA, UK
☎ 020 7229 2093
info@rainforestconcern.org
www.rainforestconcern.org

Company Description: Rainforest Concern is a non-political charity dedicated to the conservation of vulnerable rainforest and the bio-diversity they contain.

Job Description: Volunteers for reforestation/trail maintenance and the establishment of organic agriculture. The work involves an element of monitoring and of physical labour, such as reforestation or compiling species lists, or trail maintenance depending on the projects being undertaken at the time. Current volunteer opportunities are in the cloud forests of western Ecuador and in Amazonian Ecuador. Volunteers are encouraged to help out with research and reserve maintenance and are invited to sponsor acres of forest in need of protection.

Requirements: No special skills are required, although Spanish would be helpful. Applicants must have a sincere interest in conservation, be over 18 and generally fit.

Additional Information: Further volunteer opportunities in endangered sea turtle conservation are available at our projects in Costa Rica and Panama.

Application Procedure: Applications can be sent to the above address at any time of year.

BUNAC Volunteer Costa Rica

Job(s) Available: Volunteer placements.

Duration: Allows participants to spend 3–6 months working as a volunteer in Costa Rica.

Job Description: Placements can be in areas such as agriculture, conservation, small business development or teaching.

Head Office: BUNAC, 16 Bowling Green Lane, London EC1R 0QH, UK
☎ 020 7251 3472
volunteer@bunac.org.uk

Requirements: Applicants are expected to speak Spanish confidently to GCSE level or equivalent and must be either a current university level student or a graduate aged 18–32.

Accommodation: Accommodation is provided as part of the programme fee however participants will be expected to make a contribution towards their food costs.

Application Procedure: For further details contact BUNAC at the above address or visit www.bunac.org.

CUBA

EMBASSY OF THE REPUBLIC OF CUBA
167 High Holbor, London, WC1V 6PA
☎ 020 7240 2488
www.cubaldn.com
embacuba@cubaldn.com

The following organisation recruits people for a working holiday scheme in Cuba.

Red Tape

Visa Requirements: any person wishing to enter Cuba must be in possession of the relevant visa. For information on how to obtain these visas please see the website of Embassy of the Republic of Cuba.

The Cuba Solidarity Campaign

Job(s) Available: Volunteers.

Duration: 3 weeks work. There are 2 working holidays organised each year, 1 in the summer and 1 in the winter.

Working Hours: Approximately 4 mornings per working week.

Pay: Summer brigade: £875. Winter Brigade: £950.

Head Office: c/o Red Rose Club, 129 Seven Sisters Road, London N7 7QG, UK
☎ 020 7263 6452
office@cuba-solidarity.org.uk
www.cuba-solidarity.org.uk

Company Description: The Cuba Solidarity Campaign (CSC) works in the UK to raise awareness of the illegal US blockade of Cuba, and to defend the Cuban people's right to self-determination. It publishes a quarterly magazine 'Cuba Si', in addition to organising meetings, cultural events, and specialist tours to Cuba.

Job Description: Volunteers are needed to take part in a scheme in Cuba involving on a self-contained camp near Havana. The work involves light agricultural work, a programme of guided visits to schools, hospitals and community projects, with excursions arranged and transport to Havana provided during time off. There are many opportunities to meet Cubans, and enjoy vibrant Cuban culture first hand.

Accommodation: Costs including flights, accommodation, full board, full programme of guided visits and 3 days of rest and relaxation in another part of the island.

Additional Information: The campaign organises the necessary visa.

Application Procedure: Contact the above address for application deadlines and further information.

ECUADOR

EMBASSY OF ECUADOR
Flat 3b, 3 Hans Crescent, London SW1X 0LS
☎ 020 7584 2648

As well as the following organisations, Concordia, UNA Exchange and Youth Action for Peace offer short-term international volunteer projects to Britons in Ecuador, while the CIEE can do the same for US citizens (see their entries in the *Worldwide* chapter for more details).

Red Tape

Visa Requirements: For voluntary work a category 12-VII visa must be obtained. These must be applied for in person at the Consulate, with a letter of invitation and other supporting documentation. This visa is granted up to a period of 1 year.

Work Permits: At the moment, the Consulate in the United Kingdom does not issue working visas. If you would like to work in Ecuador you will need to process this visa directly in Ecuador in person or by the employer.

Voluntary Work and Archaeology

Fundacion Golondrinas/ The Cerro Golondrinas Cloudforest Conservation Group

Job(s) Available: Volunteers required to help conserve 25,000 hectares of highland cloud forest on the western slopes of the Andes.

Duration: Minimum stay 2 weeks. We prefer that volunteers stay for 1 month to be able to fully connect with our projects. Volunteers are accepted all year round.

Head Office: c/o Calle Isabel La Católica N24-679, Quito
☎ +593 2 2226602
manteca@uio.satnet.net (subject: volunteer)
www.fundaciongolondrinas.org

Cost: about $280 per month. We do offer discounts to those who choose to stay for more than 2 months or who apply to a specific volunteer position.

Company Description: Fundacion Golondrinas is a non-governmental non-profit organisation. Fundacion Golondrinas proposes management alternatives in the conservation of natural resources in the Lower Rio Mira Valley, taking technological and social realities into consideration.

Requirements: Some experience of horticulture/permaculture, and advanced Spanish. Aged 18–60.

Accommodation: Provided.

Additional Information: The Golondrinas Foundation's Scientific Studies, Thesis and Practicum Programme allows both national and international undergraduate or graduate students to conduct a project that contributes to the knowledge of the socio-cultural and ecological problem in the region of influence where the Golondrinas Foundation carries out its activities and offers feasible alternatives to improve the situation in the area. The price for students is $5 per day for 3 meals. Students must submit a written report of the activities realised during their stay and collection of data or a practicum report with related instructions and information.

Application Procedure: Contact Foundation at least 2 months in advance of desired dates of placement. Volunteers must arrange their own travel, visas and field kit. For details of work and kit requirements contact the above address.

Rainforest Concern

Job(s) Available: Volunteers (18).

Duration: Minimum period of work 7 days. Required at any time.

Cost: For costs and availability please see the website for individual project contact details.

Head Office: 8 Clanricarde Gardens, London W2 4NA, UK
☎ 020 7229 2093
info@rainforestconcern.org
www.rainforestconcern.org

Company Description: Rainforest Concern is a non-political charity dedicated to the conservation of vulnerable rainforest and the biodiversity they contain.

Job Description: Volunteers for reforestation/trail maintenance and the establishment of organic agriculture. The work involves an element of monitoring and of physical labour, such as reforestation or compiling species lists, or trail maintenance depending on the projects being undertaken at the time. Current volunteer opportunities are in the cloud forests of western Ecuador and in Amazonian Ecuador. Volunteers are encouraged to help out with research and reserve maintenance and are invited to sponsor acres of forest for protection.

Requirements: No special skills are required, although Spanish would be helpful. Applicants must have a sincere interest in conservation, be over 18 and generally fit.

Additional Information: Further volunteer opportunities in endangered sea turtle conservation are available at our projects in Costa Rica and Panama.

Application Procedure: Applications can be sent to the above address at any time of year.

EL SALVADOR

EMBASSY OF EL SALVADOR
8 Dorset Square, London NW1 6PU
☎ 020 7224 9800

Teaching and Language Schools

Centro De Intercambio Y Solidaridad

Job(s) Available: Teachers (7).

Duration: Minimum period of work 10 weeks, with 1 week vacation in San Salvador. Positions available 12 January to 13 March, 29 March to 29 May and 14 September to 17 November 2008.

Working Hours: 16–20 hours per week, teaching Monday, Tuesday and Thursday, 5.15pm–7pm, plus staff meetings and preparation time.

> **Head Office:** Colonia Libertad, Avenida, Bolivar #103, San Salvador
> ☎ +503 22265362
> ✉ cis-elsalvador@yahoo.com
> 🖳 www.cis-elsalvador.org

Company Description: A multi-faceted organisation that supports education and social justice and promotes solidarity and cultural exchange across borders between the Salvadoran people.

Job Description: Classes are small with 6–9 students per class. Additional teaching and volunteer opportunities are available. TEFL and popular educational methodology training provided. Volunteers receive a 50% discount on Spanish classes and 2 free weeks in the afternoon political-cultural programme to learn more about El Salvador and its history.

Requirements: Minimum age 18. Spanish and ESL training not necessary but useful. Fluent English necessary.

Accommodation: Accommodation and board available for $70 per week with host family. Includes breakfast and dinner. Lunch costs $1.50–$3 per day.

Application Procedure: Apply to the English school co-ordinator at least a month prior to start date. Interview not required but application and reference letter are. Applicants must qualify for a tourist visa in El Salvador.

MEXICO

EMBASSY OF MEXICO
16 St George Street, London W1S 1LX
☎ 020 7499 8586
🖳 www.sre.gob.mx/reinounido

Paid employment is difficult to find in Mexico and must be approved by the Mexican Government before a visa will be issued to enter Mexico. Permits are generally issued to people who are sponsored by companies in Mexico. Visitors entering Mexico as tourists are not permitted to engage in any paid activities under any circumstances though this does not stop private language schools employing English teachers who have tourist visas. This is illegal.

There are a growing number of opportunities for voluntary work in Mexico. British applicants can find voluntary work in Mexico through Outreach International (www.outreachinternational. co.uk), Concordia, UNA Exchange or Youth Action for Peace, US nationals through the CIEE (see the *Worldwide* chapter for details).

Voluntary Work and Archaeology

American Friends Service Committee

Job(s) Available: Volunteers.

Duration: Work generally lasts for 7 weeks from early July to late August.

Pay/Cost: Limited scholarships available some years. Participants are responsible for their own travel costs and must make a contribution to cover orientation, food, accommodation, health and accident insurance. Please note that no paid jobs are available in Mexico or US through the AFSC or SEDEPAC.

Head Office: 1501 Cherry Street, Philadelphia, Pennsylvania 19102, USA
mexicosummer@afsc.org
www.afsc.org/latinamerica/int/mexicosummer.htm

Job Description: Volunteers to work in indigenous villages in Mexico learning from an intercultural exchange while contributing to communities with work projects and cultural workshops.

Requirements: Applicants should be 18–26 years old and speak Spanish.

Accommodation: Included in cost.

Application Procedure: For details American applicants should write to the above address enclosing an international reply coupon before 1 March or apply via the website. European applicants should apply directly to SEDEPAC, Apartado Postal 27-054, 06760 Mexico DF, Mexico (sedepac@laneta.apc.org)

Concordia Mexico

Job(s) Available: International volunteer projects.

Duration: Short-term.

Cost: Volunteers pay a registration fee of £150, plus a preparation weekend fee of £30 and fund their own travel and insurance. There is also an extra fee payable to the in-country host of approximately £130.

Head Office: 19 North Street, Portslade, Brighton BN41 1DH, UK
01273 422218
info@concordia-iye.org.uk
www.concordia-iye.org.uk

Company Description: Concordia offers volunteers the opportunity to take part in international short-term volunteer projects in over 60 countries worldwide.

Job Description: The work is community based and ranges from nature conservation, renovation, construction and social work including children's play schemes and teaching.

Requirements: Minimum age 19. Volunteers have to attend a preparation weekend with dates available every year in February, June and July; for more information visit the website or contact the office at the above number.

Accommodation: Board and accommodation are free of charge.

Application Procedure: For further information on volunteering or coordinating please check the website or contact the international volunteer co-ordinator at the above address.

Industrial and Office Work

Pro World Service Corps

Job(s) Available: Interns.

Duration: Minimum period of work 2 weeks.

Working Hours: 4–6 hours per day.

Cost: Fee of £995 ($1,795) required for first 2 weeks, £195 ($345) for each week thereafter. Cost includes full room and board with a local family, domestic transportation, Spanish classes in Peru and Mexico, cultural and adventure activities, project funding and support and health and travel insurance.

Head Office: Globe II Business Centre, 128 Maltravers Road, Sheffield S2 5AZ, UK
☎ 0870 750 7202

Head Office: PO Box 21121, Billings, MT 59104-1121, USA
☎ +1 877 4296753
✆ info@myproworld.org
🖥 www.myproworld.org

Company Description: Promotes social and economic development, empowers communities and cultivates educated, compassionate global citizens. Participants will work abroad with the community and one of the affiliated non-governmental organisations (NGOs), government social programmes, or a Pro World initited project. Projects are determined by community need and participants' skills and interests. Programmes are offered in Peru, Belize and Mexico.

Job Description: Interns are needed for public health care, public health education and assistance, health research, environmental conservation, environmental tourism, cultural and museum work, archaeology, construction, education and teaching, women's rights, human rights and social assistance.

Accommodation: Included in cost.

Application Procedure: Apply to Adam Saks, placement advisor 1 to 3 months before participation. Phone interview necessary once accepted.

Teaching and Language Schools

Ahpla Institute

Job(s) Available: English teachers (35).

Duration: Teachers are expected to work a minimum of 6 months.

Working Hours: 7am–9am and 5pm–7pm.

Pay: 122 pesos per hour (approximately £5.88).

Requirements: Applicants must be educated, flexible, willing to work with a team and travel. Good people and communication skills are a must.

Head Office: Juan Escutia No. 97, Colonia Condesa, C.P. 06140 D.F Mexico
☎ +52 5286 9016, ext. 113
✆ kallen@ahpla.com
  ahpla@ahpla.com
🖥 www.ahpla.com

Accommodation: Ahpla Institute offers no help with accommodation or flights.
Application Procedure: Applications to Karen Julie Allen, operations manager.

Culturlingua Language Center

Job(s) Available: English teachers.
Working Hours: 30 hours per week, 6 daily classes Monday to Friday.
Company Description: Culturlingua is a small, privately owned institution dedicated to teaching both English and Spanish.

Head Office: Morelos 636 Sur, C.P. 59680 Zamora, Michoacàn Mexico
☎ +52 351 5123384
✒ info@culturlingua.com
🖥 www.culturlingua.com

Requirements: Native English-speaker with TESOL, ESL or any teacher's certificate. Must be adaptable to teach children, adolescents or adults.
Accommodation: Accommodation can be provided.
Application Procedure: Applications to the above address/email at any time.

Dunham Institute

Job(s) Available: English teachers (3).
Duration: To work minimum 5 months.
Working Hours: 3-4 hours in the afternoon teaching. Study Spanish in the mornings.
Pay: No salary is provided.

Head Office: Avenida Zaragoza 23, Chiapa de Corzo, Chiapas Mexico
☎ +52 29 160961
✒ dunhaminstitute@yahoo.com

Requirements: English teachers required with ESL certificate, must be a native English speaker.
Accommodation: Accommodation with a local family and 2 hours of Spanish tuition a day.
Application Procedure: Applications to Joanna Robinson, academic co-ordinator at above address.

Teachers Latin America

Job(s) Available: Various positions (25).
Duration: Minimum period of work 4 weeks.
Pay: $600-$1,000 per month.
Company Description: A TEFL organisation specialising in job placements around Latin America.
Job Description: Each position differs, applicants

Head Office: Alvaro Obregon 153 Suite 305, 06700
☎ +52 555 5118149
✒ teachers@innovative-english.com
🖥 www.innovative-english.com

will be given job or internship details based on where they would like to work. The website details several of the positions.
Requirements: Minimum high school qualification and teaching credential (TEFL or CELTA). Other experience considered. High degree of fluency in English required.
Accommodation: Accommodation and board available but to be paid by candidates, $150-$300 per month.
Application Procedure: To apply contact Guy Courchesne, employment advisor. Telephone or email interviews only.

PERU

EMBASSY OF PERU
52 Sloane Street, London SW1X 9SP
☎ 020 7838 9223
💻 www.peruembassy-uk.com
📧 postmaster@peruembassy-uk.com

The following organisations have vacancies for paying volunteers/suitably qualified employees in Peru.

Red Tape

Visa Requirements: British, Irish and EU nationals do not need a visa when travelling to Peru. Once in Peru visitors are allowed to remain for 90 days, after that time you must renew your visa. Volunteers who do not receive a wage can travel on a tourist visa. However anyone hoping to take up paid employment in Peru requires a working visa.

Work Permits: Resident working visas have to be requested by the employers in Peru. Once the visa request has been granted by Peruvian migratory authorities you can apply at the consulate. All visas have to be applied for in person. Once an application is approved by the Consul General it takes a minimum of 24 hours to issue it.

Industrial and Office Work

Pro World Service Corps

Job(s) Available: Interns.
Duration: Minimum period of work 2 weeks.
Working Hours: To work 4 to 6 hours per day.
Cost: Fee of £995 ($1,795) required for first 2 weeks, £195 ($345) for each week thereafter. Cost includes full room and board with a local family, domestic transportation, Spanish classes in Peru and Mexico, cultural and adventure activities, project funding and support and health and travel insurance.

Head Office: Globe II Business Centre, 128 Maltravers Road, Sheffield S2 5AZ, UK
☎ 0870 750 7202

Head Office: PO Box 21121, Billings, MT 59104-1121, USA
☎ +1 877 429 6753
📧 info@myproworld.org
💻 www.myproworld.org

Company Description: Promotes social and economic development, empowers communities and cultivates educated, compassionate global citizens. Participants will work abroad with the community and one of the affiliated NGOs, government social programmes, or a Pro World initited project. Projects are determined by community need and participants' skills and interests. Programmes are offered in Peru, Belize and Mexico.

Job Description: Interns are needed for public health care, public health education and assistance, health research, environmental conservation, environmental tourism, cultural and museum work, archaeology, construction, education and teaching, women's rights, human rights and social assistance.

Accommodation: Included in cost.

Application Procedure: Apply to Adam Saks, placement advisor 1 to 3 months before participation. Phone interview necessary once accepted.

Voluntary Work and Archaeology

Kiya Survivors

Job(s) Available: Volunteers.

Duration: Placements of 2, 4 or 6 months' duration starting in September, January and May.

Cost: Cost ranges between £900 and £2999. A full 4 month placement would be £2699 and includes flight Lima to Cusco, 2 nights in Lima, transfer to project, 6-week Spanish course, accommodation in a volunteer family house or home, a 2-day Inca trail and trip around the Sacred Valley; a horse-riding excursion and tourist ticket with access to all local ruins and museums. Volunteers buy their own insurance and food.

Company Description: Kiya Survivors' unique Rainbow Centre, in Peru's sacred Valley is just an hour's drive from Cusco, the center provides invaluable help for children who have been abused, neglected or who have special needs for whom there is virtually no help.

Requirements: Volunteers aged from 18–80.

Accommodation: Accommodation included in cost. The volunteer house has cooking facilities and local markets provide cheap fresh food.

Application Procedure: Contact Alexis Argent at the above address or email.

> **Head Office:** Suite 41, 41–43 Portland Road, Hove BN3 5DQ, UK
> ☎ 01273 721092
> ✉ alexis@kiyasurvivors.org
> 🖥 www.kiyasurvivors.org

Bunac Volunteer Peru

Job(s) Available: Volunteer placements.

Duration: Allows participants to spend 2–3 months working as a volunteer in Peru.

Job Description: There is a great need for volunteers with specific practical skills for example IT. Placements can also be education or based on manual/unskilled labour.

Requirements: Applications are expected to have Spanish language skills to approximately GCSE level or equivalent. The programme is open to students, non-students and graduates.

Accommodation: Accommodation is provided with a host family as part of the programme fee as are all support services in the UK and in Peru for the duration of your trip.

Application Procedure: For further details contact BUNAC at the above address or visit www.bunac.org.

> **Head Office:** BUNAC, 16 Bowling Green Lane, London EC1R 0QH, UK
> ☎ 020 7251 3472
> ✉ volunteer@bunac.org.uk

USA

AMERICAN EMBASSY
24 Grosvenor Square, London W1A 1AE
☎ 020 7499 9000
🖥 www.usembassy.org.uk

Despite a slowing economy relative to most other countries the USA has low unemployment and there is still a strong demand for workers to fill a wide variety of specialised summer jobs. Opportunities for summer work in the United States are so numerous that apart from those listed below, there are thousands on websites including www.j1jobs.com, www.coolworks.com, www.apexusa.org, www.greatcampjobs.com and www.seasonalemployment.com/summer.html to name but a few. National and state parks in the USA list their recruitment needs on their sites.

The website www.nps.gov/parks.html gives a list of all such parks from A to Z and their contact details.

Placing an advertisement in an American paper may lead to the offer of a job. *The New York Times* (www.nytimes.com) is published by A.O. Sulzberger, of 229 West 43rd Street, New York, NY10036. It has a UK office at 66 Buckingham Gate, London, SW1 6AU, UK (020 7799 2981).

Au pairing in the US differs from au pairing in Europe since the hours are much longer and, if the au pair comes from the UK, there is no language to learn. The basic requirements are that applicants be between 18 and 26, speak English, show at least 200 hours of recent childcare experience and provide a criminal record check.

Voluntary work in the USA can be arranged through the Winant-Clayton Volunteer Association (entry below), Youth Action for Peace, UNA Exchange, Concordia, International Voluntary Service, the CIEE, and Service Civil International (see the *Worldwide* chapter for details).

Red Tape

Visa Requirements: since the introduction of the Visa Waiver Program, the tourist visa requirement is waived in the case of 28 nationalities, including British and Australian citizen passport holders. Nationals of the 29 countries may enter the US for up to 90 days for tourism or business, provided they meet all of the regulations for visa free travel. Note: Certain travellers are not eligible to travel visa free, for instance those who have been arrested and/or convicted of an offence. The Rehabilitation of Offenders Act does not apply to US visa law. For a full list of the 29 visa free countries, including the criteria which must be met to travel visa free, and further information on those not eligible to travel under the Visa Waiver Program, contact your nearest Embassy or Consulate, or visit the Department of State's website (http://travel.state.gov or www.usembassy.org.uk).

Since 1 October 2004 visitors from 27 countries including Britain have been digitally photographed and electronically fingerprinted by US immigration before being given permission to enter the USA. Anyone entering the US to work requires the appropriate work visa. Under no circumstances can a person who has entered the US as a tourist take up any form of employment paid or unpaid.

Residence Permits: Anyone seeking to take up permanent residence in the U.S. requires the appropriate immigrant visa. In general immigration is family or employment based. For further information, contact your nearest Embassy or Consulate, or visit the Department of State's website as above.

Work Permits: Anyone taking up temporary employment, whether paid or unpaid, requires the appropriate work visa. There are a number of possible visas for temporary workers, au pairs, exchange visitors and cultural exchange visitors on EVPs (recognised Exchange Visitor Programmes such as BUNAC and Camp America. Most of the opportunities listed in this chapter are covered by the J-1 Exchange Visitor visa, which is arranged by the organisations with entries. Employment-based H-2B visas are available through major employers of seasonal workers (as in ski resorts) only after the employer receives Labor certification from the Department of Labor (which takes 3–6 months).

Au Pair: J-1 visa available through officially approved exchange visitor programmes overseen by the Public Affairs Division of the Department of State.

Voluntary Work: Individuals participating in a voluntary service programme benefiting US local communities, who establish that they are members of and have a commitment to a particular recognised religious or non-profit charitable organisation may, in certain cases, enter the US with business (B-1) visas, or visa free, if eligible, provided that the work performed is traditionally done by volunteer charity workers, no salary or remuneration will be paid from a US source other than an allowance or other reimbursement for expenses incidental to the stay in the United States, and they will not engage in the selling of articles and/or solicitation and acceptance of donations. Volunteers should carry with them a letter from their U.S. sponsor, which contains their name and date and place of birth, their foreign permanent residence address, the name and address of their initial destination in the U.S., and the anticipated duration of the voluntary assignment.

Agricultural Work

WWOOF Hawaii (Willing Workers on Organic Farms)

Job(s) Available: Volunteers on organic farms in Hawaii.

Duration: Opportunities may be available all year round.

Pay: Pocket money is not usually provided.

Cost: Hawaii membership is $20 plus postage. Cash or cheques are accepted, or through Paypal. WWOOF will then send you the WWOOF Hawaii booklet.

> **Head Office:** 4429 Carlson Road, Nelson, British Columbia V1L 6X3, Canada
> ☎ +1 250 354 4417
> ✉ wwoofcan@shaw.ca
> 🖥 www.wwoofhawaii.org

Company Description: US youths and hundreds of people from all over the world go 'wwoofing' every summer. Farm hosts are available in most states and on 5 of the Hawaiian islands.

Job Description: Volunteer experiences range from small homesteads to large farms. Duties include general garden work, etc.

Requirements: Minimum age of 16. If not a US citizen, only EU nationals with valid tourist visas need apply.

Accommodation: Board and lodging are provided free of charge.

Application Procedure: Applications can be made online, or send full name, mailing address and registration fee.

Hotel Work and Catering

Resort America – Camp America

Job(s) Available: Supportive roles including catering and administration at holiday resorts or hotels in the USA.

Duration: Applicants must be available to leave the UK between 1 May and 27 June for a minimum of 12 weeks.

> **Head Office:** Dept. SDA, 37 Queen's Gate, London SW7 5HR, UK
> ☎ 020 7581 7373
> 🖥 www.campamerica.co.uk

Pay: Pocket money of $1,375 (dependant on age and experience).

Company Description: Resort America, a programme of Camp America, is open only to full-time students who want to work in supportive roles including catering and administration at holiday resorts or hotels in the USA.

Requirements: Experience in leisure and hospitality management, food and beverages supervision and entertainment is preferable.

Accommodation: Participants are offered free return flights from London and other selected airports worldwide to New York and transfer to the camp where the applicant is placed, free accommodation and meals, up to 10 weeks of travel time after camp, 24 hours support and medical insurance, Cultural Exchange US visa sponsor.

Application Procedure: The application process for this programme closes in December. Early application advised. Camp America host recruitment fairs allowing participants to meet face-to-face with Camp Directors. For the latest event information and to request a brochure, please visit www.campamerica.co.uk or call 020 7581 7373.

Sports, Couriers and Camping

Goal-Line Soccer INC

Job(s) Available: Football coaches.

Duration: Placements are from the beginning of July and last 5 weeks; or longer if participant wishes.

Pay: $300+ per week.

Job Description: Qualified coaches with coaching certificates from recognised national soccer associa-

> **Head Office:** PO Box 1642, Corvallis, Oregon 97339, USA
> ☎ +1 541 7535833
> ✆ info@goal-line.com
> 🖳 www.goal-line.com

tions are required to teach football to American children and play exhibition games against local teams. Coaches stay with American families and are offered opportunities. Placements are mainly in the West Coast states of Washington and Oregon. There are opportunities to take part in other recreational sports such as water-skiing and golf.

Requirements: Applicants should be over 21. There is a registration fee of $200. A 4-day orientation at Oregon state university is given prior to commencing placement.

Application Procedure: Applications to Tom Rowney at the above address. Interviews are held in the UK

Summer Camps

Camp America

Job(s) Available: Camp America is looking to recruit skilled people for a variety of job choices available all over the USA, from Camp Counsellor roles to Camp Power or Resort America positions.

> **Head Office:** Dept. SDA, 37A Queen's Gate, London SW7 5HR, UK
> ☎ 020 7581 7373
> 🖳 www.campamerica.co.uk

Duration: *Camp counsellors:* Applicants must be available to leave the UK between 1 May and 27 June for a minimum of 9 weeks.

Pay: Pocket money, which ranges from $525 to $1,100 (depending on age and experience).

Company Description: Camp America is one of the world's leading summer camp programmes, offering its counsellors over 40 years of experience placing people from Europe, Asia, Africa, Australia and New Zealand at American summer camps. It takes pride in evaluating the background, training and main skill areas of applicants to help them find the right placement.

Job Description: *Camp counsellors:* required to undertake childcare and/or teaching sports activities, music, arts, drama and dance.

Requirements: Experience and qualifications in sport coaching, religious counselling, teaching, childcare, healthcare and life guarding is preferable.

Accommodation: Counsellors are offered return flights from London and other selected airports worldwide to New York and transfers to particular camp, free accommodation and meals, up to 10 weeks travel time after camp, plus 24-hour support and medical insurance, Cultural Exchange US Visa sponsor.

Application Procedure: Early application is advised. Camp America host recruitment fairs allowing participants to meet face-to-face with camp directors. For the latest event information and to request a brochure, please visit www.campamerica.co.uk or call 020 7581 7373.

CCUSA

Job(s) Available: Camp counsellor, support staff.
Duration: From May/June to August/September. Minimum period of work 9 weeks.
Working Hours: Work weekly shift patterns which vary from camp to camp.
Pay: *Camp counsellor:* $750–$1900. *Support staff:* $1250.

Head office: Ist floor North, Devon House, 171/177 Great Portland street, London, W1W 5PQ UK
☎ 020 7637 0779
🖥 www.ccusa.com

Company Description: CCUSA has been sending young people to work on international work/travel placements since 1986. CCUSA is a visa sponsoring company and find the best job on an individual basis.

Job Description: Working at an American summer camp is a fun and rewarding experience. If you want to do something completely different with your summer and are keen for a new challenge then contact CCUSA.

Requirements: Fluent English is necessary. *Camp counsellor:* enthusiastic with a love of children. *Support staff:* hardworking and enthusiastic.

Accommodation: Included.

Additional Information: CCUSA also offer programmes in Australia, New Zealand, South Africa, China and Russia. Programmes include: *Work Adventures Down Under:* work in Australia and/or New Zealand for up to 2 years in each country. Must be aged 18–30 and UK passport holder (or passport holder of country with reciprocal visa arrangements). *Camp Counsellors Russia*: work in Russia at a children's summer camp for 4 or 8 weeks from June or July. Flights and insurance included in package – do not have to speak Russian. *Volunteer Adventures South Africa:* Work in one of 17 projects in South Africa, with something to suit all tastes from re-habilitating street children, to caring for babies with HIV to rescuing penguins trapped by oil spills. *Camp Counsellors Canada:* Work in Canada in a children's summer camp for between 9 and 11 weeks starting from June or July. Camp placements tailored to suit your experiences and preferences. *Work and Play Canada:* Spend 6 months in the skifields of Canada. Currently work with Whistler Blackcomb, Lake Louise and Big White resorts. Jobs start November/December. *Teach and Travel China:* A choice of 2 programmes, either work with children on Chinese summer camps for up to 6 weeks, or work in a Chinese High School for 6 months.

Application Procedure: Apply from September to April to the London office on 020 7637 0779. Foreign applicants are welcome to apply but it is down to the discretion of the US embassy whether a visa is granted.

Camp Kirby

Job(s) Available: Lifeguard (2–3), creative arts counsellor (1), rock climbing instructor (1), archery instructor (1), nature counsellor (1), outdoor living skills instructor (1).

Duration: From 8 July to 18 August.

Head Office: 4734 Samish Point Road, Bow, Washington 98232 USA
☎ +1 360 733 5710
info@campfiresamishcouncil.org
www.campfiresamishcouncil.org

Company Description: Since 1923 Camp Kirby has been providing children the opportunity to grow, make friends, have fun, and come home with memories to last a lifetime. Camp Kirby's 47 acres, including beautiful, pristine forest and over 11 miles of beach, is located on Samish Island in Skagit County. Owned and operated by Camp Fire USA, Camp Kirby is constantly growing to meet the needs and excite the imagination of Kirby campers.

Requirements: *Lifeguard:* must hold current lifeguard certification. Open water and small craft certification or experience is preferred. *Outdoor living skills instructor:* previous camping/outdoor experience and food handlers permit required. OLS certification and/or previous knowledge of outdoor survival skills is helpful.

Application procedure: Please see website.

Camp Power

Job(s) Available: General maintenance roles at American summer camps.

Duration: Applicants must be available to leave the UK between 1 May and 27 June for a minimum of 9 weeks.

Head Office: Dept. SDA, 37a Queen's Gate, London SW7 5HR, UK
☎ 020 7581 7373
www.campamerica.co.uk

Pay: Pocket money $850–$1,300 (dependant on age and experience).

Company Description: Camp Power, a programme of Camp America, is open only to full-time students who want to work in general maintenance roles at American summer camps.

Job Description: Typical job roles involve assisting in kitchen/laundry duties, administration and general camp maintenance. This supportive role represents an ideal camp alternative for those not wishing to work directly with children.

Requirements: Experience in administrative roles, maintenance, health care and catering is preferable.

Accommodation: Participants are offered free return flights from London and other selected airports worldwide to New York and transfer to their camp, free accommodation and meals, up to 10 weeks of travel time after camp, 24 hour support and medical insurance, Cultural Exchange US visa sponsor.

Application Procedure: Early application advised. Camp America host recruitment fairs allowing participants to meet face-to-face with camp directors. For the latest event information and to request a brochure, please visit www.campamerica.co.uk or call 020 7581 7373.

BUNAC Kamp

Job(s) Available: KAMP is a low cost fare-paid programme for summer camp staff who are not afraid of work in an ancillary capacity. Working in the kitchen and maintenance areas, staff do not look after children and have access to many of the camps' facilities during time off.

Head Office: BUNAC, 16 Bowling Green Lane, London EC1R 0QH, UK
☎ 020 7251 3472
camps@bunac.org.uk

Duration: 2 months.

Cost: The programme fee is approximately £141.

Job Description: BUNAC places applicants, arranges the special work/travel visa, flight and travel to camp. In addition, participants are given free board and lodging at camp, a salary and up to 6 weeks of independent travel afterwards.

Requirements: The programme is open to those who are currently enrolled at a British university, studying full-time at degree (or advanced tertiary or postgraduate) level. Gap year students are not eligible.

Accommodation: Provided.

Application Procedure: Applications to the above address.

BUNAC Summer Camp USA

Job(s) Available: Over 5,000 people in US summer camps.

Duration: 9 week work period.

Cost: The programme fee is approximately £141.

Job Description: A low-cost, non-profit camp counsellor programme run by BUNAC (the British Universities North America Club). Provides job, work papers, flights, salary, board and lodging, and a flexible length of independent holiday time after the work period.

Requirements: Applicants must be aged 18 or above, have experience of working with children and be living in the UK at the time of making their application.

Accommodation: Provided.

Application Procedure: For details contact the above address or visit the website.

Head Office: 16 Bowling Green Lane, London EC1R 0QH, UK
☎ 020 7251 3472
📧 camps@bunac.org.uk
🖥 www.bunac.org

Geneva Point Centre

Job(s) Available: Camp counsellors, Elderhostel dining staff, volunteer opportunities.

Company Description: At Geneva Point Centre we believe that all persons are called to wholeness of spirit, mind and body, so that they may become effective stewards and leaders in a complex world. Geneva Point is a conference centre and camp serving Christian and non-profit groups for conferences, retreats, personal and family events and camps. Groups looking for an ideal site for their next event are encouraged to consider Geneva Point Centre.

Application Procedure: Contact Greg by email at widman@genevapoint.org. For camp counsellors and dining staff ask for Abbie. For volunteers ask for Jess or Greg.

Head Office: 108 Geneva Point Road Moultonboro, NH 03254
☎ +1 603 2534366
📧 register@genevapoint.org
🖥 www.genevapoint.org

UK Elite Soccer

Job(s) Available: Seasonal soccer coach (40), summer soccer coach (70).

Duration: *Seasonal:* March to November 2008, July to November 2008. *Summer:* 2 months, July and August 2008.

Working Hours: *Seasonal:* Full-time, 20+ hours per week. *Summer:* Full-time, 20+ hours per week.

Pay: *Seasonal:* $9,000 salary, $11,000 expenses. *Summer:* $1,700 salary, $4,000 expenses.

Company Description: The 'Leaders in Youth Soccer Education'. We provide the best quality soccer programmes in the USA with the highest trained and most diverse staff of any organisation in the field.

Requirements: Fluent English is necessary. *Seasonal:* Coaching qualifications, teaching qualifications. *Summer:* experience working with children, full clean driving license preferred.

Accommodation: Board and accommodation provided.

Additional Information: All general information can be found on www.UKElite.com and visit the employment homepage.

Application Procedure: Apply to Jobs@UKElite.com or contact David Boyd +1 973 6319802 ext.209 or Andy Broadbent ext.206. Interviews will take place in November. Foreign applicants welcome to apply.

Head Office: 210 Malapardis Road, Suite 201, Cedar Knolls, NJ 07927
☎ +1 973 631 9802
📧 AndyB@UKElite.com
🖥 www.UKElite.com

Voluntary Work and Archaeology

Gibbon Conservation Center

Job(s) Available: Voluntary primate keepers (up to 3 at any time).

Working Hours: 6.30am–5pm, 7 days a week; opportunities for time off depend on the number of volunteers.

Head Office: PO Box 800249, Santa Clarita, CA 91380
☎ +1 661 2962737
✉ gibboncenter@earthlink.net
🖥 www.gibboncenter.org

Company Description: This non-profit organisation houses the largest group of gibbons in the Western Hemisphere. It is devoted to the study, preservation, and propagation of this small ape.

Job Description: Voluntary primate keepers to work with gibbons at the centre. Duties include preparing food and feeding, changing water, cleaning enclosures, observing behaviour (if time permits), entering data into computer (Apple Mac), maintaining grounds etc.

Requirements: Minimum age 20. Applicants must be well motivated, love animals, be capable of retaining unfamiliar information, get along with a variety of people, be in good physical condition and able to work outside in extreme weather conditions. They will need to have the following medical tests: stool cultures, ova and parasite stool test, standard blood chemistry and haematology, tuberculosis (or written proof from a doctor certifying that they have been vaccinated against tuberculosis) and Hepatitis B. Also required are vaccinations against tetanus (within the last 5 years), rubella, measles and Hepatitis B (if not already immune).

Accommodation: Volunteers must make their own travel arrangements and buy their own food locally; accommodation is provided.

Application Procedure: Applications to Dorothy Agins, volunteer co-ordinator at the above address/email.

The International Volunteer Programme

Job(s) Available: Volunteers.
Duration: Between 4 and 12 weeks
Working Hours: Full-time.
Cost: Between $1200 and $3300 depending on duration, location and possible language classes.

Head Office: San Francisco Bay Area Office, 678 13th Street, Suite 200, Oakland, CA 94612 USA
☎ +1 510 4330414
✉ ivpsf@swiftusa.org
🖥 www.ivpsf.com

Company Description: The International Volunteer Programme was founded in 1991 by La Société Française de Bienfaisance Mutuelle with the assistance and cooperation of the French Consulate in San Francisco, the University of California at Irvine, and le Comité de Jumelages de Troyes. The IVP is a non-profit organisation that promotes volunteering in Europe, the US and Latin America.

Job Description: Volunteer programmes are designed to facilitate a hands-on service and international exchange opportunities, with the aim of fostering cultural understanding at the local and global levels. IVP currently offers volunteer positions in France, Spain, the UK, the US and Costa Rica.

Accommodation: Bed and full board included in price.

Additional Information: Further information including costs of programmes can be obtained from the website or contact at the above address.

Application Procedure: Application forms available from www.ivpsf.org/volunteers.html. Need to apply 3 months in advance.

Kalani Oceanside Retreat

Job(s) Available: Opportunities for volunteering exist in food service, grounds/maintenance, and housekeeping.

Duration: Volunteers must stay a minimum of 1 to 3 months.

Working Hours: 30 hours of volunteer time per week.

Pay/Cost: The cost of the Resident Volunteer Programme is $1500 for the 3-month term.

Company Description: Kalani Oceanside Retreat is a non-profit, inter-cultural conference and retreat centre located on the Big Island of Hawaii with twenty acres of pristine land, surrounded by tropical forest and the Pacific Ocean.

Job Description: The retreat centre operates with the assistance of approximately 50 resident volunteers who help to provide services to the guests of the Retreat.

Requirements: Volunteers must be at least 18 years old and in good health. Experience in the area for which the applicant volunteers is preferred.

Accommodation: In exchange for volunteering participants receive meals, shared lodging, and a week long vacation during the 3-month placement.

Application Procedure: Application form and free brochure are available from the above address.

> **Head Office:** RR 2 Box 4500, Pahoa, Hawaii 96778
> ☎ +1 808 9650468 extension 117
> 🖰 volunteer@kalani.com
> 🖥 www.kalani.com

Au Pairs, Nannies, Family Helps and Exchanges

Au Pair in America

Job(s) Available: Au pairs.

Duration: Visa-supported 1-year stay. Opportunity to extend their year for another 6, 9 or 12 months.

Pay: up to $200 per week for qualified nannies and a minimum of $157.95 per week for standard au pairs.

Job Description: Choose from a wide range of approved families from across the USA. A 4-day orientation is provided on arrival in the USA. Full local counsellor support is provided throughout the year to introduce friends and give guidance with every aspect of the stay.

Requirements: Applicants aged 18–26. Applicants must hold a full, valid driving licence and have at least 200 hours of recent childcare experience.

Accommodation: Full board and lodging.

Additional Information: Benefits include a full round trip airfare, medical insurance and part-time college course, $500 study allowance, 2 weeks paid holiday, travel month and the security of a safe and legal programme.

Application Procedure: Contact the above address for further details.

> **Head Office:** 37 Queens Gate, London SW7 5HR, UK
> ☎ 020 7581 7322
> 🖰 info@aupairamerica.co.uk
> 🖥 www.aupairamerica.co.uk

Childcare America

Job(s) Available: Au pair and nanny stays in the USA.
Duration: Visa-supported 1 year stay.
Pay: Families provide full round trip air fare, medical insurance and part-time college course plus 2 weeks paid holiday. Salary up to $200 per week for qualified nannies and a minimum of $157.05 per week for au pairs.

Head Office: Childcare International Ltd, Trafalgar House, Grenville Place, London NW7 3SA, UK
☎ 020 8906 3116
✎ sandra@childint.co.uk
🖳 www.childint.co.uk

Company Description: Childcare America offer a to applicants aged 18–26 with good childcare experience. Full local counsellor support is provided to introduce friends and give guidance with every aspect of the stay.
Job Description: Choose from a wide range of approved families from across the USA. A 4 day orientation is provided in the USA.
Requirements: Applicants must drive.
Application Procedure: By post to the above address.

Educare America

Job(s) Available: Child care positions.
Duration: 1 year.
Working Hours: 30 hours per week.
Pay: $118.46 per week.
Company Description: The Educare Programme offers the opportunity to work and study in the United States.

Head Office: Au pair in America, 37 Queens Gate, London NW7 3SA, UK
☎ 020 7581 7322
✎ info@aupairamerica.co.uk
🖳 www.aupairamerica.co.uk

Job Description: It provides the opportunity for young people to spend a year in the States caring for school-aged children for while attending an American college. Families provide air fare, medical insurance, 2 weeks paid holiday and a salary. Full year-round local counsellor support is also available.
Requirements: Aged 18–26. Full driving licence is essential.
Application Procedure: For programme information please contact the above address.

Other Employment in the USA

BUNAC Work America

Job(s) Available: The programme enables participants to take virtually any summer job in the US.
Duration: A special work and travel visa allows students to work and travel from June to the beginning of October.
Cost: The programme fee is about £259.

Head Office: BUNAC, 16 Bowling Green Lane, London EC1R 0QH, UK
☎ 020 7251 3472
✎ workamerica@bunac.org.uk

Job Description: Work America is a general work and travel programme open to students through BUNAC. Provides the opportunity to earn back living and travelling costs. BUNAC provides a Job Directory, which is packed with jobs from which to choose and arrange work before going.

Requirements: The programme is open to those who are currently enrolled at a British university or college studying at degree (or advanced tertiary or postgraduate) level; unfortunately gap year students are not eligible.

Application Procedure: Visit www.bunac.org for more details. Early application is strongly advised.

CIEE (Council on International Educational Exchange) ____

Duration: A student's work experience can last for up to 4 months and they can travel around the US for a further month. For US students going abroad it varies according to visa restrictions.

Pay: Cost of participation varies depending on the type and length of program.

Head Office: 300 Fore Street, Portland, ME 04101, USA
☎ +1-207-553-4000
   +1-800-40-STUDY (Toll-free)
✆ info@ciee.org, contact@ciee.org
▣ www.ciee.org

Company Description: The Council on International Educational Exchange is the leading US non-governmental international education organisation. CIEE creates and administers programs that allow high school and university students and educators to study and teach abroad. It also sponsors numerous international exchange opportunities for young people to live, study, train, work and travel in the United States.

Application Procedure: For more information please contact CIEE at the above address.

Internship USA Programme ____

Job(s) Available: Course-related work experience/ training placements.

Duration: period of up to 12 months in the US, with an optional travel period following placement.

Cost: Participants pay an administrative fee of £430 with £35–£40 increments for each additional month of stay.

Head Office: IST Plus Rosedale House, Rosedale Road, Surrey TW9 2SZ, UK
☎ 020 8939 9057
✆ info@istplus.com
▣ www.istplus.com

Job Description: This scheme enables students and recent graduates to complete a period of course-related work experience/training in the US.

Requirements: Minimum age 18. Applicants must be enrolled in full-time further or higher education (HND level or above). Students may participate after graduation as long as the application is submitted while still studying. Participants must find their own training placements, related to their course of study, and either through payment from their employer or through other means, finance their own visit to the United States.

Additional Information: IST Plus' US partner provides the legal sponsorship required to obtain the J-1 visa, as well as orientation materials covering issues such as social security, taxes, housing, American culture and transportation; plus 24-hour emergency assistance with any problems whilst in the United States and comprehensive insurance. See www.istplus.com for more details.

Application Procedure: Applications can be made at any time of year, but should be made 8–12 weeks before desired date of departure.

Portals of Wonder

Job(s) Available: Artistic helpers and performers. internships.

Duration: Minimum commitment from 3 to 16 months.

Working Hours: 10am–7pm, 4–5 days a week.

Pay: Internships are unpaid.

Head Office: 212 East 83rd Street – 4D, New York, NY 10028 USA
☎ +1 646 3304773
candidate@portalsofwonder.org
www.portalsofwonder.org

Company Description: Portals of Wonder is an exciting, dynamic, volunteer driven charity, working to put smiles on faces of terminally ill and disenfranchised children. By lending your valuable skills and expertise together with many others who share the Portals of Wonder mission, thousands of lives are affected.

Requirements: Ability to work in the US.

Accommodation: Help in finding accommodation may be given.

Application Procedure: First contact is by email only. Send cover letter, CV, business writing samples (for example fundraising and marketing plans, business plans, sponsorship proposals, budgets etc), references related to credits listed in your CV and availability (start and end dates, times and hours per week). Submit as an MS Word attachment and cut and paste into an email to candidate@portalsofwonder.org. Put the word internship and position title in the subject line. For security reasons attachments will not be opened. They will be used for reference after internship begins. Please include a direct telephone number.

ASIA

BANGLADESH

HIGH COMMISSION FOR THE PEOPLE'S REPUBLIC OF BANGLADESH
28 Queen's Gate, London SW7 5JA
☎ 020 7584 0081
🖳 www.bangladeshhighcommission.org.uk
🖰 bhclondon@btconnect.com

Red Tape

Visa Information: In order to do voluntary work in Bangladesh, you must first obtain an NGO visa. To do this you must submit a letter of invitation from the concerned Bangladesh organisation and a Visa application form to the Bangladesh High Commission or relevant embassy.

The following organisation offers the opportunity to do voluntary work in Bangladesh.

Bangladesh Work Camps Association (BWCA)

Job(s) Available: Volunteers.

Duration: BWCA conducts short-term workcamps with a duration of 10–15 days each year from October to March, and from 1 to 6 weeks from October to February. A Round The Year Programme (RTYP) is also available to medium-term volunteers staying for a minimum period of 3 months.

Head Office: 289/2 Workcamp Road, North Shajahanpur, Dhaka-1217, Bangladesh
☎ +880 2 935 8206/935 6814
🖰 bwca@bangla.net
🖳 www.mybwca.org

Working Hours: 30 hours per week.

Pay: Camp is $200 per camp per person. Volunteers must pay all other expenses including insurance and travel. RTYP registration is $250.

Company Description: Bangladesh Work Camps Association (BWCA) promotes international solidarity and peace through national/international workcamps for volunteers in rural and urban areas of Bangladesh.

Job Description: The projects organised include environmental and health education, literacy, sanitation, reforestation, community work, development and construction, etc. At least 30 volunteers a year are recruited onto one of the 3 international workcamps.

Requirements: Volunteers aged 18–35, must be able to speak English, be adaptable to any situation and be team-spirited.

Accommodation: Accommodation and simple local food is provided for $2 a day. Volunteers must provide own sleeping bag/mat.

Application Procedure: Applications to BWCA 3 months in advance of scheduled Camp/Programme date. Applications must come through a BWCA partner organisation in the applicant's country; if this is not possible individual, direct applications may be accepted and should be accompanied by a payment of $25. Application form available at www.mybwca.org/BWCA_APP_FORM.rtf.

EMBASSY OF THE PEOPLE'S REPUBLIC OF CHINA
49-51 Portland Place London W1B 1JL
☎ 020 7299 4049
🖥 www.chinese-embassy.org.uk
📠 visa@chinese-embassy.org.uk

British nationals can find voluntary work in China through the UNA Exchange see the *Worldwide* chapter for details. Americans can check programmes such as Volunteers in Asia (VIA, Stanford University; www.viaprograms.org) which sends volunteer teachers to China and Vietnam and Princeton in Asia (www.princeton.edu/~pia); though these programmes are likely to be for longer than a summer. However, VIA in particular is looking for ways to expand volunteering in China. The following organisations offer the opportunity to work in China.

Red Tape

Visa requirements: Visas are required for any visit to China. Applicants must submit an application form and supporting documents to the visa office of the Chinese Embassy in the UK (London) or to the Chinese Consulate-General (Manchester or Edinburgh). An interview may be required by the visa officer.

Voluntary Work and Archaeology

Earthcare

Job(s) Available: About 150–200 volunteers are recruited annually.

Duration: Minimum period of voluntary work is 2 weeks at any time of year.

Cost: Expenses must be covered by the volunteer.

Company Description: Earthcare, a local Chinese

Head Office: GPO Box 11546, Hong Kong
☎ +852 25780434
📠 care@earth.org.hk
🖥 www.earth.org.hk

charity, aims to promote the concepts of benevolence and compassion in traditional Chinese teaching to establish a green lifestyle, environmental conservation, humane education and the protection of animals.

Job Description: Volunteers to help in the following areas: fundraising, computer/data processing/maintenance, administration, clerical work, campaigning, animal care/treatment, publishing/printing, photography and filming, multimedia design and application, public relations and education. Campaigns include: banning bear farming and advocating herbal alternatives to animal derived remedies in Chinese medicines.

Requirements: Applicants must be able to speak English, any knowledge of Cantonese would be a bonus.

Accommodation: Very simple accommodation can be provided but all other expenses must be met by the volunteer.

Application Procedure: Applications to the above address.

International China Concern (ICC)

Job(s) Available: Volunteers (20–30) to fulfil a variety of roles: Administration assistant, accounts assistant, physical or occupation therapy co-ordinator, special education teachers, special needs nursing carer.

Duration: Volunteers are required from 6 months to 2 years.

Pay/Cost: Volunteers must be self-supporting.

Head Office: PO Box 20, Morpeth NE61 3YP, UK
☎ 01670 505622
✆ uk@intlchinaconcern.org
▱ www.intlchinaconcern.org

Company Description: ICC is a charitable organisation involved in projects in China's government orphanages. By bringing care and improvement of conditions ICC aims to make a difference to the lives of China's orphans. ICC is a bridge between China and the West to channel finances and resources.

Job Description: *Duties include correspondence and book keeping.*

Requirements: Knowledge of Mandarin Chinese is helpful but not essential.

Application Procedure: For more information, please visit the website.

Teaching and Language Schools

English First

Job(s) Available: English language teachers (75).

Duration: The minimum contract term is for 2 months during the Chinese school summer holidays.

Working Hours: 40 hours per week with 24 contact teaching hours, 5 days a week.

Pay: EF offers a competitive salary (paid in local currency).

Head Office: 26 Wilbraham Road, Fallowfield, Manchester M14 6JX, UK
☎ 01612 561400
✆ recruitment@englishfirst.com
▱ www.englishfirst.com

Company Description: English First is part of EF Education and is a world leader in language learning with over 200 schools worldwide. EF Education is a multi-national group with some 20,000 employees at work in 48 countries. English First's Teacher Recruitment and Training department trains and recruits English language teachers to work both at home and abroad.

Job Description: English First is looking for enthusiastic and committed teachers to teach EFL to mono-lingual Chinese students aged between 8 and 25 and to participate in the students' activity programme in various locations throughout China.

Requirements: Candidates must have or be willing to undertake a TEFL/TESL Certificate (EF can provide training in 10 European cities).

Accommodation: Free accommodation, working visa, health insurance and a generous flight allowance provided.

Application Procedure: Closing date for applications 31 May. Candidates are requested to register their details via www.englishfirst.com. All academic staff are recruited through EF's Online Recruitment Centre.

IST Plus: Teach in China

Job(s) Available: TEFL teachers.

Duration: 5 or 10 months teaching English in a university, college or school in China. IST Plus sends

Head Office: IST Plus Rosedale House, Rosedale Road, Surrey TW9 2SZ, UK
☎ 020 8939 9057
✆ info@istplus.com
▱ www.istplus.com

participants on this programme in late August and early February in accordance with the Chinese semester system.

Cost: Participants are responsible for paying their outward air fare and programme fee to IST Plus to cover the costs of arranging the placement, processing all paperwork required for visas and work permits, visa fees, the training centre and 24-hour emergency support while in China. Return fare is paid by the host institution on completion of a 10 month contract.

Company Description: Sending more graduates to China than any other organisation, IST Plus is an organisation helping people develop skills and acquire knowledge for working in a multicultural, interdependent world.

Job Description: Successful applicants attend a one-week training course on arrival in Shanghai; focusing on learning Chinese, understanding Chinese culture and acquiring the basic skills to teach English. Participants are awarded a TEFL Certificate upon completion of their teaching contracts.

Requirements: There is no age limit, and teaching/TEFL qualifications are not required in order to apply.

Accommodation: Host institutions in China provide private accommodation (usually a teacher's apartment on or near the campus), and a monthly salary, which is generous by Chinese standards.

Application Procedure: Applicants are encouraged to return forms and application materials at least 3 months beforehand in order to ensure that a suitable placement is found. US applicants should apply to the CIEE in the US (for address see the Worldwide chapter).

INDIA

OFFICE OF THE HIGH COMMISSIONER FOR INDIA
India House, Aldwych, London WC2B 4NA
☎ 020 7836 8484
🖳 www.hcilondon.org

Despite its vast size India offers few opportunities for paid temporary work, particularly for those without any particular skill or trade to offer an employer: there are untold thousands of Indians who would be delighted to do any unskilled job available for a wage that would seem a pittance to a westerner. Anyone determined to find paid employment there should explore the possibility of working for tour operators who specialise in organising holidays to India.

There are, however, a number of opportunities for taking part in short-term voluntary schemes in India. The worldwide fame of *Mother Teresa's Missionaries of Charity* in Calcutta means it has no shortage of volunteers to take on part-time work to care for and feed orphaned children, the sick and dying, mentally or physically disabled adults and children or the elderly at its children's home in Calcutta (Shishu Bhavan, 78 A.J.C. Bose Road), in the Home for Dying Destitutes at Kalighat and other houses run by the Missionaries of Charity in Calcutta and other Indian cities. However no accommodation can be offered. To register, visit the Mother House at 54A A.J.C. Bose Road, Calcutta 700 016. Further information is also available from their London office at 177 Bravington Road, London W9 3AR (020 8960 2644).

Council International Volunteer Projects and Service Civil International can place Americans on voluntary schemes in India, and Concordia and UNA Exchange can offer similar placements for Britons: see the *Worldwide* chapter for details. Please note that as is normal with short-term voluntary opportunities, those taking part must pay for their own travel expenses, and will often be required to put something towards the cost of board and lodging, though generally in India this is a modest amount. The organisation Aid India (www.aidindia.org) carries volunteer requests on its website.

Visa Requirements: a tourist visa is required by all non-Indian nationals entering India.

Residence Permits: those planning a stay of over 3 months must register with the Foreigners Regional Registration Office within 14 days of arrival and be able to provide evidence of how they are supporting themselves. It is not possible to change a tourist visa to a long stay visa within India.

Employment Visas: any foreigner taking up paid employment in India must have a valid work permit before they enter the country: they should apply (ideally in person) to the nearest Indian consulate, enclosing a copy of their contract.

Voluntary Work: details of the voluntary work to be undertaken should be sent to the Indian Consulate at least 2 months in advance as they have to be forwarded to India. If you do want to attach yourself to a voluntary organisation for more than three months, you should aim to enter India on a student or employment visa (see Indian Embassy website).

Voluntary Work

Concordia India

Job(s) Available: Volunteers.

Duration: Short-term.

Cost: Volunteers pay a registration fee of £150, plus a preparation weekend fee of £30 and fund their own travel and insurance. There is also an extra fee payable to the in-country host of approximately £120.

> **Head Office:** 19 North Street, Portslade, Brighton BN41 1DH, UK
> ☎ 01273 422218
> ✆ info@concordia-iye.org.uk
> 🖥 www.concordia-iye.org.uk

Company Description: Concordia offers volunteers the opportunity to take part in international short-term volunteer projects in over 60 countries worldwide.

Job Description: The work is community based and ranges from nature conservation, renovation, construction and social work including children's play schemes and teaching.

Requirements: Minimum age 19. Volunteers have to attend a preparation weekend with dates available every year in February, June and July; for more information visit the website or contact the office at the above number.

Accommodation: Board and accommodation are available free of charge.

Application Procedure: For further information please check the website or contact the International Volunteer Co-ordinator at the above address.

Dakshinayan

Job(s) Available: Volunteers.

Duration: Between 4 weeks and 6 months. Help is needed throughout the year.

Working Hours: Volunteers normally work 4–6 hours per day, 6 days a week.

> **Head Office:** F-1169, Chittaranjan Park, First Floor, New Delhi – 110019, India
> ☎ +91 983 6596426
> ✆ info@dakshinayan.org
> 🖥 www.dakshinayan.org

Pay/Cost: Dakshinayan charges a fee of $300 per month. Volunteers are expected to cover all expenses to and from the project.

Job Description: Volunteers to work with a registered trust engaged in providing education assistance to tribes in the Rajamhal Hills and the surrounding plains. Education is of primary level and volunteers are expected to assist in teaching English or arts and crafts, sports, poetry or singing.

Requirements: No formal teacher training is needed. Minimum age 18. All applicants must be socially sensitive and willing to work in remote locations. Knowledge of Hindi an advantage though not mandatory.

Accommodation: No expenses are paid. Cost includes food and accommodation while at the project, and there is no additional fee. Living conditions on most rural development projects are very basic.

Application Procedure: Applications at least 30 days in advance of desired departure date, to Siddharth Sanyal, executive trustee, at the above email address.

Joint Assistance Centre (JAC)

Job(s) Available: Any number of volunteers are accepted.

Duration: Help is needed from volunteers for periods of 3–26 weeks, around the year. Volunteers must be able to work for a minimum of 3 weeks. Longer term placements in other projects according to skills/interests are also arranged.

Head Office: PO Box 6082, San Pablo CA, USA
☎ +1 510 237 8331
✆ jacusa@juno.com
🖥 www.jacusa.org

Working Hours: 8 hours per day, 5 days a week with free days by mutual arrangement.

Pay/Cost: Participants are required to send a processing fee of $50 with their application to JAC USA. They will then contribute a further $150 for each month.

Company Description: JAC offers a unique opportunity to carry out humanitarian works in close unison with local agencies as well as the UN and other international groups.

Job Description: Volunteers can perform various jobs for community projects. Many tasks are available, including helping with office work, editing, writing, teaching, social work, joining youth workcamps, construction work, helping run seminars and giving demonstrations and lectures on English first aid and other skills. There are opportunities for learning natural cures (chromopathy), yoga and meditation.

Requirements: No special qualifications required. Minimum age 18.

Accommodation: Simple but safe and secure accommodation is provided in huts or tents, in the slum or rural areas. Cost covers food, accommodation, administration, and airport pickup.

Application Procedure: Contact the above address for application forms.

Nomad Travel

Job(s) Available: Volunteers.

Duration: Minimum period of work 6 weeks. Work is available all year round.

☎ 0845 310 4470
✆ katherine@nomadtravel.co.uk
🖥 www.nomadtravel.co.uk

Company Description: Help is needed on the West Bengal/Sikkim borders, in the foothills of the Himalayas, approximately 3 hours from Darjeeling. This is a small clinic set up in Karmi Farm to help the indigenous population with day-to-day healthcare and childcare.

Job Description: Volunteer nurse/doctors to help in rural communities. The clinic currently caters for 210 families from the surrounding area. There is also outreach work. Situated in the foothills of the Himalayas, transport is all on foot. The main illnesses are skin disorders, chest problems, dehydration, childhood illnesses. Midwifery plays a big part. People turn up at the clinic any time night or day. However, there are long spells when it is quiet.

Accommodation: Comfortable accommodation and organic food provided.

Additional Information: Funds are raised in the UK to pay for board and lodging and pharmaceuticals.

Application Procedure: Applications should be made to Cathy Goodyear at any time.

Rural Organisation for Social Elevation

Job(s) Available: Volunteers (1–10).

Working Hours: 5 hours per day, 5 days a week.

Cost: Volunteers must pay their own travel costs and about £4.50 (350 Rupees) a day towards board and lodging costs, administration, guide, rent and ROSE's school expenses. One off registration fee of 3500 rupees.

Company Description: ROSE is a small charity, based in a beautiful location at the foot of the Himalayas. It provides volunteers with the opportunity of experiencing true rural Indian life while providing education and improving local sanitation and health care facilities. ROSE offers many opportunities for students to conduct research in various subjects such as geography, anthropology, development, conservation and environmental studies as well as in the education development programme.

> **Head Office:** Vill.–Sonargaon, P.O. Kanda, Bageshwar, Uttaranchal
> ☎ +91 596 324 1081 (international) +95 596 324 1097 (local). Please note that it may be difficult to get through. Keep persevering.
> ✉ jlverma_rosekanda@hotmail.com (infrequent internet access)
> ▭ www.rosekanda.info

Job Description: Volunteers to carry out work in rural areas including teaching English to children, construction, poultry farming, environmental protection, organic farming, agricultural work, recycling paper to make hand-made greetings cards, office work, compiling project proposals, reports and healthcare. Groups of volunteers can be organised into workcamps lasting 10 to 30 days, but individuals are also welcome to apply.

Accommodation: Accommodation in a family house provided in addition to 3 delicious meals a day.

Additional Information: International phones and internet facilities are available in Bageshwar (1 and a half hours by bus).

Application Procedure: Application form available at www.rosekanda.info/ApplicationForm.pdf

Skillshare International

Job(s) Available: Projects cover a wide range of activities and general management, agricultural, technical, educational and medical skills are all required.

Duration: Placements are usually for 2 years.

> **Head Office:** 126 New Walk Street, Leicester LE1 7JA, UK
> ☎ 01162 541862
> ✉ recruitment@skillshare.org
> ▭ www.skillshare.org

Cost: Skillshare offers a modest living allowance, flights/travel to the placement, medical cover, and pre and post placement grants to assist with relocation. The living allowance is adequate to cover your living costs whilst in the country of placement but not adequate for savings or meeting other costs you may have in your country of residence.

Company Description: Skillshare recruits professionals to share their skills and experience with local communities to further economic and social development in Botswana, Kenya, Lesotho, Mozambique, Namibia, South Africa, Swaziland, Tanzania, Uganda, India and Nepal. Its vision is a world without poverty, injustice and inequality where people, regardless of cultural, social, and political divides come together for mutual benefit living in peaceful co-existence.

Requirements: Applicants should be aged 21, have relevant qualifications and experience, particularly in training others.

Application Procedure: An information pack is available from the above address.

JAPAN

EMBASSY OF JAPAN
101–104 Piccadilly, London W1J 7JT
☎ 020 7465 6500
💻 www.uk.emb-japan.go.jp
🖅 info@jpembassy.org.uk

The range of short-term casual jobs open to Westerners in Japan is extremely limited, even with unemployment in Japan having rapidly fallen in recent years. However, longer-term opportunities do exist, particularly in the area of teaching English: it has been estimated that 11% of all Japanese people attend English 'conversation classes'. A native English-speaker therefore possesses a marketable skill if he or she has a degree; experience or qualifications in teaching English as a foreign language are added advantages. One way of finding a teaching job is to advertise in the English-language *Japan Times* (www.japantimes.co.jp).

For further information on teaching work in Japan see *Teaching English Abroad* (see *Useful Publications*). Anyone who is serious about wanting to spend some time in Japan should read *Live and Work in Japan* (David and Elisabeth Roberts, Crimson Publishing 2008), a thorough guide for anyone hoping to live and work there.

There is a support organisation for those wishing to visit Japan on a working holiday visa – the Japanese Association for Working-Holiday Makers with offices in Tokyo, Osaka and Kyushu (Tokyo office: Sun Plaza Seventh Floor, 4-1-1 Nakano, Nakano-ku, Tokyo 164-8512; +81 3 3389 0181; www.jawhm.or.jp).

CIEE and Service Civil International can help US residents to fund voluntary work in Sapan. Concordia, Youth Action for Peace, UNA Exchange and International Voluntary Service can help UK residents. See their entries in the *Worldwide* chapter for details.

Red Tape

Visa Requirements: nationals of the UK, USA, Ireland, Germany, Switzerland and Austria can visit Japan as tourists without a visa for up to 3 months and extend this to 6 months. Most other nationalities can visit for up to 3 months, as long as they have a return or onward ticket and sufficient funds.

Work Permits: A position must be secured and working visa obtained before you enter the country. Applications for working visas must be submitted to the Consulate in person. If you a certificate of eligibility from Japan a visa can be issued in three days.

Working Holiday Visas. Holders of British, Australian, Canadian and New Zealand passports can apply for working holiday visas: these must be applied for at the Japanese Embassy of their home country. The rules are generally the same, but full details can be obtained from the nearest Japanese Embassy or consulate. There is a small, non-refundable processing fee for a working holiday visa. Working Holiday Visas are available to British citizens between April and the following March; applications are accepted from April. Application forms and explanatory material can be obtained from the Japanese Consulate-General in London or Edinburgh (www.uk.emb-japan.go.jp).

Japanese Working Holiday visas are single entry, so if you have to leave Japan for any reason you must obtain a re-entry permit from the competent immigration authorities before leaving. Travellers who stay in Japan longer than 90 days have to register with the local municipal office, and keep them informed of any subsequent change of address. They can also register with their embassy or consulate on arrival or later during their stay but this is not obligatory. For clarification of these points and news of any changes in the regulations please contact the nearest Japanese Embassy or consular mission.

Voluntary Work: a Volunteer Visa Scheme allows British nationals to undertake voluntary work in Japan, working for charitable organisations for up to a year. Work should be unpaid but pocket money and free board and lodging are permitted. Details and application forms are available from the Consulate General of Japan in London and Edinburgh.

Teaching and Language Schools

The Japan Exchange and Teaching (JET) Programme

Job(s) Available: Positions in Japan promoting international understanding at a grass-roots level and improving foreign language teaching in schools.
Duration: Departure the following July/August after applying between September and November.
Pay: Participants are provided with return air travel, an annual salary of ¥3,600,000 plus the experience of a lifetime.

> **Head Office:** JET Desk, Embassy of Japan, 101-104 Piccadilly, London W1J 7JT, UK
> ☎ 020 7465 6668
> ✆ info@jet-uk.org
> 🖳 www.jet-uk.org

Company Description: Now in its 21st year, the Japan Exchange and Teaching (JET) programme has placed over 44,000 participants from over 44 countries into Japan.
Requirements: UK nationals from any degree discipline can apply through the website between September and November.
Application Procedure: Only UK passport holders can apply through the UK JET office. If you do not hold a UK passport but are interested in the programme, please visit www.mofa.go.jp/j_info/visit/jet/apply.html for a list of countries offering the programme, or please contact the Embassy of Japan in your home country. Contact the above address or email for more information.

Shin Shizen Juku (New Nature School)

Job(s) Available: Volunteers (up to 4) required.
Duration: Minimum period of volunteering 6 weeks.
Working Hours: Hours and programme vary from day-to-day but there is plenty of time for recreation.

> **Head Office:** Tsurui-Mura, Akan-Gun, Hokkaido 085-1207, Japan
> ☎ +81 15 4642821
> ✆ ja8nb@zpost.plala.or.jp

Company Description: SSJ belongs to the UNESCO movement for peace on earth.
Job Description: Kind, honest, responsible and enthusiastic applicants wanted to teach English to Japanese people.
Requirements: An interest in learning Japanese is encouraged. An international driver's licence essential.
Accommodation: Free food and accommodation are provided, in return for English language teaching and gardening work.
Application Procedure: Applications with a photo to Hiroshi Mine, manager, at the above address.

EMBASSY OF THE REPUBLIC OF KOREA
60 Buckingham Gate, London SW1E 6AJ
☎ 020 7227 5500/2
🖳 www.koreanembassy.org.uk
🖰 koreanembinuk@mofat.go.kr

Red Tape

Visa Regulations: Most Europeans and Americans may travel to South Korea without a visa. However the length of time that a visitor may stay varies from 1 month to 3 months, with a special status of 6 months awarded to Canadians. Young Australians and New Zealanders are eligible for a working holiday visa for Korea. The Ministry of Education in Korea administers the English Programme in Korea (EPIK) through its embassies in the UK, the USA, Canada and Australia. Details of the scheme are given below.

Work Permits: if possible, you should obtain a work visa (E2) which is available only to graduates with a 4-year BA or BSc. The E2 is valid only for employment with the sponsoring employer. You can obtain the permit in advance or you can enter on tourist visa, find a job and then leave the country while the permit is being processed. However, this takes about six weeks and may not be worthwhile for a summer job.

Teaching and Language Schools

English Program in Korea (EPIK)

Job(s) Available: English teachers in Korea.

Duration: Contracts are for 1 year.

Working Hours: 8 hours per day, 5 days a week. Excluding Saturdays, Sundays and Korean national holidays. Total instructional hours will not exceed 22 hours per week.

Pay: KRW2,700,000–KRW1,800,000 depending on experience and qualifications.

Head Office: Education Director, Korean Embassy, 60 Buckingham Gate, London SW1E 6AJ, UK
☎ 020 7227 5547
🖰 education-uk@mofat.go.kr
🖳 www.epik.go.kr

Requirements: English speakers with an undergraduate degree. 10 day orientation must be completed (unpaid).

Accommodation: Furnished apartment provided free of charge.

Application Procedure: UK applications to the above address. Americans should contact one of the dozen Korean consulates in the USA. Other nationalities can apply to the EPIK office in Korea, Center for In-Service Education, Korean National University of Education, Chongwon, Chungbuk 363-791.

Voluntary Work

Concordia Korea

Job(s) Available: International volunteer projects.
Duration: Short-term.
Cost: Volunteers pay a registration fee of £150 and fund their own travel and insurance.
Company Description: Concordia offers volunteers the opportunity to take part in international short-term volunteer projects in over 60 countries worldwide.

Head Office: 19 North Street, Portslade, Brighton BN41 1DH, UK
☎ 01273 422218
✆ info@concordia-iye.org.uk
🖳 www.concordia-iye.org.uk

Job Description: The work is community based and ranges from nature conservation, renovation, construction and social work including children's play schemes and teaching.
Requirements: Minimum age 18.
Accommodation: Board and accommodation are free of charge.
Application Procedure: For further information on volunteering or coordinating please check the website or contact the International Volunteer Co-ordinator at the above address.

NEPAL

NEPALESE EMBASSY
12A Kensington Palace Gardens, London W8 4QU
☎ 020 7229 1594
🖳 www.nepembassy.org.uk
✆ eon@nepembassy.org.uk

Nepal is one of the most promising destinations for young people who want to spend a few months as a volunteer in a developing country. However, people who find voluntary openings in Nepal may face a visa problem. The first tourist visa will be issued for 60 days (£20 single entry and £55 multiple entry). Processing takes a few days. A tourist visa can be extended from the Department of Immigration and Pokhara Immigration Office for a total of 120 days. An additional 30 days visa may be granted on reasonable grounds from the department.

Over the course of a visa year, a tourist cannot stay in Nepal more than cumulative 150 days. People who overstay their visas have in the past been fined heavily or even put in prison. More information is available at www.nepembassy.org.uk. This applies to all except Indian nationals who do not require a visa to visit Nepal. An impressive range of non-governmental organisations makes it possible for people to teach in a voluntary capacity. Although volunteers must bear the cost of travel and living expenses, the cost of living is very low by western standards.

Concordia, UNA Exchange and Youth Action for Peace can arrange short-term voluntary work placements in Nepal. See their entries in the *Worldwide* chapter for more details. The following organisations are also looking for volunteers to work in Nepal.

Voluntary Work

New International Friendship Club Nepal (NIFC-Nepal)

Job(s) Available: Volunteers. Teacher also needed for schools.

Duration: Workcamps last 15 days, medium-term placements 2-6 months.

Working Hours: Approximately 36 hours per week, 6 days a week.

Head Office: PO Box 11276, Maharajgunj, Kathmandu
☎ +977 1 4427406
nifc@mos.com.np
www.geocities.com/nifcnepal

Cost: $150 registration fee (covers a 3 day cross-culture course in Kathmandu).

Company Description: Friendship Club Nepal is a small Nepali-run NGO organising regular workcamps to assist rural communities.

Job Description: Volunteers are required to participate in both research and physical workcamps. Research work usually involves investigating and writing a report on the development situation (health, education, environment or agriculture etc) in a rural area. A physical workcamp might involve construction or agriculture.

Requirements: Volunteers should be aged between 17 and 65. Proficiency in English is essential.

Accommodation: Basic Nepalese style food, accommodation and boiled water will be provided during workcamps and placements. Usually no beds are available, but mats will be provided and volunteers should bring a sleeping bag. $100 a month covers food and accommodation. Volunteers should arrange their own travel, visa and insurance.

Application Procedure: Recruitment throughout the year; preferably apply at least 2 months in advance of intended departure date enclosing a CV.

Kathmandu Environmental Education Project (KEEP)

Job(s) Available: Volunteers to teach English.

Duration: Minimum of 2 months. Registration fee is $50.

Pay/Cost: Volunteers are required to be totally self-funding.

Head Office: PO Box 9178, Thamel, Kathmandu
☎ +977 1 421 6775/776
volunteer@keepnepal.org.np
www.keepnepal.org

Job Description: Volunteers are sought to go to various villages in Nepal to teach English to lodge owners, trekking guides and porters and also to work as teachers in government schools. KEEP also sends volunteers to NGOs operating in the fields of conservation or health and community development according to the interest and experience of the volunteers.

Accommodation: Accommodation is with mountain families.

Application Procedure: Applications to the above address.

Insight Nepal

Job(s) Available: Volunteer teachers (25).

Duration: Volunteer placements for 6 weeks and 3 months can be arranged. Work available all year round except in October.

Working Hours: 5-6 hours per day, 5-6 days a week.

Head Office: PO Box 489, Zero KM, Pokhara, Kaski,
☎ +977 61 530266
insight@fewanet.com.np
www.insightnepal.org.np

Company Description: Insight Nepal was established with a view to providing an opportunity to those who are interested in gaining a unique cultural experience by contributing their time and skills for the benefit of worthwhile community service groups.

Job Description: Volunteer Teachers to teach various subjects in primary, secondary and vocational schools or development projects in Nepal.

Requirements: Applicants should be aged 18–60 and educated to at least A level standard. Experience of teaching is helpful but not essential. Applicants with games, sporting and artistic skills preferred.

Accommodation: A host family provides accommodation and all meals. The project also includes a 1-week trekking and 3-day Jungle Safari.

Application Procedure: Please send your applications on line.

Volunteer Nepal

Job(s) Available: Volunteers.

Duration: 2–4 weeks. Workcamps take place in February, May, August and November. There are also longer projects needing 2–6 months commitment.

Working Hours: There is 4 hours of physical work in the mornings Monday to Friday and the afternoons are for seminars, lectures and discussions.

Company Description: Volunteer Nepal, National Group is a community-based, non-governmental, non-profit organisation that coordinates local and international workcamps with community groups or institutions in need of voluntary assistance.

> **Head Office:** c/o Anish Neupane, PBN 10210 KTM, Bagmati Zone 84 De Beauvoir Road, Reading, Berkshire RG1 5NP, UK
> ☎ +977 1 661 3724
> ⌨ info@volnepal.np.org
> volunteer@volnepal.np.org
> 🖷 www.volnepal.np.org

Job Description: Volunteers are needed to teach in schools and be involved in health, agriculture, engineering, research and other programmes. There are 6–20 volunteers per workcamp.

Additional Information: Travel and tours in Nepal also arranged.

Application Procedure: For further details and costs, contact the above address.

SRI LANKA

HIGH COMMISSION FOR THE DEMOCRATIC SOCIALIST REPUBLIC OF SRI LANKA
13 Hyde Park Gardens, London W2 2LU
☎ 020 7262 1841–7
🖳 www.slhclondon.org
⌨ mail@slhc-london.co.uk

Red Tape

Visa Requirements: British Nationals travelling to Sri Lanka as tourists need not obtain a visa prior to departure. A visa will be issued for a period of 30 days on arrival at the port of entry in Sri Lanka. Before the expiry of initial period of visa, an extension of the duration of your stay may be granted by the Department of Immigration and Emigration in Colombo. As volunteers are used informally to help with social, economic and technical development activities in villages, this works reasonably well for both parties. Volunteers usually pay something towards their keep while volunteering. This also applies to the nationals of most EU countries, USA, Canada, New Zealand and China.

Working Holiday Scheme: As a citizen of a commonwealth country you may be eligible to apply for a UK Working Holiday Visa.

Voluntary Work

Samasevaya

Job(s) Available: Volunteers.

Duration: Placements are available all year round and normally last one month but this period can be extended.

Cost: Volunteers are requested to pay $90 per month for their food; all other expenses, including entry visa must also be met by the volunteer.

> **Head Office:** National Secretariat, Anuradhapura Road, Talawa NCP
> ☎ +94 25 2276266
> ✉ samasev@sltnet.lk

Company Description: Samasevaya works towards peace through organising development programmes.

Job Description: About 10 volunteers a year are recruited to assist with the work on these projects.

Requirements: Minimum age 18 and volunteers must be in good health and prepared to work in rural areas.

Accommodation: Simple accommodation is provided.

Application Procedure: Applications to the national secretary at the above address.

VESL (Volunteers for English in Sri Lanka)

Job(s) Available: Volunteers (English Teachers) (20).

Duration: *English teachers:* 3 month projects starting throughout the year with summer schools starting in July.

Working Hours: 2–4 hours teaching per day, 5 days a week.

> **Head Office:** 68 Derinton Road, London SW17 8JB, UK
> ☎ 0845 094 3727
> ✉ info@vesl.org
> 🖥 www.vesl.org

Cost: Covered by fundraising; no volunteer should need more than £950 to cover project set-up, food, accommodation, insurance, training, backup and support costs.

Company Description: VESL sends volunteers throughout the year to run educational programmes in rural Indian and Sri Lankan communities, and trained UK teachers to run workshops for local teachers. Placements range from 2 weeks to 3 months or longer including 4 week summer schools in July and August to 3 month placements teaching and working alongside established NGOs.

Job Description: Volunteers English teachers required to run a summer English programme in Sri Lanka and India.

Accommodation: Covered by costs.

Application Procedure: Application details can be obtained from the website or enquiries@vesl.org.

THAILAND

ROYAL THAI EMBASSY
29–30 Queen's Gate, London SW7 5JB
☎ 020 7225 5512
🖥 www.thaiembassyuk.org.uk
✍ csinfo@thaiembassyuk.org.uk

In addition to the conservation project listed below, Concordia, UNA Exchange and Youth Action for Peace (see Worldwide section) offer British volunteers the chance to work in Thailand. English teaching jobs can be found on the website of the *Bangkok Post*, an English language newspaper, at www.bangkokpost.net.

Red Tape

Visa Requirements: A foreigner holding a Thai tourist visa is not permitted to work as an English teacher in Thailand, even on a voluntary basis. Applicants from English speaking countries wanting paid employment in Thailand must apply for a type B non-immigrant visa from the Royal Thai Embassy. With this visa it is possible to stay for up to 90 days; on arrival a work permit must be applied for at the Ministry of Labour. For voluntary work, a Type O visa is required; the applicant will be permitted to stay for a maximum of 90 days. Any person wishing to exceed that time must apply to the Office of Immigration Bureau. Most foreign nationals must apply for their visa before entering the country; however there are a few countries whose citizens may apply for a 15-day visa once inside Thailand.

Teaching and Language Schools

IST Plus

Job(s) Available: TEFL teachers.
Duration: Opportunity for graduates to spend 5 or 10 months teaching English in primary and secondary schools in Thailand. IST Plus sends participants on this programme in late October and early May in accordance with the Thai semester system.

Head Office: IST Plus Rosedale House, Rosedale Road, Surrey TW9 2SZ, UK
☎ 020 8939 9057
✍ info@istplus.com
🖥 www.istplus.com

Pay: A monthly salary which is generous by local standards.
Cost: Participants are responsible for paying their outward air fare and a programme fee to IST Plus to cover the costs of arranging the placement, processing all paperwork required for visas and work permits, visa fees, the training centre and 24-hour emergency support while in Thailand. Return fare is paid by the host institution on completion of a 10-month contract if the participant starts in May.
Company Description: IST Plus is an organisation helping people develop skills and acquire knowledge for working in a multicultural, interdependent world.
Job Description: Successful applicants attend a one-week training course on arrival in Bangkok focusing on the language and culture and acquiring the basic skills to teach English. Participants are awarded a TEFL Certificate upon completion of their teaching contracts.
Requirements: There is no age limit, and teaching/TEFL qualifications are not required in order to apply.

Accommodation: Host institutions provide private accommodation (usually a teacher's apartment on or near the campus).

Application Procedure: Applicants are encouraged to return forms and application materials at least 3 months beforehand in order to ensure that a suitable placement is found. US applicants should apply to CIEE in the USA.

Voluntary Work

The Wild Animal Rescue Foundation of Thailand

Job(s) Available: Volunteers.

Duration: The minimum stay period is 3 weeks.

Company Description: The Foundation is dedicated to the protection and provision of welfare to all wild animals in need and operates 2 sanctuaries in the south of Thailand.

Head Office: 65.1 Third Floor, Sukhumvit 55, Klongton, Wattana, and Bangkok 10110
☎ +66 2 7129515
volunteer@warthai.org
www.warthai.org

Job Description: At both projects, volunteers are involved in the day-to-day operation of the unit including food preparation, cage cleaning and maintenance, assisting with health inspections, behavioural observation and educating people who call at the visitors centre.

Requirements: Volunteers should be in good physical condition and be able to live and function in field station conditions. Enthusiasm and an ability to live and work with people of different cultures are essential.

Application Procedure: For current placement rates and opportunities, please contact us, preferably by email.

THAILAND

ASIA

AUSTRALASIA

AUSTRALIA

AUSTRALIAN HIGH COMMISSION
Australia House, Strand, London WC2B 4LA
☎ 09065 508 900
💻 http://www.uk.embassy.gov.au

The short length of this chapter does not bear any relation to the vast range and number of temporary opportunities available in Australia: there are many, as unemployed Australians don't want to do the jobs that working holiday visa visitors are willing to do. However, there are a few factors to bear in mind when considering Australia as a destination for a summer job. The first factor is the reversal of seasons: the Australian summer takes place in what is winter to much of the rest of the world and so jobs on their fruit harvests and at the peak of their tourist industry occur at the wrong time of year for anyone hoping to find work between July and September. There is also the financial factor: the cost of a return ticket to Australia makes going there for a paid job for just a few weeks very uneconomic – even though in real terms the cost of getting to Australia is at its cheapest ever, the cost is still such that it makes better financial sense to stay for months rather than weeks.

Luckily for the foreigner, Australia has a reciprocal working holiday scheme with certain countries that can ease the formalities for those going there to pick up casual work. Some guidelines for those hoping to do so are given below, but working holidays in Australia are covered in greater depth in, *Work Your Way Around the World* (see *Useful Publications* section), in the information available from Australian High Commissions and Embassies or through the Australia Government Immigration website at www.immi.gov.au. A third point to consider is that Australia is one of the most popular destinations for working travellers, and you need to begin the application process well in advance of your intended travel: 88,000 (and rising) people apply for visas every year and the processing usually takes at least 5 weeks. The fee at present is £85. It is important to remember that your First Working Holiday Maker visa can only be obtained in your country of origin, you cannot apply for a WHM visa once you are in Australia, although you can renew it.

Although Australia now has a declining unemployment rate, job-seekers must be prepared to devote time and energy to the job hunt. One tip is to look for work away from the big cities, where other new arrivals from overseas may be competing for the same jobs. A valuable source of rural jobs is Employment National (EN; +61 1 300720126; www.employmentnational.com.au), the government's privatised job agency. Enquiring in one office will allow you to uncover harvest work near one of the more than 200 other offices across the country. Employment National encourage working holidaymakers to contact their specialist fruit and crop-picking department or to check their website, which has details of the EN offices all over the country and the types of work that these may offer.

The fruit harvests of northern Victoria employ a massive 10,000–12,000 people in the Australian summer (January to March). The city of Shepparton is in the Goulburn Valley, about two hours north of Melbourne with easy accessibility via rail or bus services. Information can be obtained from the Northern Victoria Fruitgrowers' Association Ltd (NVFA), PO Box 612, Mooroopna, Vic 3629 (+61 3 58253700; administrator@nvfa.com.au; www.nvfa.com.au) and The Victorian Peach and Apricot Grower's Association (VPAGA) PO box 39 Cobram, Vic (+61

3 58721729). There is also a National Harvest Hotline number; +61 1 300720126. This number gives the option of states and areas within Australia where current seasonal work is available. By following the prompts, callers are able to obtain accurate updated information to a particular area or are able to speak directly with a person in a particular area.

Searching the web for employment leads is especially productive in Australia. There are dozens of routes to finding out about job vacancies. A wide search can be done by looking at Employment under Google's regional directory at http://directory.google.com/Top/Regional/Oceania/Australia. Before leaving home, you might like to register (free) with www.gapwork.com which is updated regularly and lists employers who hire working holidaymakers. See www.jobsearch.gov.au for a government source of information with details of the National Harvest Trail. One of the best sites is a free service by the Wayward Bus Company (www.waywardbus.com.au/seaswork.html) which has an index of actual employers, hostels and pubs recommended for job-seekers and agents. If in Queensland check the adverts in *Queensland Country Life* magazine (www.queenslandcountrylife.com). The magazine also has an online jobs guide (www.jobsguide.com.au). Some properties also function as holiday ranches and they often take on domestic staff and guides.

A publication called *Workabout Australia* (Barry Brebner, Vacation Work 2004) shows areas where fruit picking and other seasonal work is available. It also gives times, transport information, accommodation information and contacts for jobs on arrival.

Hard-working travellers can earn A$100 a day doing harvest work, although A$9 an hour would be more typical. The cost of living in Australia is a lot lower than in Britain so those wages go further than it sounds if you convert them into sterling at the current rate (£1 is worth A$2.30 at the time of writing).

Some city-based employment agencies deal with jobs in outback areas, primarily farming, station, hotel/motel and roadhouse work. In Western Australia, Pollitt's (+61 8 93252544) say that experienced farmworkers and tractor drivers are paid A$12–A$14 an hour for 10–12 hours per day, seven days a week at seeding time (April to June) and harvest time (October to December). Housekeeping, nannying and cooking positions are available for two to three months at a time throughout the year. The standard wage is A$300 a week after board, most of which can be saved. For work in outback roadhouses and hotels, previous experience in kitchen, food and beverage service is essential to earn A$400 a week after lodging. The three-month commitments enable travellers to experience the regional country towns while saving most of their earnings.

In urban areas the usual range of jobs exists (bar, restaurant, office and factory work), available through the many private employment agencies such as Bligh, Adecco and Drake Personnel. It is also worth investigating tourist areas such as the coastal and island resorts of Queensland for jobs in hotels, restaurants, etc especially during the Australian winter from June to October.

One of the best sources of job information for working holidaymakers in Australia is the extensive network of backpackers' hostels, some of which employ young foreigners themselves and all of which should be able to advise on local possibilities. One such is Brook Lodge Backpackers (3 Bridge Street, Donnybrook, WA 6239; +61 8 97311520; info@brooklodge.com.au; www.brooklodge.com.au) in Western Australia, which provides accommodation and can arrange hourly or weekly contract seasonal work including seasonal work in the apple harvest between November and May. Details of lodges like this can be found on the internet at http://backpackingaround.com, a website set up by backpackers which carries job and visa information as well as links and info on accommodation around Western Australia. Another useful source is the work exchange called Workstay Australia, which is based in Western Australia and can be found at www.workstay.com.au. There is a membership fee and members are guided to a network of hostels when work is available. The group HNH Travellers Australia (18 Withington

St, East Brisbane, Queensland 4169; +61 7 34115955; www.hnh.net.au) can arrange fruit-picking in some areas. They offer a Travellers Discount Card for A$5 which will enable travellers a 10% discount at restaurants along with corporate car hire rates etc.

Either before you leave or once you are in one of the major cities, get hold of the free 200-page booklet *Australia and New Zealand Independent Traveller's Guide* published by the London-based travel magazine *TNT* (www.tntmagazine.com) It includes a section on work and some relevant advertisements as well as travel advice.

Most newspapers advertise jobs on one or two days each week - varying from paper to paper and state to state. *The Sydney Morning Herald* can be contacted at www.smh.com.au. *The Australian* at www.theaustralian.com.au, and *The West Australian* at www.thewest.com.au.

Information and application forms for visitor and working holiday visas may be obtained in the UK from the High Commission's designated agent, Consyl Publishing. For an application form and a free copy of *Travel Australia*, a newspaper aimed at those planning a working holiday in Australia, write to Consyl Publishing, 3 Buckhurst Road, Bexhill on Sea, East Sussex TN40 1QF, UK (01424 223111; consylpublishing@btconnect.com; www.consylpublishing.co.uk); enclose an A4 stamped addressed envelope.

Red Tape

Tourist Visa Requirements: All intending visitors require either a visa stamped in their passport or an Electronic Travel Authority (ETA) which is a paperless visa. Tourist visas are issued for 3 or 6 months, under special circumstances a stay of up to a year may be considered. ETAs are obtained through the Australian immigration office, airlines, travel agents or specialist visa agencies. An ETA is valid for 12 months and covers multiple entries into Australia for no more than three months each. You can now apply online at www.eta.immi.gov.au, there is a service charge of A$20. Major airlines may offer a free ETA service if you purchase an air ticket through their reservations offices. Those with ETAs and tourist visas are not permitted to work, although limited volunteer work with no form of compensation may be allowed on a tourist visa.

Working Holiday Visas The Australian Government operates a working holiday scheme for passport holders of the following countries: United Kingdom, Republic of Ireland, Belgium, Canada, Cyprus, Denmark, Estonia, Finland, France, Germany, Italy, Japan, Republic of Korea, Malta, the Netherlands, Norway, SAR Hong Kong and Sweden. To be eligible for a 12 month, working holiday visa you must satisfy the following criteria: be aged between 18 and 30, have no dependent children, intend to travel and holiday in Australia with the option of taking incidental work to supplement your holiday funds but are prohibited from working for one employer for more than a total of six months, are in possession of reasonable funds (Generally, A$5,000 may be regarded as sufficient) for normal maintenance purposes for the initial part of the proposed holiday period and sufficient for airfare. People who have worked as a seasonal worker in regional Australia for a minimum of three months while on their first Working Holiday visa, may be eligible to apply for a second Working Holiday visa. There is a non-refundable processing fee for a working holiday visa, currently A$190. Current information is available by calling the Australian Immigration and Citizenship Information Line on 0906 550 8900.

During those 12 months of the visa's validity you may leave and re-enter the country as many times as you wish. Most WHM applicants have been able to lodge their visa applications electronically over the internet via www.immi.gov.au. An e-WHM will be processed within 48 hours.

Agricultural Work

Go Workabout

Job(s) Available: Farm work/fruit picking (200), hospitality (bar, waiting staff, chefs etc) (50).
Duration: All year round. Minimum period of work 1–3 months.
Working Hours: *Farm work/fruit picking:* 40–50 hours per week. *Hospitality:* 40–50 hours per week.
Pay: *Farm work/fruit picking:* A$15–A$20 per hour. *Hospitality:* A$18–A$25.
Cost: The total price for the package is A$685.

Head Office: 61 The Boulevard, Floreat Perth, Western Australia, 6019
☎ +61 8 93839982
info@goworkabout.com
www.goworkabout.com

Company Description: Go Workabout arranges jobs in Australia for working holiday makers before they leave their home countries. The organisation also provides assistance with all the administration issues involved (eg visa, tax file number, accommodation) to give the traveller a 'kick start' to their working holiday in Australia. All of the jobs come packaged with the 'Complete Working Holiday Maker Starter Pack'. This pack includes the arrangement of your working holiday visa, tax file number, bank account, mailing service, accommodation and starter pack booklet (and job of course).
Requirements: *Farm work/fruit picking:* Minimum age 18. Must be prepared to work outdoors. No experience necessary. *Hospitality:* Relevant hospitality experience necessary.
Accommodation: Available at cost of A$50 to A$125 per week.
Additional Information: Gw also fully assists fully qualified carpenters and form workers.

Plunkett Orchards

Job(s) Available: Fruit pickers (40), fruit graders (10).
Duration: From January until April. *Fruit pickers:* 1 week minimum. *Fruit graders:* 4 weeks minimum.
Working Hours: 6.30am–2pm, 6 days a week.
Pay: *Fruit pickers:* A$28 per bin harvested, can pick between 2 and 10 bins a day depending on experience and fitness. *Fruit graders:* A$15.93 per hour.

Head Office: 255 McIsaac Road, Ardmona Victoria 3629
☎ +61 3 58290015 (business hours only)
info@plunkettorchards.com.au
www.plunkettorchards.com.au

Company Description: Plunkett Orchards is a friendly, professional, family-owned business that employs travellers each year to work on the annual harvest of apples, pears and peaches. Plunkett Orchards is 2 hours north of Melbourne and temperatures can reach up to 40 degrees during harvest time.
Requirements: Must be motivated and in good physical condition. On the job training is provided, no previous experience necessary.
Accommodation: Board and lodging is available for A$70 per week.
Application Procedure: Applications invited from 1 November, details from website.

RJ Cornish

Job(s) Available: Fruit pickers (200).
Duration: Work period is from late January to mid-March.
Working Hours: 6 days a week, 7.30am–4pm (weather and crop permitting).
Pay: Australian Workers Union rates are paid per bin of fruit harvested.

Head Office: RMB 2024, Cottons Road, Cobram, Victoria 3644
☎ +61 3 58722055
picking@rjcornish.com
www.rjcornish.com

Company Description: RJ Cornish and Co is a family-owned and operated business located at Cobham on the Murray River on the border of Victoria and New South Wales. One of Australia's largest producers of apples, pears and canned peaches, so employment is also fruitful.

Requirements: The work is heavy physical labour and may be unsuitable for some people. New pickers will participate in an induction programme which covers picking skills as well as health and safety prior to starting work.

Accommodation: Accommodation (2 or 3 persons per room) and meals are available for approximately A$115 per week.

Application Procedure: Apply online at www.rjcornish.com/readandapply.html

Outback International

Job(s) Available: Jobs for farmers, tractor drivers, cotton workers, cooks and seasonal staff.

Duration: Farm workers are required all year, while cooks, housekeepers and nannies are needed between February and October. Minimum period of work 2 weeks.

> **Head Office:** PO Box 1392, Rockhampton, Queensland 4700
> ☎ +61 7 49274300
> ✉ admin@outbackinternational.com
> 🖳 www.outbackinternational.com

Working Hours: 8–12 hours per day, 5–7 days a week.

Pay: *Farm staff:* around £6–£8 per hour. *Cooks, housekeepers and nannies:* £160–£200 per week.

Company Description: Outback International is an Australia-wide rural employment agency. The experience of working within the primary industries overseas aims to broaden your knowledge of technology and work practices.

Job Description: *Farm staff:* numerous vacancies for personnel to operate farm machinery, drive tractors/harvesters, or work on irrigation schemes. *Cooks, housekeepers and nannies:* to work on outback farm stations.

Requirements: It is essential that applicants speak English. *Farm staff:* applicants must have an agricultural background. *Cooks, housekeepers and nannies:* applicants should have experience of cooking, housework and childcare.

Accommodation: Board and lodging is usually included, but this depends on the location.

Application Procedure: Applications are invited at any time to the above address.

Torrens Valley Orchards

Job(s) Available: Fruit picking and packing.

Company Description: Farm business that has used a lot of student and backpacker workers over the last 16 years particularly during the cherry harvest.

> **Head Office:** PO Box 1659, Gumeracha, South Australia 5233
> ✉ tvo@hotkey.net.au
> 🖳 www.tvo.com.au

Requirements: Workers should be quick, polite, clean and look after the facilities provided.

Accommodation: Hostel type accommodation for travellers.

Additional Information: Owner organises trips to barbecues, football, beach etc. The farm is 30 minutes from Adelaide on the local bus.

Application Procedure: Apply to Tony Hannaford at the above mail or email address.

Visitoz

Job(s) Available: Guaranteed employment opportunities for working holidays in Australia.

Duration: Staff are needed around the year but working holiday regulations limit the time with any one employer to 6 months. For those completing 3 months outback work a second visa is on offer which can be taken straight away or at any time before the participant's 31st birthday.

Head Office: Springbrook Farm, 8291 Burnett Highway, Goomeri, Queensland, 4601
☎ +61 7 41686185
info@visitoz.org
www.visitoz.org

Pay: Varies according to the work, the skills and the state of employment, but the minimum is about A$350 per week, plus food, accommodation and tax paid. This is money that you can SAVE as there is nothing to spend it on. After 3 months or so money has built up in the bank and the participant can take a holiday and enjoy all that Australia had to offer young people.

Cost: Participants in the scheme must pay for their own air fare, visa costs and the Visitoz training fee of A$1790 which also covers being met at the airport on arrival, 3 days jet lag recovery at a beach resort, 5 days on the training farm and help with the Red Tape paperwork once in Australia.

Company Description: VISITOZ offers an introduction to Australia for those who would like to have a working holiday in Australia. This is coupled with a 9 day introduction which includes a short course in either agricultural or hospitality skills. Well paid jobs are guaranteed for the whole of the 365 days of the visa, plus a friendly helping hand from the Burnet family on Springbrook Farm. The Burnets moved from Argyll to Queensland in 1991.

Job Description: Work can be provided as tractor drivers, stockworkers, horse riders, hospitality workers, on cattle and sheep stations, and as mothers' helps and distance education teachers. Employment is guaranteed.

Requirements: Applicants must be aged 18–31 and all are assessed and/or trained for the job required.

Application Procedure: For further details contact Dan and Joanna Burnet, or their son William and his wife Jules based in the UK. William on 07966 528664 or will@visitoz.org, and jules@visitoz.org.

Sports, Couriers and Camping

Thredbo Resort

Job(s) Available: Cashiering and sales staff (5), ski hire staff (8), room attendants, childcare, lift attendants, chefs/commis/demis chefs.

Duration: The period of work is from around 1 July to 28 September (depending on snow), with a minimum period of work of 12 weeks.

Head Office: Kosciusko Thredbo Pty Ltd, PO Box 92, Thredbo, New South Wales 2625
☎ +61 2 64594100
recruitment@thredbo.com.au
www.thredbo.com.au

Working Hours: Hours of work vary between 28–38 per week according to position.

Pay: *Cashiering and sales staff:* £853 per month. *Ski hire staff:* £945 per month. *Room attendants:* approximately £920 per month. *Childcare:* depend on qualifications, from approximately £1,062 per month. *Lift attendants:* approximately £943 per month. *Chefs/commis/demis chefs:* approximately £1,200 per month.

Company Description: Thredbo is Australia's premier ski resort, with a season from mid-June to the end of September. They employ over 700 staff in winter, and have a ski village population of over 4,400.

Job Description: *Cashiering and sales staff:* to sell ski lift passes, ski school products and assist in retail. *Ski hire staff:* to fit customers with skis and snowboards and hire out clothing and equipment. *Room attendants:* to do all aspects of cleaning hotel rooms and apartments. *Childcare:* trained and untrained staff who are prepared to assist in all aspects of caring for children 6 months to 5 years. *Chefs/commis/demis chefs:* to work for the Thredbo Alpino Hotel, including bistro, à la carte, fine dining and conferences.

Requirements: *Cashiering and sales staff:* applicants should have sales and cash handling skills, accurate balancing and computer experience. *Ski hire staff:* should have some cash handling experience and be willing to work split-shifts. *Room attendants:* friendly and courteous disposition required. *Lift attendants:* must be willing to work outdoors in all weather conditions. Some heavy work required. Good customer service skills.

Accommodation: Board and lodging is available for a cost of £57 per week.

Application Procedure: Applications to the above address are invited from January and close in early-April, with interviews in Sydney, Brisbane and Thredbo in early April.

Voluntary Work and Archaeology

Australian Koala Foundation

Job(s) Available: Volunteers.

Duration: Volunteers for office duties are generally required from March to October each year.

Company Description: The Australian Koala Foundation (AKF) is a non-profit, non-government funded conservation organisation whose central aim is the conservation of Australia's unique koala habitat.

> **Head Office:** GPO Box 3659, Brisbane, Queensland 4001
> ☎ +61 7 32297233
> akf@savethekoala.com
> www.savethekoala.com

Job Description: Volunteers can also assist with general office duties, especially during the major public awareness and fundraising campaign – Save the Koala – held in September each year.

Requirements: Minimum age 18. Applicants should advise the AKF of any specialist areas of expertise or interest they may have.

Additional Information: Check out the website for upcoming fieldtrips.

Application Procedure: Contact Lorraine O'Keefe, administration and finance, at GPO Box 2659, Brisbane, QLD 4001, Australia, to discuss the voluntary opportunities available.

Conservation Volunteers Australia (CVA)

Job(s) Available: Volunteers.

Duration: CVA offers overseas volunteers the Conservation Experience 6 weeks package.

Pay: Volunteering with CVA costs approximately A$30 a night.

Company Description: Conservation Volunteers Australia is Australia's largest practical conservation organisation. CVA welcomes everyone who is enthusiastic about the outdoors and hands-on conservation.

> **Head Office:** CV International Booking Office, PO Box 423, Ballarat, Victoria 3353
> ☎ +61 3 53302600
> bookings@conservationvolunteers.com.au
> www.conservationvolunteers.com.au

Job Description: Volunteers are part of a team of 6 to 10 people under the guidance of a CVA team leader. Projects undertaken by CVA include: tree planting, native seed collection, endangered flora and fauna surveys, constructing and maintaining walking tracks in national parks, weed control. Projects are run in every state and territory of Australia throughout the year and include some of Australia's most beautiful locations.

Accommodation: Cost includes all meals, project related travel and accommodation and recreational activity on alternate Sundays.

Application Procedure: For more information visit the website or email or write to CVA.

Other Employment in Australia

Camp Counselors Australia

Job(s) Available: Work Experience Down Under is a high quality programme that helps young people to work and travel in Australia.

Duration: For up to 12 months.

Application Procedure: For details contact the above addresses; US citizens should contact CCUSA/Work Experience Down Under, 2330 Marinship Way, Suite 250, Sausalito, CA 94965; downunder@ccusa.com.

> **Head Office:** Devon House, 171/177 Great Portland Street, London W1W 5PQ, UK
> ☎ 020 7637 0779
> ✉ info@ccusa.com
> 🖳 www.ccusa.com

Bunac Work Australia

Job(s) Available: BUNAC offers a work and travel scheme to Australia.

Duration: For up to a year. Departures from the UK are year round.

Cost: Programme costs are £395.

> **Head Office:** 16 Bowling Green Lane, London EC1R 0QH, UK
> ☎ 020 7251 3472
> ✉ downunder@bunac.org.uk

Job Description: The package includes a working holiday visa, airport transfer. 2 nights' accommodation in Sydney, and orientation with guidance on jobs, housing, health, taxes, etc plus back-up services. Participants have the option to travel on a BUNAC group flight with an organised stopover in either Hong Kong or Bangkok or arranging independent travel.

Requirements: Applicants must be aged 18–30 inclusive, citizens of the UK, Ireland, Holland, Sweden, Denmark, Norway or Canada, and will need to be able to show that they have reserve funds of at least £2,000.

Application Procedure: For further details contact Work Australia at the above address.

Work and Travel Australia Programme

Job(s) Available: Opportunities in casual work, internships and teaching positions across the world.

Duration: Visa valid for 12 months from entry to Australia. Wide variety of work available, for up to 6 months per position.

Cost: Programme fee starts at £320 (and rises in increments for every month's additional stay) and includes all services and 2 nights accommodation.

> **Head Office:** IST Plus Rosedale House, Rosedale Road, Surrey TW9 2SZ, UK
> ☎ 020 8939 9057
> ✉ info@istplus.com
> 🖳 www.istplus.com

Company Description: IST Plus is an organisation offering people opportunities in work. This programme allows participants to travel in Australia, taking up work along the way to support themselves. IST Plus offer assistance at every stage, from obtaining the visa, to helping find work and accommodation in Australia. Ongoing services include mail receiving and holding, 24 hour emergency support, and access to office facilities and free internet at their partner's resource centre in Sydney.

AUSTRALIA

AUSTRALASIA

Requirements: This programme is open to British, Canadian, Dutch and Irish passport holders resident in the UK as well as certain other nationalities, aged 18–30, who have not been on a working holiday to Australia before.

Application Procedure: Applications to the above address.

NEW ZEALAND

NEW ZEALAND HIGH COMMISSION
New Zealand House, 80 The Haymarket, London SW1Y 4TQ

☎ 020 7930 8422

🖳 www.nzembassy.com/home.cfm?c=14

✒ aboutnz@newzealandhc.org.uk

New Zealand offers many job opportunities just as its massive neighbour Australia does. If you intend to work in New Zealand you will require a visa, but some visas such as Working Holiday visas are very easy and cheap to obtain; you don't need a visa if you go to New Zealand on holiday for up to 6 months and hold a UK passport.

The UK Citizens' Working Holiday Scheme allows Britons aged 18–30 to be employed in temporary jobs in New Zealand for up to two years. The scheme has proved so successful in allaying seasonal shortages of labour that the yearly ceiling of working holiday visas has been removed completely and applications are welcomed throughout the year to the New Zealand Immigration Service. Even if you are not in your home country you can apply online and pay by credit card (about £50) at the time of application. This entirely online application procedure was introduced in 2005 and keeps in touch with Working Holiday Makers by email, sending them information about jobs and requesting feedback to keep the service up to scratch. You do not need a job offer when applying as the scheme allows you to pick up temporary work while holidaying in New Zealand.

Other working holiday schemes are open to Irish, Canadian, Japanese and Malaysian nationals who must apply in their country of nationality and whose visa is for up to a year. The expense of getting to New Zealand, means that many people who visit New Zealand to work are more concerned with the cultural than the financial aspects of their trip. Opportunities vary from region to region depending on the local employment situation. While wages are lower on average than in Australia, the cost of living is comparatively cheaper.

Either before you leave or once you are in one of the major cities, get hold of the free 200-page booklet *Australia and New Zealand Independent Traveller's Guide* published by the London-based travel magazine *TNT* (www.tntmagazine.com).

If you want to place an advertisement stating that you are looking for work, try the *New Zealand Herald* (www.nzherald.co.nz).

Red Tape

Visa Requirements: New Zealand has Visa Waiver agreements with 30 countries so citizens of the UK, Ireland, USA and most European countries do not need a visa for bona fide tourist or business visits of up to 3 months (6 months for UK citizens). On arrival, visitors must have valid passports, return tickets and evidence of sufficient funds (about £300 per month of stay). Renewals of permits will be considered to allow stays of up to a maximum of 12 months: approval is not automatic.

Residence Visas: People wishing to reside permanently in New Zealand can make a prior application to a New Zealand overseas post, or can apply while on a temporary permit in New Zealand.

Work Visas and Permits: Recent changes to immigration rules make it possible for people on working holidays to apply to extend their stay or even for residence without having to leave the country. Applicants with skills in demand may apply for a new work permit option that will be valid for up to six months at one of the seven Immigration Service offices in New Zealand. Permission may be given if there are no local residents available to take up the work offered. Work permits are required for au pairs and any form of voluntary work. The government of New Zealand has a programme enabling the young people (aged 18–30) of 30 countries to take working holidays in New Zealand, countries include the UK, many other EU nations, Japan and the USA. The Working holiday Permit must be obtained before the applicant leaves their home country but it is not necessary to have already found employment. American students are eligible to apply for a six-month work permit from the CIEE, BUNAC USA or CCUSA.

It should be noted that the above rules are liable to sudden change; all visas, including visitor visas, are charged for. There is a charge for all permit applications. For further information, contact the New Zealand Immigration Service: Immigration New Zealand (London Branch), 80 Haymarket, SW1Y 4TE, London, UK (020 7208 3886; www.immigration.govt.nz)

Agricultural Work

Farm Helpers in New Zealand (FHiNZ)

Job(s) Available: Farm stays.

Duration: The stay, which can be from 3 days to several months, depends on the needs of the farm.

Working Hours: Free farm stays to visitors in exchange for 4–6 hours help per day.

Company Description: FHiNZ is a voluntary group of over 180 farms throughout New Zealand.

Head Office: 31 Moerangi St, Palmerston North
☎ +64 6 3541104
✆ info@fhinz.co.nz
🖳 www.fhinz.co.nz

Requirements: No experience is necessary and all equipment is provided. Visitors need to each have a membership booklet (revised every month), with full details of all the farms, the family and what kinds of work visitors will be helping with. These are $25 each, valid for 1 year and available either by mail order or through some agents.

Accommodation: Board and lodging is provided in the family home in return for daily farm work dependent on season and type of farm. Most farms will collect visitors from the nearest town at no cost.

Application Procedure: For more information contact the address above.

Pukenui Holiday Park

Job(s) Available: Recruits for mandarin gangs and pickers for orchards.

Duration: January to February, March to April and June to August. Minimum period of work is 2 weeks.

Working Hours: Employees work 8 hours per day (weather permitting) 5–7 days a week.

Head Office: RD4, Kaitaia, Northland
☎ +64 9 4098803
✆ pukenuiholidays@xtra.co.nz
🖳 www.northland-camping.co.nz

Pay: You can expect to earn NZ$90-NZ$110 per day. For details of wages please contact Pukenui Holiday Park at above email address.

Company Description: The Pukenui Holiday Park recruits for the mandarin gangs for Kerifresh, and pickers for orchards in the area. They organise accommodation, transport and work equipment. Pukenui is on SH1F en route to Cape Reinga, in the far North of New Zealand. There is a public bus that leaves daily from Auckland to Kaitaia and a bus is arranged from Kaitaia to Pukenui before each season starts.

Accommodation: Board and lodging is available for NZ$84 per week for camping and NZ$98 per week for a bed with full facilities in a shared room. Both prices include transport to the orchard.

Application Procedure: Applications at anytime, preferably 2 to 4 weeks prior to commencement of work.

Other Employment in New Zealand

Bunac

Job(s) Available: BUNAC offers a work/travel scheme entitled *Work New Zealand*, which enables participants to work and travel in the South Pacific.

Head Office: 6 Bowling Green Lane, London EC1R 0QH, UK
☎ 020 7251 3472
✆ downunder@bunac.org.uk
🖳 www.bunac.org

Duration: Up to 1 year.

Cost: The programme cost is £395 plus visa.

Job Description: Choose any type of job, anywhere in New Zealand. The package includes airport transfer on arrival, 2 nights' accommodation, a guaranteed job, arrival orientation and support services throughout the stay.

Requirements: The programme is open to students and non-students aged 18–35 who hold a British or Irish passport. Those who have already used their once-in-a-lifetime, 2-year Working Holiday Visa are welcome to apply for BUNAC's exclusive, 1-year IEP visa.

Application Procedure: For further information contact BUNAC at the above address or through their website www.bunac.org.

Work and Travel New Zealand Programme

Job(s) Available: This programme allows participants to travel in New Zealand, taking up work along the way to support themselves.

Head Office: IST Plus Rosedale House, Rosedale Road, Surrey TW9 2SZ, UK
☎ 020 8939 9057
✆ info@istplus.com
🖳 www.istplus.com

Duration: Visa valid for 12 months from entry to New Zealand. Wide variety of work available, for up to 3 months per position.

Cost: Programme fee is £195 and includes all services and 2 night's accommodation.

Company Description: IST Plus offers assistance at every stage, from obtaining the visa, to helping find work and accommodation. Ongoing services include mail receiving and holding, 24-hour emergency support, and access to office facilities and free internet at their resource centre in Auckland.

Requirements: This programme is open to British, Irish, Canadian residents of the UK, aged 18–30, who have not been on a working holiday to New Zealand before. Other nationalities may be eligible.

Accommodation: 2 nights accommodation included in cost.

Application Procedure: Applications all year round, at least 8 weeks before planned departure for New Zealand.

Useful Publications:

Work Your Way Around the World
Susan Griffith
Vacation Work 2007

A unique and acclaimed guide for the working traveller. With round the world trips becoming increasingly popular as air fares fall, this comprehensive guide offers up-to-date information about the kind of temporary work available in countries across the world.

Teaching English Abroad
Susan Griffith
Vacation Work 2006

Fully revised edition of the definitive and acclaimed guide to short and long-term opportunities for trained and untrained teachers across the world. Including listings of recruitment organisations and useful websites, this guide contains a directory of more than 380 courses for training as an EFL teacher as well as 1,150 language school addresses to contact for jobs.

Hands-On Holidays
Guy Hobbs
Vacation Work 2007

The definitive guide to rewarding short-term breaks. Traditionally rewarding travel has meant putting your life on hold, but hands-on holidays last from just a few days to a month so are perfect for students during their summer vacation. They offer a real opportunity to get involved, to learn and contribute, and to enjoy a more authentic travel experience. This book contains up-to-date details of organisations, charities and holiday ideas that you wont find anywhere else.

The Au Pair & Nanny's Guide to Working Abroad
Susan Griffith and Sharon Legg
Vacation Work 2006

Fully revised edition of the detailed guide for anyone looking for short or long-term work as a nanny or au pair around the world.

The Directory of Jobs & Careers Abroad
Guy Hobbs
Vacation Work 2006

The definitive guide to finding work around the world. The Directory of Jobs & Careers Abroad provides essential information on career opportunities in over 50 countries worldwide. Aimed at everyone from school leavers to fully qualified professionals, it lists the professions and trades in demand overseas and gives all the facts on over 35 different specific careers including teachers, nurses, journalists, computer operators and engineers.

Working in Tourism
Verité Reily Collins
Vacation Work 2004

Offering job opportunities which range from seasonal work to permanent employment, examples of jobs that are featured include sports instructors, tour guides and administration. There are also special employment features on summer camps, cruise ships, beach resorts and theme parks.

Guide to Volunteering for Development
World Service Enquiry 2007

With over 350 aid, development and gap-year organisations the 2007 *Guide to Volunteering for Development* is packed with ideas on how anyone, aged from 16 to 70, can be involved in development, volunteering, a gap-year, join a local group or find an organisation that sends volunteers and much more. Available to order from www.wse.org.uk

Prospects Work Experience
www.prospects.ac.uk

A magazine published every October and available free of charge to students from your careers service, university job shop or for a small charge, by ordering online. The magazine contains articles and information that will help you to get the most out of your work experience and help you in developing your ideas about your career.

The Archaeological Fieldwork Opportunities Bulletin (AFOB)
Archaeological Institute of America 2007

The Archaeological Fieldwork Opportunities Bulletin (AFOB) is an annual resource designed as an excellent starting point to plan an archaeological vacation. AFOB provides an extensive list of projects that offer opportunities to excavate in the United States and abroad. This fully indexed edition contains more than 200 fieldwork opportunities, listed under major geographic regions. All the information is available online from www.archaeological.org. Print version available in the UK from www.oxbowbooks.com.

Guide to Summer Camps and Summer Schools, 30th edition
Porter Sargent Publishers 2007

This 30th edition covers the broad spectrum of recreational and educational summer opportunities. Featuring more than 1750 camps and schools, as well as programe for those with special needs or learning disabilities, this is a comprehensive and convenient resource.